A Korean Confucian's Advice
on How to Be Moral

KOREAN CLASSICS LIBRARY: PHILOSOPHY AND RELIGION

A Korean Confucian's Advice on How to Be Moral

Tasan Chŏng Yagyong's Reading of the Zhongyong

translated, annotated, and with an introduction by
Don Baker

University of Hawai'i Press/Honolulu
Korean Classics Library

© 2023 The Regents of the University of California
All rights reserved
Printed in the United States of America

First printing, 2023

Library of Congress Cataloging-in-Publication Data

Names: Chŏng, Yag-yong, 1762–1836, author. | Baker, Don, translator, annotator, writer of introduction. | Chŏng, Yag-yong, 1762–1836. Chungyong kangŭibo. English. | Chŏng, Yag-yong, 1762–1836. Chungyong Ch'aek. English.
Title: A Korean Confucian's advice on how to be moral : Tasan Chŏng Yagyong's reading of the Zhongyong / translated, annotated, and with an introduction by Don Baker.
Other titles: Korean classics library. Philosophy and religion.
Description: Honolulu : University of Hawai'i Press, 2023. | Series: Korean classics library: philosophy and religion | Includes bibliographical references and index.
Identifiers: LCCN 2022043561 (print) | LCCN 2022043562 (ebook) | ISBN 9780824893620 (hardback) | ISBN 9780824894344 (pdf) | ISBN 9780824894351 (epub) | ISBN 9780824894368 (kindle edition)
Subjects: LCSH: 880-01 Chŏng, Yag-yong, 1762–1836. Chungyong kangŭibo. | 880-02 Chŏng, Yag-yong, 1762–1836. Chungyong ch'aek. | Confucian ethics—Korea. | Neo-Confucianism—Korea.
Classification: LCC B5254.C563 K67 2023 (print) | LCC B5254.C563 (ebook) | DDC 181/.112—dc23/eng/20221209
LC record available at https://lccn.loc.gov/2022043561
LC ebook record available at https://lccn.loc.gov/2022043562

Korean Classics Library: Philosophy & Religion

Series Editor:
Robert E. Buswell, Jr., University of California, Los Angeles

Series Editorial Board:
Donald Baker, University of British Columbia
John B. Duncan, University of California, Los Angeles
Sun Joo Kim, Harvard University
Namhee Lee, University of California, Los Angeles
James B. Lewis, Oxford University
A. Charles Muller, Tokyo University
Young-chan Ro, George Mason University
Kenneth R. Robinson, The Aichi University Institute of International Affairs
Edward Shultz, University of Hawai'i, Mānoa

Senior Editor: Jennifer Jung-Kim, University of California, Los Angeles

This work was supported by the English Translation of 100 Korean Classics program through the Ministry of Education of the Republic of Korea and the Korean Studies Promotion Service of the Academy of Korean Studies (AKS-2010-AAA-2101).

University of Hawai'i Press books are printed on acid-free paper and meet the guidelines for permanence and durability of the Council on Library Resources.

Contents

Acknowledgments ix

Part I. Translator's Introduction 1
1. Tasan Chŏng Yagyong and the *Zhongyong* 3
2. Why Translate These Particular *Zhongyong* Commentaries? 15
3. Tasan's Approach to Confucian Scholarship 19
4. Tasan's Approach to the Cultivation of a Selfless Orientation 28
5. Tasan and the Problem of Moral Frailty 41
6. Reading These Discussions of the *Zhongyong* 57
7. Notes on the Translation of Key Terms 63

Part II. Translation: Chungyong ch'aek
(*Responding to Royal Inquiries regarding the Zhongyong*) 81

Part III. Translation: Chungyong kangŭibo
(*A Discussion of the Meaning of the Zhongyong, Revised*) 99
Introduction 101
Zhongyong I: 1 103
    That which Heaven has conferred on us is called our innate ability to act appropriately.
Zhongyong I: 2 110
    We cannot distance ourselves from the Dao for even one second.
Zhongyong I: 4 113
    When joy, anger, sorrow, or pleasure have not yet begun to stir.
Zhongyong II 124
    Confucius said, "An exemplary person is someone who is consistently appropriately focused and composed."
Zhongyong III 129
    The Master said, "Constant Focus and Composure—surely this is perfection!"
Zhongyong IV 130
    Among human beings, there is no one who does not eat or drink.
Zhongyong VI 132
    There was Shun: He indeed was greatly wise!
Zhongyong VII 133
    All men say, "I am wise."
Zhongyong VIII 135
    Hui was a man who chose the Way of equanimity and constancy.

Zhongyong IX	136
All-under-Heaven, states and families can be peacefully ordered.	
Zhongyong X	138
Zilu asked about strength.	
Zhongyong XI	141
Some go to where they can hide from public view and behave in peculiar ways.	
Zhongyong XII	144
The Dao which the superior person pursues extends far and wide [*fei*] and yet is hidden [*yin*].	
Zhongyong XIII	149
The Dao is not far away from ordinary people.... When hewing an axe handle, simply hew an axe handle.	
Zhongyong XIV	152
The exemplary person does what is appropriate for whatever position he finds himself in.	
Zhongyong XV	154
When traveling a long distance, we must start from somewhere nearby. When ascending to someplace high, we must begin from down below.	
Zhongyong XVI	156
In the way it displays its power, how great is the Spirit.	
Zhongyong XVII	165
Great, indeed, was Shun's filial piety!	
Zhongyong XVIII	166
It was only King Wen who was without grief.	
Zhongyong XIX: 3	170
In spring and autumn, they would renovate their ancestral temples and arrange the ritual vessels properly.	
Zhongyong XIX: 4	175
The rituals of the ancestral temple provide the occasion for maintaining the proper *zhao* and *mu* order.	
Zhongyong XIX: 5	188
To stand in the positions of the forebears and carry out their ritual obligations.	
Zhongyong XIX: 6	189
The *jiao* sacrifices and the *she* sacrifices were ways to pay ritual homage to the Lord on High.	
Zhongyong XX: 1	195
Lord Ai asked about how to govern properly.	
Zhongyong XX: 4	198
Proper governing depends on who is doing the governing.	
Zhongyong XX: 7	200
An exemplary person, therefore, cannot do otherwise than cultivate a moral character.	

Zhongyong XX: 8	202
There are five aspects of the Dao everyone must conform to.	
Zhongyong XX: 9	208
Some understand with a natural ease.	
Zhongyong XX: 10	210
The Master said, "To love learning brings one close to acting wisely."	
Zhongyong XX: 12	213
For All-under-Heaven, all states and households, there are nine cardinal rules.	
Zhongyong XX: 16	226
In all undertakings, you must prepare in order to be successful.	
Zhongyong XX: 18	227
Acting in an unselfishly cooperative and appropriately responsive manner is the Dao of Heaven.	
Zhongyong XXII	234
In All-under-Heaven, only he who is completely unselfishly cooperative and appropriately responsive...	
Zhongyong XXIII	238
Those below that level are those who are able to extend their efforts to that which is most detailed and complicated.	
Zhongyong XXIV	241
The Dao of being perfectly selflessly cooperative and appropriately responsive makes it possible to see what lies ahead.	
Zhongyong XXV	244
To act in an unselfishly cooperative and appropriately responsive manner actualizes one's full potential.	
Zhongyong XXVI: 1	247
Therefore, those who act in a perfectly unselfishly cooperative and appropriately responsive manner never stop doing so.	
Zhongyong XXVI: 7	249
The Dao of Heaven and Earth can be completely encapsulated in a single word.	
Zhongyong XXVI: 10	253
The *Book of Songs* says, "That which Heaven confers—Its majesty is eternal."	
Zhongyong XXVII:1	254
Great, indeed, is the Dao of the Sage!	
Zhongyong XXVII: 6	256
The exemplary person, therefore, respects his innate potential for acting appropriately and follows the path of study and inquiry.	
Zhongyong XXVII: 7	263
This is the reason he is not arrogant when occupying a high office.	
Zhongyong XXVIII: 1	264
The Master said, "The foolish nonetheless like to use their own judgment."	

Zhongyong XXVIII: 5   270
    The Master said, "Let me say something about the rituals of Xia."
Zhongyong XXIX: 5   275
    This is why, when the true ruler takes action, the people of that age take this to be the Dao of All-under-Heaven.
Zhongyong XXX   276
    Confucius carried on the work of Yao and Shun as if they were his own ancestors.
Zhongyong XXXI   279
    In All-under-Heaven, only someone who is a perfect Sage...
Zhongyong XXXII   280
    In All-under-Heaven, only someone who displays the highest level of unselfishly cooperative and appropriately responsive behavior...
Zhongyong XXXIII: 1   282
    The *Book of Songs* says, "Over her brocade garments she wore a plain coat with no lining."
Zhongyong XXXIII: 2   286
    The *Book of Songs* says, "Although the fish lie on the bottom to hide, they are still clearly visible."
Zhongyong XXXIII: 3   287
    The *Book of Songs* says, "If someone spies on you in your own home, make sure there is nothing going on to be ashamed of even in the darkest corner."
Zhongyong XXXIII: 4   288
    The *Book of Songs* says, "Silently, without a word, he enters and offers the sacrifice; at that time there is no discord."
Zhongyong XXXIII: 5   289
    The *Book of Songs* says, "He doesn't make a public display of his ethical virtuosity, yet all the noblemen take him as an exemplar."
Zhongyong XXXIII: 6   291
    The *Book of Songs* says, "I admire the way you radiate moral power without proclaiming it loudly or making a big display of it."
Zhongyong XXXIII: 6   292
    The Book of Songs says, "Moral authority is light, like a feather."
Discussing Zhu Xi's Preface to *Zhongyong zhangju*   295
Discussing the Divisions of the Text   302
A Record of the Discussion of the *Zhongyong*
    at the Brilliant Governance Hall   303

  Glossary of Names, Places, and Terms   309
  Notes   349
  Works Consulted   443
  Index   459

Acknowledgments

This work has its roots in 1970s Seattle, when, as a graduate student in Korean history at the University of Washington, I first began delving into the writings of Tasan Chŏng Yagyong under the demanding but wise guidance of James Palais. In the decades since then, I have continued to explore the abundant resources in Tasan's collected works and have published articles on his philosophy, his religious orientation, his medical writings, and his life in general. I have also, over the years, translated into English bits and pieces of his writings. However, even though I realized a philosopher is best presented in his own words rather than in secondhand descriptions, I refrained from translating major portions of his works because I was aware how much work translation entails.

Reading a text written in literary Sino-Korean [Literary Sinitic] is much easier than translating such a text into English for a couple of reasons. First of all, often the key terms in these texts have such a wide range, and so many different layers, of meaning that it is difficult to pin them down with one English translation. Of equal importance is the intertextuality of traditional Sino-Korean writing. Tasan's writings, like the works of his fellow Confucians throughout East Asia, are filled with references not only to the Confucian classics but also to later commentaries on those classics. Scholarly English translations require that such citations be identified, a time-consuming task that I did not think I had time for.

However, thanks to encouragement from the Academy of Korean Studies in Korea as well as from Robert E. Buswell, John Duncan, Jennifer Jung-Kim, and others associated with the Korean Classics Library: Philosophy and Religion project at UCLA, I finally decided to tackle a sizeable slice of Tasan's philosophical musings. With financial support from the Academy of Korean Studies, I was able to enlist the help of two University of British Columbia (UBC) graduate students in this project. Christopher Lovins, then a doctoral student in Korean history, was the first to help me determine what Tasan is saying and where he found the citations he used to support his arguments. Later in this project, Clayton Ashton, then a doctoral student in early Chinese thought, joined Christopher in helping me locate Tasan's sources as well as transform Tasan's arguments into something English-language readers could understand. Without their help, I would not have been able to finish this translation within a reasonable period of time.

Our task was made easier by three incredibly helpful websites. One is ctext.org, which saved us many hours by making so many important Chinese Confucian documents in Literary Sinitic searchable. Also helpful was db.itkc.or.kr, the database of searchable Korean classical texts maintained by the Institute for the Translation of Korean Classics in Seoul. I want to thank the people who maintain those two essential websites. The third useful internet resource was the Erudition database of classical Chinese texts (*Zhongguo fangzhi ku he jiben guji ku*), to which the UBC library permitted access. It was invaluable in tracking down the many Chinese sources Tasan drew from. I am grateful to my UBC colleague Bruce Rusk for informing me of the existence of that electronic resource.

I also have to thank the many scholars whose studies of Tasan have helped me over the years to gain a better grasp of Tasan's overall philosophy. Among scholars writing in English, I am particularly grateful to Michael Kalton and Mark Setton. The number of scholars writing in Korean who have helped me both with their publications and with conversations about Tasan's thought and his significance is, of course, much greater. I cannot possibly name them all. Among those who have been the most helpful are Yi Ŭlho, Kŭm Changt'ae, Cho Kwang, Ch'oe Sŏgu, Choi Young-jin, Chŏng Ilgyun, Chŏng Pyŏngnyŏn, Chung So-Yi, Han Hyong-jo, Kim Sŏnhŭi, Lee Seung-hwan, Paek Minjŏng, Pak Chongch'ŏn, Pak Sŏngmu, Song Young-bae, Yi Hyangman, and Yi Kwangho. I also need to express my appreciation to the Tasan Cultural Foundation for their support of my research on Tasan over the years, and for the hard work they dedicated to producing the recent definitive collection of Tasan's complete works. Finally, I want to say how much I appreciate the comments of the two anonymous individuals who were asked to review this manuscript before publication. They pointed out mistakes, which I have corrected, and also made suggestions for making this text more reader-friendly, which I have adopted.

Scholars never work in isolation. Instead, we always draw on the work of others. That is why I am very grateful to all those before me, both in Korea and in the English-speaking world, who have clarified the origins of Tasan's philosophy and illuminated the distinctiveness of his intellectual journey. However, I also have to add that I alone am responsible for any errors of interpretation or translation that appear in this work.

I cannot leave this acknowledgments page without expressing gratitude to my wife, Yumi, who allowed me to spend much time on this project that she would have preferred I spend in more family-oriented activities. And she tells me not to forget to thank the family dog, who often begged me to stop working and take him for a walk but acquiesced with no more protest than a sad look in his eyes and a downward turn of his tail when I said "Not now. I'm busy translating something." That dog, Gucci by name, is no longer with us but if he were, I am sure he would be proud that his patience allowed me to finish this work.

This work was supported by the English Translation of 100 Korean Classics program through the Ministry of Education of the Republic of Korea and the Korean Studies Promotion Service of the Academy of Korean Studies (AKS-2010-AAA-2101).

I. Translator's Introduction

1

Tasan Chŏng Yagyong and the *Zhongyong*

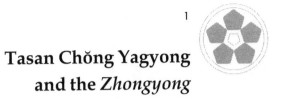

Who was Chŏng Yagyong (1762–1836), and why should we take the time to read his early nineteenth-century commentary on a Chinese Confucian work that is at least two thousand years older than that? That two-part question requires a two-part answer. First, we need briefly to survey his life and how that affected the way he thought. Second, we need to embark on an exploration of his philosophy, highlighting his originality and his relevance to the contemporary world. Even though we can explore only one corner of the multifaceted philosophy of Tasan, you will at least get a glimpse why he is one of the best-known and most studied writers from the thousands of years of premodern Korean history, and why he is worth reading today.

Tasan means "Tea Mountain." It is the best known of Chŏng Yagyong's pen names, adopted from the hill on which he lived, and grew tea, for the last ten years of his exile along the southwestern coast. Another pen name he used is Yŏyudang, which is why the collection of his complete works, all thirty-seven volumes of it in the 2012 edition, is called "The Complete Works of Yŏyudang."[1] Yŏyudang was the name he gave his study when he returned home from his "tea mountain" after spending more than seventeen years in exile. It means "the hall for cultivating a cautious and apprehensive attitude."[2] As will become clear in the pages that follow, "caution" and "apprehension" were key terms in his moral psychology, since Tasan believed a person had to remain constantly cautious and apprehensive lest they fail to do what they were supposed to do, or they do what they were not supposed to do.

Tasan was born in 1762, the youngest of four sons of Chŏng Chaewŏn (1730–1792) by a primary wife. The Chŏng family was Namin, the "Southerner faction," which meant that they were *yangban*, members of the Confucian scholar elite of Chosŏn Korea (1392–1910), but they were frustrated

3

for much of the eighteenth century by the Noron (Patriarchs) faction's control of the government bureaucracy. The Namin and the Noron were philosophical as well as political rivals, and the Noron did their best to keep Namin out of any significant government posts. However, King Chŏngjo (r. 1776–1800), like his grandfather King Yŏngjo (r. 1724–1776), preferred to choose the most qualified people to work under him rather than have the Noron tell him whom he could and could not appoint to public office. He attempted to pursue a nonpartisan policy of "grand harmony" in which factional affiliation would not be grounds for disqualification for appointment to a senior government post. As a result, though the Noron continued to dominate the bureaucracy under both King Yŏngjo and King Chŏngjo, a few Namin began to be appointed as well. One such fortunate Namin was Tasan's father, who was appointed to a series of administrative posts, rising as high as magistrate of Chinju in the far south.

While alternating between life as a scholar in the countryside near Seoul and as a government official, Chŏng Chaewŏn managed to sire five sons, four by a primary wife and one by a concubine. The oldest of the legitimate sons was Chŏng Yakhyŏn (1751–1821), whose mother died when he was less than two years old. Chŏng Chaewŏn then remarried, this time to a woman descended from the famous scholar Yun Sŏndo (1587–1671), who is considered one of the more prominent early members of the Namin faction. That second union produced Chŏng Yakchŏn (1758–1816), followed by Chŏng Yakchong (1760–1801), and then Tasan in 1762. Tasan also had a younger stepbrother named Yakhoeng (1785–1829). However, Yakhoeng was not only the son of his father's secondary wife; he was also much younger than Tasan. Tasan therefore was not very close to him and tells us little about that youngest of his brothers.[3]

Tasan's mother died when he was only eight years old, in 1770. His father lived for another twenty-two years, dying in 1792, which meant that he lived long enough to see Tasan pass the civil service examinations and begin to climb the bureaucratic ladder. Before that, however, Tasan married. At the age of fourteen, he wed a fifteen-year-old girl from the P'ungsan Hong clan, another prominent Namin family. Remarkably, they stayed married for sixty years, with his wife dying in 1838, a couple of years after Tasan died at the age of seventy-five.[4]

Tasan and his wife had nine children (six boys and three girls), but only three survived beyond the age of five. In other words, two out of three of Tasan's children died in their infancy.[5] Though such a high mortality rate was not unusual for a pre-industrial society such as Chosŏn dynasty Korea, it was painful, nonetheless. After he recounted this tragic history in a note he wrote to be placed in the grave of the last of his children to die young,

Tasan asked rhetorically, "What have I done to offend Heaven that I would lose two out of every three of my children?"[6]

Shortly after he married, Tasan embarked on a serious pursuit of a better understanding of his Namin Confucian tradition. In 1777, when he was sixteen, he began studying the writings of Sŏngho Yi Ik (1682–1764), a leading thinker of an earlier generation of Namin scholars. Though he did not accept everything Yi Ik wrote, he may have been influenced by Sŏngho's moral pessimism and by Sŏngho's distrust of the body. At times, Sŏngho appears to suggest that the goal of moral perfection is out of reach for the average person, though mainstream neo-Confucianism teaches that all human beings have the potential to become sages. He said, for example, that the *ki* [C. *qi*, psychophysical endowment] of a sage is different from the *ki* of any ordinary person. That, he argued, is obvious from the fact that the *ki* of a sage is so clear and pure that not only does it not hinder the operation of *li* [the moral principles that stimulate and direct moral behavior], a sage's *ki* can manifest as appropriately selfless motions.[7]

Sŏngho was so concerned about how the *ki* of ordinary people can keep them from behaving as they should that he called for what was, in the neo-Confucian tradition, an unusual asceticism. He encouraged husbands and wives to sleep in separate rooms in order to make it easier for men to resist the pull of the flesh. He also suggested that men eat less than one full bowl of rice at every meal so that they would be accustomed to leaving physical desires less than completely satisfied.[8] Such restrictions on normal human emotions were very difficult for human beings to adhere to consistently. Nevertheless, a much stronger distrust of the human body and the emotions it generated than is normally seen in Confucianism became a distinctive feature of the Namin approach to Confucian attitudes toward the cultivation of a moral character. Tasan later carried this concern over human moral frailty even further than Sŏngho had.

Before that happened, however, in 1779 Tasan followed his father to Seoul and was allowed to enroll in the National Confucian Academy, the Sŏnggyun'gwan. In 1783 he passed the examination that allowed him to bear the proud title of a "classics licentiate" (*saengwŏn*). While studying for higher-level exams, which he needed to pass to qualify for an important government position, he had an encounter with a non-Confucian philosophy that would have an impact on both his thinking and his career for the rest of his life.

In April (by the lunar calendar) in 1784, Tasan and his brother Yakchŏn joined their friend Yi Pyŏk (1754–1786) at a memorial service for Yi's sister. (She had been married to Chŏng Yakhyŏn, Tasan's eldest brother, but she had died in 1780.)[9] On their way back to Seoul from that traditional

Confucian ritual in the countryside, Yi Pyŏk shared with Tasan and Yakchŏn what he had learned from the Catholic books their friend Yi Sŭnghun (1756–1801), who was married to Tasan's sister, had recently brought back from Beijing. After they reached Seoul, Yi Pyŏk showed them some of his collection of Catholic works, including the introduction to Catholic teachings by Matteo Ricci (1552–1610), *Tianzhu shiyi* [The true significance of the Lord of Heaven], and a guide to Catholic ethics, *Qike* [Seven victories], by Diego de Pantoja (1571–1618). Tasan later confessed that he and Yakchŏn found what Yi Pyŏk told them that day fascinating, and those books a pleasure to read. He wrote that they were intrigued by what Yi, and those books, said about the creation of the universe, about the difference between material and spiritual beings, and about life and death.[10] Tasan was only twenty-two at that time.

Later that year Tasan and his brother Yakchŏn joined a nascent Korean Catholic community. There were no Catholic missionaries in Korea yet (the first missionary, a Chinese priest, would not arrive in Seoul until 1795). However, Yi Sŭnghun had been baptized a Catholic while he was in Beijing the previous year (he had accompanied his father on a diplomatic mission there). When he returned to Korea, he began telling his friends and relatives about his new beliefs. Yi Sŭnghun and those friends and relatives soon formed the nucleus of Korea's first Christian community. Among them were Yi Pyŏk, Tasan, and Yakchŏn, who were all baptized by Yi Sŭnghun. Yakchŏn then went on to bring his cousin Yun Chich'ung (1759–1791) and his younger brother Yakchong into that Catholic community.[11]

In 1790, however, Korea's Catholics, who were on their own without a priest to guide them, learned via a letter from the bishop in Beijing that Catholics were not allowed to use a spirit tablet (a tablet on which were inscribed the names of the deceased being honored) in an ancestral memorial rite. Since that tablet was an essential part of that obligatory ritual display of filial piety and was mandated by the government, upon learning this news Yi Sŭnghun withdrew from active leadership of the Church, turning his responsibilities over to someone Yi Pyŏk had converted, Kwŏn Ilsin (1742–1791).[12] Chŏng Yagyong and his brother Yakchŏn also withdrew from further participation in Catholic activities after the announcement of the ban on Confucian ancestor rites, although their brother Yakchong, the last of the three brothers to convert to Catholicism, remained an active leader of the Church until his execution in the persecution of 1801.[13] Yi Pyŏk was saved from having to choose between his Confucian ritual obligations and his new faith, having passed away four years earlier, in 1786.[14]

At the same time that Tasan was helping found the Korean Catholic Church, he was also making progress in his official studies of Confucianism at the National Confucian Academy. In 1784, King Chŏngjo announced a set of seventy questions on the *Zhongyong* for the students at that academy to respond to. Tasan, who was only twenty-three at the time, went to his older and more experienced friend Yi Pyŏk (who was then thirty-one) to seek his advice on how to answer those questions. Yi Pyŏk was busy reading the Catholic books Yi Sŭnghun had just brought back from Beijing, but he took time out to help his young friend. The result was an essay that won the praise of the King as the best any of the students had written. Thirty years later, when Tasan revised that essay on the *Zhongyong*, he recalled with pride the compliment his collaboration with Yi Pyŏk had earned, and he grieved that Yi was no longer alive to discuss the classics with him.[15]

In 1787, a couple of years after Tasan had come to the favorable attention of King Chŏngjo, he came under criticism from a fellow student for his interest in Catholicism. Yi Kigyŏng (1756–1819) discovered that Tasan, in addition to studying Confucian texts, had been meeting with Yi Sŭnghun and a few others at a house outside the school grounds under the pretext of engaging in some friendly poetry-writing competition. Rather than writing poems, however, they had been reading more Catholic books and talking about Catholic ideas.[16] This was not the first time Yi Kigyŏng had heard of Tasan's interest in Western ideas. He and Tasan had once been close friends and, in 1784, Tasan had lent Yi copies of *Tianzhu shiyi* and *Shengshi chuyao* [The teachings of the Church in everyday language] by Fr. Joseph-Anne-Marie de Moyriac de Mailla (1669–1748), two basic introductions to Catholic thought by Jesuit missionaries in China, and encouraged Yi to read them. Yi Kigyŏng looked over those books and told Tasan then that he had found that those books were worthless collections of absurdities.[17]

He was rather surprised, therefore, when he stumbled upon that reading circle in 1787. He tried to convince Tasan that he and the others should stop reading such material but was unsuccessful, at least at first. A couple of years later, Tasan eventually realized that Catholicism had some non-Confucian elements in it and that made it dangerous both for himself and for the Confucian moral principles he held dear. As he wrote the king a decade later, in 1797, "The books that I read did not challenge the way we honor our ancestors with ritual. I was startled when I found out that was part of Catholic teachings. How could I not but feel a chill in my bones when I learned how immoral those Catholics were?"[18] Before he came to that conclusion, however, he read enough to impact the way he read classical Confucian texts.

Tasan read those Catholic books at a formative age, when he was still in his twenties. A glance at what he wrote both then and later shows that he was influenced by what he read, often apparently without being himself aware of the Catholic role in stimulating the formation of some of the original ideas in his philosophy. For example, as early as 1784, when he answered the questions posed by the King on the *Zhongyong*, Tasan used language and concepts that resembled those he had encountered when he read Ricci's *Tianzhu shiyi* and other Catholic works. He insisted that, contrary to the standard neo-Confucian assumption, yin and yang cannot serve as the origin of the material world because they are not material entities themselves but are only names for certain patterns in nature. He also argued that the Five Processes (*ohaeng*) could not have created the multitude of things, either, since the universe is more complicated than they could have produced on their own. Moreover, he adopted the Riccian argument that human beings have an immaterial component that cannot be explained as a product of the interactions and transformations of material forces. (In Tasan's case, that "immaterial component" referred to the innate potential to act appropriately (human nature) we all have as human beings.)[19]

In more evidence of borrowing from Matteo Ricci and other Catholic missionaries in China, he writes about heavenly spirits he says are immaterial ("without physical form") servants of *Sangje*, the Lord on High.[20] Similarly, in answers Tasan gave in 1791 to questions about another ancient Confucian classic, the *Book of Songs*, he refers to spiritual beings in ways that are closer to the way Catholic missionaries talked about them than to the way neo-Confucians used such terms. He interprets those poems as talking, not about an impersonal heaven, but about actual spirits observing human behavior. Moreover, he says that when sages die, they join *Sangje* above.[21]

Tasan never admitted possible Catholic origins for those ideas of his. Nor did he change his views on those topics as he grew older and farther away from his active involvement with Korean's small Catholic community. However, we know that after he turned thirty years of age, Tasan never again attended Catholic meetings or encouraged people to read Catholic writings, unlike what he had done with Yi Kigyŏng earlier. We do not know exactly when he severed his connection with those who, unlike Tasan, never abandoned their youthful interest in Catholicism, but it must have been before 1791. That was the year his maternal cousin Yun Chich'ung became a martyr for the Catholic faith.

Yun, known to Catholics as Paul Yun, had been converted to Catholicism by Chŏng Yakchŏn. Yun was first person in the Korean Catholic community to suffer the loss of a parent after a letter had arrived from the bishop in Beijing informing Korea's Catholics that the Pope had banned as idolatrous the use of a spirit tablet in an ancestral memorial service. Yun accepted that order from the Pope as though it were the word of God Himself. For his fidelity to the demands of his new faith, he was beheaded on the charge of modifying the Confucian mourning ritual for his recently deceased mother by discarding her spirit tablet.²² If Tasan had not realized it already, that was a clear sign that he had to choose between being a Catholic and being a Confucian, with the first choice possibly leading to death, and the second hopefully to a long career as a public servant. Tasan made the choice to remain a Confucian, although he still was not able to enjoy the long civil service career he had hoped for.

That hope was rooted in the fact that, in 1789, he had passed the higher-level civil service examination and had begun to be appointed to government posts, despite the fact that he was Namin, and the Noron still dominated the bureaucracy. Passing that high-level examination was quite an accomplishment, since only 199 men passed that "palace examination" over the entire twenty-five years of Chŏngjo's reign. Other versions of the higher-level civil service examinations were given more often and therefore had more passers but, nonetheless, less than thirty-three men a year on average managed to pass such an examination while Chŏngjo sat on the throne.²³

Moreover, Tasan earned one of the highest grades on the civil service examination that year. King Chŏngjo was impressed enough to make him one of the *ch'ogye munsin,* a group of officials at the beginning of their careers whom the King personally selected and then trained in his particular philosophy of Confucianism, particularly as it pertained to the responsibilities of the ruler and relationship of the ruler to his subjects. Over the next eleven years, Tasan served in a number of government posts, including acting as eyes-and-ears of the King as a secret inspector, being responsible for the construction of a new palace/fortress south of Seoul in Hwasŏng (now Suwŏn), holding important posts in the Office of Special Counselors, and rising as high as Third Minister in the Board of Punishments. He had to accept expulsion from the capital a couple of times, once because he had angered the King, who fired him but brought him back after ten days, and once because the King tried to protect him against accusations of involvement in the illegal entrance into Korea in 1795 of Fr. Zhou Wenmo (1752–1801), a Chinese priest sent to minister to Korea's infant church. The King at that time sent him to serve as the master of a post station out in the countryside.

Tasan took advantage of his posting in the countryside to prove that he was an ardent Confucian and was opposed to Catholicism. To prove the second point, Tasan reported to King Chŏngjo that he "uncovered who the Catholics were and threatened them with dire punishment if they did not mend their ways. I encouraged them to perform proper ancestor ritual and lectured them on what was wrong with Catholicism and what was right about our Way. I even forced all the Catholic virgins to get married."²⁴ To prove the first point, he called together a group of leading local Confucian scholars and held a ten-day seminar in a Buddhist hermitage to discuss technical points in Confucian philosophy and ritual, including the proper placement of the spirit tablet.[25] He also engaged in an intensive study of the writings of T'oegye Yi Hwang (1501-1570), beginning each day by waking up before dawn and then reading, and meditating on, some of what T'oegye had written before he began carrying out his official duties of that day. He called the notes he took on his meditations on T'oegye's philosophy "Tosan sasungnok" [Notes on taking Tosan Yi Hwang as a model for self-cultivation].[26]

All this effort to prove that he was a Confucian to the core came to naught. Even the detailed explanation he sent to King Chŏngjo in 1797 that, although he had been "contaminated" by Catholic ideas for a few years when he was in the twenties, he had realized that Catholicism, with its disregard for the proper ritual manifestations of filial piety, was evil and therefore he had adhered to Confucian ideas and practices ever since was not enough to save him from arrest and exile in 1801 on the charge of having been associated with the illegal Catholic community.[27] As long as King Chŏngjo was on the throne, Tasan was relatively safe.[28] The King was not particularly fond of Catholics or Catholicism. After all, he had approved the execution of Tasan's cousin Paul Yun Chich'ung in 1791. However, King Chŏngjo, in addition to wanting to take advantage of Tasan's obvious talent and intelligence, wanted to minimize infighting among his officials. Since most of the *yangban* Catholics were members of the Namin faction, he was concerned that the Noron would use that fact to try to get him to expel Namin from their official posts and rely on Noron officials only. The King, therefore, kept the persecution of Catholics to a minimum.

That policy ended when King's Chŏngjo's life ended in July 1800. A child king, King Sunjo (r. 1800-1834), replaced him on the throne. Since the new King was only ten years old when his father died, the Dowager Queen issued orders in his name for a few years. She, in turn, relied on her relatives in government, and they were Noron. A full-scale assault on Catholics, not just those in the government but wherever they could be found, was launched early in 1801. Not long after his still Catholic brother Yakchong was captured in Seoul, Tasan himself was arrested in February on the grounds that he was a menace to society because of his previous membership in the Catholic community, and also because he was suspected of still harboring Catholic ideas and secretly supporting Catholics, including his brother Yakchong. After a few days of interrogation (which in those days included beatings we would consider torture today), he was sent into exile to the district of Changgi, along Korea's southeastern coast. His brother Yakchŏn was also exiled at that time. Their brother Yakchong, though, was executed, as were many others who had been part of the early Catholic community. Tasan was allowed to live probably not only because he denounced Catholic teachings, but also because he also informed on former friends who had maintained ties with the infant Korean Catholic Church longer than he had or played a more significant role in its birth than he had.[29]

Tasan's exile in Changgi did not last very long. In September of that same year, Hwang Sayŏng (1775–1801), who was the son-in-law of his oldest brother, Yakhyŏn, was captured with a letter written on silk so it could be placed inside clothing and smuggled out of Korea and handed to the Portuguese bishop in Beijing, Alexandre de Gouvea (1751–1808). That letter included a plea that, if it proved to be the only way to stop the government's attacks on the small Catholic community, a European military force be sent to Korea to force the Chosŏn government to stop persecuting Catholics.[30] The discovery of Hwang's letter raised the level of the threat Catholicism posed beyond the realm of ritual misbehavior to the level of a threat to the territorial integrity of the dynasty. That necessitated more interrogations to find out more about who was and who was not a Catholic, and what did even the non-Catholics with Catholic relatives and friends know. Tasan was called up to Seoul to face further brutal interrogation. Again, he escaped execution, this time because there was no evidence that he had anything to do with the letter Hwang had written. Instead, he was again sent into exile, this time to a different location, Kangjin on Korea's southwestern coast. His brother Yakchŏn suffered a similar fate, spending the fourteen years that remained in his life on the remote island of Hŭksan-do.[31]

Tasan, more fortunate than Yakchŏn, managed to live long enough to be pardoned, released from exile, and allowed to return to his home near Seoul. However, before that happened, he had to spend seventeen years away from his family, his friends, and the intellectual stimulation of life among the scholar-official elite in Seoul. When he was forced into that long exile, he was only forty years old, an age when normally he could have expected that, before too long, he would have been appointed to one or more of the most powerful positions in the government. He returned home an old man of fifty-seven, with no chance to return to the life of a scholar-official that he had enjoyed for eleven years, between 1789 and 1800.

Though those seventeen years were frustrating for Tasan, we have reason today to be grateful to the government of King Sunjo and his Noron officials for sending Tasan into exile at that relatively isolated site along the distant southwestern coast of the Korean peninsula. Even though Tasan was kept away from the intellectual stimulation of the Seoul area from late 1801 until the fall of 1818, he had books to read and time to read them. That gave him what a modern-day professor might call a very long sabbatical.

It was during that enforced sabbatical that Tasan wrote the commentaries that attract so much attention these days.

It took Tasan a while to settle into a quiet scholarly life in Kangjin, but once he did, he became quite productive. In 1803 he finished a lengthy discussion of mourning ritual, then followed that up with a study of the *Book of Changes* in 1808. In 1808 he moved to the hut on what he called "Tea Mountain" and became even more productive. In 1809, he put together his thoughts on the *Book of Songs*. Then in 1810 and 1811 he finished a couple of studies of the *Book of Documents;* following that, in 1812, he compiled a study of the *Spring and Autumn Annals*. Finally, he turned his attention to the core of the neo-Confucian canon, the Four Books, finishing his commentary on the *Analects* in 1813, and his commentaries on *Mencius, Zhongyong,* and *Great Learning* in 1814.[32]

At first those commentaries were read by few beyond the immediate members of his family, since he had been expelled from the respectable intellectual circles in Seoul. In fact, during his own lifetime, and for decades after his death in 1836, he had almost no impact on what other Koreans were thinking. It wasn't until 1883, almost a half century after he had left this earth, that a copy of Tasan's collected writings was placed in the Kyujanggak, the Royal Library of Chosŏn. None of Tasan's writings were made available to the general public until the next century. In the first decade of the twentieth century, editions of his *Mongmim simsŏ* (An essential guide for district magistrates) and his *Hŭmhŭm sinsŏ* (A new guidebook for forensic medicine) were published. Shortly afterward they were joined by his *Kyŏngse yup'yo* (A guide to statecraft). Finally, in 1934–1938, a century after his death, his complete collected works, in multiple volumes including his philosophical essays and commentaries on the classics, were published.[33] This belated interest in Tasan arose when Koreans were grappling with the struggle to adapt to the modernizing world and discovered what they saw as sprouts of modernity in Tasan's writings, viewed as proof that Korea had not needed to depend on foreign forces to modernize. Tasan's writings came to be seen by many as showing how to remain Korean while modernizing. Tasan has since become a cultural hero, with a major road named after him in Seoul and a statue of him on Namsan, the mountain that rises in the middle of Seoul.

Thanks to the many years he spent in exile, Tasan became arguably the most prolific writer of the entire Chosŏn dynasty. Not only did he write a lot, he wrote about a lot of different things. The latest published version of his complete works fills thirty-seven volumes and includes book-length volumes on government administration, forensic medicine, historical geography, and the Confucian classics.[34] It also includes essays on history, language, and philosophy, and, of course, as is standard in the complete works of any respectable Confucian scholar, two volumes of poetry.

It is only to be expected, therefore, that many scholars would be inspired to study Tasan's writings, and that they would disagree on how to characterize his ideas. There is general agreement that he is a leading representative of what Korean scholars term the "practical learning" [*sirhak*] school. Even though he died in 1836, long before Korea began its march to modernity, he is seen as offering ideas and advice that were practical solutions to the problems of his day and are also useful for Koreans in the twenty-first century. However, there is disagreement over exactly what sort of ideas he had and what sort of advice he had to offer. He wrote so much about so many different things that it is relatively easy for scholars to find whatever they are looking for in Tasan's writings.

Those who believe he was a Catholic, and therefore a harbinger of modernity since Catholicism is seen in Korea as a modern religion, find evidence in his writings that he was, indeed, a Catholic believer. His theistic commentaries on the Confucian classics, such as his commentaries on the *Zhongyong*, are particularly useful for those who want to make that argument. On the other hand, those who believe he was primarily a Confucian find the fact that he wrote commentaries on all the Confucian classics, and also wrote manuals for government officials as well as essays on various other mainstream Confucian topics, evidence that he was solidly within the broad Confucian camp. Those who believe he was a *sirhak* thinker who wanted to modernize Korea find evidence in his criticism of the Confucianism of his day, his call for a more equitable distribution of land ownership, his appreciation of the usefulness of recent technology, and in the ideas expressed in a brief essay of his arguing that political leaders should represent the people. Those who argue that, to the contrary, he was a traditional Confucian thinker note that he saw no significant role for commerce or industry in his vision of a just agrarian society, that he actually wanted to strengthen the monarchy rather than weaken it, and that even his calls for land redistribution drew on descriptions of land distribution found in the ancient Confucian classics.

In the translation in this book of one of his two major commentaries on the *Zhongyong*, he will be revealed as neither a completely mainstream Confucian nor a practicing Catholic. He remained within the broad parameters of Confucian thinking, including retaining reverence for the Confucian classics as the best guide to moral principles as well as defining those moral principles in terms of interactions between one human being and another rather than in terms of obedience to the will of God. However, he also redefined some core neo-Confucian terms, such as *li* and *ki*,[35] and borrowed concepts from Catholic books he had read in his youth, such as the notion of free will,[36] to reinterpret the Confucian canon and create a Confucianism that pushed the boundaries of what Confucianism could be. If we concede Catholic elements in his thinking, we have to say that he was more of a Catholic Confucian than he was a Confucian Catholic. For him, Confucianism took priority. His Confucian values determined what Catholic ideas he could accept rather than Catholic teachings determining what Confucian beliefs and values he held on to. We also need to note that he himself denied that, except for a few years of youthful indiscretion, he was influenced by Catholicism at all.

When Tasan finally returned to his wife and family in 1818, we see no evidence that he tried to contact any of the survivors of Korea's persecuted Catholic community. Instead, we see him continuing his Confucian scholarly pursuits. His guide to forensic medicine, *Hŭmhŭm sinsŏ*, was not finished until almost a year after he was back in his home village. The same year, 1819, he also finished a relatively short work on Sino-Korean terminology used incorrectly in Korea (by which he meant Koreans did not use those terms the way the Chinese had). In 1821 he finished another guide to ritual, this one a guide to the rituals used to welcome envoys from China. (That same year he wrote a "tombstone inscription" — actually, an epitaph too long to fit on a tombstone — for Yakhyŏn, the last of his legitimate brothers to pass away, and the only one of the four never accused of involvement with Catholicism.) In 1822 Tasan had passed his sixtieth year and decided that he had written all the treatises he needed to write on philosophy, government, and other Confucian topics. He also wrote his own "tombstone inscription" that year, but he had to add a supplement later when he lived longer than he expected. He also lived long enough to produce, in 1834 when he was seventy-three years old, a revision of an earlier study of the *Book of Documents* as well as a revision of one of his studies of the *Book of Songs*.

He had time to work on those manuscripts because, even though he had been pardoned in 1818, he was never again able to serve in any government posts. (His name was put forward for appointment to a government post a few times, but his enemies blocked those initiatives every time.) On February 22, 1836, by the lunar calendar, after a short illness Tasan Chŏng Yagyong died at the age of seventy-five, ending a life of great frustration for him but also leaving a treasure trove of writings to be discovered by those in later generations who want to learn more about both philosophy and politics in Korea in the decades leading up to the dawning of modern Korea.[37]

Why Translate These Particular *Zhongyong* Commentaries?

Of all the volumes Tasan produced, why choose these relatively short pieces, *Responding to Royal Inquiries Regarding the Zhongyong* (*Chungyong ch'aek*) and *A Discussion of the Meaning of the Zhongyong, Revised* (*Chungyong kangŭibo*), for translation into English? One reason is that his most well-known work on politics and public administration has already been translated.[1] It seems, therefore, that, in order to let the English-language scholarly world know that Tasan was as much interested in philosophy as he was in politics and government administration, some of his philosophical works should be made available in English as well.

Such a project should begin by translating one or more of Tasan's commentaries on one of the Four Books, since the *Analects, Mencius, Great Learning* [*Daxue*], and *Zhongyong* constitute the core of the neo-Confucian philosophical canon. However, his commentaries on both the *Analects* and the *Mencius* require many volumes to be fully translated. An annotated translation of Tasan's commentary on *Mencius* into Korean consumes almost six hundred pages.[2] An annotated translation into English would require many more pages than that. The annotated Korean translation of Tasan's commentary on the *Analects* is even longer. It takes up five volumes.[3] Moreover, Hongkyung Kim, at Stony Brook University, is already working on a complete annotated English translation of Tasan's *Nonŏ kogŭmju* [Ancient and recent annotations to the Analects of Confucius]. As I write this, early in 2021, he has already published four volumes of what he plans to be a six-volume project.[4] Rather than burden a reader who is just getting to know Tasan with too many more dense pages to wade through, I have decided to choose something equally important but shorter to translate and annotate.

That leaves the *Daxue* and the *Zhongyong*. Both are much shorter than either the *Analects* or *Mencius*. Moreover, Tasan wrote more than one commentary on each of them. I chose to focus on his commentaries on the

Zhongyong because that text focuses on the moral psychology of Confucianism, which is particularly relevant to the modern age.

Tasan argued that, though both the *Daxue* and the *Zhongyong* focus on how to cultivate a "sincere" heart-mind (for Tasan, as for most Confucians, "sincerity" referred to a mental attitude which, instead of prioritizing individual benefit, was oriented instead toward thinking and acting the way we should think and act as members of the human community concerned about the common good), they are quite different texts. The *Daxue*, he believed, was written as a guide to the education of crown princes and others who would assume important roles in government.[5] The *Zhongyong*, on the other hand, provided advice for anyone who wanted to cultivate a sincere, and therefore moral, heart-mind.

Tasan also argued that the *Daxue* and the *Zhongyong* approached the cultivation of a sincere heart-mind in quite different ways. The *Daxue* took as its starting point the investigation of "things" (processes and events as well as actual things we interact with), a call to investigate both what had happened in the past (as recorded in canonical history books) as well as what was going on around us at the present time in order to identify guidelines to appropriate actions and interactions in any situation in which we may find ourselves. The *Zhongyong*, on the other hand, emphasized cultivating a constant awareness that the Lord on High (K. *Sangje* / C. *Shangdi*) was watching us, which, he believed, would stimulate an attitude of awe, caution, and apprehension, motivating us to engage in the strenuous effort necessary to cultivate and maintain a sincere heart-mind.[6]

In the busy world we live in today, we are constantly bombarded by audio and visual stimuli. As we go about our everyday life, we are unable to avoid being stimulated by music, advertisements, emails, and information on our smart phone screens. As a result, it has become more difficult than ever for us to concentrate on the tasks that confront us. In order to harmoniously and productively interact with the swarms of people who surround us, we need to cultivate the ability to focus, to pay attention to what is happening to us and around us. In order to do that, we need to avoid being distracted and keep our emotions under control. That is precisely the skill the *Zhongyong* teaches us to cultivate.

One of the two commentaries translated here, the *Chungyong ch'aek*, is much shorter than Tasan's two other commentaries on the *Zhongyong*. I chose to include a translation of that shorter work for readers who might want a quick overview, in Tasan's own words, of how he understood the *Zhongyong*. But why, of the two longer commentaries, did I choose the *Chungyong kangŭibo*, rather than *Chungyong chajam* [Admonitions for myself on reading the *Zhongyong*], to translate in full? (Though a translation of

Chungyong chajam is not included in this volume, to help the reader get a more complete picture of how Tasan read the *Zhongyong*, when Tasan makes a comment in *Chungyong chajam* that supplements or complements a comment made in *Chungyong kangŭibo*, I summarize that comment from *Chungyong chajam* in an endnote to a relevant section of the translation of *Chungyong kangŭibo*.) Unlike the *Chungyong chajam*, the *Chungyong kangŭibo* is more than just a simple commentary in which Tasan engages with what previous generations of scholars said that text means. He does that in *Chungyong kangŭibo*, of course, but he also does more than that.

Chungyong kanguĭbo was originally written as a response to questions posed by King Chŏngjo when Tasan was still a student at the National Confucian Academy in 1784. As a result, Tasan not only shows us how he read that text but also shows us how King Chŏngjo read it as well (or, in a few cases, how he challenged Tasan and the others by deliberately putting forward a provocative reading of particular passages to see how agile they were in responding to his provocation). In addition, when he first wrote his answers to the king's questions, Tasan consulted with his friend Yi Pyŏk. Yi Pyŏk is a significant figure in Korean philosophical and religious history since he played a crucial role in the formation of Korea's first Catholic community. However, he died in his thirties and did not leave much behind in the way of written records giving us access to his thinking. Tasan's accounts of his discussions with Yi Pyŏk, as recorded in the *Chungyong kangŭibo*, therefore give us insight into the thinking of Yi Pyŏk we cannot find elsewhere.

One more reason for focusing on the *Chungyong kanguibo* is that Tasan revised it two times, once in 1793 after participating in a discussion on the *Zhongyong* led by King Chŏngjo, and again in 1814 when he was in exile and was consolidating his thoughts on the various Confucian classics.[7] Since Tasan points out places in his text in which he corrected what he had written earlier, we are able to get a glimpse into how his thinking changed over the years.

In *Chungyong kangŭibo*, Tasan reveals why he placed so much importance on that particular text that he wrote three commentaries on it, and he revised one of those commentaries two times. He read that text as a practical guide to the project that concerned him the most: how to become a moral person, a person who consistently acts the way he knows he should act. He spent a lot of time and energy on the *Zhongyong* because he believed it tells us why we find it so difficult to consistently act the way we know we should act and also tells us the most effective way to overcome that moral frailty. (Human moral frailty was one of Tasan's guiding assumptions, a concern he made explicit several times.)

We can also see in Tasan's commentaries on this text the realistic approach of his moral psychology. For example, he makes clear that he disagrees with what he thought the dominant form of neo-Confucianism in Korea advised: that we should try to completely empty our heart-minds of all specific content. He writes that those neo-Confucians are wrong when they advise us to eliminate all thoughts and emotions. In his view, they are wrong because not only is that an impossible goal, it also would not be very useful. Instead, he suggests that we cultivate what he considers the best thoughts and emotions for helping us keep our self-centered emotions from distracting us so that we can focus on what we are supposed to focus on.[8]

He argues that reminding ourselves that the Lord on High is aware of our every thought and action will stimulate the emotions of caution and apprehension, and those emotions will inspire us to interact harmoniously, appropriately, and productively with our fellow human beings. We can see in his commentary that he moves away from the traditional focus on abstract universals, which he believed had weakened the moral force of neo-Confucian philosophy, toward a greater emphasis on the concrete particulars we encounter in everyday situations and the specific thoughts and emotions we need to navigate through them successfully. He adopts that practical stance in order to provide a philosophical foundation for what he believes are more realistic and more effective ways of cultivating a moral character that will be reflected in the ability to consistently act appropriately.

Tasan's Approach to Confucian Scholarship

Despite his many deviations from mainstream neo-Confucianism in Korea, which are obvious in his commentaries on the *Zhongyong* as well as in his commentaries on the other works in the Confucian canon, Tasan remained a Confucian. That is clear in the way he wrote philosophy, as well as in the sources he turned to for answers to philosophical and moral questions, the questions he asked those sources to answer, and the criteria he applied to the answers he found to determine if those answers were the type of answers he was looking for.

First of all, it is important to note that Tasan wrote in *hanmun* (Literary Sinitic), not in *han'gŭl*, the Korean vernacular script. I have never seen even one piece of writing by Tasan in *han'gŭl*. Even though, when he was in exile, he may have written letters to his wife in *han'gŭl*, the only versions of those letters we can see today are in *hanmun* in his collected works. Some claim that he wrote a few *sijo* poems, which are normally composed in Korean, not Literary Sinitic, but, if he did, those poems do not appear in his collected works. The many poems that appear in *Yŏyudang chŏnsŏ* [The complete works of Yŏyudang Chŏng Yagyong] are all in *hanmun*. No one suggests that any of his philosophical writings were in *han'gŭl*, even in draft form. If he wrote anything in the Korean vernacular script, his descendants and disciples did not consider it of sufficient intellectual weight to include in what they called the complete collection of his writings. Moreover, we can be sure that, when he was in a philosophical mood, he thought and wrote with the terminology and grammar of *hanmun*, not *han'gŭl*.

The language he used for his philosophical musings is important because, though the language people use does not dictate exactly how and what they can think, it strongly influences the sorts of ideas they find easier to entertain, the sorts of questions they are more likely to raise, and the sorts of answers they not only find easier to understand but also find more persuasive. It is, of course, possible to bend a language so that it can express thoughts that do not fit neatly into the grammatical and lexical restrictions of that language, but, at the same time, the language people write in channels the way people express their ideas. People find it easier to articulate ideas that fit easily into the grammatical structures of the language they are using.

Literary Sinitic grammar has three important grammatical features that are clearly reflected in neo-Confucian philosophical discourse of the sort Tasan engaged in. First of all, Literary Sinitic does not require a clear distinction between singulars and plurals. This allows for abstract concepts that refer to both differentiated particulars and an all-encompassing universal. *Li* (dynamic normative patterns) is one obvious example. It is easy in Literary Sinitic to write about *li* both as the universal cosmic network of patterns of appropriate interactions and as the more narrowly defined various specific *li* that determine how any individual entity within that cosmic network should behave. This blurring of the distinction between singulars and plurals allows abstractions, such as *li* and *ki* (C. *qi*—the matter-energy which constitutes the stuff *li* organizes into the universe composed of the specific objects and processes necessary for interactions to occur), to move more easily between the individual and the universal than can be done with a language that requires grammatical markers to distinguish the singular from the plural. Tasan fought against this homogenizing tendency by differentiating between specific concrete examples of such universals, such as the *ki* of the individual human body, and cosmic *ki* that animates the entire universe. He labeled cosmic *ki* "primal matter and energy" (K. *wŏn'gi* / C. *yuanqi*). *Ki,* in its primordial state, takes no fixed form. He differentiated that original *ki* from *ki* that has "congealed into the various separate and distinct entities that make up the universe today."[1] He focused more on specific configurations of *ki* than on cosmic *ki,* but he had to do so with a written language that made his philosophical project more difficult.

A second feature of Literary Sinitic relevant to philosophical discourse is that it does not clearly distinguish between nouns and verbs morphologically. That makes it possible for Sinographs that usually serve as nouns to function as verbs without changing their shape, blurring the distinction between what something is and what it does. An example would be the Confucian injunction to "relative our relatives" (K. *ch'inch'in* 親親 / C. *qinqin*). The Sinograph *ch'in* is used twice, but its use as a noun meaning "a relative" is preceded by the same Sinograph used as a verb to mean "treat a relative as you should treat a relative." (In other words, treat your father like you should treat your father.")[2] This blurring of the distinction between nouns and verbs results in a tendency to conceive of reality more in term of functions (verbs) than substances (nouns), focusing more on what happens rather than on what is. That is one reason neo-Confucianism was not as concerned with inert substances as Western philosophy, written in Indo-European languages, is. Moreover, this focus on action rather than existence, on what something did rather than on what it was, made it easier, in fact actually encouraged, thinking of interconnections, of things influencing each other through their interactions, instead of concentrating philosophical thought on isolated static entities.

The third feature that is central to the way writers who philosophize in Literary Sinitic phrase their questions and their answers is the blurring of the distinction between the descriptive and the normative. As can be seen in the phrase cited in the preceding paragraph, the Sinograph "relative," when used as a verb, means to treat a relative as you *should* treat that relative. *Li*, mentioned earlier, defines both why something is what it is, and why it should do what it should do. We see this blurring of the distinction between the descriptive and the normative in the early insistence by Confucius on the "rectification of names," in other words, that someone should not be called a ruler unless they acted the way a true ruler should.[3] We also see it in the neo-Confucian dyad *soyiyŏn/sodangyŏn* (C. *Suoyiran/suodangran*), the reason why something is defined the way it is, and the reason why things should function the way they should function.[4] As the Confucian injunction and the neo-Confucian dyad show, it is obviously possible to distinguish between the descriptive and the normative, between "the is" and "the ought." However, because the normative connotations of a term are often implicit and do not require a morphological signal to tell a reader that a name can also be an injunction, sometimes the distinction between the descriptive and the normative is blurred.

Tasan pushed against these tendencies, influenced possibly by the grammatical structure of the language he spoke (Korean makes it easy to distinguish plurals from singulars, to clearly distinguish between nouns and verbs, and to distinguish between statements and commands) and also possibly by the Catholic books written in Literary Sinitic he had read which also tried to point to distinctions normal Literary Sinitic did not call our attention to morphologically.

Because of the time and place in which he lived, Tasan was nevertheless forced to work within the Confucian intellectual universe not only in the language he wrote in and which influenced the way he expressed his thoughts, but also in the sources he used. Like generations of Confucian philosophers before him, Tasan did not claim to propose new philosophical approaches or concepts. He knew that, if he wanted his ideas to be taken seriously, they had to be presented as based on a close reading of the Confucian canon. That is why, though we can find some of his philosophical musings in some short essays he wrote as well as in letters he wrote to fellow Confucian-scholar friends, the clearest explications of his philosophy appear in his commentaries on the classics. He wrote lengthy commentaries on the ritual and history classics produced in ancient China but also dedicated much of his attention to the Four Books. The fact that he paid so much attention to the Four Books (*Analects, Mencius, Daxue,* and *Zhongyong*), and that he wrote two commentaries each on the latter two, shows that, though he may have rejected some of the central tenets of neo-Confucianism, he still worked within the philosophical framework it had constructed.

Daxue and *Zhongyong* were not considered separate "books" until Zhu Xi (1130–1200), the man given the greatest credit for erecting the intellectual edifice we now call "neo-Confucianism," extracted them from the *Book of Rites* [*Liji*] and placed them alongside the *Analects* and the *Mencius* as the most important works in the Confucian canon. Tasan accepted that neo-Confucian emphasis on those four texts. He also relied on major early Confucian and later neo-Confucian commentaries on them in his attempt to understand them. He could, and often did, disagree with what those commentators wrote, but nevertheless he felt compelled to refer to them. In his intellectual environment, to philosophize without reference to the Confucian canon and the commentaries on it would not be considered philosophy at all and would not attract the attention of other scholars Tasan hoped to sway to his philosophical outlook.

We can also see evidence that Tasan operated within a Confucian universe in the sorts of philosophical questions he addressed. For Tasan, as for neo-Confucian thinkers in general, philosophy was not an abstract search for the truth about what was and was not real. Instead, it was concerned primarily with ethical wisdom, in the sense of identifying guidelines on how to become a moral person. In particular, Tasan shared the mainstream Confucian concern for two interrelated goals: *sugi* (C. *xiuji*—cultivation of a moral character) and *ch'iin* (C. *zhiren*—managing one's interactions with others in an appropriate fashion). He believed that a Confucian was obligated to become the best person he could be, with the implicit assumption that a good person was a selfless person, someone who always thought in terms of, and acted in accordance with, the needs of their community rather than pursuing their own individual self-interest. Such a person would therefore be the best-qualified person to serve as a government official. *Ch'iin* literally means to govern others, and Tasan shared the Confucian belief that, in order to govern others appropriately, it was necessary to put the needs of the governed above the desires of the governing. *Sugi* and *ch'iin* were therefore related: those who had cultivated a moral character were the most qualified to serve in leadership positions, and those who served as leaders in a society should be people who had cultivated the proper moral character to do so effectively.

Tasan shared the Confucian assumption that the most effective way to become the sort of moral person who was qualified to assist the king in governing (true Confucian that he was, Tasan remained a believer in monarchy) was to engage in an intensive study of the Confucian classics, including the classics that contained explicit instructions on ritual and etiquette.

> When the core message of the classics is illuminated, then the essence of the Dao is manifest. Once the Dao is clear, then you can cultivate your heart-mind and rectify it. Once you have rectified your heart-mind, then you can act in a virtuous manner. That why I say you have to put all of your energy into studying the classics....
>
> When you engage in an illuminating study of ritual, then you will be able to focus on interacting with your fellow human beings appropriately and playing your proper role in society. Of the six major areas of rituals, that most important is mourning ritual. To understand ritual texts correctly, you have to read them over and over again, taking into account the way earlier generations of scholars have interpreted them. You have to pay special attention to Du You (735–812)'s *Tongdian* [Comprehensive Guide to Institutions] and then you should look at Zhu Xi's *Zhuzi jiali* [*Family Rituals*].[5]

It is important to note here that, although Tasan departs from traditional neo-Confucian philosophy in insisting that there is a Lord on High (*Sangje*) who watches our every thought and action, Tasan is less concerned about ritual interaction with that Lord on High (he believed such ritual interaction with the supreme supernatural personality was reserved for state officials acting in a public capacity) than he is with rituals that promote appropriate interactions with our fellow human beings. It is also important to note the emphasis he places on correct mourning rituals, and even on Zhu Xi's guidelines for those rituals. Nothing could be more Confucian than this.

Tasan, again thinking like a typical Confucian, understands ritual in a much broader sense than that implied by the English term "ritual." In his world, the term we translate as "ritual" refers not only to ceremonies, such as the rites with which we mourn our ancestors, but also to the politeness and sense of propriety we are supposed to display in our everyday interactions with our relatives, friends, neighbors, superiors, and subordinates. In such interactions, instead of "ritual" we should instead speak of "etiquette," but with the understanding that such relatively informal interactions are also governed by explicit rules. Those norms tell us how to act in accordance with the specific role in society we are playing in each concrete situation, taking into account not only any status differences between ourselves and the people we are interacting with but also what we should do in that situation to promote the common good rather than our own personal benefit.

Tasan was very much aware, as he made clear in his commentary on the *Zhongyong* as well as in his other writings, that it is not easy always to ensure that concern for the common good guides our actions. His commentaries also reveal that his primary concern in his explorations of the Confucian classics was to find in them practical advice on how to cultivate and nurture that moral state of mind, and how to develop the ability to consistently act in accordance with it. This ethical motive combined with a respect for what he believed was the original meaning of the classics (before, in his view, their message had been distorted by neo-Confucians) defined the path Tasan took that led him to some strikingly original interpretations of the *Zhongyong* and other classics, though both his ethical motive and his respect for the classics were characteristic of traditional Confucian scholarship as well.

In Tasan, as well as in the generations of Confucian scholars who preceded him both in China and in Korea, we can find four assumptions (often implicit rather than explicit) that determine the acceptability or unacceptability of interpretations of classical texts, which is the form philosophical assertions were expected to take.

First of all, interpretations of classical texts were acceptable interpretations only if they could be seen as encouraging acceptable behavior, with acceptable behavior understood in Confucian terms as behavior that was in accordance with the standard social norms of the times as well as privileging what was best for one's community over what was best for oneself personally.

Only those claims that encouraged proper behavior, or at least did not discourage such behavior, could be entertained as acceptable. The traditional Confucian values of loyalty, filial piety, propriety, and selfless dedication to the collective good were the touchstones, forming the court before which interpretations had to come to plead their case for acceptability. This moral pragmatism is evident in the way Tasan read the classics. As we will see in his argument for a belief that a Lord on High watches us at all times, Tasan argued for a theist reading of the Confucian classics on the grounds that belief in such a Lord on High would inspire us to greater efforts to think and act appropriately.

Equally critical was a grounding in a plausible reading of the Confucian canon. Tasan disagrees with the neo-Confucians from China's Song dynasty onward who argued that they had uncovered the true message of the classics that had been hidden for millennia. He rejected their imposition of their concept of *li* onto those ancient texts, as well as their insistence that those texts tell us that human beings are virtuous by nature, as distortions introduced by Buddhism. Instead, Tasan called for a return to what he considered was the way those texts had been read when they were first composed in the time of sages.

Textual coherence was the assumption that informed his attempt to recover what he considered the original meaning of those revered texts. He assumed that, though the various Confucian classics had been written by different people and in different centuries, they used the same key terms in the same ways. Once he uncovered what a term meant in a specific context in one canonical text, he assumed it meant the same thing in a similar context in another canonical text. For example, he read the reference in the first line in the *Zhongyong* to Heaven instilling in each and every one of us "human nature" (K. *sŏng* / C. *xing*, the ability to be aware of the appropriate way to behave and to be able to act in accordance with that awareness) as simply another way of stating what the *Book of Documents* says in its "Announcement of Tang" section, "the Lord of High has conferred a moral sense on even the inferior people."[6] Since both sentences tell us that we have received the moral side of our nature from on high, even though one says we received it from heaven and the other said we received it from the Lord on High, they both should be read as references to the Lord on High, with "Heaven" in this instance being nothing more than a metaphor for the Lord on High.[7]

Similarly, he concludes that the attitudes of awe and apprehension the *Zhongyong* encourages us to cultivate in our heart-minds is the same as the reverence and watchfulness King Wen of Zhou is said in the *Book of Songs* to have shown toward the Lord on High.[8] Tasan reads into a text composed centuries later the anthropomorphic deity of earlier texts.

The behavioral criteria for the acceptability of interpretations of the classics and the plausibility of those interpretations were interrelated. The type of behavior interpretations of the Confucian classics were expected to encourage was deemed acceptable because it was ordained by the classics. And, in addition to compatibility with a reasonable exegesis of the grammar and terminology of the passage under consideration, one reason a moral reading of the classics was considered plausible was because the classics were expected to teach human beings the proper way to behave.

In addition to appearing both moral and plausible, acceptable interpretations were also expected to have a Chinese pedigree. Though Tasan clearly was influenced by the Catholic books he read in his youth, he was usually careful to avoid specific terminology distinctive to Catholic texts. For example, he always referred to the Lord on High with the term *Sangje*, found in the Confucian classics, rather than using the Catholic equivalent, which was "Lord of Heaven" [K. *Ch'ŏnju* / C. *Tianzhu*]. And he never used the Catholic word for sin [K. *choe* / C. *zui*] when he discussed behavior that was immoral.

Moreover, even when he espoused such Catholic-influenced ideas as his assertion that the Lord on High was as an actual, conscious, all-knowing being[9] and that human beings could choose whether to act appropriately or not (in other words, that they had free will),[10] he grounded such assertions in original but nonetheless plausible readings of passages he located in classical Chinese Confucian texts. He did not even try to justify his exegesis with references to what his Korean predecessors had written about those same texts. Though he showed that he was well versed in what T'oegye Yi Hwang (1501–1570) and Yulgok Yi I (1536–1584), among others, had written, when he referred to Korean commentaries he did so only to reinforce interpretations he assumed he had already validated through his explication of ancient Chinese classics. He knew that unless he could make a persuasive argument that his ideas were not new but instead were simply a restatement of what sages in ancient China had written, no one, not even his own children, would take his ideas seriously. In fact, he was so deeply embedded in the Confucian intellectual universe that even he himself would not have considered many of the ideas he espoused worth entertaining unless he had convinced himself that they had ancient Chinese roots.

The fourth criterion is related to the third: acceptable philosophical arguments had to not only have Chinese roots, those roots had to be ancient. In a brief essay Tasan wrote on the Thirteen Classics, he said that all true learning has its roots in the time of Confucius and Mencius. Unfortunately, he added, it is human nature to be attracted to what is new and to lose interest in what is old, therefore much of that sagely learning from over two thousand years ago has been buried under layers of contradictory interpretations added by the generations that followed.[11] He saw his task as excavating the original teachings so that they could again serve as reliable guides to the pursuit of a moral character and the construction of a harmonious society. Because of his criticism of much of what appears in not only Song but also Tang and Han commentaries on those classics, even though he also read those commentaries carefully and clearly learned much from them, he is often described as dedicated to *susa* learning, the pre-Han Confucian tradition.[12] In Tasan's eyes, the older the better, and even though many of his interpretations would have appeared novel to his contemporaries, he insisted both to them and to himself that he was doing nothing more than uncovering what the sages of old really meant.

The patina of age, like a Chinese pedigree, was a necessary but not a sufficient condition for an interpretation of the classics to be acceptable. More important was moral applicability and hermeneutic plausibility. His primary concern was morality. He looked to the classics for advice on how to cultivate a moral character so that he could be the person he knew he should be, and wanted to be. We can call this moral pragmatism, since the truth value of interpretative statements was determined by whether or not they were seen as promoting proper behavior.

Tasan combined this pragmatism with respect for the past and for the texts it produced. He did not believe the Confucian canon was divinely revealed. Instead, he believed that the sages who wrote those ancient Chinese texts were sages because they could see much better than others could how we should behave. By understanding exactly what the sages wrote, we can see the way they saw and therefore gain the wisdom to act properly. It is this perceived need to learn exactly what the sages of ancient times actually meant that led Tasan to put so much emphasis on hermeneutics as a philosophical tool.

However, the question Tasan most often asked himself in testing the validity of his readings of the Confucian canon was: Had he read the texts in such a way that they encouraged proper behavior? If he concluded that the answer was yes, to him that meant he had read those texts correctly, that he had correctly identified the message the sages intended to convey in those ancient Chinese texts.

Tasan was not unusual in asking such questions of the texts, such as the *Zhongyong,* that he analyzed. In fact, his approach was a typical neo-Confucian approach (though he did put more stress on the original meaning of his texts and less on later commentaries than most other Confucians of his time did). Nevertheless, Tasan came away from his years of immersion in those texts with a very different way of reading them, one that attracts many scholars today because of its perceived relevance to the modern age as well as because of its originality. Though Tasan himself would not have wanted to be described as an original thinker (he believed he was simply passing on the wisdom of others who had lived more than two millennia earlier), we can see much evidence of his creative hermeneutics in the two of his discussions of the *Zhongyong* that are translated in this volume. Tasan was a Confucian thinker, but he was also an original thinker. We can see both qualities on display in those discussions.

4

Tasan's Approach to the Cultivation of a Selfless Orientation

Tasan, as we saw earlier, was an unusually prolific scholar. He wrote so much on so many different topics that it would be very difficult, if not impossible, to summarize his entire corpus in a chapter or two.[1] Fortunately, there is no need to do that to help readers understand these translations of two of his more philosophical works. Instead, it is only necessary to introduce some major features of his moral philosophy, especially those aspects of his thought that, because they differed from the Cheng-Zhu neo-Confucian thinking that occupied the mainstream in Korea, shaped the creative way he read the *Zhongyong*.[2]

The first noticeable feature of Tasan's thought is his unusual emphasis on human moral frailty, on how difficult it was to consistently adhere to the high standards Confucianism set for moral conduct. I noted earlier that Tasan had inherited much of his approach to Confucianism from T'oegye Yi Hwang and Sŏngho Yi Ik. They provided much of the philosophical foundation for his insistence that the standard Confucian claim that human beings possessed an innate power to act appropriately at all times was misleading in that it implied that all we had to do was recover that innate power to be the sages Confucianism told us we should be.

Sages, as both Tasan and neo-Confucians in general understood them, were those who always and everywhere acted appropriately, no matter what sort of situation they found themselves in, because they were free of the biases created by selfish emotions and concern for personal benefit and could therefore identify which actions would benefit the greater good and would then act in accordance with that selfless vision. Such consistent concern for the common good was expected to stimulate all those around them to also put their selfish interests aside and pursue cooperation and harmony instead. The result was supposed to be not solely a society in which all human beings played their proper roles and therefore harmony and peace prevailed in all under heaven but one in which even nature responded to the harmony thus established within the human community by functioning as it was supposed to function, with no droughts or floods or other natural threats to the human community.

This vision of sagehood was supported by the mainstream Cheng-Zhu neo-Confucian understanding of *li*. As pointed out earlier, *li* referred to the moral principles that define, stimulate, and direct appropriate human behavior. However, *li* meant much more than that. *Li* also referred to the totality of the dynamic patterns of appropriate interactions within both the human community and the universe in general. As was pointed out earlier, *li* was both a singular and a plural noun. As a singular noun, it referred to the all-inclusive network of intertwined appropriate interactions that constituted the entire universe. As a plural noun, it referred to the various *li* that make up that network. In other words, when used in a plural sense, *li* referred to individual examples of appropriate interactions. It was in that plural sense that mainstream neo-Confucians said that *li* constitutes human nature and informs the human heart-mind, directing it to act appropriately.

Each human being, because each human being occupied a distinctive node within the overall cosmic network (every human being had a different set of interactions he or she engaged in), had his or her own *li*, his or her own guiding principles. In fact, neo-Confucians went so far as to say that a person's *li* was complete within their own heart-mind, since, in their view, the heart-mind was the "vessel" that contained human nature, and human nature itself was nothing other than *li*.[3] As Zhu Xi noted, "*Li* was not a separate thing in front of us; instead, it resides in our heart-minds."[4] That means that *li* fills an individual's heart-mind, providing the patterns defining and directing appropriate interactions. Therefore, all human beings needed to do was identify the *li* in the various people, objects, and situations in which they found themselves and allow that *li* to resonate with their own internal *li*, stimulating them to act appropriately.[5] Neo-Confucians recognized that our psychophysical endowment, primarily our body and the emotions it generates, often blocks our internal *li* from fully engaging with the external patterns defining appropriate interactions and therefore we often do not act appropriately. However, they insisted, we are all capable of doing so and need only nurture our innate moral orientation (which, they believed, was best done through education and self-discipline) to achieve sagehood.

Ethical Virtuosity as Extraordinary Rather Than Ordinary

Despite this moral optimism, all neo-Confucians were aware that they themselves were not sages nor was anyone in their circle of acquaintances a sage.

Since neo-Confucianism was ultimately a moral philosophy aimed at the attainment of sagehood, this was a serious conundrum. They therefore had to find an explanation for their failure to achieve the goal their philosophy promised them was within their grasp. The solution was to blame *ki*. *Ki*, like *li*, is a difficult term to confine to one English equivalent, since it is applied to both matter (both amorphous and well-defined) and the energy that keeps that matter in motion. Moreover, both the primal, amorphous matter-and-energy out of which the universe is formed and the physical constitution of the individual material objects that constitute the universe, as well as the energy that animates those individual objects, are referred to as *ki*.

Neo-Confucians took advantage of this ambiguity in the meaning of *ki* to explain how *ki* interfered with the smooth operation of *li*. The moral vision of neo-Confucianism sees an ideal universe as one in which all individual entities cooperate with each other by playing their assigned roles within the cosmic network of *li*. That requires those individuals to function more as parts of a whole than as separate and distinct individuals. However, it is the very nature of *ki* that it coagulates into separate and distinct individuals. As pointed out by Yulgok Yi I (1536–1584), a man considered, alongside T'oegye and Tasan, to be one of the three most important philosophers during the Chosŏn dynasty, *li* is universal, penetrating everywhere and linking everything to everything else, but *ki* is limited and limiting, forming specific individual configurations.[6] If morality is defined as acting as parts of a whole rather than as distinct individuals, then *ki*, with its differentiating impact, must be held responsible for failures to do so.

The question then became how this individualizing role of *ki* should be dealt with. This question formed the basis for the most important Confucian philosophical debate in Korea over the course of the entire Chosŏn dynasty, the Four-Seven Debate. Though that debate over the relationship between the Four Sprouts of Virtue and the Seven Human Emotions is often interpreted today as a meaningless manipulation of metaphysical abstractions, it is more accurately understood as a debate over the best approach to understanding and overcoming human moral frailty.

T'oegye insisted that emotions which prompt us to act properly (the Four Sprouts) must be clearly distinguished from those emotions (the Seven Emotions) which can mislead us into putting our individual interests ahead of the interests and needs of others. The Four Sprouts (K. *sadan* / C. *shiduan*) are those instinctive human tendencies to commiserate with others, to be ashamed when we know we have done something we should not have done, to show respect and deference toward those we should respect and defer to, and to recognize the difference between right and wrong. Mencius pointed to these Four Sprouts of Virtue as evidence of the innate moral orientation of human beings.⁷ The Seven Emotions (K. *chiljŏng* / C. *qiqing*) are those fundamental feelings ascribed to human beings in the *Book of Rites:* joy, anger, sorrow, fear, love, hatred, and desire.⁸ T'oegye drew a sharp line between the Four Sprouts and the Seven Emotions in order to distinguish between those sentiments which can be trusted and those feelings which can lead people astray. In a famous letter to Ki Taesŭng (1527–1572), T'oegye penned these often-quoted and often-debated lines: "In the case of the Four Sprouts of Virtue, *li* issues them and *ki* follows along, while in the case of the Seven Emotions, *ki* issues them and *li* mounts them."⁹

This standard translation of those lines obscures the implications for moral cultivation of that formula. Only those who know that T'oegye is talking about *li* as the dynamic normative force that directs men away from the pursuit of individual self-interest into their proper roles in society can understand why he insists that it is *li* rather than *ki* which generates the Four Sprouts of Virtue. Only those who know that he is talking about *ki* in terms of its individualizing impact that separates human beings from one another and encourages them to pursue their own selfish self-interest can understand why he insists that it is *ki* rather than *li* that generates the more self-centered Seven Emotions.

T'oegye was making a practical rather than a metaphysical point. He was encouraging Ki Taesŭng to beware of feelings such as joy, anger, love, or hate which reflect self-interest and to cultivate instead feelings such as commiseration and shame, feelings which show a regard for others. T'oegye asserted, "In the case of the Four Sprouts of virtue, *li* issues them and *ki* follows along," in order to warn his friend to beware of selfish desires even when he was motivated primarily by moral impulses. However, some of Korea's neo-Confucians, including Yulgok, worried that T'oegye's advice to carefully distinguish between our thoughts and motives generated by *li* (the Four Sprouts) and thoughts and motives generated by *ki* (the Seven Emotions) threatened the essential unity of the universe. Since the ultimate goal of neo-Confucian moral endeavors was to act in unity with the cosmos, some feared that T'oegye's advice, despite the fact that it was well-intended, could actually end up introducing fissures into a universe that was supposed to operate as a unified whole. In correspondence with a disciple after T'oegye's death, Yulgok warned:

> T'oegye's approach splits man in half, putting his original nature in the east and his physical nature in the west. If we accept his analysis, we would also have to separate the moral heart-mind from the human heart-mind, saying that the moral heart-mind originates in the east and that the human heart-mind originates in the west. Does that make any sense?...Such

wild talk, at odds with the way things really are, can only led to behavior equally off the mark.... Positing such a split in human nature actually makes it much more difficult to act appropriately in our relationships with our fellow human beings.[10]

Both T'oegye and Yulgok agreed that how successful *li* is in providing direction is what determines the difference between good and evil. Any stirring of the heart-mind which is aligned with a pattern of appropriate interactions, any emotion which resonates with the cosmic network of harmonious interactions, is good. Any stirring of the heart-mind contrary to such a pattern, any emotion which works against that web of selfless harmony, is evil. But, since it is *ki* that stirs in both cases, Yulgok argued that it is a mistake to declare, as T'oegye did, that good is generated by *li* and evil by *ki*. In Yulgok's view, T'oegye's singular focus on the patterns of appropriate relationships as determining the good overlooks the equally salient fact that it is the appropriate interaction of individual elements within those patterns, elements composed of *ki,* which make up those patterns.

Though Tasan was open to Yulgok's ideas to a certain extent, he was a member of the Namin faction, which looked to T'oegye rather than Yulgok for guidance. He also shared Namin membership with Sŏngho Yi Ik, who, as we saw earlier, carried T'oegye's concern about the individualizing effect of *ki* further than T'oegye had and ended up championing what can arguably be called a Confucian ascetism. Tasan may have found the writings of T'oegye and Sŏngho persuasive not only because, as a Namin, he had been taught to do so, but also because he had come to share their recognition that it is not as easy to be moral as mainstream neo-Confucianism appeared to him to assert.

In 1795 Tasan left us a record of what he found attractive in T'oegye's writings. That was a year in which Tasan, according to his "Tosan sasungnok" [Notes on taking Yi Hwang as a model for self-cultivation], started each day by waking up at dawn and, after washing up, reading from the letters of T'oegye. Only then would he begin his official duties for the day. He took the notes we see in the "Tosan sasungnok" to help him in his efforts at moral cultivation.[11]

There are three points in the "Tosan sasungnok" we should take pay attention to. First of all, Tasan finds his own recognition of human moral frailty confirmed by T'oegye. Tasan noted that T'oegye had written that when we make mistakes, we have to try and try again to ensure that we do not make such a mistake again, since by doing that we finally become close to being the moral person we should be. However, Tasan asked, "can there really be a human being who doesn't slip up sometimes?"[12]

Second, Tasan finds Toegye's distinction between *li* and *ki* helpful for moral cultivation. Tasan writes that he agrees with T'oegye that we are influenced by both *li* and *ki*, and that *li* should be respected and *ki* should be viewed with disdain. Moreover, he agrees that since *ki* generates strong self-centered desires, we have to put effort into acting in accordance with *li* and training our *ki* to let *li* be in control. Tasan argues further that the difficulties we face in consistently acting the way *li* tells us to comes from the fact that *li* lies within *ki* like a resident living in a house. Just like we have to fix up the homes we live in, so, too, we have to work on improving our *ki*.[13] T'oegye therefore confirms for Tasan his recognition that consistently doing the right thing is not easy but instead requires a lot of effort.

Third, Tasan expresses his agreement with T'oegye's call for quiet sitting with a reverent attitude. He notes that, as he understands T'oegye, T'oegye is not calling for withdrawal from life. Rather, T'oegye recognizes that quiet sitting as well as examining ourselves while we are active are both necessary and, in fact, are inseparable. We have to calm our heart-minds by cultivating a reverent attitude so that we can be watchful over what we do or say when we are involved with the world around us later. Tasan also notes that he agrees with T'oegye that the best way to sit quietly is to cultivate an attitude of *kyŏng* (C. *jing*), which can be translated as either "mindfulness" or "reverence." Tasan adds that a reverent attitude is the foundation from which virtuous action can emerge.[14] I will return to the stress on the importance of a reverent attitude shortly, when I explain why Tasan came to believe in the actual existence of a Lord on High.

However, first we should examine Tasan's recognition of human moral frailty as well as how he tried to explain it. Confucians had long recognized that it was not easy to consistently act the way they knew they should act. After all, the ancient *Book of Documents* had included the phrase "the Human Heart-mind is dangerous. The Dao Heart-mind is difficult to discern."[15] This was explained by neo-Confucians as warning us that it is easy to be led astray by our self-centered thoughts and desires and that we have to concentrate to hear and heed what our conscience (our human nature) is telling us to do. Nevertheless, since Confucians assumed that we all have an innate tendency to follow our conscience, so that if we only know how we should act we will naturally do so, they thought that all we needed to do to become morally perfect, to become a sage, was to study and discipline our heart-mind and our body so that we would be able to hear and heed what our conscience was telling us. Tasan, however, believed, based on his own personal experience at trying to live a moral life, that it was not that easy.

In his discussion of the *Zhongyong*, he argues that *yong* (庸), the second character in the title of this classic, refers to consistency in the performance of ethical virtuosity, which is not an easy task. He notes that "In the *Zhongyong*, we can find the line 'the Dao cannot be departed from even for an instant.'" However, he adds, we also find lines that tell us "rare are those who can act in accordance with the Dao," and "there are those who cannot follow it for even a month."[16] Together, those lines are read by Tasan as saying that we are supposed to constantly act appropriately, yet consistently acting appropriately is difficult rather than natural and requires more than mere knowledge of how to behave.

In Tasan's opinion, Zhu Xi made a mistake when he said that the *Zhongyong* was telling us to act in accordance with the patterns of appropriate interactions in everyday life. (This is how Tasan understood Zhu Xi's statements that "the Dao is nothing other than the principles which govern what we should do in our everyday interactions"[17] and that "being consistently focused and composed refers to the patterns of ordinary appropriate behavior.")[18]

> The average person thinks that "the patterns of ordinary appropriate behavior" refers to the types of behavior they see in everyday life. They are surprised to hear people using that phrase to discuss the human ability to adhere to the Dao. They expect the Dao to be quite different from the type of interactions they are accustomed to. Indeed, if the Sages had taken the way the average person normally behaves and set that up as the Dao which is the model for guiding All-under-Heaven and regulating the lives of everyone, would we not see everyone adopting vulgar customs and lowering themselves to the level of the corrupt world, imitating the actions of village hypocrites?[19]

In Tasan's view, to act morally we have to rise above the ordinary. That requires us to work harder at being moral than we normally do as we go about our everyday life.

He insists, "Following the moral side of one's nature requires effort. It is fair to say that the moral side of human nature is fundamentally good and pure. However, equally natural human inclinations regularly lead people to sink into evil. We must devote all of our energy to following our moral human nature."[20] In a more concrete statement of his recognition of human moral frailty, Tasan adds that consistently doing the right thing and sticking to the moral path is as difficult as climbing up a steep hill. However, following our preference for physical pleasure is as easy as rolling down that same hill.[21] This is quite different from the usual neo-Confucian assumption that "with sincerity very little effort is required" to act appropriately in whatever situation we find ourselves in.[22]

Tasan's unusual (for a Confucian) emphasis on how difficult it was to be moral led him to challenge two key assumptions of neo-Confucian metaphysics and psychology. Neo-Confucians believed that everything in the universe was connected to everything else through the universal web of intertwined appropriate interactions (*li*). That meant that human beings, though they often acted otherwise, were actually embedded in the very moral fabric of the cosmos. In fact, since *li* was present within the human nature and the heart-mind that defined them as human beings, human beings were assumed to be essentially moral beings. Therefore, acting appropriately simply meant acting naturally.

However, claiming that human beings were integrated into the moral fabric of the universe made it difficult to explain why human beings so often failed to act morally. There was a strong tension in mainstream neo-Confucianism between the assumption that the cosmos, human beings included, was one vast moral network and the recognition that human beings frequently behaved in immoral ways and therefore behaved as though they were apart from, rather than a part of, that network. The Four-Seven Debate, the debate over the relationship of the Four Sprouts and the Seven Emotions respectively to appropriate behavior, arose as one attempt to resolve that contradiction. As we saw a few pages earlier, when T'oegye tried to pull *li* and *ki* apart in an effort to explain why we act contrary to our own true nature, Yulgok complained that was a threat to the moral necessity to rise above a self-centered outlook and envision both our own heart-minds and the world about us as so tightly connected and interwoven that they constituted a unified web of intertwined entities existing and acting together.

Extricating Human Beings from the Universe

Tasan's solution to this Confucian dilemma was a radical one: he challenged both the unity of human psychology (going much farther than T'oegye had done in that regard) and the unity of the cosmos. In the apt phrasing of one North American scholar of Tasan's philosophy, Tasan "extricated man from the universe."[23] He had concluded that was the only way to explain why human beings, more often than not, failed to act in harmony with their social and natural environment.

To do that, first he had to dismantle the neo-Confucian holistic vision of the universe. Tasan launched a frontal assault on the core neo-Confucian notion that human beings form one *ch'e* [C. *ti*] with the universe. That notion is rooted in Zhang Zai's *Western Inscription* and its call for us to see everything in the universe as connected to us in such a way that we should treat everyone and everything with the same selfless concern we should display in interacting with members of our own families. Zhang's actual statement was "That which extends throughout the universe I regard as my *ch'e*.... All people are my brothers and sisters, and all things are my companions."[24] This statement of the interconnectedness of everything, and its moral implications, came to be phrased as "heaven and earth and all things form one *ch'e*" and "the myriad things form one *ch'e*."[25] The term *ch'e* literally means "body," but in this phrase it is often translated as substance. That is a somewhat misleading translation, since *ch'e* here does not refer to anything tangible. Instead, it is a reference to the unity resulting from the fact that everything in the universe shares in the productive potential of the cosmos, and everything is linked to everything else through participation in the all-encompassing network of patterns of appropriate interactions.

Tasan was not bothered by the ethical implications of this statement. He shared the assumption that we should always think and act as members of a community and therefore should be concerned about the common good rather than thinking and acting as separate and distinct individuals concerned more about what is best for ourselves. However, he was bothered by what he saw as the ontological implications of this statement.

Tasan chose to read *ch'e* in its literal meaning of "body." Tasan may have been influenced by Matteo Ricci's introduction to Catholicism, the *Tianzhu shiyi*, a work Tasan read when he was in his early twenties.[26] In that introduction to Catholic theology, Ricci explicitly denounced the neo-Confucian notion that all things form one substance (which is what Ricci thought *ch'e* meant). Ricci argued that if there were no real substantial differences between fathers and sons, rulers and subjects, and elders and juniors, then Confucian moral principles were meaningless, since those principles consisted primarily of rules governing how human beings should interact with other human beings as separate and distinct individuals within a hierarchical social order.[27] In addition to being influenced by Ricci, Tasan may also have interpreted the term *ch'e* in that context the way he did because he favored a literal reading of Sino-Korean characters when a literal reading appeared to him to be most appropriate in that particular context. Tasan believed that, in this context, *ch'e* should be understood as "body," with "body" understood as implying the physical potential to act appropriately. Since different types of entities have very different potential ways of acting, Tasan appears to have found it hard to accept the assertion that they all shared the same *ch'e*. Whatever his reason, Tasan rejected the mainstream neo-Confucian assertion that all things were connected by a common *ch'e*.

Tasan insisted that it is contrary to both the words of the classics and the reality of the physical universe to say that all the things in the universe share one "*ch'e*." "How could that mean that I have the same potential as the grasses and trees or as the birds and beasts?" he asked. He notes that he never saw such an expression anywhere in the classics. He says it is acceptable to say that all men are brothers, as the *Western Inscription* says, but it is not acceptable to say we have the same *ch'e* as plants and animals.[28] Instead, the world is composed as separate entities, with human beings very different from animals, both humans and animals very different from plants, and all three very different from inanimate objects such as rocks and water.

Tasan shared Ricci's Christian focus on the world we live in and act in as composed of separate and distinct entities rather than accepting the mainstream neo-Confucian assumption of an underlying unity because of his own personal experience with self-cultivation. In mainstream Cheng-Zhu neo-Confucianism, since human beings, like everything else in the universe, are inextricably intertwined with the cosmic network of appropriate relationships that constitutes the universe, human nature is essentially good. In other words, it is in our very nature to act in accordance with the cosmic network in which we are embedded.

However, Tasan, in reflecting on his own attempts to consistently adhere to the demanding moral principles of Confucianism, realized that he interacted with people and the world around him as a separate and distinct individual. That was the only way he could explain his inability to live up to his own high moral standards. He found it a challenge to coordinate his thoughts and actions with the universal network of appropriate interactions he was supposedly an integral part of. Tasan seized upon the notion of individual entities, and therefore individual potential, as a way to explain his own moral frailty and that of humanity in general. Our tendency to act on our own rather than as part of a community suggested to Tasan that we are more separate and distinct individuals than the assertion that "all things share one *ch'e*" implies.

Once he had adopted a perspective emphasizing differences and individuality rather than commonality, Tasan found that other neo-Confucian terms also had to be redefined. *Li*, for example, could no longer serve as the glue that kept everything in the universe connected to everything else. As noted earlier, the term *li* in classical Sino-Korean can be either singular (the one *li* that unites everything in the universe in an all-encompassing network of patterns of appropriate interactions) or plural (with each thing in the universe having its own *li* for its particular role in that network). Tasan insisted on using *li* only with the plural meaning. He wrote that there is no one universal *li* for the entire cosmos. Rather, each and every distinct thing has its own *li*.[29] Such metaphysical pluralism has practical implications. It is much easier to act appropriately in particular situations if we have specific *li* to guide us rather than try to find guidance from *li* that are so general that they apply to every possible situation.

Tasan also unraveled the mainstream neo-Confucian link between unconscious appropriate action by natural objects within the natural world and conscious appropriate action by human beings. He distinguishes the Dao as the Patterns of Cosmic Harmony from the Dao as the path human beings should follow from their birth until their death. The two, he writes, are totally different, despite the fact that they are written with the same Sinograph. He insisted that the Dao of Cosmic Harmony, of yin and yang, has nothing in common with the Dao of human behavior. Tasan warned against being confused by the neo-Confucian use of the term "Dao" for both the path nature followed and the path men should follow. He maintained that the patterns of proper behavior men must work hard to align their thoughts and actions with have nothing in common with the patterns of movement naturally followed by objects such as the sun and the moon. To confuse the two, because they happen to be called by the same name, is to downplay how much more difficult it is for a human being to be good than it is for the moon to follow its regular path through the sky.[30]

In his rejection of the neo-Confucian holistic vision that assumes that all things share the same *ch'e,* and that the Dao of nature is the same as the Dao of human beings, Tasan shows that he prefers the more concrete and specific to the universal and what he considers the vacuous and imprecise. He also displays a willingness to think analytically in order to identify differences in situations in which neo-Confucians often focused on pointing to unity.

One significant example of Tasan's interest in breaking things down into their component elements rather than emphasizing how those component elements work together in a unified fashion is his treatment of human nature, that which makes human beings human beings rather than animals or plants. Since Tasan believed that human beings do not share the same *ch'e* or the same *li* with other things, and he believed that there was more than one Dao in the universe, he was able to look at human nature and see that it, too, is best analyzed into different components rather than treated as a unified whole. He used the same Sinograph (K. *sŏng* / C. *xing*) that is normally translated in a neo-Confucian context as "human nature." Neo-Confucians used that term in the narrow sense of both the tendency and the ability to exercise ethical virtuosity. Tasan believed that was an oversimplification of what actually made human beings, human beings rather than animals.

The neo-Confucian narrow definition of human nature, Tasan argued, overlooks the fact that there are contrary tendencies within the heart-mind of every human being. That is a dangerous mistake to make because only if we recognize that there are opposing tendencies within us can we ensure that we push the tendency to act inappropriately aside so that the correct tendency generates our thoughts and directs our actions.

Tasan noted in his autobiographical epitaph that he has argued that it is a mistake to say that our heart-mind is pure goodness. Instead, he writes, "our heart-mind allows us to act both appropriately and inappropriately. Moreover, it is difficult to do the right thing, but it is much easier to violate our moral standards and act in a way we should not."[31]

Mainstream neo-Confucians, as noted a few pages earlier, recognized that there are two aspects of our heart-mind, a "Dao Heart-mind" that tells us to act appropriately and a "Human Heart-mind" that encourages us to pursue individual self-interest. However, they tended to treat the moral "Dao Heart-mind" as the only true human nature. In Tasan's view, that would mislead us into thinking that it was easier to be moral than it actually was. If we only had to act to accordance with our true nature, and our true nature was moral, then all we had to do to be moral was act naturally.

In his discussion with King Chŏngjo about the *Zhongyong,* Tasan challenges this standard neo-Confucian understanding of human nature. He writes that the phrase in the first chapter that "That which Heaven has conferred on us is called our nature [*xing*]" should not be narrowly read as referring only to our ability to act appropriately. Instead, it should be interpreted in light of how Mencius uses the term *xing*. Tasan says Mencius clearly uses that term to mean "human inclinations," both moral inclinations and preferences for physical pleasure.[32] Tasan points out that those two inclinations, the aspiration for the good of morality and the proclivity for the good of physical pleasure, are often in conflict. For example, he pointed out that if someone offers us a gift that could be interpreted as a bribe and, therefore, we know it would be wrong to accept it, we are torn between a yearning for the pleasure that gift would give us and the desire to act appropriately and decline it. Similarly, if we find ourselves in a difficult situation but we know we should deal with that situation, we nevertheless are tempted to simply flee and abdicate our responsibilities.[33]

This conclusion that human beings, though they have only one heart-mind, are often conflicted leads him to the logical conclusion that human beings are not ethical virtuosos from birth. In other words, he insists that ethical virtuosity is not natural in the sense of being innate. We are not born acting morally. In fact, he argues, no one can be called moral until he or she acts in a moral manner. Only after you act benevolently toward another human being can you be called benevolent. Only after you entertain a guest with proper etiquette can you be called polite. Only after you act ethically can you be called righteous. And only after you show that you can distinguish between what is right and what is wrong, and then act accordingly, can you be called wise.[34] The most we can say, he argues, is that human beings have from birth an instinctive attraction toward the moral good, along with a natural longing for the pleasurable.[35]

If human beings are not naturally moral, and, in fact, are torn between conflicting desires, then is it possible nonetheless for human beings to achieve the Confucian goal of being able to consistently think and act appropriately? Tasan is still Confucian enough to answer in the affirmative, though he notes that living a moral life is not as easy as mainstream Neo-Confucians would have us believe. As noted earlier, he points out that in actuality consistently doing the right thing and sticking to the moral path is as difficult as climbing up a steep hill, and following our preference for physical pleasure and personal benefit is as easy as rolling down that same hill.[36] Such an accurate observation of actual human tendencies is a prime example of Tasan's practical and realistic spirit. He insists on looking at human beings as they actually are rather than how we wish they were.

Mainstream neo-Confucianism assumed that to ensure that you acted appropriately at all times you needed to study the Confucian classics so that you would learn the right way to act.[37] You also needed to train your body and your heart-mind to subdue or even eliminate self-centered emotions so that you would be able to see the moral lessons in those classics clearly and could also see clearly how those lessons should be applied in whatever situation you found yourself in. In other words, education, as well as clarity of vision, was all you needed to live a moral life, as long as you were determined to do so. Tasan argued that it was not that easy.

Tasan and the Problem of Moral Frailty

To Tasan, saying all you needed was education, clarity of vision, and determination to live a moral life sounded simplistic. As we just saw, he concluded, based on his own personal experience as well as on his reading of the Confucian classics, that there are, in practical terms, two sides of human nature. This led him to the logical conclusion that being moral requires more than just a determination to act appropriately. It requires choosing between acting appropriately and acting inappropriately.

Mainstream Confucians talked about the need to resolve to do what is right. The Sinographs for resolve (K. *ipchi* / C. *lizhi*, literally "establish your will") imply determination, making up your mind to do what is right rather than choosing between alternatives, one moral and one not. Tasan recognized from his own personal experience that it was more difficult than that. For example, he writes "that there may be times when we find some delicious-looking food placed in front of us. That may cause our mouths to water and we will want to eat it. However, that may be food we are not supposed to eat. If we make the decision to not partake of that forbidden food, then we are acting in accordance with the conscience Heaven has endowed us with."[1] ("The conscience Heaven has endowed us with" is a translation of *ch'ŏnmyŏng* [C. *tianming*], literally, "the moral principles Heaven has ordained for us," implying also the ability Heaven has bestowed on us to recognize those moral principles.) Tasan points out that it takes a deliberate choice to refrain from eating that food. Therefore, we cannot say that human beings naturally act appropriately. In fact, if we look around us and see how other people behave, as well as how we ourselves behave, we cannot help but conclude that rather than naturally acting appropriately, we are actually quite morally frail, prone to self-centered and therefore inappropriate and immoral behavior.

Tasan argues out that the main reason we cannot say that we naturally act appropriately is that, unlike animals, we human beings have been given free will, the ability to choose to do what is right or to not do what we should do. A term he coined for "free will" is literally "the power of self-control" (K. *chaju chi kwŏn* / C. *zizhu zhi quan*).² The Sinograph he used for "power" here also appears in another term he used to describe the unique human ability to weigh the alternatives in a particular situation and then determine the most appropriate way to act.³ That term (K. *kwŏnhyŏng* / C. *quanheng*) can be used to mean to "weigh the pros and cons of something" as well as to "consider the alternatives in a situation you find yourself in order to determine the appropriate way to behave in that situation." Tasan choose the components of his neologisms carefully. He wanted to emphasize that we have the ability to think before we act, weighing the various alternatives before us to see which course of action is the more appropriate in the specific circumstances facing us. He also points out that the power to choose is real. We are often faced with two contradictory inclinations, one for what will benefit us personally in the short term and one for what is both better for us in the long term and serves the common good. We are not like animals, whose actions are determined by instincts. We have the power to decide for ourselves what to do. Moreover, that is a power we must exercise properly if we want to fulfill the potential for virtue that we were born with.⁴

Free will had not been a part of Confucian or neo-Confucian discourse before Tasan introduced it. Instead, neo-Confucians had talked of the need to "make our intentions sincere" as a necessary prerequisite for rectifying our heart-minds, a line they took from the opening chapter of the *Daxue*. ("Sincere" [K. *sŏng* / C. *cheng*] here means the absence of selfish concerns and biases.) Rectifying our heart-minds was, in turn, a prerequisite for acting appropriately. They had also talked of the will controlling the body, drawing on a line in *Mencius*,⁵ but the term used for will in this passage means to be determined to act properly rather than to freely weigh alternatives and then decide to do what is right. Since neo-Confucians believed that human beings were instinctively inclined to act appropriately, they also believed that if we only erased selfish biases from our heart-minds, we would see clearly what the right course of action in any situation was. There was no need for any agonizing over what to do. Once we saw clearly the right course to take, and were determined to follow that course, weighing of alternatives was unnecessary.

When Tasan discussed this passage in *Mencius*, he glossed "will" as "what you want to do" rather than "what you decide to do." He said that when Mencius declared that our will controls our bodies, he was telling us that we should always be conscious of which emotions are "willing" us to act so that we can calm any self-centered emotions to keep them from stimulating us to act inappropriately. In other words, Tasan argues that Mencius is telling us to think before we let our will tell us how to act.⁶

Tasan then declares that those who debate whether human beings are innately good or bad are ignorant of the fact that at birth we have preferences and inclinations, but we have not yet acted in accordance with those natural tendencies. We cannot yet be called good or bad at birth. It is what our preferences are preferences for, and whether they are nurtured or disregarded, which determines whether a person can later be said to be a good person. If we are drawn to a moral good, and act in accordance with that inclination, we act appropriately and therefore can be called good. However, if we let a selfish yearning for personal pleasure or benefit determine our behavior, then we will act in inappropriate ways and can be labeled a bad person. At birth, we are merely endowed with the potential to act either way.

Tasan asserts that if human beings are ethical virtuosos from birth, as he thought neo-Confucians implied, then for people to act appropriately and morally would be as easy as it is for water to roll downhill and for fire to flame upward. If that were the case, acting appropriately would be no great accomplishment. We would no more praise a person for being moral than we would praise a deer for acting in accordance with its nature and living in a forest rather than a village. However, Heaven has endowed human beings with the ability to make their own decisions. If they choose to do what is right, then they can do what is right. But if they prefer to act in an immoral fashion, then they can do that as well. This is what makes human beings different from animals. And that is what makes living a moral life an accomplishment, and that is the reason we condemn those who act immorally.[7]

Tasan then goes on to warn against an oversimplified picture of what leads human beings toward a virtuous life and what draws them down into vice. He decries the tendency to blame all our faults on our bodies and the physical desires for food, sex, and comfort they generate. He points out that our immaterial heart-minds are not completely blameless. If all evil comes from things material, then, he asks, how can we explain the existence of troublesome and even malevolent spirits? Moreover, human beings can be led astray by such emotions as inordinate pride and arrogance. Such emotions come from our heart-minds, not our bodies. We cannot blame our bodies when we get angry because someone has criticized our scholarship or our writing skills. It is our pride based in our heart-mind, he argues, that causes us to get angry in such a situation.[8]

Tasan depicts a world that was much more dangerous than Confucians normally assumed it was. As Tasan saw it, not only were we not born already ethical virtuosos, we could not simply relax and let our innate moral orientation direct our thoughts and actions since it had to vie with selfish tendencies that were as much a part of us from birth as our longing to live moral lives was. Instead, we had to choose over and over again between a moral good and a tempting alternative. Moreover, we could not rely on simply disciplining our body to keep us on the right track, since our heart-mind could also lead us astray.

To make matters more dangerous, not only are human beings born with both a longing for the moral good and a yearning for personal pleasure and personal benefit; humans are also a combination of the material and the spiritual (the nonmaterial). Mainstream neo-Confucians dismissed any sharp distinction between the material and the spiritual side of life. They believed that every entity in the phenomenal world, from spirits to human beings, was formed from *ki*, matter-energy. Tasan disagreed. He argued that human beings were a unique, subtle mixture of the material and the spiritual.[9] In mainstream neo-Confucian writing, the spiritual could refer to simply a more ethereal form of *ki*.[10] That is not how Tasan used that term. He drew a clear line between the material and the spiritual realms. In discussing Chapter XVI of the *Zhongyong*, a chapter that discusses the power of spiritual beings, Tasan states explicitly, "spirits have no bodies. They have no physical constitution. Even the smallest physical object has more mass than spirits do."[11] In another commentary on that chapter, he states that spirits are neither *li* nor *ki*.[12] This is a radical challenge to mainstream neo-Confucian thinking, which divided all there was into the realm of that which had form (the realm of *ki*) and that which was above the realm of forms (the realm of *li*) and left no room for anything that was neither *li* nor *ki*.

By dividing human beings into material and spiritual components, and by positing that there was a third realm beyond *li* and *ki*, Tasan threatened the very foundations of the neo-Confucian moral vision. Neo-Confucians valued unity above all. They understood unity as the intertwined, harmonious interactions of all that was, working together for the common good. Understood this way, unity equaled morality (that is why "harmonious" is part of that definition. Harmony was a key Confucian ethical value). Anything that threatened unity, anything that threatened to break up the universe into separate and distinct realms, would render the pursuit of the common good more difficult and was therefore a danger to the very foundations of moral behavior.

Tasan shared the neo-Confucian assumption that moral behavior meant interacting with everyone around us in such a way that we put any concern for personal advantage aside and pursued the common good so that a harmonious society, one in which we all played our respective roles to the best of our abilities, resulted. However, he came to believe that we all too often failed to cooperate and interact appropriately with others because we mistakenly believed that all we had to do to be moral was recognize our place in the cosmic network of appropriate interactions (the network formed by *li*) and let our own true nature, as defined by *li*, direct our thoughts and behavior. The assumption that we were an integral component of an all-encompassing moral network blinded us to how difficult it actually was to act appropriately. Thinking it was supposed to be easier to be moral than it actually was, we failed to exert the necessary effort needed to overcome our own selfish tendencies.

In order to point us in what Tasan believed was the right direction, the direction that would help us overcome our moral frailty, Tasan broke away from neo-Confucianism in two more major areas. He demoted *li*, denying it the core role it played in the neo-Confucian universe. And he added to that universe a conscious supernatural personality, the Lord on High.

He zeroed in on the standard neo-Confucian interpretation of the line in *Mencius* that reads, "Order and righteousness delight our heart-minds like meat delights our mouths."[13] Cheng Yi (1033–1107) had claimed that "order" means "patterning principle" (it is written with the same *li* Sinograph) and therefore is the same thing as righteousness. That interpretation leads further to the identification of both patterning principle and righteousness with the innate human ability to act appropriately, since they all "delight out heart-minds." Tasan insists such an interpretation of that line is a misunderstanding of the Sinograph *li*. Showing his preference for a literal reading of the meaning of a Sinograph, he writes that *li* originally referred to the patterns in a piece of jade. It was extended to mean appropriate patterns, since jade carvers were supposed to follow the natural patterns in the pieces of jade they were carving. It thus came to be used to mean natural patterns, and action that is in accord with those patterns, and was used with that meaning in the *Zhongyong,* in the *Book of Changes,* and by Mencius. Tasan argues, however, that it is quite a leap from that concrete meaning of that term to use it for the cosmic immaterial force paired with *ki*, cosmic material force. It is also quite a leap to use that term for the moral potential heaven has endowed us with, and to contrast it with the *ki* that generates the Seven Emotions. He insists there is no basis in the ancient texts for thus equating *li* with human nature.[14]

A few pages later, Tasan again accuses Song neo-Confucians of imposing interpretations on the *Mencius* that the text itself does not support. Commenting on the statement by Mencius that "To fully fathom one's heart is to understand one's nature. To understand one's nature is to understand heaven,"[15] Tasan charged Cheng Yi with distorting what Mencius was actually saying. Tasan noted that, starting with Cheng Yi, generations of Confucian scholars have used that statement to support their assertion that everything in the universe, no matter whether it is material or immaterial, conscious or unconscious, is embraced by the one universal *li*, which is identified with "one's heart-mind" and "one's nature" and even with Heaven. However, Tasan points out, this is a relatively late development in Confucianism, derived from the way Buddhists talk, and has no warrant in the language of the Confucian classics. Besides, he asks, how could an all-embracing *li*, which would be immaterial, have no emotions, and be unconscious, possibly function as the *li* of entities that take a concrete material form, are conscious, and have emotions? Rather than a universal *li*, there must be separate and distinct *li* for the various separate and distinct entities and processes in the cosmos.[16]

Tasan went even further in demoting *li* from the central role it played in neo-Confucian moral metaphysics. In delving into the intricacies of the debate in Korea over whether the Four Sprouts and the Seven Emotions should be treated as separate, such that the Four Sprouts (the four fundamental virtuous instincts) are seen as generated by *li* and the Seven Emotions by *ki* (T'oegye's position), or whether the Four Sprouts should be treated as a subset of the Seven Emotions and therefore *ki* alone should be granted generative power (Yulgok's position), Tasan adopted a position closer to Yulgok's. However, his terminology went far beyond what Yulgok had been willing to say. Tasan stated that, unlike *ki*, *li* was nothing more than an attribute, dependent on something substantial. "*Ki* is something that exists on its own, and *li* can only be found in connection with something else."[17] By demoting *li* to the status of the insubstantial, he undermined the traditional order that viewed *li* as superior to, and in command of, *ki*.

In another departure from the usual way neo-Confucians thought of *li*, Tasan, just as he did with the Dao, argued that *li* should be divided into the *li* as a cosmic force, in which case his definition above, that *li* is dependent on *ki*, applies, and *li* as an independent moral force, which, he argued, is a more useful way to think of *li* when we are trying to distinguish between moral and immoral thoughts springing up in our heart-mind.[18] This is more evidence that Tasan is more interested in how he can apply philosophical concepts to specific situations, especially moral practice, than he is in trying to continue the neo-Confucian project of constructing a unifying vision of the cosmos. His personal moral experience told him that it was useful to think of *li* having its own generative power within his heart-mind, though *li* was dependent on *ki* in the external material world. That is the pragmatic reason for the way he conceived the single Sinograph *li* to be dependent on the context in which it was applied.

However, though granting that it was useful to think of *li* as having moral generative power when we were trying to distinguish between moral and immoral thoughts and emotions, he refused to go further and join what he saw as a mainstream neo-Confucian tendency toward identifying *li* with human nature and the heart-mind. He insisted that Zhu Xi, as Tasan understood him, was wrong when he said that the heart-mind is *li,* and *li* is nothing other than the human nature Heaven has endowed us with. Instead, Tasan argued, though what Heaven has ordained for us (guidelines for appropriate behavior) and conferred on us (the ability to know those guidelines) can be known by our heart-mind, it does not constitute our heart-mind. Instead, our moral heart-mind is our capacity to actualize our natural tendency to prefer the good and dislike that which is not good.[19] Heaven has provided as the moral side of our human nature guidelines for what we should desire, and it has given our heart-minds the ability to recognize those guidelines, but it has not made them the sole determinant of what we think and do. We have to use another function of our heart-mind to choose to act according to those guidelines Heaven has given us. To do so, we have to overcome the other side of our nature, the side which tells us to pursue pleasure and personal benefit. *Li* helps us in that project by serving as moral guidelines, that's all. In Tasan's philosophy, *li,* which in mainstream neo-Confucianism has served as one of the two forces forming the universe and the only force giving it moral import, has been demoted to nothing more than passive moral principles.

Overcoming Moral Frailty with Confucian Theism

If we do not naturally act appropriately all the time, and if we cannot even trust our heart-mind to always tell us the right way to behave, then what can we do to ensure that we lead as moral a life as possible? Tasan again comes up with an untraditional answer, grounded in his untraditional reading of the Confucian classics. He says that we need to be shamed into doing the right thing instead of acting inappropriately. And the only way we can be sure that we will be ashamed every time we do something wrong is if we keep in mind that, always and everywhere, we are being watched to see if we think and act properly. Who can possibly watch us always and everywhere? There is only one possible answer: the Lord on High, whom he called by the ancient Confucian name *Sangje* (上帝 / C. *Shangdi*).

Tasan, as we saw in chapter 3, believed that the only acceptable ideas were those grounded in a plausible reading of the Confucian classics. That caused somewhat of a problem for his call for belief that there was a supernatural personality called the Lord on High. The Four Books, which he accepted as the core Confucian texts, rarely mentioned a personal deity. They did not mention *li,* in the neo-Confucian sense, either. However, he had used the failure of the Confucian classics to refer to *li* as a key metaphysical concept as part of his argument against granting *li* the important role neo-Confucians awarded it. Therefore, if he wanted to claim that his philosophy was drawn from the Confucian classics, he had to find passages in those classics that could be read as supporting belief in the existence of a supernatural personality above.

To do that, he looked at Confucian texts that predated the Four Books. Reversing the neo-Confucianism tendency to impose on the oldest Confucian classics a metaphorical meaning of terms like *Sangje* and Heaven, Tasan insisted that they should be read literally as referring to an actual supernatural personality dwelling in heaven above. Tasan extrapolated from explicit references to the Lord on High in such ancient texts as the Book of Documents [*Shangshu*] to later texts, such as *Mencius* and *Zhongyong,* in which a reference to a powerful anthropomorphic force above is not as clear.

For example, Tasan interjects spiritual beings into the passage in the *Zhongyong* that reads, "the man of noble character exercises utmost restraint and vigilance towards that which is inaccessible to his own vision, and he regards with fear and trembling that which is beyond the reach of his hearing."[20] Tasan explains that this passage should be understood as follows:

> As for what is "inaccessible to his own vision" and what is "beyond the reach of his hearing," that refers to the spirits who observe us from above.... There is an old saying that "In a dark room, you may deceive yourself, but the spirits' eyes can see right through the dark."[21] This is the way to interpret what this classic is saying here. If Heaven did not watch over us both when we are quiet and when we are active, there would be no need to remain circumspect and attentive after we finished practicing quiet sitting.[22]

Tasan applies the same interpretive strategy to his reading of the opening passage of the *Zhongyong*. He reads the line saying, "That which Heaven has conferred on us is called our innate ability to act appropriately [human nature, *xing*]," as stating that Heaven, which he reads as a reference to the Lord on High, endows every human being with a tendency to prefer the good over the nongood. It is that desire for the good that he says is referred to in this reference to "human nature."[23]

To support his reading of such references to Heaven as actually references to a supernatural personality called the Lord on High, Tasan had to go beyond the Four Books and look at all Thirteen Classics. In the Confucian classics predating the Four Books, there are several explicit references to a Lord on High. The Four Books, however, tended to talk of Heaven rather than the Lord on High. Tasan claimed that references to Heaven in the Four

Books were just another way to refer to the Lord on High. "We call the Lord on High who rules over the universe 'Heaven' metaphorically, just as we refer to the king of a country as simply 'the state' because it would be rude to refer to him by his full title."[24] Tasan may have been pointed in that direction by Matteo Ricci, who used those same lines from the oldest Confucian classics to argue that Chinese had once believed in a personal Lord on High. After all, Tasan had confessed in a letter to his king in 1797 that "I was infected with Catholic ideas when I was young, delighting with them as a child would with a toy."[25] But he may also have reached that conclusion on his own, because there are a few other Confucian scholars who took those references to the Lord on High literally, even though they had not been exposed to Ricci's proselytizing writings.[26]

One such Confucian who included the Lord on High in his philosophy was Yun Hyu (1617–1680), who was a member of the same Namin faction (which sided with T'oegye rather than Yulgok) as Tasan was. Yun died over a century before Catholicism emerged in Korea, so it is highly unlikely that he was influenced by Catholic ideas. However, Yun was convinced that the ancient Chinese had believed in a living God. For example, Yun wrote, "Ancient people experienced fear and trembling, and were uneasy in mind; they behaved prudently as if they were being watched from above or on all sides, and used to speak of 'the Lord on High' in everything."[27] This is language very similar to the language Tasan used to describe how people should feel and act once they realized that a Lord on High actually existed.

We will never know the exact process by which Tasan became a theist, because Tasan does not tell us if his conclusion that the Lord on High was an actual supernatural personality was a result of his own reasoning based on his own experiences with self-cultivation or if he became convinced that God existed when he encountered arguments for God's existence others had written. What we do know, however, is that Tasan clearly believed that a supernatural personality existed and oversaw human affairs. Moreover, we know how Tasan justified that conclusion. He insisted we need belief in a supernatural overseer as an incentive to make sure we follow our natural preference for the moral good rather than our equally natural inclination toward physical pleasure.

Tasan did not put much weight on the argument from order, that the existence of order in the universe tells us that there must be an external Orderer, which Matteo Ricci and other Catholic proselytizers in China thought was such an important argument.[28] Instead, Tasan favored a pragmatic argument. He argued that we should believe that God exists and watches our every thought and deed because, if we believe that, then we are more likely to behave properly.[29]

It is in his justification for belief that the Lord on High is an actual supernatural personality that we see evidence that Tasan, though he challenged many of the core concepts of neo-Confucianism, remained within the parameters of Confucian thinking. His argument for the existence of the Lord on High was a very Confucian argument.

Tasan wrote, "Abiding in reverence [K. *chugyŏng* / C. *zhujing*] is the foundation of morality. It is what makes it possible for us to act properly."[30] But reverence for what? In mainstream neo-Confucianism, the character translated here as "reverence" (K. *kyŏng* / C. *jing*) is better translated as "mindfulness," since it refers to an inner state of calm readiness to accept guidance from the *li* in the world around us and in our human nature. However, Tasan insisted that understanding of *kyŏng* was not very helpful, since it does not tell us where to direct our reverence. He insisted that reverence always requires an object of reverence. It can be reverence for Heaven, reverence of one's ruler, reverence for one's parents, reverence for one's older brother, reverence for elders, reverence for guests, or simply reverence manifest as respectful attention while dealing with matters at hand. In every instance, however, true reverence denotes a reverent attitude toward someone or something.[31]

That something toward which we should direct ultimate reverence is the Lord on High. Tasan recognizes that Confucians are sometimes told that they should show reverence for Heaven. However, as already noted, he insists that, in that context, Heaven is just another way of referring to the Lord on High.[32] We need to keep in mind, he says, that it is not the blue sky above we should revere. Instead, it is the Lord on High.

And why should we revere the Lord on High? Tasan gives a very pragmatic answer:

> There is no human being born on this earth without base desires. What keeps us from following those desires and doing whatever we feel like doing? It is the fear that our misbehavior will be noticed. Noticed by whom? Whose gaze keeps us in a state of constant caution and apprehension? We are cautious and apprehensive because we know there are law enforcement officers responsible for making sure rules are followed. We are cautious and apprehensive because we know our sovereign can punish us if we behave improperly. If we did not think there was someone watching us, would we not simply abandon all sense of moral responsibility and just do whatever we felt like doing?...
>
> But what makes us behave properly even in the privacy of our own room and make sure that even our thoughts are proper thoughts? The only reason why an exemplary person is watchful over his thoughts and

behavior even in the privacy of his own room is that he knows that there is a Lord on High watching him. If we think that the term *Lord on High* is nothing by a metaphor for *li*, then we would not be cautious and apprehensive. *Li*, after all, is not a conscious being. It is unable to inspire caution and apprehension.[33]

Tasan goes on to add, "Heaven's penetrating intelligence is able to look right into our heart-mind. There is nothing it cannot see. There is nothing that we do or think that Heaven does not know about. Even the bravest person cannot help but feel apprehensive when he realizes this."[34]

It is clear that Tasan's theology, if we can call it that, is a pragmatic theology. He believes that there is a supernatural personality in heaven above not because such a God is necessary to explain order in the universe or because God has given us proof in miracles or in writings such as the Bible that He exists. Tasan believes we should believe in the Lord on High because such a belief will inspire us to exert the effort needed to always think and act the way we should think and act. In the world as he saw it, in which human beings are not integrated into the tightly knit fabric of the universe but instead are autonomous individuals who are capable of knowing what is right but are also capable of acting contrary to that knowledge, we need a stimulus to push us in the right direction. That stimulus, he argued, is the belief that we cannot escape the gaze of the Lord on High. He had come to the conclusion that such a belief is necessary if we are to overcome the natural human tendency to pursue the good of physical pleasure and personal benefit rather than the common good which is the goal we should all pursue.

Cultivating Composure and a Selfless Orientation

Tasan did not think that maintaining an attitude of caution and apprehension out of awareness that the Lord on High was aware of our every thought and action was the ultimate goal the *Zhongyong* was directing us to pursue. Such caution and apprehension were a means to an end. That end was maintaining focused composure so that we would be able to act appropriately in all circumstances in which we find ourselves and could avoid being led astray by self-centered emotions.

The term the *Zhongyong* uses for "focused composure" [*Zhong*] literally means "being centered" or "hitting the mark." Tasan, and other commentators before him as well, interpreted this as meaning always acting appropriately in any situation you find yourself in, neither overreacting to it nor falling short of what you should do.³⁵ To be able to act appropriately consistently, you need to stay composed and focused so that you can see clearly what you need to do in order to promote the common good. As Tasan noted, "an exemplary person always looks into his own heart-mind before he takes any action. If he can see that he is not calm and composed, he has to make an effort to calm himself down and regain composure."³⁶

Tasan is realistic. He does not say we should totally empty our heart-minds by shutting down all thoughts and emotions. He argues:

> This talk in the *Zhongyong* of the emotions before and after they are activated refers to the exemplary person reaching the height of appropriate responsiveness and cooperativeness by being watchful over himself when no one else can see what he is doing or thinking. It had nothing to do . . . with stilling all emotions. It is a mark of Buddhists that, when they discuss the heart-mind, they insist on stilling all emotions. . . . The way followers of true Sagely learning should regulate their heart-minds is by thinking carefully about what they are doing rather than trying to still all emotions whatsoever. They should try to cultivate an attitude of caution and apprehension instead of trying to empty their heart-minds of all thoughts.³⁷

Tasan believed that some Cheng-Zhu Confucians advised us to clear our heart-minds of all emotions.³⁸ He counters that is an impossible task. He suggests instead that we cultivate what he considers the best thoughts and emotions (caution and apprehension) for helping us keep our other emotions from distracting us so that we can focus on what we are supposed to focus on. He also argues that a cautious and apprehensive heart-mind will keep us from putting our personal wants first and will therefore make it possible for us to interact harmoniously and appropriately with our fellow humans. Furthermore, he points out, Zhu Xi himself appears to argue that same point in his *Questions and Answers on the Zhongyong*.³⁹

Tasan assumes that the impossibility of eliminating all emotions is what makes us morally frail. There is no sanctuary from emotions, since we are a combination of a heart-mind and a body. However, we can overcome moral frailty by ensuring that we cultivate the correct emotions. One way to cultivate such emotions is to constantly remind ourselves, whether we are practicing quiet sitting alone or are out in the world interacting with our fellow human beings, is to remember that the Lord on High is watching us. That will give us the incentive to exert the effort necessary to put the common good ahead of any pursuit of personal benefit. However, that is not the only way to cultivate a selfless orientation. We can reinforce our recognition that we are a member of a community and are not isolated individuals by performing rituals properly.

Tasan devotes dozens of pages to ritual in his commentary on the *Zhongyong*. He does that not just because Chapters XVIII and XIX involve discussion of proper ritual behavior. Tasan shared the Confucian assumption that proper ritual performance is important for a couple of reasons. First of all, the role we play in a ritual is determined by our status in society at the time, particularly our position in government and in our family. Accordingly, proper ritual performance reinforces our recognition of the different gradations within the social and family hierarchies. Tasan, as did Confucians in general, assumed that you can have a harmonious society only when the various members of that society played their assigned roles. Moreover, Tasan assumed that those roles were all different, varying according to the age, gender, and political and family responsibilities of its members. Ritual manuals took those differences into account and provided detailed instructions on who should do what in a ritual. Tasan insisted we should learn those instructions and act in accordance with them. By doing that, we would ensure that the ritual proceeds as it should, and therefore that everyone is able to play their proper role and interact harmoniously with those around them.

The second reason Tasan shared the Confucian concern for proper ritual is related to the first reason: as a participant in a ritual, we are required to put our personal desires aside and instead do whatever that specific ritual role requires us to do. Engaging in ritual practice, therefore, cultivates a selfless orientation, teaching us to think of what the community to which we belong requires of us rather than what we personally want. As Tasan pointed out, "ritual is the means by which we cultivate self-control and gain control over our bodies. We study and practice ritual in order to discipline ourselves."[40]

The term translated here as "ritual" can also be translated as simply "etiquette." It means either appropriate actions in informal interactions with actual living human beings or appropriate actions in formal interactions with human beings or with spiritual beings such as ancestors or Heaven. Tasan makes clear that there is a difference between family rituals, such as those honoring ancestors, and state rituals, such as those honoring the spirits which protect the ruling family and the country. He insists that rituals honoring Heaven are not for everyone. In fact, only the Son of Heaven can offer ritual obeisance to Heaven. As Tasan points out, "the 'Royal Regulations' chapter of the *Book of Rites* says that the Son of Heaven sacrifices to both Heaven and Earth. Among the three sacrificial rituals for Heaven, Earth, and human beings, only the sovereign may sacrifice to both the Celestial Spirit and the Gods of the Earth. The feudal lords do not dare to sacrifice to the Celestial Spirit. They offer sacrifice only to the Gods of the Earth."⁴¹

However, we are all required to act properly in all our interactions, including our interactions with ancestors and other spiritual beings, even if we are not high enough in status to sacrifice to Heaven. Ritual handbooks tell us how in act in many specific situations. In other situations, those for which we lack detailed guidelines, to direct our interactions we have to rely on the cultivation of the selfless orientation we have honed during ritual performances as well as draw on the composure and concern for the common good (Tasan often labels such concern sŏ — "empathy" [C. shu]) we have cultivated by keeping in mind that the Lord on High is watching us. If we are able to do that, we will then "hit the mark" the Zhongyong tells us we should hit. We will act appropriately in every situation we find ourselves in.⁴²

If we are able to cultivate the ability to consistently act appropriately (an ability Tasan insists requires a lot of effort to acquire), then we will be "sincere." The Sinograph sŏng (C. cheng, a different Sinograph than the one used for human nature and also pronounced sŏng in Korean but pronounced xing in Chinese) is usually translated as "sincerity," but that translation is misleading. It has a much broader range of meaning than that. As Tasan himself explains,

> Sŏng/cheng means things performing the way they should perform. That is why it is said that sŏng means to make yourself do what you should do and make things do what they are supposed to do.... Without sŏng, there is no way you can make your intentions appropriately selfless. Without sŏng, there is no way you can rectify your heart-mind. Without sŏng, there is no way you can cultivate a moral character. Without sŏng, there is no way you can promote order in your family and bring peace to all under heaven.⁴³

The Zhungyong does not mention sŏng/cheng, which I translate as "attitudes and actions that are appropriately responsive and unselfishly cooperative," until its second half. However, Tasan argues that sŏng nevertheless is the core message of that classic and permeates every chapter. In fact, he insists that earlier references to being watchful over your own thoughts and actions even when no other human being can be aware of what you are thinking or doing is a reference to sŏng, since that will lead to you being appropriately responsive and unselfishly cooperative.⁴⁴

Tasan goes on to argue:

> Being appropriately responsive and unselfishly cooperative is the foundation of the entire universe. It is being appropriately responsive and unself-

ishly cooperative that makes it possible to maintain composure and act harmoniously. It is being appropriately responsive and unselfishly cooperative that makes it possible to understand the various transformations that give rise to heaven and earth.... It is being appropriately responsive and unselfishly cooperative that makes it possible to correct things that are off center and return them to their proper place so that they function exactly as they are supposed to function.[45]

Not only will you have the appropriate selfless attitude when you have a heart-mind that is *sŏng*, you will also see clearly how you should act in every situation you find yourself in. Tasan explains that when you are appropriately responsive and unselfishly cooperative, you are in tune with everything around you, and therefore you see clearly what you should do in every situation. Conversely, when you see clearly what you should do in every situation you find yourself in, then you are able to act appropriately and unselfishly in all those situations.[46]

As Tasan explains, the core message of the *Zhongyong* is that we need to cultivate the ability to consistently act in an appropriately responsive and unselfishly cooperative manner. In order to act in such a fashion, we need to be composed and collected so that our actions are determined by what we know is the right way to behave rather than letting our selfish emotions and desires for personal benefit and physical pleasure lead us astray. If our actions are appropriately responsive and unselfishly cooperative, we will live and act in harmony with those around us. We will be a sage, which is the goal of neo-Confucian self-cultivation. Tasan promises us that a sage, someone who has refined his character to the extent he is aligned with Heaven, will have a positive impact on everyone and everything around him such that everything will interact the way it should, and he can be said to have accomplished what Heaven accomplishes: without taking any deliberate actions to do so, he can bring the universe into a perfect harmonious order.[47] This, Tasan believes, is the message of the *Zhongyong*.

It is clear from Tasan's understanding of the *Zhongyong* that he remained a Confucian, but a Confucian who differed from his fellow Confucians on exactly how best to reach their common Confucian goal of sagehood. They, too, shared his practical orientation, his assumption that the purpose of philosophizing was to define proper behavior and to find the best way to cultivate the moral character that would allow them to act in accordance with the guidelines of proper behavior they discovered. However, he was even more practical than most of them were, in that he constructed a moral psychology based on the way the world actually is rather than the way it should be. He saw how difficult it was for human beings to consistently behave the way they knew they should behave. He also saw that human beings are more likely to behave appropriately when they know they are being watched. He therefore proposed that those who wanted to live moral lives abandon the *li*-centered metaphysics of mainstream neo-Confucianism and instead act on the assumption that there was a Lord on High watching their every thought and action. If they did that, then they would have a better chance of reaching the moral goal the *Zhongyong* told them was within their grasp. They would maintain a constant focused composure that would allow them to consistently harmonize their actions with the actions of those around them and always act in an appropriately responsive and unselfishly cooperative manner. This is the message Tasan wants us to take away from his commentary on the *Zhongyong*.

Reading These Discussions of the *Zhongyong*

Both of Tasan's discussions of the *Zhongyong* translated below are presented as questions from King Chŏngjo with Tasan's answers to those questions. When they discussed the *Zhongyong*, both King Chŏngjo and Tasan assumed that their audience had, as they had, memorized that classic as well as all the other works in the neo-Confucian canon. That is why they felt no need to cite an entire chapter before they asked a question about it or discussed what it meant. They knew that if they only cited a key passage from a particular chapter, their audience would instantly know what that entire chapter said. That left them free to discuss not only the passage cited but also anything else in that chapter, as well as refer to what Zhu Xi said in his commentaries on that chapter. (Of particular importance were Zhu Xi's *Zhongyong zhangju* [The *Zhongyong*, in chapters and phrases] and *Zhongyong huowen* [Questions and answers on the *Zhongyong*].)

Modern readers are unlikely to have memorized the entire *Zhongyong*. I could have made it more convenient for them by including a complete translation of that text alongside the two commentaries by Tasan on the *Zhongyong* translated here. However, for a couple of reasons, I decided not to do so. First of all, Tasan and his king did not discuss every single line in the *Zhongyong*. It is therefore not necessary to include a complete translation. But, more important, Tasan had his own distinctive way of reading the *Zhongyong*. Most English translations follow Zhu Xi's interpretation, which Tasan disagreed with on several key points. In order to highlight Tasan's originality, I have decided to translate only those portions of the *Zhongyong* King Chŏngjo or Tasan actually cite.

In the longer commentary translated here, the *Chungyong kangǔibo*, I do as Tasan did and indicate which section of the *Zhongyong* is being discussed by introducing the discussion of that passage with a key phrase from that passage. Those section headings for the *Chungyong kangǔibo* translation in this book are the same exact phrases Tasan used to introduce those sections. A few of those sections are devoted to an entire chapter in the *Zhongyong*. In those cases I add to Tasan's section title the Roman numeral for that chapter as provided in James Legge's translation of the *Zhongyong* in his *The Chinese Classics,* volume 1. However, Tasan often breaks up the discussion of lengthy chapters and treats different paragraphs in those chapters separately. In such cases, in addition to the Roman numeral for the chapter in the *Zhongyong* in which that paragraph appears, I add the Arabic numeral Legge gives for that particular paragraph.

For example, *Zhongyong* XIX: 6 is the sixth paragraph in the nineteenth chapter of the *Zhongyong* in Legge's translation. Tasan's discussion of *Zhongyong* XIX: 6 in *Chungyong kangŭibo* is introduced with a phrase taken from that paragraph: "The *jiao* sacrifices and *she* sacrifices were ways to pay ritual homage to the Lord on High." The translations of the section headings often differ from Legge's translations, since I want to show in the translations how Tasan read those lines.

Tasan does not break the shorter *Chungyong ch'aek* into sections marked off by quotations from the *Zhongyong*. There are, therefore, no such chapter and paragraph headings in the translation of *Chungyong ch'aek*.

Readers may feel that the king and Tasan often jump from one subject to another. That is because they often focus on particular phrases within a specific chapter of the *Zhongyong* rather than discuss that chapter as a whole. Readers puzzled by an apparent series of unrelated subjects within a single chapter of this translation should look at the text of the *Zhongyong* itself to see the context in which the phrases discussed appear.

Readers should feel free to consult any of the many English translations of the *Zhongyong* that are widely available. They should be aware, however, that often the translation I provide of a passage under discussion may differ significantly from the way that passage is rendered in the translation they consult. That is because I have tried to reflect Tasan's understanding of the specific passages translated. Tasan often explains why his interpretations differ from those of Zhu Xi, and the translation here takes that into account.

A reliable translation for how the *Zhongyong* was understood by most Confucians would be Ian Johnston and Wang Ping, trans., *Daxue and Zhongyong* (Hong Kong: Chinese University Press, 2012). They not only provide the original Literary Sinitic of both a Han dynasty version of the *Zhongyong* and Zhu Xi's version; they also provide important excerpts from the Han dynasty commentary of Zheng Xuan (127–200) as well as from a commentary of Zhu Xi (1130–1200), along with translations of those commentaries. Another useful translation of the *Zhongyong* can be found in Andrew Plaks, *Ta Hsüeh and Chung Yung (The Highest Order of Cultivation* and *On the Practice of the Mean* (New York: Penguin Books, 2003). A somewhat idiosyncratic translation is available in Roger Ames and David L. Hall, trans., *Focusing the Familiar: A Translation and Philosophical Interpretation of the Zhongyong* (Honolulu: University of Hawai'i Press, 2001). Ames and Hall, with their decision to use a philosophical language of "focus and field," come closer to the way Tasan read the *Zhongyong* than the other translations do. Another advantage to the Ames and Hall text is that, like the Johnston and Wang volume, it includes the original text of the *Zhongyong* so readers can easily see what is being translated.

Readers comfortable in Korean might want to look at Pak Wansik, ed., *Chungyong* (Seoul: Yŏgang Publishing, 2008). Pak includes Zhu Xi's *Zhongyong zhangju* [The Zhongyong, in chapters and phrases] and *Zhongyong huowen* [Questions and answers about the Zhongyong] in the original along with the Korean translation. Those who want to consult a Korean translation of Tasan's "A Discussion of the Meaning of the *Zhongyong*, Revised" should look at Chŏnju University Institute for Honam Studies, ed., *Kugyŏk Yŏyudang chŏnsŏ Kyŏngjip I: the Taehak and the Chungyong* [A Korean translation of the Complete Works of Yŏyudang Chŏng Yagyong: On the Classics, volume I, the *Daxue* and the *Zhongyong*] (Chŏnju, Korea: Chŏnju University Press, 1986). Like this English translation, that Korean translation does not include the complete original text of the *Zhongyong*.

For an enlightening discussion of how the assumptions of the translator affect a translation, see Wang Hui, *Translating Chinese Classics in a Colonial Context* (Bern: Peter Lang, 2008). Wang examines two different nineteenth-century translations of the *Zhongyong*, both by James Legge.

For official titles I have drawn on Charles O. Hucker's *Dictionary of Official Titles in Imperial China* (Stanford, CA: Stanford University Press, 1985), as well as on Benjamin A. Elman and Martin Kern, eds., *Statecraft and Classical Learning: The Rituals of Zhou in East Asian History* (Leiden: Brill, 2010) and, for Korean terms, the online glossary maintained by the Academy of Korean Studies (http://glossary.aks.ac.kr). I also found a website maintained by Ulrich Theobald, *ChinaKnowledge.de: An Encyclopaedia on Chinese History, Literature and Art*, to be useful for identifying individuals and important works. That website is available at http://www.chinaknowledge.de. The China Biographical Database Project also proved helpful for identifying Chinese individuals Tasan mentions. That database is available at https://projects.iq.harvard.edu/cbdb/home.

Since Tasan regularly refers to other Confucian classics, I have also found very useful the translations of the Chinese classics by James Legge as found in *The Chinese Classics, with a translation, critical and exegetical notes, prolegomena and copious indexes* (reprint; Taipei: Wen Shih Che Publishing,

1972), *The I Ching: The Book of Changes* (New York: Dover Publications, 1963), and, with Ch'u Chai and Winberg Chai, *Li Chi: Book of Rites, An Encyclopedia of Ancient Ceremonial Usages, Religious Creeds, and Social Institutions* (New Hyde Park, NY: University Books, 1967). In addition, I have referred to the translation of the *Analects* by Edward Slingerland: *Confucius: Analects, with Selections from Traditional Commentaries* (Indianapolis: Hackett, 2003), the translation of *Mencius* by Bryan W. Van Norden: *Mengzi, with Selections from Traditional Commentaries* (Indianapolis: Hackett, 2008), the translation by Arthur Waley and Joseph R. Allen of the *Shijing* with the title *The Book of Songs: The Ancient Chinese Classic of Poetry* (New York: Grove Press, 1996), the translation of the *Yili* by John Steele: *The I-li or the Book of Etiquette and Ceremonial* (London: Probsthain and Company, 1917), the translation of the *Yijing* by Richard John Lynn: *I Ching: The Classic of Changes* (New York: Columbia University Press, 1994), and the recent translation of the *Zuozhuan* by Stephen Durrant, Wai-yee Li, and David Schaberg: *Zuo Tradition: Zhozhuan Commentary on the Spring and Autumn Annals* (Seattle: University of Washington Press, 2016). I refer readers to these English translations in the endnotes, but I don't always reproduce those translations word-for-word. Instead, I try to translate those texts the way I believe Tasan would have read them.

In his longer commentary translated here, the *Chungyong kangŭibo*, Tasan draws on the work of a large number of earlier Chinese commentaries while comparing what he and those commentators say with what is said in the Confucian classics themselves. He assumes his readers would be familiar with those commentaries and the contents of those classics, so he does not provide much, if any, bibliographical information. For example, he often cites a commentator by his surname or his literary name only. (For instance, the famous Qing scholar Mao Qiling [1623-1716] is identified simply as Mao.) However, it was important to me to track down who those sources were and where Tasan found their statements. Literary Sinitic is a highly contextual language and it is easy to misunderstand a sentence or paragraph if it is taken out of context.

I found two electronic resources particularly helpful in identifying the sources Tasan used. One is an incredibly comprehensive online collection of philosophical and historical sinographic material from ancient times through the early Republican era. Without https://ctext.org I would not have been able to look at many of the sources Tasan looked at, since some of those sources are not available in my university's library. This site also made it much easier to locate a particular passage from one of the longer classics, such as the *Liji* (Book of Rites) or the *Chunqiu zuozhuan* (the Zuo commentary on the Spring and Autumn Annals), since all its texts are searchable. To locate particularly obscure commentaries, I turned to another source, fortunately available via the University of British Columbia library. The Erudition database (*Zhongguo jiben guji ku* 中國基本古籍庫) has over ten thousand titles in its database. Short phrases (of the sort Tasan often borrows for his own commentary) can be searched for and, if found, displayed in the context in which they appeared. Without those two electronic sources, I would not have been able to show how well-versed Tasan was in the Chinese commentarial tradition, and I also would have had a lot more difficulty trying to understand what Tasan was arguing for and against.

When Chinese classics and later works by Chinese scholars are cited, I use the pinyin transliteration of their titles to reflect their Chinese pronunciation. However, when the titles of those same works are part of the title of a work by a Korean writer, I transliterate the entire title according to the McCune-Reischauer transliteration method to reflect the Korean pronunciation that would have been used by the Korean author. For example, *Zhongyong* appears as *Chungyong* when it is the part of a title of a Korean-authored work, such as Tasan's *Chungyong kangŭibo*.

I do the same with the many Chinese personal names that appear in Tasan's commentaries. I provide them in pinyin transliteration, except when they appear in the title of a Korean-authored work. For example, I write Zhu Xi as Zhu Xi, not Chu Hŭi (the Korean pronunciation of his name). I do the same with most key philosophical and historical terms. When those terms appear in a Chinese context (such as in a discussion of Chinese history or Chinese philosophy), I transliterate them according to Chinese pronunciation. Most of the names and terms that appear in this translation, therefore, are written as they are pronounced in Chinese, even though Tasan and his king would have read them with their Korean pronunciation. I use Chinese pronunciation in order to signal to the reader that Tasan was working primarily with Chinese texts and Chinese commentaries on those works. Though Tasan never visited China, his philosophy was built on a Chinese foundation. Transliteration representing Chinese rather than Korean pronunciation reflects his greater reliance on Chinese rather than Korean sources.

However, when key terms are used in a purely Korean context or have become so widely used in Korea that they have become Koreanized, I normally transliterate them according to the Korean pronunciation. One exception to transcribing Sinographs according to their Korean pronunciation when they are used in a Korean context is *Dao*. The Korean pronunciation of that Sinograph meaning the Way is *Do*. However, *Dao* is so widely used in English discussions of East Asian thought that I decided to use the more familiar transliteration. Two more exceptions to transcribing Sinographs according to their Korean pronunciation when they are used in a Korean context are the words for "human nature" (K. *sŏng* / C. *xing*) and "sincerity" (K. *sŏng* / C. *cheng*). Since "human nature" and "sincerity" are pronounced the same in Korean, to avoid confusing those two terms, when I transliterate rather than translate them I use the Chinese pronunciations of *xing* and *cheng*, respectively.

On the other hand, except when citing a Chinese source, I use the Korean pronunciation of *ki* for the Sinograph meaning matter-energy. The Chinese pronunciation is *qi*, but *ki* was a very important term in Korean philosophical discussions and was at the center of some unique Korean contributions to Confucian philosophy, such as the Four-Seven Debate. I also employ *li* for the Sinograph meaning "dynamic patterns," even though in some Korean contexts that Sinograph is pronounced *i*. However, it is pronounced *li* in other Korean contexts, and using *li* avoids possible confusion with the first-person pronoun.

Material within the body of the translations that appear within parentheses are the parenthetical remarks of Tasan himself. That includes remarks in which Tasan notes that he has left out paragraphs that he had included in earlier versions of these texts. (I do not know what he left out, since I do not have the earlier versions of those texts.) When I have felt the need to add clarifying notes of my own to the body of the text rather than place those notes in endnotes, I have used brackets instead of parentheses.

Notes on the Translation of Key Terms

7

I often depart from the usual translation of key terms in order to reflect in this translation how I believe Tasan understood the *Zhongyong* and what he meant in his commentaries on it. When I revert to a standard translation, I am reflecting the way King Chŏngjo (who was more mainstream in his interpretation of the classics than Tasan was) or another commentator understood the passage in question.

It is also important to keep in mind that Sinographs are so versatile in the way they can be used and are so broad in the range of meanings they can express that limiting one Sinograph to only one translation would often distort what it means in a specific context. Not only can the same Sinograph be a noun in one context and a verb, adjective, or adverb in another, it can also be best translated by one English noun, adjective, verb, or adverb in one context but by a different noun, adjective, verb, or adverb in a different context. I have decided, therefore, to use a range of possible translations for the key terms in this text.

Here are the key terms as I have determined Tasan understood them:

體用 *ch'eyong* [C. *tiyong*]: potential and actualization of that potential. These two terms, when they appear together, are often translated as "substance" or "essence" and "function" respectively, often with the nuance of "a core and its manifestation." However, in this translation I depart from that usual translation to reflect how I have observed Neo-Confucians using that dyad.

Ch'e literally means "body" and *yong* literally means "to use or apply." Since the human body is what gives human beings the potential to interact with the world around them, "potential" rather than "substance" often appears to be a better translation of *ch'e* when it is paired with *yong* in the action-oriented philosophy that is neo-Confucianism. A human being cannot engage in any action without a body. Actions are the practical application of the potential for action the body provides. This means that a body and the actions done by that body are inseparable. Similarly, when neo-Confucians speak of *ch'eyong,* they refer to two aspects of the same process or event, the unactivated and the activated. In such instances, *ch'e* refers to what something can and/or should do (its normative potential) and *yong* to what it actually does (the actualization of that potential).[1] Since key neo-Confucian terms often have normative connotations, *ch'e* should in those contexts be understood as "the innate potential to act and interact appropriately." In contexts in which *ch'e* is best understood as potential, the *ch'e-yong* dyad should be translated as "potential and its actualization" or "potential and its implementation." In other contexts, however, *ch'e*, especially when it appears apart from that dyad, should be translated simply as "body" or even as the verb "to embody." Similarly, *yong* on its own can sometimes, depending on the context, be translated as application or as to use or apply.[2]

Tasan gives us an example of Zhu Xi using *ch'eyong* / C. *tiyong* in the sense of potential and actualization: "When the heart-mind of the sage is not yet activated, it is like the not-yet-activated potential [*ch'e*] of a spotless mirror or still water to reflect whether is nearby. As soon as the heart-mind is activated, it is like the actualization [*yong*] of the reflecting potential of a spotless mirror or still water."[3] In other words, a mirror that is not using its potential to reflect things around it can be described as *ch'e,* while a mirror which has activated its potential to reflect its surroundings can be described as *yong*.

Tasan disagrees with this description of the heart-mind of a sage as perfectly still when unengaged but does not disagree with the distinction made here between potential and actualization. As Tasan later points out:

> This talk of potential and its actualization is not explicitly mentioned in the ancient classics. Yet things certainly can be said [depending on the context] to have unactualized potential as well as to exhibit the actualization of their potential. The Dao of Heaven extends far and wide, both potentially and actualized. The Dao of Heaven is hard to see and therefore can be said to be hidden, but we can still say it has potential for manifestation as well as actually being manifest.[4]

Another example of Tasan using *ch'eyong* as potential and the actualization of that potential appears in his account of a 1790 meeting presided over by King Chŏngjo in the Brilliant Governance Hall. Asking to explain a passage from the *Zhongyong,* Tasan reports that he replied: "Composed and focused" in the term "composed, focused, and cooperative" is a reference to potential [*ch'e*]. "Composed and focused" in the term "he is appropriately composed and focused in whatever situation he finds himself" is a reference to the actualization [*yong*] of that potential. What they refer to are different, but fundamentally their meaning is the same."⁵

In other words, when you are composed and focused in preparation for dealing with a certain situation, you are in a *ch'e* state, since you have not yet activated your potential to deal with that situation appropriately. But when you remain composed and focused while you are dealing with that situation, your potential to act in a composed and focused manner has been activated and therefore you are in a *yong* state. Yet "composed and focused" means the same in each state, since potential and actualization of that potential are simply two sides of the same coin.

造化 *chohwa* [C. *zaohua*]: This term is sometimes translated as "creation." That translation is not incorrect, in that "chohwa" refers to the totality of all that has come into being. However, the English term "creation" implies an external creator, a concept absent in the way this term was understood by mainstream neo-Confucians. Literally "creating transformations," this term as normally used does not require a subject since the transformations are believed to be self-generated. It is, therefore, more accurate to translate this term in those contexts as "the creative transformations that produce the visible world." However, Tasan sometimes points out that those creative transformations are not random. Rather, they are manifestations of the Dao of Heaven and as such should be seen as evidence that above all, and external to, those transformations is Heaven, the personification of perfectly selfless and harmonious action.⁶

天 *Ch'ŏn* [C. *tian*]: In order to be faithful to Tasan's preferred word choices, I usually translate Ch'ŏn as "Heaven." However, "Heaven" should be read in this translation as synonymous with Sangje / C. Shangdi, the Lord on High, which is Tasan's name for the supernatural personality he believes watches us from above. As Tasan explained, "When we speak of Heaven as a ruler, we are referring to Sangje. Sangje is called 'Heaven' just like we talk about the king as the state because we do not want to show disrespect by using his personal name. The blue sky we see above us is nothing more than a roof over our heads. That is not Sangje. That sky above is just another physical object, like dirt, water, or fire."⁷

天命 *ch'ŏnmyŏng* [C. *tianming*]: This term is often translated as "mandate of Heaven." Tasan usually understands it as "what Heaven has conferred." Tasan explains in *Chungyong chajam* that the word "confer/ordain" (*myŏng*) has two meanings. In some contexts, it means the directives Heaven gives us through our conscience. In such contexts, it can be translated as "mandate," referring to what Heaven has ordained, the rules defining appropriate interactions. However, in other contexts, it refers to Heaven endowing us with the conscience that leads us to desire the moral good and detest the moral evil. In those contexts, "what heaven has conferred" is a better translation. In some contexts, it can even be translated as "conscience." In that sense, it is same as the moral side of our human nature, the Dao Mind that not only enables us to identity the way we should behave but guides us to act in accordance with that knowledge. This is how Tasan understands the opening line of the *Zhongyong*: "That which Heaven has conferred on us is our innate ability to act appropriately." In line with that interpretation, Tasan insists that "the Dao Mind and the Mandate of Heaven should not be viewed as two separate things."[8]

中 *chung* [C. *zhong*]: literally, "in the center." However, it normally has a more dynamic nuance in the *Zhongyong* and in commentaries on the *Zhongyong*. There it often refers to "centering," maintaining a mental state of calm and composure. In such instances, it is sometimes translated as equilibrium, equanimity, or even imperturbability, depending on the context. "Equilibrium" is the translation James Legge, probably the most influential translator of the *Zhongyong* into English, settled on late in his career, though in his influential early translation of the *Zhongyong*, he translated it as "the mean."[9] There are places, however, in which I follow his earlier view and translate it as "centered," since in those instances it means to be on target, neither going too far nor stopping short.[10] When you are *chung*, you are not pulled away from the pursuit of the common good by any self-centered emotions. In Tasan's view, you still have emotions, but they are appropriate emotions, those which stimulate you to think and act with the common good in mind.

As Roger Ames and David Hall point out, by extension it can also mean focused, in the sense of focusing on the appropriate way to behave without being distracted by any self-centered emotions.[11] Therefore there are situations in which it should be translated as "calm and focused" or "composed and focused."[12] An extended translation of its meaning in that context would be "focused on what is appropriate in a particular situation."

忠 *ch'ung* [C. *zhong*]: frequently translated as loyalty. That translation does not always convey the broader import of that Sinograph's meaning. The Sinograph shows graphically, as Roger Ames points out, "putting one's whole heart and mind into what one is doing."[13] It can be translated as "acting conscientiously," "being steadfast," or as "doing one's best." Tasan often pairs *ch'ung* with *shin* (信 trustworthy). When that pairing appears in a discussion of how an official should behave, that phrase can be translated as "loyal and trustworthy," as long as "loyal" is understood as conscientiously doing your best to carry out the duties of whatever post you hold.¹⁴ However, in other contexts in which it is paired with trustworthy, such as when discussing how people should behave in general, it should be translated as "conscientious."¹⁵ Similarly, when it is paired with reciprocity/empathy (恕 Sŏ [C. *shu*]) in discussing proper behavior in general, it is best translated as "conscientious."¹⁶

道 *Dao* [K. *to*]: Dao literally means "a path, a way," or "to walk a path, to follow a way." In a philosophical context, it has a normative sense: "the path you should follow."¹⁷ It can also mean the way the various entities and processes in the universe act and interact, when they are acting and interacting appropriately. It is often left untranslated, since it has such a broad range of reference, referring not only to the way human beings should behave but also to the way the various components of the universe should harmoniously interact always and everywhere. However, when it is used in the more limited sense of the way a person should act in a particular situation, I sometimes translate it as "Way," with the initial capital letter signifying its significance.¹⁸ When I transliterate it rather than translate it, I use the Chinese pronunciation of "Dao" rather than the Korean pronunciation of "To" because it is as Dao that it is best known in Western scholarship.

The Dao of Heaven, the Celestial Dao, is the way things naturally perform when they are able to interact without impediment.¹⁹ The Dao of human beings refers to what human beings are supposed to do (i.e., align their thoughts and actions with the Dao of Heaven).²⁰ However, Tasan warns, "We should not draw too sharp a line between the Dao of Heaven and the Dao of human beings," since they both refer to acting in an unselfishly cooperative and harmoniously cooperative manner, though for the former that happens unconsciously and for the latter that only happens if we make a decision to act in that fashion.²¹

人倫 *illyun* [C. *renlun*]: This term is often translated as "The Five Cardinal Relationships," meaning appropriate interactions between sovereigns and subjects, fathers and sons, husbands and wives, older and younger brothers, and friends. However, it also has the broader meaning of those norms which define all appropriate interactions within the human community. I therefore sometimes translate it as "Appropriate Ways of Interacting among Human Beings."²²

仁 *in* [C. *ren*]: A common translation is "benevolence," but that does not capture the full force of this term.²³ It means to be fully human, in other words, to act always as a member of the human community rather than as a separate and distinct individual with personal wants and needs that you want fulfilled even at the expense of the common good. In the Confucian world view, human beings are only fully human when they act as human beings should act. That means human beings need to actualize their humanity through appropriate interactions with their fellow human beings. Being fully human means to act in the manner that is appropriate for whatever role you are supposed to play. As Tasan explains it, "*In* always implies a relationship between two people. Acting out of filial piety in serving a parent is *in*. Showing fraternal respect for an older brother is *in*. Being conscientious in serving your sovereign is *in*. Being trustworthy with a friend is *in*. Showing compassion when you are a government official is *in*."[24]

In a broader sense, *in* could be translated as unselfish, as altruistic, as acting with due regard for fellow human beings, or as "fully human," since human beings, if they act in accord with their true human nature, will act with more regard for the common good than for personal benefit and will therefore play whatever role they are supposed to play. Henry Rosement and Roget Ames suggest a translation that differs slightly from my translation of "fully human." They suggest instead "consummate person or conduct."[25]

However, when *in* appears in a traditional list of virtues, such as *in, ŭi, ye, ji* (C. *ren, yi, li, zhi* — 仁 義 禮 智), I sometimes translate it as "benevolence" to show that it is referring to one of four possible modes of thinking and acting appropriately, which are distinguished as characterized by benevolence, righteousness, propriety, and wisdom.

氣 *ki* [C. *qi*]: I chose to transliterate *ki/qi* according to its Korean pronunciation, because this term is still in frequent use in Korea today and that is the pronunciation contemporary Koreans prefer.

Ki refers to both the primal amorphous matter-and-energy out of which the universe is formed, and to the physical constitution of the individual material objects that constitute the universe as well as the energy that animates them. In human beings, since it is through the *ki* that constitutes their physical organs that they are able to perceive and to comprehend the world around them, *ki* can in references to human beings be translated as "psychophysical nature."

It is important to remember, however, that *ki* can be so ethereal as to be invisible. In mainstream Cheng-Zhu neo-Confucian thought, ghosts and spirits, especially the spirits of ancestors, are thought to be such ethereal forms of *ki*. Tasan, however, drew a sharp distinction between the *ki* that constitutes the material world (defined as that which has a visible form) and the invisible spiritual world. He insisted that spirits were immaterial and therefore were not *ki*.[26] He also departed from the mainstream neo-Confucian assumption that rarefied forms of *ki* were an integral part of consciousness. For him, consciousness was an immaterial process and therefore was not part of the *ki* realm.²⁷ Because *ki* has such a broad range of meanings, we often simply transliterate it rather than translate it.

鬼神 ***kwisin*** **[C. *guishen*]:** Since this term is still in common use in Korea, I transliterate it according to the Korean pronunciation rather than the Chinese pronunciation.

Though this term is normally translated in a neo-Confucian context as "ghosts and spirits," Tasan often used it to refer to a specific type of spiritual being which is quite different from a ghost. He believed that there were spiritual beings who assisted the Lord on High in governing the universe, more akin to the angels found in Christianity than to ghosts. For that reason, in his writings, *kwisin* should normally be translated as "spirits" or "spiritual beings" rather than "ghosts." To preserve Tasan's reverence for the deceased, we also translate his references to what he calls "human spirits" as "spirits" or "ancestral spirits" rather than use the less respectable term of "ghost."²⁸

Tasan usually uses *sin* by itself, without *kwi* preceding it. This term can refer to a single spiritual being such as Sangje, in which case we translate it as "the Spirit."²⁹ However, sometimes we need to translate it in the plural, as "spirits," when he is referring to those celestial spirits who serve as Sangje's assistants. And, in other cases, Tasan uses *sin* to simply mean "consciousness," in which cases I translate it that way rather than as "spirit."³⁰

敬 ***kyŏng*** **[C. *jing*]:** Depending on the context, this term can be translated either as "reverence" or as "mindfulness." In traditional Confucian contexts, it usually means a respectful attitude toward someone, such as the Supreme Lord on High (who, Tasan believed, in ancient China was often viewed anthropomorphically), political superiors, and older family members. It could also refer to the respectful attitude you should display toward the object of a ritual (such as an ancestor) while you are participating in that ritual.

In Cheng-Zhu neo-Confucianism, though *kyŏng* maintained the notion of reverence toward something or someone external to you, it also came to be used to describe an internal state of mind. In that context, it is best translated as "mindfulness," or "seriousness," since it refers to introspection to ensure that you do not let yourself become distracted by thoughts of personal benefit but instead maintain a quiet and calm mind so that you can focus on whatever task is at hand. It was assumed that, when you were properly mindful, you would perceive the world around you on its own terms and would not impose your own biases and misperceptions on it. Such mindfulness within would allow you to interact respectfully, and therefore appropriately, with the external world and with the people within it.³¹

Tasan put more emphasis on reverence than on mindfulness because he believed that *kyŏng*, to be true *kyŏng*, needed an object for its reverence.³² He understood *kyŏng* to imply paying close attention to something so that you can respect it for what it is, and you can deal with it as it should be dealt with. Obviously, he insisted, you cannot pay close attention to something unless you have something to pay attention to. In Tasan's view, when there is no immediate task to concentrate on, you should focus your attention on the fact that you are constantly being watched by the Lord on High. That will allow you to maintain the attitude of *kyŏng*, of calm concentration and reverence, which is the foundation for appropriate behavior. Because of Tasan's emphasis on *kyŏng* as reverence for the Lord on High, he often used *chung* / C. *zhong* (中) where other neo-Confucians may have used *kyŏng* when talking about the concerns of daily life, since for him *chung* meant calm and focused concentration on something we should be mindful of so that we could respond appropriately.

理 *li* [C. *lǐ*]: "Dynamic normative patterns." I chose to transliterate this Sinograph as *li*, although in some Korean contexts it is pronounced as *i*. That same Sinograph is also pronounced in other Korean contexts as *li*. Moreover, it is pronounced *li* in Chinese contexts. In addition, transliterating it as *li* rather than *i* avoids possible confusion with the first-person pronoun.

The traditional translation of *li* as "principle" hides its dynamic nature. In mainstream neo-Confucian philosophy, it is better understood as the dynamic patterns defining and directing appropriate interactions both in the human realm and in the natural world. It can both be singular, referring to the entire cosmic network of appropriate interactions, and be plural, referring to the specific patterns that shape *ki* into individual objects that interact with other individual objects, and also prescribes how they should interact. Moreover, those patterns should not be understood as static structures. *Li*, as used in neo-Confucian philosophizing, retains its original verbal connotation of "ordering."³³ Though it usually appears as a noun, we should not forget its verbal origins. When a translation instead of transliteration is needed, I use "dynamic patterning" or "patterning principle" instead of using "principle" alone. In mainstream neo-Confucianism, *li* was the primary formative force in the universe, actively giving shape and direction to *ki*. It also constituted the moral patterns that both defined and directed appropriate human behavior.³⁴

Tasan dethroned *li* from that crucial position and defined it instead as dependent on *ki*.³⁵ Moreover, he gave Heaven, instead of *li*, the credit for instilling in us the moral direction human beings need. He argued that *li* was too impersonal a concept to provide a foundation for morality or inspire us to exert the effort necessary to act appropriately. "*Li* has no consciousness and therefore is unable to inspire the awe and apprehension necessary to motivate us to be watchful over our thoughts and actions even when no human being can know what we are thinking or doing."[36]

In Tasan's philosophy, *li* retained its meaning of the patterns defining appropriate interactions but the additional meaning of also directing those appropriate interactions was much weaker in Tasan's understanding of *li* since he denied that *li* played the active role mainstream neo-Confucianism thought it played. As Tasan conceived it, *li* was simply principles rather than dynamic patterning.

上帝 **Sangje [C. Shangdi]:** This term literally means "the Lord on High" and is translated as such. It could also be translated as "the Lord Above." Departing from mainstream neo-Confucianism, which defined Sangje as a metaphorical way of referring to *li* as the formative force in the cosmos, Tasan insisted that Sangje was an actual supernatural being to whom sacrifice was due. "There are three levels of spirits to whom we offer sacrifice. The first are called the celestial spirits, the second are called terrestrial spirits, and the third are called human spirits.... As for the various celestial spirits, they are essentially immaterial beings serving as the immediate subordinates of the Lord on High [*Sangje*]."[37] To reinforce that point, Tasan adds, "when the celestial and terrestrial spirits line up to form a bright array, the greatest and most respected among them is none other than *Sangje*."[38] That is why it is only by serving Sangje sincerely and reverently, with a heart-mind energized by awe and apprehension, that we can become fully human.[39]

Although Tasan believed that Sangje was the supreme supernatural being, I avoid translating Sangje as "God" in order to distinguish Tasan's concept of the supreme supernatural personality from the more complex Christian concept of God, which implies a much greater involvement in the material universe and in human affairs than Tasan attributed to Sangje.

心 *sim* **[C. *xin*]:** heart-mind. When used to refer to the actual physical organ in the chest, I translate it simply as heart. However, Tasan much more frequently used this term to refer to the functions of *sim*. In those cases, I translate it as heart-mind, since it combines both the thought processes associated in English with the mind as well as the emotions and feelings associated in English with the heart.

When *sim* is seen as the generator of emotions and feelings, it is conceived as defined by both *li* and *ki*. Selfish emotions emanating from the heart-mind are evidence, in Tasan's view, of the influence of the individualizing effect of *ki*. On the other hand, when moral emotions, such as love for our parents, emanate from the heart-mind, that is evidence that the heart-mind is in accord with *li*.[40] When *sim* is seen as the site of understanding, judging, and deciding, then, in Tasan's view, it is best discussed apart from *ki*.[41]

Tasan distinguishes between our physical body, which is formed from *ki,* and our immaterial side. We use the term *sim*, he points out, to refer to an actual physical organ within our body. However, it is our immaterial side, for which the term *sim* has been borrowed, which allows us to understand the world around us, determine the most appropriate way to interact with that world, and then decide to act in accordance with that judgment.[42] In this sense, the heart-mind can be equated to consciousness. It is this immaterial organ of ours which both perceives the world around us and stimulates us to interact with it the way we should.[43] This is the heart-mind that "unites and commands human nature and feelings."[44] Whereas Cheng-Zhu neo-Confucians tended to place more emphasis on the unifying function of the heart-mind, bringing human nature and human feelings into harmony, Tasan emphasized the moral responsibility of the heart-mind to direct our human nature and our feelings, as well as our subsequent actions, to ensure they were properly directed.[45]

Tasan assumed that the *li* in our basic human nature has to be actualized through our heart-mind in order to direct our behavior. That is why it is said that the heart-mind "unites and commands human nature and feelings." Tasan insisted that it is important to distinguish between human nature, on the one hand, and the heart-mind, on the other. They have completely different functions. One way to distinguish them is to think of them as two different stages of *li:* potential and activated. When Tasan said that human nature includes *li*, he was saying that the patterns of appropriate interactions constitute our fundamental potential to become fully human (through acting appropriately). The key word here is "potential." Our human nature includes our ability to actualize *li* and act appropriately. However, it also includes our tendencies to pursue selfish interests. That is where the heart-mind comes in. The heart-mind is able to recognize appropriate patterns of behavior and also is able to generate emotions and feelings as well as direct actions in accordance with those appropriate patterns of behavior. The heart-mind is the controller that decides which part of our human nature is activated. Tasan wrote that we can say that we should follow what the moral part of our nature tells us to do. But we cannot say we should just do whatever our heart-mind suggests. Instead, we need to use our heart-mind to decide which side of our nature we should follow. That is why the heart-mind is said to "unite and command human nature and feelings."[46]

This gives the heart-mind two important moral functions: cognition and volition. It is the heart-mind that recognizes the specific *li* that tell us how to act appropriately in any given situation, and it is the heart-mind that directs us to act in accordance with those *li*. Both cognition and volition are essential for the *li* that we are endowed with as human beings to be actualized.[47]

慎獨 *sindok* [C. *shendu*]: *Sindŏk* is a reference to the Confucian ethical practice of being careful about what you think or do even when no one can observe what you are thinking or doing. Often translated as "being watchful over yourself even when you are alone," Tasan says it means being watchful over your private thoughts and actions at all times, even when you are in public.[48] Tasan's reading is closer to the original meaning of this phrase.[49] However he adds that we need to be watchful over our thoughts and actions at all times because, wherever we are and whatever we do, even when no other human being can see what we are doing or thinking, the Lord on High is still observing our every thought and action.[50]

恕 *sŏ* [C. *shu*]: Often translated as "empathy" or "reciprocity," this Sinograph should be understood as "putting oneself in another's shoes."[51] Another possible translation for that character could be "being considerate in your dealing with others" or "acting with empathy in your dealings with others." It is one way of expressing the ethical imperative to put the needs of others ahead of your own desires.[52]

Tasan notes that if you want to follow the path (Dao) of consistent focus and composure, you have to be able to put yourself in others' shoes. Without an empathetic attitude, he argues, acting appropriately in your interactions with others will be impossible. He then goes on to define what he means by "putting oneself in another's shoes." He defines *sŏ* as extrapolating from what you know is best for yourself to see what is best for others, and then acting accordingly.[53]

性 *sŏng* [C. *xing*]: On those few occasions when I choose to transliterate rather than translate this term, I will use the Chinese pronunciation of *xing* in order to avoid confusion with the term 誠 meaning "appropriately responsive and unselfishly cooperative," also pronounced *sŏng* in Korean.

Xing is normally translated as "human nature" or simply "nature," with the implied meaning of "what things are when they are what they should be." Tasan has a more complicated reading of this term. As he uses it in reference to human beings, it means all the innate tendencies human beings are born with. That can refer only to "the innate tendency of human beings to act appropriately," in other words, to act with the common good rather than personal self-interest in mind, which is the way Cheng-Zhu neo-Confucians use that term. In that sense, it also means the potential to behave in accordance with that tendency and act appropriately. But, as Tasan defines it, it can also refer to "the innate tendency of human beings to pursue what is beneficial or pleasurable for them personally."[54] "Tendency" can be replaced with "desire" in those definitions, since Tasan made clear that he believed human beings as human beings have both a desire to act appropriately and a desire for pleasure and personal benefit.[55]

His understanding of human nature is therefore very different from the standard neo-Confucian understanding, which is that human beings are naturally moral. He agrees that Heaven has endowed human beings with the desire to live moral lives, and the ability to do so, but adds that Heaven-endowed human nature coexists with a physical nature that pulls us in self-centered directions. As he put it, all living things are born with inclination toward what is pleasurable, "like a pheasant being drawn toward a hill, a deer drawn toward a field, or an orangutan being drawn toward some wine." But living things are also endowed with an inclination toward what is needed for the realization of that thing's full potential, "like millet needing a dry field or rice sprouts needing water."[56] In human beings, however, unlike in other living things, those inclinations do not automatically direct behavior. Moreover, human beings, as beings endowed with self-consciousness, unlike animals and plants, are aware of frequent conflicts between what they would enjoy doing and what they should be doing. Instead of doing whatever feels natural, Tasan argues that we have to choose to act in such a way as to realize our potential to become fully human.[57]

In other words, rather than being naturally virtuous, Tasan insists, human beings have both the natural potential to act appropriately and the natural potential to act inappropriately. Unfortunately, it is much easier to follow the path of pleasure and personal benefit rather than the path of appropriate behavior.[58] It is that moral path which, by aiming at the common good, allows us to fully actualize our potential as human beings. However, following the moral side of our nature[59] requires effort. It is fair to say that the moral side of human nature is fundamentally good and pure. He agrees with mainstream Confucianism on that point. However, he believes mainstream Confucians have overlooked the fact that equally natural human desires regularly lead people to sink into evil. Consistently acting appropriately does not mean simply acting naturally, if by naturally we mean doing whatever we naturally want to do. Instead, we must devote all of our energy to following the inclinations of our moral human nature and avoiding what the selfish side of our nature is telling us to do.[60]

Tasan emphasizes that human nature is the potential to act appropriately. The key word here is "potential." As he sees it, human beings are not born virtuous. Their potential to act in a virtuous manner can be actualized only by exerting the effort necessary to cultivate ethical virtuosity. This means that human nature cannot be simply equated with *li*. Instead, it should be understood as the potential to act in accordance with *li*. Our human nature includes our ability to recognize *li* and act appropriately, but it also includes emotions and feelings that can stimulate us to act contrary to *li*. (Such morally questionable emotions and feelings come from the human heart-mind.) That is why our human nature cannot be equated with *li*.

Similarly, Tasan argues, Dao cannot be said to be another way of referring to our *xing*. Dao (K. *to*) means a path, in the normative sense of the path we should follow. In other words, it is another way of referring to the way we should behave. The way we should behave (the Dao) is not the same as our ability to behave that way (*xing*). We should not confuse the two.[61] Human nature includes the ability of the heart-mind to choose to follow the Dao. It is not the Dao itself.

Tasan repeatedly warns against conflating terms he believes should be distinguished. That includes distinguishing the Dao from *xing*, and a natural inclination toward the moral good (one aspect of *xing*) from actually acting in a way that conforms to the moral good. He insists, "only after you truly know what Heaven and the Dao are can you be fully cognizant of your true human nature. Only after you have come to be fully cognizant of your true human nature can you serve your parents properly and therefore cultivate your own moral character."[62] In other words, only if you understand that Heaven is not *li*,[63] but is instead the Spirit who observes your every thought and action (Sangje), and understand that the Dao is the way Heaven wants you to behave, can you understand your true nature, which includes your Heaven-bestowed ability to choose to follow the Dao Heaven has ordained for you. Only after you have grasped those essential concepts will you understand how to cultivate a moral character through such actualizations of *li* as serving your parents properly.

誠 *song* [C. *cheng*]: When I transliterate this term rather than translate it, I use the Chinese pronunciation of *cheng* rather than the Korean pronunciation of *sŏng* to avoid confusion with term for "human nature," also pronounced *sŏng* in Korean. When I translate this term, I usually do not use the usual translation of this Sinograph as "sincerity," which has the limited meaning of honesty, of doing what you said you were going to do. That English translation fails to express the full import of the way that Sinograph is used in mainstream neo-Confucian thought as well as in Tasan's writing. In fact, "sincerity" is not even an accurate translation of that Sinograph in early Chinese texts.[64] James Legge came to realize that late in his career, changing his translation of that term from "sincerity" to "perfection of nature."⁶⁵ Legge's later translation reflects his realization that *cheng* refers to attitudes and action that are appropriately responsive and unselfishly cooperative.

Tasan made clear that he shares this more expansive notion of *cheng* when he wrote that "we can see the utmost *cheng* of Heaven in the way the stars, the moon and the various stars stay in their assigned places in the sky and in the way grasses and animals populate the earth."⁶⁶ None of these examples of *cheng* refer to mere consistency of speech and action. Instead, they are examples of things behaving the way they should behave within the interactive environment in which they are found. That is what *cheng* means.

In a human context, *cheng* means to think and act in all interactions as a responsible member of the human community rather than as a self-centered individual. In other words, it means to think and act in an unselfishly cooperative and appropriately responsive manner. A person who is fully *cheng* is free of all selfish concerns and biases and therefore is able to fully actualize his or her moral nature. It is therefore similar in import to *in* but *in*, as its graphical representation of "two people" implies, is used in reference to a relatively narrow context of personal moral attitudes and actions within the human community (hence the common translation of "benevolence"). *Sŏng* refers to a broader range of attitudes and actions that, as its Sinograph implies, completes both people and things, ensuring that they are what they are supposed to be, and do what they are supposed to do.

As Tasan explains, the Sinograph *cheng*, which he understands as referring to acting in an unselfishly cooperative and appropriately responsive manner, is pronounced the same as a different *cheng* (成 K. *sŏng*) meaning to be complete or to become complete. He writes that this is not a coincidence because a person cannot become completely human (the second *cheng*) without acting in an unselfishly cooperative and appropriately responsive manner (the first *cheng*).⁶⁷

This broader range of meaning, embracing much more than mere sincerity, is the reason *cheng* is sometimes translated as "complete authenticity," as "integrity," or even as "creativity,"⁶⁸ and why the *Zhongyong* says it is only someone who is perfectly *cheng* who not only can reach his or her full potential but can help everything else reach its full potential as well and therefore bring the entire cosmos into perfect productive harmony, with all things playing their assigned roles.⁶⁹

I try to translate sentences in which *cheng* appears in such a way as to express that broader meaning of *cheng*. For example, I translate 誠身 (*sŏngsin* / C. *chengshen*) as "make ourselves (literally, our bodies) unselfishly cooperative and appropriately responsive" (behave the way we should behave)⁷⁰ rather than "make ourselves sincere," and I translate 誠意

(sŏngŭi / C. chengyi) as "make our intentions unselfishly cooperative and appropriately responsive"[71] rather than "make our intensions sincere."

Even though the Sinograph *cheng* does not appear in the earliest chapters of the *Zhongyong*, Tasan argues that nevertheless it is implied in the core messages of every chapter. For example, he writes, "Although the opening chapter does not contain the Sinograph *cheng*, it does discuss being watchful over yourself when no one can know what you are doing and thinking and therefore it refers to the same thing as the Sinograph *cheng* does. We therefore cannot say it does not discuss acting in an unselfishly cooperative and appropriately responsive manner."[72]

It is this expansive meaning of *cheng* which Tasan sees as the core message of the *Zhongyong*. He writes, "Acting in an unselfishly cooperative and appropriately responsive manner is the Dao of Heaven. Learning how to act in an unselfishly cooperative and appropriately responsive manner is the Dao of human beings."[73] As Tasan reads it, the *Zhongyong* is a guide to aligning our own thoughts and actions with the Dao of Heaven. Such alignment, to him, is the very definition of being moral: acting in an unselfishly cooperative and appropriately responsive manner.[74]

對越 *taewŏl* [C. *duiyeu*]: This term is understood by Tasan as "be reverent toward, and mindful of, that which is above you." It can also be translated as "be aware that you are in the presence of...," "looking upward with reverence toward...," or "reverently mindful of the presence above of...," with the understanding that what is above is Heaven, the Lord on High. Tasan believed we should always look upward toward the Lord on High with a reverential attitude, remaining always mindful of that constant all-seeing presence above us. He criticized scholars of more recent generations for not realizing that phrase is telling them to "turn their heart-mind with reverence toward the Lord on High."[75]

德 *tŏk* [C. *de*]: Usually translated as "virtue," this Sinograph is another example of the standard translation failing to convey the full importance of the term. In a Confucian context, *tŏk* is shorthand for both actually acting appropriately as well as having the ability to act appropriately. It can therefore be translated as "ethical virtuosity."[76]

To make translating that term accurately more challenging, in some contexts it can also refer to power, especially power manifest in the ability to produce appropriate interactions in a wide variety of situations. This is the sense in which Tasan understands it when he reads the *Zhongyong* passages about the *tŏk* of spiritual beings. For example, Tasan writes that we see the power of the Spirit (Sangje) when we observe that "the sun and moon move through their regular course without any deviations, that the four seasons follow one another in an orderly fashion, that the transformations of things that generate the visible universe are so productive, that everything has its particular role to play in the cosmic network."[77]

Tasan also uses the Sinograph *tŏk* to refer to the power of Sangje to inspire us to overcome our moral frailty and live a moral life. "The power [德] of the *Zhongyong* is that it teaches us that the ability to consistently act appropriately depends on maintaining an attitude of cautious apprehension even when we think no one can see what we are thinking or doing. We can maintain such an attitude even when we think no one knows what we are thinking or doing only if we take the existence of the Spirit seriously and hold Him in awe. Without a Lord on High, there is nothing to be in awe of and apprehensive of. The power [德] of this Spirit is the foundation of our Way."[78]

However, in Tasan's writings, *tŏk* more frequently refers to human ethical virtuosity. That is where we see another example of Tasan's originality. Tasan makes clear that one reason he disagrees with the usual Confucian assumption that human beings are innately virtuous is that he insists you cannot say someone is an ethical virtuoso unless they actually act in a morally appropriate manner. He writes that "there can be no ethical virtuosity without ethical action. If you do not act in a filial, fraternal, diligent, or trustworthy manner, or do not act in a benevolent, righteous, polite, or wise manner, how can you possibly be said to exercise ethical virtuosity?"[79] In an even more explicit challenge to the traditional Confucian understanding of *tŏk*, he writes, "Only after you have acted in a benevolent manner, acted morally, acted politely, or acted wisely can you be said to be benevolent, moral, polite, or wise. Such ways of acting are concrete displays of ethical virtuosity, not something you possess from birth [性]."[80] He adds that you do possess from birth the ability to recognize what it means to act benevolently, morally, politely, and wisely, and the ability to decide to act accordingly, but you cannot be said to be benevolent, moral, polite, or wise until you actually act benevolently, morally, politely, and wisely.

道心人心 **Tosim, insim [C. *daoxin, renxin*]**: Dao heart-mind, human heart-mind. Tasan's understanding of these key terms does not differ significantly from the mainstream view. He agreed with King Chŏngjo when the King, citing Cheng Yi, said that when we talk about the Dao heart-mind, we are talking about acting in accordance with the patterns of appropriate behavior grounded in Heaven, but when we talk about the human heart-mind, we are talking about the influence of our physical desires. However, Tasan added that it is only selfish desires, not desires in general, that lead us astray, since we can be said to also desire the moral good.[81]

Tasan also agreed that a human being has only one heart-mind. As he saw it, Dao heart-mind and human heart-mind refer to two different orientations of the heart-mind, not to two different heart-minds. He did point out, however, that we talk about "conquering the self." We can talk that way, he argues, because of the two sides of who we are, our Dao heart-mind and our human heart-mind. The problem is, he notes, is that the human heart-mind is actually stronger than the Dao heart-mind, so we have to make a firm decision to follow what the Dao heart-mind tells us to do rather than go in the direction the human heart-mind tempts us to go.[82] That is what is meant by "conquering the self."

Tasan also explains that the reason why the human heart-mind is said to be dangerous is that we, as human beings, can choose to do what is right or choose to act selfishly and therefore inappropriately. In fact, he writes, that is the ultimate reason there are problems in this world: we make the wrong choices. And the reason we often make the wrong choice is because the Dao heart-mind is much more subtle than the human heart-mind and therefore it is more difficult to heed what the Dao heart-mind is telling us to do.[83]

靈明 *Yŏngmyŏng* [C. *lingming*]: *Yŏng* means spiritual as well as intelligent. It can also refer to the power to understand or influence something. *Myŏng* means cognitive clarity in this context. *Yŏngmyŏng* is therefore best translated in this work as "spiritual insight" or "penetrating intelligence." Sometimes the best translation is simply "consciousness."[84]

For example, Tasan writes, "Heaven gives human beings intelligence [靈明]. That is what makes it possible for us to act benevolently toward our fellow human beings, to act in an appropriate and proper manner, to treat our fellow human beings the way they should be treated, and to act wisely." And, he adds, it is our consciousness, our penetrating intelligence, that differentiates us from animals.[85] He also uses that term when he says that Heaven [Sangje] is able to see directly into our heart-mind. There is nothing we can hide from Him, he warns, because Heaven is conscious [靈明].[86]

II. Translation:
Chungyong ch'aek

Translation: *Chungyong ch'aek* [Responding to Royal Inquiries regarding the *Zhongyong*]

Source: Yŏyudang Chŏnsŏ [*The complete works of Yŏyudang Chŏng Yagyong*], I: 8, 27a–31b

KING CHŎNGJO POSED THE FOLLOWING QUESTIONS IN REGARD TO THE ZHONGYONG:

This book by Zisi contains in its entirety both the fundamental principles of the mental discipline passed down by a thousand wise men and how those principles are to be put into practice. I would like you to expound on what the *Zhongyong* teaches in all its subtlety and profundity.

I RESPONDED AS FOLLOWS:

In my humble opinion, the *Zhongyong* should be read paired with Book X of the *Analects of Confucius*, the chapter "Village Community."[1] Why do I say that? In that chapter of the *Analects*, the cultural refinement displayed by the Sage shows how the Dao should be manifest in our behavior. The *Zhongyong* shows us the sage within us, the power of the Dao that is complete within our heart-mind. If someone wants to know what really constitutes the heart-mind of a sage, then he cannot ignore the *Zhongyong*.

Generally speaking, the disciples of Confucius only learned from him what they saw and heard, which was how to maintain a proper demeanor and how to act properly. But Zisi absorbed the teachings of Confucius as part of his family heritage, learning from the son of Confucius himself.[2] As a result, he was able to learn what Confucius made known only to those closest to him, the fundamental principles that provided the foundation for what he taught in public. In the *Analects*, Zigong[3] says that he was able

83

to personally observe the cultural refinement with which Confucius demonstrated his teachings but was not able to hear Confucius say anything about human nature and the Dao of Heaven.[4] If those who want to learn the Dao learn how to behave in public by modeling their behavior on what is described in Chapter X of the *Analects,* and also learn how to cultivate the power within that allows them to behave properly in public by applying the lessons learned from reading the *Zhongyong,* then they will have no trouble being true students of Confucius.

(I omit a second paragraph of my response here.)

The King asked:

The *Zhongyong* opens with the line "What Heaven bestows is called our nature."[5] This raises the question of whether the Five Primary Virtues [benevolence, righteousness, propriety, wisdom, and trustworthiness] are exactly the same in human beings and in animals.

Maintaining an attitude of caution and apprehension[6] is essential to moral cultivation but recognition of that has led to debates over what the relationship is between the heart-mind when it is active and the heart-mind when it is quiet. Why is this?

The three cardinal points in the opening section are human nature, the Dao, and instruction. However, the next line talks about the Dao only. Why is that?

The Seven Emotions are joy, anger, sorrow, delight, love, hate, and desire, but the fourth line in this section only mentions four of those [joy, anger, sorrow, and delight].[7] Why is that?

Before those emotions are activated, they are called "human nature," but after they are activated, they are called "emotions." What unites and commands human nature and emotions is the heart-mind.[8] Maintaining composure is the great foundation. Harmony is what results when the Dao pervades the cosmos.[9] That through which the Dao is manifested is *ki* (C. *Qi*).[10] However, this classic doesn't mention the heart-mind or discuss *ki.* Why is that?

I responded:

Let me address first the question of whether the Five Primary Virtues [the five primary ways of displaying ethical virtuosity] are the same in human beings and in animals. Your humble servant suggests that, although we use the same Sinograph when we refer to the "nature" of animals, "nature" in this passage refers to what Heaven bestows as human nature [C. *xing,* the natural desire to response appropriately in whatever situation we find ourselves in]. You cannot have the Five Primary Virtues [displays of appropriate behavior] until after "human nature" [the desire to act appropriately] has been conferred. You cannot confuse "human nature" with the nature of animals.

As for the question of whether caution and apprehension are operative both when the mind is calm and when the mind is active, in my humble opinion, in that interval between when a thought enters your mind and when you decide what to do, if you do not keep in mind that you are being observed by a spirit, then you will fail to act properly. If, on the other hand, you remember that you are being observed, then you will want to watch out for any mistakes in attitude or behavior. This will naturally lead to caution and apprehension operating both when your mind is calm and when it is active.

As for the second line mentioning the Dao only and leaving out any reference to human nature or education, in my opinion that is because the Dao encompasses both the nature above and education below. The Dao is that which makes human beings truly human and makes things what they truly are. This line therefore focuses on the Dao as the key to understanding everything else.

As for why the fourth line mentions four emotions only, in my opinion we talk of seven emotions because the "Evolution of Propriety" [*Liyun*] chapter of the *Book of Rites* mentions seven specific emotions.[11] However, that is not a number set in stone. There are emotions that do not appear in that list of seven. For example, shame is not on that list. Neither is regret. And both envy and frustration are left off that list. These are all different from the seven emotions listed in the *Book of Rites* and cannot be subsumed under them. It is clear, therefore, that the list of seven emotions listed in the *Book of Rites* is not an exhaustive list. Therefore, there is no need to be concerned that the *Zhongyong* mentions only four emotions, since even if it mentioned seven, it still would have left some emotions out.

As to why this classic does not focus on the heart-mind explicitly or discuss *ki*, the way I look at it is that the natural tendencies with which each individual human being has been endowed from birth comprise "human nature." When it is active, human nature is called the heart-mind. However, the fundamental point of the discussion in this section is "what is bestowed by Heaven." Therefore, to speak here of human nature [the natural inclinations all human beings possess] only in reference to that which human beings are endowed with at birth is appropriate. However, when we talk about a human being acting in an appropriate manner, then we can talk about manifestations of *li*. And when we talk about a human being's physical body, then we can talk about manifestations of *ki*. Since this section is more concerned with heavenly principles [the principles ordained by heaven that define appropriate attitudes and actions], it is natural that it talks of composure and harmony instead of *li* and *ki*.

THE KING ASKED:

Achieving a state of composure and a state of harmony requires sustained effort. The result of this composure and harmony is that everything in the universe is in its proper place and everything that exists is supported and nurtured.[12] Can you explain how one heart-mind in one body is able to have this sort of amazing, intricate relationship with the entire cosmos and everything within it?

The *Zhongyong* says that King Shun[13] of old held firm to the mean [*zhong*, i.e., the text uses the first Sinograph in *Zhongyong*], but it does not say anything about his being consistent in doing that [it doesn't use the second Sinograph in *Zhongyong*].[14] It also says Confucius talked about both being composed and centered [*zhong*] and being consistent in doing that [*yong*], while not saying anything about harmonizing with people and things around you.[15] Why, then, does Zisi so closely link being composed and centered with harmonizing in the opening chapter of the *Zhongyong*?

An exemplary person acts in a precisely appropriate manner according to the particular situation he finds himself in at a particular time.[16] Why is the most difficult aspect of acting appropriately determining how to act according to the particular situation one finds oneself in?

An inferior person thinks that he, too, is consistently right on the mark. Why was it necessary to make it explicit that he is acting contrary to how the *Zhongyong* tells him to act?[17]

The meaning of *zhong* in *Zhongyong* becomes clear over the course of reading this text, but *yong* does not appear [except when it is paired with *zhong*] other than when it is used to mean "consistently" in the phrase "consistently acting appropriately" and to mean "reliable" in the phrase "reliable when speaking."[18] Why is that?

The notion of having the Dao pervade the entire cosmos appears in every section of this classic. However, the term "great foundation," meaning the great foundation of the cosmos, only appears a couple of times.[19] Can you explain that?

I RESPONDED:

In regard to the question about how the heart-mind in the body of one individual can influence the myriad transformations that fill the cosmos, your humble servant interprets that statement in the *Zhongyong* this way: The effort sages put into achieving perfect composure and harmony in their thoughts and conduct aligns them with the balance and harmony we see in the operation of the Dao of heaven. Moreover, heaven and human beings are so closely connected that what one does affects the other. When sages act properly, they reinforce the proper functioning of the cosmos. Accordingly, the *Zhongyong* says composure and harmony put everything in the universe in its proper place and ensure that everything that exists is supported and nurtured. Although putting everything in its proper place and ensuring that everything is properly supported and nurtured means managing the myriad transformations of *ki*, and that takes a lot of effort, successful efforts at achieving composure and harmony can have that outcome. That is why the *Zhongyong* says that the successful efforts of sages have such a positive effect on the universe.

In regard to whether Zisi describes Shun and Confucius differently, as I see it, saying "held firm" is the same as saying "grabbed and held on to." What he says about Shun implies consistency [there was no need to add the term *yong*, which in this context would mean "being consistent"]. [As for Zisi reporting that Confucius talked about both being composed and centered and being consistent in doing that, but did not say anything about harmonizing with people and things around you,] in the *Zhongyong* there is a line saying that "an exemplary person interacts harmoniously without ever being distracted away from doing so.... He maintains a strong focus and composure without wavering."[20] This is recorded as what Confucius said. This is no different from what Zisi says elsewhere when he links composure with harmony in his own words.

As for what we mean when we talk about an exemplary person being consistent in acting appropriately [no matter what situation he finds himself in], as I see it, the appropriate way to act is different in every situation in which we find ourselves, because every situation is different. It's just like when you try to use a pair of scales to weigh something. To determine its exact weight, you have to adjust the position of the weight marker between the two scales in accordance with how heavy or light that object is until you find just the right spot. The reason it is so difficult to consistently act appropriately according to the particular situation you are in [neither doing too much nor not doing enough] is the same reason it is so difficult to determine how much an object weighs — you have to make sure you hit the right spot and are not even the least bit off in either direction.

As for the question about an inferior person acting contrary to how the *Zhongyong* says he should behave, when Wang Su edited the *Book of Rites*,[21] for some reason or another he inserted the Sinograph that makes it explicit that an inferior person acts inappropriately. However, that is not necessary since it is clear that the text says that an inferior person, someone who engages in inappropriate behavior, does not behave the way he is supposed to behave, even though he may think that is what he is doing. Therefore, leaving out the Sinograph that means "acting contrary to" does not cause any misunderstanding.

As for the Sinograph meaning "consistency" [the syllable 庸 yong in Zhongyong], its meaning is implied in places where that Sinograph itself does not appear. Yong in this text means "consistently" or "for a long time." In the Zhongyong, we can find such lines as "the Dao cannot be departed from even for an instant,"[22] "rare are those who can act in accordance with the Dao,"[23] and "there are those who cannot follow it for even a month."[24] Those lines clearly refer to consistency, or the lack thereof, in maintaining a focused composure.

Finally, as to why the term "great foundation" appeared only a couple of times in this text, in my opinion "great foundation" does not refer to something separate and distinct from what is discussed elsewhere in this text. Rather, that term is simply a more elegant way of saying "focused composure." The many instances in this text in which the Sinograph *zhong* appears, therefore, can be taken as references to the "great foundation."

The King Asked:

The *Zhongyong* just as it is, in its entirety, provides the best guidelines for acting appropriately. There is no part within it that is better than any other part. Therefore, there does not appear to be any reason [for Yan Hui] to "select from it."[25] There is no specific part of this text which stands out [more than any other part] as a crutch for anyone to "rely on." The text should simply say here "he relied on the *Zhongyong*" [rather than say "he selected from it."][26]

Wisdom and stupidity refer to knowledge. Worthiness and incompetence refer to action. However, this text collapses them both into references to action.[27] Why is that?

We are told that with wisdom, benevolence, and valor, ethical virtuosity is possible.[28] Nevertheless, we are also told that maintaining consistent focus and composure is impossible.[29] But didn't the wisdom of Great Shun manifest itself in his applying focused composure in whatever situation he found himself in? Didn't the true humanity of Yan Yuan[30] manifest itself in his choosing to maintain focus and composure?

That which extends far and wide but is subtle and hard to see[31] is *li*.[32] However, the fact that hawks fly and fish jump is due to their *ki*.[33] But can we refer to *ki* to elucidate *li*? Wouldn't that be contradictory?

Spirits and ghosts are *ki*, but when we talk about *tŏk* [virtue and power],³⁴ we are talking about *li*. Yet we talk about spirits and ghosts displaying their *tŏk*.³⁵ Isn't that hard to swallow?

The one thread running through everything is steadfastness and conscientiousness combined with empathy. If those are the principles you live by, though the Dao may seem far away, it actually will be close by.³⁶ This advice was provided for those in the beginning stages of applying what they learn so that they would realize that the Five Fundamental Human Relationships,³⁷ from the very first, are not something that is high and far away. This being the case, when this text refers to the need to climb to a height from a low point, is it only referring to starting from proper relations between husbands and wives and between older and younger brothers?³⁸

The *Daxue* of Zengzi³⁹ and the *Zhongyong* both talk about rectifying our character and our heart-mind. But they are somewhat different in that the *Zhongyong* tells us to cultivate our ability to act appropriately but the *Daxue* tells us to cultivate appropriate intentions.⁴⁰ A discussion of the "Nine Cardinal Rules"⁴¹ can also be found in the *Kongzi jiayu* [*Sayings of the Confucian School*]⁴² but the writing style is not the same in those two sources. One goes on and on. The other is brief and to the point.⁴³ Isn't this enough to make you a little suspicious?

I RESPONDED:

Your Highness asked why the *Zhongyong* would talk about selecting a part of it. In your humble servant's opinion, the phrase you cite does not mean to extract something from within the text of the *Zhongyong* and discard the rest. Let's look at lines that read "a person who is sincere [naturally appropriately responsive and unselfishly cooperative in whatever situation they find themselves in]⁴⁴ can act with composure and focus without having to try very hard to do so.... A person who wants to become appropriately responsive and unselfishly cooperative should grab onto the good and not let go."⁴⁵ Generally speaking, "to select" means to study so that you learn what you should do and then you work hard in order to act the way you have learned you should act. That is the reason Yan Yuan dedicated himself to learning.⁴⁶ And that is the reason Confucius allowed Yan Yuan the latitude to "select the good." But if someone is already appropriately responsive and unselfishly cooperative, then he will naturally act in accordance with how the *Zhongyong* says he should act. There is no need for him to pick out particular bits of advice from the *Zhongyong*. That is how Great Shun was always able to be right on target in whatever he did.

As for saying that the *Zhongyong* does not have a specific section for you to "rely on" to the exclusion of other sections, in your humble servant's opinion, the *Zhongyong* does not provide one way and one way only to act in a focused and composed manner every time and everywhere. Instead, in every situation there is an ethical and appropriate way to behave specific to that situation. In the eyes of a sage, the appropriate course to follow in whatever situation he finds himself in is obvious. It is like the way a carpenter uses a measure to determine how wide and long an object is. That tells him where the exact center of that particular object is. He relies on that to proceed with his task, to ensure that he does not produce something that is unbalanced or lopsided.

As for wisdom and sageliness, in your humble servant's opinion, cognitive clarity and appropriate actions are inextricably linked. If someone does not know clearly how they should behave and therefore does not act properly, then the reason they acted improperly is that they did not know what to do. If someone does not do what they are supposed to do and therefore does not gain the cognitive clarity appropriate action would give them, then the reason they do not have cognitive clarity is that they did not act like a sage would act. Knowledge and action, therefore, go together.

As for the wisdom of Shun and the true humanity of Yan Hui, it consisted of their being consistently focused on acting appropriately. In your humble servant's opinion, since wisdom, benevolence, and valor are all full actualizations of the power to interact appropriately in a wide variety of situations,[47] it is possible to accomplish anything with them. Therefore, since Shun and Yan Hui possessed those virtues [modes of ethical virtuosity], they were able to consistently act precisely the way they should act.

However, your humble servant thinks that, in regard to the three actions mentioned in Chapter IX [pacifying the world, declining ranks and emoluments, and stepping on unsheathed blades], they should not be interpreted as corresponding to three modes of ethical virtuosity [acting wisely, acting benevolently, and acting courageously] respectively.[48] In particular, the phrase "ranks and emoluments may be declined"[49] should not be interpreted as referring to "acting out of benevolence."[50]

As for the references to the *ki* of hawks and fish to explain *li*, here is my opinion. Your humble servant thinks that the Dao of the exemplary person, when it is applied on a large scale, reaches out to encompass all the myriad things and events in the entire cosmos. When it is applied on a small scale, it is concentrated in the smallest of things and events. We can see it, and apply it, in the interactions of the average man and woman. That is what is meant by "extends far and wide." However, even the sage cannot always know or apply that which is so small that it is almost hidden. This metaphorical reference to hawks and fishes, therefore, is simply a sigh of admiration in contemplation of that which is hidden. It is talking about it as that which is high and mysterious, as well as that which is deep and minute. There is no need to talk about it in terms of *li* and *ki*.

As for explaining spirits in terms of *li* and *ki*, in your humble servant's opinion, spirits do not have any material form. By their very definition, they are things which are not the least bit material. That is why you cannot talk about them in terms of *ki*. I venture to suggest, therefore, that there's no problem with using the phrase "displaying their power to act appropriately"[51] in reference to them.

As for saying that "steadfastness and conscientiousness along with empathy are not far from the Dao,"[52] your humble servant believes that the one thread running through everything is steadfastness and conscientiousness accompanied by empathy.[53] Someone who is studying to become a better person should stress learning how to be considerate in their dealings with others since that will lead to them becoming fully human. How can doing that be something that is difficult to do and out of reach? The early Confucians talked about the one thread running through everything. I am not convinced that they were talking about something that was grandiose and mysterious. The Five Fundamental Human Relationships are not something high above us or far away from us. Your humble servant believes that they can be found in something as close at hand as the relationship between a husband and a wife and between an older and a younger brother. They are right next to us. On the other hand, spirits, which are hard to see yet obvious, are high above us and far away. That is why this passage says that they move us to offer sacrifices to them.[54]

As for as the statement in the *Zhongyong* about rectifying our character so that we are appropriately responsive and unselfishly cooperative, and the statement in the *Daxue* about making our intentions appropriately responsive and unselfishly cooperative, they do not refer to the same thing. Your humble servant thinks that the *Daxue* uses the expression "make our intentions appropriately responsive and unselfishly cooperative" as a reference to the starting point for rectifying ourselves to function appropriately in the world around us.[55] The *Zhongyong*, on the other hand, uses a somewhat similar expression to refer to looking inward, into our own heart-mind, in order to rectify our inner orientation.[56] That's why these two similar expressions do not really mean the same thing.

As for why the two versions of the Nine Cardinal Rules are somewhat different, your servant believes that the *Kongzi jiayu* is something that Wang Su [195–256] constructed by putting together some older material. The "Lord Ai asks" [*Aigong wen*] chapter in *Kongzi jiayu*, in which the Nine Cardinal Rules appear, is just a few paragraphs that were tacked on and made to look like an actual exchange of questions and answers. It cannot be trusted to be accurate.[57]

THE KING ASKED:

Are the ability to act appropriately due to the clear understanding of how we should behave that we gain from acting in a *cheng* manner [58] and the ability to act appropriately because Heaven endows us with that ability[59] the same or different?

Are what we learn by cultivating a clear understanding of how we should behave, so that we become appropriately responsive and unselfishly cooperative,[60] and what we learn through the self-discipline of cultivating the proper way to behave[61] the same or different?

Why are the "Dao of Kings" and the "Dao of Men" lumped together?[62]

Are the two terms "never ceasing" and "does not cease" interchangeable?[63]

The terms "large and substantial" and "high and brilliant" refer to both earth and Heaven. So why do we see the discussion conclude by referring only to "what Heaven has arranged"?[64]

The three thousand rules of etiquette and the three hundred rules of rituals are truly quite minute and detailed.[65] So why does this section [which mentions them] begin by saying "Large indeed"?[66]

Placing "respecting your innate power to act appropriately" and "following the path of inquiry and study"[67] at the forefront of plumbing *li* and investigating things, and cultivating the greatest clarity of moral insight while keeping consistently focused and composed, is that what the title of this work as well as its various chapters are telling us?

The *Zhongyong* says that passing on the teachings of the Yao and Shun as if they were his direct ancestors and holding high for all to see the exemplary actions of King Wen and King Wu, that is the way Confucius ensured the correct transmission of the Way. It also says that aligning himself with the seasonal changes in Heaven above and harmonizing with changes in the land and sea below, that was the way Confucius acted in an appropriately ethical manner.[68] What is the reason for this high praise for Confucius?

The *Zhongyong* mentions the "lesser natural powers" which are like a flowing river and the "greater natural powers" which produce significant transformations. What does "powers" refer to here?[69] And what is the difference between the "person who displays the highest level of unselfishly cooperative and appropriately responsive behavior"[70] and the "perfect sage"?[71]

In this work, twice Confucius is referred to by his personal name Zhongni.[72] Also, the *Book of Songs* is cited in a confusing way. Sometimes the citation is introduced with "The *Book of Songs* says…" Other times, the citation is introduced with "It is said in the *Book of Songs*..."[73] Does this difference mean anything?

Some commentators break the *Zhongyong* into six major divisions. Others break it into only four. Which is most appropriate when determining the correct way to read it aloud and when analyzing it line by line?

Starting from the inner chapters and reading outward or starting from the outward chapters and reading inward, starting from the end or starting from the beginning, what is the best way to read it meticulously?

When there are abstruse explanations that obfuscate, then does it matter if the odes themselves and the way this text uses those terms precisely coincide or not?

The Dao is very subtle in that it has no sound, scent, or material form. So how can we say that Non-Polarity[74] truly derives from this Dao?

(The paragraph that followed this is missing.)

I RESPONDED:

(I omit two paragraphs here from my original response.) [Tasan deleted his answers to the first four questions in this section.]

Heaven and earth are usually discussed together, but this text suddenly focuses only on "what Heaven has arranged." Let me try to explain why. Your humble servant would like to suggest that the term "heaven" in the phrase "*cheng* [being appropriately responsive and unselfishly cooperative]... is so lofty and brilliant, it has the same power as heaven"[75] is a reference to the vast blue sky. The reference later in that same chapter to Heaven in the phrase "what Heaven has arranged, how profound it is"[76] uses the term Heaven in another sense, as a reference to Heaven who rules the universe with penetrating intelligence. Heaven in that sense cannot be paired with the earth. This means that references to heaven and earth together are references to the great expanse of the physical universe, with its mountains and rivers, while references to Heaven alone are often praise of the creative work Heaven does in effectively managing the transformations that constitute the universe. The reason why the Lord of the Earth is not included in the reference to the winter sacrifices in the southern suburbs to Heaven and the summer sacrifices in the northern suburbs to the spirits of the soil is precisely because in ancient times there were no rituals specifically to honor the earth alone.[77]

(I omit two paragraphs here.) [Tasan again deletes his responses to several of the king's questions.]

Your humble servant would like to suggest that there is an explanation for why the *Zhongyong* appears to be a jumble of different themes. The

Zhongyong should actually be divided into ten sections. The first section is like the Imperial Pivot reference in the "Great Plan with Nine Divisions" section of the *Book of Documents*.[78] The next four sections deal with the generation of the various things in the universe. They point our attention toward Heaven on High. The following four sections deal with the three thousand rules of etiquette that teach us how to interact with our fellow human beings and how to behave appropriately. The last section sums up the entire discussion. There is no need to break the text down further into various chapters.

(I omit seven paragraphs here.) [Tasan again, for reasons unknown to us, deletes several paragraphs from his original essay, which he wrote in 1790, when his philosophy was not yet fully developed.]

As for saying "that which makes no sound and has no scent"[79] is a reference to Non-Polarity your humble servant thinks "that which makes no sound and has no scent" is a description of the silent and motionless way Heaven effectively sustains and manages the transformations that constitute the universe. The terms "Non-Polarity" and "Supreme Polarity" (C. *taiji* / K. *t'aegŭk*) are actually nothing more than references to primal matter and energy (*ki*) as a formless mass.[80] It is said that, originally, *ki* took no particular form but then it congealed into the various separate and distinct entities that make up the universe today. Since I am not very intelligent, I really cannot confirm if that is the way the universe originated or not.

(I omit the paragraph that followed.) [Here Tasan deletes an answer to a question from King Chŏngjo, which he also deleted.]

The King asked:

Why is it that the state of the world has been gradually declining, such that there are not as many moral people today as there were in times past, and scholars of today do not illuminate matters as well as scholars did in times past? There appear to be plenty of people delving into obscure issues and doing all sorts of strange things, and there appear to be plenty of people willing to join with others in various disgusting activities. They remind me of Zimo, whom Mencius described as being too inflexible in his determination to hold on to focus and composure,[81] and Hu Guang, who was far too flexible in the way he applied the teachings of the *Zhongyong*.[82]

When I look at the way the sages of old established the great foundation for a moral society and compare it to the way things are today, it appears to me that people today not only misunderstand the sages just like that person from Yan who misread the letter from Ying,[83] they have gone even farther off the proper path, so far from where they should be that I cannot even say how heretical they are. Those who call themselves Confucian scholars these days claim to be engaged in the study of the Confucian classics and they intone the words of Confucius and Zisi, but they do the opposite of what Confucius and Zisi taught. They prattle on about the basic meaning of Heaven, human beings, human nature, and what Heaven has conferred in such grandiose terms that it would appear they are describing brilliant flower petals falling down from Heaven, but if you observe how they actually behave, you will see that nothing they do is in accord with the moral principles taught in the Confucian texts they study. When it comes time to prepare to engage in the actual affairs of the world, they have no idea how to maintain their innate ability to act appropriately. When they are by themselves and no one else can see them, they have no idea how to engage in self-examination so that they can identify any moral deficiencies and take steps to overcome them. When they sit quietly, as though they are meditating, they have a blank look on their face and look like nothing more than a boulder stuck to that spot. When they are in motion, they behave with reckless abandon, like a wild horse that has slipped its reins.

The moral principles of Heaven are disappearing from view day by day, as self-centered human desires move to the fore. The great foundation supporting a moral society is dissolving, and appropriate behavior is growing rare. We have reached a stage in which a trait seen in lesser human beings, the lack of concern for proper behavior, has become commonplace.

If we want to reverse course, eliminate all these problems, and change the prevalent way of behaving up to now, we need to read those Confucian texts in such a way that we understand what they are actually saying, and, then we need to set our minds on always and everywhere doing what is right. If we cultivate ethical virtuosity and focus our attention solely on the Dao, and exert ourselves in the same way the sages of the ancient past as well as the sages of more recent centuries have done, then we will return to the Dao [the proper Way]. But how can we do that?

I RESPONDED:

As to why the more recent generation of scholars worry about cramming bits and pieces of knowledge into their heads but do not put enough effort into behaving in accordance with the Dao they claimed to have learned, and why they seek only shadows rather than substance, there are a couple of reasons. They do not realize that the call to "be reverent toward, and mindful of, that which is above you,"[84] is asking them to turn their heart-mind with reverence toward the Lord on High. And they do not realize that "making their intentions unselfishly cooperative and appropriately responsive" means that, when they meet an exemplary person, they will have nothing to be ashamed of.⁸⁵ If we do as the scholars of today do, it is like driving a chariot toward Yue in the south when you are supposed to head north, or like when the man of Yan misunderstood the message from Ying. We will not achieve the result we desire.

The essential teachings of the *Zhongyong* in their entirety and how those teachings should be implemented overall cannot be broken up into separate and distinct lessons. Instead, we should extract the one core message that underlies everything written in the *Zhongyong*. That core message can be summed up in one phrase: act in an appropriately responsive and unselfishly cooperative manner. How can we do that? The only way to do that is to work hard at cultivating an attitude of caution and apprehension. If we work hard at cultivating such an attitude, then the Dao of the *Zhongyong* can be revived.

Why do I say that? Let's think about it this way. When people are able to help each other live better lives and are able to keep from doing harm to each other, it is because a wise king rules over them. If they do not have such a king, then all the otherwise good people will turn on each other and will openly engage in such immoral behavior as stealing from those around them. Such chaos would just go on and on. However, despite such behavior, we know that the only reason they appear to have such evil within them, the only reason they appear to have such a rotten core, is that there is no wise king watching over them and therefore their heart-minds are not enlightened by wise governance. They act the way they do because there is no law enforcement system to point them in the right direction and no government to punish them when they do wrong. They behave in such an unacceptable fashion because no one is watching them from above. They are as brazen as they are because there is no one around to stop them.

Why is it that people will not act in an appropriate manner unless someone above is watching them? The heart-minds of human beings are such that they are inclined to act in a foolish and headstrong manner. If there is no one who can enlighten them to the proper norms of behavior, then they will just act any which way they please without any regard for the consequences. Even when they put on a show of good behavior, in their heart-minds they still are basically immoral.

However, if you get them to engage in a serious effort to learn what really matters so that in their heart-minds they become truly cautious and apprehensive, if they can see what Heaven, humanity, human nature, and that which Heaven has conferred truly are, and if you get them to feel the same reverence for the Lord on High that the wise sages of old felt, then they will be both circumspect and diligent instead of being thoughtless and lazy. Then, when they engage in quiet-sitting, they won't have blank looks on their faces, looking no different from a large rock. And when they are up and about, engaging in some important business, they won't act with reckless abandon like a horse that has slipped its reins. By keeping in check the selfishness of human desires, they will preserve the concern for the common good that is the core of the principles conferred by Heaven.

Then the great foundation of the *Zhongyong* will be completely revitalized and the Dao will prevail. What has been lost will be restored and the Way once followed will be followed again. Would that not be an occasion of great happiness for those of us who are dedicated to Confucian learning?

However, a heart-mind governed by an attitude of apprehension needs an object for it to be apprehensive about. A cautious and apprehensive heart-mind cannot be cautious and apprehensive about nothing. It is necessary to comprehend that which Heaven has mandated in order to be able to act in accordance with it. People need to first identify the normative patterns of things and events. Then they need to apply those patterns of appropriate interactions in everyday life so that they are actualized through personal experience. In order to investigate the normative patterns of things and events and come to an understanding of the basis for them, they need to devote themselves to constant inquiry and study so that they trace them back to their source. They need to gain a thorough understanding of what things really are and how they should function. They should not spare any effort in the drive to gain this insight. Once they have achieved this, they will be able to clearly distinguish between good and evil and will be able to identify the causes of good fortune and misfortune as easily as they can spot their hand in front of their own face. They will have reached the point in which they are cautious without having to make a special effort to be so, and are naturally apprehensive without making a deliberate effort to be so. They will be able to spontaneously act in accordance with the principles of Heaven. Wouldn't that be wonderful?

Respectfully submitted by your humble servant.

III. Translation:
Chungyong kangŭibo

Translation: *Chungyong kangŭibo* [A Discussion of the Meaning of the *Zhongyong*, Revised]

Source: Yŏyudang Chŏnsŏ [*The complete works of Yŏyudang Chŏng Yagyong*] II: 4, 1a–67b

Introduction

In spring of 1783, the *kyemyo* year of the reign of Emperor Qianlong (r. 1735–1796), I passed the Classics Licentiate exam and was able to enter the National Confucian Academy. In the summer of the next year, 1784 (when I was twenty-three years old), the King (Chŏngjo. r. 1776–1800) sent to the Academy a list of seventy questions on the *Zhongyong* and ordered each student to answer every one of them.

At that time my friend Kwangam Yi Pyŏk (1754–1786), now deceased, was studying in the Sup'yo Bridge area of Seoul.[1] (He was thirty-one at the time.) I went to visit him to ask his help in answering those questions. Kwangam was happy to see me and discuss those questions with me. We worked together to compose the first drafts of my answers. When I returned to my room and looked over what we had produced, I was impressed with what we had done. The arguments were well-reasoned and supported by pithy phrasing. Adding a few of my own thoughts, I refined the arguments and polished the language a bit, and then submitted it.

A few days after the King had carefully looked over the answers all of us had submitted, First Royal Secretary Kim Sangjip (1723–?) asked Royal Secretary Hong Inho (1753–1799), "Who is this Chŏng Yagyong? How does he know so much?" That same day, during the morning Lectures on the Royal Mat, the King had remarked, "Overall, the answers by the students at the National Confucian Academy were not well-grounded nor were they very creative. But this fellow Yagyong—his answers really stand out. He is quite a profound thinker." The King especially liked what I wrote about the debate among Korean Confucians over whether *Li* or *Ki* activates the Four Sprouts of virtue. There was no other reason for him to praise my answers in this way.

Three years later, in the summer of a *pyŏngo* year, Kwangam passed away. Eight years after that, in the fall of 1793, a *kyech'uk* year, when I was staying in the Myŏngnye district in Seoul, I cleaned up my answers to those questions. Looking them over, however, I had realized that there were some places in which I had not been very precise and moreover there were times I had imposed some interpretations on the text that the text itself did not support.

In the winter of 1801, the *sinyu* year of the reign of Emperor Jiaqing (r.1796–1820), I was sent into exile in Kangjin. Fourteen years later, in the summer of 1814, a *kapsul* year, for the first time a Censor memorialized the throne with a request that my exile be ended.[2] The order freeing me from exile was prepared but its release was postponed. At that time, I was living on Tea Mountain [Tasan] and had just written the two-volume-long "Admonitions for Myself upon reading the *Zhongyong*" [*Chungyong chajam*]. After that, I turned to that text I had first written in 1784 and revised it, correcting those statements in which I had gone beyond what the *Zhongyong* actually said. Going through the *Zhongyong* chapter by chapter, I also added some information on issues the King had not asked me about, but which needed to be clarified. This revised version of the "A Discussion of the Meaning of the *Zhongyong*" comes to six volumes.

It has been a long time since the late king was able to walk this earth. I will never hear his voice again. He will have no more questions for me to answer. Moreover, when I count how long it has been since I last talked with Kwangam, I realize it has been thirty years. If Kwangam were still alive, in ethical behavior and learning I would not even come close to his achievements. When I see how I mixed some of the ideas in the original manuscript together with some new ideas of mine, I can see that it needs to be cleaned up a bit. I can't help but sigh when I think of how different this text would be if it were not for the fact that one of us is alive but the other is gone. When I hold this manuscript in my hands, I cannot keep from crying.[3]

Written on Tea Mountain on the last day of the seventh month of the *kapsul* year (1814).

Zhongyong I: 1

> That which Heaven has conferred on us is our innate ability to act appropriately.[1]

Zhu Xi wrote, "Heaven generates the myriad things with yin and yang and the Five Processes. When *Ki* then coagulates into specific shapes, Heaven endows it with the appropriate *Li*."[2]

My comment:

The terms "yin" and "yang" arise from the sun shedding its light on something or, when it is blocked, creating a shadow. That which appears dark is called "yin." That which appears bright is called "yang." However, neither yin nor yang is an actual object with tangible shape and weight. Those terms are nothing more than labels for light and dark. Accordingly, they cannot serve as the father and mother of the myriad things.

From the far north to the far south, in every country on earth, whether they are in the east or the west, the sun rises and sets at different times. But in all those countries the overall amount of "yin and yang" every day is the same. There is not one iota of difference. Moreover, the amount of daytime and night-time and the number of cold days and hot days even out over time. That is why the sages of old, in creating the *Classic of Changes*, took the interaction of yin and yang as the Dao of Heaven. The Dao of Heaven is nothing other than the Way of the Changes. If yin and yang were actual physical objects, then Fu Xi would not have been able to use them to construct the eight trigrams.

Those eight trigrams can be divided into four that suggest stability and four that suggest movement from one stage to another. The four that are stable represent Heaven, Earth, Water, and Fire. The ones that are not represent Wind, Thunder, Mountains, and Marshes.

The "Biaoji" [Record of examples] chapter in the *Liji* [Book of rites][3] says that Heaven and Fire are to be respected and we should not draw very near to them while we should draw near to Water and Earth rather than keep a respectful distance from them.[4] This tells us that there are some things that are noble and some things that are base. Heaven and Fire join forces to generate Wind and Thunder. Earth and Water interact to produce Mountains and Marshes. Through such transformations the myriad things emerge. Wise men in the distant past observed this and distinguished the light and clear from the heavy and murky by describing the former as "yang" and the latter as "yin." These were figures of speech and didn't refer to any actual material substance.

Moreover, when scholars in the past talked of "heaven," they used that term to refer to two totally different things. "Heaven" was used in a general sense to refer to everything above the earth. They also used the term "heaven" more narrowly for the large, deep blue circular sky above. When we use the term "heaven" to refer to the deep blue sky, then we can say that, though it is bright and clear, it contains both yin and yang. That's why we call the sun "the Great Yang" and call the moon "the Great Yin." The Great Yang is pure fire. The Great Yin is pure water. Similarly, the Five Stars [the five visible planets, that is to say Venus, Mars, Mercury, Jupiter and Saturn], though they all are lined up in the sky and shine down on the earth below, each has its own respective nature. Some are cold, some are hot, some are dry, some are wet, some are windy, and some are rainy. Some are responsible for the five metals [gold, silver, copper, lead, and iron] and the eight minerals of the alchemist [cinnabar, realgar, orpiment, malachite, mica, sulphur, rock salt, and potassium nitrate]. Others are responsible for the hundred grasses and the hundred trees. Birds, beasts, and insects, large and small, all receive the allotment of *ki* they need to be born and grow. So, when we look around us, we see that the firmament above and the ether below as well as water, fire, earth, rocks, the sun, the moon, and the stars all are constituent elements of the physical world. Moreover, can't we use copper, iron, plants, and trees to make many other things?

Now let me try to explain further. It is said that heaven uses yin and yang, water and fire, copper and iron [metal], and pine and cypress trees [wood] to produce the myriad things. That is really hard to comprehend. If you look at the individual components in that statement, you can see that is contrary to reason. Even if you lump all those various components together in trying to explain the origin of the entire material world, it still doesn't make any sense. Moreover, when Heaven creates plants and animals, it immediately gives them the patterns by which they live, grow, and reproduce such that each particular type of plant or animal reproduces its own kind. Each one is created with its own distinctive nature and destiny appropriate to its kind complete within it.

That is not the way it is with human beings. When the myriad of human beings on this earth first emerges from the womb, they are each endowed with the power of penetrating intelligence.[5] That makes them far superior to the multitude of other things on this planet and puts them in a position in which all those other things are for human beings to use and enjoy.

Now, some people say that human beings and animals are alike in their adherence to the Five Primary Virtues [benevolence, righteousness,[6] propriety, wisdom, and trustworthiness].[7] Then which would be the master and which the servant? After all, humans and animals are not equals. Could Heaven above possibly have endowed both humans and animals with the same innate ability to act appropriately? Besides, the names we give to appropriate behavior—benevolence, righteousness, propriety, and wisdom—are derived from what human beings do. Those terms do not refer to some mysterious principles deep in the human heart-mind.[8] All that Heaven gives human beings is penetrating intelligence. That is what makes it possible for us to act benevolently toward our fellow human beings, to act in an appropriate and proper manner, to treat our fellow human beings the way they should be treated, and to act wisely.

If we assume that Heaven above has endowed human beings with benevolence, righteousness, propriety, and wisdom so that it is complete within their nature, then we are mistaken. If this were the case, then wouldn't animals also be endowed with the Five Primary Virtues by Heaven?[9] Buddha preached that humans and animals have the same basic nature. That is why, according to the Buddha, when men die, they can reincarnate as an ox, and a dog can reincarnate as a human. Human beings and animals alike are reincarnated over and over again. This goes on forever, generation after generation. Su Wenzhong [Su Shi, also known as Su Dongpo, 1037–1101] was a strong believer in this. That is why he wrote poems such as "The Red Cliffs." That is also why he wrote the stone tablet for Han Wengong (Han Yu, 768–824) in the temple in Chaozhou. He was quite sly, though, when he expressed his Buddhist ideas, so most people didn't notice the Buddhist elements in his thinking.

It was generally the case that, when the intellectuals of the Song dynasty discussed human nature, they all tended to commit the same offense. Although they put a lot of effort into searching for the Way out of a desire to act properly, they ended up clashing with what Confucius actually taught. They were not bold enough to faithfully follow the path Confucius laid out. Would later scholars forgive me if I were just like them?

The four primary virtues of benevolence, righteousness, propriety, and wisdom can be divided into those that are more active and those that are less active. (Zhu Xi classified being fully human [benevolence] and displaying proper concern for ritual and social status [propriety] as active and associated them with being assertive, and classified behaving appropriately in human interactions [righteousness] and acting with discernment [wisdom] as less active and associated them with being compliant.)[10] However, that is not necessarily so. The *Book of Changes* says, "The sages determined what the Dao of Heaven was, which they defined in terms of yin and yang, what the Dao of earth was, which they defined in terms of hard and soft, and what the Dao of Man was, which they defined in terms of benevolence and righteousness."[11]

Here the soft and yin are associated with benevolence, and the hard and yang are associated with righteousness. We need to be flexible, therefore, in how we deal with these terms. We shouldn't arbitrarily place them in two different categories. If you give your life to save others, that's benevolence, but such an event falls under the category of yin. If you serve your parents well, that's also benevolence, but it would fall under the category of yang. If you sacrifice your life out of righteousness, that should be classified as active and assertive, but if you act in accordance with your older brother's wishes out of righteousness, that should be classified as passive and compliant. Propriety in mourning and propriety as a soldier should be associated with yin, but propriety when you are receiving a guest or when you are celebrating a joyous occasion should be associated with yang. So how can we say that benevolence and propriety should only be associated with the active and assertive while righteousness and wisdom should only be associated with the passive and compliant? That is not the way things are at all.

THE KING ASKED:

Heaven transforms and gives birth to the Ten Thousand Things by means of yin and yang and the Five Processes. *Ki* coagulates into specific material entities, and then those objects are endowed with the appropriate *Li*. Given that we say *ki* first constitutes material objects and then they are endowed with *li*, is it appropriate to conflate "our inborn tendency to act appropriately" and "our physical endowment"?

I RESPONDED:

Because the Dao of Heaven is so vast and the *li* of the Ten Thousand Things so subtle and hidden, it is not easy to infer what those *li* are. Furthermore, the Five Processes are but five among the Ten Thousand Things. Since they are all just things, isn't it a little difficult for five things to give birth to ten thousand things?

The "Ceremonial Uses" [a chapter of the *Book of Rites*] says, "Human beings are the most refined *ki* produced by the Five Processes."[12] This one phrase is something the previous generations of Confucian scholars took as their guiding principle. However, how can we be sure that this assumption has any logical basis, when we don't see any metal, wood, or any other of the Five Processes when we cut open something made of flesh and blood and look inside it? Moreover, the core nature of a thing is something that doesn't have any material form or physical characteristics. If we say that the core human nature [C. *xing*, the innate tendency to act appropriately] can be found within the physical characteristics of a thing, what does that imply? If we take the innate tendency to act appropriately as something separate and distinct from what Heaven has ordained, and in doing so we establish a human nature that is the nature of the material components of a thing, we are making a claim that ancient records do not support, and such a claim is beyond my comprehension.

The *Book of Documents* says, "The Lord on High has conferred on the common people a moral sense. This is their constant nature."[13] Is this not the nature that Heaven has conferred? Because of the mysterious combination of spirit and material form in human beings, human nature cannot be separated from *ki*.[14] But this classic [the *Zhongyong*] says that human nature is good and not evil. Therefore, when it says we must follow our human nature, how could it be asking us to follow our physical endowment?

THE KING ASKED:

As for the Sinograph "follow" in the phrase "to follow human nature," Zhu Xi glossed it as "to follow a path."[15] Also, in his *Zhongyong huowen* [Questions and answers on the *Zhongyong*], he refutes what various other schools say by illuminating the fact that they do not show us how to engage in self-cultivation but instead talk about other things.[16] His argument is truly unassailable. But as for "moral cultivation" in the phrase "cultivate the Way," he did not say that referred to self-cultivation per se but said instead that it referred to "an existing moral character" as revealed in ritual, music, punishment, and government. He wrote that is how you illuminate "your moral character."[17] So does that mean that "cultivating the Way" does not mean the work of cultivating the self?[18]

I RESPONDED:

Following the moral side of one's nature[19] requires effort. It is fair to say that the moral side of human nature is fundamentally good and pure. However, equally natural human inclinations regularly lead people to sink into evil. We must devote all of our energy to following our moral human nature. If later we find that we have aligned ourselves with the Way, then following our moral nature would have produced a positive result. Although Zhu Xi took "follow" to mean "to follow a path," when he discussed human nature overall, he lumped it together with the nature of animals. That is why Zhu Xi said, "Following the way the ten thousand things behave naturally is called the Dao." This character "following" is not the one that means "to exert a lot of effort."[20] Further, he also said "there are those who take following one's nature as acting in accordance with the *li* of their nature which they have been endowed with by Heaven. If that is the case, then the Way would only come into existence through people."[21] From this we can see that what he means by following one's nature is nothing more than acting naturally. I fear that this is not in harmony with the practice of the sages of old, which was "to restrain oneself and return to propriety."[22] It sounds, rather, like the crazy teachings of Daoists like Zhuangzi,[23] which are totally unreliable.

Moreover, the reference to "moral cultivation" does not imply an existing "moral character." "Moral cultivation" meant to command, "to make conform to a pattern," to decorate and put in order. I investigated this in the ancient dictionary of Cangjie,[24] the *Shuowen Jiezi* of Xu Shen,[25] and the restored version of that dictionary by Xu Xuan.[26] I couldn't find the term "an existing moral character" associated with the term "moral cultivation" in any of those works. It's not easy to understand why Zhu Xi said what he said.

Here is my humble suggestion. Zhu Xi, when discussing human nature and the Dao, is conflating humans with animals. We cannot use "moral cultivation" in talking about plants or animals. Therefore, he talked instead about "causing to act with in accordance with their nature." [In other words, to play their appropriate roles.] However, "instruction" refers to instructing people, and so this chapter of the *Zhongyong* says, "cultivating the Dao is called Instruction." Therefore, cultivating the Dao is not a case of cultivating the self. It is instructing others how to engage in self-cultivation. The *Zhongyong* is the book that establishes this sort of instruction.

Zhu Xi said, "Although human nature and the Dao are essentially identical, they operate differently depending on the physical temperament through which they operate. Therefore, human beings cannot avoid making mistakes of either going too far or not going far enough. The Sage, however, is one who does what is appropriate for human beings to do, and therefore can be said to have a moral character."[27]

As I see it, in regard to the mistakes of going too far and not going far enough, it is only people who make such mistakes and not animals. In actuality, people are able to move around as they wish but all animals are able to do is predetermined. If what animals do is predetermined, how could animals either go too far or not go far enough? Roosters crow at dawn, dogs bark at night, tigers attach and bite, bulls charge and butt, bees guard their queen, and ants gather and swarm. Even after a thousand years their ways do not change, nor do they differ over a distance of ten thousand *li*. How can they go too far or not go far enough? Moreover, the trees and grass flourish in the spring and wither in the fall. First their flowers bloom and then they bear fruit. Everything that is not human has a set nature. There is not a hair's difference between the various members of the same species.

How can we compare the sickness that afflicts us humans to what we see in animals? Animals follow what Heaven has ordained for them. Among all living creatures, only we humans, although we may try to control our behavior so that we always act the way we should act, find that, unlike animals, we find it difficult to always do so. What Zhu Xi says about human nature and the Dao always conflates human beings with animals. Therefore, much of what he says on this raises obstacles to understanding that are difficult to overcome.

Zhu Xi says that animals and other animate beings also have a moral character, in the sense of there are proper ways for them to behave. That is why, according to the *Zhouli* (Rituals of Zhou), there are officials in charge of training wild animals and of cultivating mountains and marshes.[28] In my opinion, we need to pay attention to where this classic says, "human beings can assist the transformations of Heaven and Earth" and "enable animals to reach their full potential."[29] Zhu Xi read these two passages and became confused by them. Every time he uses the four words "bestowed,"[30] "nature," "Dao," and "instruction," he conflates human beings with things. But that which is referred to as "the nature which Heaven has bestowed" is moral human nature [C. *xing*]; the Dao of acting in accordance with one's natural desire to behave appropriately is the Dao for humans, and the instruction in cultivating this Dao is instruction of humans. If human beings consistently act in accordance with their moral human nature, then all the animals as well will act in accordance with the nature they have been given. If the Dao of human beings is clarified for all to see, then we can participate in the transformations of everything else. How can we, when we are just in the beginning stages of learning to recognize the Dao and nurturing our nature, get birds and beasts to act appropriately and also get trees and grass to fulfill their potential so that both animals and plants thrive and multiply?

As the *Book of Songs* says, "My person is rejected / What avails it to care for what may come after?"[31]

Zhongyong I: 2

> We cannot distance ourselves from the Dao for even one second.[32]

Zhu Xi said, "The Dao consists of the normative principles for engaging appropriately in everyday affairs. They power our moral nature and are complete within our heart-mind."[33]

Let me now address the practice of using one word to stand for another word. Their basic meanings must be similar in order to allow them to be interchangeable. If their meanings are not originally similar, how can we force a Sinograph to stand in for another in a situation in which it is not appropriate for it to do so? The Dao means a path, and a path is something people follow. Confucius, therefore, said, "Who is able to leave a room without going through the door? How is it, then, that no one follows this Dao?"[34] This makes clear that from birth to death, there is but one path, one Dao, to follow.

However, if you think that the natural desire to act appropriately that is your fundamental nature is what constitutes your heart-mind, then that would mean human nature would be the Dao, and the heart-mind would also be the Dao. When these terms overlap like this, there is no way to differentiate them. Moreover, Zhu Xi's *Zhongyong Zhangju* says, "There are no things in which the Dao is not present."[35] But that would mean animals and plants also have the Dao and that the *Zhongyong* is not a book only for instructing human beings but also for instructing birds and beasts and for instructing trees and grasses. This would mean that only after such instruction would the Dao be fully actualized. How could such a situation be possible?

Zhu Xi says in his *Zhongyong zhangju*, "Do not dare to neglect even that which is unseen and unheard."[36] He also says in his *Huowen*, "Be cautious and apprehensive before what you yourself cannot see and what you yourself cannot hear." He adds in this same section of *Huowen* "What others cannot see but you alone see and what others cannot hear but you alone hear — in such cases people generally neglect common sense."[37]

As I understand these two statements from *Huowen*, the first one refers to what we can neither see nor hear while the second one refers to what others can neither see nor hear. Which one of those statements should we rely on as a guiding principle?

In the first case, if there is nothing to be seen nor even any disquieting signs of any kind, then to feel apprehensive for no reason is almost a sort of mental illness. In the second case, if there is something that only I am aware of and nobody else knows anything about it yet, then who is the one who should be apprehensive about it? If I am apprehensive about something, why should I care whether or not others see it or hear it? And if there is something that makes others apprehensive even though they cannot see it or hear it, why should I be apprehensive as well? Neither one of those interpretations is very convincing.

If you use these statements to cultivate an appropriate attitude of apprehension, then, though you spend your whole life trying to cultivate a sincere attitude of apprehension, in the end you will not experience even a moment of true apprehension. The fact that a petty person lacks any moral scruples is precisely because he relies on this sort of mistake. That is why Confucius said, "The petty person does not understand what Heaven has ordained and so does not regard it with apprehension"[38] (the "Jishi" chapter of the *Analects*). How can this reference to what can neither be seen nor heard be anything other than a reference to what Heaven has ordained?[39]

THE KING ASKED:

Is it correct to understand "feeling apprehensive" as an attitude we should cultivate when we are engaged in quiet sitting, or should it be understood as an attitude we should cultivate both when we are sitting quietly and when we are actively dealing with various affairs? If we talk about it in terms of what is written in the *Zhongyong* itself, then it seems appropriate to think about it in terms of when we are still, yet Zhu Xi in his reply to Lü Ziyue[40] understands it as underlying both action and quietude. I wonder if Zhu Xi's *Zhangzhu* also looks at feeling apprehensive as underlying both action and quietude.

I RESPONDED:

The *Zhangju* says that in the heart-mind of an exemplary person we can always find feelings of reverence and apprehension.[41] How can these two words "always find" not be understood as referring to both action and quietude? I also think that when the passage refers to "what is not seen" and "what is not heard," it is not talking about only what other people are unaware of. It is said that "the spirits of heaven and earth are arrayed in all their glory,"[42] yet spirits are things that take no physical form and make no sound. Therefore, when a passage later in the *Zhongyong* refers to "looking at them and yet not seeing them, listening to them and yet not hearing them,"[43] this is what it is talking about. These two passages clarify and reinforce each other.

As for "what is inaccessible to his own vision" and "what is beyond the reach of his hearing," that refers to the spirits who observe us from above, so how could they be called some kind of a material object?[44] There is an old saying that, "In a dark room, you may deceive yourself, but the spirits' eyes can see right through the dark."[45] This is the way to interpret what this classic is saying here. If Heaven did not watch over us both when we are quiet and when we are active, there would be no need to remain circumspect and attentive after we finished practicing quiet sitting. Moreover, when this text says, "what is hidden," this does not mean a secret place, and when it says, "what is subtle," this does not mean "insignificant things." This chapter says, "There is nothing more manifest than what is subtle."[46] The chapter on the spirits says, "That which is imperceptible is obvious!"[47] The chapter referring to the *Ode* of the embroidered robe says, "The gentleman knows how what is subtle becomes manifest,"[48] and the "broad and hidden" chapter says, "The Way of the exemplary person reaches far and wide and yet is hidden."[49] All these taken together mean that what is not seen and not heard is that which is hidden and subtle. Truly, what people do not see are the bodies of spirits and what people do not hear are the sounds of spirits, since these are the most hidden and the most subtle.[50] Yet the intimidating authority of the way in which they watch over us makes it appear that they are above and all around us. This is what this chapter means by "There is nothing more apparent than what is so subtle it can hardly be seen, and nothing more manifest than what is subtle." This being the case, "feeling apprehensive" is applicable to both when we are active and when we are still. We cannot say that the original text says otherwise.[51]

Zhongyong I: 4

> When joy, anger, sorrow, or pleasure have not yet begun to stir.

Zhu Xi said, "joy, anger, sorrow, and happiness are emotions. When they have not yet been activated, they constitute human nature."[52]

As I see it, Zhu Xi, in his *Zhongyong zhangju*, reads this section as a general discussion of the nature and emotions of everyone who lives under heaven,[53] while in *Huowen*, he says the ability to be composed and focused and interact harmoniously comes from feeling cautious and apprehensive.[54] These two meanings are at odds with each other and cannot both be true. This has been a cause of all manner of discord. Generally speaking, from the very beginning, there were already a lot of mistakes made in the Cheng school.[55] When Zhu Xi wrote *Huowen*, he pointed this out in great detail, and I will not go into it again now. But Zhu Xi himself made some mistakes in what he wrote about the Cheng school. Although he concludes it "throws the Way into disorder and leads people into error" (see *Huowen*),[56] he does not completely eliminate all of its basic assumptions or all of the claims arising from those assumptions. Therefore, sometimes he appears to be talking about ordinary people, though at other times he appears to refer to exemplary men only. Sometimes he takes our inborn ability to act appropriately to be an ability our innate heart-mind has potentially as well as in actual practice and other times he takes it to be the result of being watchful over ourselves when no one can tell what we are doing or thinking. He appears to go back and forth. This lack of coherence in his views is a cause of deep lament for scholars.

In ancient times Duke Liu Kang said, "People receive the imperturbability [中] of Heaven and Earth upon being born." (See the *Discourses of the States*.)[57] In this case, imperturbability means the fundamental human emotional orientation of focused composure. That is similar to what is said in the *Discourses of Wu*: "Heaven imparted a moral heart-mind to Wu."[58] But this is different from the imperturbability in "imperturbability and harmony" [中和]. This second meaning of imperturbability refers to neither being off the mark nor leaning off center. It is necessary to work hard at it to achieve that sort of composure. How could this be the same thing that the teeming masses have from birth? The *Classic of Rites* says, "Their heart-minds calm and composed, they reported to Heaven."[59] (See the "Liqi" chapter.) "Their heart-minds calm and composed" here means they were free of any distractions from selfish thoughts and were totally dedicated to the task at hand. If you keep a close watch over your own thoughts and feelings even when you are alone, then you will be able to achieve such a state of mind. After you are able to be appropriately responsive and unselfishly cooperative, you are then able to maintain a state of perfect calm and composure. How could this be an ability the hoi polloi possesses?

The *Book of Changes* says, "Their numbers are exactly determined, and the emblems of all things under the sky are fixed."[60] This means the yarrow stalks and the hexagrams they form are objects which can neither think nor move on their own. If they are things which are lifeless and without intentions, then how can we wake up in the morning, throw the stalks, and then interpret the four different ways they fall as telling us the direction the universe is moving? They are essentially different from what our heart-minds and bodies are. They cannot be described as imperturbable.

(The *Classic of Music* says, "People are born calm and composed. This is their celestial nature. When people encounter and respond to things, that is when we see the desires that constitute their physical nature."[61] This was also a doctrine of vulgar scholars at the beginning of the Han dynasty. The ancient classics did not display any interest in such things.)

Moreover, originally this talk in the *Zhongyong* of the emotions before and after they are activated refers to the exemplary person reaching the height of appropriate responsiveness and cooperativeness by being watchful over himself when no one else can see what he is doing or thinking. It had nothing to do with the patterns of yarrow stalks or of stilling all emotions. It is a mark of Buddhists that, when they discuss the mind, they insist on stilling all emotions. The various gentlemen of the Cheng school thought the teachings of the two schools, Confucianism and Buddhism, complemented each other. The Cheng brothers and their followers took this passage distinguishing between the emotions prior to and after activation as proof that their approach was correct, though the way followers of true Sagely learning should regulate their heart-minds is by thinking carefully about what they are doing rather than trying to still all emotions whatsoever. They should try to cultivate an attitude of caution and apprehension instead of trying to empty their heart-minds of all thoughts and emotions.

That is why Confucius warned against studying without thinking and thinking without studying.[62] King Wen was extremely careful when he reverently served the Lord on High.[63] I have never heard that he took sitting still with a totally blank mind as the basic function of our heart-mind. Mencius said, "It is the purpose of the heart-mind to think. If you think, you will know what to do."[64] I have never heard him say "It is the purpose of the heart-mind to be quiet. If your heart-mind is still, then it will respond to things and events appropriately." The line in this classic refers only to "when joy, anger, sorrow, or happiness have not yet begun to stir." How can we in any way think that phrase means to eliminate all thoughts and emotions? Even when there are not yet any inklings of joy, anger, sorrow, or happiness in our heart-minds, why should we avoid feeling cautious and apprehensive? The ability to have a composed and focused mind and interact harmoniously originates from a foundation of being watchful over ourselves even when no one else can see what we are thinking or feeling.[65] Zhu Xi's *Huowen* discusses this in detail.

Jiu Fan says in the *Discourses of Jin*, "Generally, those who lead states think only of how to regulate sorrow, happiness, joy, and anger. If a ruler, in order to protect the court, uses the regulation of emotions to guide the people so that they are not filled with excessive grief at funerals, this might turn out to cause problems. People might then enjoy funerals, mourn births, and delight in disorder. This completely undermines the point of regulating happiness, sadness, joy and anger. How can this be used to guide the people?"[66] What men of old had to say about the regulation of happiness, sadness, joy, and anger was simply this and nothing more. This is not the same as what scholars in more recent times have said. The *Zhongyong* is an ancient work. We must read it the way it was understood at the time it was written.

The King asked:

When we see this same phrase "not yet begun to stir" in Zhu Xi's *Yulei* [Classified conversations] and in his *Complete Works,* it often varies in meaning. Sometimes he seems to say the ability to keep our emotions from being activated is the same from Yao and Shun all the way down to the man in the street.[67] Sometimes he seems to say that people as lowly as servants also have times when their emotions have yet to be activated,[68] while other times he seems to say that even when the emotions of an ordinary person have yet to be activated, his heart-mind is already a disorderly mess.[69] And at still other times he seems to say that keeping emotions in the state of nonactivation means to become as unperturbed as stones.[70] When we look at those earlier statements, then the later statements must be wrong. We also have to take into account Zhu Xi's response to a letter from Lin Zezhi, in which Zhu Xi writes "when our emotions are in the state of nonarousal, that does not mean no one is in charge."[71] So in trying to understand what the state before emotions begin to stir means in the end, which saying of his should we take as our guide?

I RESPONDED:

An average person also has times when his emotions are not yet aroused and times when his emotions are aroused. However, maintaining composure when his emotions have not yet stirred, and being able to interact harmoniously when his emotions have been activated, are not things the average person can achieve. When this classic says [in this chapter], "Aim at being inwardly composed and outwardly harmonious," the Sinograph "aim at" means "to exert a lot of effort to achieve that goal."[72] Maintaining composure and focus and acting harmoniously both take a lot of effort to maintain. How could the average person possess the ability to maintain composure and always act harmoniously? Zhu Xi, in his *Zhongyong zhangju*, takes composure and harmony as the basic nature of an ordinary person, while in his *Huowen*, he takes them as something an exemplary person cultivates through a lot of effort. Generally speaking, it's not always clear what the Cheng school is saying. That's why Zhu Xi sometimes follows them and sometimes he doesn't, contradicting himself. I take doing all you can to be inwardly composed and outwardly harmonious as what an exemplary person, who watches over himself even when no one can see what he is doing or even just thinking, does. It is better, therefore, to follow what Zhu Xi says in *Huowen*.[73] How could being as disorderly as mud is or as inert as a stone is serve as the great foundation of All-under-Heaven? (My original answer contained an error that I have now corrected.)

THE KING ASKED:

Can we talk about working on cultivating a moral character when our emotions are not yet aroused or is it better not to talk about exerting ourself in such a situation? Master Cheng discussed "trying to achieve composure before joy, anger, sadness, and happiness have been aroused."[74] Master Zhu taught at one time that "we have to work on cultivating a moral character even when our emotions are in a state on nonarousal if we want to achieve our goal,"[75] but, elsewhere, he taught that it is obvious that we cannot exert any effort toward cultivating a moral character when our emotions are not activated since the very act of exerting any sort of effort is a sign that our emotions have already been activated.[76] We see, therefore, a contradiction between what Master Cheng said and what Zhu Xi said at one point. What advice should we follow? I responded:

"Before the emotions have stirred" refers only to the emotions of joy, anger, sorrow, and pleasure not yet stirring. Before those emotions begin to stir, we are not like a lifeless corpse or a dry and shriveled tree without any thoughts or concerns. We can still be cautious and apprehensive. We can still investigate patterns of appropriate interactions. We can still think about what is important and what is not. We can still evaluate the changes in the world around us. So how can it be said there is no need to exert any moral effort when our emotions have not yet been aroused?

Becoming focused and composed is the culmination of what sages work toward. How can it be reasonable to think that you can reach such a height if you do not exert the effort necessary to cultivate a moral character?

The sages took watching over oneself carefully even when no one was aware of what they were doing or thinking as the way to regulate the heart-mind.[77] When you can do that to the greatest extent possible, then you won't be perturbed by anything that happens around you. When your emotions do not entangle you in the world around you, you can be said to be focused and calm. I chose, therefore, to follow Zhu Xi when he says that people ought to put a lot of effort into cultivating a moral character even when their emotions have not been aroused. (My original answer to this question was mistaken. I have corrected it.)[78]

THE KING ASKED:

When Zhu Xi discusses the state before the emotions have stirred, sometimes he considers the "Yang returning" *fu* hexagram appropriate while other times he considers the "pure Yin" *kun* hexagram appropriate. Among these two, which do we think we should accept?

I RESPONDED:

Master Cheng considers the "Yang returning" hexagram appropriate while Zhu Xi considers the "pure Yin" hexagram appropriate. We can see this explained in his *Huowen*.[79]

I think the pure Yin hexagram refers to pure stillness and the Yang returning hexagram refers to the beginning of movement. We can take this as a metaphor for not-yet-activated and activated emotions. However, the pure Yin hexagram cannot really be taken to mean composure and the Yang returning hexagram cannot really be taken to mean harmony. The patterns of the *Book of Changes* are the patterns of the *Book of Changes,* and the *Zhongyong* is the *Zhongyong*. I'm afraid there is no need to use the one to refer to the other.

THE KING ASKED:

The term "not yet begun to stir" was certainly a new term that had not been used before Zisi wrote this classic, but when Zisi began using it, no one talked about what this new term meant back then. Why is this the case?

I RESPONDED:

"Not yet begun to stir" means the same thing as being watchful over oneself when no one else can know what you are thinking or feeling. This is why Zhu Xi said you have to exert a lot of effort even during those times when your emotions had not yet begun to stir. (My original answer contained an error that I have now corrected.)

Zhu Xi pointed out that Master Cheng had said, "The heart-mind of the sage is like a spotless mirror or still water." Zhu added, "When the heart-mind of the sage is not yet activated, it is like the not-yet activated potential of a spotless mirror or still water to reflect whatever is nearby. As soon as the heart-mind is activated, it is like the actualization of the reflecting potential of a spotless mirror or still water."[80]

As I see it, this talk of the heart-mind being like a spotless mirror and still water comes from Buddhists. They say that the heart-mind has an innate potential to be empty of all specific content, and to be totally quiet and still, and that makes it like a mirror or still water. But that which is unable to think or be concerned about anything will, by virtue of that fact, be neither cautious nor apprehensive. People can reach such a state of perfect reflectivity only if they are perfectly still without the slightest bit of mental or physical movement.

A sage, however, is still cautious and apprehensive even when his other emotions have not yet begun to stir. He examines everything he encounters in order to understand their underlying patterns of appropriate interactions so intently that he can go all day without eating and go all night without sleeping as he continues to ponder the most appropriate way to behave. This is what Confucius was like. How could the metaphor of a spotless mirror and still water refer to a man who is like Confucius?

Moreover, as for a spotless mirror and still water, they can be called empty yet illuminating but cannot be said to be in a state of composure. Composure, referring to the state of being "centered" and focused, refers to being right on target, neither being off the mark nor leaning off-center. One must evaluate situations and things and judge them according to the normative principles inherent in them. Once the parameters of the situation are all in array in your heart-mind, you will not be subject to missing your mark, leaning to one side or another, or be overly stimulated by the things around you. Then you can say you have reached a state of composure. That can be called the Great Foundation.

Also, once you have properly identified one by one the situations in which it is proper to feel joy, anger, sorrow, or pleasure and have confirmed through personal experience what Heaven has conferred [recognition of the proper way to behave],[81] then and only then can you be said to have achieved a calm focus. If, on the other hand, you take a still and empty mind as your goal, once a single thought sprouts, before you have had a chance to check and see if it is good or evil, it will already become fully activated. This is not what we can call "the proper potential of the still water and reflecting mirror." Instead, it is simply sitting in Buddhist meditation and doing nothing.

If the ten thousand things under heaven were to suddenly pass before you without your having had a chance to evaluate them, how could the pleasure, anger, sorrow, or joy they evoke be directed appropriately? Lü Dalin (1044–1093) wrote, "You can only experience composure once you have emptied your heart-mind."[82] Zhu Xi said, "There is hardly a man among them not mired in Buddhism."[83] (See *Huowen*.) Though he is sharp in his criticism of Buddhism, looking at what he says about a spotless mirror and still water there can be no doubt that Zhu Xi was influenced by it to some extent. That is why he largely missed the point here. As for the emotions not yet having begun to stir, how could you say the emotions of joy, anger, sorrow, and pleasure not yet being activated is the same as the heart-mind not recognizing anything, or thinking or being concerned about anything?

Yang Guishan [Yang Shi, 1053–1135] said, "Only when you use your heart-mind before joy, anger, sorrow, and pleasure have begun to stir to look into what is going on around you, will what composure really means reveal itself to you. If you are not single-minded in this, how can you hold fast to it?"[84] (He also said, "Hold fast to it and do not lose it. If you do that, then you will be free of the selfishness of human cravings, and your emotions will be properly expressed. When your emotions manifest themselves properly, you will surely never lose your composure. Confucius's lament over the death of Yan Hui[85] and Mencius's joy at Yuezhengzi being offered a high-ranking post mean that the emotions of sadness and joy are acceptable.[86] After all, Confucius and Mencius felt such emotions!")[87]

Zhu Xi said, "If what Yang Guishan said is correct, then when it would be appropriate for a Sage to feel joy, anger, sorrow, and pleasure, his heart should be cool like a tree or rock, and his outward expression should be equally impassive. But that would not be the case with a heart-mind which responded appropriately. Generally speaking, most of what Yang says is mixed up with Buddhism and Daoism and therefore much of it misleading like this." (See *Huowen*.)[88]

As I see it, Yang was saying that we should make an effort to maintain a state of composure before our emotions have begun to stir. This is as much at odds with the teachings of the Buddha as burning coals are in conflict with ice. I do not know why Zhu Xi corrected Yang on this point. Zhu Xi takes the state before emotions have begun to stir as the true human nature. He also called that pre-activated state that which we are potentially capable of, before that potential is actualized. Therefore, whenever he mentions the not-yet-activated state, he says in that state the heart-mind is completely calm and clear like still water or a spotless mirror.

Yang Guishan, on the other hand, says we should try out best to maintain an inner composure before our emotions are activated. That's why Zhu Xi criticized him the way he did. But the teachings of Buddhism do not include anything about the activation and pre-activation of emotions. Buddhists try to not make any sort of conscious effort to do anything. And Buddhists try not to hold on to anything. How could anyone say that Yang Guishan is anywhere near Buddhism?

As for being able to maintain a state of inner composure, that comes after we have learned to watch over our own thoughts and actions even when no one else can know what we are thinking or feeling.[89] When you watch over your own thoughts and actions even when no one else can know what you are thinking or feeling, you are exerting the sort of effort Yang is talking about. Exerting yourself in such a way will ensure that you stay composed and focused. It is in the very nature of things that it happens this way. If we must wait until our emotions are already activated before we decide which of those emotions are good emotions and then try to maintain our inner composure, then I fear we will not be able to keep from making a few mistakes of either going too far or not going far enough. How could there be anything wrong with what Yang Guishan said?

Zhu Xi once said, "If you are cautious and apprehensive so that you do not deviate from the straight and narrow the slightest bit, and keep to this path without any lapses, you can maintain your composure." (See *Huowen*.)[90]

As for the phrase "if you are cautious and apprehensive so that you do not deviate from the straight and narrow the slightest bit, and keep to this path without diverging at all," how can this not refer to maintaining your inner composure? ("Keep" means "hold fast.") This seems to be in accord with what the Zhu Xi school says about holding on to our inner composure before our emotions are activated, so why does Zhu Xi refute it as being Buddhist or Daoist?

The state of inner composure is so delicate, so difficult to see or hold onto, that if you fail to apply your heart-mind to choosing the correct course and to exert the necessary effort to hold fast to it and maintain it, you will inevitably find you will not be able to automatically do what you are supposed to do. Zhu Xi took the spotless mirror and still water as metaphors for the undisturbed composure of not-yet-activated emotion. I fear this is similar to Buddhist teachings about emptiness and stillness. Yang Guishan was not wrong here.

Zhuangzi said, "When a man would display anger and yet is not angry, the anger comes out in that repression of it."[91] Yang Guishan quotes this as evidence that composure lies in the emotions not being fully activated, but this is a mistake. When Confucius and Mencius, before their emotions had begun to stir, discovered that their disciples were wise enough to transmit the Way and put it into practice, they loved and cherished them. At that time, in their heart-minds they were fair and impartial without any taint of selfishness. (This is maintaining composure when the emotions have not yet stirred.) When Confucius heard that Yan Hui was dead, he wept bitterly. (This is a proper expression of sadness.) When Mencius heard that Yuezhengzi was going to be put in charge of a government, he was so filled with joy that he was unable to sleep. (This is a proper expression of joy.) How could anyone be as inert as a tree or a rock after his emotions have begun to stir? What Zhuangzi speaks of is not a natural human emotion.

Zhu Xi said, "The Ten Thousand Things under heaven and on earth all have the same basic potential that I have to interact appropriately with everything there is." (See the *Chapters and Phrases*.)[92]

He also said, "If you cannot maintain composure within and harmony without, then the mountains will collapse, and the rivers will dry up. Then how can Heaven and Earth be in their proper places, how can the not yet born and the very young take their proper place in the natural order, and how can the Ten Thousand Things flourish?"[93]

As I see it, we find not a single instance of the phrase "the Ten Thousand Things all have the same potential" in the ancient classics. Zixia merely said, "Everyone within the Four Seas is the gentleman's brother."[94]

How could that mean that I have exactly the same potential as the grasses and trees or as the birds and beasts? The sage who is composed and in harmony with what is going on around him may sit in the back room of his home manifesting joy, anger, sorrow, and pleasure in their proper measure, but he is not playing his proper role. If he does not plan to actually do anything, then Heaven and Earth will certainly not be in their proper places and the Ten Thousand Things will certainly not flourish. If he is the ruler, he must behave like Yao and Shun. If he is a high official, he should behave like Gao, Kui, Ji, and Xie.[95] Then and only then could the southern official Zhong [Gou Mang—the sky god] take proper charge of Heaven and the northern official Li [Zhu Rong—the fire god] take proper charge of Earth. Then and only then could Xi and He create the calendar, Yu bring the waters under control, and the Lord of Millet (Houji) make the soil productive. Only then could Shun order Yi to set some fires in Yu to clear out the brush in the mountains and dry up the marshes.[96]

If you know the distinctions between superior and inferior, grasses and trees, and birds and beasts, then Heaven and Earth will be in their proper places and the Ten Thousand Things will flourish. Although sometimes what Heaven ordains for you may not be all you want it to be, and it may seem you have exhausted all your resources and have nowhere to go but down, or sometimes something starts out promising but does not come to fruition, nevertheless, if you continue to do what you are supposed to do in the larger scheme of things, everything will be in its proper place and the Dao will prevail in the world. This is what the sages said, but many men of the Song and Yuan dynasties, not playing their proper role in the larger scheme of things, did not actualize the Dao. When they talked about the things of Heaven and Earth being in their proper places and the Ten Thousand Things flourishing, they focused entirely on the ability of their minds to respond to and understand things and did not go out and act in the world according to what they learned. They said a lot of grandiose things that lacked anything of real substance for us to hold on to. Much of what they said was like this.

Cai Qing (1453–1508) said, "Originally there was a list of seven basic emotions. Why in this chapter are only the four emotions of joy, anger, sorrow, and pleasure mentioned? Let me suggest that pleasure has been combined with love, sorrow with fear, and anger with hatred. Desires are part of everything on earth and can be found everywhere. If we want to make this list of emotions even shorter, we can say there are only joy and anger." (See Cai Qing's *Sishu mengyin*.)[97]

As I see it, we should look at the Seven Emotions this way. The first time we see a list of emotions is in the "Ceremonial Usages" [*Liyun*] in the *Book of Rites*. There we can see a list of seven emotions, but there that list starts with joy, anger, sorrow, and fear rather than with the usual first four of joy, anger, sorrow, and pleasure.[98] In "Symposium in the White Tiger Hall," Ban Gu (32–92) lists only six emotions: pleasure, anger, sorrow, joy, love, and hatred.[99] Both in the past and today there have been many cases of listing just six emotions. Kong Yingda's preface to *Mao's Book of Songs* says, "The Six Emotions are oriented correctly in your heart-mind and then get pushed and pulled here and there when they encounter the hundred things."[100] The "Biography of Yi Feng" chapter of the *History of the Former Han Dynasty* says,

"The five natures [i.e., the five virtues] will not harm each other, though the six emotions will wax and wane."[101] Lu Ji's *Wen fu* [*Rhapsody on literature*] says, "My Six Emotions are blocked, I cannot move forward, and my spirit is stalled."[102] How could Heaven have set the number of emotions at only seven? Besides, in addition to the Six Emotions and the Seven Emotions, there are also other various emotions such as remorse, resentment, arrogance, and fastidiousness. How can we say there are only seven emotions? When this classic says, "joy, anger, sorrow, and pleasure," it is using one or two to refer to the others. What Cai says is somewhat off the mark.

Zhongyong II

> Confucius said, "An exemplary person is someone who is consistently appropriately focused and composed."

Zhu Xi wrote, "Can the grandson use his grandfather's courtesy name? The section of the *Book of Etiquette and Ceremonial* that tells you what to say when you prepare the spirit tablets of recently deceased family members for ritual offerings includes the lines, 'We place your tablet alongside that of your noble grandfather of such-and-such a courtesy name.'[1] You may, therefore, address an elder by his courtesy name. That is why Zisi uses Confucius's courtesy name.[2] Moreover, Confucius never held a rank that would have given him a posthumous title. If his sons and grandsons did not use his courtesy name to distinguish him from other members of his family, what would they call him?"[3]

In my opinion, the men of old originally did not regard courtesy names as taboo. In fact, they sometimes took the courtesy names of their grandfathers and used them as their lineage names. Gongzi Zhan's grandson actually used Zhan as his lineage name, Zifu Jiao's grandson actually used Zifu as his lineage name, and Zijia Ji's grandson actually used Zijia as his lineage name.[4] So how could there have been any taboo against using courtesy names then? However, the line in that ancient text that reads "we place your tablet alongside that of your noble grandfather of such-and-such a courtesy name" is referring only to the sort of rituals discussed in the "*shiyu li*" chapter [of the *Book of Etiquette and Ceremonial*].

Zhu Xi said, "*Yong*, in *zhongyong*, refers to the normative patterns of interactions in everyday life [*pingchang zhi li*]."[5]

The way I see it, it is very difficult to identify the principles that should direct our interactions in everyday life. The average person thinks that "the patterns of ordinary appropriate behavior" refers to the types of behavior they see in everyday life. They are surprised to hear people using that phrase to discuss the human ability to adhere to the Dao. They expect the Dao to be quite different from the type of interactions they are accustomed to. Indeed, if the Sages had taken the way the average person normally behaves and set that up as the Dao that is the model for guiding All-under-Heaven and regulating the lives of everyone, would we not see everyone adopting vulgar customs and lowering themselves to the level of the corrupt world, imitating the actions of village hypocrites?

There are three possible meanings to *chang* [the *chang* that appears in *pingchang zhi li*]: consistent, regular, and ordinary. By "consistent," I mean what we see in some passages about consistency in the *Book of Documents*. For example, in the "Counsels of Gao Yao" chapter, we see "When someone displays these virtues consistently, is that not good?"[6] In the "Establishing Government" chapter, we see the line "May future rulers be able to employ men who are consistently virtuous!"[7]

The term "regular" refers to the rules that have been normative for ten thousand generations. These are the five precepts that form the basis for the "five primary virtues."[8] They are the well-established regulations of the ancient codes.

But, as for "ordinary," let's look at what Mei Ze writes in his commentary on the *Book of Documents:* "Barbarians within three hundred *li* follow the ordinary teachings."[9] Let us also look at what is recorded in the "Zhongchang Tong [lie]chuan" section of the *History of the Later Han Dynasty:* "Conforming to ordinary customs,... that is what we can see even in remote villages. That is not good enough to merit being one of the three great officers of the land."[10] How could what is ordinary be the height of ethical virtuosity? Therefore, why should a ruler, who needs to select the worthy and the virtuous to help him govern, choose those who are ordinary rather than those scholars who are "extraordinary," "unusual," "different from the ordinary," or "surpassing the ordinary"?

According to the Buddhist work "Record of Pointing at the Moon,"[11] the Chan monk Zhaozhou asked his teacher Nanquan, "What is the Way?" Nanquan is said to have answered, "The ordinary heart-mind is the way." We do not find this sort of talk in the ancient classics.

The *Book of Changes* includes the lines "He will not fail to consistently act appropriately" and "She will never change but will consistently act appropriately,"[12] so consistency is an ancient concept. That is why we see the procedures of the ancient past being consistently applied in the ancient classics and rituals. Their consistency and invariability were treasured. This is the same meaning of "consistency" we see in the "Counsels of Gao Yao."

A later section of this classic says the gentleman is "consistent in practicing virtue and consistently careful about what he says."[13] The *Book of Changes* says the gentleman is consistently reliable when he talks, and consistently careful when he acts.[14] "Reliability in speaking" means displaying consistency in what you say. "Consistently virtuous" means acting appropriately all the time. [This is similar to what Mencius said about pursuing the regular path of virtue without any deviation.][15] "Consistency in actions" means to be consistent in how you behave. Mencius said, "I am consistent in showing respect for my elder brother."[16] Being "consistent in showing respect" means to always be respectful.

From all these examples, we can see that what we are supposed to do every day is consistently act appropriately.[17] How could that be taken as merely what we ordinarily do? Anyway, maintaining composure and imperturbability at all times is the primary principle governing all appropriate interactions under heaven. If we say that what the *Zhongyong* is talking about is nothing more than the normative patterns of interactions seen in everyday life, then later generations would dismiss it as beneath discussion, which would be unfortunate. Certainly, this is not what the *Zhongyong* is trying to teach us.

Moreover, the *Zhongyong* talks about holding firm to ethical virtuosity while managing the affairs of the world. It says nothing about either "ordinary virtue" or "ordinary conduct." If what it is talking about is nothing more than the patterns of ordinary interactions of everyday life, then Confucius would have said, "the patterns of a gentleman's ordinary interactions of everyday life." Zhu Xi's language is not clear, and moreover I fear that the term "patterns of interactions" does not really belong here.

You Zuo (1053–1123)[18] said, "When we are talking about the relationship between the innate ability of human beings to act appropriately and human emotions, we talk about a calm and composed heart-mind manifesting harmonious emotions. When we are talking about actually acting appropriately, then that implies consistently maintaining a composed heart-mind."[19] Zhu Xi said, "The character 'composure' in the title of the *Zhongyong* in actuality combines the meanings of composure and harmony."[20] (He means that *zhong*, the first Sinograph, meaning "composure," in the title *Zhongyong*, combines two meanings, "not-yet-activated" and "already activated.")

In my opinion, the Great Officer of Music distinguished composure, harmony, respect, and consistency as four different virtues.[21] How can they be mixed all together as You Zuo describes? *Zhong* refers to both composure and harmony. But *yong* means consistency only. We are told that when your emotions have not yet begun to stir, you need to maintain composure, and once your emotions have been activated, you need to ensure that they are calm and appropriately focused.[22] We have to recognize the two Sinographs that can be read literally as "composed and harmonious" mean the same as the single Sinograph "composed."[23]

THE KING ASKED:

The phrase "going overboard and not going far enough" certainly directs us to the main point of the *Zhongyong*. Yet when it comes to the words "not being off the mark nor leaning off-center," the *Zhongyong* itself only contains the words "not leaning off-center" and does not have the phrase "not being off the mark." Why did Zhu Xi always make sure to discuss both "not being off the mark" and "not leaning off-center" together?[24] Saying "Not being off the mark nor leaning off-center" before your emotions have begun to stir, and "not going overboard and not going far enough" complement each other. So those two phrases "not being off the mark" and "not leaning off-center" must each indicate something different. Can you clarify how these two phrases are not redundant?

I RESPONDED:

Although the words "being off the mark" are not in the actual text of this particular text, they have their roots in the "Establishing the Pivot" section of the Great Plan.[25] Yao and Shun maintained balance and composure and displayed no biases or favoritism, without leaning one way or another. This was how they were able to establish themselves as the Pivot around which everything else revolved. We cannot say Zhu Xi had no grounds for adding the words "not drifting to one side." Let's talk about how to set up a sundial. We must place the base of the gnomon right in the middle of the sundial so that it is not offset the slightest to the east or to the west. This is the meaning of "not being off the mark." The gnomon itself must reach directly skyward and not lean one way or the other. This is the meaning of "not leaning off-center." "Not being off the mark" refers to the location of its base and "not leaning off-center" refers to its orientation. How could each not indicate something different?

THE KING ASKED:

Although someone may have the potential to exercise the ethical virtuosity of an exemplary person, they may not yet have reached the level of being focused and composed all the time, of always thinking and doing what is appropriate for a particular time and place. This is something those of us who are lesser men than the great worthies cannot avoid. The tone of the line "the exemplary person therefore maintains an appropriate balance and composure at all times" certainly implies this. The line that follows, "the petty man is the opposite of being consistently calm and unperturbed," means that a person can be said to have the heart-mind of a petty man if he fails to maintain a composed and focused heart-mind, even if he has not reached the point of behaving without restraint.[26] Why should we wait until he acts without restraint before we declare that he had failed to maintain focus and composure?

Lü Dalin and various other Confucian scholars all follow the Zheng Xuan commentary, reading that phrase "a petty man is not consistently calm and unperturbed" as meaning that a petty man only thinks that he is maintaining focus and composure consistently.[27] They therefore assume that the heart-mind of a petty man is revealed in his acting without restraint. The Cheng brothers and Zhu Xi all follow [what they assume is] Wang Su's correction of this line.[28] Although we also see an argument to this effect in *Huowen*, the Zheng commentary appeared before Wang wrote anything, so the Sinograph meaning "the opposite of" cannot be Wang's interpolation. There is no way for us to determine who added that Sinograph. In *Huowen*, Zhu Xi several times clarifies what he sees as the psychology of a petty man. This reveals what Zhu Xi was getting at.[29] Can we combine what Zheng and Wang say and not have to throw one out?

I RESPONDED:

"The exemplary person therefore maintains composure and balance in every situation" is similar to what the *Book of Changes* says: "With a dragon's virtue, he is perfectly centered."[30] In *Chapters and Phrases*, Zhu Xi distinguishes two grades of human beings, but that is going beyond what the text actually says.[31] And why is there any need to add "therefore" in distinguishing between an exemplary person and a petty person?[32] We call someone an exemplary person only after he is able to be focused and maintains composure at all times. We call someone a petty person after we see that he is not careful about what he says or does. That's all there is to it. It is not the case that an exemplary person and a petty person are originally two different grades of human being.

When it comes to the good and bad points in the way Zheng and Wang read this text, I think the petty person is someone who is unable to be calm and unperturbed and likewise cannot display consistency. It makes no sense, therefore, to refer to the consistently calm and unperturbed state of a petty person. Without the Sinograph meaning "the opposite of" added to the original line in this chapter, this line would not make sense and would not fit well with what precedes it and what follows it. I'm afraid that we have no choice other than following the correction ascribed to Wang.[33]

Zhongyong III

> The Master said, "Constant Focus and Composure—surely this is perfection!"

THE KING ASKED:

What does this classic mean in this chapter when it says, "There are very few people who are able to be consistently composed and focused so that they act and think precisely the way they should act and think"? Zhu Xi said there are reports that Master Cheng explained that this means few people are able to consistently maintain composure over a long period of time but that was the result of an error in recording what he taught, so, according to Zhu Xi, there is no need to take this interpretation seriously.[1] Still, in their discussions of this line Lü Dalin, Hou Zhongliang, and their followers take the phrase "unable to maintain composure consistently for even a month"[2] from later in the *Zhongyong* as evidence that people cannot maintain composure and focus consistently. Doesn't this imply that maintaining a composed state of mind is something people are not able to do at all?

I RESPONDED:

The *Analects* say, "The common people rarely maintain composure for long."[3] That line lacks the character "able to," Therefore, shouldn't we take the phrase "people rarely" to mean that, not that they are unable to do so, but it is rare for people to maintain a state of composure consistently? If so, then we should follow what Master Cheng says about the difficulty the average person has in consistently maintaining composure. Generally speaking, *yong* means constancy. The "Counsels of Gao Yao" [a chapter of the *Book of Documents*] provides several examples of the focused composure and harmony of ethical virtuosity, and links them with consistency.[4] The "Great Officer of Music" section in the *Zhouli* taught the ethical power of composure, harmony, respect, and *yong* [constancy].[5] Zheng Xuan's commentary pointed out that *yong* here means consistency.[6] This is the way we should understand *zhongyong*, but Zhu Xi said that *yong* refers to the ordinary. Therefore, when he looked at this passage, he rejected Master Cheng's reading of it as referring to consistently maintaining composure. Because he did not understand that the correct reading was consistency, he was confused about this.

Zhongyong IV

> Among human beings, there is no one who does not eat or drink.

THE KING ASKED:

The first lines in this chapter discuss not acting properly and not understanding the Dao, and so it would certainly be appropriate if the following lines discuss knowing the Dao as well as acting in accordance with it. Yet those lines only discuss knowing the Dao. Why is this?

I RESPONDED:

I think it is appropriate to link the "there is no person who does not eat and drink" line together with the section that follows it. Together, they discuss both knowledge and action, so there is no need to split this passage off and make it its own chapter.[1] As for the sequence of chapters in the *Zhongyong*, sometimes we have a reference to the words of Confucius followed by those of the author and other times we see the point the author wants to make, followed by a reference to the words of Confucius. There are many situations of this kind.[2]

THE KING ASKED:

Of all the lines in the thirty-three chapters of the *Doctrine of the Mean*, the phase "Alas! No one walks the correct path [Dao]!" is peculiar in that it alone makes up an entire chapter [Chapter V]. If we connect this one sentence to the end of the previous chapter, together they would talk about both knowledge and action, so why does Zhu Xi say this phrase must be treated as its own separate chapter?

I RESPONDED:

Your Majesty makes a very good point. If this chapter were connected to the one preceding it, it would be much better. If we do not do that, then we at least could join it with the "there is no person who does not eat and drink" line in order to discuss both knowing and acting. This would also not distort the meaning.

Feng Wenzi[3] said, "An ancient interpretation drawing on the *Book of Jin* says Zhang Hua was able to distinguish different types of fish and Shi Kuang was able to tell what sort of wood was used for the fire that cooked the food. Fu Lang was Regional Inspector of Qing Province. He was able to taste food so well that when he ate chicken, he knew if it had roosted partially exposed to the elements, and when he ate duck, he knew whether it had been a black or white duck. Examples like help us understand how difficult it can be to understand the *Zhongyong*. An equally difficult passage appears later when the *Zhongyong* discusses declining ranks and emoluments and trampling unsheathed blades under the feet.[4] This use of relevant examples makes it somewhat easier to understand."

Now as I see it, when it comes to people's recognizing what something should taste like, the best example is Yiya.[5] The reason Yiya is renowned for his recognition of what tastes good was that he was skilled at cooking, and he was skilled at cooking because he was able to properly blend the five flavors. He added ingredients for flavors that were too weak, and reduced ingredients whose flavors were too strong. (The *Sayings of Master Yan* [*Yanziyu*]).[6] Knowing how to make something taste just right is indeed a matter of avoiding both going too far and not going far enough. The old explanation is wrong.

Mao Qiling said, "There is no person who does not recognize differences in how things taste. Therefore, the 'Xue Ji' chapter of the *Book of Rites* says, 'However fine the viands be, if one does not eat, he does not know their taste.'[7] If you eat something and do not know what it tastes like, then this is certainly because you are paying attention to something else. According to the *Analects*, 'Confucius is the type of person who is so passionate that he forgets to eat,'[8] meaning he focused all his attention on studying. 'When a gentleman is in mourning, he gets no pleasure from eating sweet foods'[9] means he focuses only on displaying loving affection for his parents. 'For three months after listening to music [of Shao] he did not even notice the taste of meat'[10] means all he cared about then was listening to the music [of Shao]. The *Daxue* says about this: 'When the mind is not focused, we eat but do not know the taste of what we eat.'[11] This is easy to understand. The *History of the Former Han Dynasty* says, 'If someone eats meat you cannot say they are unable to recognize the taste of horse liver.'[12] There is no problem understanding this as well. Moreover, it is widely recognized that 'there is no person who does not eat or drink.' However, that statement that 'there are few people who are able to truly know the taste of food' means there are a lot of people who do not know what things should taste like as opposed to the few who do. This is something that is hard to understand."[13]

As I see it, there is no one who does not eat or drink, yet if Yi Ya alone is praised for knowing what things should taste like, that means there are only a few people who are able to distinguish the different subtle ways different things should taste.[14] Those who know taste are the same kind of person as Yi Ya is. This requires no further explanation.

Zhongyong VI

There was Shun: He indeed was greatly wise!

THE KING ASKED:

In defining the phrase "two extremes," why is it that the *Zhongyong zhangju* does not use the words "going too far and not going far enough" but instead talks here of "larger and smaller, thicker and thinner"?[1] Isn't being right on target in between the one extreme of going too far and the other extreme of not going far enough? When Zhu Xi in the *Huowen* discusses Master Cheng's distinction between "grasping" and "keeping hold of," he says that "one extreme is going too far and the other is not going far enough,"[2] though in the *Zhongyong zhangju* he talks of larger and smaller, thicker and thinner. What, in the end, is the reason for this?

I RESPONDED:

When it comes to the rites, what is appropriate for one's rank is right on target. If the coffin of a high official should be five *cun* thick, then "thicker" would be a coffin of greater than five *cun* and "thinner" would be a coffin of less than five *cun*. When it comes to clothing, being the right fit for the body is what is meant by being right on target. If a dwarf's clothes should have a length of three *chi*, then "larger" would be greater than three *chi* and "smaller" would be less than three *chi*.[3] If you think this way, you will never go to either of the two extremes when it comes to size and thickness. This is what Zhu Xi meant. But we have to be flexible when we apply the labels of large, medium, and small when we are talking about the general public. When talking of ten people, sometimes all ten will be big and stout and sometimes all ten will be small and reedy.

How would Shun handle something like this? When it comes to relative length and thickness, he would advise us to use our own heart-mind to evaluate the specifics of the situation to see what being right on target is in that situation. Only after that should we take into account what others have had to say about it. Reject what they say if they advise us to veer toward either extreme. But if their advice is in accord with a consistent focus on what is appropriate, then follow their advice. If we do that, we will be sure not to miss being right on target. Zhu Xi took the two extremes to be nothing more than two extremes in how people talk. I fear this is difficult to understand and I, your subject, cannot believe this absurdity.[4]

Zhongyong VII

All men say, "I am wise."

Zhu Xi said, "People all can recognize a dangerous situation. However, they do not know how to avoid it."[1]

Cai Qing said, "Where profit lies, there may be danger lying hidden, so you can fall into a trap. Those who know where danger may lie but not how to avoid it are like those who follow a steep path over a mountain in the hope that thereby they will escape danger."[2]

As I see it, although Confucius did not use the term "recognize a dangerous situation," in ancient times they clearly recognized dangerous situations. What kind of man would not try to avoid such a thing? It is merely because they did not see clearly what lies ahead that they did not know how to avoid it. Confucius said, "The petty person does not understand the Mandate of Heaven, and thus does not regard it with awe."[3] Indeed, it is because he does not understand it that he does not regard it with awe.

Hou[4] said, "How can one choose both to be consistent and to navigate between the extremes in different situations? There are two different things to choose there."[5]

Zhu Xi said, "Hou went too far there. He did not take into account how the moral principles of the classics are implemented in actual practice."[6]

As I see it, what Hou said is extremely clear and indeed is not at odds with what we see in the *Zhongyong zhangju*. I do not understand why Zhu Xi took him to task about this.

The King asked:

The "people" referred to in this chapter are the common people. How can it be saying that the average person can choose the Way of consistent composure and focus and keep to it? Within one month, of course, there might be a few days on which some people might be able to resolve to be consistently composed and focused and keep to that resolution. These, therefore, would be those deemed the Worthies. However, how can we talk about the way the Worthies do that in the same breath in which we discuss the common herd? As this passage refers to both those who are Worthies and the average person, how do we know what is appropriate for each?

I RESPONDED:

The line in this chapter of the *Zhongyong* saying "Choosing to be consistently composed and focused but being unable to sustain this for a full month" is like another line from another classic, the one that reads "When sent abroad as an envoy, they are unable to engage in repartee."[7] Generally it is said that although someone may decide to be consistently composed and focused, he may find he cannot do so for a full month. This is like a person who, despite being sent abroad as an envoy, is unable to engage in repartee. This is basically all it says. But Zhu Xi goes on to say that although people generally may be able to decide to be consistently composed and focused, they are usually unable to act on that decision.[8] I fear this is not the actual meaning of this passage.

This chapter of the *Zhongyong* says simply "not know how to avoid something." Zhu Xi claims that means "They recognize that disaster is about to happen but do not know how to avoid it."[9] That is another example of Zhu Xi missing the point. I cannot believe his absurd interpretation.

Zhu Xi said, "This phrase 'a period of a month' means one full month."[10]

Mao said, "The phrase 'a period of a month' is not one full month. The character 'a period' here means a recurring period, so it should be read as 'a period of months.'[11] Therefore, in the *Analects of Confucius*, 'a period of months' is understood as referring to one year,[12] meaning 'from the tenth month to the tenth month.' If it were referring to one month, how could it be a recurring period? 'This period' means one year. The *Book of Documents* says, 'Three hundred sixty and six days.'[13] This is the period named a 'year.' The *Zuozhuan* says, 'Shusun Chuo rose at dawn and stood waiting for further orders.'[14] 'Dawn' here means a series of mornings, therefore 'one 'day' can also mean a period of time. 'A period of a month' sometimes means one month and sometimes one year. This is like the *Analects* saying, 'some attain it only for a few days or for a few months.'"[15]

However, I read "a period of a month" as referring to a full month. In the summer of the eighth year of Lord Xi, the Di invaded Jin. The *Zuozhuan* says, "This was to avenge the Caisang campaign. That invasion came a full month after that."[16] In the spring that year, Jin had defeated the Di at Caisang. Spring is in the third month and summer is in the fourth month. Guo She had said, "Within the period of a year, the Di will be here again," but the Di thereupon arrived after a period of only a month. This book therefore records that Di's vengeance was swift. Mao's explanation is absurd.[17]

Zhongyong VIII

Hui was a man who chose the Way of equanimity and constancy.

The King asked:

Yan Hui's ability to choose the proper course of action and keep to it can be seen in the *Analects*. How was he able to choose it, and how could he keep to it?

I responded:

Since he spent whole days talking with Confucius without disagreeing with him, how could he be unable to choose the proper course of action?[1] Since "for three months at a time his heart-mind did not stray from concern for the common good,"[2] how could he be unable to keep to the proper course of action?[3]

Zhongyong IX

All-under-Heaven, states and families can be peacefully ordered.

Zhu Xi said, "These situations each call for acting wisely, acting unselfishly, and acting courageously, but they each tend to emphasize one at the expense of the other."[1]

Let me point out that when it comes to ruling a state, the person doing that is not necessarily wise, nor is the person who declines emoluments necessarily doing so with selfless motives, so the three situations[2] mentioned in this chapter did not necessarily imply that the actor in those situations is acting wisely, acting unselfishly, or acting courageously. There are times, of course, when declining emoluments is doing exactly what should be done in that situation. Similarly, courageously stepping on the bare blades of a sword can be an example of what should be done in a particular situation.

Bo Yi[3] gave up his claim to the throne, and Bi Gan[4] had his heart torn out. Can we say that they emphasized one of those virtues at the expense of the others and therefore are examples of going to an extreme instead of focusing on what was the most appropriate action to take in a particular situation? Knowing what one ought to know means you can focus on what is appropriate to do in every situation. Being courageous when one ought to be courageous is an example of acting appropriately according to the situation you are in. How can acting out of wisdom or courage mean that you are going to an extreme? Moreover, if you say that those who bring order to All-under-Heaven, the state, or families are emphasizing one virtue at the expense of the others, doesn't that imply that what the *Daxue* teaches does not match what the *Zhongyong* teaches? If we say acting fully human, driven by concern for the common good, is one-sided, then even when Yan Hui did not stray from thinking and acting unselfishly for three months, we still could not say he had succeeded in consistently acting appropriately!

Some cases in which emoluments are declined are right on target and others miss the mark. Some cases of trampling bare blades under the feet are appropriate and others are not. Those who rule states and families are not necessarily the equals of Yao or Shun. This is the point this classic is making.

The King asked:

Zhongyong zhangju discusses in detail the meaning of the line in this chapter "focus and composure cannot be maintained," yet when Master Cheng discussed it, he linked it to his discussion of self-restraint as the most difficult thing for people to do.⁵ Even if self-restraint is the most difficult task for a person to accomplish, how can anyone think that it is impossible to consistently act appropriately?

| RESPONDED:

The Cheng brothers and Zhu Xi always call overcoming the flaws in their physical endowment "self-restraint." In *Huowen,* therefore, we also find references to physical endowment.⁶ Generally people's deviating from the Mean [the proper course of action] is normally due to their emotions pulling them off-kilter, and usually their physical endowment is the reason they are pulled to one way or the other by their emotions. This is why the Cheng brothers and Zhu Xi talked about self-restraint meaning overcoming the flaws in one's physical endowment. Does not the *Zhongyong zhangju* identify the selfishness manifest in human desires with the desires generated by the human physical endowment?⁷ But if we gain a clear understanding of the patterns of appropriate actions, that will allow us to choose the appropriate course of action and stick firmly to it. So how can we place all the blame on our physical endowment?

Zhongyong X

Zilu asked about strength.

Zhu Xi said, "The Sinograph 'blocked' [塞 C. *sai* / K. *saek*] means 'not being able to achieve what you want to achieve.' When the government is guided by the Dao, the exemplary person does not change even if he is unable to fully realize the values he champions."[1]

Let me comment on this statement. Zhu Xi means that if you acquire wealth and power, you should not change the principles you lived by when you were poor. But the Dao of being consistently composed and focused is such that when you have wealth and rank, you should act as someone who has wealth and rank, and when you are poor and humble, you should act as someone who is poor and humble. This is what is called acting appropriately according to the situation you are in. Zhu Xi did not need to say what he said.

Someone said, "The Sinograph 'to be complete' [塞] here means to be sincere. (The 'Counsels of Gao Yao' talk of 'boldness combined with sincerity.')[2] When a government adheres to the Dao and is determined to implement it, there may be some who display baseless arrogance. An exemplary person will not do so."

Lou Xiangming[3] said, "Straighten yourself out and you will be strong. *Xunzi* says, 'Lead the assembled officers and various functionaries so that you combine the strength of all of them, and then straighten out the ruler.'[4] The character 'straighten out' was often represented by a similar Sinograph that means bridge. Here it means to make strong-willed."[5]

As I see it, the "Way to be a Minister" chapter of the *Xunzi* is saying, "make him as strong and straight as a bridge." (The Sinograph "bridge" is used for the Sinograph "straighten out" here.) Generally speaking, "straight" means as straight as an arrow flies.

THE KING ASKED:

Is the phrase "interacting harmoniously" in this chapter the same as or different than "interacting harmoniously" in the phrase "being composed and focused and interacting harmoniously" we saw in Chapter I?

I RESPONDED:

Being composed and focused is a great way to exercise ethical virtuosity, but if you try to stay composed and focused over a long period of time, you can easily find yourself leaning off-center a bit. Interacting harmoniously is a great way to exercise ethical virtuosity, but if you try to interact harmoniously over a long period of time, you can easily find yourself being pulled along with what is going on around you. If you do not lean off-center and do not let yourself be pulled along by what is going on around you, then you can be composed and focused and harmonize with everything around you and can do that consistently. The phrases "activated" and "not yet activated" refer to being composed and focused, on the one hand, and interacting harmoniously, on the other. This chapter also links being composed and focused, on the one hand, with interacting harmoniously, on the other, so how can you say there is a big difference in how the Sinograph meaning "interacting harmoniously" is used?

THE KING ASKED:

After you have managed to avoid leaning off-center, then you can be said to be right on the mark. That being the case, the phrase "being right on the mark" already includes the notion of not leaning off-center. So why is the line that reads "being right on the mark" followed by "not leaning off-center"? Someone said that "being right on the mark" means "standing upright." What do you think about that?

According to *Huowen*, the phrase "being right on the mark and not leaning off-center" should be understood as saying that if you are right on the mark and do not lean one way or another, then you certainly will be upright. It goes on to say that whether you are upright or lean off-center is determined by whether you are tenacious or weak.⁶ The material in *Zhongyong zhangju* predates the material in *Huowen*. Is that why *Zhongyon zhangju* fails to explain the deeper meaning of this passage?

I RESPONDED:

I have already explained the meaning of "being right on the mark and not leaning off-center" with an analogy to a gnomon. Generally speaking, even if that gnomon is placed exactly where it is supposed to be but the gnomon itself is not straight, then it will not give you the correct time. Only after you have made sure that the gnomon is both where it is supposed to be and does not lean one way or another will the gnomon be perfectly upright. So clearly "being right on the mark" means the same thing as "being upright."

As for relating this to being tenacious or strong, what is said here is very insightful. If you are not tenacious in your effort to act appropriately, then you will not be able to be right on the mark. Or, if you are fortunate enough to be right on the mark in a particular situation, you will not be able to keep that stance for very long. Even though you may be headed in the right direction, you will not be able to consistently do so. That is the main point of this chapter. It really is a pity that we do not see this point in *Zhongyang zhangju*.[7]

Zhongyong XI

> Some go to where they can hide from public view and behave in peculiar ways.[1]

Zhu Xi said, "Lü Dalin follows Zheng Xuan's commentary in reading *su* [素 C. *su* / K. *so*, the first Sinograph in the statement ascribed to Confucius in this chapter] as 'going toward.'[2] (Lü said, "*su* should be read as another Sinograph also pronounced *su* which appears in the compound 'going toward home.' This is the same *su* that is used in the phrase 'act according to your proper station in life' [which appears in Chapter XIV]").[3] I am not comfortable with reading it that way. The commentators in the past wrote that this phrase means that people who lack the ability to display ethical virtuosity hide from public view. That appears to be closer to the actual meaning.[4]

"Lou Xiangming said, "In the past, *su* was understood as 'to go toward.' In the *Simafa*[5] we find a phrase using that Sinograph meaning 'advance toward where the enemy is heading [*su*],' which means 'attack in that direction.' That is why Zheng Xuan interprets this line in the *Zhongyong* as referring to a person who goes toward a spot in which he can hide so that he can engage in strange practices.[6] But how could this be what an exemplary person would do? The actual meaning of this phrase becomes clear when we note that later in this chapter there is praise for someone who 'withdraws from the world to live in obscurity.'"[7]

In my opinion, Zheng Xuan's commentary leads us in the wrong direction and Lü's interpretation is incoherent. Neither are worth passing on to future generations.

The King asked:

As for reading *su* in the phrase "go to where they can hide from public view," Zhu Xi's *Huowen* says that "the ancients read this as saying a person who is unable to display ethical virtuosity hides from public view. That is roughly what this means here." He also says, "the later phrase 'withdraw from the world to live in obscurity,' when you look back at what precedes it, supports this interpretation."[8] Moreover, the *History of the Former Han Dynasty* has a similar phrase, but with a different Sinograph [*suo* 索] that is written almost the same as the Sinograph used here. (See the *Yiwen zhi*.)[9] That phrase is not exactly the same as the one we see in this text, so we cannot be absolutely sure what the phrase in *Zhongyong* actually means. However, *Zhongyong zhangju* states definitively that there is a mistaken Sinograph here.¹⁰ Yet, in a letter to Huang Zhiqing, Zhu Xi says that phrase should be written exactly the way it appears in the *Zhongyong*.¹¹ So even though he wrote in *Zhongyong zhangju* that we should correct the Sinograph *so*, isn't it the case that we should stick with the way that phrase was originally written?

| RESPONDED:

As for the phrase "hide from public view," it can mean an unwarranted retreat from public life. If you eat well without working hard to earn that food, that's called unwarranted feasting. If you collect a high salary even though you do not hold a high rank, that's called unwarranted profiting. If you act like a king even though you are not one, that's called unwarranted ruling. The basic meaning of unwarranted is the same in all those cases. But if you say that those who lack the ability to display ethical virtuosity and therefore decide to hide from public view are guilty of "unwarranted seclusion," then doesn't that imply that all those who are able to display ethical virtuosity have to hide from public view? And would that also mean that all who retreat from public life and therefore lack both high rank and wealth are able to display ethical virtuosity?

There is a slight mistake in the old understanding of this line. That's why Zhu Xi followed it in some respects but disagreed with it in others. Long ago there were examples of people, such as Bo Yi and Yu Zhong,¹² who felt they had no choice but to withdraw from public life when they felt their moral principles were threatened. However, if someone goes into seclusion without a good reason for doing so and then engages in strange behavior, then that can be called seeking seclusion for seclusion's sake. Liu Xin¹³ used that term for those who withdraw from public life to pursue immortality in the mountains. Zhu Xi, however, understand "to withdraw from public view" as a reference to Zou Yan's "occult technique for predicting the future."¹⁴ But pursuing the principles behind the obscure and arcane is not always the wrong thing to do and does not need to be dismissed as a waste of time.

There are times when an exemplary person is justified in looking into the obscure and the arcane. Look at what the *Book of Changes* advises: "delve into mysteries and search for what is hidden, hook up what lies deep, and reach for what is distant, in order to determine good fortune and bad fortune."¹⁵ Withdrawing from public life to uncover the heretofore undiscovered can sometimes be what a sage needs to do. Confucius wrote in *The Great Treatise on the Book of Changes* that pursuing the unknown is something very much worth doing. So why does this chapter then link withdrawing from public life in order to search for what is hidden with engaging in "strange behavior"? Some who withdraw from public life to engage in "strange behavior" should not be criticized for wanting to withdraw into seclusion and live their lives without drawing any attention from others. That is a perfectly acceptable way to behave. Some of the other chapters in this classic make this perfectly clear. We should take what Zhu Xi wrote in his letter to Huang Zhiqing as definitive. (My original answer was mistaken. I have now corrected it.)[16]

Zhu Xi said, "If you respect the Dao and act accordingly, then you will be able to choose the proper course of action. But if you quit before you carry through on that choice, that shows that you are not strong enough."[17]

I do not find anywhere in the classics that statement that someone who is unable to carry through on what they recognize is the Way they should behave cannot be called an exemplary person. Such a person might give up simply because they are exhausted and are on the verge of a physical collapse. To understand what this chapter actually means, you need to compare it with what is said in the "Biao Ji" ["Record of Examples"] chapter in the *Book of Rites*.[18] Also note what I say in *Admonitions for Myself upon Reading the Zhongyong*.[19]

Zhu Xi said, "Shun is known for his wisdom, Yan Hui is known for acting unselfishly, and Zilu was known for his courage."[20]

As I see it, though Yan Hui was known for acting unselfishly, in this classic it is his consistently calm and composed state of mind that is highlighted, not his benevolence.[21] However, Zilu's courage is not tempered by a calm and composed mind, nor can he be said to be as wise as Shun. These men are treated like the three legs of a tripod. In his earlier discussion of the line "declining ranks and emoluments and stepping on the bare blade of a sword,"[22] Zhu Xi took wisdom, benevolence, and courage as separate qualities which together make up what it means to be a person of good character. That would mean wisdom, benevolence, and courage are the core of a consistently focused and composed heart-mind. I'm afraid that is hard to understand.

Zhongyong XII

> The Dao which the superior person pursues extends far and wide [*fei*] and yet is hidden [*yin*].

Zhu Xi said, "*Fei* [費] refers to its actualization being wide-ranging. *Yin* [隱] refers to its potential being difficult to discern."[1]

As far as I know, this talk of potential and its actualization [K. *ch'eyong* / C. *tiyong*] is not explicitly mentioned in the ancient classics. Yet things certainly can be said [depending on the context] to have unactualized potential as well as to exhibit the actualization of their potential. The Dao of Heaven extends far and wide, both potentially and actualized. The Dao of Heaven is hard to see and therefore can be said to be hidden, but we can still say it has potential for manifestation as well as actually being manifest.[2] Therefore this classic says, "If an exemplary person speaks of the greatness of the Dao of Heaven, he means there is nothing able to contain it. If an exemplary person speaks of the smallness of the Dao of Heaven, he means there is nothing able to cut it up and make it smaller."[3]

Zhu Xi said, "The Dao of the exemplary person is nearby. It can be found in the dwellings of ordinary men and women."[4] (See *Zhongyong zhangju*.)

He also said, "This is something even uneducated people can know." (See *Huowen*.)[5]

He also said, "The *Book of Changes* opens with a discussion of how male Heaven and female Earth relate to each other, while the *Book of Songs* begins with a poem about the cry of an osprey praising the beauty of a noble lady. The *Book of Documents* records the marriages of Yao's daughters to Shun, while the *Classic of Rites* is concerned with the great rite of marriage. These are all references to the Dao."[6]

As I see it, when Zhu Xi is talking about the uneducated, he is talking about ordinary men and women. But when he talks about the starting point of appropriate human interactions, he brings up the idea that "Heaven is masculine, and Earth is feminine." In one case he is talking about the average person. In the other case, he is talking about morality. That's like confusing apples and oranges. It is difficult to understand what he is saying.

The *Book of Changes* says, "There were Heaven and Earth, and then husbands and wives came into existence. Once husbands and wives existed, soon there were fathers and sons."[7] Morality begins with interactions between husbands and wives. That is why Zhu Xi says human morality has its roots in the lives of ordinary men and women. However, the reference in this chapter to men and women is just a general reference to the uneducated masses. To talk about them in the same breath as the sages is questionable, especially if it leads to talking about ordinary husbands and wives as though they were Heaven and Earth, the foundation of the universe!

When the *Book of Changes* refers to Heaven and Earth, in neither the core text itself nor in the commentary does it say they are husband and wife. And what matters to Yao in the *Book of Documents* is not necessarily his daughter's marriage but choosing the right successor. How can we regard ordinary men and women as the starting point of these four classics [*Book of Changes, Book of Songs, Book of Documents, Book of Rites*]? Saying that the Dao has its starting point in the relationship between husbands and wives is done simply to make it easier for the average person to understand what morality is.

THE KING ASKED:

Although the two phrases "consistently composed" and "extending far and wide yet hidden" do not mean the same thing, the Dao of the exemplary person is nothing more than being consistently composed and focused. When we talk about constant focus and composure, therefore, can we look at it as extending far and wide yet remaining hidden? When we talk about that which extends far and wide and yet remains hidden, can we look upon it as the same thing as being consistently composed and focused? Consistently composed and focused means one thing, and "extending far and wide yet hidden" means something else, so shouldn't it be unacceptable to force them together like this?

I RESPONDED:

As for the phrase "extending far and wide yet hidden," it simply means that you can never separate yourself from the Dao. Why do I say this? "Extending far and wide" means that it is so large that there is nothing in the universe that can contain it and there is nothing beyond it, either. "Hidden" means it is so minute that nothing in the universe can break it into smaller pieces. Moreover, it is so small that there can be no empty spaces inside it. At the same time, it is also so large that nothing can contain it. But as something so large that it has nothing beyond it as well as so small that it has no empty spaces within it, there can be nothing within the realm of the transformations created by Heaven on High that it does not include. So that means there is no place on heaven or earth where the Dao is not present.

Let me try to clarify what I am saying here. Even though the Dao is so large that it embraces everything, if there were a crevice somewhere inside it, then it would be possible for the Dao to be absent in that spot. Even though the Dao may be extremely minute, if it has a crack in it somewhere, then it would be possible for that crack to be separate from the Dao. But what does it mean to say something is so large that it has nothing else outside it or that it is so small that it has nothing else inside it? It is like a fish in water. Does it not have water all over the scales on its outside and all through the organs on its inside? Where can it go where it would be away from water?

Generally speaking, the Dao of human beings consists of being composed and focused on the task at hand at all times. What extends far and wide yet is hidden is the Dao of Heaven. To cultivate the Dao [to cultivate your ability to act appropriately at all times], you have to understand what Heaven is. That is why we first speak of being composed and always focused on the task at hand, and then we speak of that which extends far and wide and yet is hidden. Although each phrase has its own specific reference, the Dao they refer to is one, not two. (I was not clear enough on this point at first, so I added this additional explanation.)

THE KING ASKED:

That which is described as extending wide and far and yet is hidden is the Dao, which is above the realm of material form. But those who discuss the patterns defining and directing appropriate interactions within the material realm say those patterns are the reasons things are the way they are and do what they do. Zhu Xi does not say that which extends wide and far is the reason things are what they are and do what they do, though he says that that which is hidden is the reason things are what they are and do what they do.[8] Why does he distinguish between those two aspects of the Dao?

I RESPONDED:

Zhu Xi took "extending far and wide" to refer to its actualization and "hidden" to refer to its potential. Its potential is hidden within, from where it guides and directs the Ten Thousand Things in order to actualize that potential. That is why he only refers to what is hidden as the reason things are what they are and do what they do.

Hou Zhongliang said, "What the Sage does not know is exemplified by Confucius's asking about propriety and about government offices. What the Sage cannot do is exemplified by Confucius being unable to obtain an official position and Yao and Shun not being able to do enough to bring relief to the masses."[9]

As I recall, Laozi[10] understood what propriety means and Tanzi[11] knew proper titles for government office, so how can we say Sages lack knowledge? Yao and Shun rose to the throne, and the Duke of Zhou ruled over All-under-Heaven, so how we say Sages are incapable? What one Sage does not know, another Sage knows. What one Sage cannot do, another Sage can do. How can the message of the classics be anything other than this?

Zhu Xi took bits and pieces of what the Chengs said and inserted them into his *Zhongyong zhangju*. But that makes it very difficult to understand![12]

Who knows what is responsible for the regular movements of the Sun and the Moon through the sky? Who knows what function is served by having the sun, moon, and the stars arrayed the way they are in the heavens? Who knows what keeps the earth in place as it floats in empty space? These are examples of what Sages do not know. Even Tang could not bring rain during a drought that lasted seven years.[13] Yan Hui died, and Confucius could not save him.[14] There are examples of what even Sages have no control over.

Zhu Xi said, "Heaven cannot contain all that it produces, and Earth cannot produce the way Heaven produces. *Yin* and *yang*, cold and heat, good fortune and bad fortune, calamities and blessings: none of these are under our total control."[15]

In my opinion, "people sometimes resent the hand Heaven deals them"[16] because of the mysterious way things change around them. They know that anything can happen. They do not mean that Heaven and Earth deliberately cause harm.

Zhu Xi said, "*Cha* [察 K. *ch'al*, examine] here means *zhu* [著 K. *chŏ*, to manifest]."[17] (Rao said, "*Cha* refers to things manifesting on their own. It is telling us that is the way things are and we cannot control them.")[18]

Someone else said, "*Cha* should be understood here as the equivalent of *zhi* [至 K. *chi*, to go as far as it can go]. The *Great Commentary to the Book of Documents* says, '*cha* is another way of referring to *ji* [祭 K. *che*, offer sacrifice], since that which becomes ultimately manifest [*cha*] is *zhi* [the finish line]. When a human life has run its full course [*zhi*], you then sacrifice [*ji*] to the dead.'"[19]

In my opinion, *cha* means here investigating what is hidden. It is the Dao of Heaven which is the most hidden. There is no way to see or hear it directly. You must look up, down, and all around.[20] Through close examination, you will see the traces of creation.[21] That is how you come to recognize the manifestations of the Dao of Heaven. *Cha*, therefore, means examining what is hidden and what is subtle, leaving nothing unexamined. Hawks and fish are particularly inspiring examples of that. I've never seen *Cha* listed with the meaning of *zhu* [to manifest] in the *Sancang*.[22]

The King asked:

The phrase "lively and animated"[23] originated in comments on the *Heart Sutra* by the "man of the Pine Creek with No Defilements."[24] The monk Zonggao[25] said, "Do not stick to established arrangements. Do not copy what other people have done. Be naturally lively and animated."[26] For this reason the Ming scholar Yang Shen wondered how the phrase "lively and animated' "by the Meditative Buddhist school could be used in explaining a Confucian classic. Someone asked Yin Hejing if Master Cheng actually used the phrase "lively and animated spirit" in talking about that poem since it is not clear if that term was being used at that time or not.[27] Yin replied, "They did not do a good job of recording what he said," yet later Confucian scholars relied upon this, saying this was from *Recorded Conversation of Yang Shi*.[28] The scholarship of Yang Shi is essentially like that of the Buddhists of the meditation school. That is why it has frequently been suggested that Yang Shi imposed his own ideas on Master Cheng's words. Why did Zhu Xi feel compelled to cite this statement in the *Zhongyong zhangju* as if it came from Master Cheng? However, if this phrase can shed light on our Confucian heritage, even though it originated from mediating Buddhists, isn't it something we should keep rather than throwing it out?

I responded:

The heart-mind of the exemplary person takes the best possible behavior as what he should emphasize. If someone hears something that he finds useful to that end, and it contains principles that are worth following, why should he ignore it just because of who said it? Moreover, Zhu Xi said, "the words 'lively and animated' are just the sort of things ordinary people say. They use this phrase, and so do we." (See the *Huowen*.)[29] Claiming this is a phrase only meditating Buddhists should use is a mistake. But since "lively and animated" means "moving around here and there," I'm afraid this is not really relevant to what extends far and wide and yet is hidden.

Zhongyong XIII

> The Dao is not far away from ordinary people.... When hewing an axe handle, simply hew an axe handle.[1]

Zhi Xi said, "If you ignore the commonplace and nearby and instead pay more attention to what is high and far away, then you do not know what the Dao is."[2]

Chen said, "This is like the Dao spoken about by Laozi and Zhuangzi, something that existed before the Supreme Polarity."[3]

In my opinion, the sentence "the Dao is not far away from ordinary people" refers to the Way I should behave personally. This has nothing to do with what Laozi and Zhuangzi say about a Dao that existed before the universe emerged. Two sentences that appear in this chapter, "The pattern is not far to seek" and one that follows, "it is as if the patterns are far apart,"[4] both use the same Sinograph that means "far." But if we say these phrases reflect the thinking of Laozi and Zhuangzi, that is ripping them out of their context, like separating a mountain from its peak.

Zhu Xi said, "The exemplary person, by acting in accordance with the Dao of human beings, is able to govern others by getting them to follow his example. If the people he governs are transformed into better people, then there is no more need for him to govern them anymore."[5]

As I see it, this passage refers only to the effort required in self-cultivation and has nothing to say about governing others. I am afraid that Zhu Xi missed the point by reading this as about governing others. The line in this chapter that says "it is by acting as a proper person that you are able to get other people to act properly" is telling us we should deal with others as we would like them to deal with us.[6] The phrase "acting as a proper person" should be understood as meaning "do what you are supposed to do in accordance with your station in life" and "take care of matters the way they should be taken care of." We should not read it in the sense of "governing the people" or "controlling criminal behavior." Serving your parents and serving your ruler are both "dealing with people the way they should be dealt with." "Hewing the axe handle" here means using an axe handle the way it should be used. "Serving others" means to interact with others the way you should interact with them. Those two phrases mean basically the same thing.

Doing your best and being empathetic in your dealings with others[7] [K. *ch'ungsŏ* 忠恕] refer to the effort exerted in developing a moral character. How can we say these two Sinographs refer to governing others or managing external affairs? This is not what this says at all.

Zhu Xi said, "As for the single thread that runs through the teachings of Confucius,[8] Master Cheng says it is to align yourself with Heaven. Zeng Shen[9] says that Confucius is pointing to something that is so profound it is beyond words so he borrowed the words 'doing your best and being empathetic in your dealing with others' to shed light on what Confucius was talking about by providing a rough approximation of that which is so profound it cannot be named."[10]

As I see it, Zeng Shen at that time made the meaning of "the single thread" clear to the multitudes. Previous generations of Confucian scholars have dismissed his explanation for, in their view, being too commonplace and close to the ground. They thought the "thread" must refer to something that surely must lie beyond appropriate interactions between one human being and another, and must be something that runs through Heaven, Earth, and the Ten Thousand Things and reaches all the way up to the lofty and the mysterious. They regarded doing your utmost and being empathetic in your dealings with others as the crude manifestations of that lofty abstraction. This is something I really dislike about more recent scholarship.[11]

Master Cheng said, "As for the Dao of serving someone above you, there is nothing better than doing your utmost. As for the Dao of dealing with your subordinates, there is nothing better than acting with empathy."[12]

He also said, "Heaven and Earth do not display empathy."[13]

As I recall, Zhu Xi discusses these two ideas in detail (see *Huowen*),[14] so I do not need to spend any time discussing them.

THE KING ASKED:

The Dao of the ruler consists of acting in accordance with the moral obligations entailed by the Five Relationships,[15] so why does Confucius in this section not mention the relationship between husband and wife? The "Far and Wide yet Hidden" chapter says that the Dao of the exemplary person is rooted in the relationship between husband and wife, and this is the closest relationship people have. If what Zhu Xi says about this section is accurate, then there must be some reason only four of the Five Relationships are mentioned. I would like to hear your explanation for this.

I RESPONDED:

The relationship between husband and wife is essentially one between just two people. People do not apply how they want to be treated by their wife to what they expect in other interactions. Since the proper roles of husband

and wife are like those of Heaven and Earth respectively, their Dao is not the same [as the Dao that applies in other interactions]. The husband should not expect others to deal with him the way his wife does. Is not this the reason Confucius did not say anything about husbands and wives in this section? Moreover, the assertion that "the starting point for appropriate human interactions is the relationship between husbands and wives"[16] is advice intended for the uneducated masses. I am afraid it cannot be the starting point for the full range of appropriate human interactions.[17]

Zhongyong XIV

> The exemplary person does what is appropriate [C. *su*] for whatever position he finds himself in.

Zhu Xi said, "*Su* [素] implies to be in a particular situation at a particular point in time."[1]

Mao Qiling said: "*Su* does not mean to be in a specific situation. That is not the way it was understood in the past. We can only see that kind of talk when Buddhists talk about three states of mind: one each for the current situation, the past, and the future. When earlier Confucians explained the classics, they did not use that interpretation. Looking at the commentary on the 'Record of Small Matters in Mourning Garments' in the *Book of Rites*, we can see a passage that says, 'there is an improper way to wear mourning clothes and there is a proper way to wear mourning clothes.'[2] *Su* [translated here as "proper"] in this context means normally or the way it should be. The *Etiquette and Ceremonial* [*Yili*] says, 'The mourner should eat cold [*su*] rice.'[3] Acording to Zheng Xuan, '*su* in this context means old. This means to eat rice the way rice was eaten in ordinary times in the past.'[4] When *su* is understood in this way, it is clear that 'appropriate for the position he is in' means to act in accordance with the position he normally holds. When the *Zhongyong* says *yong* [ordinarily] and when the *Mencius* says 'normal'[5] — this is what they mean."[6] (Zhang Taizhan said, "if he acts in a natural, easy-going fashion, then a rural gentleman can harvest more than ten bags of barley and he will then find it easy to attract a wife.")[7]

As I understand it, the word *su* refers to the state of mind you should have at a particular time and in a particular situation.[8] Some scholars have claimed that it is easy to see this *su* as being the *su* that means to act as you normally should act. That is why it is explained by Zhu Xi as a reference to how you should act in a particular time and place. Although we cannot say that a philological analysis of ancient texts will always allow us to avoid imposing on a term an incorrect reading, when the meaning of a classical text is quite clear, we need to beware of being led astray by the loose interpretations of later readers. In doing proper exegesis, you cannot force a meaning on a term when that reading is not supported by the *Sancang*, the *Erya*, or the *Shuowen*.[9] And, logically speaking, even if it is something Buddha has said, if it seems reasonable, why should we reject it?

The King asked:

I read Hou Shisheng's discussion of the monk Changzong[10] in *Huowen*,[11] but in the end I am not persuaded by it. The Buddhist he refers to was just playing with language, using our terminology with his own meanings. He really tried to twist our words to his advantage. He used our terminology to ask questions such as "When you acquire some knowledge, what exactly do you acquire?" However, what harm can this do? Since we Confucians say that everything is already complete within our heart-minds, was he not justified in asking us what we acquire when we acquire knowledge?[12]

I responded:

Hou Shisheng understood the knowledge that is inscribed on our heart-minds as what we know without having to say it aloud.[13] He thought that we become aware of that innate knowledge and acquire ethical virtuosity through everyday conversations and everyday actions. But that is not what Changzong was saying. That's why Zhu Xi criticized him.

Your humble subject would like to point out that this chapter of the *Zhongyong* says, "Everywhere an exemplary person goes, he is secure in his own knowledge of how to behave appropriately."[14] That is why it also says, "he does not desire to go beyond what is appropriate to his station." The single Sinograph *su* is the foundation of acquiring ethical virtuosity. It means to act appropriately in any situation you find yourself in without any concern for personal benefit. Feeling comfortable in your awareness of your own social position, you have no desire to go beyond it. As for what Changzong says about ignoring your position in society to seek fulfillment elsewhere, that is a typical of the sorts of mistakes Buddhists make.

Lü Wancun[15] said, "the sentence 'everywhere an exemplary person goes, he knows how to behave appropriately' does not mean that he does whatever everyone around him is doing, such as removing his formal clothing when he enters a country of barbarians.[16] *Huowen* says, 'our heart-mind does not lack what we need to guide our behavior.'[17] This is nothing more than the ability we have been given to make correct decisions. If that is not the case, then what kind of knowledge would be knowledge that does not need to be spoken aloud? Is this not an example of 'everywhere an exemplary person goes, he knows how to act appropriately'? Is not this the perfect retort to Changzong's question?"[18]

Zhongyong XV

> When traveling a long distance, we must start from somewhere nearby. When ascending to someplace high, we must begin from down below.

THE KING ASKED:

When it comes to the sentence "when traveling a long distance, we must start from somewhere nearby; in ascending to someplace high, we must begin from down below," why is this only illuminated with references to our relationships with our wives, children, elder brothers, and younger brothers? Among the Five Relationships, why does it exclude the relationships of ruler-subject and friend-friend? Why does it appear to treat those two relationships as already high and far away?[1]

I RESPONDED:

The Five Cardinal Relationships and the Five Cardinal Duties in the Book of Yu in the *Book of Documents*[2] are based on relationships among fathers, mothers, elder brothers, younger brothers, and children. We can find the same idea in the *Zuozhuan*.[3] In the *Daxue* when it says "make manifest for all to see illustrious ethical virtuosity," it is referring specifically to the three virtues of filial piety, brotherly affection, and parental love.[4] When someone is not interacting harmoniously within the Six Relationships, he dare not interact with people outside his family.[5] This is the Dao of ancient times. The difference between a ruler and a subject is quite high. Friends can appear to be far away. Isn't the reference to what is nearby and what is down below a reference to those close relatives who make up our Six Relationships?[6]

Zhu Xi said: "If people are able to live harmoniously with their wives and children and interact appropriately with their siblings, then their parents will be happy and at peace. Zisi cited this ode to illuminate the fact that 'when traveling a long distance, we must start from somewhere nearby; in ascending to someplace high, we must begin from down below.'"[7]

Rao Lu said: "Matters related to your wife and children are a lower level obligation. Submitting to your parents is a higher obligation. This is the meaning of 'when traveling a long distance, we must start from somewhere nearby; in ascending to someplace high, we must begin from down below.'"[8]

Huang Xunrao said: "Your wife, your children, and your older and younger brothers are examples of what is nearby and a lower obligation. Your mother and father are examples of a more distant and higher obligation."⁹

Mao Qiling said: "The terms 'high' and 'low' are used to point out that our obligations to our parents are at a higher level than our obligations to our wife and our children. But if we use the terms 'far away' and 'nearby' to imply that our parents are far away from us, and our wife and children are nearby, then this is contrary to the Way we should think and behave. I'm afraid that is not what Zisi meant."¹⁰

As I see it, in preparation for discussing the significance of serving the spirits in the next chapter, this text first discusses the relationships between fathers and sons, and between older and young brothers. The text is not dividing the members of one family into the near and the far. What Mao Qiling said is completely correct.¹¹

Zhongyong XVI

In the way it displays its power,[1] how great is the Spirit.[2]

Master Cheng said, "ghosts and spirits are terms used to refer to the way heaven and earth were brought into existence They are the residual traces of the transformations that produce the visible world." Master Zhang[3] said, "ghosts and spirits are the natural activities of *yin* and *yang*."[4]

As I see it, the section on the "Overseer of Ritual Affairs" in the "Spring Offices" volume in the *Zhouli* explains that there are three levels of spirits to whom we offer sacrifice. The first are called the celestial spirits, the second are called terrestrial spirits, and the third are called human spirits. The celestial spirits are the Lord on High of the vast heavens [昊天上帝 K. *Hoch'ŏn Sangje* / C. *Haotian Shangdi*], the Sun, the Moon, the stars, Sizhong, Siming,[5] the Master of Wind, and the Master of Rain. The terrestrial spirits are the gods of Soil and Grain, the gods of the Five Sacrificial Rites, the gods of the Five Sacred Mountains, the gods of Hills and Forests, and the gods of Rivers and Marshes. The human spirits are those honored in ancestral shrines, such as the kings of earlier dynasties, and deceased paternal and maternal ancestors.[6] As for the order of sacrificing to them, although there are three levels, in reality only the celestial spirits and the human spirits need concern us.

Why is this? Rushou[7] is one of the gods of the Five Sacrificial Rites and therefore is clearly one of the terrestrial spirits. But Shi Yin [Scribe Yin] claims in the *Chunqiu waizhuan*[8] that Rushou is a celestial spirit. If that were the case, then Gou Mang, Zhu Rong, Xuan Ming, and Hou Tu would also be celestial spirits.[9] As for Zhong, Gai, Xiu, and Xi, they are the four uncles of Shaohao.[10] Then there are the god Li, who is the son of Zhuanxu; the god Goulong, who is the son of Gonggong; the god Zhu, who is the son of Lie Shan; and the god Qi, who is the son of Gaoxin. In the five sacrifices to the gods of Soil and Grain, these are the spirits who are sacrificed to, so we can see that the various gods of Soil and Grain are actually the spirits of humans.[11]

Heaven as a celestial spirit has dominion over each of the domains of water, fire, metal, wood, soil, grain, mountains and streams, and forests and marshes. Human rulers likewise are responsible for their human subjects. This is how responsibilities were divided. However, later generations treated human beings who, as subjects, had done meritorious service as the equal of celestial spirits. At the altars to the gods of Soil and Grain, and during the worship of the gods of the Five Sacrificial Rites, and during the worship of the gods of Mountains and Streams, they are called gods of the

Earth, though actually they are all either celestial spirits or human spirits. Human spirits are nothing more than the spirits of dead people. "The way heaven and earth functions" or "the natural activities of *yin* and *yang*"[12] are not what the *Analects* is referring to when it mentions human spirits.

As for the various celestial spirits, they are essentially immaterial beings serving as the immediate subordinates of the Lord on High [*Sangje*]. (See the commentary on the *Rites*.)[13] Lined up to form a bright array,[14] each one of them has its own title and its responsibilities. The Grand Invocator in the Ministry of Ritual was actually in charge of these matters (the *Zhouli* distinguishes six different ways of referring to spiritual beings when addressing them).[15] How can we put aside what these ancient texts actually say and instead impose novel interpretations on them?

There are some who suspect that spirits are residual traces of the transformations that generate the visible world and others who suspect that "spirits" are nothing more than the natural activities of *yin* and *yang*.[16] This would have them hovering between existence and nonexistence and banish them to the realm of illusion. That would mean the practices of the kings of old of serving the spirits would no longer have any relevance for later generations. What does "residual traces" mean, anyway? They are like the imprints left behind by footsteps. If we see footprints of large men, we know large men walked this path before us. If we see footprints of small children, we know small children have walked this path before us. Residual traces, therefore, are like footprints. It is certainly unreasonable to consider the footprints they left behind to actually be those large men and small children. So how can we say these residual traces of the transformations that generate the visible world are the same things as actual spirits?

If you say that heaven and earth overall are the products of the fruitful activities of the spirits and you say that transformations of *ki* that generate the visible world are the residual traces of spirits, how can you then say those mere residual traces and activities are the spirits themselves?

The "two *ki*" refers to *yin* and *yang*.[17] *Yin* is nothing more than a shadow where the sun's rays do not reach, and *yang* is nothing more than the rays of the sun. Although these two phenomena alternate, darkening and brightening in turn, giving us what we call day and night and which we call hot and cold, as material phenomena they lack even an iota of cognitive capability. They are unable to know anything or to sense anything. That means they are far below even the level of birds and beasts, or insects and worms. How could managing the transformations that generate the visible world be something they have the inherent ability to do? And how could they "stimulate the people of this world to fast and purify themselves, and dress themselves in fine clothes in order to offer them sacrifices?"[18]

The men of old served Heaven with sincere heart-minds. With sincere heart-minds, they served the Spirit. From the earliest stirrings of their every action and every thought, they asked themselves if those incipient thoughts or actions were genuine or deceptive, were good or evil. They exhorted themselves to engage in self-reflection, saying, "Heaven watches everything we do."[19] Therefore their ardent determination to be cautious and apprehensive even when no human being could observe what they were doing or thinking was truly for the sake of aligning with the way Heaven acted appropriately.

These days people regard Heaven as *li* and spirits as the way *li* operates. Spirits are also regarded as nothing more than the traces of the transformations of things and as the natural activities of *yin* and *yang*. People assume this without thinking it through clearly. It is as though they do not know anything about spirits at all. So, when they are alone in their dark rooms, they ignore their own conscience and indulge in all sorts of inappropriate thoughts and actions as though they have nothing to fear or dread. Though they study the Dao until the end of their lives, they are unable to come even close to the level of Yao and Shun. This is all because of a lack of clarity in their understanding of what a spirit is.

A line later on this classic says, "To [have the way we behave] be affirmed before the various spirits and therefore be without any doubt [about how we should behave] is to know the will of Heaven. To be prepared to wait a hundred generations for a sage without misgivings is to know what it is to be truly human."[20] Does not this passage suggest that sages are human beings, but the Spirit is Heaven?

Chen[21] said, "The Son of Heaven sacrifices to Heaven and Earth. The Feudal Lords sacrifice to the gods of Soil and Grain. The Great Ministers sacrifice to the gods of the Five Sacrificial Rites. The Nobles sacrifice to their ancestors."

As I see it, you cannot say of the spirits of Soil and Grain, the gods of the Five Sacrificial Rites, and the ancestors that "they inform all things so they cannot be other than what they are"; you cannot say of them that "they stimulate the people of this world to fast and purify themselves"; and you cannot say of them that "they make visible what is so subtle it can hardly be seen, so that what things truly are cannot be obscured."[22] These sentences praise the power of Heaven and provide the basis for being watchful over your every thought and action even when no one else can tell what you are doing or thinking. What more needs to be said?

Zhu Xi said, "The coagulating and dispersing of *yin* and *yang* is always substantial. Accordingly, manifestations of this are necessarily visible."[23]

I would like to point out that the first chapter of the *Zhongyong* says,

"There is nothing more apparent than what is so subtle it can hardly be seen." This chapter has the line "make visible that which is so subtle it can hardly be seen" and in the last chapter [XXXIII] we can find the line "an exemplary person recognizes the manifestations of that which is so subtle it can hardly be seen." These passages clarify each other. Similar passages must be understood together. The common thread running through them must not be ignored. Only if you understand them in their entirety can you really understand what they are telling you. If you are blocked from understanding part of them, then you will not understand them at all. There are not two different ways to read these lines. Zhu Xi at the beginning of his commentary on the *Zhongyong* explains that which is so subtle it can hardly be seen as the minor affairs of human beings.[24] At the end, he says it refers to what goes on inside our heart-minds (he writes that "making visible that which is so subtle it can hardly be seen means all that is within informs all that is without."[25] And, in commenting on this chapter, he says it refers to the actual patterns directing the interactions of *yin* and *yang*.[26] Those three explanations contradict each other. Could this canonical work really vary this much in how it uses the same terms? I'm afraid that cannot be the case.

That which you look for but cannot see, and that which you listen for but cannot hear, and therefore that which is the most hidden and subtle in All-under-Heaven is none other than the Spirit. The fact that Heaven acts as it should act without being distracted by thoughts of personal benefit, that all things cannot be other than what they are supposed to be, that the sun and moon move through their regular course without any deviations, that the four seasons follow one another in an orderly fashion, that the transformations of things that generate the visible universe are so productive, that everything has its particular role to play in the cosmic network: this is how it manifests its power and renders it visible. This display of order in the universe is what stimulates the people of this world to fast, purify themselves, and offer sacrifices as though there is Something above. What other reason could they have for doing that, other than the fact that they cannot ignore that all these physical processes take place the way they are supposed to take place?

The celestial Dao takes no material form, yet we can definitely see it in the way it keeps the cosmos operating the way it should. What does this imply for human beings, who are material beings? This invisible celestial Dao is the reason an exemplary person is cautious even when no one can observe his innermost thoughts.

Zhu Xi said, "As for what the term 'spirits' means, what Confucius told Zai Yu can be found in the 'Meaning of Sacrifices' chapter of the *Book of Rites*.[27] Zheng Xuan explained what Confucius said, so that has already been clarified. He explains that our *yang* spirit [which ascends to heaven after we die] makes its presence felt when we use our mouths and nose to inhale and exhale, and our *yin* spirit [which descends to the earth after death] is revealed in the ability of our eyes and ears to clearly perceive things around us. In this way, he explains spirits in terms of flesh and blood."[28]

In my opinion, the "Meaning of Sacrifices" chapter in the *Book of Rites* was written down generations later, and you can be sure that is not as trustworthy a record as the *Analects* is. Moreover, what is being discussed here is basically human spirits and not celestial spirits. The celestial spirits and human spirits are discussed in the *Zhouli* as two fundamentally different things.[29] How can they be thrown together as the same sort of thing?

Generally speaking, "rendering visible that which is so subtle it can hardly be seen" can be said to be a manifestation of the power of Heaven. The previous chapter [Chapter XV] uses the phrases "traveling a long distance" and "ascending to someplace high" to tell us that we have to start acting appropriately in the Six Relationships[30] by beginning with what is nearer and what is lower. It follows that the meaning of the references to what is high and what is a long distance away must lie in the chapter that follows [that is to say, this chapter, Chapter XVI]. This is the first proof that there is some power greater than the power we humans possess.

The power of Highest Heaven knows no limits, having no external or internal boundaries.[31] Therefore it follows that the rituals directed toward it are without exception impressive, since what they are directed toward is the great beyond. This is the second proof.

The reason why this text says the Dao cannot be departed from for even a moment is that "the Dao informs all things so that they cannot be other than what they are."[32] In other words, the animating and sustaining power of Highest Heaven fills the various things in the universe so completely that they cannot ignore it without losing their identity. This is the third proof.

In chapters that follow this one, the *Zhongyong* makes several references to the ceremonies of ancestral temples. Such references are linked to the statement "The *jiao* [郊] sacrifices and the *she* [社] sacrifices were ways to pay ritual homage to the Lord on High [*Sangje*]. The ceremonies of ancestral temples were means of sacrificing to their ancestors."[33] If the reference to "sacrificing to the ancestors" were not also a reference to the power of Heaven, why would the two statements be linked so closely? This is the fourth proof.

In a later chapter the *Zhongyong* says, "To [have the way we behave] be affirmed before the various spirits and therefore be without any doubt [about how we should behave] is to know the will of Heaven. To be prepared to wait a hundred generations for a sage without misgivings is to know what it is to be truly human."³⁴ The sage is clearly a human being, so how can the Spirit above him [before whom he confirms the proper way to behave] not be Heaven? This is the fifth proof. (All these proofs are based on what I heard from Yi Pyŏk.)

If we regard the various spirits as nothing more than the natural activities of *yin* and *yang*, then all the various spirits such as those of the mountains and streams, soil and forests, such as *chi* demons, *mei* demons, *wang* demons, and *liang* demons,³⁵ must somehow exist as nothing more than various products of *yin* and *yang*. Yet does this chapter not say, "In the way it displays its power, how great is the Spirit"? Does it not say, "It informs all things so that they cannot be other than what they are"? Does it not say, "It is as if the Spirit is far above us"?³⁶ Is there not a good reason such statements appear in this chapter?

THE KING ASKED:

The *Zhongyong* does not use the phrase "the power of spirits." Instead, it refers to spirits "displaying their power." Why is this? If spirits are not *li*, then they must be conscious forms of *ki*. That is why Zhu Xi took the Sinograph for power in this phrase as a reference to the character of spirits and the effect they are able to have.³⁷ If we analyze what this passage is trying to tell us, then we have to admit that it must be a reference to "the power of spirits." That phrase should be followed by the phrase "the character of spirits and the effect they are able to have." But, instead, this chapter only uses the term "displaying their power." It should have added that what they display is their character and their ability to make an impact. What is it actually trying to tell us here?

I RESPONDED:

Spirits are definitely not *li*.³⁸ Are they then *ki*? We human beings have a physical endowment, a tangible form of *ki* spirits lack. That intangible spirits are the natural activities of *yin* and *yang*, the two basic modes of *ki*, is something your subject finds hard to believe. Zhu Xi takes their character and their efficacy as the power they possess. But then he says that spirits are nothing more than the natural activities of *yin* and *yang*. However, to praise the power of spirits, you have to do more than simply talk about their character and their efficacy in terms of *ki*.

I, your subject, say, on the contrary, that the line "the people of this world fast and purify themselves, and dress themselves in fine clothes in order to offer sacrifices" is a reference to the sacrifices to Heaven. The learning of the exemplary person begins with serving his parents and is fulfilled by serving Heaven. When the previous chapter, therefore, talks about "what is near" and "what is below" and about "far away" and "someplace high," I'm afraid this cannot be understood as referring to *yin* and *yang*.

THE KING ASKED:

In the *Zhongyong*, we can find many instances in which the term meaning "power" [or "ethical virtuosity," 德 *tŏk*] is used. In every case we can read it as a reference to nothing other than "patterning principle" [*li*]. But this chapter explicitly mentions only *ki*. Why is that?

Zhu Xi said, "It is the basic condition of spirits that their character is such that they are able to stimulate the people of this world to fast and purify themselves, and to dress themselves in fine clothes in order to offer them sacrifices. This is how their power produces results." He also says, "That spirits can be neither seen nor heard is their fundamental character. We see their efficacy in their informing all things so that things cannot be other than what they are." On top of that, he says, "In their character and efficacy we can see the innate ability of *yin* and *yang*. Their power is the power of heaven and earth."[39] When we take this into account, how can we not say the basic character as well as the effective power of spirits is a manifestation of *ki*? But Zhu Xi also regarded the power of spirits as the concrete manifestation of *li*. If we say, then, that spirits are concrete manifestations of *li*, then shouldn't we talk about the power of spirits in terms of *li*? It looks like Zhu Xi has contradicted himself. What do you think?

I RESPONDED:

These phrases "character" [性情][40] and "efficacy" [功效][41] do not appear in any of the canonical texts. I am afraid, therefore, that these words of Zhu Xi, even though they have some contradictions that might appear interesting to explore, are not really worth examining in detail. Speaking broadly, spirits are neither *li* nor *ki*. Why does everyone think we have to engage in verbal contortions and talk about them in terms of *li* and *ki*?

The *Book of Changes* says, "What we cannot comprehend about the movements of yin and yang we call spirit."[42] But it also says, "The alternation of *yin* and *yang* is called the Dao."[43] This is nothing more than a reference to divination with milfoil stalks to determine the strong and the weak. What does this have to do with spirits? What does it have to do with the Dao of Heaven?

The *Songs of Chu* says, "No one among the multitudes knows the alternation of *yin* and *yang*."[44] These lines mean *yin* and *yang* come and go suddenly without warning. How can it follow from this that *yin* and *yang* are spirits? Spirits cannot be defined in terms of *li* and *ki* or identified with *yin* and *yang*. I, your humble subject, say that when the celestial and terrestrial spirits line up to form a bright array, the greatest and most respected among them is none other than Sangje. King Wen with great circumspection and reverence did his best to serve the Lord on High.[45] When the *Zhongyong* encourages an attitude of caution and apprehension, how can this not be teaching us to do our best to serve the Lord on High?

When people today read this passage, they doubt whether Sangje exists or not and just push him aside into a dark corner. That is why nothing is done as it should be done, neither the duty of a ruler to maintain an attitude of apprehension and awe nor the duty of a scholar to be cautious even when no one can see what he is thinking or doing. Generally speaking, when someone is alone in a dark room, and he can do anything he wants and, he thinks, in the end no word of it will get out, will he be consistently cautious and apprehensive? It is unreasonable to expect him to do that.

An unexpected solar or lunar eclipse [reminding us that Sangje is in charge] stimulates feelings of caution and apprehension. It is viewed as a portent that is an admonishment to the ruler. However, if the exact time of that eclipse has been predicted [and we therefore are not reminded that Sangje is in charge], then it is seen as a natural phenomenon and does not inspire any extra caution or apprehension.

If scholars are wise and astute, will they not trust what this passage says and cultivate a deep sense of caution and apprehension? If we study the *Zhongyong* and plumb its deepest meaning, we will therefore make a sincere effort to maintain an attitude of caution and apprehension. Generally speaking, in the *Zhongyong* every section starts with what Heaven has mandated and returns to what Heaven has mandated at the end. That is why we see both the trunk and the branches of the Dao in this work. In the first chapter, it begins with what Heaven has conferred [our conscience], our innate ability to act appropriately, and the Dao [telling us what appropriate behavior is], and goes on to show that those three can be found even in what is hidden and obscure. In the end, it tells us that these all are what Heaven has conferred and that therefore they can be found everywhere since they pervade everything. The latter chapters of this text discuss things on their own doing what they should do and therefore causing other things to do what they should do. This has an impact on the entire world as well as on the state. It leads to understanding Heaven and all that it embraces. The *Zhongyong*, therefore, shows us the trunk and the branches of the Dao.

(Looking at how I interpret the *Zhongyong* above, I can see that there is a lot I picked up from Yi Pyŏk.)

THE KING ASKED:

As for looking for spirits and not being able to see them, listening for them and not being able to hear them, and their informing all things so that things cannot be other than what they are, this is the profound and mysterious manifestation of *ki*. This is not a reference to the Dao as both far-reaching and hidden. Yet Zhu Xi explicitly took being neither seen nor heard as "being hidden" and informing all things as "being broad and wide."[46] Why did he do this?

I RESPONDED:

The power of the *Zhongyong* is that it teaches us that the ability to consistently act appropriately depends on maintaining an attitude of cautious apprehension even when we think no one can see what we are thinking or doing. We can maintain such an attitude even when we think no one knows what we are thinking or doing only if we take the existence of the Spirit seriously and hold Him in awe. Without a Lord on High, there is nothing to be in awe of and apprehensive of. The power of this Spirit is the foundation of our Way. The *Zhongyong* therefore says "The Dao which the superior man pursues extends far and wide, and yet is hidden."[47] Zhu Xi understood being far and wide to mean being spread everywhere and therefore noticeable everywhere. He also understood hidden to mean not being able to be either seen or heard. If we try to put into practice the essential and subtle message here, how can we doubt its applicability?[48]

Zhongyong XVII

Great, indeed, was Shun's filial piety!

THE KING ASKED:

Although Yan Hui died young, we can say he is still among us.[1] Although Confucius did not obtain appointment to a high office, it is said that Heaven supported and nourished him. Statements to that effect by Yang Shi and Hou Zhongliang did not harm Yan Hui or Confucius but, on the contrary, enhanced their reputations. Yet Zhu Xi harshly criticized Yang and Hou for speaking thus.[2] Why did he do that? Later scholars thought this went too far but then they themselves went even farther and criticized even the way Zhu Xi explained the classics. This is truly absurd. Nevertheless, are there not some points he makes in his writings that merit further discussion?

I RESPONDED:

Yang Shi was guilty of using Daoist terms when he wrote that, though Yan Hui died young, he was still among us. Hou Zhongliang drew on the words of Mencius and Zhu Xi when he wrote that Confucius was assigned a special mission by Heaven. Although such a statement is not inaccurate, he failed to express the deeper meaning of what this classic is telling us. This is why Zhu Xi criticized both of them.

"Zhongni [Confucius] carried on the work of Yao and Shun as if they were his own ancestors. He modeled his behavior on that of Wen and Wu."[3] Yet he was not appointed to high public office. It might appear at first glance, therefore, that this classic is expressing disappointment in Confucius. But we ought to look at this in a more realistic manner. Let us look at it in terms of the times in which Confucius lived. Kings Wen and Wu sat on the throne when Heaven and Earth had not yet gone into decline. Yet Bi Gan had his heart cut out.[4] Kija was branded a criminal, and Bo Yi starved to death.[5] Was there any reason for them to suffer these fates? Generally speaking, the Dao of the exemplary person is nothing more than doing good. Whether he obtains office or reputation is not what an exemplary person concerns himself with. Therefore Zhu Xi, in his *Zhongyong zhangju*, does not discuss this question of whether the world was unfair to Confucius. This is a sign of Zhu Xi's wisdom.[6]

Zhongyong XVIII

It was only King Wen who was without grief.

THE KING ASKED:

Confucius said that Shun "was certain to gain renown,"¹ and that Wu "never lost the distinguished reputation he enjoyed all over the world."² Yet Rao Lu says that these two phrases do not have the same meaning. He says the difference between them is between being true to one's innate ability to act appropriately and working to recover that ability.³ What is the meaning of this?

I RESPONDED:

The two phrases are different in their implications. One is talking about gaining something, that's all. The other is talking about not losing something, which means to hold on to something that is easy to lose and not lose it. As for reputations, there are "good reputations," "great reputations," "flourishing reputations," and "distinguished reputations." Those are all the different types of reputations. But the phrase "distinguished reputation" means he was distinguished, that's all.

THE KING ASKED:

This chapter says, "King Wu was old when he received the mandate. The Duke of Zhou carried on the excellent ways of Wen and Wu. He posthumously raised King Tai and King Ji to the status of kings." The "Great Treatise" chapter [Chapter XIV] of the *Book of Rites* says, "King Wu won the battle at Muye and retired from the battlefield. He elevated Dan Fu to King Tai, raised Li to King Ji, and raised Chang to King Wen posthumously."⁴ The "Successful Completion of War" chapter of the *Book of Documents* says, "On the day Ding-Wei, he [King Wu] sacrificed in the ancestral temple of Zhou," and announced to the rulers of the various states that his ancestors were now to be known as King Tai and King Ji.⁵ A prayer cited in the "Metal-bound Coffer" section of the *Book of Documents* begins with the phrase "If you three kings [King Tai, King Ji, and King Mun]..."⁶ What the "Great Treatise" says can be excused as something that was added later. What the "Successful Completion of War" says also can be said to be a later addition. But the prayer cited in the "Metal-bound Coffer" chapter is what the Duke of Zhou personally ordered to be written down. Why is it that the *Zhongyong* and the *Book of Documents* differ on this point?[7]

I RESPONDED:

As for what King Wu did at Muye, the Duke of Zhou was at his side. When they returned to Zhou, it was the Duke of Zhou who organized all the ritual sacrifices, major and minor. King Wu merely bowed his head and folded his arms, and all was accomplished. As for that matter of posthumous kings, that was the work of the Duke of Zhou. That is why this classic says what it says. Moreover, it just says "King Wu was old when he received the mandate," nothing more. Does it ever say that once King Wu was already dead, the Duke of Zhou then went on to elevate the status of those three kings posthumously? Your humble servant does not think these two classics contradict each other here.

Zhu Xi said, "The *Rites of Zhou* says that when there is a sacrifice to the Former Kings, the *gunmian* [a crown and gown befitting a ruler] is worn, and when there is a sacrifice to the Former Lords, the *bimian* [robes suitable for feudal lord] is worn. That is why, for sacrifices to the Former Lords, they relied on the way it was done in the past and wore only the formal clothing suitable for feudal lords. *Bimian* are the formal dress of the feudal lords. That is why they are worn in the sacrificial ritual the Son of Heaven performs to honor the Former Lords. It would surely not be right to wear the formal dress appropriate for the Son of Heaven when paying ritual respect to the Former Lords."[8]

Gu Linshi[9] said, "The *bimian* is the proper formal dress for the Former Lords. Someone added that 'This is the way the rites [for them] should be done.' But if we dare to say that the Son of Heaven, when he is paying ritual respect to the Former Lords, should wear the formal dress of the feudal lords, then would it not follow that a son who is a high official, in a mourning ritual for a father who was an ordinary scholar-official, should wear the formal dress of an ordinary scholar-official? This would be a mistake."[10]

In my opinion, although the text in the "Wardrobe Overseer" [*sifu*] section of the *Rites of Zhou*[11] says something like this, in the text of the "Chariot Decorator" [*jinche*] section,[12] we are told that the sacrifices to the Former Lords used a "jade path [C. *yulu* 玉路]." The text of the "Keeper of Seal Tablets" [*dianrui*] section tells us that it was common for sacrifices to the Former Lords to use jade libation ladles.[13] And if we look at the text of the "Grand Music Master" section [*dasiyue*],[14] we would think that the sacrifices to the Former Lords included the *dawu* dance [dance of the great warrior]. (Zheng Xuan's commentary says, "The ancestors are called the Former Kings and the Former Lords.")[15] We cannot take the single word *bimian* and say that it was always used in the rituals of the feudal lords in the ancient past.

Zhan Qin of Lu[16] said, "The people of Zhou regarded King Wen as their ancestor." (See the "Discourses of Lu" section of the *Discourses of the States* [*Guoyu*][17] and the "Rules for Sacrifices" [*Jifa*] section of the *Book of Rites*.)[18] This makes it clear that the people of Zhou understood that King Wen was their grand progenitor. Zhan Qin was of noble lineage and so there is no reason for him not to know who the grand progenitor of the Zhou court was. Ban Gu's *Bai hu tong*[19] therefore says, "Houji[20] was the founder and King Wen was the grand progenitor." Zheng Xuan's commentary on the "Yong" ode also regards King Wen as the grand progenitor.[21] Even though it is quite obvious that is what those texts say, it is only since the *Classic of Filial Piety* that we have seen a sentence saying explicitly: "The Duke of Zhou honored King Wen in the ancestral hall."[22] Some earlier scholars argued that Houji was the grand progenitor of Zhou. That is incorrect.

Nevertheless, Zhu Xi's *Diagram of the Arrangements in the Imperial Ancestral Temple* [*Miaozhitu*][23] puts Houji in the seat of the grand progenitor and King Wen and King Wu in the *zhao* and *mu* rows below him.[24] However, did not Zhu Xi tell us to use the rites appropriate for the feudal lords when sacrificing to the Former Lords? Isn't Houji the only one among them who is a Former Lord? Should we then treat Houji as someone who was raised to royal status posthumously?

The *Zhouli*, in the *shoutiao* [On being responsible for the ancestral tablets] section, says, "The person in charge of the ancestral shrines is responsible for the tablets of the Former Kings and Former Lords." Zheng Xuan annotated this line by saying, "The spirit tablets of the Former Lords are kept in the shrine to Houji. The spirit tablets for Former Kings are kept in the shrine for King Wen and King Wu."[25] This makes it clear that Houji is a Former Lord. He was enfeoffed as a Former Lord. To treat him as the grand progenitor with a ritual appropriate for the Son of Heaven, even though he was a feudal lord, is to miss the point of this ritual.

Zhu Xi said, "They stopped wearing mourning clothes for feudal lords after a year. For high officials, they stopped even before that."[26]

Mr. Lin said, "Generally speaking, this is what the Sages say. What Zhu Xi says in his *Chapters and Phrases* is based on *Etiquette and Ceremonial*."[27]

As I see it, what *Etiquette and Ceremonial* says about reducing the time a high official has to wear mourning clothes is as follows; high officials wear mourning clothes for a full year when mourning for someone from a family of the same rank. However, the time for wearing mourning clothes should be reduced to nine months for mourning family members of ordinary scholars, from paternal uncles and aunts on down.[28] We cannot say that mourning for high officials did not have to last for a full year. However, this rule [of reducing the length of mourning for those of lower rank] was not created by the people of early Zhou. That is why Xianzi Suo said, "I have heard that the ancients did not reduce the period of time mourning clothes were worn [according to the rank of the family head]. They treated everyone as a relative should be treated. Thus Bowen, of Teng, wore a year's mourning for Meng Hu, who was his uncle, and the same for Meng Pi, who was also his uncle."[29] (For more detailed information in this, see my "Tan Gong chamo" [corrections to the maxims in the "Tan Gong" section of the Book of Rites].)[30] This makes clear that, according to the ritual practices of ancient times, high officials did not have to shorten their period of mourning. Isn't what the Zhongyong says here based on ancient ritual practice?[31]

Zhu Xi said, "In mourning for fathers and mothers, we mourn the same regardless of any differences in status. We should apply what we ourselves do and extend it to others."[32]

As I see it, the basic requirements for rituals honoring ancestors and for mourning etiquette are totally different. Ancestor rites take the highest rank as the baseline [for determining how many ancestors should receive ancestor memorial offerings], and work their way down from there. Therefore, the Son of Heaven offers sacrifices up to the seventh generation, the feudal lords to the fifth generation, the high officials to the third generation, and the ordinary scholar-officials to the first generation. Mourning etiquette takes the lowest rank as its base line and works its way up from there. Therefore, for ordinary officers mourning clothing are worn for only three or five months. For high officials, mourning clothings are worn for a full year. For the Son of Heaven, mourning clothings are worn for a full three years.[33] This is how the requirements differ.

We can say, therefore, that in the case of the sacrificial rites, it would be acceptable to apply what we ourselves do and extend it to others. In the case of mourning etiquette, however, if we apply what we ourselves do and extend it to others, can we say that the ordinary scholars and common people should extrapolate from the sorrow they feel in their own heart-minds and, concluding that they and the Son of Heaven feel the same about the loss of a relative, wear mourning clothes for three full years? The transformations of the Ten Thousand Things starts from the Son of Heaven, so does it make any sense for ordinary scholars and the common people to say that their feelings are the same as the feelings of the Son of Heaven?

It is true that the Dao of conscientiousness and empathy must be taken seriously. We should take what we approve of and what we disapprove of and draw on that to extrapolate how other people judge things, assuming that they approve of what we approve of, and they disapprove of what we disapprove of. However, I am afraid that is not relevant to what is discussed in this chapter.

Zhongyong XIX: 3

> In spring and autumn, they would renovate their ancestral temples and arrange the ritual vessels properly.

Zhu Xi said, "The ancestral memorial service utensils are important ritual implements that were preserved by previous generations from ancient times. For example, there are those utensils called the 'red knife' [*chi dao* – a treasured sword], the great standard [*da xun*], the celestial sphere [*tian qiu*], and the Yellow River diagram [*Hetu*] from Zhou."[1]

Mao Qiling said, "The ancestral utensils are such sacrificial utensils of the ancestral shrines as the *zunlei* [wine jar], *zhandan* [wine cup], *zisheng* [millet cup], *biandou* [bamboo and wood dishes for holding dried offerings], and the like. The 'Chunguan zongbo' [Overseer of Ritual Affairs of the Spring Offices] chapter of the *Zhouli* says, 'arranging those vessels properly and then announcing that everything is ready' is what is meant by 'arranging the ritual vessels.' Zhu Xi's references to the 'red knife' and 'the great standard' in *Zhongyong zhangju* are mistakes. The precious utensils that the Zhou officials in the Celestial Bureau had charge of were only the ones that they would bring out for special ritual feasts. During the seasonal sacrifices of the Spring and Autumn period, there were no such rituals as these."[2]

Let me point out that the "Dianyongqi" [Director in Charge of Instruments and Valuable Ritual Objects] section of the "Overseer of Ritual Affairs in the Spring Office" [Chunguan zongbo] chapter of the *Zhouli* clearly states, "For the sacrifices, set out the usual ritual vessels."[3] What Mao Qiling says is not necessarily so.

The "Chunguan zongbo" chapter of *Zhouli* says, "The Celestial Bureau is in charge of the ancestral shrines.... It has a storehouse for precious objects and ritual vessels. If there are major sacrifices or important funerals, the officials there bring them out and put them in the appropriate places. After the ritual is over, they put them away in the storehouse again." (Zheng Xuan commented, "They are displayed for great funerals and for both the *di* sacrifice [to the imperial ancestors] and the *xia* sacrifice [to the immediate ancestors of the ruler] in order to enhance the dignity of the imperial clan.")[4]

The "Spring Offices" section of the *Zhouli* says, "Those in charge of the usual ritual implements are in charge of the musical instruments as well as the other usual ritual implements. Therefore, for the ancestral sacrifice they set out the usual ritual implements and utensils. This is also done for a banquet."[5] (What is meant by "the usual ritual utensils" are *gongqi* [utensils that display the achievements of the imperial family]. Zheng Xuan said,

"These are the ritual implements obtained when attacking another state, such as Chong and Guan tripods as well as captured weapons with inscriptions carved on them.")[6]

As I see it, Zheng Xuan understood the term "major sacrifices" as referring to the *di* and the *xia* sacrifices, but to perform the *di* sacrifice once every five years and the *xia* sacrifice every three years or to perform the *xia* sacrifice once every five years and the *di* sacrifice every three years are the mistaken ideas of Han dynasty scholars. According to the "Royal Regulations" chapter of the *Book of Rites*, the Son of Heaven should perform the *xia* sacrifice [honoring the ancestors] in summer, autumn, and winter. The feudal lords should perform it in autumn and winter. Each of these *xia* sacrifices is a major sacrifice.[7] What the *Book of Rites* calls the "major banquet-ritual" is held every year.[8] How could those objects, utensils, and vessels the *Zhouli* calls precious refer exclusively to things that should be set out only on rare occasions? What Zhu Xi said about this is in error.

The "Places in the Hall of Distinction" chapter of the *Book of Rites* says, "They had the Chong and Guan tripods, the great jade hemisphere, and the tortoise-shell of Fengfu. These are all articles belonging to the Son of Heaven. They also had the lance of Yue; and the great bow — military weapons of the Son of Heaven (Chong, Guan, Fengfu, and Yue are all names of states)... the peal of bells of Chui, and the multitoned *qing* [stone or jade chimes] of Shu."[9]

In the *Zuozhuan*, Ji Tan of Jin[10] is quoted as saying, "When the feudal lords were awarded their fiefs, they all were presented with illustrious utensils from the royal household to use in their altars to the Gods of Soil and Grain."... [T]he King [Jing of Zhou] said, "*Shufu* [younger uncle] Tangshu was the younger brother of King Cheng of the same mother. How could he have not received his fair share? The drums and Grand Chariot of Mixu are things King Wen took to celebrate his victory. The armor of Quegong was what King Wu wore when he defeated the Shang.... Later King Xiang's two great chariots, his bronze axe, his black millet wine, his vermilion bow, and his elite *hubi* [tiger runner] warriors were all things taken as war booty by Lord Wen.... To have one's power reinforced with sacrificial utensils and have one's chariots bedecked with regalia... is what is called good fortune."[11] (This was in the 15th year of Lord Zhao.)

Also, there is the case of Diviner Bao[12] having a conversation with Chang Hong [a minister of King Jing of Zhou] and pointing out that King Cheng gave the Lord of Lu a grand chariot, a great banner, a jade semicircle of the Xia dynasty, and a *fanruo* of the state of Fengfu.[13] (*Fanruo* is the name of a great bow.)... He gave Kang Shu a grand chariot, a *shaobo* flag (this is a large flag embroidered from various pieces of silk and is mostly white), a *qianfa* flag (this is a red flag), banners plain and decorated with feathers (these are silken banners), and a *dalü* bell.... He gave Tang Shu a grand chariot, a drum of the state of Mixu, some *quegong* (this is the name of a set of armor), and a *guxian* (this is a bell).[14] (This was in the 4th year of Lord Ding.)

"Also, when the earl of Zheng entertained the king, the king gave him a girdle with decorative mirrors that had once belonged to the queen."[15] (This was during the 21st year of Lord Zhuang.)

"Moreover, Gongshu Wenzi brought up the matter of Lord Wen's three-legged cauldron from Shu, Lord Cheng's jeweled tortoise shell, and Lord Ding's belt."[16] (This was in the 6th year of Lord Ding.)

The *Discourses of Lu* says, "King Wu overcame Shang, extended the Dao to the nine tribes of eastern barbarians and the eight tribes of southern barbarians, and gave Chen some of the arrows that had been presented in tribute by the Sushen."[17]

According to the *Zuo zhuan*, the great bronze tripod of Gao was moved [by Lord Huan] to his ancestral shrine. Zang Aibo spoke up against that move, saying, "When King Wu overcame Shang, he moved its nine cauldrons to Luoyi[18] [and was criticized for doing that]."[19]

The people of Jin used a precious piece of carved Chuiji jade as a bribe to gain access to the road passing through Yu.[20] They had seized that jade carving during an attack on Chuiji.

Yue Yi (reporting in a letter to King Hui of Yan) said, "The ritual implements of the Qi state are now being kept in Ningtai, the *Dalü* bell is being kept in Yuanying, and the tripod has been returned to Moshi."[21] These are all examples of ritual implements that were captured after attacking another state. Whenever there is a ritual sacrifice, each of these various utensils is set out and displayed. That is why it is said that the utensils that reflect the achievements of the ruling family are displayed during the ritual sacrifices.

Zhu Xi said, "The 'ritual garments' [mentioned in this chapter] were the clothes that had been left behind by the ancestors. When they performed memorial sacrifices, they put them out for presentation to the young man who represented the deceased during the mourning ritual."[22]

Mao Qiling said, "There was a shrine called *shoutiao*[23] where ritual clothing was kept. When there was a memorial ritual, robes were taken from that shrine and given to the impersonator to wear over his other clothes. This is clearly what the word 'ritual garments' means in this chapter. But Zhu Xi in *Zhongyong zhangju* understood this to be a reference to actual clothing of the deceased being presented to the young man to wear when he impersonated the deceased ancestor. His implication that the young man representing the deceased ancestor wore those clothes is a mistake."[24]

In my opinion, there are two uses for the "clothes left behind by the ancestors." One way they were used is being laid out before the spirit tablet.

Zheng Xuan's commentary in the section on "the Master of Ritual Dress" says specifically that clothes left behind by the deceased can refer to the ritual clothing [C. *dianfu* 奠服] that is placed before the spirit tablet. The other use is being worn by the person who represents the deceased. In his commentary in the "Shoutiao" section, he says "clothing left behind by the deceased" can refer to the outer garments of the deceased which are worn by the impersonator of that esteemed ancestor.²⁵ This being the case, we can see that it is only in the "*Shoutiao*" section that the term "clothes left behind by the deceased" refers to the clothes worn by the impersonator. That section distinguishes them from those clothes that are laid out before the spirit tablet. Zhu Xi, in his *Zhongyong zhangju*, is not far off the mark.

Moreover, the clothes the impersonator wears are the outer garments of that dead person being impersonated. This refers to the type of clothing he wore when he was alive that was appropriate for his position in the government. These indicated his most respected status. (The outer garments of a deceased king are known as *gunmian*, those of a deceased lord are known as *bimian*, those of deceased great ministers are known as *xuanmian*, and those of deceased ordinary officials are known as *juebian*.) Zhu Xi did not mean they were to wear only those outer garments without also wearing ordinary garments underneath them. Mao did not understand the significance of the outer garments, so he made this absurd attack on Zhu Xi. He should be ashamed of himself.

Zhu Xi said, "The appropriate foods for ritual offerings differ according to the four seasons. For example, in spring lambs and suckling pigs, fried with fat and incense, are appropriate offerings."²⁶

Mao Qiling said, "In springtime, lambs and suckling pigs, fried and blended together with fat and incense, as well as pheasant and fish, fried and blended together with the fat of a strong-smelling dog—those are gourmet dishes offered to the queen and crown prince.²⁷ Can they be used for the sacrifices? The *Neiyong* [Palace Cooks] section of the 'Tianguan zhongzai' [Prime Minister in the Celestial Offices] chapter of the *Zhouli* only says you should slice the meat up well. It says nothing about how you fry and blend it.²⁸ Why is that? It is because the spirits do not like the taste of food that has been fried and blended. It is too messy."²⁹ Mao also said, "The 'Royal Regulations' chapter of the *Book of Rites* clearly specifies offerings of scallions in spring, wheat in summer, millet in autumn, and unhulled rice in winter.³⁰ In the 'Proceedings of Government in the Different Months' chapter, for the fresh offerings for the four seasons, it clearly specifies offerings of sturgeon, wheat, millet in fall, and cherries.³¹ When we compare this to what Zhu Xi says in the *Zhongyong zhangju*, we can see that he has some basis in those texts for what he writes, but these crops are for offerings to the gods, not for offerings to the ancestors."³²

In my opinion, the foods appropriate for the different seasons are the ones mentioned in "Royal Regulations" and the "Proceedings" chapters of the *Book of Rites*. When Mao Qiling says that fried lambs and suckling pigs are not appropriate for offering to the ancestors, he is correct, but when he goes further and says he suspects that none of the foods used for ritual offerings to the gods can be used as ritual offerings for ancestors as well, is he not reading more into that text than what it is saying? The common people understand presenting offerings to the gods to be the same as presenting offerings to their ancestors and therefore the scallions and wheat they provide as offerings for the gods are also used by the nobility in ritual offerings to their ancestors. Why should we treat those items as belonging to totally different ritual categories? The various items mentioned in the "Proceedings" can serve as ritual offerings to both gods and ancestors. It was not the way of the sage kings of the past to treat those foods as so special that they could not be associated with ancestor memorial rites or with the new moon offerings. Later generations of Confucian scholars made a mistake when they interpreted the "Proceedings" chapter in the *Book of Rites* as saying that, besides the offerings used for seasonal ancestor memorial rites and new moon rituals, there are special items used only for offerings to the gods.

Zhongyong XIX: 4

> The rituals of the ancestral temple provide the occasion for maintaining the proper *zhao* and *mu* order.

Zhu Xi said, "The spirit tablets in the ancestral temple are arranged such that the left is *zhao* and the right is *mu*. The spirit tablets of the descendants of the lineage progenitor have to be placed in the *zhao* or the *mu* line according to which generation they belong to."[33]

Zhao Ge'an[34] said, "In the rites in the ancestral shrines it is not only the dead who are placed in the proper *zhao* and *mu* order. The living should be positioned according to the *zhao* and *mu* order as well."[35]

Cai Qing said, "Arranging according to *zhao* and *mu* applies only to the living. *Zhongyong zhangju* says, 'The spirit tablets in the ancestral temple are arranged such that the left is *zhao*, and the right is *mu*.'[36] This is essentially the reason the living should also be assigned to *zhao* and *mu* places. If the spirit tablets of the dead are already arranged in the proper *zhao* and *mu* order, then from the time the shrine was established the order would already be set and so there would be no need to re-arrange the tablets when a sacrificial rite is performed." (See Cai Qing's *Sishu mengyin*.)[37]

As I recall, the *Rites of Zhou* says that the Vice-Minister of Rites should distinguish between the *zhao* and the *mu* sides in the ancestral shrine.[38] Earlier scholars understood this to mean that it was important to pay close attention to placing the tablets on their proper spot on the *zhao* and the *mu* sides in ancestor memorial rites. Therefore, Zhu Xi came up with the idea that the spirit tablets of the sage kings of old should be arranged in the proper *zhao-mu* order. But the phrase "paying close attention to placing the tablets on their proper spot on the *zhao* and *mu* sides" is not found anywhere in the ancient classics. What the *Zhongyong* says is merely that the living should be lined up according to the proper *zhao-mu* order. That is all it says. The meaning of this passage can be seen in greater detail in "A Summary Account of Sacrifices" in the *Book of Rites*.

"A Summary Account of Sacrifices" says, "At the sacrifice the parties taking part in it were arranged on the left [*zhao*] and right [*mu*], according to their order of descent from the common ancestor, and thus the distinction was maintained between the order of fathers and sons, the near and the distant, the older and the younger, the more closely related and the more distant, and there was no confusion. Therefore, at the services in the grand ancestral temple, all in the two lines of descent were present, and no one failed to receive his proper place in their common relationship. This was what was called showing the distance gradually increasing between relatives."[39] It also says, "Whenever they came to the general circulation of the cup (this is the wine cup given to meritorious subjects), those whose place was on the left [*zhao*] stood in one row, and those whose place was on the right [*mu*] stood in the other row. The members of each row had places according to their age; and in the same way were arranged all the assistants at the service. This was what was called exhibiting the proper order of the old and young."[40]

Cai Qing said, "As for placing some people in the *zhao* line and others in the *mu* line, it is not as simple as having one line on the left and one line on the right. For example, the Duke of Zhou's line was on the left as was the *zhao* line of King Wen. The various sons of King Cheng were in King Cheng's *zhao* line, and the various sons of King Wu were in Wu's *mu* line, on Wu's right. Also, King Kang's various sons were in King Kang's *mu* line, on Kang's right." (See the *Sishu mengyin*.)[41]

As I see it, according to the text of "A Summary Account of Sacrifices," arranging people into *zhao* and *mu* lines is only for the rites at the shrine of the lineage progeniture. The rituals in the shrines of the common people do not have this arrangement.

The *Zuozhuan* records Gong Zhiqi saying, "Da Bo and Yu Zhong were in King Tai's *zhao* line.... Guo Zhong and Guo Shu were in Wang Ji's *mu* line."[42] (See Lord Xi's 4th Year.)[43] The *Zuozhuan* records Fu Chen saying that [the ruling lineages of] "Guan, Cai, Cheng, and Huo[44] (along with Lu, Wei, Mao, Dan, Gao, Yong, Cao, Teng, Bi, Yuan, Feng, and Xun)[45] were in King Wen's *zhao* line, and [the ruling lineages of] Yu, Jin, Ying, and Han were in King Wu's *mu* line."[46] (See "Lord Xi's 20th Year.")[47]

As I understand it, when a ritual was held at the shrine of the dynastic founder to sacrifice to the spirits of various earlier rulers, the spirit tablets were placed in their proper positions in *zhao* lines on the left and *mu* lines on the right. The feudal lords of Wu and Yu [虞] as the direct descendants of King Tai were in the front, starting the *zhao* line. Next came the descendants of the two Guos, who started the *mu* line as the direct descendants of Wang Ji. Lu, Wei, Cao, and Teng followed in the *zhao* line of King Wen. After them were Yu [邗], Jin, Ying, and Han, in King Wu's *mu* line. Whose spirit tablets were in the *zhao* line and whose were in the *mu* line was determined by who the king was when the founder of that lineage was awarded a fiefdom. It did not make any difference if they were in the grandfather or grandson generation, or even in the father or son generation, of the current ruler.

That is why the *Zuozhuan*'s account of an agreement reached at Gaoyou [in the 4th year of Lord Ding] says that Diviner Tuo[48] argued for determining where a lineage representative would stand according to when the lineage founder was granted his fiefdom, and said that no one should be concerned about whether the current ruler was in a higher generation or a lower one than the members of those other lineages. The Cao lineage has been said to belong in the *zhao* line for the descendants of King Wen, and the Jin lineage has been said to belong in the *mu* line for the descendants of King Wu[49] for a hundred generations, without any changes in that ranking. If, because of how far down they are in the list of generations, the rulers of Lu and Wei are pushed into the lower *mu* line, and, because of their lower number in the list of generations, the rulers of Yu and Jin are moved up into the *zhao* line, would that be acceptable?[50]

The rulers in those days all inherited their status from their ancestors and received the mandate to sit on their throne. This is why the Son of Heaven referred to the feudal lords of the same clan as older paternal uncle and younger paternal uncle and to those of different clans as older maternal uncle and younger maternal uncle. They are all relying on the precedents established by the sage kings and rulers of the past. It was not asked who was from a senior line or a junior line at that time. Instead, the rule was that those in a direct line of descent from the dynastic founder were placed in the front [*zhao* line] and those in a secondary line of descent from the dynastic founder were placed behind them [in the *mu* line]. That is why "A Summary Account of Sacrifices" mentions the importance of "distinguishing the close and the distant."[51]

If the *zhao* and *mu* lines established by the kings and rulers of old originally were intended to assign lineages to their proper lines as determined by one criterion alone, such that fathers would be in the *zhao* line, their sons would be in the *mu* line, grandsons would be in the *zhao* line, and great-grandsons would be in the *mu* line, that order would be fixed and unalterable. That is what Gong Zhiqi [of Yu] and Fu Chen [of Zhou] appear to have said.[52]

But there is another criterion sometimes used in assigning people to *zhao* and *mu* lines. According to that criterion, if a king hands over power to his grandson, then he should be in the *zhao* line and his grandson should be in the *mu* line. If an elder brother hands over the throne to a younger brother, then the elder brother should be in the *zhao* line and the younger brother in the *mu* line. This criterion is based on the order of legitimate succession to the throne. That is why when Xiafu Fuji was the officer in charge of the ancestral shrine, and he wished to honor Lord Xi by moving him ahead of his normal place in the traditional generational order, the Minister in Charge of Sacrifices told him this was not the proper procedure for sacrificial rites. (See the *Discourses of Lu*).[53] Guliang[54] noted, "If you do not follow proper protocol, then you confuse the *zhao* and *mu* lines." (Second year of Lord Wen.)[55] Lord

Min was the younger brother and Lord Xi was the older brother.[56] Whether the younger brother ascended the throne before the elder brother or the elder brother ascended the throne before the younger brother has no connection to the *zhao* and *mu* lines. But Zuo[57] and Guliang, in their commentaries, said this has to be explained in terms of the *zhao* and *mu* order. Does that make any sense? Kong Yingda said, "They are using *zhao* and *mu* incorrectly."[58] Indeed, they are misusing those concepts here.

According to Zhu Xi's *Diagram of the Zhou Ancestral Temple*, *zhao* is always on the left and *mu* is always on the right.[59] When one generation is on the left, the next generation is on the right. That pattern of alternation does not change. Thus, when we trace the Zhou royal lineage from Houji[60] down to Wang Ji,[61] and from King Wen[62] down to King Yi,[63] we can see that they all passed down their thrones to one son only, therefore their succession was not problematic. That is why the *Diagram of the Zhou Ancestral Temple* has *zhao* and *mu* alternating by generations.

If brothers follow each other on the throne as was the practice during the Shang—starting with Wo Ding, and again with Da Ding, there were three generations in which the kingship passed down from elder brother to younger brother; starting with Yang Jia there were four generations of brothers on the throne[64]—then having an elder brother in the *zhao* line and his younger brother in the *mu* line, or a younger brother in the *zhao* line and his elder brother in the *mu* line, is something that could not be avoided.

All we have to do is look at how the Zhou ancestral temple was actually arranged to see examples of such deviation from the generational order. We can see that after King Yi died, his maternal uncle King Xiao inherited his throne, and when King Xiao died, [another] King Yi inherited his throne.[65] This led to a reversal of the normal generational order of the father's generation preceding the son's generation, but the *zhao* and *mu* lines still reflected the actual line of succession to the throne. (King Yi was in the *zhao* line, and King Xiao was in the *mu* line.) But, when King Xiao died, [another] King Yi succeeded him on the throne (this King Yi was the son of the earlier King Yi).[66] That meant that the first King Yi and the second King Yi, even though they were father and son, were in the *zhao* line, on the left. (Zhu Xi's *Diagram of the Zhou Ancestral Temple* has King Yi and King Xiao both in the *zhao* line on the left.) From Houji and Puku[67] on down, the *zhao/mu* division is said to have been fixed and unalterable, but in one morning it turned upside down without anyone being able to question it.

When we get to Eastern Zhou, we can see King Ping (r. 770-720) and King Huan (r. 719-697) passing the throne from grandfather to grandson. (King Huan was the son of Crown Prince Xiefu). King Kuang (r. 613-607) and King Ding (r. 606-586) were older brother and younger brother. This confusion in generational succession to the throne threw the *zhao* and *mu* lines out of their normal sequences. After that, it was impossible to return to the original generational alternation of *zhao* and *mu*. That is why Zuo and Gu interpreted the *zhao* and *mu* lines as based on who sat on the throne first and who sat on it later. This is essentially what the distinction between *zhao* and *mu* was all about then. They were not making something up here.

The "Minor Scribe" section of the "Chunguan zongbo" [Overseer of Ritual Affairs] section of the *Rites of Zhou* says, "they are assigned to the *zhao* and *mu* lines in generational order.... When there is a major sacrifice, the scribes read from the written guidelines the *zhao-mu* order in which the sacrifices to the different spirits are to be brought out." Zheng Sinong[68] commented that this means that the scribe has to read out the proper *zhao-mu* order so that the sacrifices can be brought out at the proper time.[69] As I read it, we can see in this text that the *zhao-mu* order is not an arrangement for the living only.

Zhu Xi said, "The ranks of those participating in the rituals in the imperial ancestral hall were lords, ministers, and high officials."[70] The Ministry of War [*xiaguan*] section of the *Zhouli* says, "The sons of officials (Zheng Shinong said 'these are the sons of the lords, the ministers, and the high officials') are responsible for ... determining relative ranking and assigning people to their proper places."[71] The "King Wen as Son and Heir" chapter of the *Book of Rites* says, "The Shuzi[72] was responsible for ensuring that other members of the royal and princely families took their proper places, clarifying the proper relationship that should prevail between father and son, as well as the order to be observed between elders and junior. When they appeared at court, if it were for a reception in the innermost courtyard of the palace, with those of the most honorable rank among them in the eastern [*zhao*] ranks, as high ministers they stood to the north of the others. The other officials were arranged according to their age. (If the ministers were all members of the same lineage, they were assigned places in the *zhao* and *mu* lines according to age.) If they were in the outer courtyard, they were arranged according to their offices. (If they were mixed together with ministers from other lineages, they were assigned places according to the relative ranking of their official posts.) When they were in the ancestral temple, they took their places as in the outer courtyard, and the superintendent of the temple assigned tasks to each according to rank and office."[73]

As I see it, though this classic refers to arranging people for the rites according to their ranks, when people are from the same lineage, they should be arranged into *zhao* and *mu* lines by generation. I am afraid this cannot be combined with ordering according to rank. (Whether you are in a *zhao* or a *mu* line is determined by your position within your family, while assigning you a place according to your rank is done according to how high your official post is.) If we are talking about people from different lineages, then whether we are talking about a morning audience or a royal banquet, participants will always be assigned places according to their respective ranks, without exception. But what should you do for the rites at the Royal Ancestral Shrine? Should participants still be assigned positions according to their rank alone? Some people bring up a case of members of the same lineage, including those who do not hold official posts, joining others in participating in a ritual. In such a case, they say, if you place them in their appropriate *zhao* and *mu* lines, then office holders from one lineage will be placed into the same lines with office holders from other lineages without any regard for official rank. In such a situation, therefore, it would be better to assign positions according to rank. That seems more reasonable to me.

Zhu Xi said, "That which needed to be taken care of in the imperial ancestral temple, which were the prayers to ancestors, had an officer to manage them."[74] The *Zhouli* says, in the "Vice-Minister of Rites" [*xiaozongbo*] section of the "Overseer of Ritual Affairs" chapter, that "The Vice-Minister of Rites is in charge of making the arrangements for the seasonal sacrifices and for managing the rites associated with them." (Zheng Xuan commented that making the arrangements for the seasonal sacrifices refers to following what the divination says regarding the timing and sequence of examining the sacrificial victim, cleansing the ritual implements, and cooking the sacrificial meat.)[75]

Mao Qiling said, "The *Book of Rites* clearly says, 'the superintendent of the temple assigned ritual duties to each according to their rank and office.'[76] 'According to rank' means distinguishing the different responsibilities of those higher and those lower in rank. 'According to office' means what each office is responsible for, such as how the *Zhouli* has the Great Steward assisting with the presentation of the jade symbols of high rank[77] and has the Minister of Rites evaluating the sacrificial animal and cauldron..."[78] If the person in charge of the prayers to the ancestors has assistants, they are only responsible for helping him with his duties in his office. They do not assist him in his ritual duties. By paying attention to what the role of each participant is, the superintendent can make sure he distinguishes the more capable from the less capable."[79] (Wenhui noted that when King Wu performed the sacrifices, Mao Shu Zheng presented the clear water, Kang Shu Feng arranged the mats, and the Grand Tutor Shangfu brought in the ox to be sacrificed.)[80]

Chen Ziceng[81] said, "The 'Meaning of Sacrifices' and 'Places in the Hall of Distinction' chapters of the *Book of Rites* say that the ruler meets the sacrificial animal at the gate and the nobles and great officers assist him and follow after him in proper order. The 'Rites in the Formation of Character' and 'Summary Account of Sacrifices' chapters say the ruler personally led the sacrificial animal with the high officials assisting and the ordinary officials carrying the dried grass behind.[82] All of these are clear proof of the proper procedures for carrying out such rituals."[83]

As I understand it, for the ancestral rites there are firmly fixed responsibilities for each role. We cannot say this is about choosing the most capable for those tasks. The Great Steward assisting with the jade credentials and the Minister of Rites evaluating the animal to be sacrificed are simply then fulfilling their assigned responsibilities. We cannot say they were given those tasks because they were the most capable at those tasks. However, when there is a great sacrificial rite, the person who is in charge of managing that ritual has a large number of assistants from among whom he can decide whom to dispatch to do what needs to be done. There are similar practices in our eastern land [Korea]. That is why we see in this chapter the line "for the various sequences in the ritual the more capable of doing those tasks are identified."

In the ancient past, in competitions in the imperial archery range, those who hit the target the most often were invited to participate in the rites. Those whose arrows seldom hit the target were not invited to participate in the rites.[84] (This is from the "Meaning of the Ceremony of Archery" chapter of the *Book of Rites*.) It was common practice to give them the opportunity to participate in the rites because their skill at archery showed that they were cultured enough to handle ritual roles. The *Odes* says, "The guests are arranged according to their merits."[85] This refers to their skill at archery.

Zhu Xi said, "The Sinograph *lü* [旅 — normally it means 'to travel around'] in this chapter means 'those assembled.'[86] The term 'to toast' here means to lead the drinking by asking others to lift their glasses of wine together in honor of someone. In the ceremony of general toasting, the younger brothers and sons of the guest and the sons of the elder and younger brothers each raised a toast to their elders, and all toasted each other."[87] As I see it, that general toasting is essentially a banquet ritual. The ritual takes the form of a drinking ceremony which includes offering toasts all around.

The "Banquet Ritual" chapter of the *Book of Etiquette and Ceremonial* discusses a host organizing a feast for guests. (In this case, the "host" is the chief steward.) The guests offer each other toasts at the top of the western steps. (They do so in the proper order.) The chief of the archers selects one of the ministers gathered there to ascend toward the host and receive a toast. (He is selected from among the high officials.) The host then offers some ceremonial food to all the ministers gathered there. (He first toasts them and then offers them that food.) The ministers ascend the steps, bow, and accept the food offered to them. (I skip some lines here.) The host then offers some food to the other officials gathered there. Those officials then ascend the steps to bow and receive the food offered to them. (I skip some lines here.) The musicians sing the "Call of the Deer."[88] (I skip some lines here.) The host offers some food to the singers. (I skip some passages here.) The host offers some food to the mid-level officials. (I skip some lines here.) The leader of the mid-level officials ascends the steps, bows, and accepts that food. (I skip some lines here.) The host next offers some food to the minor officials gathered on the steps. (This part of the rite is the same as the rite offering a toast to the mid-level officials.) Following this, the host offers some food to the senior officials of the left and right, and to the retainers. (This part of the rite is the same as that for the minor officials.)[89]

The "Meaning of the Banquet" chapter of the *Book of Rites* says, "The mats were arranged so that the nobles of lower status occupied the place next in honor to those of higher status; the ministers of state, in the place next to the nobles of lower status. The mid-level officers and minor officials also took their places below them in the appropriate order. The cup being presented to the ruler, he begins the general toasting, and offers the cup to the nobles. They continue the ceremony, and offer the cup to the ministers of state, who offer it in turn to the mid-level officers, and these finally offer it to the minor officials. The stands and dishes, with the meat of the animals and the savory dishes, were all proportioned to the differences of rank in the guests, and thus the distinction was shown between the noble and the not-so-noble."[90]

Mao Qiling said, "The purpose of the wine cup ritual is to bestow the blessings of the spirits equally to all those within the chamber. As for the ceremony of general toasting, it is to bestow the blessings of the spirits equally to all those in the lower hall. In a sacrifice, the spirits are treated as superior, and those who sacrifice are treated as subordinate to them. The impersonator of the dead ancestor[91] himself drains the cup and causes equal blessings to be imparted to those within the chamber. The lower ranks then receive toasts offered by the higher ranks. When presenting the cup, the host is treated as the most esteemed person within the chamber. But in toasting, the older and the younger, as well as all those in the chamber and those in the lower hall, all receive a toast. That is why this chapter has the line "the toasting reached even those of the lowest status." The *Zeng yun*[92] explains that the term "toasting" here means "to receive a toast."[93]

Lou Xiangming said: "General toasting can also be written as 'passing around the cup in turn.' According to the 'Rites of the Single Beast Offered as Food for the Ancestor' chapter of the *Book of Etiquette and Ceremonial,* when there is an animal sacrifice, then all the guests, from the noble to the multitude and from the old to the young, pass around the cup. An explication of this passage notes that here 'passing around the cup' [旅] means 'the multitude toast each other in turn' [行 K. *haeng* / C. *xing*]. The toasts are offered in such an order as to show respect for differences in status.[94] According to the "Great Archery Contest" chapter of the *Book of Etiquette and Ceremonial*, when there is an archery competition amongst the nobles, then it is said that they pass the wine cup around. An explication of this passage notes that here 'pass the wine cup' [旅] means to do so in the proper order [序 K. *sŏ* / C. *xu*].[95] Generally, though there is no explicit mention of the multitude, we should read the line in this chapter of the *Zhongyong* that says during the general toasting 'inferiors participating in toasting their superiors'[96] to refer to the lower-ranking receiving cups from the higher-ranking in order to offer them a toast. The normal order in toasting is for those of lower ranks to offer toasts to those of higher ranks. To have the higher ranks give cups to the lower ranks as well is to ensure that even the lowest-ranking participate in this ritual."[97]

As I understand it, the procedure for general toasting is that it begins from the ruler to the guest, then to the highest-ranking officials, and then on to the mid-rank officials, to the lower-level officials, then to minor officials, and finally to the lowest-ranking officials. This clearly begins from the noble and reaches to the base, starts from the high and arrives at the low. That is why the *Zhongyong* says, "those of lower status participate in toasting their superiors." I simply do not understand how anyone can continue to debate the meaning of these millennia-old words. Those old rites and sacrifices of the Son of Heaven and the feudal lords do not exist these days, but we still model our formal banquets on what is said in those classic texts, so we can extrapolate from them the proper procedures for our ritual banquets.

The "Banquet Ritual" chapter of the *Book of Etiquette and Ceremonial* says the chief steward is the person presiding over this ritual.[98] The chief steward was the equivalent of a high minister today. Because of the exalted position of a high minister, for him to walk down the steps and wash his cup himself and then offer it to the musicians, then to the mid-level officials, the minor officials, and finally to the low-ranking officials is an example of benevolence toward inferiors. It is referred to as "bestowing a favor." On the other hand, when someone of lower rank offers a cup to someone of higher rank, this is called "making an offering." These days do we ever see someone in the highly respected position of a high minister "offering" a toast to musicians and mid-level officials or offering a toast to the minor officials? Who has heard these days of the noble offering a toast to those of lesser status? The line in the *Zhongyong*, "Those of lower status participate in toasting their superiors," makes it clear that offering is by those lower to those higher. Yet various groups of scholars both in the past and today have misconstrued this text. Xiaoshan [Mao Qiling] reads the character meaning "offered a toast" as meaning "received a toast." That is indeed a mistake.

I would also like to point out that saying that toasts are offered by the "multitude" is rooted in examples we can see in the three ritual manuals.[99] We see many references to people bowing to and greeting each other. Zhu Xi's telling us that the "multitude" is involved in the round of toasts draws deep from examples found in the classics. Yet Lou distorts what the ancient commentaries say. The ancient commentaries use the words "to do in the appropriate order" [序] and "to carry out" [行] two or three different times here. Can they all refer to everyone present offering toasts to each other?

The "Rites of the Single Beast Offered as Food for the Ancestor" chapter of the *Book of Etiquette and Ceremonial* says, "The host washes the cup and gives it to the eldest of the brethren of the deceased, washes it (I skip some sentences here), and then offers wine to all of the other brothers." (Zheng Xuan comments, "Giving it to those lower than you after washing it without fail is a way to display the benevolence of the spirits.")[100] The youngest of the brothers then lifts the cup to the eldest of the brethren, like the etiquette of the host toasting the guest. (Jia Gongyan[101] says, "This is what is called passing around the toasting cup.") The chief guest sits down, receives the cup, and toasts the senior descendant. (I skip some lines here.) Then the senior among the guests receives a toast, as was done earlier. (I skip some lines here.) The guests and the younger descendants toast each other as they did at the beginning until they have all had enough to drink. (I skip some lines here.) The eldest of the descendants toasts the guest, like the ceremony of the guest toasting the brethren. (I skip some lines here.) The guest, the elder of the descendants, and the younger of the descendants all raise a toast to their eldest brother.[102]

Mao Qiling said, "The rites of the Son of Heaven and the feudal lords have been lost and have not been passed down to us today. Now the only traces we have of the old rituals we have are the rituals of the officials. As a result, the various rituals are all jumbled together, and it is difficult to distinguish which rites are appropriate for which ranks.

"Generally speaking, there are three stages to these rites. The guest offers up wine three times and only after that does he present the cup to others. This is one stage. After the cup has been passed on, then there is a general round of toasting. The guest then recovers the cup and offers it to the eldest of the brethren. The eldest of the brethren accepts the cup and offers a toast to the participants in general. Then the guest, the eldest of the brethren, and the other participants all toast each other. This is another stage. For the final round of toasting, many toasts are offered without worrying about counting how many. This is one more stage. If the cup is offered up but is not then passed around, so that only one toast is offered rather than several, then this does not count as a formal rite."[103]

As I see it, handing over the cup is the beginning of the general toasting and the unlimited toasting is the end of the general toasting. Mao's dividing them into three different stages is absurd. The cup is offered and then there is a toast. The toast is repeated again and again countless times. How can he say there are three different stages? Although the procedure for the officials' rituals are not those of kings or feudal lords, they are all cases of a host showing respect for elders, and interacting with various brethren and their sons, and with groups of guests and the sons of those guests. Compared to the host, they are all either younger or simply lower in status.

A respected senior giving cups to those younger as well as others of lower status uses the same sort of ritual seen in the "Meaning of the Banquet" chapter of the *Book of Rites* by chief stewards offering cups to musicians and ordinary officials. And the same sort of ritual described in that chapter for the lower-ranking participating in toasting their superiors is what is used today for similar situations. The subcommentary[104] on the "to provide and present" entry in the "Shigu" [Explanation and exegesis] chapter of the *Erya* says, "In all references to someone respected, you say 'present.'" When the "Summary of the Rules of Propriety" chapter of the *Book of Rites* talks of presenting someone carriages and horses,[105] would it still call this "presenting" if it were the highly respected or the noble giving something to someone who was of low rank or worse?

Zhu Xi said, "As for the ritual of rounds of toasting, the lower-ranking participate in toasting the higher-ranking and they encourage one another to drink. First someone like a Township Guardian lifts up the cup. Then a second person might offer a cup to the guest but the guest declines to drink from it. He then offers it to the officials. One of the officials accepts it and then offers it to an elder. Next it is presented to the person who cleans it. This is what is called extending courtesy down to the lowliest."[106]

Mao Qiling said, "In the case of the chapters 'The Village Drinking Ceremony,' 'The District Archery Ceremony,' and 'The Offering of a Single Beast in Sacrifice' in the *Book of Etiquette and Ceremonial*, they start with one person lifting the cup and move on to general toasting. When a rite begins with two people lifting a cup, it moves on to unlimited toasting. It is only in the 'Assistant Clears Away' chapter that we see an oversimplified version of the way the impersonator is treated.[107] Therefore, it is only when two people lift up the cup to initiate a general round of unlimited toasting that it becomes a general toasting. These are references to what we can call a major sacrificial ritual or a proper ritual. There is no need to go on like Zhu Xi did."[108]

Let me note that this commentary of mine is on the *Zhongyong*, not on *Etiquette and Ceremonial*. However, let me also point out that there is no need to argue over the difference between one person lifting the cup or a group of people doing so. Moreover, as for the high great ministers toasting the impersonator of the dead ancestor but the lower-ranking officials not doing so, Mao makes a mistake when he says that is an over-simplification of that ritual.

As for the drinking ceremony described in the chapter on ritual sacrifices of the smaller animals in the *Book of Etiquette and Ceremonial*,[109] it is also the case that the host washes and then offers the cup to the brethren, washes the cup and offers up the cup to the guests in the inner hall, and then washes the cup and offers up the cup to the general participants. After this, the guests and the brethren toast one another, and they do so countless times. Whether the person standing in for the dead is offered a toast or not, the ritual is the same. In order to show respect for the senior officials (the smaller sacrificial animals are for the rituals for the senior officials), below them toasts are offered by the sons of the brethren and even by the lowest of the general participants. This is what is meant by "inferiors participating in toasting their superiors."[110] Why should we even question this reading?

Zhu Xi said, "As for what is meant by 'hair color as it relates to the banquets,' after the sacrificial rites finish and the banquet begins, then a distinction is made between old and young by the color of their hair and the seating is arranged accordingly."[111]

Xu[112] says, "We cannot understand these days what ritual Zhu Xi is referring to when he says, 'when the sacrificial rite is over and the banquet begins.' However, in 'Chu Ci' in the *Book of Songs* we can find the general idea of what he was talking about. That poem says, 'The august Dead One then rises... / The Spirits and Protectors have gone home.' After this, it says, 'While the uncles and brothers all go to the private feast.'[113] You can get a rough idea from this what a ritual banquet is."[114]

Mao Qiling said, "There is nothing in the ritual texts about sitting people by the color of their hair.[115] Generations of scholars, therefore, have all had to guess what this means. But now, when I look carefully at this phrase, it seems to me that it is saying that when the sacrificial rite is over, then it is time for the ritual of bestowing toasts. Here the ninth of the ten relationships in the 'Summary Account of Sacrifices' chapter of the *Book of Rites* comes into play.[116] At the end of the series of toasts, ending up in the unlimited toasting, we can see that those in whose honor the cup is lifted are in order of seniority. To lift the cup means to bestow a toast. That this means a ritual feast to bring blessings is clear in the 'Fu Yi' poem in the *Book of Songs* in which we are told that offering a toast to the stand-in for the deceased is called 'feasting and drinking.'[117]

"When this passage in the *Zhongyong* mentions hair, it refers to using hair color to sit the old and the young in order of seniority. The 'Ritual Overseer' section in the 'Autumn Officers' chapter of the *Zhouli* says that when the king holds a feast, the feudal lords are arranged according to hair color.[118] When it mentions teeth, it means that whether people are placed in the *zhao* or *mu* line depends on their relative age. 'A Summary Account of Sacrifices' says, 'the *zhao* line makes up one row, and the *mu* line made up another row. *Zhao* and *mu* placement were determined by relative age.'[119] Different lineages had their own order of seniority. Those in charge of arranging the rituals took this into account. That is what is called having the proper arrangement of putting the old before the younger. What the ritual classics refer to is only the proper order of seniority within individual lineages."[120]

I notice that the accounts of the rites of the smaller animals and of the single sacrificial animal [in the *Book of Etiquette and Ceremonial*] both lack the phrase "bestowing the cup." The term "bestowing the cup" is found only in the sacrificial rite of the Son of Heaven and the feudal lords. These rites are after the sacrifices, so the ninth relationship mentioned in the "Summary Account of Sacrifices" applies here.[121] What Mao Qiling said is completely correct, and Hu's reading of the *Chu ci* ode is absurd.

"A Summary Account of Sacrifices" says, "Whenever they came to the general bestowing of toasts, those whose place was on the *zhao* line stood in one row, and those whose place was on the *mu* line stood in another row. The members of each row were placed according to their age; and in the same way were arranged all the superintendents at the service. This was what was called exhibiting the proper order of the old and young."[122]

As I understand it, this reference to the ninth relationship applies to the *zhou* and *mu* lines of the same lineage. The various superintendents are for the different lineages. The different superintendents are responsible for arranging the nobles according to their ages and arranging the lower-ranking officials separately according to their ages. The fact that this is not made explicit in this classic is because the description of proper ritual behavior was abbreviated.

Zhongyong XIX: 5

> To stand in the positions of the forebears and carry out their ritual obligations

Zhu Xi said, "'Those who are held in high esteem' and 'those who are held dear' are the ancestors of former kings, their descendants, and their subjects."[123]

Zhang Taizhan[124] said, "In the ancestral shrine 'those who are held dear' refers to your male and female ancestors. Examples of this are those whose tablets are in your ancestral shrine and those in your family mausoleum."[125]

As I see it, there is no greater display of filial piety than loving those whom you hold dear. Filial love for your father, therefore, must include loving your brothers. Filial love for your grandfather must include loving your uncles, his brothers. Filial piety toward your great-grandfather must include loving his brothers as well. If you want to have a loving family, therefore, you must show filial piety through ritual toward all your relatives. This is how the officials show that they are filial. The way to have a realm that is filled with joy is to show respect through ritual for the former rulers. This is the filial piety of the feudal lords. The way to have All-under-Heaven filled with joy is to serve through displays of ritual respect the former kings and to serve through displays of ritual respect the Lord on High. This is the filial piety of the Son of Heaven. "Repairing the ancestral shrine, arranging the ritual utensils properly, providing the proper ritual clothes, and offering the proper ritual food"[126] are the way to show respect for those who deserve respect. "Standing in the *zhao* or *mu* lines, offering toasts all around, taking our places as ritual participants according to rank as well as according to age"[127] is the way to show love for those you hold dear. What Zhang says is totally absurd. We should follow what Zhu Xi said.[128]

Zhu Xi said, "This sums up this chapter and the one preceding it, which both tell us to continue to act in accord with the ancestors' wishes and to carry on with what the ancestors were doing."[129]

In my opinion, "to act in accord with the ancestors' wishes" and "to carry on with what the ancestors were doing" are references to King Wu and the Duke of Zhou.

The clauses in this chapter of the *Zhongyong* that follow "in spring and autumn"[130] should begin a separate chapter and should not be bundled together with what immediately precedes it.[131] I explain this in my "Admonitions for Myself upon Reading the *Zhongyong*."[132]

Zhongyong XIX: 6

> The *jiao* [郊] sacrifices and the *she* [社] sacrifices were ways to pay ritual homage to the Lord on High.

Zhu Xi said, "The *jiao* sacrifice is the sacrifice to Heaven. The *she* sacrifice is the sacrifice to the gods of the soil. The only reason 'and the God of the Earth' was not written after 'the Lord on High' is simply to make the sentence shorter."[133]

Zhu Xi said, "*Zhouli* does not say anything about sacrifices to the God of the Earth. Wufeng[134] said 'there is no altar to Heaven in the north. All that is there is an altar to the gods of the soil. That is where you should sacrifice to the gods of the soil.' This is good advice."[135]

Let me point out that, although in the "Grand Overseer of Ritual Affairs" section in the "Spring Offices" volume in the *Zhouli* the celestial spirits and the gods of the soil are treated as distinct from one another,[136] the Ten Thousand Things all have the same essential origin. Fundamentally, there are not two roots from which the various things have emerged. The spirits of the sun, moon, stars, and other celestial bodies, as well as the spirits of rain, wind, and of Siming [the star presiding over human destiny], and the five spirits of soil and grain, the spirits of the seasonal rituals, along with spirits of the five sacred peaks and mountain forests as well, are all intelligent spirits serving Heaven. The only difference among them is in what they are responsible for, with some responsible for celestial matters and others responsible for things on earth. That is why some spirits are called celestial spirits and others are said to be the terrestrial spirits.

According to the *Zuo Commentary on the Spring and Autumn Annals*, Cai Mo[137] made it clear that Gou Mang, Rushou, and three others are the five spirits who receive seasonal sacrifices (Lord Zhao yr 29).[138] According to the records of "discourses of Zhou" in the *Guoyu*, the Royal Secretary Guo informed the King that Zhu Rong[139] had descended to Mt. Chong.[140] The Royal Secretary called him an intelligent radiant spirit.[141] The "discourses of Jin" in the *Guoyu* reports that the scribe Yin called Rushou a celestial spirit.[142] This makes clear that the spirits who receive sacrifices at the five seasonal sacrifices and at the Altars to the Gods of Soil and Grain are nothing other than celestial spirits.[143] All the spirits, whether above or below, act in accordance with the commands of the Lord on High and help him manage the Ten Thousand Things. The king offers sacrifices to them in gratitude. This is nothing other than "paying ritual homage to Heaven." That is why the *Zhongyong* says in this chapter "the *jiao* sacrifices and the *she* sacrifices were ways to pay ritual homage to the Lord on High."

The fact that the phrase "and the God of the Earth" does not follow "The Lord on High" does not mean that Houtu [the God of the Earth] is implied nonetheless and is only absent because this sentence is abbreviated.[144] However, the God of the Earth is the god sacrificed to at the *she* sacrifice. And the God of the Earth is also one of the five gods who receive regular seasonal sacrifices (Lord Zhao yr. 29).[145] There appears to be some duplication of the rituals to that spirit, or that text is talking about different spirits with the same name. I am unable to figure this out now.

The sacrifices to the gods of the earth also are most certainly linked to the enshrinement of human spirits. Goulong was enshrined as a god of the soil. Jiqi was enshrined as a spirit of grain. Chong was enshrined as Guo Mang. Gai was enshrined as Rushou. Xiu and Xi were both enshrined as Xuan Ming.[146] Li was enshrined as Zhu Rong.[147] (Lord Zhao yr. 29.) Therefore the "Zhengyi" [correct readings] Commentary on the *Spring and Autumn Annals* says that being enshrined together means that they can be offered sacrificial food together under the names of the spirits they were enshrined as[148] (Lord Zhao yr. 29). You can see for yourself that such deification of human beings has occurred. The *jiao* rites definitely included enshrined sages alongside the Lord on High. The *Gongyang Commentary* [*Gongyangzhuan*] points out, "Those who come from within are unable to act unless they are linked to something beyond them; those who come from without have to have a someone in charge. Otherwise, they will not stay within their limits"[149] (Lord Xuan yr. 3). Is not that what this means?

As for this notion of *jiao* sacrificial ritual being held in the northern suburbs, this is the mistaken interpretation of Zheng Xuan.[150] The Musician-in-Chief playing at the square altar for sacrifices to Earth [in the northern suburbs] was essentially part of a ceremony to drive away spirits who caused disease or natural disasters. It was not a sacrificial ritual. Zheng Xuan was careless when he described this as a sacrifice to the God of the Earth. There are actually three sacrifices to gods of the earth. The first is to Mt. Kunlun,[151] a god of the great earth, who is sacrificed to in the northern suburbs. The second is said to be to the spirit of the Divine Land [China], to whom sacrifice is made at the time of the *taicou* tone, that is, the first month of the lunar year.[152] The third is to the God of the Earth, to whom sacrifice is made at the Altars for the Gods of Soil and Grain. The reason we have seen all sorts of improper, strange, and poorly organized rituals is that the people who standardized ritual procedures in later generations all relied on Zheng Xuan and so repeated his mistake. They respected him and followed his advice, and that is why we have ended in this disastrous situation of no longer having proper *jiao* and *she* sacrificial rituals.

The "Royal Regulations" chapter of the *Book of Rites* says that the Son of Heaven sacrifices to both Heaven and Earth.[153] Among the three sacrificial rituals for Heaven, Earth, and human beings, only the sovereign may sacrifice to both the Celestial Spirit and the Gods of the Earth. The feudal lords do not dare to sacrifice to the Celestial Spirit. They offer sacrifice only to the Gods of the Earth. Zheng Xuan misunderstood this text. That is why Zheng thought that there was an additional sacrifice to Earth other than the *she* sacrifices at the Altars of the Gods of Soil and Grain. Is not this a mistake?

When the "Shuogua" [Explaining the trigrams] chapter of the *Book of Changes* says, "Qian is the father" and "Kun is the mother,"[154] it is using those terms symbolically. It does not mean that those hexagrams are mothers and fathers. Similarly, we associate certain hexagrams with horses and oxen and with heads and bellies[155] but that does not mean they are actually those material entities. *The Classic of Filial Piety* is a composite text of uncertain authorship [and uses similarly symbolic language]. It goes so far as to say that when the king demonstrates filial piety toward his father he is serving Heaven, but when he demonstrates filial piety towards his mother he is serving Earth.[156] An apocryphal supplement to the *Spring and Autumn Annals* even has the words "The sun is like our brother, and the moon is like our sister."[157] The Ancient Kings said nothing like this.[158] Zhu Xi suspected that the *Classic of Filial Piety* contained statements added later, insisting that the *jiao* sacrifices which this text says were carried out in the northern suburbs did not happen the way this text says they did.[159] This superb insight surpasses what others have said, both long ago and more recently, but what he said about this is not widely known.[160] Alas! How can we bear this? (I discuss this more in detail in my *Ch'unch'u Kojing* [An evidentiary investigation of the *Spring and Autumn Annals*]. This is just a brief summary of what I wrote there.)[161]

Zhu Xi said, "The term *di* refers to the grand sacrificial ritual in the Son of Heaven's ancestral temple and is based on sacrificial rituals which the founding emperor himself instituted in the ancestral temple and so matches what the founder did. The term *chang* refers to the autumn sacrifice. The four seasons all have sacrifices, but only *chang* is mentioned here as an example of a seasonal ritual."[162]

Let me point out that what is written about the *di* sacrifice is so complicated and difficult to unravel that it can hardly be understood. The first type of *di* sacrifice is to the Five Emperors. The "Vice-Minister of Rites" chapter of the "Spring Offices" section of *Zhouli* says, "The sacrificial rites to the Five Emperors are carried out in the four different outlying areas."[163] The "Grand Minister of Punishments" chapter of the "Autumn Offices" section says, "When there is a sacrifice to the Five Emperors, an oath is administered to the various officials on the archery range."[164] It also is written, "The horns of the sacrificial bull at the *di* sacrifice should be no larger than a cocoon or chestnut." In addition, it says the king had to personally use his own bow and arrow to kill the animal to be sacrificed.[165] It is also reported that King Ding of Zhou said that in a *di* sacrifice the sacrificial animal had to be steamed whole.[166] This is the first type of *di* sacrifice.

Second, there is the *di* sacrifice of expressing gratitude to the origin of one's ancestral line. The "Great Treatise" and "Record of Small Matters in Mourning Clothing" chapters of the *Book of Rites* say that, in the *di* sacrifice, "the place of honor was given to him from whom the lineage sprang, and that founder then was paid ritual homage along with the other ancestors."[167] The *Discourses of Lu* and the "Rules for Sacrifices" chapter of the *Book of Rites* say that Yin [Shang] and Zhou focused the *di* sacrifice on their prime ancestor, who was Ku.[168]

The third type of *di* sacrifices were seasonal offerings. *The Zuo Commentary to the Spring and Autumn Annals* mentions a *di* sacrifice to Lord Wu. (Lord Zhao 15).[169] Moreover, the "Meaning of Sacrifices" and "Royal Regulations" chapters, in the *Book of Rites,* sometimes say "spring *di* sacrifice" and other times "summer *di* sacrifice."[170] I think these are references to the regular sacrifices for the four seasons. Besides these examples, there are still many other different ways to refer to a *di* sacrifice. (I examined this carefully in my *Ch'unch'u Kojing*. My findings are only summarized here.)

It is worth noting that the "placing something in the palm of one's hand" passage from this text is the same as a passage we can see in the *Analects,* except that the *Analects* says "the *di* sacrifice" only instead of saying "the *di* and *chang* sacrifices."[171] It would seem that to understand the meaning of the *di* sacrifice, we have to dig deeper and explore farther than we do in trying to grasp the meaning of other rituals.[172]

Zhu Xi understood *di* in this text to have the restricted meaning of a grand sacrifice of gratitude to the origin of the imperial lineage. However, various other canonical texts link the *di* sacrifice and the *chang* sacrifice together as regular seasonal sacrificial rituals. He should not base his understanding of the *di* sacrifice solely on what is said in this text. Moreover, he should not think that *chang* stands alone as the name for sacrificial rituals for the four seasons. I'm afraid that is not the way it is.

The "Single Sacrificial Animal at the *Jiao* Sacrifices" section of the *Book of Rites* refers to "the different character of the spring *di* and the fall *chang* sacrifices."[173] "The Meaning of Sacrifices" section of the same classic says, "There is a *di* sacrificial ritual in the spring, at which music is played. In the fall there is a *chang* sacrificial ritual without any music."[174]

"A Summary Account of Sacrifices" says, "The summer sacrifice is called *di*; the sacrifice in autumn is called *chang*. . . . The *di* sacifice takes place when *yang* is at its height [and all nature is flourishing]. The *chang* sacrifice takes place when *yin* is its strongest [and nature has begun to retreat]. That is why it is said that there is nothing more important than the *di* and *chang* sacrifices. In ancient times, it was during the time of *di* sacrifice that official titles, and the robes that went with them, were conferred. This was in conformity with the *yang* tone of that time. During the time of the *chang* sacrifice, assignments of rank land were made and the work to be done preparing the land for the winter was assigned. This was in conformity with the *yin* tone of that time.... The *di* and *chang* sacrifices, therefore, are of great significance. They are the foundation of a strong government. It is essential that they be understood properly."[175] The "Zhongni at Home at Ease" section of this classic says, "The significance of the *jiao* and *she* sacrifices is that they are how we show we know how to treat the spirits the way they should be treated; the significance of the *di* and *chang* sacrifices is that they are how we show we know how to treat our ancestors the way they should be treated.... A clear understanding of the significance of the *jiao* and *she* sacrifices, and of the correct procedures for the *di* and *chang* sacrifices, would make governing a state as easy as putting something in the palm of one's hand."[176]

In my opinion, when we look at some of these various texts, we can see that they use *di* and *chang* as the names for the seasonal sacrifices in the spring and fall. This is quite different from how the *Analects* uses *di*.[177] The Analects uses *di* with a deep significance, but these other texts give it a shallower reference. The term certainly does not mean the same thing in all of these texts. Nowhere else is the importance of both the *di* and the *chang* sacrifices as the foundation of a strong government laid out as clearly as in those two chapters of the *Book of Rites*, "A Summary Account of Sacrifices" and "Zhong-ni at Home at Ease." Those who are interesting in learning should look into this.

Zheng Xuan's commentary says, "*Shi* [示][178] here is read like *zhi* [寘] in 'place it on the river bank.'... Placing something in the palm of one's hand is said to be easy."[179]

According to Bao Xian's commentary on the *Analects,* this passage should be read as "Confucius told a certain person that someone who understands the *di* sacrifice would know how to rule All-under-Heaven. They would find it as easy as pointing to something in the palm of their hand is easy."[180]

Zhu Xi said, "The Sinograph *shi* [display] here is the same as the different Sinograph pronounced *shi* [視] that means to look at. This phrase, therefore, means easy to see."[181]

Zhang Taizhan says, "Zheng Kangcheng[182] explicated *shi* as *zhi*. Bao Xian in his ancient commentary also said that placing something in the palm of the hand is what Confucius is talking about. But Zhu Xi said that *shi* refers to looking at the palm of your hand. That is the first sign we see of later generations of scholars becoming careless in the way they explained that passage, and failing to be in any way at all as careful and conscientious as Han dynasty scholars were. Where in the world do you have someone saying 'I see something in the palm of my hand' when there is nothing there to see? When there is nothing there, you cannot say that there is."[183]

Let me point out that the *Book of Songs* has a line with *zhi* in it that is read as "I laid it there on the path."[184] Another poem in that classic, one that uses the *shi* [display] Sinograph, is read as "will put me on the perfect path."[185] In the ancient commentaries, *shi* and *zhi* were seen as interchangeable. When Xunzi said "expose them to the shaping frame,"[186] he used *shi* [display] to mean *zhi* [put there], so *zhi* has the same meaning as *shi*. In my opinion, the ancient commentators had sound reasons for their interpretations. We have no grounds for challenging them today.

THE KING ASKED:

The preceding chapters did not say anything about running a kingdom. It is only when we reach the end of this chapter that it begins to talk about governing. What is the connection between what this text says earlier and what it says at the end of this chapter?

I RESPONDED:

When Shun, King Wen, King Wu, and the Duke of Zhou were in charge of their realm, they looked to Heaven above for direction and they nurtured filial piety down below. They did not plan on governing, yet they ended up in charge. This is what is meant by saying that you first receive what Heaven has conferred [i.e., your knowledge of what is appropriate behavior along with your ability to act appropriately], then you use what Heaven has given you to actually act appropriately, and, as a result, you end up governing a realm. This becomes clear in the chapters that follow.

Zhongyong XX: 1

Lord Ai[1] asked about how to govern properly.

Mao Qiling said, "*Fang* is a wooden tablet. *Ce* is a bamboo slip. The 'Interstate Missions' chapter of the *Book of Etiquette and Ceremonial* says, 'If there are less than a hundred characters, record them on wooden tablets. If there are one hundred characters or more, record them on bamboo slips.'"[2]

Zheng Xuan said, "*Pulu* [K. *p'olo*. It appears in the phrase from this chapter "governing is acting like a *pulu*"] refers to the bollworm wasp."[3]

Zhu Xi said, "Shen Kuo took *pulu* to mean *puwei* (rushes and reeds)."[4] (Zhu Xi noted [in *Huowen*] that Shen Kuo's words are a reference to the line "It is the Dao of the earth to stimulate plants to grow quickly" in this chapter of the *Zhongyong*.)[5]

Someone remarked, "The 'Tenth Month' section of the 'Xiaxiaozheng' chapter of the *Records of Ritual Matters by the Elder Dai* says, 'a black pheasant went into the Huai River and became a giant shape-shifting mussel.' The comment on that line says that 'shape-shifting mussel here means *pulu*.'[6] If that is the case, then it looks like we should take *pulu* to simply refer to any kind of a metamorphosis. Explanations dating far back in time, such as this one, are never made without some evidence to support them." Zhu Xi responded, "If we take *pulu* to be a 'giant shape-shifting mussel,' we cannot say that *pulu* means something else as well. So, if we take *pulu* to mean a metamorphosis, then we should not say it also means the same thing as bollworm wasp."[7] (See *Huowen*.)[8]

Some New Words for Breaking into Laughter[9] says, "A gourd with a slender waist is called *pulu*. A wasp with a slender waist is also called a *pulu*."[10]

Mao Qiling said, "The *Erya* explains that the bollworm wasp is the same as the mud wasp. Each seizes bollworm larvae and then transforms them into replicas of itself.[11] One of the 'Minor Odes of the Kingdom' says, 'The bollworm moth has offspring, and the bollworm wasp carries them away.'[12] The annotations of Kong Yingda say, 'Skillful administrators of government nourish other people as if they were their own children, just as the bollworm wasp does with the larvae of the bollworm.'[13] Mao also points out that Zhu Xi in his *Zhongyong zhangju* suggests that *pulu* should be read as 'rushes and reeds.' But rushes and reeds are not the same thing, and a wasp is not a reed. Besides, Zhu Xi confuses two similar Sinographs here, both pronounced *lu* but one meaning rushes [蘆] and the other meaning a bowl for holding cooked rice [盧]."[14]

In the *Kongzi jiayu*, the Master says, "It is the Dao of Heaven to animate the myriad entities. It is the Dao of Earth to stimulate plants to grow quickly. It is the Dao of humans to govern properly. Government then should be like a bollworm wasp. It should take things and transform them into what they should be."[15]

Mao Qiling said, "The reference to the bollworm wasp most certainly should not be taken as imparting the same idea as 'stimulates plants to grow quickly.' However, the addition of the phrase 'transforming' is certainly a reference to the actual bollworm wasp." Mao also said, "Han Wo's[16] poem 'At Ease in Poverty' says, 'Through the crack of the window can be seen horses flying in the sunlight. In the bamboo tube on the table-top *pulu* grow.'[17] This is saying that, in the reflected sunlight, dust can be seen floating in the air and, in the shaft of the bamboo brush, bollworm wasps make their nests. The men of Tang wrote poems as if they recognized bollworm wasps, but people today do not know what they are."[18]

THE KING ASKED:

In the scholarship of the last few centuries, there is much that we can rely on. Nevertheless, why did Zhu Xi reject the explanation provided in the distant past and instead insist on following Shen Kuo's interpretation [that this is a reference to rushes and weeds rather than to bollworm wasps]? In *Huowen* he argues that [other than the *Erya*] "no other reliable source tells us to read *pulu* as bollworm wasp,"[19] but isn't what the *Erya* says sufficient grounds for reading it that way?

I RESPONDED:

Bollworm wasps are insects so the passage about the Dao of the Earth stimulating plants does not apply to them. Moreover, Zhu Xi did not trust the *Kongzi jiayu* at all but instead rejected it as a forgery by Wang Su. He therefore gave extra weight to the words of Shen Kuo. The way most plants change and grow is not like at all like the speed with which rushes and reeds grow. So "stimulating plants to grow quickly" could refer to rushes and weeds.

However, rushes and reeds essentially are two different things. The "Treatise on Foods and Commodities" in the *History of Jin*[20] says, "When dikes deteriorate, good farmland turns into nothing but rushes **and** reeds."[21] The "Shi Jilong House Records" section of the *History of Jin* says, "Rushes **and** reeds, as well as fish and salt, were only preserved for use as offerings at the annual sacrifices."[22] Liu Xin's *fu* poem has a line, "Dark forests, rushes, reeds, rushing water, and clear springs" in which they are all different things.[23] However, the *Huainanzi* says, "Sometimes they bend and at other times they stretch. They can be weak and yielding like rushes and reeds"[24] as though they are the same thing. The poem "Southeast Fly the Peacocks"[25] has lines reading, "The rushes and reeds are as strong as silk thread / So it is impossible to move a rock." It also says, "However strong the rushes and reeds are, they can disappear in just a day."[26] This is saying the rushes and reeds can cut through a rock like a needle can thread silk. This poem also suggests that rushes and reeds are the same thing. But Cai Qing writes that saying rushes and reeds are the same thing is like saying a gourd and a willow tree are the same thing, and how can that make any sense?[27]

Considering all this, "rushes and reeds" should not be spoken of as though they are references to the bollworm wasp. Yet the *Bencao Gangmu* [Compendium on *Materia Medica*] of Li Shizhen (1518–1593) says that bollworm wasps are the same thing as the mud wasps who bear their own young.[28] That makes it hard to understand the reference to bollworm wasps as raising bollworm larvae as their own offspring. (Previously, I misunderstood this passage, but I have now corrected myself.)[29]

Zhongyong XX: 4

Proper governing depends on who is doing the governing.

(What follows should be a separate chapter since it does not belong with the prior section [the one entitled "Lord Ai Asked about How to Govern Properly"]. I suspect that, in the *Kongzi jiayu,* this material was modified in such a way as to make it appear to be part of the conversation with Lord Ai. It is a mistake to treat these two sections as actually part of the same chapter.)[30]

Zhu Xi said, "In assuming that government depends on the quality of the men doing the governing, the *Kongzi jiayu* says, 'Conducting government properly depends on filling posts with the right people.' This statement is particularly germane. In this chapter the 'right people' [Ren 人 literally, "human beings"] means worthy ministers. *Shen* [身 literally, "body"] indicates the ruler himself."[31]

In my opinion, the statement that government depends on the quality of the men who govern should be interpreted in line with the sentence [in the *Book of Changes*], "when an exemplary man is not present, that it is useless to try to implement the Way."[32] In other words, it is a reference to the rulers themselves. I'm afraid this should not be read as a reference to filling posts with the right people. Zhu Xi dismisses the *Kongzi jiayu* overall as a forgery, yet now he contradicts himself and accepts what it says.

Generally speaking, when it comes to selecting officials, it is necessary to look how well they have cultivated their character. This text certainly does not mean by "fill posts with the right people" that a king simply takes a group of people and chooses among them. The four Sinographs "human being" [人], "the self" [身], "the Dao"[道], and "being fully human" [仁] that appear in this passage are strung together like a string of pearls that look like they can be taken apart and dealt with one by one. But if you try to do that, you destroy the meaning they get from the context they are in. You can end up taking "human being" to mean worthy ministers and taking "the self" to refer to the ruler. If you do that, you take them out of context and distort what they mean here. The result would not make any sense.[33]

Zhu Xi said, "Benevolence [仁] is the heart-mind of Heaven and Earth, that which begets all things as well as that which people acquire by being born."[34]

As for the meaning of the Sinograph 仁, this classic tells us what it means. It explicitly states, "To be *'ren'* [仁 K. *in*] is to be fully human; the key point is to treat your relatives as you should treat your relatives."[35] This is clear and straightforward. There is no need for a more convoluted explication. In the ancient seal script, *ren* was written with the "human being" character doubled. A father and a son are two people, an elder brother and a younger brother are two people, a ruler and a subject are two people, and an official and a commoner are two people. In every instance, *ren* refers to two people each completely fulfilling their obligations and playing their proper roles in their relationship. That is why it also means "being fully human." What does "the heart-mind of Heaven and Earth, that which begets all things" have to do with such personal matters? All a son has to do is act out of filial love toward his parents. If he says "I, by means of the heart-mind of Heaven and Earth, that which begets all things, am filial to my parents," would that make any sense? All an official has to do is serve his sovereign with utmost dedication and loyalty. Would it make any sense for him to say "By means of the heart-mind of Heaven and Earth, that which begets all things, I am devoted to my ruler"? I'm afraid this would do more harm than good to the way people should behave.

This classic says, "To be '*ren*' is to be truly human." "Being truly human" refers to acting appropriately and unselfishly in interactions with other people. That is why it is written to show two people interacting. There should be righteousness between a ruler and a subject in fulfilling their respective obligations, trust between friends, and compassion and understanding between officials and commoners. These are all examples of the way people should interact with proper regard for their respective roles and obligations. Being a filial son and dutiful younger brother is the root of being fully human. That is why this classic includes the sentence "the key point is to treat your relatives as you should treat your relatives."

Righteousness refers to nothing more than acting appropriately in a wide variety of situations. Respecting those who deserve respect is the key to acting appropriately. That is why there is a sentence in this passage reading "The key point is to respect those who are worthy of respect."[36]

Zhongyong XX: 7

> An exemplary person, therefore, cannot do otherwise than cultivate a moral character.

Zhu Xi said, "If a person wants to become human by treating his family members in every respect the way they should be treated, he must draw on his ability to act appropriately by honoring those who are worthy of respect; then he will come to understand what it means to be a real human being."[37] Chen commented, "If we have teachers and friends who are worthy of our respect, then the Dao of treating relatives appropriately is fully clarified. However, if we spend our time with people of unseemly character, then we will dishonor both our parents and ourselves."[38]

As I recall, the "Record on the Subject of Education" chapter of the *Book of Rites* says, "A teacher is not one of the categories in the five degrees of mourning clothing; but without his help you will not be able to wear the clothes you are supposed to wear in mourning your relatives."[39] This is the basis for Zhu Xi saying what he said. But truly understanding Heaven is the foundation of self-cultivation. Once you truly understand what Heaven is, then it is only natural that the first thing you will do is serve your parents as a way to cultivate your own moral character. To say that in addition to understanding Heaven you also need to find a good teacher is to misunderstand what comes first and what comes later. It is acceptable to say that if someone truly understands what Heaven is, then they will not fail to show respect for those who are worthy of respect. But to say that after you come to understand Heaven, you first show respect for those who are respectable and then you serve your parents does not make any sense.

Those who understand human beings know what makes a human being fully human.[40] Only after you truly know what Heaven and the Dao are can you be fully cognizant of your true human nature [*xing*, your innate ability to act appropriately]. Only after you have come to be cognizant of your true human nature can you serve your parents properly and therefore cultivate your own moral character.[41]

THE KING ASKED:

When this chapter talks about treating relatives the way relatives should be treated, showing respect for those who are worthy of respect, and playing your proper role within the social hierarchy, this is precisely the ethical virtuosity displayed in acting in a benevolent manner, acting in accord with righteousness [acting appropriately], and acting politely. But why is there no explicit reference to acting wisely here?[42] A few lines later, however, the text talks of knowing what it means to be a human being and of understanding what Heaven is. That implies wisdom. If we put the first half and the second half of this section of this chapter together, therefore, then would not we have the complete set of the four ways of acting appropriately: acting benevolently, acting righteously, acting politely, and acting wisely? However, the term used here for "to know" [知] is associated with sensory perception, which is the ability of our psychophysical nature to perceive things. Acting wisely [智], on the other hand, is one of the ethical powers of our human nature. Is it acceptable here to use the Sinograph meaning "to know" in place of the Sinograph that means "to act wisely"?

I RESPONDED:

Acting in a benevolent manner, acting appropriately, acting politely, and acting wisely correspond to the forms of the *zhen, dui, li,* and *kan* trigrams in the *Book of Changes*.[43] When Mencius talked of the Four Sprouts [the four instinctive impulses that inspire appropriate behavior], he did so to clarify that we have an inner moral nature.[44] The four ways of displaying ethical virtuosity certainly provide the basic contours of the Dao of human beings. But if we look in the time-honored classics, we can see that sometimes they only mention acting in a benevolent manner, and other times they stop after explicitly referring only to acting benevolently and appropriately. That is because it is not necessary to mention all four ways of displaying ethical virtuosity every time. This particular classic also stops short after making an explicit reference to acting benevolently and appropriately. But shouldn't the wisdom implicit in knowing what it means to be a real human being and truly understanding Heaven be understood as the wisdom that is included in the usual list of four ways of acting appropriately?[45]

Zhongyong XX: 8

There are five aspects of the Dao everyone must conform to.

Zhu Xi said, "The Dao everyone must conform to is defined in the *Book of Documents* as the Five Cardinal Patterns of Appropriate Interactions."[46]

Mao Qiling said, "In ancient times the term 'Five Appropriate Interactions' referred only to the appropriate interactions involving fathers, mothers, elder brothers, younger brothers, and children. The patterns governing behavior in those five types of interactions were called the Five Precepts. They were nothing more than rectitude for fathers, maternal affection for mothers, fraternal affection for elder brothers, fraternal respect for younger brothers, and filial piety for children. When these patterns defining appropriate attitudes and appropriate interactions are taken seriously, then the cosmos operates harmoniously. Moreover, proper relations between sovereigns and subjects, between husbands and wives, and between friends brings harmony into the human realm. It is in this context that we can read, in the 'Canon of Shun' chapter of the 'Book of Yu' section in the *Book of Documents,* that Shun said, 'The people are not adhering to the five cardinal patterns of appropriate interactions,'[47] and, in the 'Lord Ya' section of the 'Canon of Zhou,' we can read that the king gave an order to 'diffuse widely the knowledge of those five basic patterns of appropriate interactions.'[48] In addition, in discussing with Xie[49] how to teach appropriate behavior to the people, Shun said, 'respectfully instruct the people about the Five Precepts.'[50]

"All the old commentaries point this out. For example, in the *Spring and Autumn Annals,* it is recorded that in the 18th year of Lord Wen, in the state of Ju the ruler Shuqi was assassinated.[51] The *Zuo Commentary* explains that, in the aftermath of this incident, Ji Wenzi, drawing on the words of Zang Wenzhong,[52] dispatched to court the scribe Ke to point out that Gaoxin[53] had eight descendants worthy of public office and had them make the Five Precepts known to the four corners of the world. After that, fathers were paragons of proper behavior, mothers were kind, elder brothers displayed fraternal affection, younger brothers were respectful, and children were filial.[54]

"These are the Five Precepts. One of those eight worthy descendants, Xie, was appointed Minister of Instruction, and so Xie instructed the people in proper behavior.[55] From the reigns of Tang and Yu[56] up through the Spring and Autumn period, it is clear that this list of the five appropriate ways human beings should relate to one another was the only such list.

"Then, during the Spring and Autumn period, Guan Zhong[57] came up with the notion that there were Six Important Familial Roles, which he listed as the relationship between the husband and the wife as well as the usual list of roles for fathers, mothers, elder brothers, younger brothers, and children. This was when the relationship between husband and wife was first added to the list of important familial roles. Shi Que, an official in the state of Wei, referred to what he called Six Instances of What Should Be. These were rectitude of a ruler, proper conduct of a subject, paternal affection of a father, filial piety of children, fraternal love of an elder brother, and deference of a younger brother.[58] This added ruler and subject to the list of roles with specific moral obligations. The 'Royal Regulations' chapter in the *Book of Rites* refers to seven precepts. These relate to the relationships between fathers and sons, elder brothers and younger brothers, husbands and wives, rulers and subjects, elders and juniors, friends and friends, and hosts and guests.[59] This adds elders and juniors as well as friends and friends to the list of important relationships. Nevertheless, here we see the roots of the notion of the five fundamental moral principles governing relationships.

"As for the ten ways of acting appropriately discussed by Yan Ying,[60] the ten ways of acting appropriately mentioned in the 'Liyun' section of the *Book of Rites*,[61] and the ten fundamental moral principles governing relationships mentioned in the 'Jitong' section of the *Book of Rites*,[62] these are all examples of the basic norms of human relationships being gradually expressed in more elaborate fashion until it became difficult to sort them all out.

"In the Warring States period, Mencius was the only one who clarified the specifics of how Xie's Five Precepts related to concrete human interactions. Mencius said, 'between father and son, there should be familial affection; between sovereign and subject, adherence to their respective roles; between husband and wife, attention to their separate functions; between old and young, maintenance of the proper order; and between frioends, fidelity.'[63] This is what is meant by the ways human beings ought to relate to one another. He called them 'proper human interactions,' and ever since that is the way the Five Cardinal Principles of Appropriate Interactions have been labeled in many works.

"But this was not something Mencius introduced. His term 'proper human interactions' means the same thing as the term 'the Five Cardinal Principles of Appropriate Interactions' that was used before the Spring and Autumn period. It is just that after the Warring States period, the preferred term became 'proper human interactions.' However, this is not exactly the same thing as the 'five aspects of the Dao everyone must conform to.' Early Confucian scholars, in commentaries on the *Zhongyong*, took 'five aspects of the Dao everyone must conform to' to be a reference to completely understanding the Dao and consistently conforming to the Dao. They did not use the term 'Five Appropriate Interactions.'[64] What Zisi says in the *Zhongyong* is not exactly the same as what Mencius said. Mencius talked about the proper relationship between the older and the younger in general, while the *Zhongyong's* five aspects of the Dao everyone must conform to includes instead the relationship between elder and younger brothers. They do not perfectly coincide.

"The reference to proper interactions between those older and those younger refers to interactions among those of different ages working together in government offices and to interactions among members of village associations who are of different ages. It does not limit itself to interaction between older brothers and younger brothers. That is why the 'seven precepts' distinguishes interactions between older and younger generations from interactions between older brothers and younger brothers.

"The ten ways of acting appropriately [in the *Book of Rites*] includes four additional ways of acting appropriately: an elder brother acting kindly, a younger brother showing fraternal respect, a senior acting generously, and a junior showing proper deference. This is not the same as the 'seven precepts.' It is clear in a number of works that there are differences in emphasis on the relationship between older and younger brothers, on the one hand, and the older and the young generations, on the other."[65]

(In his commentary, Zheng Xuan says that "the five aspects of the Dao that everyone must conform to" means that "we are required to consistently act in accordance with the Dao, the Way that even a hundred monarchs cannot change."[66] Kong Yingda adds that "the reference to 'five' here refers to the five fundamental moral principles governing interactions human beings should always conform to. Such interactions lead to all interactions progressing harmoniously.")[67]

Mao Qiling also wrote, "In the Spring and Autumn period, Zangsun Chen and Jisun Xingfu [two scholar-officials] were both known for being wise. Ke, a scribe at the time, was well acquainted with tales from the past. That's why their records of what the Five August Emperors[68] said about the Five Precepts all agree.

"[In his commentary on the *Book of Documents,*] when the 'Books of Yu' section of the *Book of Documents* says, 'Shun carefully set forth the beauty of the five cardinal patterns of appropriate interactions,'[69] Kong Anguo[70] wrote 'the five cardinal patterns of appropriate interactions are the Precepts of the Five Constant Moral Obligations, which are rectitude for a father, compassion for a mother, fraternal affection for an elder brother, deference for a younger brother, and filial piety for the children.'[71]

"As for the line 'The people are not adhering to the five cardinal patterns of appropriate relationships,'[72] in his commentary 'The Correct Interpretation [of the Shangshu],' Kong Yingda explained that the 'five cardinal patterns of appropriate relationships' refers to the proper attitudes and behavior for people acting as fathers, mothers, older brothers, younger brothers, or children. 'The Correct Interpretation' goes on to say that in the line 'respectfully instruct the people about the Five Precepts,'[73] the Five Precepts refers to rectitude, compassion, fraternal affection, deference, and filial piety.[74] Moreover, the line in 'Counsels of Gao Yao' [in the *Book of Documents*] saying, 'we are charged with enforcing the five cardinal patterns of appropriate interactions'[75] and the line in the 'Officers of Zhou,' and 'Lord Ya' sections [of the *Book of Documents*], saying 'diffuse widely the knowledge of the five cardinal patterns of appropriate interactions,'[76] are all explained the same way. In no instance are the relationships between sovereigns and subjects, fathers and sons, elder brothers and younger brothers, husbands and wives, and friends called the Five Cardinal Patterns of Appropriate Interactions. And from the Han and Tang dynasties up to, but not including, the Song dynasty, no one understood the five aspects of the Dao everyone must follow as merely the Five Cardinal Patterns of Appropriate Interactions."[77]

(Yan Ying's "ten ways of acting appropriately" are a sovereign commanding and a subject respectfully obeying, a father acting with compassion and a child responding with filial piety, an elder brother loving his younger brother and the younger brother respecting his elder brother, a husband promoting harmony in his household and a wife being cooperative, the mother-in-law acting just as she should act and a daughter-in-law listening to her mother-in-law.[78] Moreover, the record of *Discussions in the White Tiger Hall*[79] includes what it calls the Three Major and Six Minor Principles, which refers to the principles governing interactions between sovereigns and subjects, parents and children, husbands and wives, elder brothers and younger brothers, as well as with paternal relatives, maternal relatives, teachers and elders, and among friends.)

"From the Song dynasty on, however, nowhere you looked would you see anyone who did not think that the five aspects of the Dao everyone must conform to was anything other than another way of saying 'The Five Cardinal Patterns of Appropriate Relationships.' They do not realize that this is not the way those terms were used earlier. Their mistake has brought almost unprecedented confusion into this world."[80]

Zhang Taizhan[81] wrote: "I suspect that the term Mencius used, 'Five Primary Relationships,' was already being used from the Spring and Autumn period. When we look at the references Zilu is recorded in the *Analects* as making to the appropriate interactions between an elder and a younger as well as about the respective duties of sovereigns and subjects, we can see that they are both called primary relationships.[82] There is no doubt that this is a reflection of the notion that interactions between sovereigns and subjects and between those who are older and those who are younger as two of the Five Primary Relationships."[83]

Mao Wenhui[84] pointed out "the ten cardinal moral principles governing relationships discussed in the 'Jitong' Section [of the *Book of Rites*] include relationships between someone older and someone younger but there is nothing said explicitly about the relationship between an elder brother and a younger brother.[85] However, in the commentaries it is made clear that the order that prevails in interactions between an older person and a younger person should prevail in interactions within the family, including between older and younger brothers. He also noted that commentaries to that text point out that the generations participating in ancestor rites are arranged in the *zhao-mu* order that reflects the proper order among fathers and sons, among distant relatives and close relatives, and between generations. This distinguishing between fathers and sons, the older and the younger, and close relatives from distant relatives would, of course, include distinguishing between older and young brothers within the general category of older and younger."[86]

I would like to point out that the way the term "the Five Cardinal Patterns of Appropriate Interactions" was used in the distant past is not the same as the way the term "five aspects of the Dao everyone must conform to" was used.

THE KING ASKED:

As for the three character traits necessary for ethical virtuosity—wisdom, benevolence, and valor—Zhi Xi thought that everywhere on earth, both in the past and today, those three are manifestations of the exact same *li* [the normative pattern governing appropriate interactions]. That would mean that acting wisely and acting benevolently represent the same fundamental way of interacting with others. But what about acting with valor? Where would that fit among the five core features of our moral nature?[87] How can it be rooted in the same basic patterns of appropriate interactions as acting wisely and acting benevolently?

I RESPONDED:

The names "benevolence," "righteousness," "propriety," and "wisdom" are applicable only to actions. Only after you have acted in a benevolent manner, acted morally, acted politely, or acted wisely can you be said to be benevolent, moral, polite, or wise. Such ways of acting are concrete displays of ethical virtuosity, not something you possess from birth. If you want to say that the dynamic patterns of appropriate interactions that make it possible for human beings to act benevolently, morally, politely, and wisely are an intrinsic part of human nature, then you are talking about the sprouts of ethical virtuosity that Mencius refers to when he discusses compassion and three other fundamental ethical inclinations as the roots of the four basic ways of responding appropriately to situations we find ourselves in.[88] However, those four basic ethical inclinations are all rooted in the unitary capacity for spiritual insight every human being is endowed with. Potential for spiritual insight [consciousness, the ability to be aware of how we should interact with people and things around us] means the ability to respond to things and events we encounter. If we calculate the various ways human beings can respond to their social and material environment, how can we limit it to only four ways? Mencius singled out four fundamental ethical inclinations for special attention, that's all. Some might add acting in such a way as not to betray the trust of others. Others might add acting with valor. But these, too, are phrases that are only applicable after someone has actually acted in a trustworthy or courageous manner. However, they all originate from movement of the one heart-mind that person has. I'm afraid that to try to match exactly the three character traits necessary for ethical virtuosity with the five primary relationships is an impossible task.[89]

Zhongyong XX: 9

> Some understand with a natural ease.

Zhu Xi said, "The one thing you need is the fortitude not to back down in the face of any obstacles you may encounter." He also said, "If you can exert yourself without ever letting up, then you are doing what you need to do to reach the one and the same goal everyone is working toward."[90]

I note that, in this classic, the phrase "one and the same" occurs many times. Usually "one and the same" is explicitly linked with sincerity [C. *cheng* — acting in an appropriately responsive, harmonious, and selfless manner]. But "one and the same" in the two sentences in this passage, unlike in other cases, is not explicitly linked with sincerity.[91] Is there any reason for that?

After all, whether you are born understanding basic moral principles, learn them only after studying them, or have to struggle to learn them, even though there is a difference in whether you reach understanding early or late in life, nevertheless, what you learn is one and the same — how to act in an unselfishly cooperative and appropriately responsive manner. And whether you find it easy to act appropriately, do so only with strenuous effort,[92] or have to struggle to act appropriately, even though there is a difference in how easy or difficult it is for you to do so, nevertheless, what you learn is one and the same — how to act in a *cheng* manner. So "one and the same" must be a reference to *cheng* here as well.

Zhu Xi said, "Understanding moral principles naturally and easily acting in accordance with them is called 'wisdom.' (This is like the great wisdom of Shun.) To have to study to learn moral principles and then make a strenuous effort to be a better person and act in accordance with them is called 'becoming fully human [仁].' (This is like Yan Hui disciplining himself and recovering his ability to act politely in order to be fully human.)[93] Having to struggle to learn moral principles and then struggling some more to act appropriately is called fortitude."[94]

Someone asked Zhu Xi, "Zhang Zhai, Lü Dalin, Yang Shi, and Hou Zhongliang all say that understanding moral principles from birth and being able to easily act in accordance with them is 'being fully human,' that coming to understand moral principles by studying them and then realizing that you will be a better person if you act in accordance with them and therefore strive to do so is 'wisdom,' and that having to struggle to learn moral principles and then struggling some more to act in accordance with them is fortitude. This sounds good to me. Why don't you agree, Master?"

Zhu Xi replied, "In previous passages in this classic, Shun is used to illuminate wisdom, Yan Hui to illuminate what it means to be fully human, and Zilu to illuminate courage. You should not take the word 'wisdom' in too narrow a sense. It simply refers to acting wisely. How can we call wise only those who have to study in order to learn moral principles and then have to make strenuous efforts to make themselves better persons so that they can act in accordance with those principles"?[95]

Let me point out that the *Analects* says instead, "Those who are fully human can easily act in a fully human manner, whereas those who are wise know that they have to work hard to order to act in a fully human manner."[96] (This is in the "*Liren*" chapter of the Analects.) The "Record on Example" [*Biaoji*] chapter of the *Book of Rites* says, "Those who are fully human can easily act in a fully human manner, whereas those who are wise know that they have to work hard to order to act in a fully human manner; and those who act appropriately because they fear they will be punished if they do otherwise have to struggle to act in a fully human manner."[97] (This is also something Confucius said.) *Records of Ritual Matters by Dai the Elder* [*Dadai Liji*] says, "Those who are fully human take pleasure in acting in accordance with the Dao. Those who are wise know that they have to make a strenuous effort to order to act in accordance with the Dao." (This is from the "Zengzi lishi" [Zengzi on correctly serving one's superiors] chapter.)[98]

If we closely examine what is said in these various classics, we can see that they all understand that acting fully human with a natural ease is to be fully human [to realize your full human potential]. Having to make an effort to act appropriately because you know you will be a better person for doing so is to show yourself to be wise. To have innate knowledge of moral principles is linked to being able to easily act appropriately. Having to study in order to understand moral principles is linked with having to make a strenuous effort to act appropriately in order to become a better person. But being fully human is just as important as acting wisely. They cannot be separated. This is what Hengqu[99] and his disciples said.[100] I suspect there is a good reason they said so and therefore there is no reason to change it.

Zhongyong XX: 10

> The Master said, "To love learning brings one close to acting wisely."

(The *History of the Former Han Dynasty* version of this sentence has Confucius saying, "To love asking questions brings one close to acting wisely.")[101]

Zhu Xi said, "The three words 'The Master said' are redundant."[102]

Mao Yuanzhong[103] said, "*Kongzi jiayu* also includes the same text we see in this passage. However, *Kongzi jiayu* begins with Lord Ai saying to Confucius, 'Your words are beautiful and excellent, indeed. My humble self is certainly not up to matching this.'[104] That is why Confucius answered the way he did.[105] ... Because Lord Ai's question is left out in the *Zhongyong* version, 'the Master said' appears to be superfluous. This statement clearly clarifies the statement by Confucius immediately preceding it. That is why previous commentators thought this phrase was redundant."[106]

In my opinion, this passage in the *Kongzi jiayu* was lifted from the *Zhongyong* and then embellished a bit. (For a full account of how Zhu Xi saw the relationship between Chapter XX and *Kongzi jiayu*, see his remarks at the end of his discussion of Chapter XX in his *Complete Works*.)[107] People like Zhu Xi have taken this chapter, all the way through the section on the Nine Cardinal Rules, as an actual record of an extended conversation with Lord Ai. That is a big mistake.

Zhu Xi originally dismissed *Kongzi jiayu* as unreliable, but then he reversed himself and accepted it, saying that Zisi left out what he thought was superfluous in the *Kongzi jiayu* of the conversation between Confucius and Lord Ai but forgot to delete this instance of those three words "the Master said." There is no evidence that is what actually happened. The *Zhongyong* is a single work. From beginning to end it flows smoothly as if it were written in a single breath. So why would almost an entire chapter be presented as a conversation with Lord Ai? And why would that conversation be this elaborate and wide-ranging? There is a record of a short conversation with Lord Ai in this text but it appears in the bollworm wasp passage only.[108] The rest of this chapter has nothing to do with the conversation Confucius had with Lord Ai.

Zhu Xi said, "This section talks of how those who have not yet realized their potential for ethical virtuosity can embark on their journey toward ethical virtuosity. According to what is said above, the three ways of understanding moral principles all make one wise. The three ways of acting appropriately all make one fully human.[109] And to come close to achieving all this, one needs fortitude [a determination to overcome all obstacles]."[110]

Let me point out that those who love studying do so in order to learn how to act appropriately. Those who exert themselves do so in order to act appropriately. Those who understand what it is to be ashamed are willing to struggle in order to understand how to act appropriately, and struggle some more in order to do so. Those who from birth understand how they should act and can naturally act appropriately are at the top of the scale in terms of acting wisely, actualizing to the fullest their humanity and displaying strong determination. Below them are those who cannot reach what that first group has achieved. The latter group is therefore said to come close to acting wisely, come close to fully actualizing their humanity, and come close to displaying strong determination. "Come close" means to almost, but not quite, reach a certain point.

Zhu Xi, in a passage earlier, wrote that those who naturally understand and naturally act appropriately are the most advanced and are called wise. Below them are those who have to study to acquire knowledge of proper behavior and have make a strenuous effort to act properly. Such people, he said, can be called fully human.[111] But in the passage cited just above Zhu Xi says that all three ways of coming to understand how to behave appropriately are manifestations of wisdom, and all three ways of managing to behave appropriately are manifestations of being fully human. He contradicts himself. I cannot follow what he is trying to say. Moreover, all three examples of "coming close to" are manifestations of strong determination. What Zhu Xi says diverges from what this classic tells us. I am afraid I cannot accept his interpretation. After careful examination of the text itself, I have drawn the chart below to show what this passage actually means.

Diagram for Zhongyong XX: 10
    Highest Level:
        Naturally Knowing How to Behave
        Easily Acting Appropriately
    Lower Levels:
        Studying to gain wisdom—
            love of learning brings one close to acting wisely
        Struggling to gain wisdom
        And struggling to act appropriately
    Knowing to be ashamed of where one falls short brings one close to having the requisite determination.
        Making a strenuous effort to act appropriately.
        Making such an effort brings one close to becoming fully human

Lou Xiangming[112] said, "Far back in the distant past, the Sinograph [li 力 — usually understood as meaning 'power' or 'to make an effort'] was understood to mean the same as the Sinograph that means 'benefit' [li 利]. That is why the term 'dexterous' [kuaili 快利] was said to mean the same as the Sinograph 力. Dictionaries cite one of the odes in the *Book of Songs* that literally says 'they work hard [力] for the people instead of relying on an official salary'[113] as an example of this usage, since they read this line in the *Book of Songs* as saying they benefited the people rather than just consuming the grain the people produced instead. Some say that benefit and power came to be written with the same Sinograph because they are homonyms."[114]

As I see it, to be wise means to clearly understand what is helpful and what is harmful. It is therefore because I regard becoming fully human as helpful for myself and for others that I work hard to order to act in a fully human manner. The sentence "work hard to fully actualize your humanity [利仁]" means "you have to make a strenuous effort to order to act in a fully human manner [利行]."[115] What Lou said is incorrect. This in explained in detail in the *Discourse on the Analects*.[116]

Zhongyong XX: 12

> For All-under-Heaven, all states and households, there are nine cardinal rules.

Zhu Xi said, "When it comes to making progress in aligning with the Dao, there is nothing more important than family. Treating your relatives with the affection due them, therefore, comes next."[117]

As I see it, as I noted earlier,[118] you must first understand what Heaven is in order to serve your parents properly. And serving your parents is the way to cultivate a moral character. That means that serving one's parents is the core of the cultivation of the self. When Zhu Xi wrote "treat your relatives with the affection due them," he was talking about how you should treat all the members of your extended family. We see proof of this when, later on in this section, the *Zhongyong* says, "If there is affection among family members, then there will be no ill will within generations, or across generations, either." If this were not the case, then there would be no reason for the *Zhongyong* to say, "respect the worthy" and immediately follow that with "treat your extended family with the affection due them."[119]

Zhu Xi explains that when this chapter says that when the ruler respects the worthy, there will be "no confusion," that means that no one will be in doubt about *li* [the proper way to behave]. He also explains that when this chapter says when the ruler respects the high officials, none of them will try to "confuse him," that means that when the ruler treats the high officials with respect, no one will try to mislead him about how to manage affairs of state.[120]

Mao Qiling said, "The ancient commentaries take 'no confusion' as referring to major affairs of state and 'not confusing' as referring to everyday affairs. So, Zhu Xi makes a mistake here. The Six Classics say nothing about *li*. Moreover, when the ancient texts record the high officials discussing what to do, we never see the word *li* mentioned. What sort of a thing is the *li* Zhu Xi is talking about?"[121]

As I see it, that phrase "no confusion" means there is no confusion about the Dao, the proper way to behave. When you discuss the Dao, you cannot avoid referring to *li* at the same time. Mao's comment here is frivolous.

Zhu Xi said, "If you encourage the Hundred Artisans to come and work in your realm, they will complement each other, and commerce will prosper. Agriculture, too, will benefit from this. The result will be that you will not suffer from any shortages of anything."[122]

As I recall, the "Dongguan kaogongji" volume of the *Zhouli* says, "The realm has six occupational categories. The Hundred Artisans is one of these." It also says, "If you closely examine the shape of things and of what they are made, you can place them in different categories according to which one of the five primary materials dominates. You can then place people under one of the Hundred Artisans categories depending on which type of tool they use."[123]

In a discussion of the "Nine Occupations" in the "Tianguan: zhongzai" chapter of the *Zhouli*, we can find the explanation that the Hundred Artisans are those who turn the eight basic natural materials into useful objects. Zheng Xuan's commentary adds that the eight natural materials are gems, ivory, jade, stone, metal, wood, leather, and feathers.[124] If the Hundred Artisans are assigned tasks appropriate to their individual skills and given an additional ration of grain for their work, then the skilled artisans in all four directions will hear about this and move to that realm to be enlisted in the ranks of the Hundred Artisans. When this results in the production of tools useful and convenient for farming, peasants will be able to grow and harvest a lot more grain with less effort. When this results in the manufacturing of better tools for weaving, then weavers can produce sufficient cotton cloth and silk fabrics with less effort. If ships and carts become easier to maneuver, then goods can be moved a great distance with less effort. If there are devices that make it easier to pull and lift heavy rocks, then dikes and roads can be made stronger with less effort. That is what Zhu Xi means when he writes "If you encourage the Hundred Artisans to come and work in your realm..., you will not suffer from any shortages of anything."

It is common in our country for carpenters and metalworkers to have only the most rudimentary knowledge of how to shape wood and metal. Moreover, officials make them work without giving them any compensation. Even worse, the officials even go so far as to flog them frequently and even break their fingers and cut off their hands when their work is not satisfactory. This scares them away from training any successors. So how can we find enough qualified artisans?

The tools used by our farmers and weavers, and our boats and carts, are unchanged from the time of Suiren.[125] The countryside is more and more turning into wasteland and as a result the size of our harvests is shrinking. When we suffer from even a single flood or drought, all we can do is complain about the way Heaven is treating us. Our people are destitute, and our state is bankrupt, and we feel helpless to do anything about it. This is because we do not have a clear understanding of what the *Zhongyong* is telling us.

Zhu Xi said, "When you are devoted to your family members, you desire that they are appointed to high offices. When you love someone, you desire their good fortune. When your brothers marry, you desire that they not move far away. Therefore, this classic advises respecting their status, making their rewards substantial, and taking into account, and respecting, their likes and dislikes equally."[126]

Let me note that, according to the "Tianguan zhongzai" chapter in the *Zhouli*, "there are eight regulations for managing the people. One of them is treating family members as family members should be treated and another is promoting the worthy."[127] That is why all the members of the royal family who are worthy are appointed to important posts. Even those who are not particularly talented, since they are treated the way family members should be treated, are still given respectable titles and given a decent stipend. As a result, even though they do not exercise any real power, they will nevertheless have no complaints. When the Duke of Zhou was Grand Intendent, the Duke of Shao was Grand Guardian, and Kang Shu and Dan Ji were Minister of Punishments and Minister of Works respectively. They were all wise men worthy of serving as high officials. However, the Duke of Zhou's five other brothers, such as Cheng Shuwu and Mao Shuzheng, though they had titles and stipends, did not hold any actual office.[128] This can be seen in *Huowen*.[129]

That is why under the Zhou system some people were provided with stipends of government land. "The Conveyance of Rites" chapter of the *Book of Rites* says, "The Son of Heaven has land on which he can settle his sons and grandsons."[130] And the discussion of the "Noblemen's manors" in the "Diguan" [Ministry of Education] chapter of the *Zhouli* notes that stipend lands were established separately from the enfeoffments of the sons and younger brothers of kings in order to provide them with grain.[131] If in the past the king's sons and younger brothers had actual government posts, and all the officials received sufficient stipend lands, why would there have been any need to create these extra stipend lands? That is why scholars of old in their commentaries on the *Record of Ritual* all said, "This means that they were only given stipends and titles but were not given actual government posts." (Mao said this.)[132]

Zheng Xuan commented, "What 'respecting, and taking into account, their likes and dislikes equally' means is to be impartial in rewarding and punishing." Zheng goes on to say that "although the affection you feel for them may not be exactly the same, the same principles defining appropriate action should be applied in every case."[133]

The *Collected Commentaries on the Four Books* [*Sishu jishuo*] says, "Respecting, and taking into account, their likes refers to how you give them rewards. Respecting, and taking into account, their dislikes refers to how you hand down punishments to them. Although your feelings toward them may not appear to be exactly the same, the same principles defining appropriate action are applied in every case."[134] (The *Zuozhuan* has the comment,

"The leader of Jin restored the Prince of Wei to his throne but did not do the same for the lord of Cao. The Jin scribe recorded that Cao and Wei were both dismissed but only Wei had his realm restored. To give different punishments for the same crime is not proper punishment.")[135]

Mao Qiling said, "Someone who is a ruler should try to make what his kinsmen like and dislike agree with his likes and dislikes. This does not mean, however, that the ruler should adopt the likes and dislikes of all his kinsmen."[136]

Feng Wenzi said, "If Lord Yi of Rong was fond of making a profit, then should the king be fond of making a profit as well? If Lord Zhuang of Zheng harbored animosity against the state of Guo, then should the King also harbor animosity against Guo? Could this be called respecting, and taking into account, the likes and dislikes of others?"[137]

In my opinion, what the father loves, the son loves as well. But this only applies to fathers and sons. It is not the way the king should think when treating other family members the way they should be treated. In discussing how to manage your family, the *Daxue* warns that "People are partial toward those they love and hold dear; they are prejudiced against those they look down upon and dislike."[138] "Respecting, and taking into account, their likes and dislikes" is how you manage your family. Isn't this the same thing as saying you should treat your family members the way they should be treated?

Zhu Xi said, "The line in this chapter of the *Zhongyong* that reads 'ensure that there are enough officials that it is possible for them to discharge their duties' means to make sure all the various officials have sufficient assistants. If high officials do not have to pay undue attention to minor matters, then you know you have enough minor officials."[139]

Chen Ziceng said, "According to the *Zhouli*, each office had both a great and a lesser official. There were sixty such offices."[140]

In my opinion, when the hundred offices of the various states were established, I do not think they were supposed to be staffed only by officials of the highest rank. To make it possible for them to discharge their responsibilities means to appoint the worthy and assigning the able to work in those offices. If the high officials staff their offices with those who are capable of doing a proper job, then those offices will be filled with the worthy and the able and everything will be managed well. If the ruler does not respect the high officials, the high officials will lack the authority to promote the worthy. This does not measure up to "making it possible for them to discharge their responsibilities." In that case, then the state will not be managed well, and it will be difficult to attract qualified officials.

Zheng Xuan said that this means that "Those officials who are loyal and trustworthy should have their stipends increased."[141]

Zhu Xi said, "The reference in this chapter of the *Zhongyong* to 'increasing the stipends for the loyal and the trustworthy' means to treat them with the appropriate lack of regard for your own personal self-interest and to compensate them generously."[142]

Mao Qiling said, "If we say that the officials' salary should be generous and substantial according to their rank, then we need to remember that in the Zhou system of officials' stipends, the stipend for lower-level officials was half that of the great officers. By the time you get down to the lowest class of officials, it would not be substantial at all. However, if all the stipends were truly substantial, then it would have to be that way starting from the bottom ranks. Since this is the case, I do not know what the reference to 'the loyal and trustworthy' means. And what time period are we talking about here? Are we talking about the time of earlier kings or of kings today?"[143]

As I see it, being loyal means being loyal to the ruler, and being trustworthy means carrying out official duties with a sincere heart-mind. The "Royal Regulations" chapter of the *Liji* says, "The feudal lord who had done good service for the people, and shown them an example of virtue, received an enhancement to his territory and rank."[144] That is the way rewards for the officials in the countryside were handled. Why should the officials at court be treated differently? The practice of later generations, however, is for one department to have many different officials, each with a different title. The system here in our country is that, in the Office for the Royal House Administration alone, we have a First Secretary, a Third Secretary, an Auditor, and a Master of the Records, all with different titles. The system of the Zhou was not like this. The Six Ministries during the Zhou had several posts in them but they only used the names of the various departments within each ministry and did not have separate names for the various posts within those departments.

For example, let's take a look at the discussion of the *sishi* [director of markets] office in the Ministry of Education of the Zhou. There are two great officers of the lower grade, four officials of the highest regular grade, eight officials of the regular middle grade, and sixteen officials of the regular lowest grade.[145] Although there is a rank order among the officials working there, they are all called director of markets. How can it be this way? If the officials of the lowest regular class are loyal and trustworthy, they will advance to the middle regular class and receive a stipend appropriate to that rank. If the officials of the middle regular class are loyal and trustworthy, they will advance to the highest regular class and receive a stipend appropriate to that rank. If the officials of the highest regular class are loyal and trustworthy, they will advance to the rank of the great officers of the lower grade and receive stipends appropriate to that rank. Those officials will not move to a different office when they are promoted. They merely receive an enhancement of their stipends. This is what the *Zhongyong* means by "increasing the stipends for the loyal and the trustworthy."

The "Celestial Ministry: The Grand Steward" chapter of the *Zhouli* says, "It is through their stipends that they are made comfortable."[146] The "Celestial Ministry: The Ordinary Grand Master" chapter says, "Assess their performance and then determine their stipend."[147] And in the "Ministry of Education: The Grand Minister of Education" chapter, it says "If you use performance to determine stipends, then the people will benefit greatly."[148] This is the way things were done.

For example, at the end of the year, a doctor's performance as a physician was examined and his stipend was determined accordingly. A doctor who made no mistakes was given the best stipend. Those who were successful in 90 percent of cases were next, then those who succeeded 80 percent of the time, then 70, and, finally, those who were successful only 60 percent of the time got the smallest stipend. So how well they did their job determined their stipend. It was done this way for doctors, and that is the way it must have been done for other officials as well. (The *Zuozhuan's* comment on the 22nd year of the reign of Lord Xiang says, "Guan Qi of Chu was favored by the Chief Minister Zinan so, though he had not been given much of a stipend, he nonetheless owned dozens of horses.")[149] "Officials" [士 — the term used in the discussion of the number of officials in the director of markets office] means "those who have been appointed to public office." It is a general term for those who serve the ruler in the upper levels of the government.

Chen said, "Order corvée labor at the proper time, and you will not exhaust the people's strength. Keep taxes to a minimum, and you will not exhaust the people's resources." See his comment in the *Questions and Answers about the Zhongyong* section in *Sishu daquan*.[150]

As I recall, *Zhouli*, in the "Treating People Fairly" section, says "it is appropriate to order three days' corvée labor during an abundant harvest year, two days in an average year, but only a single day in a lean year."[151] The "Royal Regulations" chapter of the *Book of Rites* says, "Only three days' labor was required by the state from the people in the course of a year."[152] Moreover, corvée labor can only be required of the people when they do not need to work on their own land. When the encampment constellation appears in the middle of the sky at dusk, only then can corvée labor be enlisted to work on the palace.[153] After the harvest is finished, then repairs can be made on the fortress walls. If the peasants are robbed of their time to tend their fields, this is what the *Spring and Autumn Annals* calls "not being timely."[154] This is what the *Zhongyong* is referring to when it advocates "ordering corvée labor at the proper time."

Zhu Xi said, "In the clause discussing how to compensate the Hundred Artisans, the character *ji* [既] should be read as *xi* [餼], meaning to give a ration of grain. *Xibing* [餼稟] means to reduce the amount of grain in the rations. *Chengshi* [稱事] is the same as the phrase in the 'Gaoren zhi' [Duties of the provisioner] section of the *Zhouli*, which says, 'Examine his crossbows to determine whether to increase or decrease his rations.'"[155] (This is based on an old annotation.)

Mao Qiling said, "Zheng Xuan also read *ji* as *xi*. That Sinograph *xi* is another name of 'stipend grain,' except that it tells you that grain is mixed with fodder. As it says in the *Discourses of the States*, 'grain for horses is nothing more than fodder.'[156] Therefore this character *ji* should be read as a different *xi* [餴], the one that appears in the *Shuowen* with the meaning of 'to give someone grain,' not as the *xi* that means grain mixed with fodder. So this means give them nothing but grain, without it being combined with fodder. Furthermore, in his *Zhongyong zhangju*, Zhu Xi follows Zheng Xuan's commentary and says that '*Xibing* means to slightly reduce their rations.'[157] *Xi* can also be read in some contexts as providing animals for sacrifices, since in those days government officials were given raw sheep or ox meat [as part of their stipend]. But this would be a mistaken reading here. Sacrificial meat is meat, and stipend grain is grain pure and simple."[158]

In my opinion, the Sinograph *shao* [稍], which Zheng and Zhu read as "to slightly reduce," here actually means the tip of a stalk of grain. In the old days, they cut off the tip of the stalk to collect the grains there and used that to provide stipends in the form of bushels of grains. That's what this phrase "to slightly reduce" means. *Xibing* does not mean necessarily that their rations were reduced.

The "Proceedings of Government in the Different Months" chapter of the *Book of Rites* says, "In the first month of winter, orders are given to the chief Director of Works to prepare a statement on the work of the craftsmen; setting forth especially the sacrificial vessels with their measures and capacity, and seeing that there are no excessive displays of ingenuity in the workmanship which might disturbs the minds of their superiors; and making the suitability of the article the first consideration. (There is a sentence of explication here.)[159] Every piece should have a name engraved on it (that means the name of the person who made it should appear on the sacrificial vessel), for reference when determining whether it was made the way it should have been made. When that item was not made the way it should have been, the craftsman responsible should be punished in order to make sure that does not happen again."[160]

Zhu Xi said, "Give a tally [as proof that they were formally received] in order to properly send off those who are departing. Provide grain to properly welcome those who are arriving. Appoint them to positions according to their ability in order to benefit from their skill. If you do this, those traveling throughout All-under-Heaven will all want to travel the road that leads to you."[161] (See *Huowen*.)

I would like to point out that earlier Confucians explained "those from afar" [a phrase that appears in this chapter] as a reference to envoys of other feudal lords making a formal call. We can see this in *Zhongyong zhangju*.[162] However, we cannot be sure if this is not a reference to someone who wants to serve the feudal lord he has come to visit (this is what *Huowen* appears to mean when it says "appoint people to positions according to their ability"),[163] or is not a reference to traveling merchants (those *Huowen* describes as "traveling throughout All-under-Heaven").[164] How can we know what this phrase is actually referring to?

If we say this is a reference to envoys from other feudal lords, then this must be referring to feudal lords he has good relations with. In that case, this statement should not be read as advising being kind to people from afar. As for people who are looking for a post in a particular realm or who are traveling merchants, they are not necessarily people from afar, either.

There were numerous occasions when a feudal lord dispatched someone on an official mission or welcomed envoys from other domains. This reference to those from afar most be a reference to those who have come [on such missions] from barbarian lands. Confucius said, "If those who are from far away do not show proper respect for you, simply refine your cultured behavior and ethical virtuosity in order to attract them."[165] (This is in the "Ji Family" chapter.) Also, people like the Yi from Huai and the Rong from Xu"[166] are called "those from afar." (See my notes on the *Analects*.[167]) The "Hounds of Lü," chapter of the Mei version of the *Book of Documents* says, "When he does not appear greedy for foreign objects, foreigners will come to his court."[168] It is not a mistake to read this line in light of these lines from these other Classics.

Generally speaking, those we call barbarians do not know how to walk the path of the Dao, do not practice proper ritual and etiquette, and do not know how to use the accoutrements of a civilized society. Therefore, they need a guide when they come to visit a civilized ruler, and someone to accompany them when they leave. (An example of this is when an envoy from Yuechang people came to offer tribute at the Zhou court. He had to be escorted by three interpreters when he traveled to and from the central states.)[169] When they use refined speech and present a pleasant appearance, even if only slightly, the court should act pleased and praise them. When they are unable to act exactly as they should act, the court should have pity on them. They should not be subjected to harsh criticism.

The "Huaifang shi" chapter of the *Zhouli* says, "The people who are in charge of welcoming those coming from distant lands to offer tribute should ensure they are sent off with the tally confirming they were formally received. While they are here, it is important to make sure they are comfortable. They should be provided with accommodations, food, and drink."[170] I note that Zhu Xi confirms this in *Zhongyong zhangju*.[171]

Huowen says, "Do you, Master, think 'be kind to those from afar' means the same as the sentence 'do not neglect strangers and travelers?'[172] Zhu Xi answered that this should be read in accordance with the reference to those feudal lords he has good relations with. In the old days, they used to say that feudal lords who came from far away should be extended hospitality first but that does not mean they should necessarily be ranked ahead of those who traveled a shorter distance. The *Book of Documents* says, 'Be kind to those from afar and cultivate the ability of those nearby.' It also says, 'This will bring the barbarous tribes to you one after another to make their submission.'[173] So this sentence 'be kind to those from afar' is indeed not limited to the four barbarians who come to pay their respects." (See *Huowen*.)[174]

As I recall, where the "Huaifang shi" chapter of the *Rites of Zhou* says, "The people who come from distant lands," Zhu Xi reads "people" as "commoners." Understood this way, this cannot refer to the feudal lords of other states. But those who brought "tribute of distant lands" were not commoners. "People" simply refers to human beings. Sometimes the ruler himself came, and other times he dispatched ministers with tribute. They were both referred to as people from distant lands. We should not read the term "people from distant lands" in too narrow a sense.

As for the statement that, if you are kind to those from afar, this will bring the barbarians to you one after another to pay their respects, how can there be barbarians the ruler should not be kind to? And, if you say that people from distant lands should not be included among those who pay their respects, then why do the classics say, "be kind to those from afar and then cultivate the ability of those nearby"?[175] Does not that give priority to being kind to those who have come from far away?

Zhen Xishan[176] said, " 'Restoring lineages that have been severed' is like what King Wu of Zhou did when he restored the royal lineages of Xia and Shang. 'Raising the fallen' is like what Lord Huan of Qi did when he enfeoffed Wei."[177]

Mao Qiling said, "When King Wu overcame Shang, he had the great-grandson of Zhong Yong, Zhou Zhang, continue the line of Tai Bo into later generations. This is 'restoring lineage legitimacy in lineages that have been broken.' When Cai Zhong had his lordship of Cai restored, this was 'raising states that had fallen.' "[178]

Zhu Xi said, "When 'bringing order where there is disorder,' one must bring about peace between superior and inferior. When 'giving support where there is danger,' one must foster empathy between larger and smaller states." (See *Huowen*.)[179]

As I recall, the Minister of War section of the *Zhouli* says, "he should wield the nine cardinal rules to rectify the subordinate fiefdoms. If they treat the worthy poorly and bring harm to the people, he should attack and punish them. If they mistreat or kill their relatives, then he must rectify that situation by viciously killing that ruler and eliminating his fiefdom."[180] This is the benevolence of bringing order where there was disorder and giving support where there was danger. After the Zhou had moved its capital eastward, the Son of Heaven was unable to restore order and end the chaos among the various feudal states. That is the reason there were a multitude instances of depravity and disorder, of killings and rebellions. The Son of Heaven was unable to provide support for feudal lords who were in trouble, so larger states swallowed smaller states, and strong ministers usurped weak rulers. The nine cardinal principles were no longer operating.

Zhu Xi wrote, "The 'Royal Regulations' chapter in the *Book of Rites* says, 'The feudal lords should dispatch a minor mission to court every year, and dispatch a major mission every three years. Once every five years they should appear there in person.'"[181]

As I recall, "The Meaning of the Interchange of Missions between Different Courts" chapter of the *Book of Rites* says, "Every year the feudal lords should send a small mission, and every three years a great one."[182] Generally speaking, for small missions high officers were dispatched, and for great missions ministers were dispatched. For a royal audience, the ruler had to go in person. But this is the way things were done under the Eastern Zhou. It was not the system of the Duke of Zhou.

Under the system of the Duke of Zhou for official ritual interactions, originally Luoyi was the center of the ruler's personal domain. It was completely surrounded by the lands of the nobility, the land that provided grain directly to the royal family, the lands of the high ministers, the lands of the great officers and the lower nobility, and the lands supporting the defense of the realm.[183] Therefore those whose lands were nearby made a formal call on the court once a year, and those a little farther away every two years. (This applies to the nobles and those who were in charge of the land providing grain for the royal family.) Those farther away were required to make a formal call every three years, and those even farther away every four years. (This applies to the high ministers and great officers and then the lower nobility.) Those in charge of lands supporting the defense of the realm were required to make a formal call every five years. (Also see the *Zhouli*, "Senior Messenger" chapter.)[184]

The five-fold system of assigning lands around the capital was abandoned when Eastern Zhou replaced Western Zhou. The rulers of the twelve strong states were all required to send emissaries to the Zhou court according to a regular schedule. How close or how far away their domain was made no difference. They were required to send a minor mission to that court every year and a major mission every three years, and a royal mission once every five years in which they had to appear at the court in person. This was the established procedure for ritual interactions among the various rulers. But it was not always enforced. Qi and Jin did not always comply with this regulation.

The "Senior Messenger" chapter of the *Zhouli* tells us that the feudal lords came to pay tribute at the court of their own accord. So the expectation that lesser rulers pay tribute to the royal court survived through the Spring and Autumn period (770–481 BCE).[185]

Mao Qiling said, "There was a set order for each person holding a fiefdom to present tribute to the Zhou court. After they were first enfeoffed, at the first of the year they were supposed to dispatch a great officer to make that presentation. After that, they were supposed to regularly dispatch great officers to present tribute. It appears that each fiefholder appeared personally at court only twice over twelve years and dispatched only six tribute missions over that same period of time. The nobles personally appeared at court in the first and seventh years and dispatched tribute missions in the second, fourth, sixth, eighth, tenth, and twelfth years. Those responsible for the lands that provided grain for the royal family appeared at court in the second and eighth years and dispatched tribute missions in the third, fifth, seventh, ninth, and eleventh years. With the exception of the years in which the Zhou ruler visited various domains in his realm, this is the order they followed. This is how they reciprocated the visits of the Zhou ruler to their realms. This is called "reciprocal visits." It is also called "reciprocal missions."[186]

In my opinion, the "Officers of Zhou" section of Mei Ze's version of the *Book of Documents*[187] clearly does not coincide with what the "Senior Messenger" section of the *Zhouli* says. So it is clear that the section in Mei's *Book of Documents* is a fabrication. Mao Qiling was troubled by this. He tried to force what is said in the "Senior Messenger" section to match what is said in the "Offices of Zhou" but in the end he could not hide the fact that they contradicted each other.

What is recorded in the "Royal Regulations" and "Meaning of the Interchange of Missions between Different Courts" chapters in the *Book of Rites*[188] are the corrupted practices of Eastern Zhou and cannot be reconciled with what is recorded in the "Senior Messenger" chapter of the *Zhouli*.[189] Nor can they be reconciled with what is recorded in Mei Ze's "Zhougwan."[190] Mao

Qiling distorted the contents of Mei Ze's version of the *Book of Documents* to try to force it into agreements with those other texts. To do that, he extracted bits and pieces from accounts of the corrupted and confused practices of the Spring and Autumn period and used them to support his argument. (I deleted part of my original argument here.) But that was a waste of ink since his argument does not hold water. I delve into this in detail in my *A Critical Look at Mei Ze's Book of Documents*.[191]

Zhu Xi said, "The line 'To be generous when sending them away but requiring little when they come' refers to providing a substantial feast when sending them off but not requiring much in the way of tribute when they arrive."[192]

Mao Qiling said, "Welcoming an arriving guest with a banquet is the polite thing to do. But that is not done for those who are departing. 'Arriving and departing' refers to the Son of Heaven over the course of twelve years making an inspection tour of the feudal lords six times and also, over the course of those same twelve years, the feudal lords presenting tribute at court six times. In addition to the six imperial visits, the Son of Heaven bestowed meat to be used in sacrificial rituals. An example of this is the Celestial Ruler providing meat to the Marquis of Jin to be used in honoring his ancestors.

"Also, he sent official congratulations on occasions of good fortune. For example, King Ding of Zhou dispatched a high official to offer congratulations to the Marquis of Jin. In the case of a death or a bad harvest, the Son of Heaven consoled the afflicted with relief measures. An example of this is when he dispatched his steward Xuan to provide items for use in a funeral. If there was a disaster or catastrophe, he sent disaster relief. An example of this is when Song was in a dire situation and relief supplies were bestowed upon them. All of these are all examples of what is meant by 'sending off.'

"When it comes to arriving, that refers to the feudal lords personally appearing at court. The nobles presented sacrificial beef and pork. Those responsible for the lands that provided grain directly to the royal family presented silk and linen. Those who came from farther away presented ritual vessels and utensils. Those who came from even farther away presented fine cotton. And those responsible for the defense of the realm on its outer border presented tortoise shells and seashells. Apart from these nine tribute items, jade and robes of silk for betrothal ceremonies were also offered as tribute. In addition, in spring and fall, horses and leather items were presented as tribute. These are all examples of 'arriving.'

"The quantity of the tribute items is not as important as the spirit behind them. As for the welcoming banquet, the chief steward and the reception overseer are responsible for the sacrificial animals and the other food to be used in the welcoming rituals, as well as for escorting the visitors to the banquet. This is the way a welcoming banquet was supposed to be handled. How could this be proper procedure for sending someone off?"[193]

As I recall, regarding the proper ritual for official visits to the court, the *Zuozhuan* says "When they arrive, there is a feast on the outskirts of the capital to compensate them for all the trouble they went to in order to come here. When they departed, they were given gifts to take with them." (*Zuozhuan* Lord Zhao's Fifth Year.)[194] That is what this classic means by "be generous when sending them away." Mao's interpretation is too complicated.[195]

Zhongyong XX: 16

In all undertakings, you must prepare in order to be successful.

Zhu Xi said, "Making oneself unselfishly cooperative and appropriately responsive requires clearly understanding the proper way to behave. Generally speaking, if you are unable to engage in the investigation of things to extend your knowledge so that you truly know the best way to behave, then you will inevitably be unable to love the good the way you love an attractive woman and will be unable to detest what is evil the way you detest a terrible stench."[196]

As I see it, to investigate things means to investigate what is essential and what is non-essential in a particular situation, and to extend knowledge means to learn what is of primary importance and what is of secondary importance in that situation. Investigating things so that you extend your knowledge is not the same as being perfectly clear about the best way to behave. If you clearly understand the proper way to behave, then you will perceive what is hidden and discern what is subtle. You will realize that Heaven can never lead you astray. Only after you truly understand Heaven can you choose the proper way to behave. If you don't understand Heaven, then you will be unable to choose the proper way to behave.[197]

Zhongyong XX: 18

> Acting in an unselfishly cooperative and appropriately responsive manner is the Dao of Heaven.

THE KING ASKED:

Learning to act in an unselfishly cooperative and appropriately responsive manner (*cheng*) stands at the very center of this work, as Zhu Xi has already fully explained in *Huowen*.[198] However, the first fifteen chapters do not explicitly mention acting in an unselfishly cooperative and appropriately responsive manner, since the character *cheng* does not appear at all until the chapter on spirits [Chapter XVI]. Moreover, from the XVIIth chapter all the way to the section preceding this one, again there are no explicit references to acting in an unselfishly cooperative and appropriately responsive manner until we get to this section. Why is that? Moreover, the chapter on spirits only has a single instance of the Sinograph *cheng*. Why does the *cheng* Sinograph appear so many times in this section?

I RESPONDED:

Although the opening chapter does not contain the Sinograph *cheng*, it does discuss being watchful over yourself when no one can know what you are doing and thinking and therefore it refers to the same thing as the Sinograph *cheng* does. We therefore cannot say it does not discuss acting in an unselfishly cooperative and appropriately responsive manner.

The chapter about Yan Hui [Chapter VIII] says that "if he encountered an opportunity to act appropriately, then he held it tight against his chest and refused to let it go." This is an example of *cheng*. The "Acting in Accordance with One's Status" chapter [Chapter XIV] says, "if the archer fails to hit the target, he looks inward and places the blame on himself." This is also an example of *cheng*. When Lord Ai asked Confucius about governing, he replied, "If you want to truly understand how to interact with your fellow human beings, you cannot not know Heaven."[199] This is also a reference to *cheng*. How can we say that the earlier chapters and sections do not discuss being unselfishly cooperative and appropriately responsive? The next section in this chapter says that the five things you have to do to actualize the Dao all boil down to one thing only. This one thing is nothing other than *cheng*. The very next sentence says that there are three ways of acting that are essential to achieving ethical virtuosity. It goes on to say that those three ways [acting wisely, acting benevolently, and acting courageously] all boil down to one way of acting.[200] This one way of acting is *cheng*.

The three ways of acquiring knowledge are not the same, but the knowledge that is acquired is one and the same. It is nothing other than knowing how to act in an unselfishly cooperative and appropriately responsive manner. The three ways people are able to act appropriately are not the same, but what they accomplish is one and the same thing.[201] Their actions are manifestations of *cheng*. The implications of the cardinal rules, mentioned in an earlier section, are unlimited, yet, when they are put into practice, they all boil down to the same thing: *cheng*.[202] So how can we say *cheng* is not discussed very much?

It is worthy of note that the effort required to watch over yourself when no other human being can see what you are doing or thinking relies on your heart-mind being aware of what is extremely subtle. When you are aware of what is extremely subtle, that means you are aware that the Spirit above is watching you. The character *cheng* was inserted into the chapter on the Spirit (Chapter XVI) to show that thinking and acting in an unselfishly cooperative and appropriately responsive manner is the key point of this entire text.

From Shun and King Wen on, whether we are talking about major core issues or minor incidental issues, whether we are talking about something that is wide-ranging or something that is narrowly focused, whether we are talking about a matter that was laid out before us in an orderly fashion or about a matter that presented a multiple array of factors to consider, there is still one thing that has been relevant in every case: *cheng*. Whether you want to engage with the outside world or are not yet ready to do so, whether your emotions are activated or your heart-mind is still, whether you are about to get up or are about to lie down, whether it is hard to see how you should behave in a particular situation or it is easy to see what you should do, in whatever situation that arises, thinking and acting in an unselfishly cooperative and appropriately responsive manner is always what you should do. Even for that one sentence "you need to prepare in order to be successful," the Sinograph *cheng* should be added mentally. Once it is added, you should repeat it over and over again. It will then become like a flower in full bloom radiating a sweet fragrance. How can the Dao of Heaven and the Dao of human beings be anything other than thinking and acting in an unselfishly cooperative and appropriately responsive manner?

Zhu Xi wrote, "The sentence 'Understanding comes from acting in an unselfishly cooperative and appropriately responsive manner' should be counted as the start of chapter XXI."[203] In my opinion, the chapter that begins with "Lord Ai asked about how to govern properly" [XX: 1] should end at the phrase "bollworm wasp [*pulu*]." The next chapter should begin with "Proper government therefore requires appointing the right men." [XX: 4.] It should be followed by a chapter composed of the discussion of the five things you have to do to actualize the Dao in the world. (XX: 8.) The distinction between "Some who understand with a natural ease and some who have to study hard to learn how to act" (XX: 9) should also be treated as a separate chapter. Following that, the section on the nine cardinal rules (XX: 12) should also be treated as a separate chapter. The same goes for the section on "In all undertakings, you must prepare in order to be successful" (XX: 16). The next chapter should begin with "Thinking and acting in an unselfishly cooperative and appropriately responsive manner is the Dao of Heaven" (XX: 18) and end with the section on "Understanding comes from acting in an unselfishly cooperative and appropriately responsive manner" (XXI). That these should be treated as separate chapters is quite clear, since each section deals with a different topic. Zhu Xi, relying too much on the *Kongzi jiayu*, took from "Lord Ai asked about how to govern properly" down to "even the weak will develop the strength to accord with the Way" as one chapter.[204] But this passage in the *Kongzi jiayu* was lifted from the *Zhongyong* and then embellished a bit. It has so many twists and turns in it that it is hard to make any sense of it.

As for the passage in Zhu Xi's Chapter XXI saying that if you are naturally unselfishly cooperative and appropriately responsive, then you will understand how to act, that is a reference to a sage. (That is the Dao of Heaven.) He also mentions those who come to understand how they are supposed to act and become selflessly cooperative and appropriately responsive, saying they do so by holding on tight to what is proper and good. (That is the Dao of human beings.) Human nature [the ability human beings have to act the way human beings should act] is the Dao of Heaven. Becoming educated [learning how we should act] is the Dao of human beings. That is what Zhu Xi's Chapter XXI says, so it clearly belongs with what is written in section XX: 18 about the Dao of Heaven and the Dao of human beings.[205] You cannot separate blood from the arteries it runs through. Nor can you separate vital substances from the bone marrow they are inextricably connected with. I have no idea why anyone could treat what Zhu Xi labels Chapter XXI as a separate chapter.

THE KING ASKED:

Two words used in this chapter, "human nature" and "becoming educated" both refer to people actualizing their true human nature. That is precisely what scholars are supposed to study how to do. What these words mean is rooted in how they are used in the opening chapter. We can say that, within what they have in common, there are differences, and, within their differences, there are commonalities. So why does Zhu Xi only talk about the differences between them?[206] Hu[207] said, "The human nature talked about here is the nature that Heaven has conferred, and being educated here means to engage in the cultivation of the Dao within oneself." Is not this precisely what Zhu Xi said but with a little more detail?

| RESPONDED:

As for the sages Yao and Shun, the human nature they received was conferred on them by Heaven. They were able to naturally act appropriately. Tang and King Wu were not that way at all. They had to learn how to cultivate their innate ability to act appropriately in order to activate their innate moral nature.[208] This being the case, what this chapter means by the two words "human nature" and "being educated" is really no different from what those two words mean in the opening chapter. But this chapter distinguishes between those who naturally know how to act and those who have to learn how to do so. On the other hand, the first chapter links human nature, the Dao, and being educated as intertwined guiding principles of self-cultivation. That is why Zhu Xi said those two characters have different nuances in this chapter than they do in the opening chapter.[209]

Zhang Zai said, "For your ability to act in an unselfishly cooperative and appropriately responsive manner to give you clear insight into how you should act, you have to first fully cultivate your human nature [*xing*, your Heaven-conferred potential for seeing how to act appropriately] by exhaustively investigating the patterns of appropriate behavior in things, processes, and events. To become unselfishly cooperative and appropriately responsive by first gaining a clear understanding of how one should act, you must first exhaustively investigate the patterns of appropriate behavior in things, processes, and events by harnessing the power of your human nature to its fullest extent."[210]

Master Cheng said, "When Zhang Zai said, 'clear understanding of how to act leads to *cheng*,' he is correct. However, when he said, '*cheng* leads to a clear understanding of how to act,' I'm afraid that is not the way it is. After all, *cheng* is precisely nothing other than understanding how you should act."[211]

Lü Dalin said, "Someone who goes directly from *cheng* to understanding clearly how to act is someone who is simply acting according to his innate nature. On the other hand, to go from understanding to *cheng* is the opposite. To be an ethical virtuoso means that you recognize and understand the normative patterns of everything under heaven as though they are right in front of your eyes without having to ponder over them or talk about them. (This refers to someone who goes from *cheng* to understanding clearly how to act.) Those who are determined to improve themselves by studying try to extend their knowledge through an exhaustive investigation of normative patterns. They can finally reach a point where they have no farther to go, since acting appropriately will come easy to them and they will encounter no obstacles to doing so."[212] (This refers to someone who starts from learning how to act to actually acting in a selflessly cooperative and appropriately responsive manners.)

You Zuo said, "Going directly from *cheng* to understanding clearly how to act comes from within. It can therefore be called human nature. Going from understanding to *cheng* requires interacting with the world around you. That is called 'becoming educated.' Those who are naturally able to act in an unselfishly cooperative and appropriately responsive manner are so by nature. That is why there is nothing they do not understand about how to interact with others. Those who over time come to understand how to act do so through self-discipline. That is why they become able to think and act in an unselfishly cooperative and appropriately responsive manner."[213]

Yang Shi said, "Going from *cheng* to moral clarity is the Dao of Heaven. That is why we say that is a manifestation of human nature. To first develop moral clarity and then to go on to be able to think and act in an unselfishly cooperative and appropriately responsive manner is called the Dao of human beings. That is why it is called 'being educated.' The Dao of Heaven and the Dao of human beings are essentially one and the same. How the heart-mind reaches that goal is different, but the destination is the same."[214]

Zhu Xi said, "Zhang Zai took human nature and being educated as two different ways of reaching the same goal, but he did not discuss the qualitative difference between sages and the merely wise. That is why he talked about gaining a clear understanding of how one should act by first being unselfishly cooperative and appropriately responsive. Although Master Cheng Yi did a good job analyzing what Zhang Zai said, he went on to say that *cheng* is precisely nothing other than understanding how you should act. I am afraid that he was unable to avoid making a mistake in saying that. Lü Dalin was correct in distinguishing between *cheng* and being educated. He made a mistake, however, in what he said about all those who are able to act in an unselfishly cooperative and appropriately responsive manner. He said that both sages and the wise will find that acting appropriately will come easy to them and they will encounter no obstacles to doing so. It appears that he missed the main point. Nevertheless, his ideas are far superior to what You Zuo and Yang Shi said."[215] (See *Huowen*.)

In my opinion, what all five men said was pretty much the same. While

Zhu Xi both praises and criticizes their specific formulations, what they are fighting over are differences as thin as a strand of hair. These are not the sort of disputes an ignorant person could engage in. The point Master Cheng Yi and Zhu Xi are making is that, generally speaking, it is through coming to understand how you should act that you become able to think and act in an unselfishly cooperative and appropriately responsive manner. (See the explication on this point.)[216] We can dismiss the contrary notion that moral clarity can arise from *cheng* rather than accompany it. A sage is someone who is able to easily act appropriately because he knows from birth how he should act. A sage does not need to wait until he has exhaustively investigated the normative patterns in things, events, and processes before he can clearly see the normative patterns in the ten thousand things. That is why you cannot say of a sage that he is first able to think and act in an unselfishly cooperative and appropriately responsive manner and after that he is able to see how he should act.

However, when we examine the final two sentences in this section [when you act with *cheng*, you have moral clarity, and when you have moral clarity, you act with *cheng*], when you look at the way the Sinographs in them are organized and how those sentences are constructed, you can see that there really is only a very small difference between them. You can go on all day saying one is correct, but the other is not, or saying that one tells us how things are but the other does not. However, you will not be able to come to an agreement that way. Generally, when you speak of the Dao of an exemplary person, you are talking about the fact that they cannot act properly if they do not know how they should act, and they cannot act the way they should act if they do not know how they should act.

This classic made this point clear in an earlier section, in which we see sentences such as "No one walks the correct path!"[217] and "There are few people who are able to truly know the taste of food."[218] The common man does not think or act in an unselfishly cooperative and appropriately responsive manner, so he can be said to lack understanding of how to behave. (This is saying that you cannot learn how to act properly unless you act properly.) At the same time, we can say that the common man does not understand how to act properly, so he fails to think or act in an unselfishly cooperative and appropriately responsive manner. (This is saying that he does not know how to act properly, so he fails to act properly.)

It is different for sages and the wise. Because they think and act in an unselfishly cooperative and appropriately responsive manner, they gain an even better understanding of how to act. And because they have a clear understanding of how to act, they are able to act in a *cheng* manner. To go from thinking and acting in a *cheng* manner to knowing how to act properly is easy. To go from knowing how to act properly to actually thinking and acting in an unselfishly cooperative and appropriately responsive manner is much more difficult.

However, although sages are born knowing how to act properly, they still have to take care that they act without any taint of selfishness whatsoever [are completely *cheng*]. If they do that, they will be able to see the normative patterns defining appropriate behavior even more clearly, and they will cling to that which is morally good even more closely. So how can we not say that, for them, thinking and acting in an unselfishly cooperative and appropriately responsive manner goes hand in hand with moral clarity, so that you cannot say one comes before the other? Although the sages Yao, Shun, the Duke of Zhou, and Confucius were sages, from the day they were born until the day they died, every day, step by step, they strove to reach even higher levels of sagacity. If sages are born knowing how to act properly yet they do not display increasing ethical virtuosity, then the sentences "The noble man never ceases to strengthen himself"[219] and "King Wen never ceased acting from the purest motives"[220] do not relate at all to their supposed Dao of Heaven.

If, on the other hand, we see an improvement in their mastery of appropriate behavior, then "when you act with *cheng*, you have moral clarity" is one way to think about them. These two sentences are certainly not all that different. But Zhang Zai saying that we have to first fully cultivate our human nature by exhaustively investigating the patterns of appropriate behavior in things, processes, and events is most definitely incorrect. What Zhu Xi says is correct.

The problem with what You Zuo and Yang Shi had to say was that it was not very sophisticated.

Zhongyong XXII

> In All-under-Heaven, only he who is completely unselfishly co-operative and appropriately responsive...

Zhu Xi said, "The nature [*xing*, innate ability to behave appropriately] of other people and things is the same as my nature, but the physical constitutions conferred on each one of us are not the same. There are significant differences. In the case of someone who is able to fully actualize his nature, it can be said that there is nothing that he is not clear about and that in any situation in which he finds himself he does nothing inappropriate."[1]

As I see it, this is a reference to the notion that "patterning principle [*li*] is the same everywhere but psycho-physical natures [*ki*] are different."[2] Zhu Xi, when he commented on the *Zhongyong* and the *Daxue*, always pointed out that *li* is the same everywhere but *ki* varies. Only when he talks about the *Mencius*, in the discussion about the ox, the dog, and the human beings, does he talk about *ki* being the same and *li* being different.[3] Hu Yunfeng explained this apparent discrepancy in detail. (See his *Minor Commentary* on the "Book of Gaozi" chapter of the *Mencius*.)[4] He echoed what Zhu Xi said.[5] Isn't it acceptable to understand words differently according to the contexts they appear in?

Zhu Xi's intention is to point out that, when we talk about what heaven has conferred on the myriad things, we should say they all partake of the same *li* [they all share in, and are essential components of, the universal network of appropriate interactions].[6] However, the physical characteristics animals are given [their *ki*], such as feathers, fur, scales, and shells, are different from what we see in human beings. That is why he says their *ki* is different.

However, the discussion in *Mencius* about differences between human beings, dogs, and oxen is not using those terms that way. Instead, it says that they all partake of the same *ki* [psychophysical stuff] that allows them to perceive their environment and move around. On the other hand, they are different in terms of their ability to act in an unselfish, righteous, polite, or wise manner. That is why we can say their *li* is different.[7] Zhu Xi has good reasons for saying in one case that *ki* is different but *li* is the same and in other cases saying that *ki* is the same and *li* is different.

In saying that *li* is the same in animals and human beings, he is not just saying that the natural potential Heaven conferred on them comes from the same source. He is also saying that *li*, the endowment of a natural ability to perceive things and interact with them appropriately, is essentially the same in humans and animals. However, because their psychophysical constitutions are very different from those of human beings, he argues that animals are unable to fully actualize their potential to act appropriately in all four major ways and are only able to do so in partial, incomplete ways.[8] This is not all that different from what Buddhists mean when they talk about the reflection of the moon in a pond [as a pale reflection of the actual moon].

Zhu Xi also accepts the concept of an "original nature" found in the *Shoulengyan*[9] and says our human nature should be called our "original nature." However, "original nature" is not what Heaven has conferred, and what Heaven has conferred is not the "original nature." I'm afraid that this is not even worth discussing. It is as ridiculous as what Zhuangzi says about tigers and wolves having proper father-son relationships.[10] This clearly is nothing more than a fable. Tigers and wolves do not even form family units. This is different from what we see in the behavior of such birds as *yuan* birds, mandarin ducks, swallows, and sparrows. Even if a tiger were endowed with the same potential for unselfish filial piety as Zhu Shouchang displayed,[11] how can it know who its father is? Moreover, tigers and wolves are fundamentally not the same beast. The tiger is a beast of brilliant colors. The wolf is a beast with a long snout. If I said these two beasts were both filial sons, it would be ridiculous to believe me.

The sentence "in any situation in which he finds himself he does nothing inappropriate"[12] truly can also refer to the concrete result of fully actualizing the nature of animals, but that does not mean the same thing as fully actualizing human nature. As for the sentence "there is nothing that he is not clear about,"[13] I'm afraid it cannot be applied to both human beings and animals. Why do I say that? If I understand my own human nature, then I understand the human nature of all human beings. I do not need to take any additional steps. When it comes to the nature of animals, if I know in general how animals tend to behave, I can rest assured that I know how to interact with them. There is no need to exhaustively investigate their behavior so that I learn every little detail of how they behave. I will still be able to control them the way Yi controlled the wild animals in the forests for Emperor Shun.[14]

THE KING ASKED:

Are the fundamental natures of human beings and animals the same or different? If we say they are different, then how can we reconcile that with the fact that in this chapter in the three different contexts in which the word "nature" appears, that term appears to mean "the fundamental nature of all things." Moreover, in the three contexts in which the Sinograph meaning "fully actualize" appears, it has the same meaning each time [of fully actualizing that fundamental nature]. How can we reconcile that with saying the fundamental natures of human beings and animals are different? What if we assume they are the same? Then, although this chapter goes on to speak of "fully actualizing the fundamental nature of animals," even the Sage cannot make an animal behave like a human being. So how can we say they share the same basic nature?

| RESPONDED:

There are three levels of fundamental nature [innate ability]. It is the nature of grasses and trees to be alive, but they are unable to perceive anything. It is the nature of birds and beasts to be alive and also to be aware of their surroundings. It is the nature of us humans to not only be alive and be aware of our surroundings but also to be able to think and to pursue the moral good.[15] Those three levels, the vegetative, the animal, and the human, are not at all the same. When this classic therefore talks about "fully actualizing their nature," it is not referring to the same potential being actualized.

For grasses and trees, getting them to actualize their full natural potential is nothing more than causing them to grow and flourish. For birds and beasts—getting them to actualize their full natural potential is nothing more than causing them to be born or hatched so that they can run or fly, as that is their nature. In ancient times, there were ways to cultivate those things that lived in mountains and forests, and in streams and wetlands. You had to prune the plants at the proper times. You also had to protect the animals from harm and not engage in overkill. That is all you had to do to make sure they all realized their full potential. The *Book of Songs* says, "Strong and abundant grow the rushes / He discharges but one arrow at five wild boars."[16] This tells us that the caretaker of the Royal Preserve was able to completely fulfil the duties of his office and cause the grasses and trees, birds and beasts to be fruitful and multiply. The Sage's helping things fully actualize their natural potential is nothing more than things like this. Is it possible to cause a horse, cow, sheep, or pig to love its parents and respect its elders, which are both things that human beings do? When Zhu Xi said that people and animals have the same fundamental nature, he was saying nothing more than that they all were endowed with that nature by Heaven. How could he have meant that it is possible to teach birds and beasts to act like human beings? (My earlier answer contained an error which I have now corrected.)

Mao Qiling said, "The 'Ceremonial Usages' chapter of the *Book of Rites* says, 'the birds do not fly from phoenixes in terror if phoenixes have been domesticated' and 'the wild beasts do not scamper away from the unicorn if the unicorn has been domesticated.'[17] This is what is meant by causing animals to reach their full potential."[18]

In my opinion, there is a lot in that passage in "Ceremonial Usages" that does not make any sense. I fear it was added by some so-called "Confucians" at the end of the Qin dynasty. When sages cause animals to actualize their basic nature, they simply cause them to be fruitful and multiply, nothing more. Is it necessary for someone to tame a fierce animal so that it no longer frightens anyone or anything before we can call them a sage? There is a line in the *Zhouli* that says one of the officials of Zhou was an animal tamer [*fubushi*] who was responsible for taming wild animals.[19] All he did, though, was nothing more than keeping those animals in an enclosure where they could be observed. If you want to take all the wild animals all over the world and transform them completely so that they conform to the way of the ancient kings, that is something even Yao or Shun would find difficult to do.[20] Therefore, when the Duke of Zhou "drove the tigers, leopards, rhinoceroses, and elephants far away,"[21] he did not even try to tame them.[22]

Zhongyong XXIII

> Those below that level[1] are those who are able to extend their efforts to that which is most detailed and complicated [曲 C. *qu* / K. *kok*].

Zhu Xi said, "The phrase 'those below that level' refers to those who are merely wise and highly capable, and also to those inferior to them in ability."[2]

As I recall, "Yao and Shun were the sages they were from birth; King Tang of the Shang and King Wu of Zhou had to recover their original potential."[3] Yao and Shun are men at the top level. Those just below them are Kings Tang and Wu. Despite this, in the end King Tang and King Wu displayed the same totally unselfish cooperation and appropriate responses we see in sages. Those who are unselfishly cooperative and appropriately responsive and therefore see clearly how they should behave are sages. However, those who see clearly the way they should behave and therefore act in an unselfishly cooperative and appropriately responsive manner are also sages. How can you say the highly capable and wise form the second level? If we say that in their early years they were merely among the wisest and most capable, but at the end of their lives they became sages, then whether we call them a sage or a wise man is determined after they die. Therefore no one can be said to be one of the wisest and most capable when they are young.

Zheng Xuan said, "The Sinograph *qu* means very small (trivial or minor) matters."[4]

Zhu Xi said, "The expression 'to extend their efforts' here means to push to the limit. *Qu* means partial. Generally speaking, everyone has the same fundamental nature [*xing*]. However, their physical endowment differs. It is only the sage who is able to fully activate his natural potential, being all that he possibly can be. The next level of people have to activate that part of themselves that constitutes the sprouts of the good, and then expand and extend it in order to become the best person they can be."[5]

Let me point out that *qu* actually means complicated. It also refers to the minute ins-and-outs of some situation. "To extend efforts to that which is most detailed and complicated" means to focus your heart-mind on even the minutest and most complicated details of situations you find yourself involved in. That is what *qu* means in the line in the *Book of Rites* that refers to the "three thousand minute rules of ritual."[6] Zhu Xi has said that human beings and animals both participate in the network of patterns of acting appropriately (*li*) but have different physical endowments (*ki*), and here as well he says that the sage and the wise and highly capable have the same *li* and different *ki*. How can we accept that? The *Book of Documents* says, "The wise, by not thinking, become foolish, and the foolish, by thinking, become wise."[7] This clearly means that the fundamental nature [*xing*] as well as the physical endowments of the wise and the foolish are essentially the same. How can we say instead that their basic physical endowments are different? Parsing *qu* as meaning partial is not supported by anything in the ancient texts.

You Zuo said, "Those who are naturally able to act in an unselfishly cooperative and appropriately responsive manner do so without having to think about it or work hard at it. They simply let their heart-mind direct their actions. 'Those below that level' refers to those who have to think before they speak. They cannot just blurt out whatever they are thinking. And when they are getting ready to do something, they have to think and decide the best way to act. They cannot recklessly act without thinking. Therefore, when this passage says 'extend efforts to that which is most detailed and complicated,' it means to reflect on even the smallest and most complicated details of what should be done. Once you have clarified the correct course of action, then you will be able to arouse the masses to act in accordance with it. Once they begin acting in accordance with this clear picture of what is proper, then it will be easy to change their habitual way of acting for the better."[8]

As I see it, although what You Zuo said is not very clear, when he talks about arousing the masses to change their usual ways of acting, he is talking about how to go about transforming the people so that their customary behavior changes for the better. This is the same goal as we see in the sentences "get other human beings to actualize their full natural potential [*xing*]" and "get animals to actualize their full natural potential." This is the fundamental point of this classic.

THE KING ASKED:

As for the Sinograph *qu* in the phrase [which some read as "that which is most detailed and complicated" and others read as "that which is only partially actualized"], when I looked in the old dictionaries, I did not see it defined as "partial." Yet Zhu Xi glosses it that way. What are we to make of this? If we read the first phrase in this section as saying that we need to extend what is partially activated so that it is completely activated, then we would expect the second phrase to say we need to "extend" our ability to act in a *cheng* manner. However, the Sinograph *qu* appears again instead of "extend." That would appear to mean "if you pay proper attention to even the minutest details, you will be able to act in a *cheng* manner." How are we to understand this? When You Zuo said *qu* means paying close attention to even the minutest and most complicated details, it looks to me that he is faithful to both the meaning of the individual Sinographs in this passage as well as to the context. Yet Zhu Xi criticizes You, accusing him of misunderstanding this passage. Is this only because they each preferred to understand that passage in their own way?

| RESPONDED:

Zhu Xi understood the chapter immediately preceding this one to be about the Dao of Heaven and this chapter to be about the Dao of human beings. The preceding chapter talks of "going from acting in a *cheng* manner to having moral clarity" and this chapter talks of "going from having moral clarity to acting in a *cheng* manner." Although there are slight differences between those two sentences, in the end they both refer to acting in a perfectly unselfishly cooperative and appropriately responsive manner. Since acting in a perfectly *cheng* manner is the same in each case, then they both end up with people who are sages. So to say that the next level, those who extend their efforts to that which is the most detailed and complicated, consists of merely the wisest and most capable but not sages, I'm afraid that is not correct.

Moreover, to say that the sage is someone who has been endowed with a perfect physical endowment but a wise and highly capable man has to work with a flawed physical endowment, so that the sage is able to be a sage because he has been endowed from birth with the ability to be everything a human being can possibly be but a merely wise and highly capable man has to begin with less than that ability fully actualized, I'm afraid, is also totally incorrect.

Zhu Xi once said that we human beings are endowed with a complete psychophysical endowment, but animals do not get everything we get.[9] But here he seems to be saying that the physical endowments of sages and the merely wisest and most capable men are not the same, with one being perfect and the other as somewhat lacking. Why is he not somewhat uneasy saying that? To gloss *qu* as partial, one-sided, or incomplete goes beyond what is seen in the *sancang*.[10] Although You Zuo's point that *qu* means "complicated and detailed" is not especially clear, still he got the basic point of this text right.[11]

Zhongyong XXIV

The Dao of being perfectly selflessly cooperative and appropriately responsive makes it possible to see what lies ahead.

Kong Yingda said, "Something that a kingdom originally had but is now different is called an auspicious sign; something it originally did not have but now has is called a good omen. He Yin (of Jin)[1] said, 'The kingdom originally had a common sparrow; now there is a red bird that comes into the kingdom, and this is "auspicious." The kingdom originally did not have a phoenix, but now there is a phoenix that has appeared, and this is 'a good omen.'"[2]

Chen Ziceng[3] points out that *Zuozhuan* says, "When things have been pushed out of place by the earth, it is a sign that something bad is going to happen,"[4] And he adds that the *Shuowen* says, "when strange things happen with clothing, songs, and vegetation, that is a bad omen. When strange things happen to wild animals and locusts, that is a sign of an impending disaster."[5] In my opinion, these statements are too inflexible.

Zheng Xuan said, "The reference [in this chapter] to the 'four limbs' refers to the four feet of the tortoise. At the spring prognostication, we look at the rear left leg; at the summer prognostication, we check out the front left leg; at the autumn prognostication, it is the front right leg we examine; at the winter prognostication, it is the rear right leg."[6]

Zhu Xi said, "The 'four limbs' refers to the dignified bearing of the movements of the ritual performer, like the way he holds the piece of jade high or low, and the way he lifts his head high or looks downward, and so on."[7]

(It is recorded in the *Zuozhuan* for Lord Ding's 14th Year[8] that "Lord Yin of Zhu paid a visit to Lord Ding's court. Lord Yin lifted the jade up high while looking upward. Lord Ding accepted the jade with his hands held low while looking downward. Zigong said, 'When you look at their actions from the perspective of ritual propriety, it appears both of these rulers will soon face death or exile.'"[9] That very same year Lord Ding died. In the 7th year of Lord Ai of Lu, Lu attacked Zhu, captured Yi [Lord Yin], the ruler of Zhu, and brought him [to exile] to Lu.)[10]

Mao Qiling said, "The *Spring and Autumn Annals* has many examples of this, like Hui of Jin receiving ceremonial jade in a lackadaisical manner, Qu Xia of Chu stepping high as he walked, Lord Chengsu in Zhou accepting the sacrificial meat without due reverence, Lord Li of Jin walking with a broad stride while staring off into the distance, Xi Yi of Jin begging the state of Lu for troops, and Xi Chou accepting an invitation to a banquet from the ruler of Wei. All of these men were arrogant and did not display proper decorum."[11]

I would like to point out that what Zheng Xuan said is too simple. Zhu Xi has corrected him.

The King asked:

What this chapter says about foreknowledge, does not, I'm afraid, match the meaning of the earlier chapters, nor does it come close to the points made in the chapters that follow. Why does it talk about this? Can you clarify how it relates to what we see in the chapters that precede and follow it?

I responded:

The previous chapter about "extending your efforts into the complicated and minute details of situations you find yourself in" is all about the difference between the Dao of Heaven and the Dao of human beings. That being the case, what is called the Dao of Heaven refers to a sage who is born knowing what to do, and what is called the Dao of human beings refers to the sage who has to learn what to do. Their ability to act in a perfectly cooperative and responsive manner matches the way heaven acts, so we call it the Dao of Heaven. It does not mean that they actually have the same power Heaven has.

Zhu Xi misunderstood the "Knowing What Lies Ahead" chapter as discussing the Dao of Heaven and the chapter that follows, "Realizing Your Full Potential," as discussing the Dao of humans.[12] This is mixing up the Dao of Heaven with the Dao of humans. If we look at [his commentary on] the last chapter of this classic [Chapter XXXIII], he appears to take the Dao of Heaven as merely the way Heaven operates.[13] I'm afraid that is a mistake. When this chapter talks of seeing what lies ahead, it is only extolling how much being perfectly unselfishly cooperative and appropriately responsive can accomplish. It is probably not necessary to link this chapter too closely with what follows it.[14]

Zhu Xi said, "Some of the things Master Cheng said drew on unacceptable teachings. (I note that Master Cheng said just because seeing what lies ahead of us is something Buddha talked about, we can't dismiss it as something that originated with some strange fellow.)[15] For example, he said people like the eccentric hermit of Mt. Shu, Dong Wujing, were able to see into the future." (See *Huowen*.)[16]

As I see it, those who are perfectly unselfishly cooperative and appropriately responsive will be able to understand the workings of heaven.[17] If they understand how heaven operates, then they will be able to know in advance what is going to happen.

The Sage is able, therefore, to "act before Heaven does without fear that Heaven will oppose him; he may act after Heaven does, but he will do so only in line with the timing of Heaven."[18] The Duke of Zhou understood Heaven. That is how he knew that Zhou would inevitably overcome Shang and did not take any prior action to agitate Shang. Guan and Cai[19] did not understand Heaven very well. They did not understand, therefore, that states rose and fell in accordance with the mandate of Heaven and tried to help Wu Geng[20] restore the Shang. What is referred to as "foreknowledge" can be seen in cases like this. As for people like Dong Wujing of Mt. Shu, they rely on all sorts of dishonest tricks and illusions. If they know something is going to happen in advance, they use that information to bewitch and delude the ignorant masses. How can you possibly speak of this in the same breath with the foreknowledge of those who are able to do so because they are perfectly *cheng* [in tune with the cosmos]? If you call what they claim to know to be "foreknowledge," you are raising Guo Pu,[21] Guan Lu,[22] and Li Chunfeng[23] to the same status as a sage who is perfectly unselfishly cooperative and appropriately responsive [*cheng*]. That is unspeakable![24]

Zhongyong XXV

> To act in an unselfishly cooperative and appropriately responsive manner [*cheng*] actualizes one's full potential.

Zhu Xi said, "Being what they should be and doing what they should do without any concern for personal benefit (*cheng*) is how things become what they should be and do what they should do." He also said, "All things-under-heaven are what they should be and do what they should do because the concrete dynamic patterns of appropriate interactions that define and direct what they should be and what they should do are already complete within them. Those defining patterning principles, therefore, are prior to the actual thing, event, or process those principles define. They provide all the dynamic patterning principles it needs. ('All it needs' means it possesses the complete set of those defining and directing principles.) Since a thing, event, or process has all the patterning principles that it needs to make it what it is and do what it does, nothing needs to be added to it."[1] ("All it needs," repeated twice by Zhu Xi in this passage, should be read here as meaning completion, as in "from start to completion.")

As I see it, the things, events, and processes referred to here are the same "thing" that is referred to in the line in the *Daxue* that says that "all things have their roots and branches." And the phrase "from start to completion" is like the next sentence in the *Daxue*, which says "all human affairs have a beginning and an end."[2] What a sage has learned is nothing more than to how to actualize his own full potential and cause other things to realize their full potential as well. The *Daxue* and *Zhongyong* do not have two different goals. If there were two goals promoted in those two works, then there would be two Dao. How could there be two Dao? People of today read the *Daxue* as concrete and practical but read the *Zhongyong* as if it were enigmatic and vague. It is truly the case that, because some earlier Confucians thought of the *Zhongyong* as making broad sweeping statements, they did not catch its meaning.

"Actualizing your full potential" is the starting point. To do that, you focus inward. "Having things actualize their full potential" is the end point. To do that, you focus on the world around you. How can it be the case that something is all it should be and should do before it is alive, and that when it falls short of being all it can be and doing all it can do that it dies?

What Zhu Xi said implies that the patterning principles that Heaven on High instills in something when that thing emerges into existence makes that thing everything it should be and should do. As a result, the patterning principles that Heaven on High endows things with have neither a beginning nor an end. They would be the same now as they were in the past. But does it make any sense to say "since the patterning principles defining and directing what something can be and should do are already complete within that thing from the beginning, that thing is accordingly already a finished product"? If Heaven became barren and the earth grew old and infertile, and no more things were being produced, the dynamic patterning principles from Heaven would be unable to be fully actualized. How can we say that, if all the dynamic patterning principles that define what something should be and should do are complete within a thing, then that thing is already everything it should be and has done everything it should do?[3]

Zhu Xi said, "The dynamic patterns directing interactions in Heaven and on Earth are real and the absurd idea that they might stop operating even for a moment has no basis in reality. Therefore, from ancient times up until now, there has been no actual thing, event, or process that is not real,[4] and in the midst of each thing, event, or process, from its beginning until its end, are [in their entirety] all the dynamic patterns that make things real [define and direct what they should be and what they should do]."[5]

As I see it, the *Zhongyong* very clearly takes actualizing one's full potential and making other things actualize their full potential as the starting point and the end point respectively. There is not one iota of difference from what the *Daxue* means when it says, "human affairs have a beginning and an end."[6] How could all the dynamic patterning principles that produce the Ten Thousand Things be already complete within me?

Mao Qiling said, "The 'Proceedings of Government in the Different Months' chapter of the *Book of Rites* says, 'withered grass becomes fireflies.'[7] This chapter means that when something has exhausted its patterning principles, it dies. When the grass has withered, therefore, it changes into fireflies. The time when one set of patterning principles has run its course and that which it was defining and directing dies is precisely the time when something else is brought to life by its own defining and directing principles. I cannot tell when a set of dynamic patterning principles will animate a thing or when those patterning principles will run their course."[8]

I would like to point out that Xiaoshan [Mao Qiling], in this case, takes the beginning and ending of things, events, and processes as the beginning and ending of the myriad things. That is a mistake.

Hu Bingwen wrote, "Zigong said, 'You learn but always feel you need to learn more—that shows your wisdom. You teach without growing tired of doing so—that shows your true humanity.'[9] The way this passage [in the *Zhongyong*] talks of wisdom and true humanity is slightly different.[10] Zhu Xi said, 'What Zigong talked about put emphasis on wisdom. What Zisi talked about put emphasis on behavior.'"[11]

In my opinion, to know how to cultivate your own person so that you become the best person you can be is what is meant by wisdom, and caring deeply about others is what acting in a fully human manner [*in* 仁] means. This is what Zigong meant when he focused on wisdom. To be earnest and sincere in the way you interact with your fellow human beings is being fully human. Having a clear understanding of what the essence of the Dao is, is what we can call wisdom. This is the key point of the *Zhongyong*.

Zhu Xi said, "When you act with wisdom and show concern for others according to the particulars of the situation you find yourself in, then you are applying wisdom and being appropriately fully human."[12]

Someone asked, "as for acting appropriately according to the particulars of the situation, are you referring to Yan Hui shutting his door rather than going out in improper dress to intervene in an argument among his neighbors, and to Yu and Houji rushing to help someone though they were not properly attired, since their caps were pulled over their unbound hair."[13] Zhu Xi said, "Yes, that is what it means."[14]

I would like to point out that this reference to "acting with wisdom and caring for others according to the particulars of the situation you find yourself in" is immediately followed, after a chapter break, by the sentence "those who act in a perfectly unselfishly cooperative and appropriately responsive manner never stop doing so." Why is that? It is because there is no time when it is not appropriate to act wisely and care for others according to the particular of the situation. (See what I say in *Chungyong chajam* about this.)[15]

THE KING ASKED:

Why does this chapter say that causing other people and things to actualize their full potential is an example of knowing what to do? Is this contrasting the Sinograph for knowing what to do [*zhi* 知] with the Sinograph for acting fully human? If that is the case, should not this text have used the Sinograph that means "wisdom" [智] rather than the one that means "knowledge"?

I RESPONDED:

"Those who act in a fully human manner [showing that they care for others] do so because they are comfortable with doing so. Those who act appropriately because they know they should do so, do so because they know that is a useful way to act."[16] "Those who truly care for others enjoy mountains. Those who are knowledgeable enjoy rivers."[17] Caring for others and acting wisely are essentially the same sort of action. Why is there any need to interpret them differently?[18]

Zhongyong XXVI: 1

> Therefore, those who act in a perfectly unselfishly cooperative and appropriately responsive manner never stop doing so.

You Zuo said, "The line that says that 'those who act in a perfectly unselfishly cooperative and appropriately responsive manner [*cheng*] will never stop acting in that fashion' is a reference to the power of Heaven. It is just like the pure power we see in King Wen.[1] However, it is not possible to be consistently perfectly unselfishly cooperative and appropriately responsive. But you can keep trying to do so. A superior person is someone who never gives up trying to act like Yan Hui, whose heart-mind for three months at a time did not stray from the path followed by someone who is fully human."[2]

Yang Shi said, "To never stop acting that way is the defining characteristic of being unselfishly cooperative and appropriately responsive. To never stop trying to act in an unselfishly cooperative and appropriate responsive manner is the way in which we internalize acting in an unselfishly cooperative and appropriate responsive manner."[3]

Zhu Xi remarked, "You Zuo's and Yang Shi's distinction between 'consistently unselfishly cooperative and appropriately responsive' and 'never stopping trying to be unselfishly cooperative and appropriately responsive' is not quite right."[4] (See *Huowen*.)

As I see it, "consistently acting in an unselfishly cooperative and appropriately responsive manner" refers to being focused and in harmony with your surroundings all the time. What "consistently" means here should be obvious. If you are not clear about what it means here, that means you have not examined this statement carefully enough and have misunderstood it.

Zhu Xi said, "If you maintain internally a selfless and appropriately responsive attitude for a long time, then the positive effect on the outside world will be far-reaching."[5]

Let me point out that the Sinograph linking two clauses with the meaning "since it is...then..." [則 C. *ze* / K. *ch'ik*] appears five times in this first section in Chapter XXVI describing the effect of constant selflessness and appropriate responsiveness. Each time that Sinograph means the same thing. These clauses are all connected, like pearls on a string. Each use of that Sinograph clarifies the connection between what precedes it and what follows it. In *Zhongyong zhangju*, Zhu Xi takes everything after the phrase "will be far-reaching," as referring only to the impact on the outside world.[6] I am afraid this is not right. If the impact is far-reaching on the outside, would it not also have a cumulative far-reaching effect internally? Zhu Xi's explanation is not quite right.

The reason for this mistake is that Zhu Xi accepted the interpretation Zheng Xuan provided: "The power of perfect selflessness and responsiveness is clearly manifest in all four directions."[7] But are not these five uses of the phrase "since it is…then…" reinforcing each other? (Zhu Xi said, "The various schools often put forward various stages of making progress toward developing moral virtuosity. But perfect selflessness and appropriate responsiveness are alone sufficient. Why do they need to add additional stages? There is no need to distinguish between within and without. There is no need to change the ancient commentary.")[8] The sentence in this chapter reading "When this selflessness and appropriate responsiveness lasts a long time, it definitely has an effect" means that if you preserve such an attitude for a long time, then it will definitely have a long-term quieting effect on your heart-mind. Therefore, you will come to have greater self-confidence and will make progress toward developing a moral character. That is why the effect is said to be far-reaching.[9]

Zhongyong XXVI: 7

> The Dao of Heaven and Earth can be completely encapsulated in a single word.

The two sections below should be separated from the rest of Chapter XXVI and treated as a separate chapter.

This section says that the reason that Heaven and Earth are so far superior to the rest of us and are so productive lies in the fact that they are not of two minds. Not being of two minds means they operate in an unselfishly cooperative and appropriately responsive manner. The sage gains his ethical virtuosity by acting in harmony with Heaven and Earth. When you discuss the ethical virtuosity of the sage, therefore, you have to talk about the Dao of Heaven and Earth at the same time.[10]

Zhu Xi said, "No one knows how they produce so many living things."[11] In my opinion, "no one knows" means "no one can calculate how much they produce."

Lou Xiangming[12] said, "The term *chen* [辰] that appears in this chapter does not refer here to the three primary types of celestial bodies, the Sun, the Moon, and the stars.[13] Nor does it in this particular context refer to the fifth hour of the day. And, in this line, it does not refer to the *chen* that is fifth of the twelve terrestrial branches used to name years, months, and hours. The *Zuozhuan* says that *chen* means where the sun and the moon cross paths on the first day of every lunar month.[14] In other words, it refers to a designated location along a celestial path.[15] This is what it means here. But the twelve designated locations are not always given in the same order.

"The cycle of Jupiter stations begins in the eleventh month under the first terrestrial branch [*diji* 地支], which is *zi* [子], and ends in the tenth month under the twelfth terrestrial branch, which is *hai* [亥] [with each month associated with one of the twelve terrestrial branches as well as with one of the Jupiter stations]. In the 'Lülizhi' [Musical pitches and the calendar] chapter of the *Book of Former Han*, we see the twelve Jupiter stations placed in the following order: *Xingji, Xuanxiao, Zouzi, Jianglou, Daliang, Shichen, Chunshou, Chunhou, Chunwei, Shouxing, Dahuo,* and *Ximu*.[16] However, in his commentary on the *Book of Documents*, Ma Rong (79–166) has that cycle begin with the terrestrial branch *zi* under the Jupiter station *Xuanxiao*. He goes on to say that Jupiter then passes through *Xingji* under the terrestrial branch *Chou* [丑] and *Ximu* under the terrestrial branch *yin* [寅] and then goes all the way back up through the rest of the list of Jupiter stations, ending at *Zouzi* under the terrestrial branch *hai*.[17] He reverses the order [of the Jupiter stations seen in the *History of the Former Han Dynasty*]. I do not know which order is correct."[18]

Mao Qiling noted, "There is a line in this chapter referring to the earth being strong enough to support Mt. Hua and Mt. Yue and contain rivers and oceans. According to the 'Zhifang shi' chapter of *Zhouli,* there are nine mountain garrisons in total, with the one in Yu Province south of the Yellow River called Mount Hua, and the mountain garrison in Yong Province directly to the west called Mount Yue.[19] The *Erya* says in regard to the Five Sacred Mountains that 'Mount Hua is south of the Yellow River. Mount Yue is west of the Yellow River.'"[20]

In my opinion, Mao has correctly identified those mountains.

THE KING ASKED:

The sentence in this chapter saying "The earth supports all the water in the rivers and seas without letting any leak out" is a good one to analyze. Water in any sort of container is a material substance. If none of it leaks out, then whatever holds it will fill up. If it fills up, it then overflows. However, since the beginning of time, thousands of rivers and streams have flowed into the oceans, yet none of that water has been seen to leak out or overflow out of those oceans. How can this be?

The popular notion that there is an outlet at the bottom of the Eastern Sea for all that water to flow through and disappear is not supported by anything we can read in the classics.[21] On the other hand, this does appear to coincide with Zhu Xi's notion that things are constantly coming and going out of existence. Zhu Xi also appears to believe that the earth floats above ocean waters flowing beneath it.[22] If we accept the former theory, then water does leak out of the sea, and if we accept the latter suggestion, then earth does not hold the oceans but rather the oceans hold the earth. Either way, that would mean Zisi was totally wrong when he writes in this chapter that the earth contains all that water without leaking a single drop.

This chapter says, "heaven is filled with small points of light," and "earth is composed of many handfuls of dirt." Zhu Xi warns that we should not take those words literally.[23] In that case, "earth supports all the water in the rivers and seas without letting any leak out" does not have to be taken literally, either. If it is true that the earth floats above ocean water, then we cannot say "earth supports the water," can we? If it is true that water escapes through a hole in the ocean floor, we cannot say "the water does not leak out," can we?

I RESPONDED:

Your humble servant would say the first thing to do would be to make clear the notion that the earth is round.[24] Then we can see that it is reasonable to say that it holds the ocean water without any leaking out. When your humble servant looked at the *Zhoubijing*,[25] I noticed that it says that beneath the North Pole, there are plants that flourish in the morning and die in the evening. It also says that beneath the Equator, there are grains that are harvested twice in a single year.[26] If something flourishes in the morning and dies in the evening, then a day and a night is as a year for it. If something is harvested twice in a single year, then the periods when the sun is at its northernmost and southernmost points are its two winters.

The *Erya* says that in the south the sun is supported by Mt. Danxue, and in the north, the North Star is supported by Mount Kongdong.[27] The Sun and the North Star both lie within the sphere that is the arc of heaven. What is beneath that arc must take the same shape. So how can we not say that the earth is round?

The *Suwen* [Pure Questions] section of the *Huangdi nejing* says, "The North Star is located in the center of Heaven."[28] This agrees totally with what the *Erya* says. Dan Juli asked Master Zeng, "I dare to ask about the many problems entailed by the notions that Heaven in round and the earth is square." Master Zeng replied, "If Heaven is round and Earth is square, Heaven would not cover the four corners of Earth."[29] This is completely in accord with what the *Zhoubijing* says.

This being the case, it is certain that the earth is round. Moreover, it fits like the missing half of a tally what this chapter says about the earth supporting Mt. Hua and Mt. Yue as well as containing the oceans and rivers. How can anyone say the earth floats in water! As for this noncanonical notion that there is a hole in the bottom of the sea through which water leaks out, it is not worth discussing. Since the earth is round, water naturally follows the curvature of the earth and flows downward, which would not happen if the earth were not round. All the water on earth flowing into the oceans is just following the curvature of the earth. Isn't that how it is able to flow continuously day and night without, in the end, filling up the oceans and rivers, causing them to overflow?

There is a reason that things that do not reproduce themselves nevertheless exist in massive quantities. Where does the water of the rivers and streams come from? The sea is not constantly overflowing, and the rivers and seas are not constantly running dry. Isn't it a fact that, though water constantly flows from here to there and back again, the total amount of water never changes? Moreover, the water in the sea is always salty and the water on land is always fresh. Surely there is some explanation for how fresh water becomes salt water. These days when we dig into mountain soil to erect a fortress, we frequently find caverns. Clearly a lot of those caverns are connected underground. We can assume that seawater enters cracks in the earth, ends up in those caverns, then gradually moves up toward the open air. It leaves its salt behind in the soil as it moves upward and becomes fresh water as it reaches open air. That is how, your humble servant has heard, that people living on the coast are able to harvest salt. They protect part of the shoreline against the morning and evening tides. The stagnant water in those salty pools gradually clears up and becomes fresh water when, after only a few years, the salt that was in that water sinks deep into the ground. Then crops can be grown in what had been a salt pond. This is indisputable proof that salt separates from water and returns to the soil from whence it came. In Zisi's time this fact was already clear. That's why he wrote, "Earth supports the rivers and seas without letting any of it leak out." (I took this argument word for word from what Yi Tŏkcho [Yi Pyŏk] wrote on this subject.)

    Zhu Xi said "*Zhen* [振] here is equivalent to 'collect.'"[30]

    As I see it, here *zhen* is equivalent to 'hold up or support.'"

Zhongyong XXVI: 10

> The *Book of Songs* says, "That which Heaven confers—Its majesty is eternal."³¹

Master Cheng said, "That which is pure is one thing only and is not mixed with anything else. That which is eternal has no breaks in its operation, nor does it have a beginning or end."³²

In my opinion, "that which is pure" refers to the ethical virtuosity displayed in composed, focused, and cooperative behavior. That which "has no breaks in its operation" is a reference to *yong* [庸 constant consistency].³³

Zhongyong XXVII: 1

> Great, indeed, is the Dao of the Sage!

Zhu Xi said, "This speaks of the Dao being so extremely small that there are no breaks in it at all."[1]

As I see it, we should say the three hundred major rules of ritual and three thousand minor rules of etiquette are important, so what does Zhu Xi mean by "extremely small" here?[2] The "Extending Far and Wide and Yet Hidden" chapter says, "to say 'small' in this context means there is nothing able to cut it up and make it smaller."[3] This tells us the Heavenly Way is subtle and hidden. Because there are things even a sage cannot know fully, in this case "extremely small" means the Dao has no material form so it cannot be taken apart and analyzed. Although the three thousand minor rules of etiquette are extremely precise and detailed, they all define actions in the material world and therefore take concrete form. That's why they can serve as specific models of behavior and can be grasped. How could they have no interruptions in their performance or be unable to be analyzed into their constituent parts?

THE KING ASKED:

This chapter says, "Major rules number three hundred and minor rules number three thousand." *Zhongyong zhangju* takes the major rules to mean the major procedures for ceremonial rituals and the minor rules to mean the minutiae of etiquette.[4] But if we go paragraph by paragraph through the various classics of ritual and etiquette, can we find every single one of those three hundred major rules of ritual and three thousand minor rules of etiquette?

I RESPONDED:

The "three hundred" rules of ritual and "three thousand" rules of etiquette are just rough approximations to suggest large numbers. They are not meant to be taken literally. The "Minister of Rites" [*dazongbo*] chapter of the *Zhouli* lists five types of ritual behavior. There are thirteen rituals for auspicious occasions, five rituals for inauspicious occasions, eight different rituals for when you receive guests from afar, five rituals dealing with military matters, and six rituals for joyous occasions with family and friends.[5] Those are the broad categories it provides for rituals and etiquette without going into a great deal of detail.

We can see a further instance of the loose use of numbers, using ten to actually indicate one, in what it says about the method of identifying the Three Omens. It says that there are 120 classic omens, with 1,200 ways of reading those omens.[6] The major rules of ritual are unalterable rules, so you cannot have too many of them. The minor rules of etiquette follow the major rules but allow ten variations per rule. That is why there are ten times as many minor rules of etiquette as there are major rules of ritual. [But these numbers should not be taken literally. They are used to simply indicate a large number.][7]

Zhongyong XXVII: 6

> The exemplary person, therefore, respects his innate potential for acting appropriately and follows the path of study and inquiry.

THE KING ASKED:

The two clauses "respects his innate potential for acting appropriately" and "follows the path of study and inquiry" are well worth examining at length. Can you provide a more detailed explanation of what it means to respect your innate potential for ethical virtuosity and how we can best go about following the path of study and inquiry? It is natural to show respect for our innate potential for acting appropriately, but if I lack the ability to do so consistently, can I nonetheless follow the path of study and inquiry? I'm afraid I do not quite understand this.

I RESPONDED:

Heaven on High has endowed us with an innate potential to act appropriately [*dexing* 德性]. How could we not respect what it tells us to do? As for following the path of study and inquiry, that is what an exemplary person should do all the time. How can we shirk that task? Anyone who is given a command by his sovereign dare not act contrary to that command. Instead, he must do as he is directed, acting appropriately and graciously. Similarly, anyone who respects the innate potential to act appropriately Heaven has endowed him with dare not violate it. Instead, he must actualize the Dao by acting in a manner befitting a fully human and honorable person. Our obligation in both situations is the same. How could anyone say they lack the ability to do this on a consistent basis?

The Sinograph *Dao* [道] here means "the course you should follow."[8] The *Book of Changes* says, "An exemplary person advances in ethical virtuosity and makes sure to do the tasks allocated to him, striving to always do so in a timely manner."[9] If he does not stay the course, how can he be sure he will act in a way that is appropriate for whatever situation he finds himself in? In ancient times, those who took studying seriously made filial piety, fraternal affection, conscientiousness, and trustworthiness its foundation. To develop culturally, they wrote poetry, read books, performed rituals, and played music. How can anyone say this is hard to understand? (Yi Tŏkcho understands the innate potential to act appropriately as Heaven's innate power to act appropriately. This is a mistake, and I have corrected it here.)

THE KING ASKED:

The line discussed just above adds the phrase "act appropriately" to "the innate tendencies of human beings." This seems redundant. That line also adds the word "inquiry" to "study." Isn't it repeating itself? I would like to hear a detailed explanation from you about the deeper meaning of what the sage wrote.

I RESPONDED:

If you act in accordance with your innate moral potential, then you will display filial love and fraternal affection, as well as act conscientiously and in a manner that shows you are trustworthy. How could this not be ascribed to an innate tendency to act appropriately? Such behavior is rooted in that which Heaven had endowed in us. How would it not be appropriate to respect it? "Study" means to study a wide range of things. "Inquiry" refers to analyzing one thing intensively. Fundamentally they are not the same thing. How could you say that phrase repeats itself?

THE KING ASKED:

The four clauses in this chapter about an exemplary person "extending his knowledge to the widest extent," "reaching toward the highest and brightest," "reviving the old," and "being appropriately solemn" all relate to "the innate tendency to act appropriately." The four clauses that follow those clauses in turn, "exhausting every angle," "following the path of constant focus and composure," "understanding the new," and "displaying the highest respect for proper ritual," all relate to "following the path of study and inquiry." Both the *Zhongyong zhangju* and the *Huowen* explain this in detail.[10] But "reviving the old" would seem to be better placed under "following the path of inquiry and study." Must we now link it instead with respecting the innate tendency to act appropriately? "Displaying the highest respect for ritual," on the other hand, would seem to be more appropriately linked with "respecting the innate tendency to act appropriately." Must we now link it instead with "following the path of inquiry and study?" And when it comes to "following the path of constant focus and composure," being linked here to "following the path of inquiry and study," I find that really aggravating.

In both truly knowing and correctly acting, so that you neither do too much nor stop short of what you are supposed to do, as well as in embodying the Dao, no matter how significant or minor [your actions may be], there is nothing to which the words "consistently focused and composed" are not applicable. Therefore, I fear it is inappropriate to restrict "consistently composed and focused" to understanding alone. However, *Zhongyong zhangju* says that you achieve ultimate understanding by sticking to the Dao of being consistently composed and focused.[11] In *Huowen*, Zhu Xi tells us that in each of those two-clause sentences, there is both what must come first and what follows.[12] This appears to clarify what Zhu Xi meant in *Zhongyong zhangju* about what is of primary importance and what is of secondary importance actually being inseparable [since one cannot be actualized without the other].[13]

If we extrapolate from the way the two clauses in the first sentence in this section fit together [the sentence that says "an exemplary person respects his innate potential for acting appropriately and follows the path of study and inquiry"], then [according to Zhu Xi] the next four sentences should also be each divided into two clauses, the first half focused on "respecting the innate potential for acting appropriately" and the other on "following the path of study and inquiry." But if what Zhu Xi is saying is actually the way this should be read, then "being consistently composed and focused" would be limited to applying to understanding, and that would relegate following the proper path to secondary status. No matter how hard I try, I cannot understand this.

On top of that, "composed and focused" in the clause "consistently composed and focused" means not only being composed and focused but also harmoniously interacting. If that is the case, then "following the path of consistently being focused and composed" should be treated as an example of "respecting one's innate potential for acting appropriately." How can I not find what Zhu Xi is saying really irritating! I would like to see if you could clear this up for me.

| RESPONDED:

There must be some reason why, in this passage, those clauses appear in the order they appear in. "Respects his innate potential for acting appropriately," "extends his knowledge to the widest extent,", and "reaches toward the highest and brightest" are all linked to the clause that follows them the same way [with the word "and" — C. *er* 而], telling us that equal emphasis is placed on both clauses in those three sentences. Why do we need to assume that the first one takes the lead and the second one follows it?

Here is what your humble servant thinks: The innate tendency to act appropriately is what Heaven has endowed us with. If you respect that innate tendency to act appropriately, you will act in a completely unselfishly cooperative and appropriately responsive manner [*cheng*]. "The widest extent" refers to knowledge that is both broad and deep. "Highest and brightest" refers to gaining the greatest possible clarity. The previous chapter starts with acting in a *cheng* manner and then moves on how that allows some to exert influence that is both broad and deep as well as gain the greatest possible clarity in order to act in tandem with Heaven. This particular chapter first discusses the innate tendency to act appropriately and then moves on to extending knowledge to the greatest extent and gaining the greatest clarity, in order to reinforce what the preceding chapter says. The logic of this is quite clear. With that understood, we can see that the first clauses in those three sentences refer to the way Heaven always acts appropriately, and the following clauses in those sentences refer to the way human beings should act. What need is there to separate the two halves of those sentences, treating "respecting the innate potential to act appropriately" and "following the path of study and inquiry" as two completely opposite ways to cultivate a moral character and forcing those two halves into looking like they contradict each other?

The Dao of the *Zhongyong* assumes understanding Heaven as the primary task to be accomplished. For that reason, with the great significance it gives to understanding Heaven, it lays out the steps people need to take to reach that goal, starting with respecting their innate potential to act appropriately, moving on to extending their knowledge to the widest extent, and then achieving the highest and brightest clarity. You have to begin with study and inquiry and delve into the minutest details before you can align your actions with the Dao of the *Zhongyong*.

The first parts of those three sentences address reaching for an ability to act appropriately, like Heaven. The second parts deal with studying things below. However, since studying takes as its final goal becoming consistently composed and focused, clearly the Dao of human beings is nothing other than being consistently composed and focused. Why should we say that being consistently composed and focused falls under the category of extending our knowledge to its greatest extent possible? (Mao Qiling asked, "How could following the path of being consistently focused and composed and performing ritual respectfully have anything to do with extending our knowledge? They are as different as black and white.")[14]

Constant composure and focus [*zhongyong*] are the final goal of our endeavors. How could they be treated as a lesser aspect of the Dao? But being composed and focused cannot be limited to merely respecting our innate potential for acting appropriately, either. Nor can these six parts of those three sentences be separated into those focusing only on understanding and those focusing only on acting. It is, however, appropriate to separate them into those focused primarily on Heaven and those focused primarily on human beings. Your humble servant who may be stupid enough to be deserving of death trusts himself on this one.

Both "broad and profound" and "the highest and the brightest" refer to the foundation for revising the old and understanding the new, as well as for being truly reverential in matters of ritual and etiquette, to have long-lasting effects. The meanings of those clauses are clarified when examined in the light of what preceded them. Being consistently composed and focused means to be always composed, focused, and acting harmoniously with everything around you. Does not "long-lasting" imply consistency and constancy? (This is basically Yi Tŏkcho's idea.)

THE KING ASKED:

The sentence talking about "respecting the innate potential to act appropriately" and the three sentences that follow all contain the word "and." When we come to the fifth and last sentence in this series, however, it has "with" [以 C. *yi*] instead of "and." Why is this? Hu says the reason for the difference is that the first four place emphasis on the second part of the sentence while the fifth places emphasis on the first part.[15] A quick glimpse at this text makes it appear likely this is the case, but in *Huowen* we can read "After reviving the old, you will understand the new, so you cannot revive the old without consequently understanding the new. Only after you are truly reverent can you perform the ritual with appropriate solemnity, and, moreover, if you are truly reverent, you cannot do other than perform the ritual with appropriate solemnity."[16] Keeping this is mind, although the fourth and fifth sentences differ slightly in how they are worded, with one ["reviving the old and understanding the new"] using the word "and" and the other ["with an appropriately solemn manner, displaying the highest respect for proper ritual"] using the word "with," the ways "reviving the old" and "with an appropriately solemn manner" are used in their respective sentences are the same.

Generally speaking, if you do not preserve your pure heart-mind, then you have no way to extend your knowledge to the widest extent. Conversely, if you preserve your pure heart-mind, you cannot help but extend your knowledge to the widest extent.[17] That is what *Zhongyong zhangju* says. That is an overall approach to understanding those five phrases. But Hu divides them into two types of statements [differentiated by where their emphasis lies]. I'm afraid that if you separate these phrases into two separate types the way he does, you cannot avoid making a mistake. Although we are only talking about a difference of just one word here, we have to be clear about what that difference means. I would like to hear what you think.

I RESPONDED:

The three terms "revive," "understand," and "display the highest respect for" that are paired with the three terms "the old," "the new," and "ritual" respectively are single Sinographs with a single meaning each. But the two Sinographs telling us we have to display the greatest respect for ritual by acting "in an appropriately solemn manner" are a compound, with two Sinographs combining to mean just one thing. That is why the two clauses in that sentence are connected by "with" rather than by "and" as in the other phrases. This was done to illuminate the fact that those two Sinographs are a compound forming just one word.[18]

Generally speaking, ritual is dependent on the person performing the ritual being truly solemn and respectful. You cannot separate the ritual from the attitude of the person performing the ritual. This is not like the old and the new, which are clearly two different things. This is why the two different words, "and" and "with," are used. Indeed, there was a good reason for doing so.

THE KING ASKED:

Is the line in this chapter that says "reviving the old and understanding the new" telling us we should seek new things to enjoy in the process of reviving the old? Or should the two words "old" and "new" be taken as totally opposed to each other?

I RESPONDED:

Combining reviving the old with understanding what is new means you are looking for new things to enjoy. So "reviving the old" already implies seeking new things to enjoy. Your humble servant suggests that "reviving the old" and "understanding the new" are saying the same thing.

THE KING ASKED:

The ten clauses [in five sentences] starting from "respects the innate potential for acting appropriately" are about the great things a sage can accomplish. Which of these clauses should those of us who are studying to improve ourselves focus on? Where should we begin our endeavor?

I RESPONDED:

"Respecting the innate potential for acting appropriately," "extending knowledge to the widest extent," and "reaching toward the highest and brightest" all lead to the level of the appropriate behavior Heaven demonstrates. "Following the path of inquiry and study," "exhausting every angle," and "following the path of consistently being focused and composed" all lead through study to the ultimate ethical efficacy. All these are the tasks of the Sage. Only the clause "following the path of inquiry and study" refers specifically to what scholars should do. The last four clauses [in the last two sentences] are admonitions to "expand our knowledge while observing proper decorum."[19] But these four clauses cannot be applied to scholars alone.

THE KING ASKED:

"Respecting your innate potential for appropriate action" refers to what you do. "Following the path of study and inquiry" refers to how you learn. And Confucius made clear that doing comes first and learning second. This cannot be telling us that doing is actually more important than the knowing, can it? If that were the case, then you would have to do something before you knew how to do it properly. Is that possible? Wang Yangming caused quite an uproar with ideas like this.[20] But is this not what he was talking about?

I RESPONDED:

The way Wang Yangming's philosophy placed action before knowledge is different from what this chapter is talking about. According to this chapter, understanding gained in reviving the old comes first, and the action of performing ritual with proper solemnity follows. Learning and doing inform each other. This is the practice of the sages of old.[21]

Zhongyong XXVII: 7

This is the reason he is not arrogant when occupying a high office.

Zhu Xi said, "Here 'to prosper' [*xing* 興] refers to being promoted to a higher office."[22]

As I see it, when this chapter says not speaking up when the Dao does not prevail at court will be enough to allow one to be left alone by others, it is referring to what an individual can do to survive. So how can the paired phrase "be enough to prosper" refer to someone else promoting him? He who finds himself in a situation that is enough for him to prosper is someone whose words of wise counsel are accepted by his ruler. That is enough for him to prosper [realize his full potential]. Someone who finds himself in a situation in which it is best to be left alone by others is someone who should keep quiet rather than showcase his brilliance [and thereby incite the envy or anger of others]. That will be enough for him to ensure his personal safety.[23]

The *Dadai liji* says,[24] "When the court is in accord with the Dao, he only had to speak to thrive there. When the court was not in accord with the Dao, not speaking was the best way to be tolerated at court. This is how Tongti Bohua acted"[25] ("Weijiangjun" chapter).[26]

Zhongyong XXVIII: 1

> The Master said, "The foolish nonetheless like to use their own judgment."

THE KING ASKED:

If "to be born in the present and yet try to restore the way things were done in the past"[1] is something we should not try to do, then does that mean that we do not necessarily need to study how to do what the Sages did, and that we should not try to govern as they did in the great dynasties of ancient times?

I RESPONDED:

Shun and the Duke of Zhou were able to occupy powerful posts and ensure that the Dao prevailed. Confucius, on the other hand, was never able to obtain a powerful post and therefore was not able to ensure that the Dao prevailed. Earlier chapters tell us that Shun and the Duke of Zhou were able to establish proper rituals, impose proper standards, and determine the proper form of writing.[2] A later chapter states that Confucius looked up to Yao and Shun as though they were his own ancestors and followed their example.[3] A Sage is someone who has the ability to establish proper rituals, impose proper standards, and determine the proper form of writing. Sages all have that potential. However, whether they can fully actualize that potential depends on fate and on the times in which they live. To be born in the present yet restore the way things were done in the past is not something someone without a powerful post can accomplish. Isn't this statement, therefore, nothing more than Confucius bewailing his fate?

Confucius loved learning so much that he never slacked off, so he was someone who was able to restore in himself the sort of personal ethical virtuosity we see in the ancient past. However, as we can see in the chapter on Confucius carrying on the work of Yao and Shun as though they were his own ancestors and emulating the standards established by King Wen and King Wu, even though he wanted to restore the way the Dao prevailed in the ancient past and transform the entire world for the better, he was unable to do so. That is why this chapter warns those who live in the present against trying to restore the ways things were in ancient times. Those who find themselves holding an exposed position in a shaky government but nonetheless try to make things conform to the Dao of the past might find themselves in a lot of trouble. If we focus on restoring personal ethical virtuosity, then we can see that Confucius was able to carry on the work of Yao and Shun as though they were his own ancestors and emulate the standards established by King Wen and King Wu.⁴

Zhu Xi said, "Rites refer to the core features of how you should interact with those both close and distant, and those both noble and base."⁵ As I see it, rites here refer to those rituals used for auspicious occasions, the rituals used when dealing with inauspicious occasions, the rituals used when receiving guests, and the rituals used on joyful occasions.

Zhu Xi said, "Proper standards here refers to protocol."⁶

Cai Qing said, "Protocol refers to standards governing chariots and banners, the style and color of official uniforms, and so forth."⁷

In my opinion, "proper standards" refer to how we should distinguish the noble from the less noble. There are many different types of chariots [depending on the status of the person using that chariot], as we can see in the *Jinche* [chariot decorator] section [in the *Zhouli*].⁸ There are also many different levels of official ritual clothing, as we can see in the *Sifu* [Wardrobe overseer] section [in the *Zhouli*].⁹ Banners also have many grades, as we can see in the *Sichang* [Overseer of banners] section [in the *Zhouli*].¹⁰ Moreover, [in receiving guests] how big the ceremonial pieces of jade, the ceremonial mats, and the horse bridles are, and how many sacrificial animals and attendants are involved, differs: the higher-ranking guests are honored with nine or seven times the basic amount, and lower-ranking guests are honored with five or three times the basic amount, as we can see in the *Daxingren* [Senior messenger] section [of the *Zhouli*].¹¹ All this is what we call proper protocol.

Zheng Xuan commented that the Sinograph *wen* [文 K. *mun*] in this chapter refers to the written script. (Zhu Xi accepted this.)¹²

Zhao De¹³ wrote, "The *Daxingren* section of the 'Autumn Officials' chapter of *Zhouli* notes, 'The musicians and the scribes were called to court to be taught how to write names properly and how to distinguish sounds.' The term 'write names' [書名 *shuming*] means to write Sinographs. In ancient times, the word 'names' meant the same as the word Sinograph [字 C. *zi*] we use today. Also, in the *Waishi* [Scribes for external affairs] section of the 'Autumn Officials' chapter of the *Zhouli*, we find a statement that they standardized writing in all four corners of the world. The subcommentary states that means that they rectified the way Sinographs were written so that people in all four corners of the world could read and write, and pronounce them, the same way.¹⁴ In ancient times, there were only a few Sinographs, so they were called 'names.' Today there are a lot more Sinographs than there used to be, so now they are called 'Sinographs.' The term 'Sinograph' has taken over."¹⁵

Mao Qiling said, "There is a minor commentary that explains that here 'writing' [書] refers to the shape of the Sinographs and 'naming' [名] refers to how they are pronounced. This is a mistake. Let me point out that the treatise section of the *Hanshu* [The history of the Former Han dynasty) says that according to the standards in ancient times, Sinographs all had to be written the same way. If someone did not know how to write a Sinograph correctly, they skipped it. That is why Confucius said, 'I have heard that there was a time when scribes who did not recognize a Sinograph would skip over it.'[16] This is called 'a skipped Sinograph.' But, if we are talking about how that Sinograph is pronounced, what does that have to do with a scribe skipping over it? This reference to distinguishing sounds should be understood as a reference to pronouncing Sinographs aloud [and should be differentiated from writing Sinographs].

"Emperor Xuan of the Han (r. 74–49 BCE) asked a man of Qi to voice the correct pronunciations of Sinographs and directed Zhang Chang[17] to accept these readings as the only correct pronunciations. This is what is meant by 'the correct sound of Sinographs.' If we examine what the *Daxingren* chapter in the 'Autumn Offices' chapter of the *Zhouli* says, that they 'were taught how to write names properly and how to distinguish sounds,'[18] then that would mean that not only would people of the various states have been taught how to write Sinographs the same, they would have been taught how to pronounce them the same as well. Obviously, 'name,' meaning written Sinographs, and 'sound,' meaning the pronunciation of Sinographs, are two completely separate things. That is why the *Waishi* section of the *Zhouli* speaks of 'standardizing writing in all four corners of the world.'[19] That is what is meant by teaching them how to write Sinographs [書名] correctly."[20]

As I see it, the four Sinographs *shu* [書 K. *sŏ*], *wen* [文 K. *mun*], *ming* [名 K. *myŏng*], and *zi* [字 K. *cha*] all refer to something different. *Shu* refers to Sinographs written with the brush. (It is composed of two parts, one referring to a hand holding a brush [聿 C. *yu* / K. *yul*] and another [者 C. *zhe* / K. *cha*] referring to doing something.) *Shu* is the same thing we mean today when we talk about writing a Sinograph. *Wen* refers to patterns in actual objects, such as seen on a tortoise shell, a leopard's skin, embroidery, and seashells. Any kind of complicated pattern like that is called *wen*. (This resembles what "The "Great Treatise" chapter in the *Book of Changes* is talking about when it says, "When things are mixed together and an elegant pattern results, it is called *wen*.")[21] Written Sinographs are also a type of pattern. That is why they, too, are called *wen*. As for *ming*, though the Sinograph used here normally means "name," it implies another Sinograph [命] also pronounced *ming* which means "decree." When something does not yet have a name, a name is decreed for it. For example, the blue sky above was given the name "heaven," and the yellow dirt below was given the name "earth."

"*Zi*" means offspring. Each Sinograph has a mother. "Tree" is the mother for the Sinographs meaning "root" (根 C. *gen* / K. *gŭn*) and "tree trunk" (株 C. *zhu* / K. *chu*).[22] "Metal" is the mother of both "forge" (鍛 C. *tuan* / K. *dan*) and smelt (鍊 C. *lian* / K. *yŏn*).[23] In the ancient past Sinographs were called *ming*, literally "names." We can see proof of that in the "Pinli" [Ceremonial of a mission] chapter of the *Book of Etiquette and Ceremonies* where it says, when discussing a formal letter that is presented to the head of a neighboring state along with a roll of silk, "If the letter contains more than a hundred Sinographs [名], it is written on bamboo tablets tied together; but if there are fewer than a hundred Sinographs [名], it is written on a square board."[24] When we see the line in this chapter that says, "they unified the way the Sinographs were written," that means that the specific pattern for a particular Sinograph was the same wherever that Sinograph was written anywhere in the world.

Zhu Xi said, "The width of paths for carts and chariots is based on the ruts left by the wheels of carts.[25] The people of Zhou placed great value on carts and chariots and so they established regulations governing the making of such vehicles and placed them under the jurisdiction of the Officers of Winter. The carts and chariots had to have axles exactly six *chi* plus six *cun* long.[26] That would made the wheels fit exactly in the ruts on the cart path. It did not make any difference if cart or chariot came from far away or nearby. Its wheels would still fit into those ruts. Everyone who manufactured carts and chariots had to follow this regulation. If they did that, their carts and chariots could travel anywhere there was a path for vehicles with wheels. There would be nowhere they could not go. However, if they ignored this regulation, not only would they face a legal penalty, they would find that if they tried to take that cart or chariot out on a road, it would not be able to stay on the path and instead would veer from one side to the other and might even end up on the side of the road. So people would be sure to all make their carts and chariots the same width even if there were no legal penalties for doing otherwise. That's why there is an old saying 'even if your gate is shut so that no one can watch you make a cart, you still have to make it the same width as other carts if you want it to be able to go anywhere at all.'

"The *Zuozhuan* says, 'The ruts were all the same distance apart, so all the dignitaries were able to come there by chariots.'[27] Writing works the same way. Sinographs have to be the same everywhere in the number of their strokes and in the shapes they take. The *Waishi* section of the *Zhouli* tells us that writing was standardized across all four corners of the world.[28] The *Daxingren* section tells us the scribes were summoned every nine years to be reminded of how to write Sinographs correctly.[29] They were this painstaking to ensure consistency in writing across the civilized world.

"Although after a while the Zhou was no longer able to maintain political dominance, and its old territory fragmented into a number of feudal states, the writing system remained unified. Then the Qin (221–207 BCE) absorbed and destroyed the last six remaining feudal states. The Qin made sure that its laws and regulations were the same throughout its realm. From this time on, the axles of all carts and chariots had to conform to the six-*chŏk* standard. As for writing, only seal script [*xiaozhuan*] and clerical script [*lishu*] style were permitted. This was the beginning of changes in the writing system promoted by the Zhou."[30]

Zhu Xi said, "'the norms of proper human interactions' [*lun*] are the essence of acting appropriately by taking into account the social hierarchy."[31] (To act appropriately by taking into account the social hierarchy means doing all the things you need to do in order to interact with others in a manner appropriate to their rank and authority. The core elements of such behavior are distinguishing superiors from inferiors and settling the people's minds by exemplifying the way rulers and ministers, fathers and sons, the noble and the base, and the exalted and the humble should interact.)

As I see it, the norms of proper human interactions define how to act in a manner appropriate for the position in society you hold vis-à-vis those you are interacting with. To differentiate your behavior according to your status and the status of those you are dealing with is precisely what we mean by proper human interactions. Look at the nine northeastern barbarian peoples and the eight southern aboriginal peoples. We can find among them fathers and sons with different surnames, cases of matrilineal rather than patrilineal succession, and situations in which young and strong are treated with more respect than the elderly are. When people act this way, we cannot apply to them [the line from this chapter that reads,] "everywhere the same ethical norms prevail."

THE KING ASKED:

This chapter says, "Although someone sits on a throne, if he does not possess ethical virtuosity, he should not dare to create new rituals and music." This being the case, if a ruler falls short of the ethical virtuosity of a sage, can he still on his own regulate ritual and music and lead military campaigns against other states?

I RESPONDED:

The ritual and music of the Shang was created by King Tang alone. The ritual and music of the Zhou was created by the Duke of Zhou alone. The rulers who followed them used these rituals and this music only and did not create their own. That is why the *Book of Songs* says, "Never erring or forgetting / Following faithfully the old standards."³² If we faithfully follow the old standards, then "ritual, music, and military campaigns against other states will be determined by the Son of Heaven only."³³

Yi Tŏkcho³⁴ remarked, "A true ruler does not have to feel that he has reached the same level as a great sage before he creates something. He should just go ahead and do it. But he has to try to create what a sage would create. How do we know that is what he should do? A sage fully understands what is good and what is bad for the people's bodies and minds, and he acts on the basis of a heart-mind that wants only the best for the people. That is why he cannot refrain from creating things [that benefit the people]. If that is not the sort of person a sage is, what is? If he truly is a sage, then his ethical virtuosity will be manifest in humility. How can someone who is humble think that he has achieved the same degree of perfection sages have achieved and can therefore create things as great as what Yao, Shun, King Wen, and King Wu created?"

Zhongyong XXVIII: 5

The Master said, "Let me say something about the rituals of Xia."

Zhu Xi said, "The Shang rites, although they have been preserved, are not appropriate for our time."[35]

Mao Qiling said, "According to the *Analects*, Confucius said, 'There are few documents in the state of Song that can tell us much about the Shang rites.'[36] Someone said, 'Zisi was hard-pressed in Song. When he wrote the *Zhongyong*, he wrote about the rites of Song as though they were the rites of Shang.' To present something under one name when it actually should be credited to another is acting like Weisheng Gao."[37]

In my opinion, to say that "Song has preserved the Shang rites"[38] is telling us only that some remnants of the Shang rites were preserved in Song. What was preserved in Song was not enough to fully reconstruct the rites of Shang.

Zheng Xuan said [in regard to a phrase in the line that immediately follows this one],[39] "The reference to the 'three important things' is a reference to the rites established by the founders of the first three dynasties [Xia, Shang, and Zhou]."[40]

Lu Deming, writing during the Tang in his *Textual Explanations of the Classics*, the old version,[41] says, "Those 'three important things' are ethical virtuosity, acting in a way appropriate for your position in society, and acting at the proper time."

Master Cheng said, "The 'three important things' are the rites of the three most exemplary kings in Xia, Shang, and Zhou respectively."[42]

Lü Dalin said, "The 'three important things' are, as mentioned in this chapter, discussing proper ritual, creating proper protocol, and establishing a proper script. Only the Son of Heaven can do these things. If he does so, then affairs of state will run smoothly, families will not have inappropriate customs, and the mistakes people make will be few."[43]

Cai Qing said, "Proper conduct, proper speech, and proper implementation are what are meant by the 'three important things.'"[44] (The next chapter has a passage that reads, "When the ruler conducts himself properly, that becomes the Dao future generations follow. When he implements proper measures, he sets the standards for future generations to follow. When he speaks, he creates the norms for future generations to follow.")

Mao Qiling said, "The 'Summary Account of Sacrifices' chapter of the *Book of Rites* says, 'In a sacrificial ritual there were three things which are especially important.' The next sentence explains that those three things are offering libations, singing in the upper hall, and dancing the martial dance.[45] Later on, it talks about acting at the proper time, acting in a way appropriate for your position in society, and ethical virtuosity. It makes no reference to creating proper protocol. Nor does it say anything about establishing the proper script. There appear to be some doubtful points in this interpretation."[46]

As I see it, what Lü Dalin said is the most reasonable. This is how Zhu Xi understood it. But to understand "the mistakes people make will be few" as "the people all over the earth will make few mistakes" is, I fear, going too far. An earlier passage says that someone who is unable to act with appropriate ethical virtuosity should not ascend to a position of authority and should not dare to institute new rituals and music. "Should not dare to institute new rituals and music" means if he does so, he will make mistakes. The one who is qualified to reign over All-under-Heaven is the one who regulates the rites and composes music, and standardizes protocol and writing. Such a person would not make any mistakes. That is what "making few mistakes" means here. Is this not what this is referring to?

The next chapter includes the sentence "People must compare the way they behave with the way the three exemplary kings [the founders of the first three dynasties] behaved so that they do not make any mistakes." This is the way to clarify the Dao, proving that it is authentic and can serve as a reliable guide.

Master Cheng said, "[In this chapter] the phrase 'what is prior' means the period leading up to and including the period of the three exemplary kings and 'what is later' refers to the period of the five hegemons of the Spring and Autumn period and the feudal lords."[47]

Lü Dalin said, "'What is prior' refers to matters of greater concern, that is to say, the fundamentals of the human nature that is our endowment from Heaven, and of the Dao of ethical virtuosity. 'What is later' refers to the matters of lesser concern such as the basis for law and punishments, and for uniform standards."[48] See *Huowen*.[49]

Zhu Xi said, "What is prior refers to the rites of Xia and Shang. Although they are wonderful, we cannot uncover much about them. What is later refers to Confucius. Although he was an expert at ritual matters, he was not able to win appointment to a respected position."[50]

In my opinion, it is appropriate to follow Zhu Xi's interpretation.

THE KING ASKED:

Although matters related to Xia and Shang are definitely worthy of study, we cannot verify details about them. Although the words of Confucius and Mencius were magnificent, they were not appointed to respected positions. If what we are told about Xia and Shang is not totally verified, and if Confucian and Mencius did not win the confidence of people in their day, then is there any way at all that anything can be verified, or anyone can be respected?

I RESPONDED:

We can admit that we do not have verified detailed knowledge about Xia and Shang but how can we say that Confucian and Mencius were not appointed to respected positions because they were not admired? What an exemplary person studies is what is admirable and good. Confucius and Mencius took what is admirable and good as guidelines for their behavior. This was all the evidence that was needed for them to win the confidence of the people of their day and be seen as worth following.

THE KING ASKED:

The first line in this passage said that the lack of validation of something is the reason it is not trusted. Why does it add later that the Dao is not contrary to the way things should be, and there can be no doubts about it?

I RESPONDED:

The foundation for implementing the Dao is to have the people follow it. The foundation for the people following it is trust in it. "The Dao is not contrary to the way things should be, and there can be no doubts about it" clarifies that it is appropriate that the people have confidence in the Dao and act in accordance with it.

Yi Tŏkcho said, "A sage has a high regard for validation that comes from the trust the people have in him. If he already has the trust of people, what harm can come from a lack of specific concrete evidence? The Dao that has been endowed by Heaven is, as this chapter says, 'rooted in a ruler's own personal behavior'[51] and 'is confirmed by the trust the people place in him.' His behavior should be 'comparable to the example set by the three exemplary kings' and be in 'conformity with Heaven and Earth.' If that is the case, no one will doubt him. He himself will provide the standard for judging. What need would there be for any other evidence?

"If that were not the case, how could we say that the Dao originates in the examples set by the three exemplary kings? Indeed, the Dao is nothing more than that which is grounded in a true ruler's own personal behavior and is confirmed by the trust the people place in him. That is why this Dao is said to the Dao endowed by Heaven. It does not make any difference whether you have the Dao 'confirmed by spirits' or 'wait for a sage to confirm it.' You will get the same result."⁵²

THE KING ASKED:

How are the meanings of "The Dao of a ruler is confirmed by the spirits"⁵³ and "He who is perfectly selflessly cooperative and appropriately responsive is like a spiritual being"⁵⁴ similar, and how are they different? Zhu Xi already in his comments on Chapter XVI explained the meaning of 'spiritual beings' and then here in this chapter he explains it again. Why does he bother to define what a spirit is again? Moreover, he already explained them as the spiritual power of *yin* and *yang* but that meaning contrasts with the use of "spirit" in the phrase "the Dao of a true ruler is confirmed by the spirits." Moreover, he ignores Master Cheng's explanation that spirits are the functioning of heaven and earth and repeats only the explanation that they are the traces of the creative transformations of things.⁵⁵ Why does he do that?

I RESPONDED:

Spiritual beings are able to foresee the future. That's why an earlier chapter, in talking about the possibility of foreknowledge, says, "He who is perfectly selflessly cooperative and appropriately responsive is like a spirit." That term refers to the same thing in both instances. That being the case, we cannot say that spirits are nothing more than the natural functioning of *yin* and *yang*. Nor can we say that they are nothing more than the functioning of heaven and earth or that they are nothing more than the traces of creation. In the "Great Overseer of Ritual" chapter in *Zhouli*, the spirits of heaven and of earth who are the subjects of sacrificial rites are all spirits who assist the Supreme Ruler.⁵⁶ The words accredited to the Royal Secretary Guo in the "Sayings of Zhou" and those accredited to the scribe Yin in the "Sayings of Jin" support this.⁵⁷

Zhu Xi said, "Spiritual beings are traces of the creative transformation of things."⁵⁸ (When asked, "When we talk about spiritual beings, do we mean that when we use tortoise shells and yarrow stalks for divination, those spirits determine whether we obtain auspicious or inauspicious readings?" Zhu Xi responded, "That is the case, but that is not the complete explanation. The tortoise shells and yarrow stalks are in tune with the interactive patterns [*li*] of those spiritual beings.")⁵⁹

Let me point out that "to test and confirm" [質 C. *zhi*] means "to verify," as in the regulations in the *Zhouli* regarding market contracts [質劑 C. *zhiji*], which are a means by which the honesty or dishonesty of an agreement is tested.[60] The heavenly spirits, that is to say those spirits in charge of celestial and terrestrial phenomena, all line up in a brilliant array to receive the mandate of Heaven in order to assist in the management of human affairs. This clearly shows that all things in heaven and on earth are linked to each other. This is what is meant by "confirmed by spirits." How can plants or tortoise shells be used to confirm whether we are acting in accord with the Dao or not? Spirits are not "traces of creation," as we have already seen.[61]

Zhongyong XXIX: 5

> This is why, when the true ruler takes action, the people of that age take this to be the Dao of All-under-Heaven.

Cai Qing said, "Proper conduct, proper speech, and proper implementation are what are meant by the 'three important things.'" (See the *Mengyin*.)[1]

Allow me to point out that it is unclear why Cai Qing says these three things are what the phrase "three important things" refers to. Those three important things he mentions apply to the line that begins with "the Dao of the exemplary ruler," which appears just above where those three things appear in this text. They have nothing to do with the preceding section, which begins with "He who would be the ruler of All-under-Heaven."

Zhu Xi said, "Chapter XXVIII of the *Zhongyong* should be understood in relation to the line in the previous chapter that says, 'when he is in a lower post, he is not insubordinate.'"[2] (He is saying it should be connected to the chapter that begins with "The foolish nonetheless like to use their own judgment" and ends with "I follow the rites of Zhou.")[3] Zhu Xi also says that Chapter XXIX should be understood in light of the line [also in Chapter XXVII] that says "When he holds a high position, he is not arrogant."[4] (He wants to link it with the chapter that begins with "He who would be the ruler of All-under-Heaven" and ends with "won praise from all under heaven.")

In my opinion, Chapter XXVIII has nothing to do with the phrase "he is not insubordinate" [from Chapter XXVII]. (Instead, it is closer in meaning to the sentence [in the opening line in Chapter XXVIII], "Though he has a low rank, he tries to act as if he is in charge.") Nor does Chapter XXIX have anything to do with the line "he is not arrogant." I have no idea why Zhu Xi says what he says.

Zhongyong XXX

> Confucius carried on the work of Yao and Shun as if they were his own ancestors.

Zhu Xi said, "When we read of Confucius [in the *Analects*] that 'he did not eat foods out of season, ... and his face took on a solemn expression when he saw lightning or heard strong winds,'[1] that tells us he would accept an appointment to an official post as long as it was appropriate to do so, but then would quickly resign that office if he concluded that was what he should do. We can tell that the phrase in this chapter that says 'Confucius harmonized his actions with the changes in the seasons so that they were appropriate for the time' means the same thing.

"When he was in the state of Lu, Confucius wore the clothing with wide sleeves that was appropriate there. When he was in the state of Song, he wore the *zhangfu* hat that was appropriate there.[2] When his talents could be used properly, he made himself available. Otherwise, he retreated to the shadows. We can see that the phrase in this chapter that says, 'he was in tune with his surroundings' is telling us the same thing." See *Huowen*.[3]

Zhu Xi also said, "The great emperors of ancient times observed the movements of the sun and calculated a calendar which they then presented to their subjects. They stepped down from the throne to pass it on to a worthy successor. They dismissed some local lords and subjugated others. These are examples of ensuring actions were appropriate for their time. They managed their territory and its wildlands such that the vegetation there and the insects therein did exactly what they were supposed to do. This is what is meant by being in tune with one's surroundings." See *Huowen*.[4]

In my opinion, the phrases in this chapter that read "above he harmonized his actions with the changes in the seasons" and "below he was in tune with his surroundings" simply mean that by acting in harmony with heaven and earth he was able to join forces with them. There is no need to break them down into separate categories.

Moreover, as for his accepting an appointment to an official post as long as it was appropriate to do so, but then quickly resigning that office if he concluded that was what he should do, as well as making himself available when his talents could be used properly and otherwise retreating into the shadows, they are similar types of behavior. I do not understand why they should be separated into actions characterized as harmonizing with the changes in the seasons and actions that are in tune with his surroundings.

Also, to say that not eating foods when they were out of season is an example of Confucius harmonizing his actions with the changes of the seasons is trivializing the way Confucius harmonized his actions with heaven above. There is a lot we can learn by delving into the ancient classics. Those texts teach us much we can apply in our everyday lives. However, if we focus too closely on the particular phrases in these passages, we will go astray and miss the overall message they are trying to impart.

THE KING ASKED:

This work cites Confucius quite a bit, but it does not say anything about the Dao of Confucius until this chapter, when for the first time it mentions how great he was. Why is that? Confucius's great accomplishment of harmonizing his actions with the changes of the seasons above and being in tune with his surroundings below — is there anything we can compare that with?

I RESPONDED:

Zhu Xi in *Huowen* said that pointing out that Confucius did not eat foods out of season, and that his face took on a solemn expression when he saw lightning or heard strong winds, is an example of Confucius harmonizing his actions with the changes in the seasons. And Zhu Xi said that pointing out that when he was the state of Lu, Confucius wore the clothing with wide sleeves that was appropriate there, and when he was in the state of Song, he wore the *zhangfu* hat that was appropriate there, is an example of Confucius being in tune with his surroundings. I'm afraid that is not the correct interpretation. The phrases in this chapter that read "harmonizing with what is above" and "being in tune with what is below" are references to the broader truths that heaven provides shelter for us with its canopy above and earth supports us with its solid ground below.[5]

Mao Qiling said, "The phrase in this chapter that reads 'the Ten Thousand Things all nurture each other [instead of harming each other]' tells us that All-under-Heaven is not a single [undifferentiated] entity. And the phrase 'people travel on parallel paths [without any conflict among them]' tells us that there is not just one Dao for All-under-Heaven."[6]

As I see it, there is just one Dao. Many sages all traveled that path, so there must be only one Dao. If the peoples of the various social classes join them in following that Dao, then there will be no conflict among them. But there are alternative "Dao," the paths [trod by followers] of Laozi and Buddha. If those following those ways try to join us on the path we are walking, how could that not result in conflicts breaking out?[7]

Zhu Xi said, "Small displays of ethical virtuosity [referred to in this chapter] are the various parts of the complete potential of human beings. Great displays of ethical virtuosity are the foundation of the multiple of interactions being proper and appropriate.[8]" Chen wrote that " 'Small acts of ethical virtuosity' refers to doing part of what you are supposed to do. 'Great acts of virtuosity' refers to realizing your full potential."[9]

As I read this chapter, everything in this chapter that follows "the Ten Thousand Things all nurture each other" is a reference to the way Confucius taught. And the phrases "small acts of ethical virtuosity" and "great acts of ethical virtuosity" refer to the different degrees of ethical virtuosity among his students.[10]

Zhongyong XXXI

In All-under-Heaven, only someone who is a perfect Sage...¹

THE KING ASKED:

If we relate being focused and right on target to being fully human and acting appropriately, then focused here refers to the great potential we have for concentrating on the task at hand and right on target refers to the wisdom we possess which tells us exactly how we should act. Zhou Dunyi in his *Explanation of the Diagram of the Supreme Polarity* [*Taijitu shuo* 太極圖說] tells us all we need to know about this. His work relates that diagram to acting with benevolence, acting appropriately, acting with a sense of propriety and respect for ritual, and acting wisely.² It says that when being focused is combined with being right on target, the result is a display of a sense of propriety and respect for ritual.³ Being focused is certainly one aspect of propriety. But should being right on target also be associated with a sense of propriety? Should not this word "being right on target" be linked to wisdom, instead? Can it also be linked with a sense of propriety? There must be an explanation that says it can. Can you explain it to me in detail?

I RESPONDED:

The *Explanation of the Diagram of the Supreme Polarity* was written over a thousand years after Zisi wrote the *Zhongyong*. When Zisi uses the words "focused" and "right on target," he is talking about a ruler. If you want to question linking the terms "focused" and "right on target" with a sense of propriety and acting wisely, as they are in that diagram, then that would be acceptable. But in this chapter of the *Zhongyong*, there is no need to doubt what they mean.⁴

Zhongyong XXXII

> In All-under-Heaven, only someone who displays the highest level of unselfishly cooperative and appropriately responsive behavior...

THE KING ASKED:

This chapter has phrases saying that someone who is unselfishly cooperative and appropriate responsive is a "bottomless abyss" [profound] and is Heaven. Those phrases should not be taken literally.[1] The Sinograph meaning "like" or "as" is left out, that's all. The text is saying that such a person is **like** a bottomless abyss [in the depth to which they can explore what is going on around them] or **like** Heaven [in the breadth of what they can understand]. In the preceding chapter, we see the expressions "as deep as a bottomless abyss" and "as broad as heaven." That is making a similar point in a slightly different way. Can you tell me why the phrasing is different even though both chapters are referring to the Dao of heaven?

There is another difference to discuss as well. The *Yulei* cites Zhu Xi saying about this chapter, "this is the difference between evaluating someone by his actions and evaluating someone for his moral character."[2] But in *Zhongyong zhangju* Zhu Xi says simply, "It does not mean that literally."[3] There we do not seeing him saying anything similar to "this is the difference between evaluating someone by his actions and evaluating someone for his moral character." Why does he offer two different explanations?

I RESPONDED:

The Sinograph *ru* [如], linked in the preceding chapter to "the abyss" and to "heaven," is used when you are comparing one thing to another and want to point out their similarities; the Sinograph *qi* [其], used in this chapter with "the abyss" and "heaven," means "the same type of thing." Although the way the differences between those two words are utilized is quite profound, I am afraid that it does not appear to me that there is very much difference between the perfect sage discussed in the previous chapter and the person discussed in this chapter who acts in an unselfishly cooperative and appropriately responsive manner. Why do we need to say they are different?

In the *Yulei*, Zhu Xi says, "People looking at how he behaves notice only that [the impact of] his appropriate behavior is as broad as Heaven and as deep and profound as an abyss. They think, therefore, that his moral character must truly be almost the same as both Heaven on high and a deep abyss."[4] This is seeing a connection between the core and how it manifests.

THE KING ASKED:

From Chapter XXI to this chapter, this text focuses on the Dao of Heaven and the Dao of human beings. However, Chapter XXI talks about both the Dao of Heaven and the Dao of human beings, Chapter XXII talks only about the Dao of Heaven, Chapter XXIII talks only about the Dao of human beings, Chapter XXIV talks only about the Dao of Heaven, Chapter XXV talks only about the Dao of human beings, Chapter XXVI talks only about the Dao of Heaven, and Chapter XXVII talks only about the Dao of human beings. These chapters alternate between talking about the Dao of Heaven first and then talking about the Dao of human beings. This is the way it should be. It is supposed to discuss the Dao of Heaven first and then discuss the Dao of human beings. That being the case, Chapter XXVIII and the chapters that follow it should do that as well. Yet both Chapter XXVIII and Chapter XXIX discuss the Dao of human beings only. The next three chapters, one after another, talk only about the Dao of Heaven. They should alternate what they talk about, and they should do so in the right order. Why are those later chapters different from the ones that precede them?

I RESPONDED:

Zhu Xi tries to point out at the end of those chapters whether a particular chapter is about the Dao of Heaven or the Dao of human beings.[5] However, the *Zhongyong* is a single work. Although it is based on the endowment we receive from Heaven, the Dao it teaches is the Dao of human beings. Earlier in the text it says, "Acting in an unselfishly cooperative and appropriately responsive manner is the Dao of Heaven. Learning how to act in an unselfishly cooperative and appropriately responsive manner is the Dao of human beings."[6] This is nothing more than the difference between "knowing it from birth" and "knowing it by studying it," that's all. We should not artificially separate the Dao of Heaven from the Dao of human beings. Moreover, what the various chapters tell us is based on our endowment from Heaven, so what they clarify is the Dao of human beings. Those two are completely intertwined. I do not know why Zhu Xi felt it necessary to treat some chapters as focusing on the Dao of Heaven and other chapters as focusing on the Dao of human beings as though they are as different as black and white. Saying one chapter is about the endowment we receive from Heaven but another is about the Dao of human beings is misleading. It is not as black and white as that.[7]

Zhongyong XXXIII: 1

> The *Book of Songs* says, "Over her brocade garments she wore a plain coat with no lining."[1]

Mao Qiling said, "The four-Sinograph phrase 'Over her brocade garments she wore a plain coat with no lining' is definitely not a line from the 'shuo ren' or the 'feng' odes.[2] Neither of those poems includes the last two Sinographs [*shangjiong* 尚絅] in that four-Sinograph phrase cited in this chapter of the *Zhongyong*. The last two Sinographs quoted here have been changed from what we see in the *Book of Songs* [*jiongyi* 褧衣]. This must be a line from a poem that has been lost.

"However, the fourth Sinograph cited here [meaning a plain coat with no lining] can be used interchangeably with another character that also means a plain unlined coat. The 'Yuzao' [jade-bead pendants of the royal cap] chapter of the *Book of Rites* points out that 'a plain garment with no lining is called *jiong* [絅].'[3] This phrase is a reference to a bride setting off for her new home, and, while she was on the road, wearing a plain, unlined coat over her embroidered silk dress. The real reason for this was to protect her silk dress from the dust of the road, but this chapter adds that 'it was because she preferred clothing that was plain and simple.' That is misunderstanding the context in which that phrase appears. Although this line does not use the exact same Sinographs we see in the *Book of Songs*, there is no real difference in meaning. If we go beyond the literal meaning of this line and say that it is talking about much more than the clothes worn by a bride, what would be the reason for it to refer to putting a plain coat with no lining over an embroidered silk gown? To say that this line is about anything other than [protecting] a bridal dress is ludicrous."[4]

Let me concur that the phrase "over her brocade garments she wore a plain coat with no lining" [*shangjiong* 尚絅] is from a poem that has been lost. But, since it is from a poem which we no longer have access to, how can we be sure it does not have a deeper meaning?[5]

THE KING ASKED:

The phrase "not monotonous," though it appears in this chapter, is not fully explained in *Zhongyong zhangju*.[6] Should we then rely on what Chen is reported to have said and understand it to refer to people not being tired of seeing it?[7] Refined patterns of things [文] as well as properly organized patterns [理] are both what they are in and of themselves. "Not monotonous," on the other hand, is the only phrase here that refers to how people feel about things. Would not it be appropriate, I venture to suggest, in this case to read the phrases that immediately precede and follow this particular phrase as having essentially the same reference as this phrase? If we understand "not monotonous" as something that is dependent on individual perception, then how could we make sense of this entire passage?

I RESPONDED:

This chapter is a general discussion of the line "the Dao of an exemplary person...is understated but not monotonous." It is referring to the Dao, that's all. There is no need to draw on Chen's interpretation that reads into it a comparison of what I and others think. The Dao of an exemplary person is the Dao in its own right. That's why it is described as "understated but not monotonous." Why do we need to bring other people into it? I'm afraid that Chen is not quite correct here.

Lü Dalin said, "If you trace back the roots of what you have learned from experience and the incisive actions you have taken, you will see that there is nothing that did not originate in your heart-mind. Is that not what is meant by the phrase in this chapter 'knowing from whence the wind blows'"?[8]

Zhu Xi said, "What people say these days shows that they have fully accepted this interpretation of what 'knowing from whence the wind blows' means, taking it as something only Master Cheng could have said. They have become accustomed to the Buddhists' talk about 'human nature being nothing more than the body's basic physical functions.' They have not noticed the mistake in Liaoweng's preface.[9] To study without clarifying the actual meaning of what you are studying, resulting in a distorted understanding—that's really pitiful."[10] In my opinion, this is just another example of the disciples of Master Cheng being infected by the ideas of meditative Buddhists.

Zhu Xi said, "The phrase 'extrapolating what is far away from what is close at hand' means to see how 'that' comes from 'this.' 'From whence the wind blows' refers to what is manifest externally being based on what is within. The 'that which is subtle becoming manifest' refers to that which is within your heart-mind becoming manifest externally."[11]

Lin said, "In the phrase 'extrapolating what is far away from what is close at hand,' what is far away refers to other people and what is close at hand refers to oneself. The 'wind' here refers to people imitating the behavior of their superiors. Also 'wind' can refer to me personally doing something which has a positive impact on others. When we say 'wind' emanates from ourselves, we are talking about what actually is generated by our heart-mind." See *Harboring Doubts*.[12]

As I see it, what Zhu Xi means is that which is far away refers to things actualizing their potential and that which is near at hand refers to actualizing your own potential. However, the "Counsels of Gao-yao" chapter of the *Book of Documents* says, "He may reach what is distant,"[13] and the *Zhongyong* talks of "extrapolating what is far away from what is close at hand." I see a contradiction here that is unsettling.[14]

Moreover, reading "wind" as a reference to what a person does, and then saying that "from whence" refers to the heart-mind of that person (Zhu Xi said, "the phrase 'knowing from whence the wind blows' is a reference to knowing whether you personally have acted properly or improperly, and whether what emanated from your own heart-mind was on target or deviated from the Dao.")[15] doesn't appear to be accurate, I'm afraid. How can we say that such expressions as "the teachings of the wind" [public morals and proper customs] and "transformations of the wind" [social customs and public mores] refer to the actions of individual people?

As for the phrase "subtle yet obvious," it appears four times in the *Zhongyong*. In each case, it refers to the Dao of Heaven seeming to be subtle yet actually being obvious. It is not the case, however, that the Dao of Heaven is obvious in every minor situation we find ourselves in. The statement that the subtle and hard-to-see can actually be obvious is intended to serve as a warning to those who act improperly because they do not realize they need to be cautious and apprehensive in everything they do.

I would also like to point out that, because Lin takes that which is far away to refer to other people and that which is near to refer to oneself, he therefore understands "wind" as a reference to harmonizing our actions with those of others and "from whence" as referring to oneself alone. But the subtle and the obvious both refer to what we ourselves do, so why does he make this sort of distinction?

That which appears to be far away is actually right at hand and that which appears to be subtle is actually quite obvious. Both are ways of referring to the Dao of Heaven.

How could "knowing from whence the wind blows" have any other meaning?

"Knowing from whence the wind blows" is referring to grasping the traces of the transformations of things and recognizing the foundations of those transformations. The sun, moon, stars, and mountains, as well as waterways, soil, and rocks, are all things that are stable. Therefore people think of them as things that will stay the way they are and will always do what they do. Although we cannot be certain when there will be rain, frost, dew, or snow, we know that the mountains and waterways will produce clouds, heaven will send down seasonal rains, dew will freeze and turn into frost, and rain will freeze and turn into snow. All of this is to be expected. But we might suddenly encounter a sudden blast of angry, howling wind and not have any idea what caused it.

The *Book of Songs* mentions "a gentle wind from the south."[16] We know only that it came from the south. We do not know what happened in the south to cause this gentle wind. The *Book of Songs* also includes the line "cold blows the northern wind."[17] We know only that it blew from the north. We do not know what happened in the north to send down this cold wind.

As for the traces of the transformations of things, they are nowhere more obvious than they are in the manifest changes seen in such winds. Therefore "knowing from whence the wind blows" and "knowing what appears subtle is actually obvious" are saying the same thing. There is no need to try to read different meanings into them.

Zhongyong XXXIII: 2

> The *Book of Songs* says, "Although the fish lie on the bottom to hide, they are still clearly visible."[18]

Zhu Xi said, "There is nothing more visible than what is hidden; there is nothing more obvious than what is subtle."[19]

As I read him, Zhu Xi takes "hidden" and "subtle" to refer to people who are in a hidden-away place or are engaged in some hardly noticeable activity. (See the introduction to *Zhongyong zhangju*.)[20] But I am afraid that is not what this line means in that ode. "The fish lie on the bottom to hide" is a reference to the fact that the Dao of Heaven is not particularly obvious at first sight; "They are still clearly visible" is a reference to the fact that the Dao of Heaven is actually quite obvious when you know where to look. The fact that what may appear hard to see is actually obvious is the reason an exemplary person watches over himself even when no one else is aware of what he is thinking or doing.[21]

Zhongyong XXXIII: 3

> The *Book of Songs* says, "If someone spies on you in your own home, make sure there is nothing going on to be ashamed of even in the darkest corner."[22]

Zhu Xi said, "The exemplary person is cautious, wary, apprehensive, and fearful. There are no times when he is not so. People do not wait until after he speaks or acts to respect him or trust him."[23]

Chen Beixi said, "The exemplary person does not wait until action is called for but approaches things with a mindful attitude beforehand. With an exemplary person, you do not need to see them speaking to know that they can be trusted."[24]

Hu Yunfeng said, "When there is movement, you can see what is moving. Therefore, the phrase in this section that says 'even though it is not seen to do anything, an exemplary person maintains an attitude of respect and mindfulness' tells us he is cautious and apprehensive toward what is not seen. When someone speaks, you can hear them. The phrase in this section 'even though it does not say anything, he trusts it' therefore tells us he is apprehensive about, and is in awe of, what is not heard."[25]

Xu Dongyang said, "An exemplary person is already trustworthy and mindful before he says or does anything."[26]

Cai Qing said, "References to being mindful and trustworthy when nothing is happening means that an exemplary person always maintains in his heart-and-mind a mindful and trustworthy stance."[27]

In my opinion, what Hu Yunfeng said is the closest to the actual meaning of that text and surpasses what the others said. The others all regard the references to words and actions as referring merely to their own words and actions [without going into how they can maintain a mindful and trustworthy stance when they are not doing or saying anything]. They are way off the mark.

Lü Dalin said, "If his heart-mind is solidly grounded, an exemplary person does not have to speak or act for people to respect and trust him."[28]

Zhu Xi said, "Lü...took the phrases 'To be respected even before he does anything' and 'before he speaks, he is already trusted' as referring to other people respecting and trusting the exemplary person [before he shows why he should be respected and trusted].... This is not the correct meaning of this text."[29]

As I see it, what Lü said is full of errors. In the next passage the *Zhongyong* talks of the "people" being encouraged by, and "people" being in awe of, the exemplary person. This passage does not have the word "people," so how can anyone say this is referring to being respected and trusted by others?[30]

Zhongyong XXXIII: 4

> The *Book of Songs* says, "Silently, without a word, he enters and offers the sacrifice; at that time there is no discord."³¹

Zhu Xi said, "*Zou* [奏-the first Sinograph in this line from this poem] means 'enter.'... This line speaks of him acting just as he should, displaying the utmost sincerity and respect, on the occasion of entering the sacrificial hall and establishing an emotional connection with the ancestral spirits. Without him saying a single word, the people [are stimulated to] change their ways on their own."³²

As I read it, this line says entering the sacrificial hall in silence touched the heart-minds of the common people so that they came to trust the celebrant. This is not a reference to "establishing an emotional connection with the ancestral spirits." (Although in the *Book of Songs* this line appears in a poem about paying ritual respect to ancestral spirits, the person who inserted that line in this work separated it from the context in which it appears in the *Book of Songs*.) In this final chapter of the *Zhongyong*, there are seven lines lifted from the *Book of Songs*. The first three are used for a discussion of self-cultivation. The next three are used for a discussion of elevating the people. The last one is used for a discussion of the integration of the Dao of Heaven and the Dao of human beings. This being the case, the reference to "silently, without a word, he enters and offers a sacrifice" has to be about touching the heart-minds of the people. It is not about stablishing an emotional connection with ancestral spirits.³³

Zhongyong XXXIII: 5

> The *Book of Songs* says, "He doesn't make a public display of his ethical virtuosity, yet all the noblemen take him as an exemplar."[34]

Zhu Xi said, "The phrase 'he doesn't make a public display' means 'how could it not be obvious to everyone?'"[35]

In my opinion, "he doesn't make a public display of his ethical virtuosity" refers to cultivating his ethical virtuosity even when he is alone. Even though he does not make a public display of his ethical virtuosity, the people nonetheless take him as a model for their own behavior. His ethical virtuosity may not be noticeable at first but day by day it becomes more obvious.

Hu Yunfeng said, "The two lines from the *Book of Songs* cited in this section are related to the lines cited in the passage two sections before this [Chapter XXXIII: 3] which say 'even though it is not seen to do anything, an exemplary person maintains an attitude of respect and mindfulness' and 'even though it does not say anything, he trusts it.' That makes the meaning of these later lines much clearer.

"To say that he trusts it before it says anything means that people will [take him as a model and] place their trust in such a person even before he himself says anything. In other words, they will cultivate their moral character without having to wait until they hear promises of rewards or threats of punishments.

"Similarly, to be respectful and mindful of something before seeing it move means he behaves in a thoughtful and respectful manner even when that which he is displaying reverence towards is not visible."[36]

As I see it, what Hu is trying to say is that this means that the Dao of Heaven does not speak, yet the exemplary person trusts it. The Dao of Heaven does not do anything, yet the exemplary person reveres it. That is the reason the exemplary person does not need to speak to have the common people trust him. And this is the reason the exemplary person does not need to make a public display of his ethical virtuosity for the common people to respect him. What Hu is saying here is very discerning and perceptive. Ordinary scholars would not be able to display such insight.

Hu Yunfeng said, "The reference to ethical virtuosity that is not openly displayed is a reference to none other than that state of equilibrium and composure in which the emotions of pleasure, anger, sorrow, and joy have not yet begun to stir. A cautious and apprehensive attitude before pleasure, anger, sorrow, and joy have begun to stir produces a mindful and respectful stance."[37]

In my opinion, what Hu says here is extremely perceptive. He is right on target. If we accept Hu's interpretation, then we have to exert a lot of effort even when our emotions have not yet been activated.[38]

Zhongyong XXXIII: 6

> The *Book of Songs* says, "I admire the way you radiate moral power without proclaiming it loudly or making a big display of it."[39]

Zhu Xi said, "This clarifies that the term 'not make a public display' in the preceding passage means to properly refrain from calling attention to your ethical virtuosity with either your voice or your demeanor."[40]

In my opinion, the phrase "not make a public display" which we saw in the preceding passage means to be low-key. The phrase "radiate moral power" means that it grows more obvious every day. The Dao of Heaven is subtle and hard to see, but an exemplary person embodies it in his actions so that it becomes visible. For the same reason, though the ethical virtuosity of an exemplary person is not meant to be conspicuous, the way the common people look up to it in admiration makes it so. This is another marvelous example of something naturally stimulating a response in something else. It is like what happens when ethical virtuosity takes root in a house in the west. The neighboring house to the east benefits as well.

Zhu Xi said, "This section of the *Zhongyong* also quotes Confucius saying that a strong voice and a stern demeanor will not serve to get people to respect you."[41]

I would like to point out that Confucius first intoned the "I admire the way you radiate moral power" ode from the *Book of Songs* and then pointed out that using a strong voice and a stern demeanor is not a very effective way to transform the people for the better.[42] As we can see in the *Analects* and *The Book of Rites*, that is essentially the way Confucius used the *Book of Songs* in talking with his disciples. (In one of the odes, there is a line that reads "I gathered the bark of the mulberry tree."[43] After intoning the ode that includes that line, Confucius went on to relate it to the proper way to govern a state.[44] There is another ode that has the line "there is a little oriole."[45] After intoning the ode that includes that line, Confucius went on to discuss knowing what goal to strive for in your pursuit of a moral life.)[46] Why should this particular ode be treated different from the rest?

The next part of this chapter of the *Zhongyong*, starting with "the *Book of Songs* says moral authority is as light as a feather," should be treated as a separate section. I'm afraid Zhu Xi made a mistake when he linked this to the earlier citations.

Zhongyong XXXIII: 6

The *Book of Songs* says, "Moral authority is light, like a feather."[47]

Zhu Xi said, "Sounds and scents[48] are composed of *ki* but take no material form. Of the various things we experience in the world around us, they are the most elusive and mystifying. You could almost say they do not exist at all. Accordingly, this is a good way to refer to the marvelous way someone not making a public display impresses people with their thoughtful and reverential manner. There is nothing beyond such moral authority. However, we can distinguish three separate degrees of moral authority."[49]

As I see it, Zhu Xi took "not proclaiming it loudly" as one level of moral power, "light, like a feather" as a second level, and "with neither sounds nor scent" as a third level. These are his so-called three degrees of moral authority. But it is Heaven on High that has neither sound nor scent, yet the exemplary person reveres it. That is why, though an exemplary person does not loudly proclaim or make a public display of his ethical virtuosity, the common people give their allegiance to him. The two phrases "loudly proclaim and publicly display" and "sounds and scents" illuminate this principle. The Dao emanates from Heaven, is manifest in an exemplary person, and finally is actualized in the transformation of the people [so that they act appropriately]. We should, therefore, speak first of the transformation of the people, then of the moral authority residing among them, and finally that it was Heaven that made that possible. This is the essential point.[50]

THE KING ASKED:

The first chapter of this work begins with our internal mental states and then it moves on to how they are manifested externally. This final chapter begins with what is external and links it to what is within us. Zhu Xi provides a comprehensive summary of this arrangement. He emphasizes that both the opening and concluding chapters deal with our internal mental states and our external behavior. I venture to point out, though we cannot say that the first chapter is only about our internal mental state while the final chapter is only about our external behavior, I'm afraid that neither can we say that the final chapter explicitly addresses our internal mental state while the first chapter explicitly addresses our external behavior. So why does Zhu Xi want to emphasize that both chapters deal with internal mental states as well as external behavior?[51]

| RESPONDED:

Zhu Xi's intent is to show that initially there is just one defining inclusive pattern of how all things are supposed to interact, that this pattern then becomes manifest in ten thousand different ways in the Ten Thousand Things, and finally that all those patterns come together to again form just one inclusive pattern. That is why the first chapter discusses the endowment Heaven has bestowed on us and expounds on that to explain how it embraces all of the Ten Thousand Things, and the final chapter discusses the people being transformed through the way Heaven operates. Both the opening chapter and the closing chapter, therefore, each have something to say about internal mental states and external actions. It is just that the first chapter deals with what is internal first and then moves on to what is external, while the last chapter deals with what is external first and then moves onto what is internal. What harm can it do to say that external behavior and internal mental states are addressed in both of those chapters?

THE KING ASKED:

The first chapter says that "when pleasure, anger, sorrow, or joy have not yet begun to stir, the heart-mind is calm and composed." This is none other than what we express as "Non-Polarity [C. *wuji* / K. *mugŭk*] yet Supreme Polarity [C. *taiji* / K. *t'aegŭk*]." The final chapter says that "The operations of Heaven on High have neither sound nor scent." This is precisely what we express as "Supreme Polarity is essentially nothing other than Non-Polarity."[52] The way Hu Yunfeng explained this is truly completely correct.[53] If we can clarify what this chapter says by using his interpretation, and come to understand what it means point by point, then the subtle and profound message of Chapter XXXIII can be thoroughly grasped. Give this some careful thought and then clarify and explain it.

| RESPONDED:

Zhu Xi in his *Questions and Answers on the Zhongyong* says caution and apprehension are the foundation for achieving a calm and composed heart-mind.[54] What he says here is extremely precise and accurate. Looking at it from this point of view, then even when we say that the emotions of pleasure, anger, sadness, or joy have not yet begun to stir, it is not the case that the heart-mind, and its ability to know, reflect, and deliberate, is totally still. How can we talk as though there is nothing at all happening in the heart-mind? "The way Heaven on High operates" means the same thing as the phrase "the operations of Heaven on High" in the "Biography of Yang Xiong" [a chapter of the *History of the Former Han Dynasty*].⁵⁵ "Operations" is equivalent to "the exercise of dominion over." That which exercises dominion does so over the transformations of the myriad things, and it does so in a totally unselfishly cooperative and appropriately responsive manner without ever stopping.⁵⁶ So how can we say that nothing is happening at all?⁵⁷

However, as for whether Non-Polarity is something real or not, your humble servant does not have any idea of what sort of thing it could possibly be. Nevertheless, how can we talk about nothing happening at all when we discuss the message of the *Zhongyong*?

(What follows is what I learned from Kwangam.)⁵⁸ Let me point out that the *Diagram of the Supreme Polarity* is nothing more than a combination of the trigrams *Kan* and *Li* [which mean water and fire, respectively].⁵⁹ The patterns (*li*) defining *Kan* and *Li* are explained in detail in the *Cantong qi* [參同契].⁶⁰ There is no need to go further and make them the foundation of all the myriad things. Unfortunately, the defining patterns of appropriate interactions Confucian scholars talk about these days are completely vacuous and have no real substance, so those scholars are forced to say that the defining patterns they put so much emphasis on emerge out of some dark and featureless Supreme Polarity. Your humble servant is not intelligent enough to understand what they are talking about. The subtle and profound message of the *Zhongyong* is found within the *Zhongyong* and is without a doubt quite clear. Why do we need to add anything about a *Supreme Polarity* to what it tells us? However, I am still carefully mulling over what this all means. As a result, I am unable to clarify and explain this at this time.

Discussing Zhu Xi's Preface to *Zhongyong zhangju*

THE KING ASKED:

Master Cheng[1] said that when we talk about the Dao heart-mind, we are talking about acting in accordance with the patterns of appropriate behavior grounded in Heaven. When we talk about the human heart-mind, we are talking about the influence of our physical desires. Zhu Xi said that even those who are the wisest of all cannot escape having a human heart-mind.[2] But why does he then attribute all human desires to the human heart-mind? The desires Master Cheng was referring to are what Mencius called the desires of the eyes, ears, nose, mouth, and the four limbs.[3] That is why Master Cheng says that even those who are the wisest of all are unable to avoid having physical desires. However, Zhu Xi takes the word "desires" in the phrase "human desires" to refer to "self-centered carnal desires" [those desires that reflect the pursuit of individual benefit]. What these two wise men say appears to be contradictory. Can you somehow reconcile what they are saying?

I RESPONDED:

What Mencius called the desires of the eyes, ears, nose, mouth, and the four limbs are certainly things that even the most sagely cannot live without. But when it comes to how we respond to these desires, if we are able to act in accordance with the principles defining appropriate behavior, then we do not have to worry about going against the morally good. However, if we act in accordance with our selfish desires, then we will fall into depravity. The *Book of Documents* therefore says, "The human heart-mind is dangerous." "Dangerous" here refers to how difficult it is [for the human heart-mind] to distinguish between good and evil. That is why Zhu Xi's commentary on the "Counsels of the Great Yu" [in which the preceding quotation appears] says, "The human heart-mind finds it much easier to pursue personal self-interest than to pursue the common good. That is why it is called dangerous."[4] Isn't what we call "easier to pursue personal self-interest" the same as "being led by physical desires"? This being the case, what Master Cheng and Zhu Xi said are complementary. As for any difference between "human desires" [欲] and "carnal desires" [慾], there is a slight difference between these two terms. But most of the ancient classics have written them both as "desire" just as they used the character "knowledge" for both "knowledge" and "wisdom." They are not very different from one another.

The Sinograph "human desires" [欲] is made up of components meaning "valley" [谷] and "to lack" [欠] respectively. "Valley" means "empty" and "to lack" means "insufficient." Generally speaking, when something feels it is missing something that it wants or needs, it tries to grab it from somewhere else and use it to make up for what itself lacks. The desires of the human heart-mind are like this. Accordingly, this Sinograph "human desires" was made by combining "valley" and "to lack." Looking at it this way, we can see that, although the Sinograph "human desires" does not include the radical for the heart-mind [which appears at the bottom of "carnal desires"], it is not much different from the Sinograph "carnal desires" in the term "selfish carnal desires." Laozi used the phrase "A valley lacks that which would fill it up."[5] That can be read as a reference to "insatiable desires."

THE KING ASKED:

A certain Korean scholar (that Korean scholar is Yulgok Yi I), in discussing the difference between the human heart-mind and the Dao heart-mind, said, "Dynamic patterns of appropriate interactions [*li*] and the psychophysical nature [*ki*] are intrinsically intermingled and cannot be separated from one another.... It is *ki* that manifests *li*, but the reason it is manifest the way it is, is *li*.... So why do people try to distinguish between manifesting via *li* and manifesting via *ki*?"[6]

Although the Dao heart-mind cannot operate apart from *ki*, nevertheless it manifests as appropriate interactions between human beings. That is why we place it in the same category as the innate potential for acting appropriately Heaven has endowed us with. Although the human heart-mind is rooted in *li* as well, it manifests through the mouth and limbs. That is why we place it in the same category as our psychophysical constitution. When Yulgok distinguishes "the reason something manifests the way it does" and "that which manifests it," he is saying that a thing or event can become visible only if there is a dynamic pattern [*li*] defining, directing, and shaping the way that thing or event becomes visible, but, if there is no psychophysical stuff for *li* to work with, then there is nothing that can be seen. This confirms that *li* and *ki* are intrinsically intermingled and cannot be separated from one another.

However, there are some who argue that the Four Sprouts are manifestations of *li* and the Seven Emotions are manifestations of *ki*. (This is the argument made by T'oegye.)[7] I would like to hear if you can resolve this difference of opinion.

I RESPONDED:

When it comes to linking the Four Sprouts to *li* and the Seven Emotions to *ki*, your humble servant harbors doubt about this. If we can avoid becoming entangled in confusing language and instead rise above the fray and sit quietly to look at it from an objective perspective, then this puzzle will be easy to unravel. *Ki* is something that exists on its own, and *li* can only be found in connection with something else. Anything so dependent on something else is contingent on that which exists on its own. This means the *li* of a thing can only be manifest after some *ki* has congealed into that thing.[8] This being the case, it must be said that *ki* appears first and then *li* uses it to become manifest. It cannot be said that *li* appears before *ki* does. Why do I say that? There is no way *li* can plant itself in itself. That means there is no way it can manifest first. Before something becomes manifest, although they may already be a patterning principle defining the way it should look and the way it should act, for that patterning principle to be manifest, there must already be some *ki* ready to be shaped and directed by *li*.

When that Korean scholar [Yulgok] says, "It is *ki* that manifests *li*, but the reason it is manifest the way it is, is *li*," he is completely correct. Who could say otherwise? Your humble servant ventures to say that the Four Sprouts and the Seven Emotions are both, in a succinct phrase, cases of "*ki* manifests itself and *li* then uses it to become manifest itself."[9] It is not necessary to place the Four Sprouts and the Seven Emotions in separate camps. This does not apply only to the Four Sprouts and the Seven Emotions. Every plant and tree that grows out of the ground, every bird that flies, and every beast that runs is a case of *ki* manifesting itself in a particular way, and *li* then taking advantage of that to make itself manifest.

Yi Tŏkcho[10] once said to me, "If we examine the original meanings of the words *li* and *ki* in an objective manner, then Yulgok's approach is certainly not far from the truth. However, if we follow the analytical approach adopted by some of those who study patterning principle and humanity's innate potential for appropriate behavior [i.e., neo-Confucians], then we have to say that *li* refers to the Dao heart-mind only, and *ki* refers only to the human heart-mind. When what the heart-mind manifests originates from the innate moral potential and spiritual insight of human beings, it is said to be a manifestation of *li*. On the other hand, when what the heart-mind manifests originates in the physical body, then it is said to be a manifestation of *ki*. If we accept this way of looking at it, it's clear that T'oegye's suggestion is a produce of profound thinking, and we cannot go along with what Yulgok said."

Back in 1784, I mistakenly clung to this interpretation. Then in the summer of 1801, when I was in exile far away from the capital in Changgi, I wrote *On Whether the Four Sprouts are Activated by Li or by Ki*[11] to explain my own thoughts on this issue.

THE KING ASKED:

A certain Korean scholar [Yulgok] drew a diagram explaining the difference between the Dao heart-mind and the human heart-mind in which he places the phrase "the moral good" directly under the Dao [moral] heart-mind. [See figures 1 and 2.] Is "moral good" on this diagram the same as the "good" we are referring to when we say the innate potential of human beings is good, or does it mean something different? Also, the human heart-mind is something that both Sages and ordinary people have in common, yet this diagram places the human heart-mind on a diagonal line that slants off to the left from the circle that includes the word *xing* [the innate potential of human beings to act appropriately] and then places the word "evil" at the end of that line. Why did he do that?

I RESPONDED:

The diagram basically focuses on the phrase "moral good," and the word "evil" is there only to provide a contrast with it. There is no doubt that the word "good" we use when we say "the innate potential of human beings to act appropriately [human nature] is good" means nothing other than "moral good." I truly do not understand why he felt he needed to add a line slanting off to the left from the circle that includes the word *xing* and then place "the human heart-mind" along that line, with leads to "evil." We should note that Zhu Xi's preface to his *Zhongyong zhangju* includes the statement "There is no human being who does not have a physical body. Therefore, even the wisest among us is unable to escape having a human heart-mind."[12] Then can we understand him, when he says that even the greatest sages among us cannot be free of a human heart-mind, to mean that there is evil within them? I'm dare to say this was not the point Zhu Xi is trying to make.

THE KING ASKED:

Further on in his preface, Zhu Xi added, "We need to closely examine the differences between these two and not confuse them."[13] What advice should we draw from this classic when we embark on this task of closely examining the differences between these two?

I RESPONDED:

"These two" means the human heart-mind and the Dao heart-mind. As for what we can take from this classic to help us closely examine the differences between those two, it is the phrase "choose to act appropriately and then hold fast to that decision."[14] That is what it means to closely examine the differences between those two.

THE KING ASKED:

Are the meanings of "being appropriately composed and focused in whatever situation you find yourself in" [shizhong 時中] and "maintaining a composed and focused state of mind" [zhizong 執中] the same or different?[15] Emperor Yao called for maintaining a composed and focused state of mine.[16] Confucius advocated being composed and focused in whatever situation you find yourself in.[17] How is the former sagely teaching any different from the latter? Moreover, when it comes to "being appropriately composed and focused on whatever situation you find yourself in" and "maintaining a composed and focused state of mind," do you prefer Zimo's "holding on stubbornly to a composed and focused state of mind"[18] or Hu Guang's "focusing on whatever situation he found himself in"?[19]

I RESPONDED:

When Confucius says of an exemplary person "he is appropriately composed and focused in whatever situation he finds himself in,"[20] he is saying that in general an exemplary person is able to tailor his actions to whatever is the appropriate way to behave in whatever situation he finds himself in. That is what makes an exemplary person an exemplary person. As for "maintaining a composed and focused state of mind," that is what an exemplary person should strive to do in whatever situation he finds himself. Such a consistent effort to maintain such a state of mind is precisely what an exemplary person does.

The first of those phrases is a more general statement about the stance people should adopt if they want to act appropriately. The second phrase is a reference to the specific effort required to do so. That is why they are phrased somewhat differently.

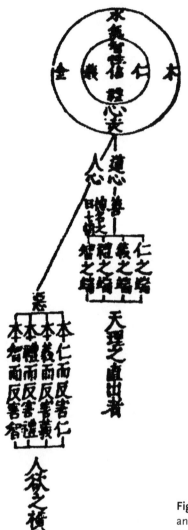

Figure 1: Yulgok's Diagram of the Dao Heart-Mind and the Human Heart-Mind. (Yi I, *Yulgok chŏnsŏ* [The complete works of Yulgok Yi I], "Insim.Dosim tosŏl" [A diagram of the Human Heart-mind and the Dao Heart-mind], XIV: 6a.)

As for Zimo, he was described as being composed and focused without taking into account the need to be flexible enough to adapt to different circumstances in different situations. On the other hand, Hu Guang was not able to maintain a consistent focus on the task at hand and on what he should do. Neither of them provides an appropriate model for maintaining focus and composure. (Looking back now on what I wrote back then, I see that I took this paragraph from something Yi Tŏkcho wrote.)

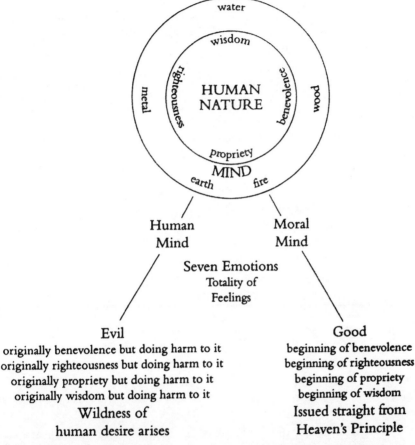

Figure 2: Yulgok's Diagram of the Human Mind and the Moral Mind. (Source: Edward Y. J. Chung, *The Korean Neo-Confucianism of Yi T'oegye and Yi Yulgok: A Reappraisal of the "Four-Seven Thesis" and Its Practical Implications for Self-Cultivation* [Albany: State University of New York Press, 1995, 198].)

Though Huangfu Xi[21] arrogated for himself the title "recluse" and Feng Dao[22] usurped the title "a man of insight," people of their day did not believe they deserved those labels, and later generations did not allow those terms to be applied to them. Similarly, though Zimo and Hu Guang take terms from the *Zhongyong* to imply that is the way they behave, how is what they did different from what Huangfu Xi and Feng Dao did?

Discussing the Divisions of the Text

THE KING ASKED:

In dividing up the chapters in the *Zhongyong*, *This is How to Read the Zhongyong* suggests dividing them into six major sections.[1] *Zhongyong zhangju*, on the other hand, divides them into four major sections. Rao Lu follows *This Is How to Read the Zhongyong*. Wang Bo[2] concentrates instead on the way this text is divided in *Zhongyong zhangju*. I am not sure if we should follow *Zhongyong zhangzu*. After Rao and Wang, some others proposed instead dividing the text into five major sections.

Most people generally follow the division into sections presented in *Zhongyong zhangju* for the chapters after Chapter XII. However, some take Chapter I as a separate section by itself, separating it from Chapters II through XI, which are put together in a separate section. That is how *This Is How to Read the Zhongyong* does it.

Is there any way to draw on how both *Zhongyong zhangju* and *This Is How to Read the Zhongyong* divide the chapters into sections to come up with a compromise?

I RESPONDED:

When you separate the chapters in a single work into different sections, it is difficult to get it right. For example, the Grand Historian Sima Qian (145 BCE–87 BCE) noted that there are three different ways to arrange the one poem "Li Sao,"[3] depending on how you read it. Consequently, scholars have continued to argue over how to interpret that poem. There is still no consensus.

As for how to link the various chapters in the *Zhongyong* into larger sections, scholars in the ancient past said absolutely nothing about that. Your humble servant does not know how many sections it should be divided into to get at the original meaning. I would like to suggest, however, that examining a book is like examining bamboo; although it may be made up of joints and sections, one would do well to look it as a whole.

A Record of the Discussion of the *Zhongyong* at the Brilliant Governance Hall.[1]

In the spring of 1790, I resigned my post as a transcriber in the Office of Royal Decrees and accepted exile to Haemi County. After ten days I was pardoned and set out on the road to Onyang, where I stopped briefly to bathe in a hot spring. I then returned to the court in Seoul. His Highness the King was at the Brilliant Governance Hall. He ordered the officials of the Royal Library to gather there to discuss the *Zhongyong*.

SUPERINTENDENT OF SCHOLARSHIP IN THE ROYAL LIBRARY O CHAE-SUN[2] ASKED:

Does the Sinograph *zhong* [中] as it appears in "he is appropriately composed and focused in whatever situation he finds himself" mean the same as it does in the phrase "composed, focused, and cooperative"?[3]

I RESPONDED:

"Composed and focused" in "composed, focused, and cooperative" is a reference to potential. "Composed and focused" in "he is appropriately composed and focused in whatever situation he finds himself" is a reference to the actualization of that potential. What they refer to is different, but fundamentally their meaning is the same.

SUPERINTENDENT OF SCHOLARSHIP IN THE ROYAL LIBRARY YI PYŎNGMO[4] ASKED:

The *Zhongyong* says "a petty person lacks any moral scruples." Why is it that he acts "contrary to the Dao of constant composure and focus"?[5]

I RESPONDED:

The exemplary person's ability to be consistently composed and focused is due to nothing other than his feeling cautious and apprehensive. Since a petty person does not cultivate such feelings, how can he be other than unscrupulous?

THE KING ASKED:

What do you have to say about the line that reads, "People are rarely able to be consistently composed and focused over a long period of time so that they act and think precisely the way they should act and think."[6]

I RESPONDED:

If we focus on "people are rarely **able to**" as the key phrase, then it does not match what the *Analects* says: "among the common people few have been able to maintain this proper way of behavior for very long."[7] However, if we take "few are able **for very long**" as the key phrase, then there is no contradiction here. When the *Zhongyong* talks about how difficult something is, it is referring to the difficulty of being consistent in doing that over a long period of time. That is why later on the *Zhongyong* says, "The common people cannot be consistently composed and focused for a whole month."[8] I dare to propose that this is the correct reading.

O CHAE-SUN ASKED:

Are being fully human, being profound, and being like Heaven equally important or do they differ in the emphasis we should place on them?[9]

I RESPONDED:

"Being fully human" refers to the foundation of ethical virtuosity, "being profound" [as deep as an abyss] refers to self-control, and "being like Heaven" refers to appearing to have achieved ethical virtuosity.

O CHAE-SUN ASKED:

If being like Heaven refers to achieving ethical virtuosity, then is there any need to make an effort to become fully human and profound as well?

I RESPONDED:

If we take into account the word "his" in the phrases "his being fully human" and "his being profound," we can see that it means "he is already fully human and fully profound." It is not appropriate to take these phrases as exhortations to separate efforts. However, if we talk about those three as though they are separate, then we should look upon being like Heaven as the ultimate accomplishment of ethical virtuosity.

Yi Pyŏng-mo asked:

If this chapter said only "he embraces all, just like Heaven does," wouldn't that include being fully human and being profound? Why was it necessary to explicitly add those other two references as well?

I responded:

If this chapter said only "he embraces all, just like Heaven does," then that would have touched only the surface. By also referring to being fully human and being profound, it amplifies the wonder of it all.

O Chae-sun asked:

Does the term "great foundation" which appears in this chapter mean the same as the "great foundation" we see in the first chapter?[10]

I responded:

It has been a long time since being composed and focused has not been seen as the main point of this text. The two-word phrase "great foundation" refers to that which functions as a pillar holding up heaven. I'm afraid I have to admit the two usages of that term have exactly the same meaning.

O Chae-sun asked:

What is the meaning of the term "to establish" in Chapter XXXII?

I responded:

If we understand that the two words "great foundation" refer to the full potential of the innate human ability to act appropriately, "to establish" here means the same as it does in the phrase in *Mencius* referring to "establishing on a firm foundation what Heaven has determined one is supposed to do."[11] If we understand "centered" in a broader sense, then we can read "to establish" as it is used in the line "to firmly establish the correct ["centered"] course for others to follow" which is in the *Book of Documents*.[12]

O CHAE-SUN ASKED:

Did the two words "be off the mark" and "lean off-center" originally have two different meanings?[13]

I RESPONDED:

The phrase "be off the mark" is a reference to the place where someone or something should stand. The phrase "lean off-center" is a reference to who or what is standing. Let's say you want to stand a gnomon upright on a stand. You need to make sure it is in the exact center of that stand. That is what is meant by not being off the mark. But if we are talking about that gnomon itself being perfectly upright, then we describe it as not being off-center. So "not being off the mark" is a reference to how it appears from a horizontal perspective. "Not leaning off-center" is a reference to how it appears from a vertical perspective. If you put that gnomon exactly where it should be on its base but the gnomon itself is not straight, then, although at the base it will be perfectly centered, it will not be where it should be at the top.

YI PYŎNG-MO ASKED:

[In Chapter XXXII] there is a two-syllable compound that has a Sinograph for "to run a thread through" followed by a Sinograph for "to pull together." What does that mean here?

I RESPONDED:

"To run a thread through" means to examine individual things and processes in order to find the normative patterns in each one. "To pull together" means to bring them together so that they coalesce. Therefore, these two Sinographs side-by-side mean to manage the patterns defining appropriate interactions in the myriad things and processes so that they all interact appropriately with each other.

O CHAE-SUN ASKED:

The single Sinograph meaning "sagely" embraces ten thousand ways of displaying ethical virtuosity, yet this text goes on to explicitly name just three characteristics of a sage: being discerning, acting intelligently, and behaving wisely. Why is that?[14]

I RESPONDED:

The Sinograph "sagely" as it appears in the two-syllable compound "the sagely and worthy" is a general term for someone who has become an ultimate ethical virtuoso. "Sagely wisdom" and other such compounds that include the Sinograph "sagely" are just ways of identifying specific ways a sage displays ethical virtuosity. This is just like the way we see sages referred to in the ancient histories as "respectful and wise, impartial and profound."[15]

YI PYŎNG-MO ASKED:

If the phrase [in Chapter XXXII] "he embraces all, just like Heaven does" is another way of referring to ultimate ethical virtuosity, then why does this chapter go on to discuss being right on the mark and not off-center by adding the phrase "how can there be anything on which he leans on for support?"

I RESPONDED:

This is simply a way of heaping praise on the great things a sage accomplishes. It is rhetorical overkill. It was not necessary to go this far.[16] To the extent that we wholeheartedly accept the leadership of such a person, however, we can be sure that we are in accord with the Dao.

Glossary of Names, Places, and Terms

Ai, Lord (r. 494–468 BCE) 哀公: a ruler of the state of Lu 魯. Also known as Jiang 蔣.
Aigong Wen Zheng 哀公問政: "Lord Ai asks about governing."
Anbin shi 安貧詩: "At Ease in Poverty," a poem by Han Wo 韓偓.
Baihutong 白虎通: "Discussions in the White Tiger Hall," a record of a discussion among officials and scholars in 79 CE.
Ban Biao (3–54 CE) 班彪: the initiator of the project that produced the *Hanshu* 漢書.
Ban Gu (32–92) 班固: the son of Ban Biao. He is the principal author of the *Hanshu* 漢書.
Bao, Diviner 祝鮑: This appears to be a copyist's error for Diviner *Tuo*, a late sixth-century BCE figure who appears in the *Spring and Auumn Annals*.
Bao Xian (6 BCE–65 CE) 包咸: a Han-era scholar-offficial who wrote an influential commentary on the *Analects*.
Beifeng 邶風: a collection of poems in the "Airs of the States" section of *Book of Songs*.
Beishan, decade of 北山之什: a section in the collection of poems called "minor odes of the kingdom" in *Book of Songs*.
Beixi 北溪: the literary name of Chen Chun (1159–1223).
Bencao Gangmu 本草綱目: *Compendium on Materia Medica*, a sixteenth-century work by Li Shizhen (1518–1593) 李時珍.
Bi 畢: a regional state in early Zhou.
Bi Gan (fl. 11th c. BCE) 比干: legendary virtuous minister in the late Shang court. He was killed when he criticized the last Shang ruler's conduct.
Biandou 籩豆: bamboo and wooden dishes used in ancestor memorial rites.
Biaoji 表記: "Record of Example" chapter in the *Liji* [禮記.*Book of Rites*].
Bimian 鷩冕: outer garments of a deceased lord.
Binfeng 豳風: the "Odes of Ben" subsection of the "Airs of the States" section of the *Book of Songs*.
Bo Yi (fl. 11th c. BCE) 伯夷: legendary figure who is said to have given up his rightful claim to the throne of a vassal state under the Shang in order to allow his younger brother, his father's favorite son, to become king. He also is said to have starved himself to death rather than live under the Zhou dynasty, which replaced the Shang, to which he had been loyal.
Bowen of Teng (fl. Zhou period) 滕伯文: a man from the regional state of Teng 滕 who appears in the "Tan Gong" 檀弓 chapter of the *Book of Rites*.
bu xiu 不朽: a Daoist term for physical immortality.
bumang 不亡: a Daoist term for physical immortality.
Cai 蔡: a regional state in early Zhou.

Cai Chen (1167–1230) 蔡沈: editor of *Shujing jichuan* 書經集傳.
Cai Mo 蔡墨: a Spring and Autumns period scribe named Mo from the fiefdom of Cai.
Cai Qing (1453–1508) 蔡清: a scholar-official during the Ming dynasty and compiler of *Sishu mengyin* 四書蒙引.
Cai Shu Du (11th c. BCE) 蔡叔度: a brother of King Wu of Zhou 周武王 and the Duke of Zhou 周公. Cai is the name of the region King Wu asked him to govern.
Cai Zhong (11th–10th c. BCE) 蔡仲: the second ruler of the state of Cai during the Zhou dynasty.
Caisang 采桑: the name of a place in the state of Jin 晉 during the Spring and Autumn period.
Cangjie 倉頡: a legendary figure who is said to have invented Chinese characters.
Cangjiepian 倉頡篇: an early dictionary, originally compiled during the Qin dynasty, in the third century BCE.
Cantong qi 參同契: "The Seal of the Unity of the Three." An inner-alchemy text from the eighth century by Wei Boyang 魏伯陽 (??–728).
Cao 曹: a fiefdom in Zhou.
Ce 策: a bamboo slip used for writing.
Cha / K. *ch'al* 察: read by Tasan in Chapter XII as meaning to investigate what is hidden. Zhu Xi read it as "to manifest" instead.
Chach'an myojimyŏng 自撰墓誌銘: "[A self-authored tombstone inscription]," Tasan's autobiography.
chaju ji kwŏn 自主之權: "the power of self-control," free will.
Chang 昌: personal name of the man who was the grandson of King Tai 太王 and became King Wen 文王.
Chang: autumn sacrifice 嘗
chang / K. *sang* 常: consistent; regular; ordinary.
Chang Hong 萇弘: a minister of King Jing of Zhou 景王.
Changgi 長鬐: a rural district along Korea's southeastern coast.
Changzong (1025–1091) 常總: a famous Chan monk during the Song dynasty.
Chanmen xiuzheng zhiyao 禪門修證指要: "Essential Pointers to Practice and Realization through the Chan Gate," by the monk Shengyan 聖嚴.
ch'e / C. *ti* 體: literally, "body." However, it is sometimes used metaphorically to refer to the core or essence of something. It can also be used as a verb meaning "embody." When used in conjunction with *yong* 用, it is often best translated as "unactualized potential," with *yong* understood as that potential actualized.
Chen 陳: a small fiefdom during the Zhou dynasty era.
chen 辰: Relying on Lou Xiangming, Tasan reads this, in this text, as a reference to the places on a sky map designated as locations the moon, Jupiter, and other celestial objects pass through on a regular basis.
Chen Chun (1159–1223) 陳淳: also known as Chen Beixi 陳北溪. Author of *Beixi's Neo-Confucian Terms Explained* (*Beixi ziyi* 北溪字義).
Ch'en Ch'un. *See* Chen Chun.

Chen Feng-Yuan 陳逢源: a contemporary scholar in Taiwan.
Chen Guan (1057–1124) 陳瓘: a Confucian official in Northern Song who associated with Cheng Hao in his youth.
Chen Li (1252–1334) 陳櫟: a Song dynasty follower of Zhu Xi's approach to Confucianism. Chen Li is often referred to as Xin'an Chen 新安陳氏.
Chen Ziceng (fl. late 17th–early 18th c.) 陳自曾: a Confucian scholar during the Qing who was an acquaintance of Mao Qiling 毛奇齡.
Chen Zhongzi (fl. Warring States) 陳仲子: a man from the state of Qi 齊 who is mentioned in Mencius.
cheng / K. sŏng 誠: "sincerity," appropriately responsive and unselfishly cooperative.
Cheng 郕: a fiefdom in early Zhou.
Cheng, King of Zhou (r. 1042/35–1006 BCE) 周成王: second actual king of Zhou.
Cheng Hao (1032–1085) 程顥: also known as Cheng Mingdao 程明道. A Song dynasty philosopher who, together with his brother Cheng Yi 程頤, laid the foundation upon which Zhu Xi erected the philosophy we now call neo-Confucianism.
Cheng Shuwu 成叔武: younger brother of King Wu of Zhou 周武王.
Cheng Yi (1033–1107) 程頤: also known as Cheng Yichuan 程伊川. A Song dynasty philosopher who, together with his brother Cheng Hao 程顥, laid the foundation upon which Zhu Xi erected the philosophy we now call neo-Confucianism.
chengshi 稱事: to weigh a situation. Used by Zhu Xi in place of another chengshi 乘事 meaning "to take a situation into account" in a paraphrase of a line from the Zhouli.
Chengsu of Zhou, Lord 周成肅公: a nobleman of Zhou 周 in the late sixth-century BCE.
Cheng-Zhu 程朱: a reference to the new approach to Confucianism created in the Song dynasty by the two brothers Cheng Hao (1032–1085) 程顥 and Cheng Yi (1033–1107) 程頤 and further developed by Zhu Xi 朱熹 (1130–1200). This became the dominant approach to Confucianism in Chosŏn.
ch'eyong / C. tiyong 體用: "substance/essence and function," unactualized normative potential and that potential actualized.
chi / K. ch'ŏk 尺: a rough equivalent of a foot.
chi / K. Li 魑: a type of mountain demon dangerous for humans.
chi dao 赤刀: "red knife," a treasured sword. Used in ancient ancestor rites.
ch'iin / C. zhiren 治人: literally, "govern others." In a broader sense, it can mean to interact appropriately with others.
Chiljŏng / C. qiqing 七情: the seven emotions: joy, anger, sorrow, pleasure, love, hatred, and desire.
Chin Sŏnghak shipto ch'a 進聖學十圖箚: "Presenting the Ten Diagrams on Sagely Learning," by T'oegye Yi Hwang 退溪李滉.
ch'inch'in / C. qinqin 親親: to treat a relative the way a respected relative should be treated.

Chinju 晋州: a town in southeast Korea.

Chixiao 鴟鴞: "Kite Owl," a poem in the "Odes of Bin" section in the "Guofeng" volume of the *Book of Songs*.

Cho Changhan (1743-?) 趙章漢: an official in the government at the time Tasan was in exile.

choe 罪: fault, crime. It is used by modern Korean Christians to mean sin.

Ch'oe Sŏgu (1922-2009) 崔奭祐: a modern scholar of Catholicism in Korea.

ch'ogye munsin 抄啓文臣: promising young officials selected by King Chŏngjo (正祖 r. 1776-1800) to work in his newly established Kyujanggak [Royal Library] to provide him information to supplement what he was being told by his senior officials.

chohwa / C. *zaohua* 造化: the transformations that generate the visible world; the totality of what is thus generated.

ch'ŏn 天: Heaven, both in the sense of the sky above and, in neo-Confucianism, the impersonal moral force otherwise known as *li* 理. Tasan, however, read 天, when it was not referring to the sky, as another name for Shangdi 上帝, the supernatural personality who endows us with a conscience and then watches what we think and do.

Chong 崇: a type of tripod used in ancestral rituals.

Chong 重: the god of wood, also known as Goumang.

Chŏng Chaewŏn (1730-1792) 丁載遠: the father of Chŏng Yagyong.

Chŏng Such'il chŭngŏn 丁修七贈言: "words of advice for Chŏng Such'il." Chŏng Such'il (???) was a younger man Tasan met while in exile in Kangjin. He is considered one of Tasan's Kangjin disciples.

Chŏng Yakchŏn (1758-1816) 丁若銓: an older brother of Tasan who shared his early interest in Catholicism, and, like Tasan, was exiled for his youthful involvement with that illegal religion.

Chŏng Yakchong (1760-1801) 丁若鍾: an older brother of Tasan. He was also drawn to Catholicism but, unlike Tasan and Yakchŏn, he remained a Catholic despite its illegality and was executed in 1801.

Chŏng Yakhoeng (1785-1829) 丁若鐄: a stepbrother of Tasan. His mother was a secondary wife of Chŏng Chaewŏn.

Chŏng Yakhyŏn (1751-1821) 丁若鉉: Tasan's older brother by a different mother. He married Yi Pyŏk's sister.

Chŏng Yagyong (1762-1836) 丁若鏞: also known as Tasan. He is the author of the commentaries on the *Zhongyong* translated here.

Chŏngjo (r. 1776-1800) 正祖: the twenty-second king of Chosŏn.

Chongshan (Mt. Chong) 崇山: a mountain said to have been located near where the capital of the legendary Xia dynasty had been.

Ch'ŏnju / C. Tianzhu 天主: "The Lord of Heaven," the Roman Catholic word for God.

Ch'ŏnmyŏng / C. Tianming 天命: understood by Tasan as "what Heaven has conferred" or "what Heaven has ordained."

Chosŏn 朝鮮: Korea. The name of the dynasty that ruled Korea from 1392 until 1910.

Chou 丑: the second of the twelve terrestrial branches.
Chuci 楚辭: "Thick Star-Thistle," a poem in the minor odes section of *Book of Songs*.
chugyŏng 主敬 C. zhujing: "abide in reverence," to sit quietly and, as Tasan understood it, remind yourself that Sangje is watching you and therefore you cultivate an attitude of caution and apprehension lest you act inappropriately.
Chui 垂: a legendary craftsman, and Director of Works, in the court of the equally legendary ancient emperor Shun 舜.
Chuiji 垂棘: a place in what is now Shanxi during the Spring and Autumn period.
Ch'unch'u Kojing 春秋考徵: Tasan's "A Detailed Examination of the Spring and Autumn Annals."
chung / C. zhong 中: centered, on target, focused, composed.
Ch'ung (C. Zhong) 忠: acting conscientiously. Being steadfast. Doing one's best.
ch'ungsŏ / C. zhongshu 忠恕: "doing your best and being empathetic in your dealings with others."
Chunguan 春官: "Spring offices," ministry of ritual affairs in *Zhouli*.
Chunguan zongbo 春官宗伯: "Overseer of Ritual Affairs" chapter in *Zhouli*.
Chungyong / C. Zhongyong 中庸: one of the Four Books of Neo-Confucianism. The title was traditionally translated as "The Doctrine of the Mean." However, recent scholarship has shown that such a translation is misleading. Tasan understood it to mean "Maintaining Consistent Focus and Composure."
Chungyong ch'aek 中庸策: "Responding to Royal Inquiries Regarding the *Zhongyong*," a short essay on the *Zhongyong* written in response to questions posed by King Chŏngjo to the junior officials in the Royal Library (Kyujanggak).
Chungyong chajam 中庸自箴: "Admonitions for Myself upon Reading the *Zhongyong*," one of Tasan's commentaries on the *Zhongyong*.
Chungyong kangŭibo 中庸講義補: "A Discussion of the Meaning of the *Zhongyong*, Revised." Tasan's longest commentary on the *Zhongyong*.
Chunhou 鶉火: one of the twelve Jupiter stations.
Chunqiu 春秋: *Spring and Autumn Annals*, the history of the state of Lu 魯 between 722 and 479 BCE.
Chunqiu ganjing fu 春秋感精符: "Tallies of Spiritual Resonance in the Spring and Autumn Annals." Considered an apocryphal text.
Chunqiu waizhuan 春秋外傳: "Unofficial Records of the the Spring and Autumn Period," another name for the *Guoyu* [國語 Discourses of the States].
Chunqiu zuozhuan 春秋左傳: Zuo commentary on the *Spring and Autumn Annals*.
Chunqui zuozhuan zhengyi 春秋左傳正義: "The Correct Meaning of the Zuo Commentary on the *Spring and Autumn Annals*."
chunshou 鶉首: one of the twelve Jupiter stations.
chunwei 鶉尾: one of the twelve Jupiter stations.
Chuyŏk 周易: the *Book of Changes*. Also known as the *Yijing* 易經.
Chuyŏk sŏŏn 周易緒言: [Introductory remarks for the study of the *Changes*]. A commentary on the *Yijing* by Tasan Chŏng Yagyong.
Chuyu 楚語: "Discourses of Chu," one of the chapters in *Guoyu* 國語.

ci 次: Jupiter stations, twelve places on a sky map through which the apparent movement of Jupiter is plotted.

ci / K. ch'ŏk 尺: a unit of length equal to a little more than a foot.

Cui Jing (fl. Tang dynasty) 崔憬: a commentator on the *Yijing*.

Cun / K. ch'on 寸: a rough equivalent of 1.3 inches.

Da Bo (fl. 11th c. BCE) 大伯: also known as *Taibo* 泰伯. He was the eldest son of King Tai 太王, who was said to be the founder of the royal lineage of Zhou.

Da Ding 大丁 (fl. 18th c. BCE): according to some later records, he was the son of the founder of the Shang dynasty but died before he could assume power. There are contemporary historians who argue, because of evidence on oracle bones, that he actually ruled for a few years.

Da Lin Zezhi 答林擇之: "A Response to a Letter from Lin Zezhi." A letter from Zhu Xi to Lin Zezhi 林擇之.

da sima 大司馬: Minister of War, in *Zhouli*.

da xun 大訓: "the great standard," an ancient utensil used in ancestor rites.

Da ya 大雅 "The Major Odes," a section of the *Shijing* [Book of Songs].

da zongbo 大宗伯: Grand Overseer of Ritual Affairs [Minister of Rites] in *Zhouli*.

Dadai Liji 大戴禮記: *Records of Ritual Matters by Dai the Elder*.

dagao 大誥: a section of the *Shangshu dazhuan* 尚書大傳 "Great Tradition of *the Book of Documents*," by Fu Sheng 伏胜.

Dahue Zonggao (1089–1163) 大慧宗杲: a famous Chan monk in Song. He is said to have pioneered the technique of asking a question with no logical answer to stimulate the listener into enlightenment.

Dahui chansi yulu 大慧禪師語錄: *Records of Chan Master Dahui*.

Dahuo 大火: one of the twelve Jupiter stations.

Daliang 大梁: one of the twelve Jupiter stations.

Dalü 大呂: the name of a bell used in rituals in Zhou times. Also, the bell that sounds the second of the twelve traditional pitches of ancient China.

Daming 大明: "Major Bright," a poem in the "Decade of King Wen" collection of poems in the major odes section of the *Book of Songs*.

Dan 聃: a regional state in early Zhou.

Dan Fu 亶父: personal name of the person who was posthumously named King Tai 太王.

Dan Ji 聃季: younger brother of King Wu of Zhou 周武王.

Dan Juli (???) 單居離: an individual who appears in the *Dadai liji* 大戴禮記.

Dang, decade of 蕩之什: a section of the major odes volume of *Book of Songs*.

Danxue 丹穴: a mythical mountain rising high into the sky in the far south.

Dao / K. *to* 道: "the Way," the way everything should act and interact with everything around it.

Daodejing 道德經 "The Classic of the Dao and Its Power," a Daoist classic, traditionally attributed to Laozi 老子.

Dasi Ming 大司命: one of the songs in the "Nine Songs" [*jiuge* 九歌] poem in *Chu ci* [楚辭].

Dasiyue 大司樂: "Grand Music Master," a section in the "Spring Offices" chapter of *Zhouli*.

dawu 大武: "Great Warrior" (dance).
daxingren 大行人: Senior Messenger, an officer in the Ministry of Justice in *Zhouli*.
Daxue / K. *Taehak* 大學: the Great Learning, one of the Four Books.
Deng-Zhang-Xu-Zhang-Hu liezhuan 鄧張徐張胡列傳: "A collection of Biographies of Deng Biao, Zhang Yu, Xu Fang, Zhang Min, and Hu Guang," a section of the *Houhanshu* 後漢書.
dexing 德性: "ethical virtuosity and human nature," the innate ability to act appropriately.
Di 狄: a non-Chinese people living to the north of China. They were considered barbarians.
Di 禘: ritual in the ancestral temple of the Son of Heaven.
dianfu 奠服: ritual clothing that was placed before a spirit tablet in an ancestor rite.
Dianming 典命: "Superintendent of Ranks and Titles," a section in the "Spring Offices" section of *Zhouli*.
Dianrui 典瑞: "Keeper of Seal Tablets" section in the "Spring Offices" chapter of *Zhouli*.
Dianyongqi 典庸器: "Director in Charge of Instruments and Valuable Ritual Objects," a section in the "Spring Offices" chapter of *Zhouli*.
diguan, junren 地官 均人: "Treating People Fairly" section in the chapter on the Terrestrial Ministry [Ministry of Education] in *Zhouli*.
diguan situ 地官司徒: "Terrestrial Ministry" [Ministry of Education], overseers of public affairs.
diguan situ-xia, zaishi 地官司徒下, 載師 "Estate Manager" section in the chapter on the "Terrestrial Ministry" [Ministry of Education] in *Zhouli*.
diji 地支: the twelve terrestrial branches, used in the sexagenary system to number days and years.
Diku 帝嚳: "Emperor Ku," a legendary ruler in ancient China. Also known as Gaoxin.
Ding, King (r. 606–586) 定王: the twenty-first king of the Zhou dynasty.
Ding, Lord (r. 509–495 BCE) 定公: ruler of the state of Lu during the Spring and Autumn period.
Ding-Wei / K. *chŏngmi* 丁未: one of the sixty combinations of "stems" and "branches" in the sexagenary cycle in traditional East Asia used for counting days and years.
Dong Wujing 董五經: a Daoist hermit during the Song dynasty.
dongguan kaogongji 冬官考工記: "Winter Ministry, the Artificer's Record," a chapter in *Zhouli*.
Donglin Changzong 東林常總: "Changzong of Donglin Temple," Changzong (1025–1091)
Du You (735–812) 杜佑: the Tang-era author of *Tongdian* 通典, "Comprehensive Guide to Institutions."
Du Zhongyong congshuo 讀四書叢說: "A Collection of Accounts of Reading the *Zhongyong*," a Song dynasty compilation by Xu Qian 許謙.
dui 兌: one of the eight trigrams used to form the hexagrams in the *Book of Changes*.

Durenshi, decade of 都人士之什: A section of the "Xiao Ya" volume of the *Book of Songs*.

er 而: Tasan reads this in Chapter XXVII as "and," linking two clauses of equal importance, though in some contexts it can be read as "and then" or even "but."

Er Cheng Yishu 二程遺書: "Writings Left Behind by the Two Cheng Brothers" (Cheng Yi 程頤 and Cheng Hao 程顥).

Erya 爾雅: The oldest dictionary of Sinographs. It is considered one of the Classics.

Fa Ke 伐柯: the "Axe-Handle" poem in the *Book of Songs*.

Fan Ye (398–445) 范曄: author of *Hou Hanshu*. [後漢書 History of the Later Han dynasty].

fang 方: In the context in which it appears in this work, *fang* means a wooden tablet.

Fanlunxun 氾論訓: "Boundless Discourses," chapter 13 of *Huainanzi* [淮南子].

fei 費: read here as "wide-ranging."

Feng 鄷: a fiefdom in early Zhou.

Feng 丰: the "Splendid Gentleman" poem in the *Book of Songs*.

Feng Dao (882–954) 馮道: a scholar-official during the Five Dynasties and Ten Kingdoms period.

Feng Weishou (fl. Song dynasty) 馮偉壽: also known as Feng Wenzi 馮文子.

Fengfu 封父: a fiefdom in ancient China mentioned in the *Book of Rites* and in the *Zuo Commentary to the Spring and Autumn Annals*.

Fu / K. *pok* 復: "returning," the 24th hexagram in the *Yijing*.

fu 賦: "rhapsody," a form of literature that is somewhere between poetry and prose.

Fu Chen (fl. 7th c. BCE) 富辰: an official in the court of King Xiang of Zhou.

Fu Lang (?–389) 苻郎: an official in Eastern Jin (317–420).

Fu Sheng (268–178 BC) 伏胜: the Former Han scholar credited with restoring the *Shangshu* [Book of Documents] after almost all copies had been destroyed by the Qin. He is given credit for *Shangshu dazhuan* 尚書大傳.

Fu Yi 鳧鷖: "The Wild Duck," a poem in the Decade of Sheng Men section of the *Book of Songs*.

fubushi 服不氏: animal tamer.

Gai 該: alternate name for Rushou 蓐收.

Ganquan-gong fu 甘泉宮賦: "Rhapsody of the Sweet Spring Palace" in *Yuding lidai fuhui* [御定歷代賦彙 Collection of prose poems by dynasty].

Gao 皋: one of the four wise officials who are said to have assisted the legendary Emperor Shun 舜.

Gao 郜: a fiefdom in early Zhou.

Gao Yao 皋陶: also read as Gao Tao. Believed to have been the Minister of Justice for the legendary Emperor Shun 舜.

Gao Yao, Counsels of 皋陶謨: a chapter in the *Yushu* volume of the *Book of Documents*.

Gaoren zhi 槁人職: "The Duties of the Provisioner," a section in the Ministry of War volume of *Zhouli*.

Gaoxin 高辛: a legendary emperor of ancient China, also known as Emperor Diku.

Gaoyou 皋鼬: name of a place in what is now Henan.

Gaozi 告子: a man who argued with Mencius.
Ge Yinliang (fl. 17th c.) 葛寅亮: author of *Sishu Hunanjiang* 四書湖南講.
gen / K. *gŭn* 根: root (of a plant). Is also used metaphorically to refer to the origin, source, or cause of something.
Gong Zhiqi 宮之奇: a high official in the state of Yu in the seventh century BCE.
Gonggong 共工: the god of water, said to be the father of Hou Tu 后土, the god of earth.
gongqi 功器: utensils that display the achievements of the imperial family.
Gongshu Wenzi 公叔文子: an official in Wei 衛 in the sixth century BCE. Also known as Gongshu Fa 公叔發. He is also mentioned in *Analects* 14:13 and 14:18 (Slingerland, 159, 161).
Gongsun Hong, Bu Shi, and Er Kuan 公孫弘卜式兒寬: all high officials in the Former Han dynasty. Er Kuan is also known as Ni Kuan.
Gongyangzhuan 公羊傳: one of three major commentaries on the *Spring and Autumn Annals*.
Gongzi Zhan 公子展: an important figure in the state of Lu 魯 during China's Spring and Autumn period.
Gou Mang 句芒: the god of wood.
Goulong 句龍: a mythical figure who was once a human being but became a god.
Gu Menglin (1585–1653) 顧夢麟: also known as Gu Linshi 顧麟士.
guan 貫: a type of tripod used in ancestral rituals.
Guan 管: a fiefdom in early Zhou.
Guan Lu (210–256) 管輅: a diviner interested in astrology, fortune-telling, and physiognomy.
Guan Qi of Chu 楚觀起: an official in the state of Chu in the sixth century BCE.
Guan Shu Xian (11th c. BCE) 管叔鮮: a brother of King Wu of Zhou 周武王 and the Duke of Zhou 周公. Guan is the name of the region King Wu asked him to govern.
Guan Zhong (c. 720–645 BCE) 管仲: known for bringing order to the warring states of China but also for leading an ostentatious lifestyle.
Guanzi 管子: "Master Guan," a collection of essays said to be by Guan Zhong.
Gufeng 谷風: "Valley Wind," a poem in the "Odes of Bei" collections of poems in the "Lessons from the States" section of the *Book of Songs*.
Gui mei 歸妹: "the marrying maiden," hexagram 54 in the *Yijing*.
Guishan xiansheng yulu 龜山先生語錄: "Recorded Conversations of Guishan Yang Shi," a collection of things Yang Shi 楊時 said to his friends and students
Guliang Chi (trad. fl. 5th c.) 梁赤縠: said to have been a disciple of Zixia, a close disciple of Confucius.
Guliangzhuan 穀梁傳: one of three major commentaries on the *Spring and Autumn Annals*.
gunmian 袞冕: clothing of a deceased king.
Guo 虢: a regional state in the Zhou era.
Guo, Royal Secretary (fl. 7th c. BCE) 內史過: an official in the Zhou domain.
Guo Pu (276–324.) 郭璞: a famous Daoist writer and expert on geomancy.
Guo She (fl. 7th c. BCE) 虢射: a leading warrior for the regional state of Jin 晉.

Guo Shu (fl. 11th c. BCE) 虢叔: the third son of King Ji and brother of King Wen of Zhou.

Guo Zhong (fl. 11th c. BCE) 虢仲: the second son of King Ji and brother of King Wen of Zhou.

Guofeng 國風: "The Airs of the States" volume of the *Book of Songs*.

guoluo 果蠃: bollworm wasp, a type of parasitic wasp which was believed to steal the eggs from the nest of the bollworm moth.

Guoyu 國語: "Discourses of the States," a collection of speeches by rulers of various states, and their ministers, during the Spring and Autumn period.

guxian 沽洗: a type of bell. It is named for its pitch, one of the twelve pitches of ancient Chinese music.

Haemi 海美: a town and military base along the coast southwest of Seoul in what is now South Ch'ungch'ŏng province. It is now part of the city of Sŏsan.

hai / K. *hae* 亥: the twelfth of the twelve terrestrial branches.

Han 漢: China, particularly China's Han dynasty (202 BCE–220 CE).

Han 韓: a state during the Zhou period, situated in what is now central China.

Han E 韓鄂: said to be the Tang dynasty author of *Suihua jili* 歲華紀麗.

Han Feizi 韓非子: "Master Han Fei," a third-century BCE writer often called a legalist for the emphasis he placed on the importance of law rather than virtue in governing.

Han Wengong (768–824) 韓文公: another name for Han Yu 韓愈.

Han Wo (844–923) 韓偓: a well-known poet in Tang China.

Han Yu (768–824) 韓愈: a famous scholar-official in Tang China, best known for his philosophical essays.

Han Yu ji 韓愈集: *The Collected Works of Han Yu*.

Hang Shijun (1696–1773) 杭世駿: editor of *Xu Liji jishuo* 續禮記集說.

han'gŭl 한글: the Korean alphabet.

Hanlin Academy 翰林院.

Hanlu 旱麓: "Foothills of Mt. Han," a poem in the "Decade of King Wen" collection of poems in the major odes section of the *Book of Songs*.

hanmun 漢文: Literary Sinitic. The language Tasan wrote in.

Hanshu 漢書: History of the Former Han dynasty.

haosheng 好生: "Loving Life," a chapter in *Kongzi jiayu* [孔子家語 The sayings of the Confucian School].

he / K. *hwa* 和: harmony, harmonizing.

He Yin of Jin (446–531) 晉何胤: He was not actually from Jin. He was from the later kingdom of Liang.

Hengqu 橫渠: another name for Zhang Zai 張載 (1020–1077).

Hetu 河圖: "Yellow River diagram." A schematic representation of numerical relationships with cosmological implications. It was believed to have appeared on the back of a dragon-horse that came out of the Yellow River.

Hong Inho (1753–1799) 洪仁浩: a scholar-official who served under King Chŏngjo (r. 1776–1800).

Hongfan 洪範: "The Great Plan," a chapter in the *Book of Documents*.

Hou Tu 后土: a deity in Chinese tradition. The Lord of the Earth, also known as the Goddess of the Soil.
Hou Zhongliang (fl. 11th c.) 侯仲良: Also known as Hou Shisheng 侯師聖.
Houhanshu 後漢書: "History of the later Han dynasty."
Houji 后稷: "the lord of millet," worshiped as the god of crops. Also known as Qi 棄.
Hu Bingwen (1250–1333) 胡炳文: also known as Hu Yunfeng 胡雲峯.
Hu Guang (91–172) 胡廣: a Han dynasty official and Confucian scholar.
Hu Guang (1369–1418) 胡廣: the compiler of *Sishu daquan* 四書大全.
Hu Hong (1106–1162) 胡宏: also known as Wufeng 五峯.
Hua, Mt. 華山: a mountain in Shanxi Province.
Huaifang shi 懷方氏: a section of Ministry of Education volume of *Zhouli*.
Huainanzi 淮南子: "The Master from Huainan," a Former Han dynasty guide to philosophy and statecraft.
Huan, King (r. 719–697 BCE) 桓王: the fourteenth ruler of Zhou, and the second king of Eastern Zhou.
Huang Gan (1152–1221) 黃榦: a disciple of Zhu Xi.
Huang Xunrao (1318–1361) 黃洵饒: also known as Huang Kuan 黃寬.
Huang Zhiqing (1152–1221) 黃直卿: also known as Huang Gan 黃榦.
Huangdi 黃帝: the mythological first emperor of China, the Yellow Emperor.
Huangdi nejing 黃帝內經: "The Yellow Emperor's Classic of Medicine," the first medical guide in China.
Huangfu Fang (1497–1582) 皇甫方: a poet and official during the Ming dynasty.
Huangfu Xi (fl. late 4th c.) 皇甫希: a self-proclaimed Daoist recluse in the Eastern Jin period.
Huangyi 皇矣: "Sovereign Might," a poem in the Decade of King Wen section of the *Book of Songs*.
Hubi 虎賁: "tiger runners," elite palace guards in Zhou China.
Hui, King of Yan (r. 545–536 BCE) 燕惠王: a ruler of the state of Yan during the Zhou period.
Hui of Jin (r. 651–637 BCE) 晉惠: a ruler of the state of Jin during the Zhou period.
Hui'an xiansheng Zhu wengong wenji 晦庵先生朱文公文集: one set of the collected writings of Zhu Xi.
Hŭijŏngdang 熙政堂: a building within the Changdŏk palace complex in Seoul.
Hŭksan-do 黑山島: an island off the southwestern coast of Korea.
hŭm / C. *qian* 欠: to lack, insufficient.
Hŭmhŭm sinsŏ 欽欽新書: "New Guidebook for Forensic Medicine," a handbook of forensic medicine by Tasan Chŏng Yagyong.
Huan, Lord of Qi (r. 685–643 BCE) 齊桓公: a ruler of the state of Qi during the Zhou period.
Huo 霍: a fiefdom in early Zhou.
Hwang Sayŏng (1775–1801) 黃嗣永: son-in-law of Chŏng Yakhyŏn, Tasan's elder brother. He became a devout Catholic and was executed for his faith in 1801. When he was interrogated in 1801 about Hwang's Catholic activities, Tasan claimed he hardly knew him at all.

Hwasŏng 華城: a fortress south of Seoul.
Illyun / C. *renlun* 人倫: In its narrow sense, this means the Five Cardinal Relationships and the reciprocal moral obligations that govern those relationships. In a broader sense, it refers to morality in general, to all the normative principles that define what is appropriate in any interaction.
in / C. *ren* 仁: being fully human, which means to act the way human beings should act, especially caring for others and their needs. In some contexts, it is better given the more limited translation of benevolence.
in, ŭi, ye, ji / C. *ren, yi, li, zhi* 仁 義 禮 智: acting in a fully human manner, acting in an appropriate manner, acting in accordance with propriety, acting wisely.
Insim. Dosim tosŏl 人心道心圖說: "A diagram of the human heart-mind and the Dao heart-mind," by Yulgok Yi I 栗谷 李珥.
ipchi / C. *lizhi* 立志: literally, "to establish your will." It is used to refer to strengthening your determination to live a moral life and to do your best to always act appropriately.
ji 稷: millet; also the name of a mythical ancient official who became the god of grain.
ji 既: Normally means "since" or "already" but is glossed in the passage that appears here as "to give a ration of grain."
ji / K. *che* 祭: "sacrifice."
Ji, King 季王: He was given the title of king after his grandson established the Zhou dynasty.
Ji Tan 籍談: an important minister of Jin in the sixth century BCE.
Ji Wenzi 季文子: an official in the state of Lu in the sixth century BCE.
Jia Gongyan (fl. Early Tang dynasty) 賈公彥: He wrote a commentary on *Zhouli*.
Jiale 假樂: "All Happiness," a poem in the Decade of Sheng Min section of the *Book of Songs*.
Jianglou 降婁: one of the twelve Jupiter stations.
jiao 郊: the outskirts of the capital. Used in *Zhongyong* when referring to a seasonal ritual held in the suburbs of the capital in which the emperor sacrificed to Heaven.
Jiaqing (r. 1796–1820) 嘉慶: the fifth emperor of Qing China.
Jieyi xinyu 解頤新語: "Some New Words for Breaking into Laughter," by the Ming poet Huangfu Fang 皇甫汸 (1497–1582).
jifa 祭法: "Rules for Sacrifices" section of the *Book of Rites*.
Jin (265–420) 晉: a powerful kingdom which emerged in the aftermath of the collapse of the Han empire and of the Wei, Shu, and Wu kingdoms which followed; also a regional state in Zhou times.
Jin Yu 晉語: "Discourses of Jin," a chapter in *Guoyu* [國語].
Jinche 巾車: "chariot decorator," a section in the chapter on "Spring Offices" [Ministry of Rites] in *Zhouli*.
Jing, King of Zhou (514–519 BCE) 周景王: the twenty-fourth king of Zhou.
Jing zhi 敬之: "Reverence," a poem in the Decade of Min Yi Ziao Zi collection in the "Sacrificial Odes of Zhou" section of the *Book of Songs*.

Jingdian Shiwen 經典釋文: "Textual Explanations of the Classics," a Tang dynasty work by Lu Yuanlang explicating important Confucian and Daoist classics.

Jinshu 晉書: The History of the Jin dynasty (265–420).

Jinxin 盡心: "Realizing the Full Potential of Your Heart-Mind," the last chapter in *Mencius*.

Jinyu 晉語: "The Sayings of Jin," a chapter in *Gouyu* 國語.

*jiongy*i 褧衣: a line from two poems in the *Book of Songs* meaning plain unlined outer garment.

Jiqi 姬棄: the god of grain. Another name of Houji 后稷.

Jishi 季氏: *Ji* family, a chapter in the *Analects*.

Jisun Xingfu (d. 568 BCE) 季孫行父: also known as Ji Wenzi 季文子. He was a high official in the state of Lu 魯.

Jitong 祭統: "Summary Account of Sacrifices," a chapter in the *Book of Rites*.

Jiu Fan (d. 622 BCE) 舅犯: also known as Hu Yan 狐偃. A high official in the state of Jin 晉.

Jiuge 九歌: "The Nine Songs," a poem in *Chu Ci* (Songs of the South).

Jiyi 祭意: "The Meaning of Sacrifices," a chapter in *Lunheng* 論衡.

Ju 莒: a state on the outskirts of Warring States China.

Juan Er 卷耳: "Cocklebur," a poem in the Odes of Zhou and the South section of the *Book of Songs*.

juebian 爵弁: clothes worn to represent deceased ordinary officials

Junya 君牙: Lord Ya. A high official in the court of King Mu of Zhou (周穆王 r. 956–918 BCE).

Kaifeng 凱風: "Gentle Wind," a poem in the "Airs of the States" section of the *Book of Songs*.

kan 坎: one of the eight trigrams used to form the hexagrams in the *Book of Changes*.

Kang, King of *Zhou* (r. 1005–978 BCE) 周康王: third ruler of Zhou.

Kang Shu 康叔 (fl. 11th c. BCE): younger brother of King Wu of Zhou 周武王

Kang Shu Feng (fl. 11th c. BCE) 康叔封: Kang Shu of the regional state of Feng.

Kangjin 康津: a town along the southwestern coast of Korea.

kapsul / C. *jiaxu* 甲戌: one of the sixty combinations of "stems" and "branches" in the sexagenary cycle in the traditional East Asian numbering of days and years.

Ke, scribe 史克: an official in the state of Lu 魯 in the late seventh century BCE.

ki / C. *qi* 氣: matter-energy, the basic animating and animated stuff of the cosmos. Functions as the individualizing force in the cosmos.

Ki Taesŭng (1527–1572) 奇大升: a young scholar-official whose exchange of letters with T'oegye Yi Hwang 退溪 李滉 sparked the Four-Seven debate in Korea. He is also known as Ki Myŏngŏn 奇明彥.

Kija (C. Jizi) (fl. 11th c. BCE) 箕子: "the marquis of Ji." He was a virtuous official under the last ruler of Shang China but left when Shang was replaced by Zhou since he felt he could not serve two different dynasties. Koreans once believed he moved to Korea and spread civilization there, but that story is no longer popular on the Korean peninsula.

Kim Sangjip (1723–??) 金尙集: an official who rose to ministerial rank under King Chŏngjo.

kok / C. *gu* 谷: valley, empty.

Kong Anguo (late 2nd c. BCE) 孔安國: said to be a descendant of Confucius. He was an early Han official and scholar who is associated with the Old Text version of the *Book of Documents*.

Kong Yingda (574–648) 孔穎達: said to be a direct descendant of Confucius. He compiled an important set of commentaries [*Wujing Zhengyi* 五經正義] on the Classics in early Tang.

Kongdong 崆峒: a mythical mountain that rises high into the sky in the far north.

konghyo / C. *gongxiao* 功效: effectiveness, effect, positive impact.

Kongque dongnan fei 孔雀東南飛: "Southeast Flies the Peacocks," a famous Han dynasty ballad by an unknown author.

Kongzi jiayu 孔子家語: "The Sayings of the Confucian School."

Kongzi jiayu tongjie 孔子家語通解: "A Complete Exegesis of the Sayings of the Confucian School."

Ku 嚳: one of the five legendary emperors of ancient China. Also known as Gaoxin and as Diku.

kuaili 快利: "dexterous," vigorously.

Kuang, King (r. 613–607 BCE) 匡王: the eighth king of Eastern Zhou.

Kuangmiu zhengsu 匡謬正俗: "Corrections of Errors and Rectification of Vulgar Readings," a seventh-century work by Yan Shigu 顏師古.

Kui 夔: one of the four wise officials who are said to have assisted the legendary Emperor Shun 舜. He is said to have invented music and dance.

Kŭkki cham 克己箴 "An Admonition on Self-Control." A short essay by Tasan Chŏng Yagyong.

Kun [K. Kon] 坤: "Earth"; one of the eight trigrams used to form the hexagrams in the *Yijing*.

Kunlun 崑崙: a legendary mountain believed to be to the far west of China and to be the capital of the legendary Yellow Emperor.

Kwangam Yi Pyŏk (1754–1786) 曠菴李檗: a close friend of Tasan Chŏng Yagyong and an important figure in the formation of Korea's first Catholic community.

kwisin / C. *guishen* 鬼神: "ghosts and spirits." Spiritual beings.

Kwŏn Ilsin (1742–1791) 權日身: one of Korea's first Catholics.

kwŏnhyŏng 權衡: "to weigh the pros and cons of something" Tasan used this to mean to consider the alternatives in a situation you find yourself in order to determine the appropriate way to behave in that situation.

kyech'uk / C. *guichou* 癸丑: one of the sixty combinations of "stems" and "branches" in the sexagenary cycle in traditional East Asian time-keeping. The fiftieth year in that cycle.

kyemyo / C. *guimao* 癸卯: one of the sixty combinations of "stems" and "branches" in the sexagenary cycle in traditional East Asian time-keeping. The fortieth year in that cycle.

Kyŏng / C. *jing* 敬: In traditional Confucian contexts, this means reverence. Neo-Confucianism added the meaning of mindfulness.

Kyŏngguk taejŏn 經國大典: "Great Administrative Code," the laws and regulations governing Chosŏn.

Kyŏngse yup'yo 經世遺表: "A Guide to Statecraft." A guide to central government administration by Tasan Chŏng Yagyong.

Kyujanggak 奎章閣: Royal Library, established by King Chŏngjo (正祖 r. 1776–1800).

Laozi 老子: also known as 老聃 Lao Dan. A legendary figure traditionally believed to have lived in the sixth century BCE. He is thought to be the author of the *Daodejing* [The Classic of the Dao and Its Power].

li 力: power, to exert effort, to make an effort.

li 利: profit, to benefit.

li 里 C. li: a village, a neighborhood; a traditional measure of distance.

li / C. *li* 理: the dynamic patterns defining and directing appropriate interactions. In neo-Confucianism, it operates as the unifying force in the cosmos.

li 離: one of the eight trigrams used to form the hexagrams in the *Book of Changes*.

Li 歷: personal name of King Ji 季王, according to the *Book of Rites*. He was the grandfather of King Wu 周武王, the founder of the Zhou dynasty, and was posthumously named a king as well.

Li 黎: also known as Zhu Rong 祝融: an ancient deity who was the spirit of fire.

Li of Jin, Lord (r. 580–574 BCE) 晉厲公: a ruler of the regional state of Jin during the Spring and Autumn period.

Li Chunfeng (602–670) 李淳風: a Tang dynasty Daoist astronomer and mathematician.

Li Dingzuo (fl. 8th/9th c.) 李鼎祚: a Tang dynasty scholar-official.

Li Shizhen (1518–1593) 李時珍: a physician and medical writer during the Ming dynasty.

lian / K. *yŏn* 鍊: to smelt metal, to temper metal with fire.

liang / K. *ryang* 魎: a type of demon.

Liang (502–557) 梁: one of the southern dynasties that arose between the fall of the Han and the rise of the Tang.

Liaoweng 了翁: the literary name of Chen Guan 陳瓘 (1057–1124).

Lie Wen 烈文: the "Renowned and Gracious" poem in the Decade of Qing Miao section of the *Book of Songs*.

Lieshan 烈山: another name for the legendary Flame Emperor Yandi 炎帝.

Liezu 烈祖: the "Glorious Ancestor" poem in the Sacrificial Odes of Shang section in the *Book of Songs*.

Liji 禮記: the *Book of Rites*, one of the thirteen Confucian Classics.

Liji sishuo 禮記集說: a 150-volume collection of commentaries on the *Book of Rites*, by Wei Shi 衛湜.

Lin Xiyuan (1481–1565) 林希元: credited with writing *Sishu cunyi* 四書存疑, "Harboring Doubts about the *Four Books*."

Lin Zezhi (1119–1176) 林擇之: a correspondent of Zhu Xi.

Liqi 禮器: "Ritual Utensils," a chapter in the *Book of Rites*.
Liqi-xia / K. *Ligi-ha* 理氣下: a chapter in Zhu Xi's *Zhuzi yulei* [The Classified Sayings of Master Zhu] on patterning principles and the matter out of which the universe is formed as well as the energy that animates it.
Liren 里仁: "A Virtuous Neighborhood," chapter 4 of the *Analects*.
Lisao 離騷: "Encountering Sorrow," a Warring States–era poem by Qu Yuan 屈原.
lishu 隸書: "script of the clerks." The cursive form of *xiaozhuan* 小篆 "small seal script."
Liu, Lady 劉氏: mother of Zhu Shouchang 朱壽昌.
Liu Kang, Duke 劉康公: a high official in Zhou during the sixth century BCE.
Liu Xin (50 BCE–23 CE) 劉歆: a well-known Confucian scholar during the Han dynasty. He was in charge of the imperial library.
lixing 利行: make a strenuous effort.
Liyun 禮運: "The Conveyance of Rites," a chapter in the *Book of Rites*.
Lou Xiangming (fl. first half of 17th c.) 樓象明: also known as Lou Zhanghuan 樓丈煥.
Lu 魯: a regional state in Zhou times.
lu 蘆: rushes.
lu 盧: a rice bowl.
lü 旅: Normally this Sinograph means "to travel around." However, it was also used to refer to a group of people who have traveled from different places and assembled in one location.
Lü, Hounds of 旅獒: a chapter in the *Book of Documents*.
Lü Dalin (1044–1093) 呂大臨: a disciple of Cheng Yi 程頤 and therefore one of the first neo-Confucians. He wrote on the *Zhongyong*.
Lu Deming (556–627) 陸德明: an imperial librarian during the Sui dynasty (581–618 CE). Known for defending Confucianism against Buddhism.
Lu Ji (261–303) 陸機: author of *Wen fu* [文賦 Rhapsody on Literature].
Lü Liuliang (1629–1683) 呂留良: also known as Lü Wancun 呂晚村.
Lu ming, Decade of 鹿鳴: a section in the minor odes of the kingdom collection in the *Book of Songs*; also a poem, "Deer Cry," in that section.
Lü Shang 呂尚: another name for Grand Tutor Shangfu 師尚父.
Lu Yuanlang (556–627) 陸元朗: also known as Lu Deming 陸德明. Author of *Jingdian Shiwen* 經典釋文.
Lü Ziyue (d. 1196) 呂子約: also known as Lü Zujian 呂祖儉.
Lülizhi 律曆志: the "Musical Pitches and the Calendar" chapter in the *Hanshu* 漢書 [Book of the Former Han Dynasty].
lun 倫: the norms defining appropriate human interactions.
Lunheng 論衡: "Balanced Inquiries," a Han-dynasty work by Wang Chong 王充.
Lunyu 論語: the *Analects* of Confucius.
Luoyi 洛邑: the old name of Luoyang 洛阳, a capital of the Zhou dynasty.
Luyu 魯語: "Discourses of Lu," a chapter in the *Guoyu* [國語].
Luzi pingyu 呂子評語: "Master Lü's Critical Observations," by Lü Liuliang (1629–1683) 呂留良.

Ma Rong (79–166) 馬融: wrote important commentaries on the *Book of Documents* and other important early Confucian Classics.

Maengja yoŭi 孟子要義: "Essential points in *Mencius*," Tasan's commentary on *Mencius*.

Mao 毛: a fiefdom in early Zhou.

Mao Huang (fl. 12th c.) 毛晃: Together with his son Mao Juzheng, he compiled *Zeng yun* [增韻 Expanded Rhymes].

Mao Juzheng (fl. 12th c.) 毛居正: Together with his father, Mao Huang, he compiled *Zeng yun* [增韻 Expanded Rhymes].

Mao Qiling (1623–1713) 毛奇齡: a philosopher in early Qing who was critical of the Cheng-Zhu reading of the Confucian Classics, particularly the way they interpreted the *Daxue* and the *Zhongyong*. He is the author of *Sishu gaicuo* 四書改錯, "Correcting the Errors in Zhu Xi's Commentaries on the Four Books," and *Sishu shengyan* 四書賸言, "Residual Remarks about the Four Books."

Mao Shuzheng (fl. 11th c. BCE) 毛叔鄭: younger brother of King Wu of Zhou 周武王.

Mao Wenhui (1656–1733) 毛文輝: a near contemporary of Mao Qiling and contributed to his *Sishu gaicuo*.

Mao Yuanzhong. (17th–18th c.) 毛遠宗: the adopted son of Mao Qiling. He contributed to the editing of Mao's complete works after Mao's death.

Maoshi Zhengyi xu 毛詩正義序: "Preface to Mao's Book of Songs," by Kong Yingda 孔穎達.

Maessi sŏp'yŏng 梅氏書平: Tasan's "A Critical Look at Mei Ze's Book of Documents."

mei / K. *mae* 魅: a dangerous forest demon.

Mei Ze (fl. 4th c.) 梅賾: forged an "old text" version of the *Book of Documents* which was accepted as genuine for centuries afterward.

Mencius (fl. 4th c.) 孟子: often considered second only to Confucius for his contributions to early Confucian philosophy. A book of that same name, containing accounts of his elucidation of how he understood the philosophy of Confucius, is one of the Four Books of Confucian tradition.

Meng Hu 孟虎: a person mentioned in the "Tan Gong" 檀弓 chapter of the *Book of Rites*.

Meng Pi 孟皮: a person mentioned in the "Tan Gong" 檀弓 chapter of the *Book of Rites*.

Mengzi hwowen 孟子或問: Zhu Xi's "Questions and Answer on the *Mencius*."

Mengzi zhangju jizhu 孟子章句集注: Zhu Xi's "A Collection of Notes, by Phrase and Sentence, on the *Mencius*."

Mianman 綿蠻: "Tender and Pretty." A poem in the Decade of Duren Shi section of the *Book of Songs*.

Miaozhitu 廟制圖: "Diagram of the Arrangements in the Imperial Ancestral Temple."

Min, Lord (r. 661–660 BCE) 閔公: a ruler of the regional state of Lu 魯.

Min Yi Xiaozi, decade of 閔予小子之什: a collection of poems in the "Sacrificial Odes of Zhou" section of the *Book of Songs*.

ming / K. *myŏng* 名: name.

ming / K. *myŏng* 命: decree, command, mandate, to assign a name, fate, life-span.

Ming (1368–1644) 明: the Ming dynasty in China.

Mingdang wei 明堂位: "Places in the Hall of Distinction," a chapter in the *Book of Rites*.

Mingxin baojian 明心寶鑒: "a precious mirror for enlightening the heart-mind." A collection of aphorisms compiled in medieval China.

Minlu 民勞: "Our People Are Exhausted," a poem in the Decade of Sheng Min section of the *Book of Songs*.

Mixu 密須: a regional state in Zhou times.

Mongmin simsŏ 牧民心書: Tasan's "An Essential Guide for District Magistrates." It has been translated into English by Choi Byonghyon as *Admonitions on Governing the People: Manual for All Administrations*.

Moshi 磨室: the name of a palace in the state of Yan.

Mozi (fl. 430 BCE) 墨子: a Warring States thinker who argued that we should care for all our fellow human beings, not just those close to us.

Mu 穆: the row on the right for spirit tablets in an ancestral shrine.

Muye 牧野: the site of the battle at which the Zhou forces defeated the Shang and established the Zhou dynasty.

Myŏngnye 明禮 a district in Seoul in Tasan's time.

Namin 南人: the Southerner faction in Chosŏn Korea politics.

Nanquan (748–835) 南泉: a well-known Buddhist monk in Tang China.

Neiyong 內饔: palace cooks.

Ningtai 寧臺: a palace in the state of Yan.

Nonga kwangji 農兒壙志: "Tomb Inscription for Nonga." Tasan wrote this for the last of his children to die very young.

Nonŏ kogŭmju 論語古今註: Tasan's *Ancient and Recent Annotations to the Analects of Confucius*.

Noron 老論: "Old Doctrine," The Patriarch faction in Chosŏn Korea politics.

O Chae-sun (1727–1792) 吳載純: a scholar-official in eighteenth-century Korea who rose as high as Minister of Personnel and Director of the Office of Special Counselors.

Ohaeng / C. *wuxing* 五行: the Five Processes, also known as the Five Agents. These are the five basic ways thing change in the cosmos: wood (slow growth), fire (rapid growth), water (slow decline), water (rapid decline), and earth (stability).

Onyang 溫陽: a town in what is now South Ch'ungch'ŏng Province famous for its hot springs. It is now part of Asan city.

Pak Wansik 박완식: the translator into modern Korean of Zhu Xi's two major commentaries on the *Zhongyong*.

pian 偏: partiality; leaning to one side; a part of [something].

Ping, King (r. 770–720 BCE) 平王: the first king of Eastern Zhou.

pingchang zhi li / K. *p'yŏngsang ji li* 平常之理: the normative patterns of interactions in everyday life.

Pinli 聘禮: "Ceremonial of a Mission" chapter of the *Yili* 儀禮 [Book of Etiquette and Ceremonial].

Pinyi 聘義: "The Meaning of the Interchange of Missions between Different Courts," a chapter in the *Book of Rites*.

Puku 不窋: also pronounced Puzhu with the same Sinographs. A legendary high official in the legendary Xia dynasty. Said to be the son of Houji 后稷 "the lord of millet."

pulu / K. *p'olo* 蒲盧: bollworm wasp.

P'ungsan Hong 豊山 洪氏: a member of the Hong family with a founding ancestor from P'ungsan.

puwei 蒲葦: rushes and weeds.

Pyŏnbang sa Tongbusŭngji so 辨謗 辭 同副承旨 疏: Tasan's 1797 "Memorial to the Throne to Defend Myself and also to Resign as Sixth Royal Secretary."

pyŏngo / C. *bingwu* 丙午: one of the sixty combinations of "stems" and "branches" in the sexagenary cycle in traditional East Asian time-keeping. This is the forty-third year in that sexagenary cycle of years.

qi 旗: identifying flag, banner.

Qi 棄: to reject; the god Qi who is the son of Gaoxin 高辛; Also known as Houji 后稷.

Qi 齊: a state during the Spring and Autumn period; a regional kingdom during the Han dynasty.

Qi / K. *ki* 氣: matter-energy, the basic animating and animated stuff of the cosmos. Acts as the individualizing force in the cosmos.

qi 其: such (a thing), come close to being like something.

Qi Fu, decade of 祈父之什: a chapter in the minor odes of the kingdom volume of *Book of Songs*.

Qi Taigong 齊太公: another name for Grand Tutor Shangfu 尚父, who assisted King Wu 武王 in overthrowing Shang and establishing the Zhou dynasty.

Qian / K. *kŏn* 乾: one of the eight trigrams in the *Yijing*. It represents heaven.

qianfa 綪茷: a red flag or banner used as a mark of official status.

Qianlong (r. 1735–1796) 乾隆: emperor in the Qing dynasty.

Qike 七克: *Seven Victories* by Diego de Pantoja (1571–1618), a Catholic missionary in China.

Qin (221–207 BCE) 秦: China's first empire but one that was short-lived.

Qing 清: the Qing dynasty, 1644–1912.

qing 磬: stone or jade chimes.

Qing Miao, decade of 清廟之什: a collection of ten poems in the "Sacrificial Odes of Zhou" section of the *Book of Songs*.

Qingmiao 清廟: "The Hallowed Temple," a poem in the Decade of Qing Miao collection of ten poems in the "Sacrificial Odes of Zhou" section of the *Book of Songs*.

Qingzhou 青州: the province of Qing in ancient northern China.

qiuguan 秋官: Ministry of Justice ("Autumn Offices") in *Zhouli*.

qiuguan dasikou 秋官大司寇: Grand Overseer of Penal Affairs in the Ministry of Justice in *Zhouli*.

qiuguan daxingren 秋官大行人: the "Senior Messenger" section in the Ministry of Justice chapter of *Zhouli*.

qiuguan sikuo 秋官 司寇: Grand Overseer of Penal Affairs in the Ministry of Justice in *Zhouli*.

qu / K. *kok* 曲: Tasan reads this term as "detailed and complicated."

Qu Ruji (1548–1610) 瞿汝稷: compiler of the *Zhiyue lu* [指月錄 record of pointing at the moon].

Qu Xia of Chu 楚屈瑕: a military commander in the regional state of Chu in the eighth and seventh centuries BCE.

Qu Yuan (4th c. BCE) 屈原: a poet and official in the court of Chu 楚 in the Warring States Period. Author of *Lisao* 離騷.

Quantangshi 全唐詩: "The Complete Collection of Tang Shi Poems" compiled early in the eighteenth century.

Quegong 闕鞏: a regional state in ancient China during the Shang and Zhou in what is now the Henan area. Also, a suit of armor of the type produced in Quegong.

Quli 曲禮: "Summary of the Rules of Propriety," first chapter in the *Book of Rites*.

Rao Lu (1193–1264) 饒魯: also known as Rao Shuangfeng 饒雙峰.

ren (K. *in*) 人: human being, both in a descriptive and a normative (someone who acts like a human being should act) sense.

Rong from Xu 徐戎: a non-sinicized people living in the state of Xu in ancient times in what is now China.

ru 如: to be like; to be similar to. Used in drawing an analogy.

Rushou 蓐收: the god of metal.

Ruxing 儒行: "The Conduct of the Scholar," a chapter in *Liji*.

sadan / C. *siduan* 四端: the "Four Sprouts," the four fundamental selfless instincts.

saengwŏn 生員: classics licentiate. The title given to someone who has passed the lower-level civil service examination on the Classics.

sai / K. *saek* 塞: to be blocked.

Sancang 三倉: "Three Storehouses," an ancient dictionary that drew on three earlier works, hence the name.

Sang Kim Wŏn sŏ 上金園書: "A letter to Kim Wŏn," a letter written by Tasan in 1796.

Sang Rou 桑柔: "The Mulberry's Tender Leaves," a poem in the Decade of Dang section of the *Book of Songs*.

Sangang liuji 三綱六紀: Three Major and Six Minor Principles section of *Baihutong* 白虎通, *Discussions in the White Tiger Hall*.

Sangje / C. Shangdi 上帝: the Lord on High.

Sangnye oep'yŏn 喪禮外編: an appendix to a discussion of mourning ritual. A lesser work by Tasan Chŏng Yagyong on mourning ritual.

Shang dynasty (trad. 17th–11th c. BCE) 商.

Shangfu, Grand Tutor (fl. 11th c. BCE) 師尚父: also known as Qi Taigong and Lü Shang.

shangjiong 尚絅: a phrase in Chapter XXXIII of *Zhongyong* meaning "plain unlined outer garment."

Shangshu 尚書: *Shujing* Book of Documents.
Shangshu dazhuan 尚書大傳: "Great Tradition of the *Book of Documents*," by Fu Sheng 伏胜.
Shangshu Zhengyi 尚書正義: a Tang-era authoritative commentary on the *Book of Documents* by Kong Yingda 孔穎達.
Shangsong 商頌: the "Sacrificial Odes of Shang" section of the *Book of Songs*.
Shao, Duke of 召公: younger brother of King Wu of Zhou 周武王.
Shao 韶: the music of the court of the legendary Emperor Shun 舜.
shao 稍: Tasan reads this as meaning, in the context it appears here, the tip of a stalk of grain.
Shaobo 少帛: a type of flag used in early Zhou times.
Shaohao 少皞: also written as 少昊, a legendary figure who is said to have been the son of the Yellow Emperor and to have also ruled as one of the Five First Emperors.
she 社: the imperial sacrifice to the gods of the soil. Tasan understood this as primarily a ritual honoring the Lord on High.
She Yi 射義: "The Meaning of the Ceremony of Archery," a chapter in the *Book of Rites*.
shen (K. *sin*) 身: In this work, it means the self. It can also mean one's individual character.
Shen Kuo (1031–1095) 沈括: a well-known philosopher, scientist, inventor, and statesman during the Song period.
Sheng Men, Decade of. 生民之什: a section of the *Book of Songs*.
Shengshi chuyao 盛世芻蕘: "The Teachings of the Church in Everyday Language," by Fr. Joseph-Anne-Marie de Moyriac de Mailla (1669–1748, a Catholic missionary in China).
Shengyan (also written Sheng Yen) 聖嚴: a twentieth-century monk who compiled the *Chanmen xiuzheng zhiyao* [禪門修證指要 Essential Pointers to Practice and Realization through the Chan Gate].
shi 示: to display by placing in the palm of your hand.
shi 視: to look at, to inspect.
Shi chong 釋蟲: "Explaining Term Related to Insects," a chapter of the *Erya* 爾雅.
Shi Jilong 石季龍: a section in the "Hereditary Houses of the Barbarian Dynasties" section in *Jinshu* 晉書. Shi Jilong (295–349) was the ruler of the Later Zhao [後趙] kingdom in the fourth century. He is also known as Shi Hu 石虎.
Shi Kuang (fl. Spring and Autumn period) 師曠: Music Master Kuang. A master musician in China in the the sixth century BCE. Also know for his discriminating palate.
Shi Que 石碏: an official in the state of Wei in the eighth century BCE.
Shi Yin (fl. Warring States period) 史嚚: Scribe Yin. A scribe in the court of Lord Zhuang, ruler of the state of Lu in the seventh century BCE.
shichen 實沈: one of the twelve Jupiter stations.
shidi 釋地: "Explaining Terms Related to the Earth," a chapter of the *Erya* 爾雅.
shigu 釋詁: the "Explanation and Exegesis" chapter of the *Erya* 爾雅.

Shiji 史記: "Records of the Grand Historian," by Sima Qian 司馬遷.

Shijing 詩經: the *Book of Songs,* one of the Thirteen Classics.

Shisanjing zhushu 十三經注疏: "Commentaries and Explanations of the Thirteen Classics." A Qing-era collection of mostly Han and Tang commentaries on the Thirteen Classics. The commentaries on the *Book of Rites,* from which the *Zhongyong* is taken, are by Zheng Xuan 鄭玄 and Kong Yingda 孔穎達.

shishan 釋山: the "Explaining Mountains" chapter in *Erya* 爾雅.

shiyu li 士虞禮: "The Sacrifices of Repose for an Ordinary Officer," a chapter in the *Yili* [The Book of Etiquette and Ceremonial].

shizhong [K. *sijung*] 時中: composed and focused on the situation at hand.

Shoulengyan 首楞嚴: a Buddhist sutra, either the *Śūraṅgama Sūtra* 大佛頂首楞嚴經 or the *Śūraṅgama Samādhi Sūtra* 首楞嚴三昧經.

Shoutiao 守祧: "Guardian of the Ancestral Shrine" section of the "Spring Offices" chapter of *Zhouli.*

Shouxing 壽星: one of the twelve Jupiter stations.

Shu 舒: a regional state in ancient China.

shu / K. *sŏ* 書: writing, a piece of writing.

Shu, Mt. 蜀山: a mountain in Sichuan province in China.

Shufu 叔父: "younger uncle," the younger brother of one's father.

Shujing 書經: *Shangshu.* the *Book of Documents.*

Shujing jichuan 書經集傳: "A Collection of Commentaries on the *Book of Documents,*" by Cai Chen 蔡沈.

shuming 書名: "to write names," in other words, to write Sinographs.

Shun 舜: a mythological early emperor of China.

Shuo Ren 碩人: the "A Beautiful Woman" poem in the Odes of Wei section of the *Book of Songs.*

Shuogua 說卦: "Explaining the Trigrams" chapter of the *Yijing.*

Shuowen 說文: abbreviated name for *Shuowen jiezi.*

Shuowen jiezi 說文解字: one of China's earliest dictionaries.

Shuqi 庶其: ruler of the state of Ju 莒 in the seventh century BCE.

Shusun Chuo (d. 517) 叔孫婼: the head of a powerful family in Lu 魯.

shuzhuan 書傳: a commentary on an "Old Text" version of the *Shangshu.*

Shuzi 庶子: an office in the Ministry of War, under the Overseer for Military Affairs.

Sichang 司常: "Overseer of Banners," a section in the chapter on Spring Offices in *Zhouli.*

Sifu 司服: "Wardrobe Overseer," a section in the chapter on Spring Offices in the *Rites of Zhou.*

Sigyŏng kangŭi 詩經講義: Tasan's *Lectures on the Book of Songs.*

Siku quanshu cunmu congshu Jingbu 四庫全書存目叢書經部: "A Collection of Works Whose Titles Appear in the *Siku quanshu*: on the Classics." The *Siku quanshu,* sometimes called "The *Emperor's Four Treasuries,*" was a late eighteenth-century compilation of what the Qing court considered the most valuable works ever produced in China. The "Four Treasuries" refers to the four categories of books in this massive collection: classics, histories, philosophy, and literature. *Siku quanshu cunmu congshu* includes works that were not included in the original *Siku quanshu* but whose titles are mentioned in that collection.

Sim much'eyong pyŏn 心無體用辯: "Discussing the Assertion That the Heart-Mind Has No Distinction between *ch'e* and *yong*," an essay by T'oegye Yi Hwang 退溪 李滉 in *T'oegye sŏnsaeng munjip* 退溪先生文集.

Sima Qian (145–87 BCE) 司馬遷: a historian in the Former Han dynasty. Author of the *Shiji* [史記 Records of the Grand Historian].

Simgyŏng mirhŏm 心經密驗: Tasan's *Personal Experience with the Classic of the Heart-and-Mind*.

Siming 司命: a star in the Wenchang cluster. It is seen as a god who oversees human destiny.

sin / C. *shen* 神: spirit. Tasan used this both to refer to the nonmaterial beings who assisted the Lord on High and to refer specifically to the Lord on High. Sometimes, however, he uses this term to refer to the immaterial consciousness of individual human beings.

sindok / C. *shendu* 慎獨: watching over your own thoughts and actions, even when no one else can know what you are thinking or doing.

Sinp'yŏn Kyŏngguk taejŏn 新編經國大典: "Newly Edited Version of the Great Administrative Code."

sinyu / C. *xinyou* 辛酉: the fifty-eighth year in the sexagenary cycle for naming years. In this work, it refers to 1801.

Sipsamgyŏng ch'aek 十三經 策: "A Discussion of the Thirteen Classics," an essay by Tasan.

sirhak 實學: "practical learning," a term often applied to writing in the second half of Chosŏn that discussed practical matters such as government administration rather than metaphysics.

sishi 司市: director of markets, an office in the Zhou Education Ministry.

Sishu cunyi 四書存疑: "Harboring Doubts about the *Four Books*," by Lin Xiyuan 林希元.

Sishu daquan 四書大全: "A Great Collection of Commentaries on the Four Books," complied by Hu Guang 胡廣.

Sishu faming 四書發明: "Clarifying the Meaning of the Four Books," by Chen Li 陳櫟.

Sishu gaicuo 四書改錯: "Correcting the Errors in Zhu Xi's Commentaries on the Four Books," by Mao Qiling 毛奇齡.

Sishu Hunanjiang 四書湖南講: "Discussions in Hunan on the Four Books," by Ge Yinliang 葛寅亮.

Sishu huowen 四書或問: Zhu Xi's "Questions and Answers about the Four Books."

Sishu jianyi 四書箋義: "Notes on the Meaning of the Four Books," by Zhao De 趙悳.

Sishu jishuo 四書集說: "Collected Commentaries on the Four Books," compiler unclear. There were many works with this title.

Sishu jizhu 四書集註: Zhu Xi's "Collection of Commentaries on the Four Books."

Sishu mengyin 四書蒙引: "Introduction to the Four Books for Beginners," by Cai Qing 蔡清.

Sishu shengyan 四書賸言: "Residual Remarks about the Four Books," a work by Mao Qiling 毛奇齡.

Sishu shengyan bu 四書賸言補: "Supplement to Residual Remarks about the Four Books," by Mao Qiling 毛奇齡.

Sishu shuoyue 四書說約: "Simple Explanations of the Four Books," by Gu Menglin 顧夢麟.

Sishu tong 四書通: "General Survey of the Four Books," by Hu Bingwen 胡炳文.

Sishu zuanshu 四書纂疏: "A Collection of Commentaries on the Four Books," by Zhao Shunsun 趙順孫.

Sizhong 司中: a star in the *wenchang* 文昌 constellation. Also, a celestial spirit.

sŏ / C. *shu* 恕: to empathize, being considerate in your dealings with others.

Sŏam Kanghak-gi 西巖講學記: "A Record of a Scholarly Discussion at the Western Hermitage," Tasan's account of a get-together with twelve other Namin in 1795 to discuss Sŏngho Yi Ik's writings.

Sŏmo Kimssi Myojimyŏng 庶母金氏墓誌銘: "an epitaph for Mrs. Kim, a secondary wife." Mrs. Kim was the secondary wife of Tasan's father.

sŏng / C. *cheng* 誠: "sincerity," appropriately responsive and unselfishly cooperative.

sŏng / C. *xing* 性: human nature. The nature of things. That which is natural. Innate potential to act the way one should act. In human beings, that which makes human beings truly human. In mainstream neo-Confucianism, it refers to the innate *tendency* to act appropriately. Zhu Xi identifies human nature with *li* [patterning principles of appropriate interactions]. Tasan redefined *xing* to mean the natural desires all human beings have for both acting appropriately as well as for pursuing what feels good and/or is personally advantageous. He denied that human nature was *li*. Instead, it includes the *potential* to align our actions with *li*.

Song 宋: (1) a kingdom during the Warring States period. (2) a major dynasty that lasted from 960 to 1276.

Song 頌: the "Odes of the Temple and the Altar" volume of the *Book of Songs*.

Sŏnggyun'gwan. 成均館: National Confucian Academy.

Sŏngho Sasŏl 星湖僿說: "The Humble Discourses of Sŏngho." A collection of short essays on a wide variety of subjects by Sŏngho Yi Ik. Also pronounced *Sŏngho saesŏl*.

Sŏngho Yi Ik (1682–1764) 星湖 李瀷: an influential scholar in Tasan's Namin [Southerner] faction.

sŏngjŏng / C. *xingqing* 性情: human nature and human emotions, character, natural temperament, or natural disposition.

sŏngnihak / C. *xinglixue* 性理學: "scholarship on human nature and patterning principle." The Korean term for the Cheng-Zhu school of neo-Confucianism.

soyiyŏn/sodangyŏn (C. *suoyiran/suodangran*) 所以然 / 所當然: that which makes things what they are, that which defines what things should be and do.

Sŏnjungssi myojimyŏng 先仲氏墓誌銘: "An Epitaph for My Older Brother," Tasan's epitaph for Chŏng Yakchŏn. 丁若銓.

su / K. *so* 素: in this text, to go toward. Tasan also understands this Sinograph to refer to the state of mind you should have at a particular time and in a particular situation.

Su Dongpo (1037–1101) 蘇東坡: one of the names used by the poet and political figure Su Shi 蘇軾.

Su Shi (1037–1101) 蘇軾: an important figure in the politics of eleventh-century China. He is best known today for his poetry.

Su Wenzhong (1037–1101) 蘇文忠: another name for Su Shi 蘇軾, the famous Song poet.

sugi / C. *xiuji* 修己: cultivate the self; cultivate a moral character.

Suihua jili 歲華紀麗: presented as a Tang dynasty text by Han E. 韓鄂 but believed by some to be a Ming-era forgery.

Suiren 燧人: a legendary figure who is said to have discovered how to make a fire.

Sunjo (r. 1800–1834) 純祖: the twenty-second king of Chosŏn. It was when he was technically the king (he was but a child at the time) that Tasan was sent into his long exile.

suo / K. *saek* 索: to try to get.

Sup'yo 水標: a bridge in downtown Seoul.

susa / C. *zhusi* 洙泗: a reference to the rivers in the area where Confucius was active. By extension, this is a reference to Confucian thought before the Han dynasty.

Sushen 肅慎: a tribe to the north of China that the Chinese considered barbarians.

Suwen 素問: The "Pure Questions" section of the *Huangdi neijing* 黃帝內經.

Suwŏn 水原: a city south of Seoul.

Taehak / C. *Daxue* 大學: The Great Learning.

Taehak Kangŭi 大學講義: Tasan's "A Discussion of the Meaning of the *Daxue*."

taewŏl / C. *duiyeu* 對越: "be reverent toward, and mindful of, that which is above you."

Tai, King (fl. 11th c. BCE) 太王: also known as Gugong Dan Fu 古公亶父. Was named King Tai posthumously. Said to be the founder of the royal family of Zhou.

Taibo 太伯: also known as Da Bo 大伯. Son of King Tai 太王 and the first king of the ancient state of Wu 吳.

Taicou 太蔟: a musical pitch associated with the first month of the year and as representing humanity in the triad of Heaven, Earth, and Humanity.

Taiji [K. *t'aegŭk* 太極]: Supreme Polarity, a cosmological concept in neo-Confucianism referring to the differentiation of primordial cosmic unity into the complementary forces of yin and yang, stillness and activity.

Taijitu shuo 太極圖說: *Explanation of the Diagram of the Supreme Polarity* by Zhou Dunyi 周敦頤.

Tan Gong 檀弓: a chapter in the *Book of Rites* named after a person who appears in that chapter.

Tan Gong chamo 檀弓箴誤: "Corrections to the Maxims in the 'Tan Gong' section of the *Book of Rites*," a chapter in Tasan's *Sangnye oep'yŏn* [An appendix to a discussion of mourning ritual].

Tang (trad. c. 1675–1646 BCE) 湯: believed to have been the first king of the Shang dynasty.
Tang dynasty (618–907) 唐: This is also a name used for the legendary emperor Yao 堯.
Tangshu 唐叔: the younger brother of King Cheng of Zhou 周成王.
Tanzi 郯子: ruler of a small principality in the sixth century BCE.
tap Ki Myŏngŏn 答奇明彦: "A response to a letter from Myŏngŏn Ki Taesŭng." Part of an exchange of letters between T'oegye Yi Hwang 退溪 李滉 and Ki Taesŭng 奇大升.
tap Sŏng Howŏn 答成浩原: "A response to a letter from Sŏng Howŏn [Sŏng Hon 成渾 1535–1598]." Sŏng Hon is also known as Sŏng Ugye 成牛溪. This is part of an exchange of letters between Yulgok Yi 栗谷 李珥 and Sŏng Hon that continued the Four-Seven debate begun by the exchange of letters between T'oegye Yi Hwang 退溪 李滉 and Ki Taesŭng 奇大升.
tap Yi Yŏhong 答李汝弘: "A response to a letter from Yi Yŏhong (Yi Chaeŭi, 1772–1839)." This is one of several letters Tasan exchanged with Yi Chaeŭi to discuss philosophical issues and how to read the Confucian Classics.
Tasan 茶山: pen name of Chŏng Yagyong (1760–1801) 丁若鏞.
Teng 滕: a fiefdom in early Zhou.
Teng Wen Gong 滕文公: "Lord Wen of Teng," a chapter in the *Mencius*.
Tian (K. *ch'ŏn*) 天: Heaven, both in the sense of the sky above and, as Tasan used this term, the supernatural personality Sangje/Shangdi 上帝, who instilled a conscience in human beings and then watched to see if they listened to their conscience. In neo-Confucianism, Heaven was an impersonal moral force identified with *li* 理.
tian qiu 天球: a celestial sphere. Used in ancient ancestor rites.
Tianchang 天長: a city in Anhui province in China.
Tianguan dazai 天官 大宰: Premier in the Celestial Offices in *Zhouli*.
Tianguan zhongzai 天官冢宰: the Prime Minister in the Celestial Offices in *Zhouli*.
Tianzhu shiyi 天主實義: Matteo Ricci's *True Significance of the Lord of Heaven*. First published early in the seventeenth century.
T'oegye sŏnsaeng munjip 退溪先生文集: "The Collected Works of T'oegye Yi Hwang."
T'oegye Yi Hwang (1501–1570) 退溪 李滉: one of the three leading Confucian philosophers of Chosŏn Korea.
tŏk / C. *de* 德: ethical virtuosity, the power to act appropriately.
t'ong / C. *tong* 統: to unify, to control.
Tongdian 通典: "Comprehensive Guide to Institutions," a Tang-era work by Du You 杜佑 (735–812).
Tongti Bohua 銅提伯華: also known as *Yangshe Chi* 羊舌赤. He was a nobleman in the state of Jin in the sixth century BCE.
Tosan sasungnok 陶山私淑錄: "Notes on Taking Yi Hwang as a Model for Self-cultivation," a short text by Tasan Chŏng Yagyong.

Tosim 道心: moral heart-mind, Dao mind. That part of our heart-mind which directs us to act appropriately.
tuan / K. *dan* 鍛: to forge metal.
Tuo, Diviner 祝佗, 祝鮀: surname of a figure who appears in *Spring and Autumn Annals*.
ŭi / C. *yi* 依: rely on.
ŭi / C. *yi* 倚: leaning off-center.
Waishi 外史: "Scribes for External Affairs" section of the Autumn Offices chapter of *Zhouli*.
wang / K. *mang* 魍: demon, mountain spirit.
Wang Bi (226–249) 王弼: the author of an influential commentary on the *Yijing*.
Wang Bo (1197–1274) 王柏: an early followed of Zhu Xi's approach to Confucianism.
Wang Chong (27–97 CE) 王充: a Han dynasty thinker who was critical of what he believed were supernatural elements that had crept into mainstream Chinese thought, contaminating Confucianism.
Wang Ji (ancestor of the Zhou royal family) 王季: also known as Ji Li 季歷.
Wang Su (195–257) 王肅: a post-Han scholar of the Classics.
Wang Yangming (1472–1529) 王陽明: also kwown as Wang Shouren 王守仁. He was an important Confucian philosopher during the Ming dynasty.
Wang zhi 王制: "Royal Regulations," a chapter in the *Book of Rites*.
Wei 衛: a regional state in Zhou times.
Wei, Odes of 衛風: a section of the "Airs of the States" section of the *Book of Songs*.
Wei Boyang 魏伯陽 (??–728): the author of *Cantong qi*, an internal alchemy text.
Wei Shi (??–1227) 衛湜: a scholar-official during the Song dynasty. He compiled *Liji jishuo* 禮記集說.
Wei Tian zhi Ming 維天之命: "The Charge That Heaven Gave," a poem in Decade of Qing Maio section of the *Book of Songs*.
weilü 尾閭: an imaginary opening in the ocean floor through which water flows out so that the ocean doesn't fill up.
Weisheng Gao 微生高: a man from the state of Lu 魯 who is mentioned in the *Analects*.
wen / K. *mun* 文: This Sinograph has a wide range of meanings. Depending on the context, it can mean script, written language, culture, patterns, or, as an adjective, refined.
Wen, Decade of King 文王之什: a collection of ten poems in the major odes section of the *Book of Songs*.
Wen, King of Zhou (r. 1049/45–1043 BCE) 周文王: not an actual king, but the father of the first king of Zhou. 文王 is also the name of a poem in the Decade of King Wen collection of poems in the major odes section of the *Book of Songs*.
Wen, Lord (r. 626–609 BCE) 文公: the ruler of the state of Lu 魯 in the late seventh century BCE.
Wen fu 文賦: "Rhapsody on Literature," by Lu Ji 陸機, a post-Han poet.

Wen Wang Shizi 文王世子: "King Wen as Son and Heir," a chapter in the *Book of Rites.*

Wenchang 文昌: a constellation in traditional Chinese astronomy. Also the god of literature.

Wenhui (fl. 16th-17th c.) 文輝: Mao Wenhui 毛文輝, a near-contemporary of Mao Qiling 毛奇齡, who contributed to the editing of Mao Qiling's *Sishu gaicuo* [四書改錯 Correcting the errors in Zhu Xi's commentaries on the Four Books].

Wenzi of Wei, General 衛將軍文子: chapter 60 of the *Dadai Liji* 大戴禮記.

Wo Ding 沃丁: Shang ruler. Said to have reigned 1720-1692.

Wojiao 沃焦: an imaginary mountain at the bottom of the southern part of the Eastern Sea.

wŏn'gi / C. *yuanqi* 元氣: matter-energy in its original indeterminate state, before it has begun to congeal into separate and distinct things and processes.

Wu 吳: a state in ancient China.

Wu, King of Zhou (r. 1099-1050 BCE) 周武王: first actual king of Zhou.

Wu, Lord. (r. 826-816 BCE) 武公: a ruler of the state of Lu 魯 in the ninth century BCE.

Wu Geng (11th c. BCE) 武庚: a scion of the Shang ruling family who joined with two brothers of the Duke of Zhou 周公 to resist the Duke of Zhou's de facto seizure of royal power.

Wudi 五帝: "The Five Overlords," a chapter in *Kongzi jiayu* [孔子家語 The sayings of the Confucian School].

Wufeng 五峯: the literary name of Hu Hong (1106-1162) 胡宏.

Wufu 五輔: "The Five Aids," a chapter in *Guanzi* 管子.

Wugouzi 無垢子: the literary name of Zhang Jiucheng (1092-1159) 張九成.

wuji / K. *mugŭk* 無極: Non-Polarity. In neo-Confucian cosmology, the original state of nondifferentiation out of which everything emerges.

Wuyu 吳語: the chapter on the state of Wu in *Gouyu* [國語].

Xi 熙: an alternate name for Zhurong. Said to be related to Shaohao.

xi 餼: to provide a ration of grain.

xi 槩: to give someone grain.

Xi, Lord (r. 659-627 BCE) 僖公: a ruler of the state of Lu 魯 in the seventh century BCE.

Xi and He 羲和: two gods who created the first calendar on the order of Emperor Yao 堯.

Xi Chou 郤犨: an official in the state of Jin in the early sixth century.

Xi Yi of Jin 晉郤錡: a sixth-century-BCE official of Jin.

xia 祫: a sacrificial ritual honoring the immediate ancestors of a ruler.

Xia 夏: according to legend, the first state in what is now China.

Xia shu 夏書: "The Book of the Xia," a volume of the *Shangshu* 尚書.

Xiafu Fuji 夏父弗忌: a master of ritual in the state of Lu 魯 in the seventh century.

Xiaguan 夏官: "Summer Offices" (Ministry of War) in *Zhouli*).

Xiaguan, sima 夏官 司馬: Overseer of Military Affairs in the Ministry of War in *Zhouli*.

Xiang (651–619 BCE) 襄王: sixth king of Eastern Zhou.

Xiang, Lord (r. 572–542 BCE) 襄公: a ruler of the state of Lu 魯 in the Spring and Autumn period.

Xiang Zhuan 象傳: "Commentary on the Images," a section of the *Yijing*.

Xianzi Suo 縣子瑣: a person otherwise unknown who appears briefly in the "Tan Gong" 檀弓 chapter of the *Book of Rites*.

Xiao, King (r. 872–866 BCE) 孝王: the ninth king of Eastern Zhou.

Xiao Ya 小雅: "Minor Odes of the Kingdom," a volume in the *Book of Songs*.

Xiaojing / K. *hyogyŏng* 孝經: "The Classic of Filial Piety."

Xiaojing zhushu 孝經注疏: the "Commentaries on, and Explanations of, the *Classic of Filial Piety* in the *Shisanjing zhushu* 十三經注疏.

Xiaomin, Decade of 小旻之什: a section in the minor odes of the kingdom collection in the *Book of Songs*.

Xiaoshan 蕭山: a way of referring to Mao Qiling 毛奇齡.

xiaoshi 小史: "minor scribe." An official position in the ministry of ritual affairs in *Zhouli*.

Xiaowan 小宛: "Diminutive," a poem in the minor odes of the kingdom in the *Book of Songs*.

Xiaozai 小宰: title in *Zhouli* for the Ordinary Grand Master in the Celestial Offices.

xiaozhuan 小篆: "seal script." An early form of writing Sinographs that became the preferred form with the Qin empire's standardization of Sinographs. Also known as 篆文 zhuanwen.

xiaozongbo 小宗伯: Vice-Minister of Rites in the Spring Offices in *Zhouli*.

Xiaxiaozheng 夏小正: "The Small Calendar of the Xia," a secion of the *Dadai Liji* 大戴禮記.

xibing 餼稟: to reduce the amount of grain in the rations.

Xici zhuan, shang 繫辭傳, 上: "Commentary on the Appended Phrases, Part One." Part of the *Yijing*.

Xici zhuan, xia 繫辭傳, 下: "Commentary on the Appended Phrases, Part Two." Part of the *Yijing*.

Xie 契: believed to be a wise official serving the legendary Emperor Shun 舜. He is seen as the ancestor of the ruling family of Shang.

Xiefu 泄父: a crown prince of Eastern Zhou in the eighth century BCE. Son of King Ping.

Ximu 析木: one of the twelve Jupiter stations.

xing 興: to prosper, to rise.

xing / K. *sŏng* 性: "human nature." That which makes human beings truly human. In mainstream neo-Confucianism, it refers to the innate *tendency* to act appropriately. Zhu Xi identifies human nature with *li* [patterning principles of appropriate interactions]. Tasan redefined *xing* to mean the natural desires all human beings have both for acting appropriately and for pursuing what feels good and/or is personally advantageous. He denied that human nature was *li*. Instead, it includes the *potential* to align our actions with *li*.

Xing Bing (932–1010) 邢昺: Northern Song author of a commentary on *Erya* 爾雅 and commentaries on other Confucian Classics, including the *Analects*.

Xingji 星紀: one of the twelve Jupiter stations.

xingli 性理: "Human Nature and Patterning Principles." An early chapter in *Zhuzi yulei* 朱子語類.

Xingwei 行葦: "Wayside Weeds," a poem in the major odes section of *Book of Songs*.

Xiu 修: an alternate name for Xuan Ming 玄冥, the god of water. Tasan, relying on the *Zuozhuan*, says he is the uncle of Shaohao 少皞, but other sources say he is Shaohao's younger brother.

Xiu 宿: lunar lodges, the twenty-eight constellations near the celestial equator the moon passes through on a regular basis.

Xu 需: "Waiting," the fifth hexagram in the *Yijing*.

Xu Dongyang (1270–1337) 許東陽: also known as Xu Qian 許謙, a reclusive Confucian scholar during the Yuan dynasty known for his explications of Zhu Xi's commentaries on the Four Books.

Xu Kai (920–974) 許鍇: Together with his brother Xu Xuan 許鉉, he produced a restored version of the *Shuowen jiezi* 說文解字 during the Song period.

Xu Liji jishuo 續禮記集說: "Supplement to the Commentaries on the Book of Rites," by Hang Shijun 杭世駿.

Xu Qian (1270–1337) 許謙: also known as Xu Dongyang 許東陽. The compiler of *Du Zhongyong congshuo* [讀四書叢說 a collection of accounts of reading the *Zhongyong*].

Xu Shen (58–c.147) 許慎: the compiler of the *Shuowen jiezi* 說文解字 during the Later Han dynasty.

Xu Xuan (916–991) 許鉉: Together with his brother Xu Kai 許鍇, he produced a restored version of the *Shuowen jiezi* 說文解字 during the Song period.

Xuan (r. 74–49 BCE) 漢宣: emperor in the Former Han dynasty.

Xuan, Lord (r. 608–591 BCE) 宣公: ruler of the state of Lu 魯 in the late seventh–early sixth centuries.

Xuan, Steward 宰咺: an official under King Ding of Zhou.

Xuan Ming 玄冥: the god of water. Also known as Xiu 修.

Xuandi chuixun. 玄帝垂訓: Also known as *wudang shan xuantian shangdi chuixun wen* 武當山玄天上帝垂訓文, "Admonition by the Emperor of Dark Heavens" is a Daoist text of the late Yuan period. The author is unknown.

xuanmian 玄冕: clothing for deceased high officials.

Xuanxiao 玄枵: one of the twelve Jupiter stations.

Xueji 學記: "Record of Studies," a chapter in the *Book of Rites*.

Xugua 序卦: "Providing the Sequence of the Hexagrams," a section of the *Yijing*.

Xun 郇: a regional state in early Zhou.

Xunzi (3rd c. BCE) 荀子: "Master Xun." Xun Kuang 荀況. He is famous for insisting that human beings are not virtuous by nature but instead have to restrain and manage their emotions in order to act properly. Tasan echoed Xunzi, though he did not mention Xunzi's name, when he argued that there are three levels of existence: existing without being able to perceive anything (like plants and trees); existing and being able to be aware of the surrounding environment (like animals); and existing, being able to be aware of the surrounding environment, and being able to decide how to interact with that environment (like human beings).

Yan 燕: a large regional state during the Zhou period.

Yan Hui (fl. 6th c. BCE) 顏回: a much-beloved disciple of Confucius who died young. Also known as Yan Yuan 顏淵.

Yan Shigu (581–645) 顏師古: author of *Kuangmiu zhengsu* 匡謬正俗 "Corrections of Errors and Rectification of Vulgar Readings."

Yan Ying (578–500 BCE) 晏嬰: Prime Minister of Qi 齊 during the Spring and Autumn period.

Yan Yuan (fl. 6th c. BCE) 顏淵: another name for Yan Hui 顏回, the favorite disciple of Confucius.

yang 陽: one of the two fundamental complementary forces in the cosmos. Yang represents what is male, forceful, active, light, hot, and dry.

Yang Jia (r. 1408–1404 BCE) 陽甲: believed to have been a ruler of Shang.

Yang Shen (1488–1559) 楊慎: a scholar-official during the Ming. He was more of a historian and philologist than a philosopher. Among his works was a study of the place names in the *Spring and Autumn Annals*.

Yang Shi (1053–1135) 楊時: also known as *Yang Guishan* 楊龜山. He studied under Cheng Yi 程頤 and Cheng Hao 程顥 and therefore was one of the first neo-Confucians.

Yang Xiong (53 BCE–18CE) 揚雄: a poet-philosopher and court official in the Former Han dynasty.

Yang Zhu (440–360? BCE) 楊朱: a Warring States period thinker about whom little is known except that he was criticized for supposedly prioritizing self-interest over the common good

Yanzi chunqui 晏子春秋: "The Spring and Autumn Annals of Master Yan" [Yan Ying 晏嬰].

Yanzi jiyu 晏子集語: "The Collected Stories about Master Yan" [Yan Ying 晏嬰]. This appears to be a reference to a work otherwise known as *Yanzi chunqui* [晏子春秋 the Spring and Autumn Annals of Master Yan].

yanzi shiji 晏子事蹟: "The Exploits of Master Yan" [Yan Ying 晏嬰].

Yanziyu 晏子語: "Stories of Master Yan." This may be Tasan's abbreviated title for the collected sayings of Yan Ying 晏嬰.

Yao 堯: a mythological early emperor of China.

yi 以: with, by means of.

Yi 益: (1) a legendary minister of the equally legendary Emperor Shun 舜; (2) another name for Lord Yin of Zhu (r. 491–484 BCE) 邾隱公, a ruler of the regional state of Zhu.

Yi 抑: "Grave," a poem in the Decade of Dang section of the *Book of Songs*.

Yi, King (trad. r. 899–873 BCE) 懿王: the ninth king of Western Zhou.

Yi, King (trad. r. 865–858 BCE) 夷王: the eleventh king of Western Zhou.

Yibal kibal pyŏn 理發氣發辨: "An Analysis of the Debate over Whether *li* or *ki* Generates the Four Sprouts," an essay by Tasan.

Yi Chiptu (1744–1820) 李集斗: a Chief Magistrate of the State Tribunal who blocked appeals for Tasan's release from exile. He held several high positions in the state bureaucracy under both King Chŏngjo 正祖 and King Sunjo 純祖.

Yi from Huai 淮夷: a non-sinicized group living along the Huai River in ancient times.

Yi Hwang (1501–1570) 李滉: one of the three leading Confucian philosophers of Chosŏn Korea. Also known as T'oegye 退溪.

Yi I (1536–1584) 李珥: one of the most influential Confucian philosophers in Chosŏn Korea. Also known as Yulgok 栗谷.

Yi Ik (1682–1764) 李瀷: a leading Confucian scholar of the Namin faction. Also known as Sŏngho 星湖.

Yi Kigyŏng (1756–1819) 李基慶: a scholar-official who had once been friendly with Tasan but became his enemy over Tasan's youthful involvement with Catholicism.

Yi of Rong, Lord (fl. 9th c. BCE) 榮夷公: a ruler of the regional state of Rong.

Yi Pyŏk (1754–1786) 李蘗: one of Tasan's closest friends. He is the friend Tasan relied on the most in writing his commentary on the *Zhongyong*.

Yi Pyŏngmo (1742–1806) 李秉模: a scholar-official in the eighteenth century and into the early nineteenth century. He held several high posts under Kings Chŏngjo 正祖 and Sunjo 純祖.

Yi Sŭnghun (1756–1801) 李承薰: He was baptized while on a trip to Beijing and began telling his friends and relatives about his new religion when he returned to Korea in 1784. He was married to Tasan's sister.

Yi Tŏkcho 李德操: another name for Yi Pyŏk 李蘗.

Yifengzhuan 翼奉傳: a biography in the *Hanshu* [The Book of the Former Han dynasty].

Yijing 易經: the *Book of Changes*. Also known as *Chuyŏk* 周易.

Yili 儀禮: "Book of Etiquette and Ceremonial." One of the three ancient ritual texts, along with the *Book of Rites* and *Zhouli*.

Yili zhushu 儀禮注疏: "Notes and Explanations of the *Yili*." Included in *Shisanjing zhushu* 十三經注疏.

yin 隱: difficult to discern. hidden.

yin [K. *ŭm*] 陰: one of the two fundamental complementary forces in the cosmos. *Yin* represents what is female, passive, heavy, cool, and wet.

Yin 殷: another name for the Shang dynasty.

yin 寅: the third of the twelve terrestrial branches.

Yin, scribe (fl. 7th c. BCE) 史嚚: a court official in the Spring and Autumn period.

yin and *yang* (K. *ŭm* and *yang*) 陰陽.

Yin Hejing (1071–1142) 尹和靖: also known as Yin Tun 尹焞. He was a disciple of Cheng Yi 程頤.

Yin of Zhu, Lord 邾隱公: fifth-century-BCE ruler of the regional state of Zhu.

Ying 郢: a regional state in early Zhou.
Ying 應: a regional state in early Zhou.
Yingshi 营室: the encampment constellation among the twenty-eight lunar lodges of traditional Chinese astronomy. Also known as Dingxing 定星.
Yiwen zhi 藝文志: "Treatise on Literature," a chapter in the *Hanshu* 漢書 that provides a bibliography of pre-Han literature.
Yiya (fl. 7th c. BCE) 易牙: a man of Qi 齊 who was known for his cooking skills and his disciminating palate.
Yŏhong Yi Chaeŭi (1772–1839) 汝弘 李載毅: a man whom Tasan met while he was in exile in Kangjin and later exchanged letters with.
yok / C. *yu* 欲: human desires, physical desires; to desire.
yok / C. *yu* 慾: carnal desires, selfish desires; to lust after.
yong 庸: consistent; constant, all the time.
Yong 雝: a poem in the Decade of Chen Gong section of the *Book of Songs*.
Yong 雍: a regional state in early Zhou.
Yong Province 雍州: one of the nine provinces the legendary Yu the Great 禹 is said to have demarcated when he divided the world into administrative regions.
Yŏngjo (r. 1724–1776) 英祖: a king in Korea's Chosŏn 朝鮮 dynasty.
Yŏngmyŏng / C. *lingming* 靈明: spiritual insight, penetrating intelligence, consciousness.
You Zuo (1053–1123) 游酢: a disciple of Cheng Yi 程頤.
Yousi che 有司徹: "The Assistant Clears Away," a chapter in the *Book of Etiquette and Cermonial* 儀禮.
Yŏyudang 與猶堂: one of the literary names of Chŏng Yagyong 丁若鏞.
Yŏyudang chŏnso 與猶堂全書: "The Complete Works of Yŏyudang Chŏng Yagyong" 丁若鏞.
Yu 禹: legendary figure who was believed to be the first person in China to control flooding and to have founded the legendary Xia dynasty.
Yu 虞: an ancient state in what is now China. This is also sometimes used as the name of the legendary emperor Shun 舜.
yu / K. *yul* 聿: a writing brush, written to depict a hand holding such a brush.
Yu 邘: a regional state in early Zhou.
Yu Meng Shangshu shu 與孟上書 書: "Letter to Prime Minister Meng," written by Han Yu 韓愈.
Yu Province 豫州: one of the nine provinces the legendary Yu the Great 禹 is said to have created when he divided the world into administrative regions.
Yu Zhong (fl. 11th c. BCE) 虞仲: also known as Zhong Yong 仲雍. A descendant of King Tai.
Yuan 元: the Yuan dynasty (1279–1368), when China was ruled by Mongols.
Yuan 原: a regional state in early Zhou.
yuan 鳰: a kind of bird.
Yuanying 元英: the name of a palace in Yan 燕.
Yuding lidai fuhui 御定歷代賦彙: "Collection of Prose Poems through the Ages."

A Qing dynasty compilation of *fu* poems [賦 prose-poems] from the Warring States period through the Ming, compiled by order of the Kangxi Emperor 康熙.

Yue 越: A non-Chinese state in the Spring and Autumn period in what is now southeastern China.

Yue, Mt. 嶽山: This would in other contexts be taken as a reference to the Five Sacred Mountains of China, but it is mentioned here as a specific mountain garrison.

Yue Yi (fl. 3rd c. BCE) 樂毅: a general of the state of Yan 燕.

Yue Yi liezhuan 樂毅列傳: biography of Yue Yi in the *Shiji* 史記

Yuechang 越裳: an ancient state in what is now southern China.

Yueji 樂記: "Record of Music," a chapter in the *Book of Rites*.

Yueling 月令: "Proceedings of Government in the Different Months," a chapter in the *Book of Rites*.

Yuezhengzi 樂正子: a disciple of Mencius. Also known as Yuezheng Ke 樂正克.

Yulgok Chŏnsŏ 栗谷全書: "The Complete Works of Yulgok Yi I" 栗谷 李珥.

Yulgok Yi I (1536-1584) 栗谷 李珥: one of the most influential Confucian philosophers in Chosŏn 朝鮮 Korea.

Yulu 玉路: "jade path," a path normally reserved for rulers.

Yun Chich'ung (1759-1791) 尹持忠: an early Korean Catholic convert and martyr, and a cousin of Tasan Chŏng Yagyong 丁若鏞.

Yun Hyu (1617-1680) 尹鑴: a scholar-official during the Chosŏn 朝鮮 dynasty. A member of the same Namin faction Tasan was a member of.

Yun Sŏndo (1587-1671) 尹善道: a scholar-official during the Chosŏn 朝鮮 dynasty. A member of the same Namin faction Tasan was a member of. Tasan was related to Yun Sŏndo through his mother.

Yushu 虞書: the "Book of Yu" in the *Book of Documents*.

Yuzao 玉藻: "Jade-bead Pendants of the Royal Cap," a chapter in the *Book of Rites*.

Yuzuan Zhuxi quanshu 御纂朱子全書: the collection of Zhu Xi's complete works compiled in the eighteenth century under imperial command.

Zai Yu (522-458 BCE) 宰予: also known as Zai Wo 宰我, a disciple of Confucius.

Zang Aibo (fl. late 8th c.-early 7th c. BCE) 臧哀伯: an official in the state of Lu 魯. Also known as Zangsun Da 臧孫達.

Zangsun Chen (fl. 7th c. BCE) 臧孫辰: an official in the state of Lu 魯. Also known as Zang Wenzhong 臧文仲.

zaohua / K. *chohwa* 造化: "the transformation of things," the totality of events and process in the cosmos.

ze / K. *ch'ik* 則: since it is.... then ...

Zeng Shen (505-436 BCE) 曾參: also known as Zengzi 曾子, a disciple of Confucius.

Zeng yun 增韻: "Expanded rhymes." Also known as *Zeng xiu hu zhu li bu yun lüe* 增修互注禮部韻略, a pronunciation dictionary compiled in the Song dynasty by the father and son Mao Huang and Mao Juzheng to indicate the proper pronunciation of Sinographs in ancient ritual texts.

Zengzi (505–436 BCE) 曾子: disciple of Confucius. Also known as Zeng Shen 曾參.
Zengzi lishi 曾子立事: "Master Zeng Answers Questions about How to Properly Serve Superiors," a chapter in the *Dadai liji* 大戴禮記.
Zengzi Tianyuan 曾子天圓: "Master Zeng Answers Questions about Heaven Being Round," a chapter in *Dadai liji* 大戴禮記.
Zhan 展: a surname.
Zhan Qin (720–621 BCE) 展禽: also known as Zhan Huo 展獲.
zhandan 琖單: a wine cup used in ancestor memorial rituals.
Zhang Chang 張敞: an official during the former Han dynasty who was known for being knowledgeable about pre-Qin Sinographs.
Zhang Hua (232–300) 張華: a government official in Western Jin, after the fall of the Han dynasty.
Zhang Jiucheng (1092–1159) 張九成: a Southern Song official known for being friendly with the prominent Buddhist monk Zonggao 宗杲. Also known as Wugouzi 無垢子.
Zhang Taizhan (fl. late17th–early 18th c.) 章泰占: also known as Zhang Dalai 章大来, a Qing scholar and disciple of Mao Qiling 毛奇齡.
Zhang Wenzhong 臧文仲: a high official in the state of Lu 魯 in the seventh century BCE. Also known as Zangsun Chen (fl. 7th c. BCE) 臧孫辰.
Zhang Zai (1020–1077) 張載: a pioneer of what became neo-Confucianism. Best known for composing the influential "Western Inscription" 西銘.
zhangfu 章甫: a type of cap used by the nobility and scholars in the state of Song 宋 in the time of Confucius. It was believed to have been worn in Shang times.
Zhangzi yulu zhong 張子語錄中: Records of what Zhangzi said-B. A collection of sayings by Zhang Zai 張載. It is included in *Zhangzi quanshu* 張子全書.[The Complete Works of Zhang Zai].
zhao 昭: the row on the left for spirit tablets in an ancestral shrine.
Zhao, Lord (r. 541–510 BCE) 昭公: a ruler of the state of Lu 魯.
Zhao De (fl. 9th c.) 趙德: A Tang dynasty scholar of the Confucian Classics. He was an associate of Han Yu 韓愈 and edited a collection of Han's writings.
Zhao Ge'an (1215–1277) 趙格菴: also known as Zhao Shunsun 趙順孫, compiler of *Sishu zuanshu* 四書纂疏 [A compilation of notes on the Four Books].
Zhaojue Chanshi (1025–1091) 照覺禪師: "Chan Master of Illuminating Awakening," This is Changzong 常總, a famous Chan monk during the Song dynasty.
Zhaozhou (778–835) 趙州: a Tang dynasty monk.
zhe / K. cha 者: a nominalizing particle, adding the meaning of someone who does or is the term it is appended to.
Zhejiang 浙江: a coastal province in China.
zhen 震: one of the eight trigrams used to form the hexagrams in the *Book of Changes*.
Zhen 振: Tasan reads this Sinograph in *Zhongyong* as "to support or hold up."
Zhen Dexiu (1178–1235) 真德秀: A high official in Southern Song, he also wrote an important commentary on the *Daxue* 大學, *Daxue yanyi* [大學衍義 Extended Meaning of the Daxue], based on how Zhu Xi had read that text.

Zhen Xishan 真西山: the literary name of Zhen Dexiu 真德秀.

Zheng, earl of 鄭伯: a relative of a ruler of the regional state of Zheng 鄭 in the seventh century BCE.

Zheng, odes of 鄭風: a subsection of "The Airs of the States" section of the *Book of Songs*.

Zheng Kangcheng 鄭康成: another name for Zheng Xuan 鄭玄.

Zheng Sinong (d. 83 CE) 鄭司農: also known as Zheng Zhong 鄭眾 a Han-era official and commentator on the Classics.

Zheng Xuan (127–200) 鄭玄: writer of influential early commentaries on important Confucian texts.

Zheng Yue 正月: "The First Month," a poem in the Decade of Qifu section of the *Book of Songs*.

Zhengmin 烝民: "A People Created by Heaven," a poem in the major odes section of the *Book of Songs*.

zhengyi 正義: "correct interpretation," a name for early commentaries on the Confucian Classics.

zhi / K. *chi* 至: to go as far as it can go, the ultimate.

zhi 寘: to place or put.

zhi 知: knowledge; to know what to do.

zhi 智: wisdom; acting wisely.

zhi 質: to test and confirm, to verify.

zhiji 質劑: commercial contracts.

zhifangsi 職方氏: "The Obligations of the Vassals." A section in the "Xiaguan" (summer offices) volume of *Zhouli*.

Zhiyue lu 指月錄: "Record of Pointing at the Moon," compiled in 1595 by Qu Ruji 瞿汝稷.

zhizhong / K. *chipchung* 執中: holding on to focus and composure.

zhizhonghe / K. *ch'ijunghwa* 致中和: usually translated as "when both focused composure and harmony are realized to their fullest extent." Tasan, however, read this as the command to "strive to fully realize focused composure and harmony."

Zhong 重: also known as Gou Mang 句芒. He is the god of wood.

Zhong Yong (fl. 11th c. BCE) 仲雍: second ruler of the ancient Chinese state of Wu 吳. Also known as Yu Zhong 虞仲. Said to be an older brother of King Wen 周文王.

Zhongchang Tong liechuan 仲長統列傳: "Biographies of Wang Chong, Wang Fu, and Zhongchang Tong," in *Hou Hanshu* [後漢書 History of the Later Han dynasty].

Zhongni yan ju 仲尼燕居: "Confucius at Home at Leisure," a chapter in the *Book of Rites*.

Zhongyong / K. *Chungyong* 中庸: one of the Four Books. Tasan understood the title to mean "Consistent Composure and Focus" or "Constantly Centered."

Zhongyong Hunanjiang 中庸湖南講: "Discussions in Hunan about the *Zhongyong*." A section of *Sishu Hunanjiang* 四書湖南講 by Ge Yinliang 葛寅亮.

Zhongyong huowen 中庸或問: "Questions and Answers on the *Zhongyong* by Zhu Xi" 朱熹.

Zhongyong huowen-xia 中庸或問 下: volume 2 of the section on "Questions and Answers on the *Zhongyong*" in *Sishu daquan* 四書大全, compiled by Hu Guang 胡廣.

Zhongyong jilüe 中庸集略: "An Edited Outline of the *Zhongyong*," by Zhu Xi 朱熹.

Zhongyong zhangju 中庸章句: "The *Zhongyong*, in Chapters and Phrases," by Zhu Xi 朱熹.

Zhongyong zhangju daquan-shang 中庸章句大全 上: volume 1 of "Great Collection of Commentaries on the *Zhongyong* by Chapters and Phrases," compiled by Hu Guang 胡廣.

Zhongyong zhangju daquan-xia 中庸章句大全下: volume 2 of "Great Collection of Commentaries on the *Zhongyong* by Chapters and Phrases," compiled by Hu Guang 胡廣.

Zhongyong zuanshu 中庸纂疏: a compilation of notes on the *Zhongyong* by Zhao Shunsun 趙順孫.

Zhongyongshuo 中庸說: "On the *Zhongyong*," by Mao Qiling 毛奇齡.

Zhou, Duke of 周公: brother of King Wu 周武王, the founder of the Zhou dynasty.

Zhou dynasty (11th c.–221 BCE) 周.

Zhou Dunyi (1017–1073) 周敦頤: an early articulator of some of the core metaphysical claims of what became neo-Confucianism.

Zhou Song 周頌: the "Sacrificial Odes of Zhou" section of the *Book of Songs*.

Zhou Wenmo (1752–1801) 周文謨: first priest ministering to Koreans in Korea.

Zhou Zhang 周章: a ruler of the state of Wu 吳 in the eleventh century BCE. He was the great-grandson of Zhong Yong 仲雍 of Wu, who was said to be a brother of King Wen 周文王.

Zhoubijing 周髀經: also kwown as *Zhoubi suanjing* 周髀算經 ["The Gnomon of the Zhou Mathematical Classic"], an early work on calculation methods.

Zhouguan 周官: "Offices of Zhou," a section of the *Shangshu*.

Zhouli 周禮: the *Zhou Book of Rites*. One of the Thirteen Classics.

Zhoumiaotu 周廟圖: "Diagram of the Zhou Ancestral Temple," a pictorial representation of the placement of ancestral tablets in the ancestral shrine of the ruling family of Zhou 周. Drawn by Zhu Xi 朱熹.

Zhoushu 周書: The "Book of Zhou" in the *Book of Documents*.

Zhouyi jijie 周易集解: "Collected Exegeses on the Zhou *Book of Changes*," compiled by Li Dingzuo 李鼎祚 (fl. 8th/9th c.).

Zhouyu 周語: chapter on Zhou in the *Guoyu* 國語.

Zhouyu-shang 周語上: volume 1 of "Discourses of Zhou" in *Guoyu* 國語.

zhu / K. *chŏ* 著: read by Zhu Xi 朱熹 in the *Zhongyong* to mean "to manifest."

Zhu 柱: the god *Zhu*, the son of the Flame Emperor Yandi 炎帝; it can also mean a post or a pillar.

zhu / K. *chu* 株: trunk of a tree.

Zhu Rong 祝融: the god of fire.

Zhu Shouchang (1014–1083) 朱壽昌: Song dynasty man known for his filial piety toward his mother.

Zhu Xi (1130–1200) 朱熹: one of the most influential philosophers in all Chinese history. He constructed a new vision of Confucianism that focused on what he called the Four Books (*Analects*, *Mencius*, *Daxue*, and *Zhongyong*). He also provided a new way to read those Four Books by interpreting them through the concepts of *li* 理 and *qi* / (氣 K. *ki*), which provided a metaphysical foundation for Confucian ethics and self-cultivation.

zhuan 傳: biography (in *The History of the Former Han Dynasty*).

Zhuang, Lord (r. 693–662) 莊公: a ruler of the regional state of Lu 魯.

Zhuang of Zheng, Lord (757–701 BCE) 鄭莊公: third ruler of the regional state of Zheng during the Spring and Autumn period.

Zhuangzi (trad. 369–286 BCE) 莊子: "Master Zhuang," a non-Confucian Chinese thinker usually considered an early Daoist for his relativism. Also known as Zhuang Zhou 莊周. *Zhuangzi* is also the name of the book purported to have been written by him.

Zhuanxu 顓頊: a mythological early emperor of China, also known as Gao Yang 高陽.

Zhuo Qiuming (556–451 BCE) 左丘明: the supposed author/editor of the *Zuozhuan* 左傳, "Zuo's Commentary on the *Spring and Autumn Annals*."

Zhuzi jiali 朱子家禮: "Family Rituals of Master Zhu," by Xhu Xi 朱熹.

Zhuzi quanshu 朱子全書: "The Complete Works of Zhu Xi," the writings of Zhu Xi 朱熹.

Zhuzi wenji 朱子文集: "The Collected Works of Zhu Xi," the writings of Zhu Xi 朱熹.

Zhuzi yulei 朱子語類: "The Classified Sayings of Master Zhu." Transcripts of discussion between Zhu Xi 朱熹 and his disciples.

zi / K. *cha* 子: the first of the twelve terrestrial branches.

Zi / K. *cha* 字: Sinograph, "Chinese character."

Zifu Jiao (fl. 7th c. BCE) 子服椒: an important figure in the state of Lu 魯 in the sixth century, during China's Spring and Autumn period. Also known as Zifu Huibo 子服惠伯.

Zigong (fl. late 5th–early 4th c. BCE) 子貢: an important disciple of Confucius.

Zijia Ji 子家羈: an important figure in the state of Lu during China's Spring and Autumn period.

Zilu (fl. late 5th–early 4th c. BCE) 子路: early disciple of Confucius.

Zimo 子莫: a person who shows up in Mencius as someone who avoided the extremes of the egocentrism of Yang Zhu and the universal love of Mozi. However, Mencius says, Zimo tried too hard to adhere to the mean and was not flexible enough.

Zinan (d. 551 BCE) 子南: the chief minister in the state of Chu.

zisheng 齍盛: a millet cup used in ancestor memorial rites.

Zisi (483 BCE–402) 子思: a grandson of Confucius who is credited with writing the *Zhongyong*.

Zixia (disciple of Confucius) 子夏: also known as *Bu Shang* 卜商.

Zongbo 宗伯: ritual official in the Spring Offices (Ministry of Ritual), in *Zhouli*.
Zonggao 宗杲: a monk also known as Dahue Zonggao 大慧宗杲 (1089–1163).
zou 奏: Normally meaning to present something to a superior, it is understood in the "Glorious Ancestors" poem in the *Book of Songs* as meaning "to enter" an ancestral shrine.
Zou Yan (305–240 BCE) 鄒衍: known for formulating yin-yang philosophy.
Zou Yu 騶虞: "The Zou-yu," a poem in the Odes of Shao and the South section of the *Book of Songs*.
zouzi 諏訾: one of the twelve Jupiter stations.
zunlei 尊罍: a wine jar used in ancestor memorial rites.
Zuozhuan 左傳: "Zuo Tradition," a commentary, traditionally attributed to Zu Qiuming 左丘明 (556 BCE–451 BCE), on the *Spring and Autumn Annals*.

Notes

Chapter 1: Tasan Chŏng Yagyong and the *Zhongyong*

1. Chŏng Yagyong. *Chŏngbon Yŏyudang chŏnsŏ* [Complete works of Chŏng Yagyong, the definitive version] (Seoul: Tasan haksul munhwa chaedan, 2012).
2. "Yŏyudang ki" [Why I named my study "yŏyudang"]. Chŏng Yagyong, *Yŏyudang chŏnsŏ* I: 13, 39b–40a. Citations in this work will be to Chŏng Yagyong, *Yŏyudang chŏnsŏ* [The complete works of Chŏng Yagyong] (Seoul: Tasan haksul munhwa chaedan, 2001). This is the version that provides the traditional pagination (the volume [*kwŏn*], and a–b page numbers).
3. See the epitaph for Yakhoeng's mother: "Sŏmo Kimssi myojimyŏng." In *Yŏyudang chŏnsŏ*, I: 16, 35a–b.
4. Kŭm Changt'ae, *Silch'ŏnjŏk iron'ga: Chŏng Yagyong* [Chŏng Yagyong: a practical theorist] (P'aju, Korea: Ikkŭllio Books, 2005), 295.
5. "Chach'an myojimyŏng" [A self-authored tombstone inscription]. In *Yŏyudang chŏnsŏ*, I: 16, 18b.
6. "Nonga kwangji" [Tomb inscription for Nonga]. In *Yŏyudang chŏnsŏ*, I: 17, 5b.
7. Yi Ik, *Sŏngho sasŏl* [The humble discourses of Sŏngho Yi Ik] (Seoul: Minjok munhwa ch'ujinhoe, 1977–1978), 26: 15b–16a.
8. *Sŏngho sasŏl*, 26: 15b–16a.
9. Ko Sŭngje, *Tasanŭl ch'ajasŏ* [Searching for Tasan] (Seoul: Chungang Ilbosa, 1995), 22.
10. Chŏng Yagyong, "Sŏnjungssi myojimyŏng" [An epitaph for my older brother]. In *Yŏyudang chŏnsŏ*, I: 15, 42a.
11. Charles Dallet, *Histoire de L'Église de Corée* (Paris: Victor Palmé, 1874), I: 38; Kang Mangil et al., eds., *Ch'uan kŭp Kugan* [Records of special investigations by the State Tribunal], vol. 25 (Seoul: Asea munhwasa, 1978), 51.
12. Ch'oe Sŏgu, "Han'guk kyohoe ŭi ch'angsŏl kwa ch'ocha'nggi Yi Sŭnghun ŭi kyohoe hwaldong" [Yi Sŭnghun and his church activities during the founding years of Catholicism in Korea], *Kyohoesa yŏn'gu* 8 (1992): 29; Cha Kijin, "Manch'ŏn Yi Sŭnghun ŭi kyohoe hwaldong kwa chŏngch'ijŏk ipchi" [Manch'ŏn Yi Sŭnghun's political stance and his activities for the church], *Kyohoesa yŏn'gu* 8 (1992): 47; Sŏ Chongt'ae and Han Kŏm, trans., *Chosŏn hugi Ch'ŏnjugyo sinja chaep'an kirok: ch'uan mit kugan* [Records of the trials of Catholics in the latter half of the Chosŏn dynasty: the Records of special investigations by the State Tribunal] (Seoul: Kukhak Charyowŏn, 2004), 940–943; Dallet, I: 34–35.
13. *Ch'uan kŭp Kugan* 25: 86–88. *Chosŏn hugi Ch'ŏnjugyo sinja chaep'an kirok: ch'uan mit kugan*: 937–940; Dallet, I: 24.

14. Dallet, I: 28–29.
15. "Chungyong kangŭibo." In *Yŏyudang chŏnsŏ*, II: 4, 1a–b; Paek Minjŏng. "Tasan ŭi chungyong kangŭi(bo) chodae naeyong punsŏk: Chŏngjo 'Kyŏngsa kangŭi. Chungyong' ŏje chomun mit kit'a chodae wa ŭi pigyorŭl chungsimŭro" [An analysis of Tasan's answers to questions on the *Zhongyong* as seen in his *Chungyong kangŭibo*: A comparison with the opinions of King Chŏngjo regarding the *Zhongyong* seen in his lectures on the Classics], *Tongbang hakchi* 147 (2009): 401.
16. Yi Manch'ae, *Pyŏgwip'yŏn* [In defense of orthodoxy against heterodoxy] (Seoul: Yŏlhwadang, 1971): 113–114.
17. Yi Kigyŏng. *Pyŏgwip'yŏn* [In defense of orthodoxy against heterodoxy] (Seoul: Kyohoesa yŏn'guso, 1979), 143; *Chosŏn wangjo sillok Chŏngjo*, 15:11, *Kapsin* (November 13, 1791).
18. "Pyŏnbang sa Tongbusŭngji so" [Memorial to the throne to defend myself and also to resign as Sixth Royal Secretary]. In *Yŏyudang chŏnsŏ* I: 9, 44a.
19. "Chungyong kangŭibo" [A lecture on the *Zhongyong*, revised]. In *Yŏyudang chŏnsŏ* II: 4, 1b–3a.
20. "Chungyong kangŭibo." In *Yŏyudang chŏnsŏ*, II: 4, 20b.
21. "Sigyŏng kangŭi" [Lectures on the *Book of Songs*]. In *Yŏyudang chŏnsŏ*, II: 19, 13a–14a.
22. Don Baker, "The Martyrdom of Paul Yun: Western Religion and Eastern Ritual in Eighteenth-Century Korea," *Transactions of the Royal Asiatic Society, Korea Branch*, no. 54 (1979): 33–58.
23. Han Yŏng'u, *Kwagŏ, Ch'ulse ŭi Sadari: Chokporŭl t'onghae pon munkwa kŭpche ŭi sinbun idong, Chŏngjo – Ch'ŏljong tae* [The civil service examination as a ladder of success: changes in the social status of those who passed the civil service examination from the reign period of King Chŏngjo through that of King Ch'ŏljong, as seen in genealogies] (Seoul: Chisik sanŏpsa, 2013), vol. 3, 14–15.
24. "Pyŏnbang sa Tongbusŭngji so." In *Yŏyudang chŏnsŏ*, I: 9, 44b.
25. "Sŏam Kanghak-gi" [A record of an academic discussion at the Western Hermitage]. In *Yŏyudang chŏnsŏ*, I: 21, 23a–38b.
26. "Tosan sasungnok," In *Yŏyudang chŏnsŏ*, I: 22, 1a–12b.
27. "Pyŏnbang sa Tongbusŭngji so." In *Yŏyudang chŏnsŏ*, I: 9, 42b–46b.
28. For a detailed account of Tasan's relationship with King Chŏngjo from 1783 up to Chŏngjo's death, see Cho Sŏngŭl, "Chŏng Yagyong kwa Hwasŏng kŏnsŏl" [Chŏng Yagyong and the construction of Hwasŏng], in Yu Ponghak, Kim Donguk, and Cho Sŏngŭl, *Chŏngjo Sidae Hwasŏng Sindosi ŭi Kŏnsŏl* [The construction of the new city of Hwasŏng during the tine of Chŏngjo] (Seoul: Paeksan sŏdang, 2001), 174–203.
29. *Ch'uan kŭp kugan* 25: 13–18 (Feb. 9, 1801); 39–41 (February 11, 1801), 61–65 (February 12, 1801), 109 (February 15, 1801).
30. Don Baker, *Catholics and Anti-Catholicism in Chosŏn Korea* (Honolulu: University of Hawai'i Press, 2017), 198–201.
31. "Sŏnjungssi myojimyŏng" [An epitaph for my older brother]. In *Yŏyudang chŏnsŏ*, I: 15, 40a–b.
32. Yi Kwangho, "Chungyong kangŭibo wa Chungyong chajamŭl t'onghayŏ pon Tasan ŭi sŏng ŭi ch'ŏrhak" [Tasan's philosophical understanding of *sŏng* as seen

through his *A Discussion of the Meaning of the Zhongyong, Revised*, and his *Admonitions for Myself upon Reading the Zhongyong*], *Tasanhak* 7 (2005): 51-52.

33. *Yŏyudang chŏnsŏ* [The complete works of Yŏyudang Chŏng Yagyong] (Keijo: Sinchosŏnsa, 1934-1938).

34. *Chŏngbon Yŏyudang chŏnsŏ* [The complete works of Yŏyudang Chŏng Yagyong, definitive edition] (Seoul: Tasan haksul munhwa chedan, 2012).

35. "Chungyong kangŭibo" [*A discussion of the meaning of the Zhongyong, Revised*]. In *Yŏyudang chŏnsŏ*, II: 4, 65a.

36. Chŏng Yagyong, "Maengja yoŭi" [Essential points in *Mencius*]. In *Yŏyudang chŏnsŏ*, II: 5, 33a-b; Ko Sŭnghwan, "Tasan Chŏng Yagyong ŭi kwŏnhyŏngnon chaehaesŏk: sŏnjin munhŏn-e taehan kojŭngŭl pat'angŭro" (A re-evaluation of Tasan Chŏng Yagyong's theory of weighing alternatives, based on a careful examination of what he wrote), *Tasanhak* 29 (December 2016): 197-248.

37. The biographical information presented in this chapter is drawn from two versions of his "Chach'an myojimyŏng" (his self-authored epitaph) included in his collected works, *Yŏyudang chŏnsŏ*, I: 16, 1a-20a. I also drew on the biographical material available in Tasan haksul munhwa chaedan, eds., *Tasanhak sajŏn* [A dictionary for Tasan studies] (Seoul: Saam books, 2019), especially the entries on Tasan and his family members, 1402-1446.

Chapter 2: Why Translate These Particular *Zhongyong* Commentaries?

1. Chŏng Yagyong, *Admonitions on Governing the People: Manual for All Administrations*, trans. Choi Byonghyon (Berkeley: University of California Press, 2010). This is a translation of *Mongmin simsŏ*.

2. Chŏng Yagyong, *Yŏkchu Tasan Maengja yoŭi* [An annotated translation of Tasan's Essential Points in the Mencius], trans. Yi Chihyŏng (Seoul: Hyŏndai sirhaksa, 1994).

3. Chŏng Yagyong, *Yŏkchu Nonŏ kogŭmju* [Ancient and recent annotations to the Analects of Confucius, translated into Korean], trans. Yi Chihyŏng (Seoul: Saam, 2010).

4. Chŏng Yagyong, *The Analects of Dasan: A Korean Syncretic Reading* I-IV, trans. Hongkyung Kim (New York: Oxford University Press, 2016-2021).

5. Ch'oe Taeu. "Taehak Kyŏngsŏl ko" [An examination of ideas about the *Daxue* as a Confucian classic], in Ch'oe Taeu, Chŏng Pyŏngnyŏn, An Poo, and Yi Ŭlho, *Chŏng Tasan-ŭi kyŏnghak: Nonŏ, Maengja, Taehak, Chungyong yŏn'gu* [Tasan's studies of the Classics: *The Analects, Mencius, Daxue*, and *Zhongyong*] (Seoul: Minŭmsa, 1989), 11-43.

6. Chŏng Pyŏngnyŏn, "Chungyong haesŏk ko: Tasan ŭi sosahakchŏk chungyong haesŏk pangpomnon" [An examination of Tasan's explication of the *Zhongyong*: His focus on serving the Lord on High], Ch'oe Taeu et al., *Chŏng Tasan-ŭi kyŏnghak*: 121-122.

7. Paek Minjŏng, "Tasan ŭi chungyong kangŭi(bo) chodae naeyong punsŏk: Chŏngjo 'Kyŏngsa kangŭi. Chungyong' ŏje chomun mit kit'a chodae wa ŭi pigyorŭl

chungsimŭro" [茶山의 中庸講義(補)』 條對 내용 분석: 正祖 『經史講義·中庸』 御製 條問 및 기타 條對와의 비교를 중심으로. An analysis of Tasan's Answers to Questions on the Zhongyong as seen in his Chungyong kangŭibo: A comparison with the opinions of King Chŏngjo on the Zhongyong seen in his lectures on the Classics]. Tongbang hakchi 동방학지 147 (2009): 400–404.

8. "Chungyong chajam," Yŏyudang chŏnsŏ II: 3, 15a.

Chapter 3: Tasan's Approach to Confucian Scholarship

1. "Chungyong ch'aek," Yŏyudang chŏnsŏ I: 8, 30b.

2. For example, see Mencius 6B: 3. Bryan Van Norden, Mengzi, with Selections from Traditional Commentaries (Indianapolis: Hackett, 2008), 161, translates this phrase as "treat one's parents as parents."

3. Analects 13:3 (See Edward Slingerland, Confucius: Analects, with Selections from Traditional Commentaries [Indianapolis: Hackett, 2003], 139).

4. Meng Peiyuan. Eric Colwell, and Jinli He, trans. "How to Unite Is and Ought: An Explanation Regarding the Work of Master Zhu," in Returning to Zhu Xi: Emerging Patterns within the Supreme Polarity, ed. David Jones (Albany: State University of New York Press), 273–297.

5. "Chŏng Such'il chŭngŏn" [Words of advice for Chŏng Such'il], Yŏyudang chŏnsŏ I, 17: 40b–41a.

6. Shangshu IV, the Book of Shang: Tanggao Book III, 2 (James Legge, The Shoo King, or the Book of Historical Documents. Chinese Classics, III [Hong Kong: Hong Kong University Press, 1970], 184).

7. "Chungyong kangŭibo," Yŏyudang chŏnsŏ II: 4, 3a.

8. Book of Songs, "Daya," "Decade of Wen Wang," "daming," 3 (James Legge, trans. The She King, or the Book of Poetry, Chinese Classics, IV [Hong Kong: Hong Kong University Press, 1970, 433]; Arthur Waley and Joseph R. Allen, The Book of Songs [New York: Grove Press, 1996], 229; "Chungyong kangŭibo," Yŏyudang chŏnsŏ II: 4, 23a.

9. "Chungyong chajam," Yŏyudang chŏnsŏ, II: 3, 5b.

10. "Maengja yoŭi," Yŏyudang chŏnsŏ, II: 5: 34b; "simgyŏng mirhŏm," II: 3, 29b.

11. "Sipsamgyŏng ch'aek" [A discussion of the Thirteen Classics], Yŏyudang chŏnsŏ I: 8, 17a.

12. See, for example, Kŭm Changt'ae, Tasan sirhak t'amgu [Explorations of Tasan's Practical Learning] (Seoul: Sohaksa, 2001), 16–20, and Han'guk ch'ŏrhaksa yŏn'guhoe, ed. Tasan kyŏnghak ŭi hyŏndaejŏk ihae [A contemporary understanding of Tasan's studies of the Confucian classics] (Seoul: Simsa Publishing, 2004), 20–22.

Chapter 4: Tasan's Approach to the Cultivation of a Selfless Orientation

1. For an ambitious attempt to survey his entire philosophy in one volume in English (translated from the German original by Tobias J. Körnter), see Shin-Ja Kim,

The Philosophical Thought of Tasan Chŏng (New York: Peter Lang, 2010). There have, of course, been several such attempts in Korean, usually by bringing together articles by various scholars on different aspects of Tasan's thought.

2. Cheng-Zhu neo-Confucianism refers to the new interpretation of the Confucian classics promoted during China's Song dynasty (960–1279) by two Cheng brothers, Cheng Hao (1032–1085) and Cheng Yi (1033–1107), and further articulated and synthesized by Zhu Xi (1130–1200). By the 15th century, under the name of *Sŏngnihak* (scholarship on human nature and patterning principle], it had become the dominant approach to Confucianism in Korea and maintained that dominance for the rest of the Chosŏn dynasty, even though during China's Ming dynasty (1368–1644) some central concepts of Cheng-Zhu neo-Confucianism were challenged by Wang Yangming (1472–1529).

3. Ch'en Ch'un, *Neo-Confucian Terms Explained (The Pei-hsi tzu-i)*, translated by Wing-tsit-chan (New York: Columbia University Press, 1986), 57.

4. Curie Virág, trans., "Moral Psychology and Cultivating the Self," in Philip J. Ivanhoe, ed., *Zhu Xi: Selected Writings* (New York: Oxford University Press, 2019), 48. This is a translation of *Zhuxi yulei* IX: 50. https://ctext.org/zhuzi-yulei/9. Accessed July 31, 2021.

5. On the heart-mind as replete with *li*, see Yong Huang, *Why Be Moral? Learning from the Neo-Confucian Cheng Brothers* (Albany: State University of New York Press, 2014), 203.

6. Yulgok Yi I, "Tap Sŏng Howŏn" [A response to a letter from Howŏn Sŏng Sŏnghon], in *Yulgok Chŏnsŏ* [The complete works of Yulgok Yi I], X: 26a.

7. *Mencius*, 6A:6.

8. *Li Chi* [Book of Rites], translated by James Legge, in *The Chinese Classics* (reprint; Hong Kong: Hong Kong University Press, 1970), I: 379.

9. "Chin Sŏnghak shipto ch'a" [Presenting the Ten Diagrams on Sagely Learning], in *T'oegye sŏnsaeng munjip* [The writings of Master T'oegye Yi Hwang], VII: 24a–b; "Tap Ki Myŏngŏn" [A response to a letter from Myŏngŏn Ki Taesŭng], in *T'oegye sŏnsaeng munjip*, XVI:32a (Seoul: Konggŭpch'ŏ Han'guk Ch'ulp'an Hyŏptong Chohap, 1997), and at http://db.itkc.or.kr, accessed December 24, 2019. Similar statements by T'oegye are available in Yi Hwang, *To Become a Sage: The Ten Diagrams of Sage Learning*, translated by Michael C. Kalton (New York: Columbia University Press, 1988), 126–127, and in Peter H. Lee, ed., *Sourcebook of Korean Civilization* I (New York: Columbia University Press, 1993), 627.

10. "Tap Sŏng Howŏn," *Yulgok Chŏnsŏ*, X: 29b–30a.

11. "Tosan Sasungnok," *Yŏyudang chŏnsŏ* I: 22, 1a–12a.

12. "Tosan sasungnok," *Yŏyudang chŏnsŏ* I: 22, 9b. Tasan is referring to *T'oegye sŏnsaeng munjip* XII: 31a.

13. "Tosan sasungnok," *Yŏyudang chŏnsŏ* I: 22, 8b–9a.

14. "Tosan sasungnok," *Yŏyudang chŏnsŏ* I: 22, 6a.

15. "Counsels of the Great Yu," *Book of Documents* (II:2, 15); Legge, *Chinese Classics* III: 61.

16. "Chungyong ch'aek," *Yŏyudang chŏnsŏ* I: 8, 28b.

17. See Zhu Xi's *Chapters and Phrases of the Zhongyong* in Ian Johnston and Wang Ping, trans., *Daxue and Zhongyong* (Hong Kong: Chinese University Press, 2012), 410.
18. Johnston and Wang, *Daxue and Zhongyong,* 412.
19. "Chungyong kangŭibo," *Yŏyudang chŏnsŏ* II: 4, 9b.
20. "Chungyong kangŭibo," *Yŏyudang chŏnsŏ* II: 4, 3a.
21. "Maengja Yoŭi," *Yŏyudang chŏnsŏ*, II: 5, 33a.
22. Ch'en Ch'un, *Neo-Confucian Terms Explained,* 193.
23. Michael Kalton, "Chŏng Tasan's Philosophy of Man: A Radical Critique of the Neo-Confucian World View," *Journal of Korean Studies* 3 (1981): 18.
24. Zhang Zai, "The Western Inscription," in Wm. Theodore De Bary and Irene Bloom, eds., *Sources of Chinese Tradition,* vol. I (New York: Columbia University Press, 1999), 683.
25. Chang Hao, "On Understanding the Nature of Humanity" and "On Humaneness," in *Sources of Chinese Tradition,* 694–695. Also see Zhu Xi's *Chapters and Phrases of the Zhongyong,* in Johnston and Wang, trans., *Daxue and Zhongyong,* 410.
26. Song Young-bae, "A Comparative Study of the Paradigms between Dasan's Philosophy and Matteo Ricci's *Tianzhu shiyi,*" *Korea Journal* 41, no. 3 (Autumn 2001): 76–78.
27. Matteo Ricci, *The True Meaning of the Lord of Heaven* [*Tianzhu shiyi*], translated by Douglas Lancashire and Peter Hu Kuo-chen, S.J., and revised by Thierry Meynard, S.J., (Boston: Institute of Jesuit Sources, Boston College, 2016), 245.
28. "Chungyong kangŭibo," *Yŏyudang chŏnsŏ* II, 4: 8b–9a.
29. "Maengja yoŭi," *Yŏyudang chŏnsŏ* II: 6, 38a–b.
30. "Maengja yoŭi," *Yŏyudang chŏnsŏ* II, 6: 39a.
31. "Chach'an myojimyŏng" [A self-authored tombstone inscription], *Yŏyudang chŏnsŏ* I: 16, 17b.
32. "Chungyong chajam" [Admonitions for myself upon reading the *Zhongyong*], *Yŏyudang chŏnsŏ* II, 3: 2b.
33. "Maengja yoŭi," *Yŏyudang chŏnsŏ* II: 6, 19a.
34. "Maengja yoŭi," *Yŏyudang chŏnsŏ* II:5, 22a–b.
35. "Maengja yoŭi," *Yŏyudang chŏnsŏ* II: 5, 32a–35b.
36. "Maengja yoŭi," *Yŏyudang chŏnsŏ* II:5, 33a.
37. Yong Huang, *Why Be Moral,* 128.

Chapter 5: Tasan and the Problem of Moral Frailty

1. "Chungyong chajam," *Yŏyudang chŏnsŏ* II, 3: 3b.
2. "Maengja yoŭi," *Yŏyudang chŏnsŏ* II:5, 33b–35a.
3. "Simgyŏng mirhŏm" [Personal experience with the classic of the heart-mind], *Yŏyudang chŏnsŏ* II: 2, 28a; Chung So-Yi, "Kyŏnggi Southerners' Notion of Heaven and Its Influence on Tasan's Theory of Human Nature," *Journal of Korean Religions* 2, no. 2 (October 2011): 122–126.
4. "Maengja yoŭi," *Yŏyudang chŏnsŏ* II: 6, 19b–21b. For more on Tasan's in-

sistence that we have to choose to act appropriately, see Baek Min Jeong, "Moral Success and Failure in the Ethical Theory of Tasan Chŏng Yagyong," *Acta Koreana* 19, no. 1 (June, 2016): 241-266.

5. *Mencius* IIA: 2:11. Van Norden, *Mengzi*, p. 38, translates this phrase as "Your will is the commander of your Qi [K. ki]. Qi fills your body."

6. "Maengja yoŭi," *Yŏyudang chŏnsŏ* II: 5, 17a-b.

7. "Maengja yoŭi," *Yŏyudang chŏnsŏ* II: 5, 34b-35a.

8. "Maengja yoŭi," *Yŏyudang chŏnsŏ* II: 5, 35a-b.

9. "Simgyŏng mirhŏm," *Yŏyudang chŏnsŏ* II: 2, 25a.

10. Joseph A. Adler, "Varieties of Spiritual Experience: *Shen* in Neo-Confucian Discourse," in Tu Weiming and Mary Evelyn Tucker, eds., *Confucian Spirituality* (New York: Crossroad Publishing, 2004), II: 120-148.

11. "Chungyong chajam," *Yŏyudang chŏnsŏ* II: 3, 16b.

12. "Chungyong kangŭibo," *Yŏyudang chŏnsŏ* II: 4, 22a-b.

13. *Mencius,* 6A: 7; Van Norden, *Mengzi*, 151.

14. "Maengja yoŭi," *Yŏyudang chŏnsŏ* II: 6, 25b-26a.

15. *Mencius,* 7A: 1; Van Norden, *Mengzi*, 171.

16. "Maengja yoŭi," *Yŏyudang chŏnsŏ* II: 6, 38a-b.

17. "Chungyong kangŭibo," *Yŏyudang chŏnsŏ* II: 4, 65a.

18. "Yibal kibal pyŏn" [An analysis of the debate over whether *li* or *ki* generates the Four Sprouts], *Yŏyudang chŏnsŏ* I: 12, 17a-18a. For a partial translation of this essay by Tasan, see "What the *i/ki* Debate Is Really All About," in Peter H. Lee, ed., *Sourcebook of Korean Civilization II* (New York: Columbia University Press, 1996), 269-271.

19. "Nonŏ Kogŭmju" [Ancient and modern notes on the *Analects*], *Yŏyudang chŏnsŏ* II: 14, 39a.

20. Andrew Plaks, *Ta Hsüeh and Chung Yung (The Highest Order of Cultivation and On the Practice of the Mean)* (New York: Penguin, 2003), 25.

21. This phrase can be found in the *Mingxin baojian* (K. *Myŏngsim pogam*) [A precious mirror for enlightening the heart-mind], section 2 (On the mandate of Heaven), where it is cited as coming from a Daoist text, the *Xuandi chuixun*. http://www.taolibrary.com/category/category86/c86017.htm. Accessed December 25, 2019. For the *Mingxin baojian,* see https://ctext.org/wiki.pl?if=en&chapter=523440 line 62. Accessed December 25, 2019.

22. "Chungyong kangŭibo," *Yŏyudang chŏnsŏ* II: 4, 5a.

23. "Chungyong chajam," *Yŏyudang chŏnsŏ* II, 3: 2b.

24. "Maengja yoŭi," *Yŏyudang chŏnsŏ* II: 6, 38b.

25. "Pyŏnbang sa Tongbusŭngji so" [A defense against accusations against me and letter of resignation from the post of Sixth Royal Secretary], *Yŏyudang chŏnsŏ* I: 9, 45b.

26. Chung So-Yi, "Kyŏnggi Southerners' Notion of Heaven and Its Influence on Tasan's Theory of Human Nature," *Journal of Korean Religions* 2, no. 2 (October 2011): 111-141.

27. Miura Kunio, "Orthodoxy and Heterodoxy in Seventeenth-Century Korea: Song Siyŏl and Yun Hyu," in Wm. Theodore de Bary and JaHyun Kim Haboush,

eds., *The Rise of Neo-Confucianism in Korea* (New York: Columbia University Press, 1985), 430.

28. Tasan did not completely ignore the argument from order, however. In his commentaries on the *Book of Changes* (Chuyŏk), when he discussed the order in the universe, he briefly mentioned that such order implies someone is responsible for that order. He labels that orderer "the Spirit." Pang In [Bang In], *Tasan Chŏng Yagyong ŭi Yŏkhak sŏŏn: Chuyŏk ŭi haesŏksarŭl tasi ssŭda* [Tasan Chŏng Yagyong's Introductory remarks for the study of the Changes: Rewriting the history of the interpretations of the Book of Changes] (Seoul: Yemun sŏwŏn, 2020), 57–61, 613–618. See also Bang In, "Chŏng Yag-yong's Cosmogonic Idea and Matteo Ricci's Influence Shown in His Interpretation of the *Zhouyi*: A Compromise between Creationism and Evolutionism," *Tasanhak* 35 (2019): 281–328. Pang here is drawing on "Chuyŏk sŏŏn" [Introductory remarks for the study of the Changes], *Yŏyudang chŏnsŏ* II: 48, 7a–b.

29. "Chach'an myojimyŏng," *Yŏyudang chŏnsŏ* I: 16, 17b.

30. "Tosan sasungnok" [A record of my admiration of T'oegye], *Yŏyudang chŏnsŏ* I: 22, 6a.

31. "Maengja yoŭi," *Yŏyudang chŏnsŏ* II: 6, 23b.

32. "Maengja yoŭi," *Yŏyudang chŏnsŏ* II: 6, 38b.

33. "Chungyong chajam," *Yŏyudang chŏnsŏ* II: 3, 4b–5a.

34. "Chungyong chajam," *Yŏyudang chŏnsŏ* II: 3, 5b.

35. See, for example, Johnson and Wang, *Daxue and Zhongyong*, 412.

36. "Chungyong chajam," *Yŏyudang chŏnsŏ* II: 3, 15a.

37. "Chungyong kangŭibo," *Yŏyudang chŏnsŏ*, II: 4, 6a.

38. That is how Tasan reads Zhu Xi's statement in *Zhongyong zhangju* that "joy, anger, sorrow, and happiness are the emotions. When they have not yet arisen, this is human nature" (Johnston and Wang, *Daxue and Zhongyong*, 411). Stephen C. Angle and Justin Tiwald, "Moral Psychology: Heartmind (Xin), Nature (Xing), and Emotions (Qing)," in Kai-chiu Ng and Yong Huang, eds., *Dao Companion to Zhu Xi's Philosophy* (Cham, Switzerland: Springer Nature, 2020), 365.

39. Zhu Xi, *Sishu huowen* [Questions and answers on the Four Books] (Shanghai: Shanghai guji chubanshe, 2001), 55; Pak Wansik ed., *Chungyong* (Seoul: Yŏgang Publishing, 2008), 383. For Zhu Xi's ambivalence about the value of sitting quietly and stilling the mind, see Masaya Mabuchi, "Quiet-Sitting in Neo-Confucianism," in Halvor Eifring, ed., *Asian Traditions of Meditation* (Honolulu: University of Hawai'i Press, 2016), 207–226.

40. "Nonŏ kogŭmju," *Yŏyudang chŏnsŏ* II: 15, 4a.

41. "Chungyong kangŭibo," *Yŏyudang chŏnsŏ* II: 4, 33a–b. The section of the Book of Rites Tasan is referring to here can be found in Legge, *Book of Rites*, I: 225.

42. For more on Tasan's understanding of ritual, see Pak Chongch'ŏn. *Tasan Chŏng Yagyong ŭi ŭirye iron* [The ritual theory of Tasan Chŏng Yagyong] (Seoul: Sin'gu munhwasa, 2008). This is a useful corrective to the common mistake of portraying Tasan as a "practical learning" thinker who had no interest in such "impractical" subjects as ritual.

43. "Chungyong chajam," *Yŏyudang chŏnsŏ* II: 3, 23b–24a.

44. "Chungyong kangŭibo," *Yŏyudang chŏnsŏ* II: 4, 44b.

45. "Chungyong chajam," *Yŏyudang chŏnsŏ* II: 3, 29a.
46. "Chungyong kangŭibo," *Yŏyudang chŏnsŏ* II: 4, 46a.
47. "Chungyong chajam," *Yŏyudang chŏnsŏ* II: 3, 24b.

Chapter 7: Notes on the Translation of Key Terms

1. Yi Hwang, "Sim much'eyong pyŏn" [Discussing the assertion that the heart-mind has no distinction between *ch'e* and *yong*], *T'oegye sŏnsaeng munjip* [A collection of the writings of T'oegye Yi Hwang] 4l: l6b–17b.
2. Cua, Antonio S., "On the Ethical Significance of the Ti-Yong Distinction," *Journal of Chinese Philosophy* 29, no. 2 (June 2002): 164–165.
3. Zhu Xi, *Sishu huowen* [Questions and answers on the Four Books] (Shanghai: Shanghai guji chubanshe, 2001), 57 (Pak Wansik, trans. *Chungyong*. Seoul: Yŏgang Publishing, 2008, 394), cited in "Chungyong kangŭibo," *Yŏyudang chŏnsŏ* II. 4, 7b.
4. "Chungyong kangŭibo" II. 4, 16a.
5. "Chungyong kangŭibo" II. 4, 66b.
6. For example, see "Chungyong Kangŭibo," II. 4: 20b–21a. For more on how Tasan explained the order we see in the "creative transformation of things," see Pang In, *Tasan Chŏng Yagyong ŭi Yŏkhak sŏŏn*, 57–61, 613–618.
7. "Maengja yoŭi," *Yŏyudang chŏnso* II: 6: 38b. Also see Chŏng Ilgyun. "Tasan Chŏng Yagyong ŭi ch'ŏn kaenyŏm-e taehan chaegoch'al" [A reexamination of Tasan Chŏng Yagyong's concept of Heaven], *Tasanhak* 32 (June 2018): 61–120.
8. "Chungyong chajam," *Yŏyudang chŏnsŏ* II: 3, 5a–b; "Chŏnmyŏng chi sŏng," Tasan haksul munhwa chaedan, ed., *Tasanhak sajŏn* [A dictionary for Tasan studies] (Seoul: Saam books, 2019), 1657–1658.
9. Wang Hui, *Translating Chinese Classics in a Colonial Context* (Bern: Peter Lang, 2008), 150–151.
10. "Chungyong chajam," II: 3, 9a.
11. Roger T. Ames and David L. Hall, *Focusing the Familiar: A Translation and Philosophical Interpretation of the Zhongyong* (Honolulu: University of Hawai'i Press, 2001), 86.
12. "Chungyong kangŭibo," II: 4, 5b–6a.
13. Roger T. Ames, *Confucian Role Ethics: A Vocabulary* (Honolulu: University of Hawai'i Press, 2011), 200–201.
14. "Chungyong kangŭibo," II: 4, 41a–b.
15. "Chungyong kangŭibo," II: 4, 53a.
16. "Chungyong ch'aek," I: 8, 28b.
17. "Chungyong kangŭibo," II: 4, 53a.
18. In "Chungyong chajam," II, 3: 13b–14a, Tasan states that the Dao of Heaven is the same as the Dao of an exemplary person, in that it refers to the proper way to behave. However, in "Maengja yoŭi," II: 6, 39a, he also notes that the Dao of Heaven is different from the Dao of human beings because the Dao of Heaven operates unconsciously.
19. "Chungyong chajam," II, 3: 28a–b.

20. "Chungyong chajam," II, 3: 22a.
21. "Chungyong kangŭibo, II: 4, 60b.
22. "Chungyong kangŭibo," II: 4, 19a.
23. Michael Nylan, "Translating Texts in Chinese History and Philosophy," in Ming Dong Gu and Rainer Schulte, eds., *Translating China for Western Readers: Reflective, Critical, and Practical Essays* (Albany: State University of New York Press, 2014), 130.
24. "Chach'an myojimyŏng," *Yŏyudang chŏnsŏ* I: 16, 17b.
25. Henry Rosement Jr. and Roger T. Ames. *The Chinese Classic of Family Reverence: A Philosophical Translation of the Xiaojing* (Honolulu: University of Hawai'i Press, 2009), 83.
26. "Chungyong kangŭibo," II: 4, 22b.
27. "Chungyong chajam," II: 3, 2b.
28. "Chungyong kangŭibo," II: 4, 20a–23b.
29. "Chungyong kangŭibo," II: 4, 21a.
30. "Simgyŏng mirhŏm," II: 2, 25a; "Chungyong chajam," II: 3, 5a.
31. Jeeloo Liu, *Neo-Confucianism: Metaphysics, Mind, and Morality* (Hoboken, NJ: John Wiley & Sons, 2018), 235–239.
32. "Maengji yoŭi," II: 6, 23b.
33. Yong Huang, *Why Be Moral,* 209–210.
34. For an illuminating discussion of the diverse ways *li* has been translated, see Galia Patt-Shamir, "Li and Qi as Supra-Metaphysics," in Kai-chiu Ng and Yong Huang, eds., *Dao Companion to Zhu Xi's Philosophy* (Cham, Switzerland: Springer Nature, 2020), 243–263.
35. "Chungyong kangŭibo," II: 4, 65a.
36. "Chungyong chajam," II: 3, 5a.
37. "Chungyong kangŭibo," II: 4, 20a–b.
38. "Chungyong kangŭibo," II: 4, 23a.
39. "Chach'an myojimyŏng," I: 16, 17b.
40. "Yibal Kibal Pyŏn," *Yŏyudang chŏnsŏ* I: 12, 17a–18a.
41. Chŏng Yagyong, "Tap Yi Yŏhong" [A response to a letter from Yi Yŏhong]. *Yŏyudang chŏnsŏ* I: 19, 30a–b.
42. Chŏng Yagyong, "Taehak kangŭi" [Discussing the meaning of the Daxue], *Yŏyudang chŏnsŏ* II: 2, 3b.
43. "Tap Yi Yŏhong," I: 19, 30a–b.
44. This phrase was used by Zhang Zai in the eleventh century and was adopted and repeated by scholars for centuries afterward as a way to explain the relationship of the heart-mind with human nature and emotions within a neo-Confucian framework. See Wm. Theodore de Bary and Irene Bloom, eds., *Sources of Chinese Tradition* I (New York: Columbia University Press, 1999), 689.
45. For Zhu Xi's understanding of the mind-heart as uniting human nature and feelings, see Angle and Tiwald, *Moral Psychology,* 381–384. For how Tasan placed more emphasis on the commanding function of the heart-mind, see Daeyeol Kim, "Reviving the Confucian Spirit of Ethical Practicality: Tasan's Notions of Sŏng

(Nature) and Sim (Heart/Mind) and Their Political Implications," in Andrew David Jackson, ed., *Key Papers on Korea: Essays Celebrating 25 Years of the Centre for Korean Studies, SOAS, University of London* (Leiden: Global Oriental, 2014), 197.

46. Chŏng Yagyong, "Sang OKim Wŏn sŏ" [A letter to OKim Wŏn], *Yŏyudang chŏnsŏ* I: 18, 40b.

47. "Tap Yi Yŏhong," I: 19, 30a–b.

48. *Tasanhak sajŏn,* 931–932; "Simgyŏng mirhŏm," II: 2, 30a.

49. Tao Liang, "The Interpretation of *Shendu* in the Interpretation of Classical Learning and Zhu Xi's Misreading," *Dao* 13 (2014): 305–321.

50. "Chungyong chajam," II: 3, 5b–6b.

51. Ames. *Confucian Role Ethics,* 194–200.

52. *Tasanhak sajŏn,* 782–784.

53. "Chungyong chajam," II, 3: 14b–15a.

54. "Chach'an myojimyŏng," I: 16, 16a.

55. Yi Sukhŭi, "Yongmang kwa yŏmch'irosŏ ŭi Chŏng Yagyong ŭi simsŏng: Sŏng.kihosŏl ŭi 'naksŏn ch'iak-e taehan yŏn'gu" [Chŏng Yagyong's notion of human nature and the heart-mind as a desire to act appropriately and a sense of shame when failing to do so: a study of his concept of human nature as the desire for the moral good and disdain for the moral bad], *Tasanhak* 27 (December 2015): 41–76.

56. "Simgyong mirhŏm," II: 2, 26a.

57. "Maengja youi," II: 5, 34b.

58. "Chach'an myojimyŏng," I: 16, 17b.

59. "Moral side of one's nature" is a reference here to *song/xing,* which, in contexts such as this, is sometimes translated as "the innate tendency to behave appropriately." However, at times, as noted earlier, Tasan uses that Sinograph to refer to what he sees as two aspects of human nature, a natural desire to do what is morally correct and an equally natural desire to do what feels good. In order to indicate that he is referring to those two aspects, I distinguish in this translation between the "moral side of one's nature" and the "physical nature." Note that in *Chungyong chajam,* II, 3: 2b–3b, Tasan states explicitly that "human nature" (*xing*) refers to the inclinations of the heart-mind. He distinguishes those natural inclinations into two kinds. The nature heaven endows human beings with at birth includes the penetrating intelligence that allows us to recognize the morally correct and desire to act in accordance with it, but it also includes a desire for the pleasurable and personally beneficial. Fortunately, the moral part of our nature (*tosim* – Dao heart-mind) also includes the ability to choose to act appropriately, as well as to decide to refrain from acting inappropriately, rather than just recognizing how we should behave and wishing we could act accordingly. That ability to choose to act appropriately rather than inappropriately makes it possible for us to behave in a moral fashion.

60. "Chungyong kangŭibo, II: 4, 3b.

61. "Chungyong kangŭibo," II: 4, 4b.

62. "Chungyong kangŭibo," II: 4, 36b.

63. "Simgyŏng mirhŏm," II: 2, 40a.

64. Michael Nylan, "Translating Texts in Chinese History and Philosophy," 130.

65. Wang Hui, *Translating Chinese Classics in a Colonial Context* (Bern: Peter Lang, 2008), 153–154.
66. "Chungyong chajam," II, 3: 25a
67. "Chungyong chajam," II, 3: 23b.
68. Ames and Hall, *Focusing on the Familiar*, 61–63.
69. *Zhongyong* XXII; Ames and Hall, 105; "Chungyong chajam," II, 3: 22a–b.
70. *Zhongyong* XX: 16.
71. "Chungyong ch'aek," I: 8, 30b.
72. "Chungyong kangŭibo, II: 4, 44b.
73. "Chungyong kangŭibo," II: 4, 60b, d.
74. "Chungyong kangŭibo," II: 4, 65a. For a detailed examination of Tasan's concept of *cheng*, see Yi Kwangho, "Chungyong kangŭibo wa Chungyong chajamŭl t'onghayŏ pon Tasan ŭi sŏng ŭi ch'ŏrhak" [Tasan's philosophical understanding of sŏng as seen through his *A Discussion of the Meaning of the Zhongyong, Revised*, and his *Admonitions for Myself upon Reading the Zhongyong*], *Tasanhak* 7 (2005): 51–79.
75. "Chungyong ch'aek," I: 8, 30b.
76. Ames, *Confucian Role Ethics*, 180–183, 206–210, prefers "excelling morally."
77. "Chungyong kangŭibo," III: 4, 21b.
78. "Chungyong kangŭibo," II: 4, 23b.
79. "Chungyong chajam," II, 3: 25a.
80. "Chungyong kangŭibo," II: 4, 38a.
81. "Chungyong kangŭibo," II: 4, 64b. For the statement by Ching Yi, see *Er Cheng Yishu*, vol. 24; Available at https://zh.wikisource.org/wiki/二程遺書/卷24. Accessed August 28, 2019.
82. "Kŭkki cham" [An admonition on self-control], *Yŏyudang chŏnsŏ*, I: 12, 27a.
83. "Simgyŏng mirhŏm," II: 2, 29b. Tasan is drawing on a famous phrase found in "Counsels of the Great Yu," *Book of Documents*, II: 2, 15; Legge, *Chinese Classics III*: 61: "the Human Heart-mind is dangerous; the Dao Heart-mind is difficult to discern."
84. *Tasanhak sajŏn*, 1070–1071.
85. "Chungyong Kangŭibo," II: 4, 2b.
86. "Chungyong chajam," II: 3, 5b.

Translation: *Chungyong ch'aek*

1. Edward Slingerland, *Confucius: Analects, with Selections from Traditional Commentaries* (Indianapolis: Hackett, 2003), 98–110.
2. It was generally assumed from China's Song dynasty (960–1279) onward that Zisi (c. 483–402 BCE) was both the grandson of Confucius and the author of the *Zhongyong*.
3. Zigong was one of the more important disciples around Confucius.
4. *Analects* 5:12 (Slingerland, 44).
5. King Chŏngjo assumes the standard interpretation of this line, which treats

nature as referring to whatever is natural, though, as is usual in neo-Confucian thinking, there are normative implications as well. In human beings, this leads to the conclusion that human nature and human moral character are one and the same and, therefore, acting morally is the natural thing to do. Tasan has a more complicated understanding of human nature, distinguishing between a natural tendency to act appropriately and an equally natural tendency to act inappropriately. He understands this line as referring to the former only. Translated the way Tasan understands it, it would read "That which Heaven has conferred on us is our innate ability to act appropriately."

6. *Zhongyong* I: 2.

7. The locus classicus for the Seven Emotions is *Liji*, "Li Yun," 18. *Sacred Books of the East*, XXVII, James Legge, *Li Chi* [*Book of Rites*] I (New Hyde Park, New York: University Books, 1967), 379. However, King Chŏngjo may have been influenced by the *Zhongyong* in his list of the seven Emotions, since the *Book of Rites* has "fear" instead of "delight." Traditional Chinese medicine has a slightly different set of seven basic emotions: joy, anger, sorrow, anxiety, grief, fear, and fright. They all agree, however, that there are seven basic human emotions.

8. Wm. Theodore de Bary and Irene Bloom, eds., *Sources of Chinese Tradition* I (New York: Columbia University Press, 1999), 689, 711. The wide range of meaning a particular Sinograph can have sometimes results in fruitful ambiguity in important phrases. The phrase "what unites and commands [統 K. *t'ong* / C. *tong*] human nature and emotions is the heart-mind" is one example. *T'ong* can mean both to unite and to control. In this important phrase, coined by Zhang Zai (1020–1077) but repeated by countless neo-Confucians over the millennia that followed, it carries both meanings. That is why de Bary and Bloom translate this phrase as "The heart-mind unites [or commands] human nature and feelings."

9. *Zhongyong* I: 5.

10. *Ki* (*Qi* in Chinese) is a difficult term to translate since it has no exact English equivalent. It refers to the basic stuff, both matter and energy, out of which the visible universe is constructed. However, *ki* can be so ethereal, as most Confucians believed was the case with ghosts and spirits, that it becomes invisible for all practical purposes. We have decided to leave it untranslated in most cases and to transliterate it as *ki*, and to ask the reader to keep in mind that it refers to the basic stuff, both matter and energy, out of which individual objects that fill the universe are composed and are animated by.

11. Legge, *Li Chi* (New Hyde Park, NY: University Books. 1967), I, 379.

12. *Zhongyong* I: 5.

13. One of the legendary sage-kings of ancient China.

14. *Zhongyong* VI. The Sinograph *zhong* is here translated as "mean," meaning, "doing exactly what is appropriate, neither going too far nor stopping short," because that is the way King Chŏngjo understands it. Tasan often uses that same term to refer to a mental state that is better translated as "composure," or "focused," since to him it often refers to a state of calm focus in which nothing disturbs you or pushes you to act in inappropriate ways so that you concentrate on what is important and what

is appropriate. In this book, it is translated either as "mean," "centered," "equilibrium," "composure," or "focused," depending on the context in which it appears.

15. *Zhongyong* II.
16. *Zhongyong* II.
17. *Zhongyong* II. Chŏngjo is referring to the Sinograph "contrary to" being inserted into that line by Wang Su (195–257) to make it say explicitly that the inferior person acts in a way that is contrary to the way the *Zhongyong* says he should act. Ian Johnston and Wang Ping, *Daxue and Zhongyong* (Hong Kong: Chinese University Press), 412.
18. *Zhongyong* XIII: 4.
19. *Zhongyong* I, XXXII.
20. *Zhongyong* X.
21. The *Zhongyong* is a chapter in the *Book of Rites*.
22. *Zhongyong* I.
23. *Zhongyong* III.
24. *Zhongyong* VII.
25. *Zhongyong*, VIII. Chŏngjo is adopting an unusual interpretation of this line. It is usually read as "selected the mean," in other words, "decided to stick to the center, neither going too far nor stopping short," not "selected something from the *Zhongyong*." Yan Hui was said to be the most gifted of the direct disciples of Confucius.
26. *Zhongyong* XI. King Chŏngjo is making a bit of a pun here, contrasting the term 依 (K. *ŭi*, to rely on) with its homonym 倚, which he uses in the preceding phrase to mean "rely on for support." 倚 is elsewhere used in a negative sense in the *Zhongyong* to mean "deviating from the norm" (*Zhongyong* X:5).
27. Chŏngjo is referring to *Zhongyong* IV, which says that the wise go too far while the stupid fall short, and worthies also go too far while the incompetent do not go far enough.
28. *Zhongyong* XX: 8.
29. *Zhongyong* IX.
30. Yan Hui.
31. *Zhongyong* XII: 1.
32. *Li*, like *ki*, is notoriously difficult to translate. The traditional translation of "Principle" hides its dynamic nature. It is better understood as the dynamic patterns of appropriate interactions both in the human realm and in the natural world. It shapes *ki* into specific objects that interact, and it prescribes how they should interact. In other words, in the mainstream neo-Confucian universe, *li* provides the "is" and the "ought" while *ki* provides the stuff *li* defines and directs.
33. *Zhongyong* XII: 3.
34. *Tŏk* is another term that is difficult to translate precisely. It normally refers to virtue, in other words to acting appropriately as well as having the ability to act appropriately, but it can also refer to power, especially power manifested by interacting appropriately in a wide variety of situations.
35. *Zhongyong* XVI: 1.

36. *Zhongyong* XIII: 3.

37. The Five Fundamental Human Relationships refer to the appropriate interactions between rulers and subjects, parents and children, husbands and wives, older siblings and younger siblings, and among friends.

38. *Zhongyong* XV: 1.

39. Zengzi (Zeng Shen) (c. 505–437 BCE), one of the most beloved disciples of Confucius, was believed to have written the *Daxue* [The Great Learning].

40. Compare *Zhongyong* XX:17 with *Daxue* (*Daxue zhangju*, Johnston and Wang, 135).

41. *Zhongyong* XX:12.

42. *Kongzi jiayu*, "Aigong Wen Zheng," 1. Both *Zhongyong* XX and *Kongzi jiayu* [The sayings of the Confucian school] have sections called "Lord Ai asked about governing" and both those chapters include Nine Cardinal Rules for governing. See Yang Zhaoming and Song Lilin, ed., *Kongzi jiayu tongjie* [A complete exegesis of the sayings of the Confucian school] (Jinan: Qi Lu shu she, 2009), 211. *Kongzi jiayu* is also available online at https://ctext.org/kongzi-jiayu. Accessed August 28, 2021.

43. The *Kongzi jiayu* version of "Lord Ai asked about governing" is somewhat longer than the corresponding chapter in *Zhongyong*.

44. In this translation, "sincere" (*cheng*) will usually appear as "appropriately responsive and unselfishly cooperative." The English term "sincerity" doesn't have the power or range the equivalent term has in the Confucian world. It is much more than simply being honest with others, doing what you say you are going to do. It extends to being appropriately responsive and unselfishly cooperative in whatever interactions you find yourself. Sometimes the translation "integrated" or possessing "integral wholeness" is used to indicate that such a person always acts as a member of a larger community rather than as an isolated individual. See the translation of the *Zhongyong* by Andrew Plaks, in *Ta Hsüeh and Chung Yung* (New York: Penguin, 2003), 107. Roger Ames, in *Focusing the Familiar: A Translation and Philosophical Interpretation of the Zhongyong* (Honolulu: University of Hawai'i Press, 2001), 61–63, prefers "creativity" to emphasize that by responding appropriately and cooperating unselfishly with both human and non-human objects we interact with, we contribute to the creation of a harmonious society and cosmos.

45. *Zhongyong* XX: 18.

46. *Analects* VI: 3 (Slingerland, 53).

47. *Zhongyong* XX: 8.

48. Here Tasan is criticizing Zhu Xi's commentary on *Zhongyong* IX. See *Sishu jizhu*, 6 (Johnston and Wang, 420).

49. *Zhongyong* IX.

50. Here Tasan is again criticizing Zhu Xi's commentary on *Zhongyong* IX. The term translated here as "benevolence" is sometimes translated here as "humanity," "benevolence," "unselfish," or even "being fully human." It means being fully human, because it means always acting as a member of the human community rather than acting as a separate and distinct individual with personal desires and needs that you want fulfilled even at the expense of the common good. Zhu Xi, in his com-

mentary on Chapter IX of the *Zhongyong,* stated that this chapter says that it appears easy to rule a country but keeping to the Way consistently is difficult. Therefore, Zhu explains, this chapter is telling us that unless we have mastered recognizing how to act appropriately and have become accustomed to acting benevolently, and unless we eradicate all our selfish desires, we will never be able to adhere to the Dao consistently. See *Sishu jizhu,* 6 (Johnston and Wang, 420–421).

51. *Zhongyong* XVI: 1.
52. *Zhongyong* XIII: 3.
53. Roger Ames, in *Confucian Role Ethics: A Vocabulary* (Honolulu: University of Hawai'i Press, 2011), suggests that the term translated here as "empathy" [恕 K. *sŏ* / C. *shu*] should be understood as "putting oneself in the other's place" (194–200). Another possible translation for that Sinograph could be "being considerate in your dealing with others."
54. *Zhongyong* XVI: 3.
55. "Making our intentions appropriately responsive and unselfishly cooperative" (*cheng*) is the third of the eight stages to cultivating a moral character capable of bring peace to the entire world. See Ian Johnston and Wang Ping, trans., *Daxue and Zhongyong* (Hong Kong: Chinese University of. Hong Kong Press, 2012), 134.
56. The expression "rectifying our character so that we are appropriately responsive and unselfishly cooperative" is the two-Sinograph combination that can be literally translated as "making our bodies sincere." However, the word for body can also simply refer to our moral character, which is the way Tasan notes it is used in the *Zhongyong*. He argues that "rectify our character" means to cultivate attitudes of caution and apprehension. "Chungyong chajam," *Yŏyudang chŏnsŏ,* II, 3: 21a–b, commenting on *Zhongyong* XX: 17.
57. *Kongzi jiayu tongjie,* 206–219. *Kongzi jiayu* is also available online at https://ctext.org/kongzi-jiayu. Accessed August 29, 2021.
58. *Zhongyong* XXI.
59. *Zhongyong* I: 1.
60. *Zhongyong* XXI.
61. *Zhongyong* I: 1.
62. This may be a reference to *Zhongyong* XX: 3, in which a reference to the "Way of Man" is included in a discussion of the way the great rulers of ancient times ruled.
63. *Zhongyong* XXVI: 1–2.
64. *Zhongyong* XXVI: 8–10. After a discussion of the respective roles of Heaven and earth in sustaining the cosmos, this section ends with a line from the *Book of Songs* that begins "What Heaven has arranged, how profound it is!" See Legge, *Chinese Classics, IV,* 570 (Ode 267); Waley and Allen, *The Book of Songs,* 291.
65. The original reference to the three thousand rules of etiquette and the three hundred rules of ritual can be found in James Legge, trans. with Ch'u Chai and Winberg Chai, *Li Chi: Book of Rites* (New Hyde Park, NY: University Books, 1967), I: 404.
66. *Zhongyong* XXVII, 1–3.
67. *Zhongyong* XXVII: 6.

68. *Zhongyong* XXX: 1.

69. *Zhongyong* XXX: 3. The word translated here as "powers" [*tŏk*] is translated in other contexts as "virtue" or "ethical virtuosity."

70. *Zhongyong* XXXII: 1.

71. *Zhongyong* XXXI: 1.

72. *Zhongyong* II: 1; XXX: 1. Confucius is normally referred to simply as "the master."

73. There are fifteen references to the *Book of Songs* in the *Zhongyong*, ten of which are introduced with "The *Book of Songs* says" and five with "It is said in the *Book of Songs*."

74. Non-Polarity (C. *wuji* / K. *muguk*) is a translation I modified from Joseph A. Adler's translation of "Nonpolar" in *Reconstructing the Confucian Dao: Zhu Xi's Appropriation of Zhou Dunyi* (Albany, NY: SUNY Press, 2014), 160. Non-Polarity is a term used in neo-Confucian cosmology to refer to the cosmos before any differentiation has yet emerged. It is not meant to be understood temporally. In neo-Confucian thinking, there was never a time when there was no differentiation. Yet, to understand differentiation, we have to imagine what it was like before differentiation. This undifferentiated oneness is called "Non-Polarity" to differentiate it from the next state, the Supreme Polarity, the name for the differentiation of Non-Polarity into yin and yang.

75. *Zhongyong* XXVI: 5.

76. *Zhongyong* XXVI: 10. This is from the *Book of Songs,* IV: 1 (Legge, *Chinese Classics, IV,* 570 [Ode 267]; Arthur Waley and Joseph R. Allen, *The Book of Songs* [New York: Grove Press, 1996], 291).

77. XIX: 6 states, in the translation by Andrew Plaks, in *Ta Hsüeh and Chung Yung*, 37, "The ceremonies conducted at the Outer Precincts and at the Altar of the Soil provide the occasions for the sacrificial worship of the Supreme Lord of Heaven."

78. Tasan is referring to the advice Kija (C. *Jizi*) is said to have given to King Wu at the start of the Zhou dynasty. The specific reference to the "Imperial Pivot" can be found in the *Book of Documents, The Book of Zhou,* Book IV, "The Great Plan" (James Legge translation, *Shoo King,* 328–333.) The Imperial Pivot can be a reference to a ruler around which everything in his kingdom revolves. In this case, Tasan uses this to emphasize that the first section of the *Zhongyong* is the core of the text and everything else in the text is simply an amplification of what is said in the first section.

79. *Zhongyong* XXXIII: 6, citing, in turn, "Major Odes," "Decade of King Wen," "King Wen," in the *Book of Songs*. Legge, *Chinese Classics IV,* 431; Waley and Allen, *The Book of Songs*, 228.

80. Like "Non-Polarity" for *wuji*, the translation of *taiji* as "Supreme Polarity" is taken from Adler, *Reconstructing the Confucian Dao: Zhu Xi's Appropriation of Zhou Dunyi*. (Albany: State University of New York Press, 2014), 113–136.

81. *Mencius*, 7A: 26.3 (Van Norden, 178).

82. Hu Guang (91–172) was a Han dynasty official who was thought at the time to be an expert on the *Zhongyong* but made a recommendation to the throne that backfired, which caused people to say that he actually did not know how to choose

the appropriate way to act at a particular time in a particular situation. Fan Ye, *Houhanshu* [History of the Later Han dynasty], chapter 44, "Deng-Zhang-Xu-Zhang-Hu liezhuan" [A collection of biographies of Deng Biao, Zhang Yu, Xu Fang, Zhang Min, and Hu Guang]. Available at https://ctext.org/hou-han-shu/deng-zhang-xu-zhang-hu-lie-zhuan. Accessed January 1, 2020.

83. In the famous story found in chapter 32 of the *Han Feizi*. W. K. Liao, trans., *The Complete Works of Han Fei Tzu* (London: A Probsthain, 1959), 318. https://ctext.org/hanfeizi/wai-chu-shuo-zuo-shang line 47. Accessed June 29, 2019.

84. "Sacrificial Odes of Zhou," "Decade of Qingmiao"; "Qingmiao" in the *Book of Songs*. (Waley and Allen, 291). Legge, *She King, Chinese Classics IV*, 569, translates the phrase 對越 [C. *dueyue* K. *taewŏl*] as "In response to him in Heaven," with "him" being a reference to King Wen. Waley and Allen, 291, translate it as "There has been an answer in Heaven." Tasan, however, used this phrase with the more imperative meaning indicated in the translation used here. He believed that there was an actual supernatural personality in heaven above, and we should always look upward toward that Lord on High with a reverential attitude, remaining always mindful of that constant all-seeing presence above us.

85. This is a reference to Chapter VI of *Daxue*, in which "making intentions appropriately responsive and unselfishly cooperative" is defined as being brutally honest with oneself. This is explained further by saying that a lesser person will try to hide his moral defects in the presence of an exemplary person, but an exemplary person makes his intentions appropriately responsive and unselfishly cooperative even when he is not being observed by anyone and therefore has nothing to hide. Johnston and Wang, *Daxue and Zhongyong*, 52.

Translation: *Chungyong kangŭibo*

1. Kwangam was his literary name. Yi Pyŏk's sister had been married to Tasan's oldest brother but she had passed away three years earlier. Yi Pyŏk is revered by Korean Catholics today as a founder of the Korean Catholic Church, since it was at his suggestion that Yi Sŭnghun (1756–1801) visited a Catholic Church in Beijing in late 1783. Yi was baptized a Catholic there before he returned to Korea. Once he was back in Korea, he began preaching his new faith to friends and relatives, including Tasan.

2. This request was made by Cho Changhan (1743–?), the Third Inspector in the Office of the Inspector-General. The State Tribunal prepared a letter of pardon but an uproar among officials who still thought Tasan was a dangerous criminal caused the Chief Magistrate of the State Tribunal, Yi Chiptu (1744–1820), to block that letter from being sent. Chŏng Yagyong, "Chach'an myojimyŏng," in *Yŏyudang chŏnsŏ* I: 16, 12a.

3. In *Chungyong chajam*, Tasan writes that he and Kwangam (Yi Pyŏk) agreed on almost every point of their interpretations of the *Zhongyong*, except on how to interpret the references to the emotions before they have begun to stir and the emotions after they have been activated. He then sighs that he is sure that Yi Pyŏk would agree

with the position he has adopted now, if only he were around to hear it! (*Yŏyudang chŏnsŏ, Chungyong chajam*, II, 3: 7b.)

ZHONGYONG I

1. "Innate ability to act appropriately" is usually translated as "nature."
2. Tasan is citing Zhu Xi, *Zhongyong zhangju* [The Doctrine of the Mean by Chapter and Phrase], 1. For this translation, we refer to the version in *Sishu jizhu* [Collected Commentaries on the Four Books], published by Dafu Shuju in Tainan, Taiwan 1991. We also refer to Johnston and Wang, Ian Johnston and Wang Ping, trans. *Daxue and Zhongyong* (Hong Kong: Chinese University of Hong Kong Press, 2012), 409.
3. The "Biaoji" chapter immediately follows the *Zhongyong* chapter in the *Liji*.
4. James Legge, trans., *Li Chi: Book of Rites,* II: 341 *Liji* in *Shisanjing zhushu* [Notes and Annotations to the Thirteen Classics] (reprint; Beijing: Chunghua Shu Ju, 1980), 1641.
5. "Penetrating intelligence" (靈明) is a term Tasan coined for the ability of the human heart-mind to understand the world around it, evaluate what it is encountering, and decide how to respond appropriately. "Penetrating," literally "ethereal," refers to Tasan's assumption that this cognitive power straddles the line between the material and the spiritual and therefore is able to reach beyond the limits of our material bodies and understand the things and events around us from their point of view rather than ours. "Intelligence" literally is the term for both shedding light on something as well as the enlightening understanding of that thing that results. Tasan explained his understanding of the heart-mind in a letter to Yi Yŏhong (Yi Chaeŭi, 1772–1839). He wrote, "The core of the heart-mind is empty of any specific content and straddles the line between the material and the spiritual. As such, it is able to ingeniously respond to all things and events. It is not a thing we can attach a name to. All we can say about it is that it is the innate tendency to take pleasure in the good and to regard doing evil as something to be ashamed of," *Yŏyudang chŏnsŏ*, I: 19, 31b, "*tap Yi Yŏhong.*" For more on philosophical exchanges between Tasan and Yi Chaeŭi, see Silsi Haksa Kyŏnghak Yŏn'guhoe, trans., *Chŏng Yagyong and Yi Chaeŭi, Tasan kwa Munsan ŭi insŏng nonjaeng* [The discussion between Chŏng Yagyong and Yi Chaeŭi on human nature] (Seoul: Han'gilsa, 1996).
6. Roger Ames, *Confucian Role Ethics: A Vocabulary* (Honolulu: University of Hawai'i Press, 2011), 201–205, suggests that "righteousness" does not convey what this term really means in a Confucian context. He suggests instead translating it as "achieving an optimal appropriateness in one's relations," or simply "appropriateness" for short. We agree with his point but will stick with the standard translation of "righteousness" when it is discussed as one of the five "virtues" to avoid confusion with our translation of the term usually translated as virtue in general as "acting appropriately" or "displaying ethical virtuosity."
7. This phrase is taken verbatim from Zhu Xi's *Sishu jizhu*, 1 (Johnston and Wang, 408).

8. In *Chungyong chajam*, II, 3: 2b, Tasan defines "benevolence" much more broadly than that English term implies. He says it refers to displaying ethicial virtuosity in all human interactions. Since he assumes a person is not fully human until he or she consistently acts the way human beings should act, we sometimes translate that term as "being fully human."

9. Zhu Xi says that is the case. He says that animals also have a virtuous nature, just like humans. *Sishu jizhu*, 1 (Johnston and Wang, 408).

10. This is a paraphrase of what Zhu Xi says in *Zhuxi yulei,* "Xingli-III" "ren-yi-li-zhi mingyi," line 54. Accessed at https://ctext.org/zhuzi-yulei/6.

11. *Yijing*, "Shuo Gua" (Explaining the Trigrams), 2, as translated by Richard John Lynn, *The Classic of Changes, a New Translation of the I Ching as Interpreted by Wang Bi.* (New York: Columbia University Press, 1994), 120.

12. Legge, *Book of Rites*, vol. I, 381.

13. James Legge, *The Shoo King, or the Book of Historical Documents (Chinese Classics III* (Hong Kong: Hong Kong University Press, 1970), 185, (Part IV: "the Books of Shang," Book III: "The Announcement of T'ang," 2.

14. See Tasan's *Simgyŏng mirhŏm* [Personal experience with the *Classic of the Heart-and-Mind]*, in *Yŏyudang chŏnsŏ*, II: 2, 25a, where he writes that human beings are formed from a union of spirit and physical form, and that is what is called the person. He then warns that it is a mistake to talk of the conscious heart-mind with just one word, like "spirit," since that does not do justice to its full complexity and to that fact that the body is inextricably intertwined with the heart-mind.

15. *Sishu jizhu*, 1 (Johnston and Wang, 408).

16. Zhu Xi, *Sishu huowen* [Questions and Answers on the Four Books] (Shanghai: Shanghai guji chubanshe, 2001), 46–48. We also refer to Pak Wansik, ed., *Chungyong* (Seoul: Yŏgang Publishing, 2008), 355–356. This Korean translation of Zhu Xi's *Zhongyong huowen* also contains the original text.

17. *Sishu jizhu*, 1 (Johnston and Wang, 408).

18. See the question raised in the *Zhungyong huowen*, in *Sishu huowen*, 48 (Pak Wansik, 363).

19. "Moral side of one's nature" is the translation here of K. *sŏng* / C. *xing,* elsewhere translated as "the innate tendency to behave appropriately." However, at times, such as in this line, Tasan uses that Sinograph to refer to what he sees as two aspects of human nature, a natural desire to do what is morally correct and an equally natural desire to do what feels good. In other to indicate that he is referring to those two aspects, we will distinguish in our translation between the "moral side of one's nature" and the "physical nature." Note that in *Chungyong chajam*, II, 3: 2b–3b, Tasan states explicitly that "human nature" [C. *xing*] refers to the inclinations of the heart-mind. The nature heaven endows human beings with at birth includes the penetrating intelligence that allows us to recognize the morally correct and desire to act in accordance with it but it also includes a desire for the pleasurable and personally beneficial. Fortunately, the moral part of our nature (K. *tosim*) also includes the ability to choose to act appropriately, as well as to decide to refrain from acting inappropriately, rather than just recognizing how we should behave and wishing

we could act accordingly. That ability to choose to act appropriately rather than inappropriately makes it possible for us to behave in a moral fashion.

20. Zhu Xi, *Zhuzi yulei* [The Classified Sayings of Master Zhu], 62, in *Zhongyong*, I, 9: "*diyizhang.*" Available at https://ctext.org/zhuzi-yulei/62.

21. *Zhuzi yulei*, 62, in *Zhongyong*, I, 16: "*diyizhang.*" Available at https://ctext.org/zhuzi-yulei/62.

22. *Analects*, 12:1 (Slingerland, 125).

23. Zhuangzi is a writer in the late fourth century BCE who is traditionally considered to be a founding figure of the Daoist tradition of valuing what is natural over artificial social norms.

24. The legendary creator of Chinese characters and of the first Chinese character dictionary, at the time of the Yellow Emperor. Dictionaries presented as expansions of his dictionary, called the *Sancang*, appeared during the Han dynasty and during the Wei and Jin dynasties that followed the Han.

25. The *Shuowen jiezi*, by the Han dynasty scholar Xu Shen, was the first comprehensive dictionary of Chinese characters.

26. Xu Xuan (916–991) together with his brother Xu Kai (920–974) produced a restored version of the *Shuowen jiezi* during the Song dynasty.

27. *Sishu jizhu*, 1 (Johnston and Wang, 408). In *Chungyong chajam*, II, 3:5a, Tasan argues that it is a mistake to say, as Zhu Xi does, that human nature, the Dao, and that which Heaven has endowed us with are all the same because they are all *li*, the normative patterns defining and directing appropriate human interactions. That, he insists, gives undeserved credit to *li* as that which motivates us to act appropriately. *Li*, he points out, is unconscious and therefore does not know what we are doing or thinking. How can something that does not know what we are doing or thinking inspire in us a feeling of apprehension that leads us to be cautious about how we behave?

28. *Zhuzi yulei*, 62, in *Zhongyong*, I, 23: "*diyizhang.* Available at https://ctext.org/zhuzi-yulei/62.

29. *Zhongyong*, XXII.

30. "Bestowed" is the same Sinograph [命] that Tasan reads elsewhere as "to confer, to endow."

31. *Book of Songs*, "Lessons from the States," "Beifeng," "Gufeng." James Legge, trans., *The She King, or the Book of Poetry* (Chinese Classics IV, Hong Kong: Hong Kong University Press, 1970), 56. Arthur Waley and Joseph R. Allen, *The Book of Songs: The Ancient Chinese Classic of Poetry* (New York: Grove Press, 1996), 31, translate these lines as "Though for my person you have no regard / At least pity my brood." Tasan, however, appears to read this line as saying that if we do not cultivate our full moral potential, then we cannot expect to be able to have a positive influence on the rest of the natural world.

32. In *Chungyong chajam*, II, 3: 4a–b, Tasan writes that the Dao we should never distance ourselves from is the Dao that is the moral nature Heaven has given us. That Dao within tells us how we should interact with our fellow human beings. In other words, it lays out the path (Dao) we should follow. We should no more ignore what

that Dao is telling us than we should ignore the commands of our king. Tasan goes on to argue that when this text talks about not distancing ourselves from the Dao for even one second, it is telling us to act appropriately consistently and constantly.

33. *Sishu jizhu*, 2 (Johnston and Wang, 410).

34. *Analects* VI: 17 (Slingerland, 58).

35. *Sishu jizhu*, 2 (Johnston and Wang, 410).

36. *Sishu jizhu*, 2 (Johnston and Wang, 410).

37. *Sishu huowen,* 51 (Pak Wansik, 370).

38. *Analects* XVI: 8 (Slingerland, 195).

39. In *Chungyong chajam,* II, 3: 5a–b, Tasan explains what Heaven has ordained is nothing other than our own Dao heart-mind Heaven endowed us with at birth. He goes on to describe it as our conscience. Heaven does not speak to us through our ears. Instead, it "speaks" to us by having our Dao heart-mind tell us how to act appropriately in any given situation, and also gives us the emotions that inspire us to act that way and that inspire us to put ourselves in someone else's shoes, so we can interact with them the way they should be interacted with. He notes that the Dao heart-mind is completely immaterial, so it should be distinguished from our physical nature. Moreover, because it is completely immaterial, we should not expect it to "speak" to us through our ears.

40. Lü Ziyue is Lü Zujian (d. 1196). Zhu Xi's reply to Lü Ziyue can be found in *Zhuzi wenji,* available at https://ctext.org/wiki.pl?if=gb&chapter=149612&remap=gb Accessed April 18, 2020.

41. *Sishu jizhu,* 2 (Johnston and Wang, 410).

42. This sentence was made famous by the Tang dynasty writer Han Yu (768-824) in his "Letter to Prime Minister Meng" [*Yu Meng Shangshu shu*] in *Han Yu quan ji jiao zhu* [Corrections and notes to the complete works of Han Yu] (Chengdu, China: Sichuan University Press, 1996), 4: 2351.

43. *Zhongyong,* XVI: 2.

44. There is ambiguity in Tasan's use of the word "spirits." It can be either singular or plural, referring to the Lord on High or referring to the many spiritual beings Tasan argues (see the discussion of Chapter XVI) act as the assistants to the Lord on High.

45. This sentence can be found in the *Mingxin baojian* (K. *Myŏngsim pogam*) [A precious mirror for enlightening the heart-mind], where it is cited as coming from a Daoist text, the *Xuandi chuixun* [Instructions revealed by the Dark Emperor]. Available at https://ctext.org/wiki.pl?if=en&chapter=523440, line 62. Accessed October 29, 2018. A version of the *Xuandi chuixun* can be found under the name *Wudang xuantian shangdi chiuxun wen* at http://www.taolibrary.com/category/category86/c86017.htm. Accessed December 25, 2019. The citation here is slightly modified from what is seen in *Mingxin baojian,* which, in turn, is slightly modified from the way it appears on the web as *Wudang xuandi Shangdi chuixun wen*. A discussion of the tradition which produced this Daoist text in the early fourteenth century can be found in Vincent Goossaert, "Modern Daoist Eschatology: Spirit-Writing and Elite Soteriology in Late Imperial China," *Daoism: Religion, History and Society* 6 (2014): 227. This

is a rare example of Tasan citing a product of Daoist religiosity. It is possible that, because it was cited in a work promoting Confucian morality, the *Mingxin baojian*, Tasan was not aware of the Daoist origins of *Xuandi chuixun*.

46. *Zhongyong*, I: 2.
47. *Zhongyong*, XVI: 5.
48. *Zhongyong*, 33: 1.
49. *Zhongyong*, XII: 1, 2.
50. In *Chungyong chajam* II, 3: 5b, Tasan states that what is the most hidden and what is the most subtle is a reference to the way Heaven operates. Heaven works behind the scenes. The exact mechanism by which Heaven has nature do what it does, such as having birds fly and fish swim, is unseen and unheard and therefore is the most hidden and the most subtle.
51. In *Chungyong chajam*, II: 4b–5b, Tasan makes an argument similar to what we see at the end of *Chungyong ch'aek*. However, in *Chungyong chajam*, he gives that argument a monotheistic twist. He argues that what is neither seen nor heard is a reference to Heaven. And he states explicitly that by Heaven he means the Lord on High. He then explains that, just as people will do whatever they feel like doing rather than acting as they should if they do not have a ruler above them to force them to be moral, people will fail to consistently act appropriately unless they are constantly aware that the Lord on High is watching them and can see everything they say, do, or even just think. Such awareness will make them apprenhensive and inspire them to be cautious about what they do or think, since, Tasan argues, the penetrating intelligence of Heaven is able to look into the innermost recesses of our heart-mind no matter where we are so that there is no place we can hide. Recognizing the need to be cautious and feeling apprehensive will motivate them to act in accordance with the moral nature Heaven has endowed them with rather than allow their selfish impulses lead them astray. Even the most courageous person cannot help but feel apprehensive and realize they need to be careful when they remain aware they are being watched at all times and in all places.
52. *Sishu jizhu*, 2 (Johnston and Wang, 410).
53. Zhu Xi wrote in *Zhongyong zhangju* that the *Zhongyong* tells us here that before these four emotions are activated, the heart-mind is in a state of perfect composure, undisturbed by any emotions, and therefore can engage harmoniously and appropriately with people and things in the world around it. That is why these four emotions can be equated with the inborn human ability to act appropriately. *Sishu jizhu*, 2 (Johnston and Wang, 410).
54. See, for example, *Sishu huowen*, 55 (Pak Wansik, 383).
55. "The Cheng school" is a reference to the brothers Cheng Hao (1032–1085) and Cheng Yi (1033–1107) and their immediate followers.
56. *Sishu huowen*, 58 (Pak Wansik, 395).
57. We were unable to find this phrase in the *Guoyu* [Discourses of the States]. Instead, we found it in *Chunqiu Zuozhuan* Chenggong, yr. 13 (Legge, *Chinese Classics V*, 379). Liu Kang is a man of the Spring and Autumn Period said to have lived around 590 BCE (Stephen Durrant, Wai-yee Li, and David Schaberg, trans., *Zuo*

Tradition: Zhozhuan Commentary on the Spring and Autumn Annals [Seattle: University of Washington Press, 2016], II: 803).

58. *Guoyu* "Wuyu," 5. Available at https://ctext.org/guo-yu/wu-yu. Accessed October 29, 2018. This is a reference to the ruler of the state of Wu during the Warring States Period.

59. *Liji*, "Liqi." Legge, *Li Chi* (Book of Rites), 1: 410 (Rites in the formation of Character, II: 12).

60. *Yijing*, "Xici zhuan, shang" (Commentary on the Appended Phrases, Part One), 10, *Book of Changes*. Translation by James Legge, I, 61 (p. 370). Richard Lynn translates this line as "As they bring out all the potential of these numbers, they also establish images for everything in the world." Richard Lynn, *The Classic of Changes, as Interpreted by Wang Bi* (New York: Columbia University Press, 1994), "Commentary, Part One," 62.

61. "Yueji" (Record of Music), 7. *Liji*. Legge, *Li Chi* (Book of Rites), 2: 96 (Record of Music, Section One).

62. *Analects* II: 15 (Slingerland, 13).

63. *Book of Songs*, "Daya," "Decade of Wen Wang," "Daming," 3 (Legge, *Chinese Classics IV*, 433; Waley and Allen, 229).

64. *Mencius*, VIa: 15 (Van Norden, 156).

65. In *Chungyong chajam* (II, 3, 6a), Tasan argues that maintaining a composed and focused heart-mind and interacting harmoniously with everything around us is not something that comes naturally. It is not part of the human nature we are born with. Instead, we have to exert a lot of effort to be able to do that. That is why we have to be constantly aware of everything we think or do to ensure we act and think as we should. It is only by being watchful over everything we think or do, even when no one else is aware of what we are thinking or doing, that we can think and act in an appropriately responsive and unselfishly cooperative manner.

66. *Guoyu*, "Jin yu," II, 17. Available at https://ctext.org/guo-yu/jin-yu-er Accessed October 29, 2018.

67. *Zhuzi yulei*, 26, "lunyu" VIII, "burenzhe bukeyi jiuchuyue zhang," 12. Available at https://ctext.org/zhuzi-yulei/26. Accessed October 29, 2018.

68. We were unable to locate the source of this exact quotation in any Song dynasty texts. The closest to this we could find is the statement that ordinary people have times when their emotions are not yet activated. *Sishu huowen*, 57 (Pak Wansik, 393).

69. *Zhuzi yulei*, 95, "*Chengzi zhi shu*" I, 3. Available at https://ctext.org/zhuzi-yulei/95. Accessed October 29, 2018.

70. *Zhuzi yulei*, 62, in *Zhongyong*, I, "*diyi zhang*," 75. Available at https://ctext.org/zhuzi-yulei/62. Accessed October 29, 2018.

71. Zhu Xi, "Da Lin Zezhi" [A response to a letter from Lin Zezhi, in *Hui'an xiansheng Zhu wengong wenji* [Collected writings of Hui'an Zhu Wengong]. Vol. 43. Accessed via the Erudition database, April 19, 2020.

72. The standard English translation of the phrase 致中和 has more passive connations. Plaks, for example, translates that phrase as "when the attributes of both the

balanced mean and harmony are realized to their fullest extent" (Plaks, 25). However, Tasan, in line with his more activist reading of this text, understands that phrase as more a command than a description, telling us what to do rather than simply telling us what we might hope to achieve. That more activist reading is supported by what Zhu Xi says in *Questions and Answers* (*Sishu huowen*, 55; Pak Wansik, 384).

73. In *Chungyong chajamm*, II: 3, 7b, Tasan cites several lines from *Huowen* (*Sishu huowen*, 54–55, Pak Wansik, 383–384) in which Zhu Xi says that it is only an exemplary person, who is cautious and apprehensive of what he can neither see nor hear, who is able to exert the effort needed to be consistently inwardly focused and composed while interacting harmoniously with everything around him.

74. Master Cheng here refers to Cheng Yi. Tasan omitted the conclusion by Cheng Yi that it is not possible to try to achieve composure before your emotions are activated, since trying itself requires activating your heart-mind. Chan, Wing-tsit, trans., *A Source Book in Chinese Philosophy* (Princeton, NJ: Princeton University Press, 1963), 565. Also see https://ctext.org/zhuzi-yulei/62/zh. Accessed April 20, 2020.

75. *Zhuzi yulei*, 59, in "Mengzi," 9: "*niushan zhi mu zhāng*," 25. Available at https://ctext.org/zhuzi-yulei/59. Accessed April 20, 2020.

76. This may refer to what Zhu Xi says in *Sishu hwowen*, 59 (Pak Wansik, 395). Also see Wing Tsit-chan, trans., Lu Zuqian and Zhu Xi, *Reflections on Things at Hand* (New York: Columbia University Press, 1967), 145–146. The king is correct in pointing out the Zhu Xi made contradictory remarks about whether or not we can make an effort toward moral cultivation even when our emotions have not yet stirred. That is because he changed his mind from believing that it is impossible to work on cultivating a moral character with an unactivated heart-mind to believing that we need to cultivate an attitude of quiet reverence even when our other emotions have not yet begun to stir. See Peimin Ni, "Moral Cultivation: Gongfu—Cultivation of the Person," in Kai-chiu Ng and Yong Huang, ed., *Dao Companion to Zhu Xi's Philosophy* (Cham, Switzerland: Springer Nature, 2020), 453–455. Also see Huang Ying-nuan, "Zhizo zi lun: Zhongyong-Weifa zhi yi qi gongfu" [What Zhu says in the *Zhongyong* about the meaning of the "unactivated state" and its relationship to the effort to cultivate a moral character], *Chung-Hsing Journal of Chinese Literature* 21 (2007): 1–20.

77. In *Chungyong chajam* (II, 3, 71), Tasan says that the Dao of the *Zhongyong* cannot be realized unless we are watchful over ourselves even when no other human being is aware of what we are doing or thinking.

78. In confessing to have once misunderstood this section of the *Zhongyong*, Tasan may be referring to what he wrote in *Chungyong chajam* (II, 3, 7b). There he said that he and Yi Pyŏk had spent a lot of time together trying to figure out exactly what sort of mental state the phrase "before the emotions have stirred" refers to. He notes that it took him thirty years to finally grasp it. He then bemoans the fact that Yi Pyŏk is no longer around to share his joy at this discovery. If Yi Pyŏk were still alive, Tasan writes, he surely would agree with Tasan's corrected understanding.

79. *Sishu huowen*, 58 (Pak Wansik, 394).

80. *Sishu huowen*, 57 (Pak Wansik, 394).

81. "What Heaven has conferred" is the phrase often translated as "mandate of

Heaven." Tasan explains in *Chungyong chajam* that the word "confer" actually has two meanings. In some contexts, it means the directives Heaven gives us through our conscience. In such contexts, it can be translated as "mandate." However, in other contexts, it refers to Heaven endowing us with the conscience that leads us to desire the moral good and detest the moral evil. In those contexts, "confer" is a better translation. *Chungyong chajam*, II, 3: 2b–4a.

82. Lü Dalin was a direct disciple of Cheng Yi.

83. *Sishu huowen*, 59 (Pak Wansik, 395).

84. *Sishu huowen*, 59 (Pak Wansik, 395).

85. *Analects,* 11: IX (Slingerland, 114).

86. *Mencius*, 6b: 13 (Van Norden, 168–169).

87. Zhu Xi, *Zhongyong jilüe* [An edited outline of the *Zhongyong*]. Accessed via the Erudition database, April 21, 2020. Yang Guishan was first a disciple of Cheng Hao and then of his brother Cheng Yi.

88. *Sishu huowen*, 59–60 (Pak Wansik, 396).

89. In *Chungyong chajam* (II, 3, 6b), Tasan argues that you will only be careful about what you do or think when no human being can be aware of what you are doing or thinking if you comport yourself as though you are always in the presence of the Lord on High [*Sangje*] and remind yourself that the spirits who assist the Lord on High can see even into a dark room in which you are all alone. Reminding yourself the the Lord on High is aware of everything you think or do will ensure that you are cautious and apprehensive about deviating from the path of appropriate thought and behavior.

90. *Sishu huowen*, 55 (Pak Wansik, 383).

91. *Zhuangzi*, "Miscellaneous Chapters, Geng-sang Chu," Book 23: 19. The translation is by James Legge. Available at https://ctext.org/zhuangzi/geng-sang-chu. Accessed October 29, 2018.

92. *Sishu jizhu*, 2 (Johnston and Wang, 410). Literally, "All the Ten Thousand Things under Heaven have the same body [*ch'e*] as I do." "Body" in this case should be understood not as body nor as substance (a common translation) but as innate potential to act and interact appropriately. However, we will see that sometimes Tasan interprets that term literally as "body" in order to raise an even stronger objection to this assertion that human beings essentially are not very different from other things.

93. *Zhuzi yulei*, 62, in *Zhongyong* I: "*diyi zhang*," 109. Available at https://ctext.org/zhuzi-yulei/62. Accessed October 29, 2018.

94. *Analects* 12:5 (Slingerland, 127). The Four Seas refers to the whole world. Zixia is the courtesy name of Pu Shang, one of the most important disciples of Confucius.

95. Gao, Kui, Ji, and Xie are the four wise officials who are said to have assisted the legendary Emperor Shun.

96. *Mencius*, IIIa, 4; Legge, *Chinese Classics* II, "The Works of Mencius," 250 (Van Norden, 70–71).

97. Cai Qing, *Sishu mengyin* [Introduction to the Four Books for beginners], III: 37. Available at https://ctext.org/wiki.pl?if=gb&chapter=701073#階翩則一汁

明蔡清撰. Accessed October 29, 2018. Also available on Erudition database in *Sishu mengyin* 14: 3. Accessed April 23, 2020.

98. *Liji*, "Liyun" (Ceremonial usages), 18; Legge, *Li Chi*, I, 379.

99. Ban Gu, *Baihutong* (Symposium in the White Tiger Hall), VIII, "*qing xing*," 2. Available at https://ctext.org/bai-hu-tong/xing-qing. Accessed October 29, 2018.

100. Kong Yingda (574–648), *Maoshi Zhengyi xu* (Preface to the Mao's Book of Songs). Available at https://ctext.org/wiki.pl?if=gb&chapter=498860. Accessed October 29, 2018.

101. *Hanshu*, "Yifengzhuan," 24. Available at https://ctext.org/han-shu/sui-liang-xia-hou-jing-yi. Accessed October 29, 2018.

102. Lu Ji (261–303), *Wen fu*, 17. Available at https://ctext.org/wiki.pl?if=gb&chapter=624701. Accessed October 29, 2018. This line was translated by Shih-hsiang Chen as "the Six senses were stranded, when the heart seems lost, and the spirit stagnant." See Cyril Birch, ed., *Anthology of Chinese Literature from Early Times to the Fourteenth Century* (New York: Grove Press, 1965), 213.

Zhongyong II

1. Zhu Xi draws on chapter 14, "*Shiyu li*" [The sacrifices of repose for an ordinary officer] of the *Yili* [The book of etiquette and ceremonies]. See John Steele, trans., *The I-li or the Book of Etiquette and Ceremonial* (London: Probsthain and Company, 1917), II, 124–25.

2. *Zhongyong* II opens with the phrase "Zhongni said." Zhongni was the courtesy name of Confucius.

3. *Sishu huowen*, 60 (Pak Wansik, 403).

4. Gongzi Zhan, Zifu Jiao, and Zijia Ji were important figures in the state of Lu during China's Spring and Autumn Period. Only the last syllables of their names were their actual names.

5. *Sishu huowen*, 60 (Pak Wansik, 404). Tasan left out part of that statement. The full statement reads "*Yong*, in *zhongyong*, refers to the normative patterns of interactions seen in everyday life which tell us to neither go overboard nor stop short of what we should do."

6. *Shangshu*, "Book of Yu," "Counsels of Gao Yao," 2. (Legge, *Chinese Classics* III, *Shoo King*, 71).

7. *Shangshu*, "Book of Zhou," "Establishment of Government," 10. (Legge, *Chinese Classics* III, *Shoo King*, 521).

8. The five precepts are for fathers to be fair, mothers compassionate, older brothers cordial, younger brothers respectful, and children filial. See *Zuo Zhuan* [Commentary on the Spring and Autumn Annals]. Legge, *Chinese Classics* V, *The Ch'un Ts'ew with the Tso Chuen*, Lord Wen, yr. 18, 280 (Durrant, Li, and Schaberg, *Zuo Tradition* [Seattle: University of Washington Press, 2016], I: 573). The "Five Primary Virtues," are the five ways of acting appropriately so that you display kindness, rectitude, decorum, wisdom, and good faith.

9. This is a reference to the *Shuzhuan*, a commentary on an "Old Text" version of the *Shangshu*, by Mei Ze (fl. fourth century), in *Shisanjing zhushu* I, 153.

10. Fan Ye, *Hou Hanshu* [History of the later Han dynasty], "*liechuan*" (biographies), "*Wang Chong, Wang Fu, Zhongchang Tong liechuan*" (Biographies of Wang Chong, Wang Fu, and Zhongchang Tong) 42: 48. The latter part of that citation is a paraphrase of the wording found in the *Hou Hanshu*. Available at https://ctext.org/hou-han-shu/wang-chong-wang-fu-zhong-chang. Accessed June 28, 2019.

11. *Zhiyue lu*, compiled in 1595 by Qu Ruji, vol. 11. Available at https://zh.wikisource.org/zh-hant/指月錄. Accessed December 11, 2022.

12. *Yijing*, "Xiang Zhuan," "hexagram 5, Xu, 2" (Lynn, *Classic of Changes*, 166, translates this phrase as "one never neglects his rightful duties), and "Xiang Zhuan," "hexagram 54, Gui mei, 3" (Lynn, 482, translates this phrase as "such a one never deviates from the norms of conduct").

13. *Zhongyong* XIII.

14. *Yijing*, "hexagram 1. Qian, 11" (Lynn, *Classic of Changes*, 133, translates this as "He is trustworthy in ordinary speech and prudent in ordinary conduct."

15. *Mencius*, Jinxin B, XXXIII: 2 (Van Norden, 193).

16. *Mencius*, Gaozi A, V: 4 (Van Norden, 148).

17. In *Chungyong chajam*, II, 3: 9a, Tasan writes that you cannot be described as an ethical virtuoso if you only think and act appropriately some of the time. You have to be consistent and always act and think the way you should act and think to merit such praise.

18. He was a disciple of the Cheng brothers.

19. Ch'en Ch'un, *Neo-Confucian Terms Explained (the Pei-hsi tzu-i)*, translated by Wing-tsit-chan (New York: Columbia University Press, 1986), 126.

20. *Sishu jizhu*, 2 (Johnston and Wang, 412).

21. *Zhouli*, "Chunguan Zongbo" [Spring Offices, Overseer of Ritual Affairs], in *Shisanjing zhushu*, I, 787.

22. This is part of a line from this chapter of the *Zhongyong*. Tasan does not mention that this line ends in the phrase "and this is called acting harmoniously."

23. In *Chungyong chajam*, II, 3, 9a, Tasan points out that the Sinograph translated here as composed also means focused. Its literal meaning is "centered," so in addition to composure it also means neither going too far nor falling short, neither being off the mark nor leaning to one side. He also makes a reference to the legendary emperor Shun telling his equally legendary successor Yu that, since the Dao heart-mind is difficult to discern while the human heart-mind is dangerous, he needs to maintain a steady course, avoiding being pulled off course by the human heart-mind. *Book of Documents*, "Counsels of the Great Yu" (II: 2,15); Legge, *Chinese Classics* III: 61–62.

24. *Sishu zizhu*, 3 (Johnston and Wang, 412).

25. *Shangshu*, "Zhoushu," "Hongfan 7" (Legge, *Chinese Classics* III, 328).

26. *Sishu jizhu*, 3 (Johnston and Wang, 412).

27. This is a reference to the commentaries of Zheng Xuan (127–200). See Johnston and Wang, 224. The original text of the *Zhongyong* does not have the character "is the opposite of" after "a petty man."

28. Zhu Xi claimed that it was Wang Su (195–266) of the Wei dynasty who inserted the Sinograph "the opposite of" in the reference to the petty man being "being consistently calm and unperturbed." In his view, that is the only way this sentence can make sense in this context. *Sishu jizhu*, 3 (Johnston and Wang, 412), However, Wang Su is now recognized as forging several "classical" texts.

29. *Sishu huowen*, 60 (Pak Wansik, 404). Zhu Xi argues that all men have the same basic heart-mind, but a petty man differs from an exemplary person in that he is incapable of looking within his heart-mind for guidance on how to behave appropriately.

30. See the Richard Lynn translation of the *Book of Changes* with the commentary of Wang Bi (226–249) and others, p. 133, for the first hexagram, *Qian:* "When there appears a dragon in the fields, it is fitting to see the great man.... This refers to one who has a dragon's virtue and has achieved rectitude and centrality (*zhong*)." This passage came to be read as stimulating others to also maintain a focused composure (*zhong*) and avoid being pulled one way or another by personal biases or self-interest. The original text, with Wang Bi's commentary, can be found in Li Dingzuo's *Zhouyi jijie* [Collected exegeses on the Zhou Book of Changes]. Available at https://zh.wikisource.org/wiki/周易集解/卷. Accessed September 5, 2020.

31. *Sishu jizhu*, 3 (Johnston and Wang, 412).

32. Tasan reads Zhu Xi as saying, "An exemplary person possesses the ethical virtuosity of an exemplary person and **therefore** [而] is able to be composed and focused when he is supposed to be composed and focused... but a petty person has the heart-mind of a petty person and **therefore** [而] is not careful about what he says or does." *Sishu jizhu*, 3 (Johnston and Wang, 412).

33. In *Chungyong chajam*, II, 3: 9b, Tasan says that, in contrast to an exemplary person, a petty person either misses the mark or leans off-center (when his emotions have not yet stirred, he is not focused) and either goes too far or not far enough (when his emotions have been activated, he does not interact harmoniously with people around him). He goes on to explain that the petty man falls short of acting how he should act because he is not aware of the importance of what he can neither hear nor see and therefore does not develop the feelings of caution and apprehension that motivate the exemplary person to always be watchful over his own thoughts and actions even when no human being can see what he is thinking and doing.

ZHONGYONG III

1. *Sishu huowen*, 62 (Pak Wansik, 408).
2. *Zhongyong*, VII.
3. *Analects* VI: 27 (VI: 29 in the Slingerland translation).
4. The "Counsels of Gao Yao" section in the *Shangshu* does not explicitly mention composure (*zhong*) and harmony (*he*) but it discusses nine appropriate attitudes and modes of behavior people are capable of (Legge, *Chinese Classics*, III, 70–71).
5. In the "Offices of Spring" section of *Zhouli*, we are told that it is the job of the

Great Officer of Music to use music and ritual to inculcate constant composure and harmony among government officials.

6. *Shisanjing zhushu* [Notes and annotations to the Thirteen Classics] (reprint; Beijing: Chunghua Shu Ju, 1980), 787.

ZHONGYONG IV

1. In *Chungyong chajam*, II, 3: 10a, Tasan briefly provides his view of the close relationship between knowledge and action. He says that if you are not clear about the appropriate way to behave, then you can be said to not know how to act. If you do not know how to act, then you will not act appropriately. Conversely, if you do not act appropriately, then you will not gain a clear understanding of how you should act. Knowledge and action, in Tasan's view, are intertwined. Knowledge that does not lead to appropriate action is not real knowledge, while action that is appropriate is necessary for more accurate knowledge of how to act.

2. Chapter IV is one of several chapters that begins with the phrase "The Master [Confucius] said." Other chapters, however, including the opening chapter, are not presented as the exact words of Confucius.

3. Feng Weishou. He was active during the Song dynasty. This passage can be found in Mao Qiling, *Zhongyongshuo*, I: 15a, as reprinted in *Siku quanshu cunmu congshu Jing bu* [A collection of works whose titles appear in the *Siku quanshu*: on the Classics], ser.1 (Jinan: Qi Lu shu she, 1997}, 173: 92.

4. Paraphrase of *Zhongyong* IX.

5. Yi Ya is mentioned by Mencius as the first person to comprehend the subtle differences between what tastes good and what does not taste as good. *Mencius*: 6a: 7 (Van Norden, 151).

6. This story of how to harmonize and modify flavors to make something more delicious, though it is attributed to Yan Ying rather than to Yi Ya, can be found in the *Zuo Zhuan* [Commentary on the Spring and Autumn Annals]. Legge, *Chinese Classics* V, *The Ch'un Ts'ew with the Tso Chuen*, King Zhao, yr. 20, 684 (Durrant, Li, and Schaberg, III: 1587).

There is a text called *Yanzi [ji]yu* [Collected stories about Yanzi] available on the web but the story that has Yan Ying talking about adding ingredients for flavors that were too weak and reducing ingredients when flavors were too strong appears in another section of the *yanzi chunqui* [The Spring and Autumn Annals of Master Yan] called *yanzi shiji* [晏子事蹟 the exploits of Master Yan], which can be found at https://ctext.org/wiki.pl?if=gb&chapter=692285#晏子事蹟. Accessed December 29, 2020. That story is also available in Olivia Milburn, trans., *The Spring and Autumn Annals of Master Yan* (Brill: Leiden, 2016), 373, 433.

7. "Record on the Subject of Education," *Liji*, XVI (Legge, *Li Chi*, II: 83).

8. *Analects* 7.19 (Slingerland, 70).

9. *Analects* 17.21 (Slingerland, 210).

10. *Analects* 7.14. Edward Slingerland, in his translation of the *Analects*, explains that the music of Shao is the name given to the music of the court of the sage emperor Shun (68).

11. *Great Learning*, 9 (Plaks, 12).

12. *History of the Former Han Dynasty*, "Records of the Confucian Scholars," 27. Accessed at https://ctext.org/han-shu/ru-lin-zhuan.

13. Mao Qiling (1623–1716), *Sishu gaicuo* [Correcting the errors in Zhu Xi's commentaries on the Four Books], vol 22. Accesssed via Erudition database June 13, 2019. Mao Qiling was a prolific writer in early Qing and is often seen as a forerunner of the School of Han Learning, which displayed a critical stance toward Cheng-Zhu neo-Confucianism. For more on Mao Qiling as a critic of Song readings of the Classics, see Lauren Pfister, "Mao Qiling's Critical Reflections on the Four Books," *Journal of Chinese Philosophy* 40, no. 2 (June 2013): 323–339.

14. In *Chungyong chajam* (II, 3: 10b), Tasan explains that "to know what something should taste like" means to know by tasting something whether it was overcooked or undercooked.

Zhongyong VI

1. *Zhongyong zhangju*, 5 (Johnston and Wang, 419).

2. *Sishu huowen*, 63 (Pak Wansik, 413).

3. A *cun* is a unit of length equal to about 1.3 inches. A *chi* is a unit of length equal to ten *cun*, which totals a little more than a foot.

4. In *Chungyong chajam*, II, 3: 11a. Tasan writes that the target is not the same in every situation you find yourself in. Instead, you have to weigh the particulars of each situation you encounter, and then make sure you do not lean too far in one direction or another but instead stay focused on the target. "The target" refers to the most appropriate way to behave in a situation you find yourself in. If you worry only about doing too much or only about not doing enough, and instead do not try to avoid both extremes, you will miss the target and act inappropriately.

Zhongyong VII

1. *Sishu jizhu*, 5 (Johnston and Wang, 418).

2. Cai Qing, *Sishu mengyin*, III: 44. Available at https://ctext.org/wiki.pl?if=gb&chapter=701073.

3. *Analects* 16.8. The translation is Slingerland's (195).

4. Hou Zhongliang (fl. 1100). He is cited in *Questions and Answers. Sishu huowen*, 63 (Pak Wansik, 415).

5. The translation reflects how Zhu Xi understood Hou's remark. Tasan understood it differently. In *Chungyong chajam*, II, 3: 11b, he argues that Hou did not mean we have to choose between being either consistent or maneuvering in order to avoid the extremes in different situations. Instead, he insists, Ho is pointing out how difficult it is when we encounter a number of possibly acceptable options in situations we find ourselves in. We have to weigh our options, choose the course of action that is the most appropriate for each situation, and then be consistent in acting in accordance with that choice.

6. *Sishu huowen*, 64 (Pak Wansik, 415).

7. *Analects* 13.5. Slingerland notes that "unable to engage in repartee" refers to the inability to use the poems in the *Book of Songs* as one must in order to function as an envoy (141).
8. *Sishu jizhu*, 5 (Johnston and Wang, 418).
9. *Sishu jizhu*, 5 (Johnston and Wang, 418).
10. *Sishu jizhu*, 5 (Johnston and Wang, 418).
11. Mao Qiling, "*Zhongyongshuo*" I: 16b (173-93).
12. *Analects* 13.10 (Slingerland, 144). The same phrase translated in the *Zhongyong* as "a period of a month" is understood by commentators to mean a year in this passage.
13. *Shangshu*, "Canon of Yao," 2. Legge, *Shoo King (Chinese Classics* III), 21-22.
14. *Zuozhuan*, "Lord Zhao," 23. Legge, *Ch'un Ch'ew with the Tso (Chinese Classics* V), 696 (Durrant, Li, and Schaberg, *Zuo Tradition: Zuozhuan Commentary on the Spring and Autumn Annals* [Seattle: University of Washington Press, 2016], III: 1617).
15. *Analects* 6.7 (Slingerland, 54). The passage contrasts the length of time that Yan Hui could keep focused and composed with the time of the other disciples.
16. *Zuozhuan*, "Lord Xi," 8. Legge, *Ch'un Ch'ew with the Tso (Chinese Classics* V), 150 (Durrant, Li, and Schaberg, I: 291).
17. In *Chungyong chajam*, II, 3: 11b, Tasan writes that the phrase "unable to sustain composure and focus for a full month" is another way of saying someone lacks the ability to be consistent. If someone is unable to consistently act appropriately, then they have failed to sustain a consistent composure and focus. Tasan reads this line as using "a full month" as a reference to consistency and "sustain" as a reference to maintaining a composed and focused state of mind.

ZHONGYONG VIII

1. *Analects* 2.9.
2. *Analects* 6.7. This translation is slightly altered from Slingerland's (55).
3. In *Chungyong chajam* II, 3: 11b, Tasan writes that, whenever he encountered a situation in which he had to choose how to act, Yan Hui would first think deeply about which moral principles were relevant in that situation. He would then decide on the best course of action and would stick to that decision without fail without being distracted by any pleasant or unpleasant emotions that might arise. That, Tasan notes, is what is known as consistency in maintaining focused composure and a harmonizing attitude.

ZHONGYONG IX

1. *Sishu jizhu*, 6.
2. Those three situations are bringing order to states and families, declining ranks and emoluments, and stepping upon the bare blades of a sword. In *Chungyong chajam*, II, 3: 11b–12a, Tasan gives three examples of people who excelled in some areas but were not models of ethical behavior. The first is Guan Zhong (c. 720-645 BCE),

who brought order to the warring states of China but openly led an ostentatious lifestyle. The second is Chen Zhongzi, another Warring States figure. He is known for leaving his family home because he believed his older brother had received an undeserved honor. He was condemned by Mencius for abandoning his family (Mencius, 3B: 10; Van Norden, 86–87). The third is Zilu, a brave disciple of Confucius who came to be considered somewhat of a troublemaker (Slingerland, 246).

3. Bo Yi is said to have been the son of the ruler of a vassal state of Shang who relinquished his claim to the throne because he knew his father preferred his younger brother. He is also known for starving to death rather than live under the Zhou dynasty, which overthrew the Shang to which he had been loyal.

4. Bi Gan is said to have been the uncle of the evil last king of the Shang. When he criticized his nephew's immoral ways, the king had his heart ripped out.

5. *Sishu huowen*, 64 (Pak Wansik, 416–417).

6. *Sishu huowen*, 64 (Pak Wansik, 416).

7. *Sishu jizhu*, 6 (Johnston and Wang, 420).

Zhongyong X

1. *Sishu jizhu*, 6 (Johnston and Wang, 422).

2. "Counsels of Gao-yao," 3, *Shangshu* (Legge, 71). The Sinograph Legge translates here as "sincerity" is the same Sinograph translated above both as "blocked" and as "complete." The original meaning of "blocked" could refer to going as far as you can and therefore doing all that you could do in a particular situation. That original meaning was expanded to also mean all you should do, and that, in turn, came to mean acting the way you should act. In other words, that Sinograph can refer to acting with "sincerity."

3. Lou Zhanghuan. Xiangming was his literary name. He lived at the time of the Manchu conquest of Ming in the first half of the seventeenth century.

4. *Xunzi*, "The Way to be a Minister," chapter 13 (Hutton, 134).

5. As cited in Hang Shijun, ed., *Xu Liji jishuo* [A supplementary collection of discourses on the *Book of Rites*], vol. 86, via the Erudition database. Accessed May 7, 2020.

6. *Sishu huowen*, 65 (Pak Wansik, 419).

7. In *Chungyong chajam*, II, 3: 12b, Tasan says that this text is called the *Zhongyong* to reinforce its message that you have to be consistently (*yong*) composed and focused on acting appropriately (*zhong*). Otherwise, you will find yourself following the crowd and drifting away from the path of appropriate interactions you are supposed to follow.

Zhongyong XI

1. In *Chungyong chajam*, II, 3: 12b–13a, Tasan explains why he disagrees with Zhu Xi's reading of this line as "some seek out strange doctrines and behave in strange ways" (*Sishu jizhu*, 7; Johnston and Wang, 434). He argues that the sentence that opens this chapter can be read as saying that some people flee society for no

good reason other than that they lack the ability to fit in. However, he points out that it can also refer to those who find themselves in morally uncomfortable situations and therefore withdraw in order to preserve their moral integrity. To support his argument, Tasan points to *Analects* 18:8 (Slingerland 218–219).

2. Johnston and Wang, 243, gives Zheng Xuan's reading of this Sinograph.

3. Found in Hu Guang (1369–1418), ed., *Sishu daquan* [The complete collection on the Four Books], "Zhongyong huowen-shang" [Questions and Answers on the *Zhongyong*, Part I]. Available at https://zh.wikisource.org/wiki/四書大全_(四庫全書本)/中庸或問卷上. Accessed May 7, 2020. Also available via the Erudition database.

4. *Sishu huowen*, 65 (Pak Wansik 420–421).

5. "Records of the Minister of War." This is an ancient military classic said to have been written during the Warring States period. Ralph D. Sawyer, trans., *The Seven Military Classics of Ancient China* (New York: Basic Books, 1993), 107–143. The Literary Sinitic original is available at https://ctext.org/si-ma-fa. Accessed May 11, 2020. We were unable to find the phrase cited here in this source.

6. Johnston and Wang, 243.

7. As cited in Hang Shijun, ed., *Xu Liji jishuo* [A supplementary collection of discourses on the *Book of Rites*], vol. 86, via the Erudition database. Accessed May 7, 2020.

8. *Sishu huowen*, 65 (Pak Wansik, 420–421).

9. The "Treatise on literature," in the *Hanshu*, "Yiwen zhi," line 676. Available at https://ctext.org/han-shu/yi-wen-zhi Accessed May 11, 2020.

10. *Sishu jizhu*, 7 (Johnston and Wang, 424).

11. Zhiqing is the literary name of Huang Gan (1152–1221), one of Zhu Xi's disciples and also his son-in-law. We were unable to find this directive in any of Zhu Xi's letters to Huang Zhiqing.

12. Yu Zhong was said to be a member of a royal family who moved far away from his father's capital to avoid competition with a younger brother who was chosen to be the next occupant of the throne. He is listed, along with Bo Yi, among the famous recluses of old. *Analects* 18:18 (Slingerland, 218).

13. Liu Xin (50 BCE–23 CE) was a renowned Confucian scholar during his time.

14. Zou Yan (305–240 BCE) systematized the art of making predictions based on the interactions of the Five Agents during China's Warring States period.

15. *Yijing* "Xici zhuan, shang," I, 11; Lynn, *Classic of Changes*, 66.

16. Tasan's defense of those who withdraw from public life to pursue obscure and arcane ideas and practices might be an indirect justification of his own youthful involvement with Catholicism.

17. *Sishu jizhu*, 7 (Johnston and Wang, 424).

18. Legge, trans., *Li Chi*, II, 330–335. This section of the *Li Chi* dwells on how difficult it is to try to become the moral person we know we should be but, it notes, "one should pursue the path of it, not giving over in the way, forgetting his age, taking no thought that the years before him will not be sufficient for his task" (335).

19. *Chungyong chajam*, II, 3: 13a–b. Here Tasan notes that the pursuit of moral perfection is a life-long task which requires a lot of effort. However, old age eventu-

ally catches up with us and we give up before we reach that goal. That should not, however, diminish our right to be considered someone who did their best.

20. *Sishu jizhu*, 7 (Johnston and Wang, 424),

21. See Chapter VIII.

22. See Zhu Xi's commentary on Chapter IX of the *Zhongyong*. *Sishu jizhu*, 6 (Johnston and Wang, 420).

ZHONGYONG XII

1. *Sishu jizhu*, 7 (Johnston and Wang, 427). The translation here differs from that of Johnston and Wang in order to show how Tasan understood this passage.

2. Tasan explains in *Chungyong chajam*, II, 3: 13b–14a, that the Dao of Heaven is the same as the Dao of an exemplary person, in that it refers to the proper way to behave. He adds that, because the Dao extends so far and wide, it is impossible to see it in its entirety. However, it can be seen in the way it operates behind the scenes in the orderly movements and creative activity of the cosmos as well as in the proper behavior of human beings.

3. This is a paraphrase of *Zhongyong* XII.

4. *Sishu jizhu*, 7–8 (Johnston and Wang 427).

5. *Sishu huowen*, 66 (Pak Wansik, 422).

6. *Sishu huowen*, 66 (Pak Wansik, 422).

7. This is a paraphrase from the "Xugua" chapter of the *Book of Changes* (Lynn, *Classic of Changes*, 106).

8. *Sishu jizhu*, 8 (Johnston and Wang, 426).

9. *Sishu jizhu*, 8 (Johnston and Wang, 427).

10. Laozi is a legendary figure traditionally believed to have lived in the sixth century BCE. He is thought to be the author of the *Daodejing* [The classic of the Dao and its power] and therefore is considered to be the founder of Daoist philosophy. In the Daoist religion in China he is seen as a divine figure. In Korea, however, the Daoist religion never established a strong presence, so he was known only as a philosopher. For Confucian respect for the ritual knowledge of Laozi, see "The Questions of Zengzi," *Liji*, V (Legge, *Li Chi*, I: 325, 340).

11. Ruler of a small principality during the Warring States period. Supposedly, in 535 BCE, he was asked by the ruler of Lu to tell him the proper names for various offices. Tanzi is said to have done so, and Confucius looked up to him for that. See *Kongzi jiayu tongjie*, 198. Also available at https://ctext.org/kongzi-jiayu/bian-wu. Accessed May 17, 2020.

12. Tasan here is commenting on Zhu Xi's insertion of what one of the Chengs said about the short excerpt from Ode 239 (in Waley and Allen, 235) which is included in this chapter of the *Zhongyong*. *Sishu jizhu*, 8 (Johnston and Wang, 428). The lines cited here say simply that hawks fly as high as heaven, while fish dive into the depths.

13. K. C. Wu, *The Chinese Heritage: A New and Provocative View of the Origins of Chinese Society* (New York: Crown Publishers, 1982), 162–163.

14. *Analects* 11:9 (Slingerland, 114).

15. *Zhongyong huowen*, 65 (Pak Wansik, 422). This is an abbreviation of what Zhu Xi is quoted as saying in that text. The full statement is "Heaven can give birth to things and provide a protective canopy over them but cannot support their materializations. Earth can support material objects but cannot give birth to them or provide a protective canopy over them. *Yin* and *Yang*, cold and heat, good and bad fortune, and calamities and blessings are all the result of movements of *ki/qi*. None of these are under our total control."

16. *Zhongyong huowen*, 65 (Pak Wansik, 422).

17. *Sishu jizhu*, 8 (Johnston and Wang, 428). Zhu is commenting on a line in this chapter which, he believes, quotes a section from "Daya," "Decade of King Wen," "Hanlu," in the *Book of Songs*: "hawks fly as high as heaven, and fish dive into the depths," to tell us that the Dao is manifest [*cha*] above and below. Legge, 445 (Waley and Allen, 235).

18. Rao Lu (1193–1264) He is also known as Rao Shuangfeng. He is said to have been a student of Zhu Xi's son-in-law Huang Gan. This statement by Rao can be found *Sishu daquan*, a Ming compilation of commentaries on the Four Books by Hu Guang (1369–1418, in the section called "*Zhongyong zhangju daquan-shang*." It is available at https://zh.wikisource.org/wiki/四書大全_(四庫全書本)/中庸章句大全上. Accessed July 6, 2019.

19. This is from vol. 5: 4 of *The Great Commentary to the Book of Documents* credited to Fu Sheng, a scholar in the early Han dynasty. We were able to locate this citation through the Erudition Database of Ancient Chinese Classics.

20. In *Chungyong chajam*, III, 3: 14b, Tasan writes that it is precisely because the Dao of Heaven is hidden and therefore not visible that an exemplary person is always careful about what he does or even thinks, even if no one around him can see what he is doing or thinking.

21. The term translated as "creation" [造化] should not be confused with the Judeo-Christian understanding of creation. It does not refer to creation out of nothing but, as the literal reading of the two Sinographs in this term show, to the transformations of the basic matter-and-energy [*ki*] of the cosmos such that it coagulates into different visible entities. However, though Tasan does not see a divine creator consciously directing the various transformations of *ki* that produce the world in which we live, he also does not believe those transformations occur in a disorderly manner. Instead, he believes they are manifestations of the Dao of Heaven, of the unselfish and unbiased way the cosmos operates when it operates as it should.

22. A dictionary named for Cang Jie, the supposed inventor of Sinographs. The *Sanchang* itself is a Jin dynasty (265–420) compilation.

23. In this chapter of *Zhongyong zhangju*, Zhu Xi cites one of the Chengs describing this poem as "lively and animated." *Sishu jizhu*, 8 (Johnston and Wang, 428).

24. That Buddhist text by "the man of the pine creek with no defilements" (Zhang Jiucheng, also known as Wugouzi) can be found at http://buddhism.lib.ntu.edu.tw/FULLTEXT/sutra/10thousand/X26n0574.pdf. Accessed May 18, 2019.

25. Zonggao is Dahue Zonggao (1089–1163), a Song dynasty Chan monk.

26. Dahui, *Dahui chansi yulu* (Recorded sayings of the Chan master Dahui), chapter 19. Cited in Shengyan, *Chanmen xiuzheng zhiyao* [Essential pointers to prac-

tice and realization in the Chan Gate] (Taipei: Fagu wenhua, 1980), 141. Available at http://ddc.shengyen.org/mobile/text/04-01/141.php. Accessed May 19, 2019.

27. Yin Hejing (1071–1172) was one of the first neo-Confucians. As noted above, Zhu Xi in *Zhongyong zhangju* reported that Master Cheng used the phrase "lively and animated."

28. *Guishan xiansheng yulu* [Recorded conversation of Yang Shi] is available at https://ctext.org/wiki.pl?if=gb&res=845306. I was unable to locate any reference in that text to that supposed statement by one of the Chengs. Accessed May 18, 2019. We can find Yin Hejing's doubts about whether one of the Chengs actually used that phrase in *Xu liji jishuo,* vol. 87. Accessed via the Erudition database. June 13, 2019.

29. *Sishu huowen,*. 67–68 (Pak Wansik, 428).

Zhongyong XIII

1. "In hewing an axe handle, hew an axe handle" is taken from the *Book of Songs,* "Guofeng" [Airs of the states], "Binfeng" [Odes of Bin], "Fa Ke" (Ode V). It is translated in Legge, *Chinese Classics,* IV, *The Book of Poetry,* 240, and also translated in Waley and Allen, 126. In Waley and Allen's translation, the line "Cut an axe-handle? Cut an axe-handle?" is followed by "The pattern is not far to seek."

2. *Sishu jizhu,* 8 (Johnston and Wang, 430).

3. We located this citation via the Erudition Database of Ancient Chinese Classics. It is found in Gu Menglin (1585–1653), *Sishu shuoyue* [Simple explanations of the Four Books], vol. 20, and in Hu Guang, *Sishu daquan,* so we are not sure which source Tasan took this statement from. Moreover, we are given only the surname of the person who made this statement, so we were unable to positively identify him. However, thanks to the *Sishu daquan* entry on the *ChinaKnowledge.de* website (http://www.chinaknowledge.de/Literature/Classics/sishudaquan.html), we know that Hu drew on the *Sishu Faming* [Clarifying the meaning of the Four Books] of Chen Li (1252–1335), so he is probably the Chen referred to here. Moreover, though there are five different men with the surname Chen cited in the *Zhongyong* section of the *Sishu daquan,* Chen Li is the person most frequently cited. See Chen Feng-Yuan, "Cong 《sishu jizhu》 dao 《sishu daquan》 – Zhu Xi houxue zhi xueshu xipu kaocha," *Chengda zhongwen xuebao* 49 (June 2015): 92–93.

4. The phrase, "it is as if the patterns are far apart," refers to an inability to see the patterns that should guide our behavior, even though they are close by.

5. *Sishu jizhu,* 8–9 (Johnston and Wang, 430).

6. Tasan gives us his understanding of this phrase in greater detail in *Chungyong chajam,* II, 3: 14b–15a. There he says this phrase means that if you are not dealing with others as you yourself want to be treated, then you need to change and start acting toward others the way you want them to act toward you. Once you do that, you can feel you have accomplished what you need to do.

7. One line in this chapter reads "Doing your best and being empathetic in your dealings with others ensures that you do not depart very far from the Dao."

8. This is a reference to *Analects* 4.15 (Slingerland, 34), in which a disciple of Confucius explains that the one thread running through his teachings is nothing

other than doing one's best while acting in an empathetic manner in your dealings with others.

9. Zeng Shen (505–435 BCE) is said to have been a student of Confucius and to have taught Zisi, who is traditionally believed to have written the *Zhongyong*.

10. *Sishu huowen*, 70 (Pak Wansik, 436).

11. In *Chungyong chajam*, II, 3: 14b, Tasan places more emphasis on empathy than on doing your utmost. He says that if you want to follow the path (Dao) of consistent focus and composure, you have to be able to put yourself in others' shoes. Without an empathetic attitude, he argues, acting appropriately in your interactions with others will be impossible.

12. *Zhuzi yulei*, "Chengzi shi shu III, 63." Available at https://ctext.org/zhuzi-yulei/97. Accessed May 19, 2019.

13. *Zhuzi yulei*, "Liqishang," "Taiji tiandi shang," 40. Available at https://ctext.org/zhuzi-yulei/1. Accessed May 19, 2019.

14. *Sishu huowen* 71 (Pak Wansik, 436–437). The point Zhu Xi makes here about the second statement is that only sentient beings can put themselves inside another being's skin and therefore only sentient beings are able to treat others the way they themselves would want to be treated.

15. The Five Relationships are the basic moral relationships between rulers and subjects, parents and children, husbands and wives, elder siblings and younger siblings, and friends. This chapter in the *Zhongyong* makes explicit mention of certain moral shortfalls: of a son not being able to serve his father the way he expects his son to serve him, a subject not being able to serve his superior the way a superior would expect his subordinates to serve him, a younger brother not being able to treat his older brother the way he in turn expects his younger siblings to treat him, and not being able to treat his friends the way he would like his friends to treat him. Nothing is said explicitly about the expectations in a relationship between spouses.

16. This is a line from Chapter XII.

17. Tasan noted in his comment on this chapter of the *Zhongyong* in his *Chungyong chajam*, II: 3: 15a, that "an exemplary person always looks into his own heart-mind and weighs the alternatives before him before he takes any action. If he can see that he is not calm and composed, he must make an effort to calm himself down and regain composure." That is how, Tasan argues, he can do his utmost and think and act with empathy.

ZHONGYONG XIV

1. *Sishu jizhu*, 9 (Johnston and Wang, 434).

2. "Commentary of Kong Yingda (574–648) on the *Book of Rites*," XXXIII, *Shisanjing zhushu* [Notes and annotations to the Thirteen Classics] (reprint; Beijing: Chunghua shuju, 1980) II: 1501 (*Sangfu xiao ji*). For the passage commented on, see Legge, *Li Chi II*, 54–55.

3. John Steele, trans., *The I-li or the Book of Etiquette and Ceremonial* (London: Probsthain and Company, 1917), II, 11.

4. Cited in *Kuangmiu zhengsu* [Corrections of Errors and Rectification of Vulgar Readings], III, 42. Available at https://ctext.org/wiki.pl?if=gb&chapter=402955. Accessed May 19, 2019. *Kuangmiu zhengsu* is a Tang dynasty work by Yan Shigu (581–645).

5. Mencius, IVB, 26 (Van Norden, 110).

6. Mao Qiling. *Zhongyongshuo* II: 8a.

7. Taozhan was the literary name of Zhang Dalai, a Qing scholar and disciple of Mao Qiling. We found this statement in Hang Shijun, ed., *Xu Liji jishuo*, vol. 87, via the Erudition database. Accessed June 13, 2019. Zhang made this statement to support the interpretation of *su* as meaning acting normally instead of doing anything special.

8. In *Chungyong chajam*, II, 3: 15b, Tasan says that this simply means that people should maintain composure and a harmonious and cooperative attitude no matter what sort of situation they find themselves in.

9. *Sancang, Erya,* and *Shuowen* are all dictionaries compiled during China's Han dynasty. They are the oldest extant Chinese-language dictionaries. *Erya* and *Shuowen* are available at http://ctext.org/er-ya and http://ctext.org/shuo-wen-jie-zi. *Sanchang* is the name given to an expanded version of *Cangjiepian*, said to have been originally compiled during the Qin dynasty.

10. Changzong (1025–1091) was a famous Chan monk in Song times. He is also known as Donglin Changzong (Changzong of Donglin Temple) and Zhaojue Chanshi (Chan Master of Illuminating Awakening).

11. Shiseng is the literary name of Hou Zhongliang (fl. 1000). This particular portion of the *Huowen* can be found in *Sishu huowen*, 73–74 (Pak Wansik, 447).

12. Pak Wansik, 450, provides a detailed account of the questions raised by Changzong.

13. This phrase draws on *Analects*, VII: 2. It is translated by Slingerland as "remaining silent and yet comprehending" (Slingerland, 64) and by Waley as "I have listened in silence and noted what was said" (Waley, *Analects*, 123).

14. In *Chungyong chajam*, II, 3: 16a, Tasan explains that "to act appropriately in whatever situation you find yourself in" and displaying ethical virtuosity are basically referring to the same thing. They both refer to maintaining a consistent focus and composure, whether you are rich and powerful or poor and powerless. People who do not realize this are unable to maintain a consistent focus and composure.

15. Lü Liuliang (1629–1683).

16. Lü Liuliang, *Luzi pingyu* [Master Lü's critical observations], 19: "*Sufu guijie.*" I accessed this text at https://ctext.org/wiki.pl?if=gb&res=205251 on May 19, 2019.

17. *Sishu huowen*, 73 (Pak Wansik, 447).

18. Tasan adds in *Chungyong chajam*, II: 3: 16a, that when you accurately match the power to act appropriately with the particulars of a situation, you are doing so on a foundation of constant focus and composure.

Zhongyong XV

1. King Chŏngjo's question arises from the fact that the Ode quoted in this chapter refers only to maintaining harmonious relationships with your wife, your

children, and your older and younger brothers. See Legge, *Chinese Classics* IV, *Book of Poetry*, 252–253, and Waley and Allen, *Book of Songs*, 135–136.

2. Legge, *Chinese Classics*, III, *Shoo King*, "The Canon of Shun," 31. (I: II, 2.)

3. Legge, *The Ch'un Ts'ew with the Tso Chuen*, Lord Wen 18th yr., 280 *Chinese Classics* V (Durrant, Li, and Schaberg, *Zuo Traditions* I: 573).

4. Here Tasan challenges Xhu Xi's reading of this phrase from the first line of the *Daxue* [Great Learning] as "letting one's inborn luminous virtue shine forth" (Daniel K. Garden, *The Four Books: The Basic Teachings of the Later Confucian Tradition* [Indianapolis: Hackett, 2007], 3). Since Tasan believed you could not be called "virtuous" until you had consistently displayed ethical virtuosity, he read this line in a more active sense. He argues it is actually saying "make manifest for all to see illustrious ethical virtuosity." Moreover, in another example of Tasan's preference for the specific and concrete over the abstract, he says that the particular forms of appropriate behavior referred to here are nothing more than treating your parents with reverence, treating your siblings with respect and affection, and caring for your children with loving-kindness.

5. Tasan explains in *Chungyong chajam*, II, 3: 16a, that the Six Relationships refer to one's father, one's mother, one's elder brother, one's younger brother, one's spouse, and one's children. The Six Relationships refer to relationships among family members only. The Five Cardinal Relationships are a different set of relationships that include the relationships among family members (parents and children, husbands and wives, elder siblings and younger siblings) but reach beyond them to also include the relationships between rulers and subjects and the relationships among friends.

6. In *Chungyong chajam*, II, 3: 16a, Tasan writes that "ascending to someplace high" tells us to look toward Heaven, since Heaven watches our every move and judges whether we are a good person or not by watching how we interact with our fellow human beings. It is through appropriate interactions with our fellow human beings that we serve Heaven.

7. *Sishu jizhu*, 10 (Johnston and Wang, 434).

8. Rao Lu's statement can be found in *Sishu daquan*, "Zhongyong Zhangju daquan –shang." Available at https://zh.wikisource.org/wiki/四書大全_(四庫全書本)/中庸章句大全上. Accessed July 6, 2019.

9. Huang Xunrao is the literary name of Huang Kuan (1318–1361). Xunrao is his literary name. This statement can be found in Gu Menglin, *Sishu shuoyue*, XX: 2, "Zhongyong I." We located this citation through the Erudition Database of Ancient Chinese Classics.

10. We were unable to locate the exact source for this statement by Mao Qiling. Mao makes a similar statement in *Zhongyongshuo*, II, 10b. There he says that parents are higher than their children, but according to this chapter what is high must start from what is low. If we read this passage as referring to familial relationships, that would imply that parents come from their children. This chapter also says that to reach somewhere far away you have to start with somewhere nearby. But, if you interpret the references in this passage as referring to your wife and children as near

and your parents as far away, that would mean you have to start with your wife and children, who are nearby, to draw closer to your parents, who are far away. In Mao's opinion, that is unreasonable.

11. In *Chungyong chajam*, II: 3: 16a, Tasan argues that this chapter is reminding us that, in order to serve the Lord on High, we have to fulfill our moral obligations here down below, since the Lord on High determines whether people are moral or not by looking at how they interact with their fellow human beings.

Zhongyong XVI

1. The term translated here as "power" is the same Sinograph often translated as "virtue" [德 K. *dŏk* / C. *de*]. That Sinograph usually refers to the ability to do what is appropriate, as well as acting in accordance with that ability, in which case it can be translated as "ethical virtuosity." In some contexts, it can be translated as "virtue" but in other contexts a translation of "power" or "ethical virtuosity" comes closer to its connotations.

2. The term translated as "Spirit" is a two-Sinograph compound which can be literally translated as "ghosts and spirits" [鬼神 K. *kwisin* / C. *guishen*]. There are instances in which it is clear that a multitude of spiritual beings, including the spirits and ghosts of ancestors, are being discussed. In such instances, "spirits" or "spirits and ghosts" is the appropriate translation. In other instances, however, that term is used by Tasan to refer to the Lord on High and his spiritual assistants. In such cases, it will be translated as "spiritual beings." Tasan also uses that term to refer to the Lord on High alone. In those cases, it is translated in the singular as Spirit, though before Tasan this term was usually understood by Confucians in the plural. King Chŏngjo appears to be using it in the traditional plural sense.

3. Zhang Zai (1020-1077). See Ch'en Ch'un, *Neo-Confucian Terms Explained (The Pei-his tzu-i)*, translated by Wing-tsit Chan (New York: Columbia University Press, 1986), 143.

4. *Sishu jizhu*, 11 (Johnston and Wang, 436). For an overview of this neo-Confucian concept of "ghosts and spirits," which views them primarily but not exclusively as natural forces rather than supernatural personalities, see Joseph Alder, "Varieties of Spiritual Experience: *Shen* in neo-Confucian Discourse," in Tu Wei-ming and Mary Evelyn Tucker, eds., *Confucian Spirituality*, vol 2 (New York: Crossroads, 2004), 120-148, and Thomas Wilson, "Spirits and the Soul in Confucian Ritual Discourse," *Journal of Chinese Religions* 42, no. 2 (November 2014): 185-212.

5. Sizhong and Siming are stars in the *wenchang* constellation of six stars, which would appear to put them in present-day Ursa Major. Siming is seen as the arbiter of human destiny. The entire *wenchang* cluster was associated with the god of literature and culture.

6. *Zhouli*, "*chunguan*," "*dazongbo*" (*Shisanjing zhushu*, I, 757-758).

7. Rushou is mentioned in the *Zuozhuan* [Lord Zhao yr. 29] as one of the five spirits worshipped at the Altars to the Gods of Soil and Grain and also, since those five spirits are correlated with the Five Agents, is linked to metal and therefore to

the earth. Legge, *Chinese Classics,* V, 729 (Durrant, Li, and Schaberg, *Zuo Tradition* III: 1699).

8. *Chunqiu waizhuan* [Unofficial Records of the Spring and Autumn Period] is another name for the *Guoyu* [Discourses of the States], This citation is to *"Jin Yu"* II (12:1). Available at https://ctext.org/guo-yu/jin-yu-er. Accessed June 5, 2019.

9. Along with Rushou, the four other gods of the Five Sacrificial Rites are responsible for the Five Agents (Metal, Wood, Fire, Water, and Earth, respectively). They were also believed to have originally lived on earth and served as government officials. Tasan therefore considers them to be human spirits rather than terrestrial spirits. Hou Tu is often mentioned alone as the primary God of the Earth. All five of these are listed as former human officials who were later "offered sacrifices as the most exalted spirits" (Legge, *Chinese Classics,* V, 731; Durrant, Li, and Schaberg, III: 1699).

10. Tasan is following the *Zuozhuan* (Legge, 729; Durrant, Li, and Schaberg, III: 1700) here. The "Wudi" [Five Overlords] section of the *Kongzi jiayu* says that Zhong, Gai, Xiu, and Xi are the younger brothers of Shaohao, not his uncles. That same text tells us those are alternative names for Gou Mang, Rushou, Xuan Ming, and Zhu Rong, respectively (*Kongzi jiayu tongjie,* 287). Hou Tu is also mentioned in this section. They are all given human ancestry and therefore, Tasan implies, should be seen as human spirits rather than as terrestrial spirits. Tasan says that, except for Hou Tu, they were all related to Shaohao, who himself was said to be descended from the Yellow Emperor and to have been one of the legendary first Five Emperors of China.

11. These last four gods are also seen as descended from legendary human beings and therefore qualify as human rather than terrestrial spirits. They are all introduced in *Zuozhuan* (Legge, 729; Durrant, Li, and Schaberg, III: 1700). That same text tells us that the five sacrifices are to Gou Mang, Rushou, Xuan Ming, Zhu Rong, and Hou Tu, respectively.

12. These are standard neo-Confucian explanations of what the term translated here as "spiritual beings" means. Zhu Xi attributed the first statement to one of the Cheng brothers and the other to Zhang Zai. *Sishu jizhu,* 11 (Johnston and Wang, 436).

13. We were unable to locate a commentary on the *Rites* that says explicitly that the celestial spirits are the assistants of the Lord on High. However, there is one commentarial note that Tasan may have read that way. See Zheng Xuan's commentary on the *"Yueling"* (proceedings of the government in various months) section of the *Liji* (Legge, I, 309) in *Shisanjing zhushu,* II, 1384.

14. Tasan borrowed the phrase "lined up to form a bright array" from Han Yu (768–824), "Yu Meng Shangshu Shu" [A letter to Minister Meng]. The exact passage says, "The various spirits of heaven and earth are lined up to form a bright array." See *Han Yu ji* [Han Yu's Collected Writings," XVIII, 5, 31, Accessed May 22, 2019, at https://ctext.org/wiki.pl?if=gb&res=464031.

15. See *Zhouli,* "chunguan" (Spring offices): Zongbo (Overseer of Ritual Affairs) (*Shisanjing zhushu* I: 809).

16. Zhang Zai is the first to articulate this identification of spirits with *yin* and *yang* and to say that what are called spirits are nothing other than the traces of the transformations of *ki* that give birth to the myriad things. Wing-tsit Chan, compiler

and trans., *A Source Book in Chinese Philosophy* (Princeton, NJ: Princeton University Press, 1963), 505–506.

17. This is a reference to the statement by Zhang Zai cited above. There it is rendered as "Ghosts and spirits are nothing more than the natural activities of *yin* and *yang*." Literally, it could be translated as "Ghosts and spirits are the positive capabilities of the two *ki*."

18. A line in this chapter of the *Zhongyong* says that it is because of the spirits that men act that way.

19. This line is from the *Book of Songs*, "Sacrificial Odes of Zhou," "Decade of Min Yi Xiaozi," "Jing zhi." Legge, *Chinese Classics* IV, 599 (Waley and Allen, *Book of Songs*, 302).

20. *Zhongyong* XXIX.

21. Ch'en Ch'un, *Neo-Confucian Terms Explained*, 152. We are not sure why Tasan attributes this phrase to Ch'en Ch'un. Ch'en is simply citing a passage from the "Wang Zhi" [Royal Regulations] chapter, section 28, of the *Book of Rites*. Legge, *Li Chi: Books of Rites*, I: 225, though Ch'en Ch'un did add that final clause about the nobles sacrificing to their ancestors.

22. These are all lines from this chapter of the *Zhongyong*.

23. *Sishu jizhu*, 11 (Johnston and Wang, 436).

24. *Sishu jizhu*, 2 (Johnston and Wang, 410).

25. *Sishu jizhu*, 29 (Johnston and Wang, 490).

26. This is how Tasan reads Zhu Xi's comment that the actual operation of yin and yang that creates the visible things and patterns in the universe is not itself visible. *Sishu jizhu*, 11 (Johnston and Wang, 436).

27. This is a reference to Legge, *Book of Rites*, II, 220.

28. *Sishu huowen*, 74 (Pak Wansik, 452).

29. *Shisanjing zhushu*, I: 757.

30. As noted above, the Six Relationships are our relationships with our immediate family members.

31. Tasan here is borrowing the phrase from the *Book of Songs* "High Heaven acts with neither sound nor smell" ("Daya," "Decade of King Wen," "Wen Wang": 7; Legge, 431 [Waley and Allen, 228]) but changed the second half of that phrase to draw on his earlier discussion of Chapter XII about the Dao being so large it has no external boundaries but also being so small it cannot be subdivided into internal parts. In *Chungyong chajam*, II, 3: 16a, he cites that entire phrase from the *Book of Songs* in support of his argument that the Spirit is invisible.

32. See *Zhongyong* I: 2 for the first part of this sentence. The second part is a line from this chapter.

33. *Zhongyong* XIX.

34. *Zhongyong* XXIX.

35. These are mountain and forest demons that were believed in popular culture to represent a source of danger for people wandering around in such environments.

36. This is Tasan's reading of a phrase that is usually understood as saying that the spirits, in the plural, are in the air directly above and around us.

37. *Sishu jizhu*, 11 (Johnston and Wang, 436).

38. Tasan considered spirits to be conscious beings. Since *li* is incapable of consciousness, as Tasan points out in *Chungyong chajam*, II, 3: 5a, spirits cannot be *li*.

39. King Chŏngjo is extracting phrases from what Zhu Xi says about spirits in a discussion of the *Zhongyong*, Chapter XVI. *Zhuzi yulei*, LXIII: 19a–26b. Available at https://ctext.org/zhuzi-yulei/63. See Chapter XVI, 24–26. Accessed May 25, 2019.

40. *Sŏngjŏng* (C. *xingqing*), which literally means "nature" (natural tendencies) and emotions, is usually translated as character, temperament, or disposition.

41. *Konghyo* (C. *gongxiao*), which literally means "the positive effect of your accomplishments," is usually translated as effectiveness, effect, or positive impact.

42. *Xici zhuan, shang* A: 5; Lynn, *The Classic of Changes*, 54.

43. *Xici zhuan, shang* A: 5; Lynn, *The Classic of Changes*, 53.

44. *Chu Ci* [Songs of the South], "Jiuge" [Nine Songs], "Dasi Ming" (The Great Master of Fate). Available at https://ctext.org/chu-ci/zh. Accessed May 25, 2019. See David Hawkes, *Ch'u Tz'u: The Songs of the South* (Boston: Beacon Press, 1962), 39–40.

45. The *Book of Songs*, "Da ya," "Decade of King Wen," Daming," 3 (Waley and Allen, 229; Legge, 433).

46. *Sishu jizhu*, 11 (Johnston and Wang, 436).

47. *Zhongyong* XII.

48. Tasan is more explicit in *Chungyong chajam* than he is in this text that the Lord on High is also known simply as the Spirit, since, like the lesser spirits, he takes no material form and has the same sort of power they have. Tasan adds that we call the Lord on High "the Spirit" when we are referring to His ability to watch over us and observe what we are doing and thinking. The Sinograph "spirit" can also be used to refer to the human ability to think and perceive. In other words, "spirit" can mean consciousness, and Tasan takes advantage of the multilayered implications of that term to refer to Sangje as "Spirit," a conscious entity (*Chungyong chajam*, II, 3:16a). He also often uses Heaven as a synonym for Sangje. As he explains in *Maengja yoŭi* [Essential points of the *Mencius*], "we call Sangje Heaven for the same reason we might informally refer to the ruler of a state as 'the state.' However, we wouldn't dare to directly address Him as such" (*Yŏyudang chŏnsŏ*, "Maengja yoŭi," II: 6, 38b).

Zhongyong XVII

1. Confucius considered Yan Hui his favorite disciple because he was the one who loved learning the most. His death at a young age caused Confucius to lament that Heaven had abandoned him. *Analects*, 117–119 (Slingerland 113–114).

2. The king paraphrased what Yang said about Yan Hui, using the Daoist phrase "he is still among us" (不朽 C. *bu xiu*). In *Sishu hwowen*, 75–76 (Pak Wansik, 460), Zhu Xi has Yang using another phrase used by Daoists to refer to physical immortality, *bumang* 不亡. Such a reference to transcending death is, in Zhu Xi's view, inappropriate for a Confucian to bring up. Both Yang and Hou said that Confucius failed to accomplish the mission Heaven had ordained for him. Hou went further

and compared Confucius to the legendary early emperor Shun, pointing out that Shun was able to govern All-under-Heaven but Confucius was never able to do that and therefore fell short of what Shun had done, and what Heaven had ordained for Confucius. Zhu Xi argued that was both a contradiction of Hou's statement that Heaven supported and nourished Confucius and also was unfair to Confucius, since Confucius lived under different conditions than Shun had faced but nonetheless, though he was not expected to become an emperor, made a major contribution to restoring proper rites and ethics.

3. *Zhongyong* XXX.

4. Bi Gan is a legendary figure who is said to have been the uncle of the last king of the Shang dynasty. When he reproached that king for his immoral ways, the king ordered Bi Gan's heart to be cut out to see if the claim that the heart of a sage had seven openings in it was true or not. He became a symbol of unyielding moral character.

5. K. C. Wu, *The Chinese Heritage,* provides a narrative of much of the mythical history of early China. On Bi Gan and Kija (C. Jizi), see 289. On Bo Yi, see 283–284. Kija was jailed for his criticism of the late Shang ruler, and Bo Yi starved himself to death rather than transfer his loyalties from the fallen Shang to the newly arisen Zhou dynasty.

6. Tasan is referring to the fact that Chapter XVII says that people such as Shun, who are paragons of ethical virtuosity, will surely gain a high rank and be widely respected. Confucius did not enjoy either of the rewards of being an exemplary person that Chapter XVII promises were his due and thus later scholars had trouble reconciling what this chapter says with the facts of the life of Confucius. For further elaboration on why this chapter caused difficulty for later generations of Confucians, see *Chungyong chajam,* II. 3:16b–17a. There Tasan points out that not only does history provide examples of virtuous individuals who did not receive a high official post and the rewards that come with it but that also some people who clearly were not virtuous (he mentions the founder of the Han dynasty as an example) reaped the rewards this chapter promises to the virtuous. It is obvious, Tasan writes, that we should not take this chapter literally.

Zhongyong XVIII

1. *Zhongyong* XVII.
2. *Zhongyong* XVIII.
3. Rao Lu is referring to *Mencius,* VII B: 33 (Van Norden, 193). Rao Lu's statement, of which this is a paraphrase, can be found in *Sishu daquan,* "Zhongyong zhangju daquan-shang." Available at https://zh.wikisource.org/wiki/四書大全_(四庫全書本)/中庸章句大全上. Accessed July 4, 2019.
4. Legge, *Book of Rites,* II: 60. Dan Fu was King Wu's great-grandfather. Li was his grandfather. Chang was his father (K. C. Wu, 299).
5. Legge, *Chinese Classics, III, Shoo King,* 309–311.
6. Legge, *Chinese Classics, III, Shoo King,* 353.

7. King Chŏngjo's question concerns the discrepancy between the *Zhongyong* saying that it was the Duke of Zhou who raised King Wu's ancestors to the posthumous status of kings while the other texts say that it was King Wu himself who did so.

8. *Zhuzi yulei,* vol. 63 ("Zhongyong II," 18). Available at https://ctext.org/zhuzi-yulei/63. Accessed May 28, 2019. Zhu Xi is referring here to *Zhouli,* "chunguan," "zongbo" (*Shisanjing zhushu* I, 781).

9. Gu Menglin (1585–1653). Linshi is his literary name.

10. *Sishu shuoyue,* vol. 2 ("Zhongyong I"). We located this citation through the Erudition Database of Ancient Chinese Classics.

11. *Zhouli,* "chunguan," "zongbo" (*Shisanjing zhushu* I, 781–783).

12. *Zhouli,* "chunguan," "zongbo" (*Shisanjing zhushu* I, 822–825).

13. *Zhouli,* "chunguan," "zongbo" (*Shisanjing zhushu* I, 776–778).

14. *Zhouli,* "chunguan," "zongbo" (*Shisanjing zhushu* I, 787–789).

15. *Zhouli,* "chunguan," "zongbo" (*Shisanjing zhushu* I, 789).

16. Zhan Huo (720–621 BCE) was an official in the state of Lu. Qin was his courtesy name.

17. *Guoyu,* "Luyu" A: 9. https://ctext.org/guo-yu/lu-yu-shang/zh. Accessed May 29, 2019.

18. Legge, *Book of Rites,* II: 202.

19. *Discussions at White Tiger Hall* (*Bai hu tong*) is a record of discussions on philosophical, political, and cosmological matters supposedly held in the White Tiger Hall in Han China in 79 CE. It can be found at https://ctext.org/bai-hu-tong/zhs. Accessed May 29, 2019.

20. Houji, "Lord Millet," is the legendary hero who was said to have introduced agriculture to China. See Legge, *Chinese Classics, IV,* 465–472, and Waley and Allen, 243–247.

21. Legge, *Chinese Classics, IV,* 589–590; Waley and Allen, 298. See the commentary in *Shisanjing zhushu* I, 595. King Wen is not explicitly mentioned in that ode of the state of Zhou.

22. *Xiaojing* [Classic of Filial Piety], X: Shengzhi ("the government of the sages"). https://ctext.org/xiao-jing. Accessed May 29, 2010. Tasan abbreviates this passage, leaving out the explicit reference to the worship of King Wen as the equal of the Lord on High. He also left out the preceding clause that says that the Duke of Zhou worshipped Houji as the equal of Heaven. Also see Henry Rosemont Jr. and Roger T. Ames, trans. *The Chinese Classic of Family Reverence: A Philosophical Translation of the Xiaojing* (Honolulu: University of Hawai'i Press, 2009), 83–84.

23. An explanation of Zhu Xi's *Miaozhitu* can be found at https://zh.wikisource.org/wiki/廟制圖考_(四庫全書本). Acccessed May 29, 2019.

24. The *zhao* row, on the left, was for the spirit tablet of the 2nd ancestor while the *mu* row, on the right, was for the spirit tablet of the son of the 2nd ancestor. The spirit tablets of descendants then alternated between the *zhao* and *mu* rows, with the grandson of the 2nd ancestor in the *zhao* row, and his son in the *mu* row, and so on.

25. *Zhouli,* "chunguan," "zongbo" (*Shisanjing zhushu* I, 784).

26. *Sishu jizhu,* 13 (Johnston and Wang, 440).

27. This is probably Lin Xiyuan (1481–1565) and may be a reference to his *Sishu cunyi* [Harboring doubts about the Four Books]. However, Erudition located this phrase in Gu Menglin's *Sishu shuoyue*, vol. 20. Gu does not attribute this statement to Lin.

28. There is a long discussion of what sort of mourning clothes to wear for whom, and for how long, in John Steele, trans., *The I-li or the Book of Etiquette and Ceremonial*, II, 9–44. Also see https://ctext.org/yili/sang-fu. Accessed May 29, 2020.

29. *Book of Rites*, "Tan Gong" (Legge, I: 152).

30. "Tan Gong chamo" is found in *Sangnye oep'yŏn* [An appendix to a discussion of mourning ritual]. *Yŏyudang chŏnsŏ*, III: 17: 21a–b. There Tasan explains that he departs from the traditional reading (which Legge relied on for his translation). Tasan insists that Bowen was not an earl, despite what was usually assumed. Instead, the Sinograph (Bo 伯), mistakenly translated here as "earl," is actually part of his name. Moreover, Tasan insists, Meng Hu and Meng Bi were both paternal uncles of Bowen. He also goes on to explain here that Xianzi Suo is referring to the mourning rituals of Western Zhou (11th century–770 BCE), which changed by the time of Confucius.

31. This chapter says that a ritual for a funeral should be appropriate to the rank of the deceased, but the mourning rituals afterward should be the ones appropriate for the status of the mourner. It also says that the high officials were to mourn for one year for other high officials.

32. *Sishu jizhu*, 13 (Johnston and Wang, 440).

33. The *Great Administrative Code of the Chosŏn Dynasty* [*Kyŏngguk taejŏn*] has detailed instructions on what sort of mourning clothes to wear and how long to wear them, depending on the rank of the deceased and the rank of the person mourning them. Yun Kugil, trans., *Sinp'yŏn Kyŏngguk taejŏn* [Newly edited version of the Great Administrative Code] (Seoul: Sinsŏwŏn, 2005), 215–229. For a detailed description of the different types of mourning clothing, see Patricia Buckley Ebrey, trans., *Chu Hsi's Family Rituals* (Princeton, NJ: Princeton University Press, 1991), 86–97.

ZHONGYONG XIX

1. *Sishu jizhu*, 13 (Johnston and Wang, 445).
2. Mao is citing from *Zhouli*, "Chunguan zongbo" (*Shisanjing zhushu* I, 769). This citation by Mao is from his *Zhongyongshuo*, III, 9a.
3. *Zhouli*, "Chunguan zongbo" (*Shisanjing zhushu* I, 802).
4. *Zhouli*, "Chunguan zongbo" (*Shisanjing zhushu* I, 776).
5. *Zhouli*, "Chunguan zongbo" (*Shisanjing zhushu* I, 803).
6. *Zhouli*, "Chunguan zongbo" (*Shisanjing zhushu* I, 803).
7. *Book of Rites*, "Wang zhi" (*Shisanjing zhushu* I, 1336). Legge, I: 226.
8. A description of the "major banquet-ritual" can be found in the *Book of Rites*, "Zhongni yan ju" (*Shisanjing zhushu* II, 1614). Legge, II, 274–275.
9. Chong, Guan, Fengfu, and Yue are all names of early states in Zhou times. *Book of Rites*, "Mingdang wei" (*Shisanjing zhushu* II, 1491). Legge, *Li Chi* (Book of Rites), II: 37.

10. Ji Tan was an important minister of Jin during the Spring and Autumn period.

11. Legge, *Chinese Classics*, V, 660 (Lord Zhao, 15th year) (Durrant, Li, and Schaberg, III: 1527).

12. The source text has Diviner Tuo [佗] instead of Diviner Bao [鮑]. Bao must be a copyist's error, confusing the Sinograph 鮀, also pronounced Tuo, with 鮑. Legge, *Chinese Classics*, V, 750 (Lord Ding, 4th year) (Durrant, Li, and Schaberg, III: 1746–1749).

13. Chŏnju University Center for the Study of Honam, ed., *Kugyŏk Yŏyudang chŏnso Kyŏngjip I: the Taehak and the Chungyong* [A Korean translation of the Complete Works of Yŏyudang Chŏng Yagyong: On the Classics, volume I, the *Daxue* and the *Zhongyong*] (Chŏnju, Korea: Chŏnju University Press, 1986), 315, explains that a "grand chariot" refers to a "golden chariot," and the "great banner" has two dragons on it.

14. Legge, *Chinese Classics*, V, 754 (Lord Ding, 4th year) (Durrant, Li, and Schaberg, III: 1748–1749). The material in parentheses are Tasan's explanations of obscure terms that appear in this passage.

15. Legge, *Chinese Classics*, V, 100 (Lord Zhuang, 20th year) (Durrant, Li, and Schaberg, I: 191).

16. Legge *Chinese Classics*, V, 761 (Lord Ding, 6th year) (Durrant, Li, and Schaberg, III: 1771).

17. *Guoyu*, "Discourses of Lu: B, 19." The Sushen were a "barbarian" tribe to the north of China. Available at https://ctext.org/guo-yu/lu-yu-xia/zh. Accessed May 31, 2019.

18. The site of the palace of rulers of Western Zhou.

19. Legge, *Chinese Classics*, V, 37–38 (Lord Huan, 2nd year) (Durrant, Li, and Schaberg, I: 76–79).

20. Legge *Chinese Classics*, V, 135 (Lord Xi, 2nd year) (Durrant, Li, and Schaberg, I: 257).

21. *Shiji* (Records of the Grand Historian), "Yue Yi liezhuan" (Biography of Yue Yi), 80:9. Available at https://ctext.org/shiji/lie-zhuan#. Accessed May 31, 2019. Yue Yi was a general of the state of Yan. *Kugyŏk Yŏyudang chŏnsŏ Kyŏngjip I*, 316, says that Ningtai, Yuanying, and Moshi are the names of palaces in Yan.

22. *Sishu jizhu*, 13 (Johnston and Wang, 445). The young man who represented the deceased was, according to the *Book of Rites*, supposed to be the grandson of the person being honoured. *Book of Rites*, chapter 22 (Legge, II, 246). See also Ebrey, xvi.

23. *Zhouli*, "Chunguan, zongbo" (*Shisanjing zhushu* I, 684).

24. Mao Qiling, *Zhongyongshuo* III, 10a. This chapter (chapter XIX) of the *Zhongyong* states only that the ritual garments were displayed. It does not say explicitly they were presented to anyone.

25. *Zhouli*, "Chunguan, zongbo" (*Shisanjing zhushu* I, 784). On p. 784, he states explicitly, "the impersonator should wear the upper garments of the deceased to make it look as if he is alive."

26. *Sishu jizhu*, 13 (Johnston and Wang, 444).

27. These foods are mentioned in *Liji* [Book of Rites], "Nei ze" [The Pattern of the Family] (Legge, I, 461).

28. *Zhouli*, "tianguan zhongzai, neiyong" (*Shisanjing zhushu*, I, 661–662).

29. Mao Qiling, *Zhongyongshuo*, III, 10b.

30. *Liji* [Book of Rites], "Wang zhi" [Royal Regulations] (Legge, I, 226).

31. *Liji* [Book of Rites], "Yue ling" [Proceedings of Government in the Different Months'] (Legge, I, 264, 271, and 274).

32. Mao Qiling, *Zhongyongshuo*, III, 11a–b.

33. *Sishu jizhu*, 13–14 (Johnston and Wang, 444). *Zhao* is literally "bright" or "illuminated" and *mu* is "somber" but in this context is often understood as "in the shade." According to Cai Qing, the founding ancestor was in the front, followed by the generations of ancestors alternating positions in line, starting with the older generation (odd-numbered) on the left (*zhao*), then the next generation (even-numbered) on the right (*mu*), and back to the generation that followed on the left, and so forth. Cai Qing, *Sishu mengyin*, vol. IV: 13. https://ctext.org/wiki.pl?if=gb&chapter=277936#蠹蟬體雪當誼高持守固繼述 Accessed June 3, 2019. Zhu Xi explains, in *Questions and Answers*, that the *zhao* line faced south and therefore was considered to be more in the light than the *mu* line. *Sishu huowen* 77 (Pak Wansik, 467).

34. Zhao Shunsun (1215–1277).

35. Zhao Shunsun, *Zhongyong zuanshu* [A compilation of comments on the *Zhongyong*], II: 47b.

36. *Sishu jizhu*, 13–14 (Johnston and Wang, 444).

37. Cai Qing, *Sishu mengyin*, IV: 13. https://ctext.org/wiki.pl?if=gb&res=745255&searchu=若死者 Accessed June 3, 2019.

38. *Zhouli*, "Chunguan zongbo" (*Shisanjing zhushu* I, 766).

39. *Book of Rites*, chapter 22 (Legge, II, 246–247).

40. *Book of Rites*, chapter 22 (Legge, II, 248).

41. Cai Qing, *Sishu mengyin*, IV: 13. Available at https://ctext.org/wiki.pl?if=gb&chapter=277936#蠹蟬體雪當誼高持守固繼述. Accessed August 30, 2021.

42. Da Bo (also known as Taibo) is the eldest son of King Tai (aka Gugong Dan Fu). Yu Zhong is the second son of King Tai. Wang Ji (King Ji), despite being the youngest son of King Tai, is said to have inherited the throne from his father because of his superior wisdom and capability. Guo Zhong is the second son of Wang Ji, and Guo Shu is the third son of Wang Ji—the eldest son being King Wen, who is said to have inherited the throne from his father, Wang Ji. Only King Wen was an actual king. King Tai and Wang Ji were raised to royal status posthumously.

43. Tasan, or his copyist, appears to have made a slight mistake here. This text appears in "Lord Xi's 5th Year." Legge, *Chinese Classics, V*, "Ch'un Ts'ew with the Tso Chuen," 143 (Durrant, Li, and Schaberg, I: 277).

44. King Wen's third, fifth, seventh, and eighth sons respectively. Since King Wen's tablet started a *mu* line, his children had to be in a *zhao* line.

45. King Wen's remaining sons. "Lu" probably refers to the Duke of Zhou (King Wen's fourth son). The other sons listed here are, in order: the sixth son, the ninth son, the tenth son, the eleventh son, the twelfth son, the thirteenth son, the fourteenth

son, the fifteenth son, the sixteenth son, the seventeenth son, and the eighteenth son. King Wen's first son died young.

46. Jin, Ying, and Han are the third, fourth, and fifth sons of King Wu, named here by the states to which they were assigned. Since King Wu started a *zhao* line, his sons had to be in the *mu* line.

47. Tasan, or his copyist, appears to have made a mistake here. This text appears in "Lord Xi's Twenty-fourth Year." Legge, *Chinese Classics V*, "Ch'un Ts'ew with the Tso Chuen," 189 (Durrant, Li, and Schaberg, I: 381).

48. Tuo is here written 鮀, though the source text has 佗. Both are pronounced Tuo. This may be a substitution for a character which had become a taboo character by the time Tasan was writing this commentary.

49. Legge, *Chinese Classics V*, "Ch'un Ts'ew with the Tso Chuen," 750 (Durrant, Li, and Schaberg, III: 1751).

50. As noted above, the rulers of Lu and Wei were believed to be direct descendants of King Wen, the father of King Wu. The rulers of Yu and Jin were believed to be direct descendants of King Wu.

51. *Book of Rites*, chapter 22 (Legge, II, 247).

52. For Gong Zhiqi, see Legge, *Chinese Classics V*, "Ch'un Ts'ew with the Tso Chuen," 143 (Durrant, Li, and Schaberg, I: 277). For Fu Chen, see Legge, *Chinese Classics V*, "Ch'un Ts'ew with the Tso Chuen," 189 (Durrant, Li, and Schaberg, I: 381).

53. The story appears both in the "Discourses of Lu" section of the *Guoyu* (Discourses of the States), https://ctext.org/guo-yu/lu-yu-shang; accessed June 5, 2020. and in Legge, *Chinese Classics V*, "Ch'un Ts'ew with the Tso Chuen," "Second year of Lord Wen," 232 (Durrant, Li, and Schaberg, I: 473–475).

54. Guliang Chi (trad. fl. 5th century BCE) is said to have been a disciple of Zixia, a close disciple of Confucius. Guliang is traditionally believed to have written one of the most influential commentaries on the *Spring and Autumn Annals*, the *Guliangzhuan*. For more on the *Guliangzhuan,* see http://www.chinaknowledge.de/Literature/Classics/guliangzhuan.html. Accessed June 5, 2020.

55. *Guliang zhuan* https://ctext.org/guliang-zhuan/wen-gong-er-nian; accessed June 7, 2020. There is a translation of this passage in Harry Miller, trans., *The Gongyang Commentary on the Spring and Autumn Annals: A Full Translation* (New York: Palgrave Macmillan, 2015), 125. Tasan's reading of this passage differs from Miller's. An explanation follows that without the proper ordering of the *zhao* and *mu* lines, the lines of succession are not clear and that will cause disorder in heaven above.

56. Lord Min (661–660 BCE) sat on the throne first and was followed by Lord Xi (659–627 BCE).

57. Zuo Qiuming (556–451 BCE) was the supposed author/editor of the *Zuozhuan*, Zuo's commentary on the *Spring and Autumn Annals* (spelled by Legge as the Ch'un Ts'ew). He is said to have been a contemporary of Confucius. See Legge, *Chinese Classics V*, "Ch'un Ts'ew with the Tso Chuen," 232 (Durrant, Li, and Schaberg, I: 473). *Zhao* and *mu* lines are not explicitly mentioned here, but Tasan understands "elevating the tablet" as placing it in the *zhao* line.

58. "Chunqui zuozhuan zhengyi" [The correct reading of the Zuo commentary on the Spring and Autumn Annals], *Shisanjing zhushu* II, 1839.

59. Zhu Xi's diagram (*Zhoumiaotu*) shows that this is from the standpoint of the spirit tablet of the dynastic founder, which is facing south. The *Zhou* line then is, in the east, on that tablet's left, and the *mu* line is in the west, on that tablet's right. That diagram is in *Yuzuan Zhuxi quanshu* [Imperial edition of the complete works of Zhu Xi], 39: 31a–32a. It is reproduced in Legge, *Book of Rites*, I, 224.

60. A legendary figure from the equally legendary ancient Xia dynasty of China. He is claimed as an ancestor by the ruling families of both the Shang and the Zhou dynasties.

61. Wang Ji was not actually a king of Zhou. He was given that title posthumously when his grandson King Wu defeated the Shang and established the Zhou dynasty.

62. King Wen was also never an actual king of Zhou. King Wu, his son, was the first member of the family to rule over the Zhou.

63. King Yi (937–892 BCE) reigned from 899 to 892 BCE. (Some sources place his reign from 899 to 873 BCE.) He was followed on the throne by his uncle.

64. These were all Shang dynasty kings, which means that their dates are all speculative. However, it is assumed that Wu Ding reigned in the eighteenth century BCE, Yang Jia in the fifteenth century BCE, and Da Ding may never have reigned at all, since he died before he could take the throne in the eighteenth century BCE.

65. They were kings in Western Zhou. The first King Yi is said to have reigned 899–873 BCE. King Xiao is said to have followed him on the throne from 872–866. He, in turn, was followed by another King Yi, who is said to have sat on the throne from 865 to 858 BCE.

66. The Sinographs for the two King Yi are different. The first King Yi (trad. 899–873) is 懿王. His son, King Yi (trad. 865–858), is 夷王.

67. Puku is said to have been the son of Houji. He is also known as Buzhu.

68. Zheng Sinong is Zheng Zhong (?–83 CE), a Han-era official and commentator on the classics.

69. *Zhouli*, "xiaoshi," "Chunguan zongbo" (*Shisanjing zhushu*, I, 816).

70. *Sishu juzhu*, 14 (Johnston and Wang, 445). The text of *Zhongyong zhangju* includes "earl," but Tasan omits this rank.

71. *Zhouli*, "xiaguan" (*Shisanjing zhushu*, I, 850).

72. Shuzi was a rank in the Ministry of War, under the Overseer for Military Affairs. That part of the government had primary responsibility for military affairs as well as for communications.

73. *Book of Rites*, Legge, I, 353–354.

74. *Sishu jizhu*, 14 (Johnston and Wang, 445).

75. *Zhouli*, "Chunguan zongbo," "xiaozongbo" (*Shisanjing zhushu*, I, 767).

76. *Book of Rites*, "King Wen as Son and Heir" [Wen Wang shizi, 16] (Legge, I, 354).

77. *Zhouli*, "tianguan zhongzai [prime minister]," "xiaozai [Ordinary Grand Master]" (*Shisanjing zhushu*, I, 654).

78. *Zhouli*, "Chunguan," "dazongbo" [Grand Overseer of Ritual Affairs] (*Shisanjing zhushu*, I, 763).

79. Mao Qiling, *Zhongyongshuo* III, 13b–14a.

80. Mao Shu Zheng (Zheng of Mao) was King Wu's younger brother and Kang Shu Feng (Kang of Feng) his younger half-brother. Grand Tutor Shangfu appears in the *Book of Songs*. He is also known as Qi Taigong and Lü Shang. He assisted King Wu in overthrowing Shang (Waley and Allen, 230; Legge, *Chinese Classics, IV*, 436). The statement attributed to Wen Hui appears a couple of paragraphs after the statement by Mao Qiling just cited, at Mao Qiling, *Zhongyongshuo*, III, 14b. Wenhui is citing a line found in *Shiji*, "Zhoubenji" [Annals of Zhou], line 17, at http://ctext.org/shiji/zhou-ben. Accessed January 1, 2016. It can also be found in Nienhauser, ed., *The Grand Scribe's Records* (Bloomington: Indiana University Press, 2018), Vol. I, 131–132. We also found this statement in *Xu Liji jishuo*, vol. 87, via the Erudition Database, where this statement is explicitly attributed to Mao Wenhui and is placed in a broader context in which Mao Wenhui uses this passage from the *Shiji* to argue for placing more importance on official rank than on generational ranking. Mao Wenhui was a near-contemporary of Mao Qiling and contributed to the editing of Mao's *Sishu gaicuo* [Correcting the errors in Zhu Xi's commentaries on the Four Books].

81. We were unable to identify Chen Ziceng other than that he was a Confucian scholar during the Qing and was an acquaintance of Mao Qiling.

82. This is a paraphrase of passages in the *Book of Rites*. Legge, I: 411–412; II: 33, 217–218, 241.

83. This statement by Chen Ziceng is found in Mao Qiling, *Zhongyongshuo*, III, 14a. It can also be found in *Xu Liji jishuo*, vol. 87, available via the Erudition Database.

84. Tasan here is relaying what is said in the *Book of Rites*, "She Yi" [The meaning of the Ceremony of Archery." Legge, II: 448.

85. *Book of Songs*, "Major Odes," "Decade of Sheng Min," "Xingwei." The translation is from Waley and Allen, *Book of Songs*, 247. See also Legge, *Chinese Classics, IV, She King*, 474.

86. Zhu Xi is referring to the line in this chapter which is translated by Roger Ames and David L. Hall, trans., *Focusing the Familiar: A Translation and Philosophical Interpretation of the Zhongyong* (Honolulu: University of Hawai'i Press, 2001), 99, as "they used the drinking pledges in which inferiors toast superiors as their way of reaching down to include the lowliest."

87. *Sishu jizhu*, 15 (Johnston and Wang, 445).

88. This is the poem "Luming" from the *Book of Songs*, "Minor Odes of the Kingdom," "Decade of Lu Ming," "Lu Ming." Waley and Allen, 133; Legge, *Chinese Classics, IV, She King*, 245–247.

89. John Steele, trans., *The I-li or the Book of Etiquette and Ceremonial*. The detailed description of the banquet rituals, which Tasan draws on here, can be found in Vol. I, 122–143.

90. *Book of Rites*, Legge, II: 456–57.

91. The impersonator normally is a grandson standing in for a deceased grandfather. *Book of Rites*, Legge, I: 337.

92. The *Zeng yun* [Expanded Rhymes] was a pronunciation dictionary compiled in the Song dynasty by the father and son Mao Huang and Mao Juzheng to indicate the proper pronunciation of Sinographs in ancient ritual texts.

93. Mao Qiling, *Zhongyongshuo*, III, 15b–16a.

94. *Shisanjing zhushu*, I: 1190. For a detailed description of the passing around of the wine cup during the sacrificial ritual, see Steele, *The I-li or the Book of Etiquette and Ceremonial*, II: 148–150. The definition of the Sinograph 旅 in this context as referring to the multitude can also be found in Johnston and Wang, 289 and 445.

95. *Shisanjing zhushu*, I: 1032. For a detailed description of the passing around of the wine cup as a part of the archery ritual, see Steele, *The I-li*, I: 155–163.

96. This line in Chapter XIX of the *Zhongyong* is usually read as "inferiors offered cups to superiors." Andrew Plaks, however, notes that there have been differences of opinion over how to read this line. To straddle those differences, he translates this line as "those of lower status are given precedence" (Plaks, 36, 92).

97. This explanation by Lou Zhanghuan (Lou Xiangming) can be found in *Xu Liji jishuo*, vol. 87, accessed via the Erudition Database, June 9, 2019.

98. The main text of the *Book of Etiquette and Ceremonial* does not provide that explanation. It is found in the commentary on that text, "Yili zhushu" [Notes and explanations of the *Yili*] (*Shisanjing zhushu*, I: 1016).

99. *The Rites of Xhou (Zhouli)*, the *Book of Rites (Liji)*, and the *Book of Etiquette and Ceremonial (Yili)*.

100. *Shisanjing zhushu*, I: 1186.

101. A mid-seventh century Tang dynasty commentator on the *Zhouli*. We have not been able to otherwise identify him. However, we found his comment in *Shisanjing zhushu*, I: 995, though it is not attributed to him there.

102. *Shisanjing zhushu*, I: 1186–1187; Steele, II: 145, 148–150.

103. Mao Qiling, *Zhongyongshuo*, III, 14b–15a.

104. This is the principal subcommentary on the *Erya*, written during Northern Song by Xing Bing (932–1010). For the Erya entry, see https://ctext.org/er-ya/shi-gu, line 154. Accessed June 19, 2020. *Shisanjing zhushu*, II: 2577.

105. "Quli," *The Book of Rites* (Legge, I: 84).

106. *Zhuzi yulei*, vol. 63 (p. 1557 of Beijing: Xinhua shudian, 1986, reprint). Available at https://ctext.org/zhuzi-yulei/63. Accessed June 9, 2019.

107. "Yousi che," *Book of Etiquette and Ceremonial*. Available at https://ctext.org/yili/you-si-che. Accessed June 20, 2020 (Steele, II: 179–214).

108. Mao Qiling, *Zhongyongshuo*, III: 16a–b.

109. Smaller sacrificial animals refers to sheep and pigs rather than bulls.

110. Tasan says he is referring to the ritual associated with the sacrificing of smaller animals, as described in the chapter with that title in the *Book of Etiquette and Ceremonial (Yili)*. However, the ritual he describes is in the next chapter of the *Yili*, the one called "The Assistant Clears Away." See Steele, *The I-Li*, II, 196–213.

111. *Sishu jizhu*, 14 (Johnston and Wang, 445).

112. This is Xu Qian (1270–1337).

113. *Book of Songs*, "Minor Odes," "Decade of Beishan," "chuci" (Waley and Allen, 195; Legge, *Chinese Classics, IV, She King*, 372).

114. Xu Qian. *Du Zhongyong congshuo* [A collection of accounts of reading the *Zhongyong*]. Accessed via the Erudition Database June 9, 2019.

115. A line in this chapter of the *Zhongyong* says, "They took into consideration

the color of the hair as their way of seating participants according to their seniority" (Ames and Hall, *Focusing the Familiar*, 99).

116. *The Book of Rites* listed ten differences among human beings to be observed in sacrificial rituals. The ninth involves "the order to be observed between old and young." Legge, *Book of Rites*, II, 245.

117. *Book of Songs*, "Major Odes," "Decade of Sheng Min," "Fu Yi" (Waley and Allen, 249–250; Legge, *Chinese Classics*, IV, *She King*, 479–481.

118. *Shisanjing zhushu*, I: 897.

119. *Book of Rites*, Legge, II: 246–247.

120. Mao Qiling, *Zhongyongshuo*, III: 17b–18a.

121. *Book of Rites*, Legge, II: 245.

122. *Book of Rites*, Legge, II: 248.

123. *Sishu jizhu*, 14 (Johnston and Wang, 445).

124. Zhang Taizhan was a scholar and official who was a disciple of the Qing scholar Mao Qiling. Taizhan was his literary name. His actual name was Zhang Dalai. No information on when he was born or when he died is available.

125. Mao Qiling cites Zhang Dalai making this remark in Mao Qiling, *Zhongyongshuo*, III: 19a. Spirit tablets are kept in the ancestral shrine, and rituals are held in their honor there, for only a few generations. After that, they are moved to the family mausoleum.

126. This is a shortened version of a line in this chapter.

127. This is also a paraphrase of a line in this chapter.

128. In *Chungyong chajam*, II: 3: 18b–19a, Tasan reinforces his agreement with Zhu Xi that this section refers to the rites in the ancestral shrine of the ruling family. He writes that the reference to those held in high esteem is a reference to the ancestors of former kings, and the reference to those held dear is a reference to the descendants of former rulers. However, he notes, the same general rule applies to commoners as well. If we care for our parents, we must love our brothers. If we care for our grandfathers, we must love our uncles as well.

129. *Sishu jizhu*, 14 (Johnston and Wang, 444).

130. These are the clauses that say we should "repair the ancestral shrine, arrange the ritual utensils properly, provide the proper ritual clothes, offer the proper ritual food...stand in the *zhao* or *mu* lines, offer toasts all around, and take our places as ritual participants according to rank as well as according to age."

131. He is referring to the references to King Wu and the Duke of Zhou as paragons of filial piety in the first two lines of Chapter XIX.

132. In his comments in his *Chungyong chajam* on Chapter XVIII of the *Zhongyong*, Tasan argues that the sentences at the beginning of Chapter XIX about King Wu and the Duke of Zhou actually belong in Chapter XVIII. Otherwise, we might get the mistaken impression that King Wu and the Duke of Zhou created those procedures for proper ritual displays of respect for ancestors. See *Chungyong chajam*, II: 3: 17b.

133. *Sishu jizhu*, 14 (Johnston and Wang, 445).

134. Hu Hong (1106–1162). Wufeng is his literary name.

135. *Zhuzi yulei*, 90. Available at https://ctext.org/zhuzi-yulei/90. Accessed June 14, 2019.

136. *Shisanjing zhushu*, I: 757.

137. Mo of Cai was a scribe who was known for his knowledge of esoteric matters such as dragons and various spiritual beings. See Durrant, Li, and Schaberg, III: 1697.

138. Legge, *Chinese Classics V*, "Ch'un Ts'ew with the Tso Chuen," 731 (Durrant, Li, and Schaberg, III: 1701). Each of those spirits is responsible for one of the Five Agents. For example, Guo Mang is responsible for wood and Rushou is responsible for metal. Also, each spirit is assigned responsibility for one of the five seasons of the year. See the "Yueling" chapter in the *Book of Rites* (Legge, I: 249–310). Also see Alfred Forke, trans., Wang Chong, "Jiyi" [The meaning of sacrifices], in *Lun-Heng: Part 1, Philosophical Essays of Wang Ch'ung* (London: Luzac & Co., 1907), I: 518.

139. Zhu Rong is one of those five spirits and is responsible for fire. This passage can be seen at https://ctext.org/guo-yu/zhou-yu-shang. Accessed June 14, 2019.

140. Chongshan is said to have been located near where the capital of the legendary Xia dynasty had been.

141. This story can be found at https://ctext.org/guo-yu/zhou-yu-shang. Accessed June 14, 2019.

142. *Guoyu*, https://ctext.org/guo-yu/jin-yu-er. Accessed June 14, 2019.

143. Earlier Tasan wrote those spirits were terrestrial spirits because they originated as human beings, and he repeats that statement in the next paragraph. However, here he grants them the label of celestial spirits because of their responsibilities.

144. In *Chungyong chajam*, II: 3:19a, Tasan points out that the ancient texts talk about rituals to show respect for the Lord on High and the celestial spirits. Moreover, rituals showing respect for the celestial spirits were actually honoring the Lord on High. Nothing is said in those ancient text about the "God of the Earth" in conjunction with those rituals. Tasan therefore argues that the lack of any mention of the God of the Earth in this line is not simply a way to shorten that sentence. He doesn't belong there.

145. Legge, *Chinese Classics V*, "Ch'un Ts'ew with the Tso Chuen," 731 (Durrant, Li, and Schaberg, III: 1699–1701).

146. Xuan Ming was a god of water.

147. These are all described in legends as particularly exemplary human beings in ancient Chinese history who were later enshrined as the spirits of the respective areas in which they excelled. Together they are responsible to the harmonious interactions of the Five Agents (soil, wood, metal, water, and fire). Legge, *Chinese Classics V*, "Ch'un Ts'ew with the Tso Chuen," 731 (Durrant, Li, and Schaberg, III: 1701).

148. *Shisanjing zhushu*, II, 2123.

149. Available at https://ctext.org/gongyang-zhuan/xuan-gong-san-nian/zh. Accessed June 14, 2019. As Tasan reads this passage, "those who come from within" should be understood as human spirits, and "those who come from without" should be understood as celestial spirits. The standard interpretation, however, takes this statement as referring to the living descendants (those who come from within) as

well as the ancestors (those who come from without) participating when a ruler sacrifices to Heaven. See Miller, trans., *The Gongyang Commentary*, 148.

150. "Xiaojing zhushu," *Shisanjing zhushu*, II: 2553.

151. Mt. Kunlun is a mythical mountain believed to be to the far west of China and to be the capital of the legendary Yellow Emperor.

152. The *taicou* pitch has been correlated with both the first month of the year and as representing humanity in the triad of Heaven, Earth, and Humanity. See Youlan Feng and Derk Bodde, trans., *A History of Chinese Philosophy*, Vol. II (Princeton, NJ: Princeton University Press, 1983), 118–121.

153. Legge, *Book of Rites*, I: 225.

154. *Yijing*, "Shuo Gua," X; Lynn, *The Classic of Changes*, 123.

155. *Yijing*, "Shuo Gua," XIII-IX; Lynn, *The Classic of Changes*, 123. "Shuo Gua" 8: "Qian has the nature of a horse; Kun, that of an ox." "Shuo Gua" 9: "Qian works like the head; Kun, like the stomach."

156. See http://ctext.org/xiao-jing for the complete text of the *Classic of Filial Piety*. This is a commonly abbreviated version of a line in Chapter XVI. Also see Rosemont and Ames, *The Chinese Classic of Family Reverence*, 114.

157. This appears to be a reference to a line in the *Chunqiu ganjing fu* [Tallies of Spiritual Resonance in the Spring and Autumn Annals]. That text itself was unavailable to us. The earliest possible reference we could find to this text making this statement is in *Suihua jili*, which is presented as having been written in the Tang dynasty by Han E (?–?), though scholars suspect it actually is a much later forgery, possibly from the Ming. (See http://www.chinaknowledge.de/Literature/Diverse/yulingzi.html.) We accessed *Suihua jili* via the Erudition database. Accessed June 14, 2019.

158. This shows Tasan's preference for precise and narrowly defined references for terms rather than allowing terms to have such a broad range of meanings that they are hard to pin down and therefore permit confused reasoning.

159. One line both Zhu Xi and Tasan found suspicious is in Chapter IX of the *Xiaojing* [Classic of Filial Piety]. That line reads "Duke Zhou performed the *jiao* sacrifice on the outskirts of the capital to the first ancestor of the Zhou, Houji, to place him on a par with *Tian*" (See Rosemont and Ames, *Chinese Classic of Family Reverence*, 110). This did not seem accurate to Tasan since Houji was the god of the earth and should not be confused with *Tian* (Heaven), especially since the god of the earth is subordinate to *Tian*.

160. Tasan is correct to say that remark purportedly by Zhu Xi is not widely known. We could not find it attributed to Zhu Xi anywhere except in this statement by Tasan. However, it was widely known that Zhu Xi believed that much of what people in his day thought of as the *Xiaojing* was not in the original *Xiaojing* but instead consisted of later interpolations. See Rosemont and Ames, 20.

161. *Yŏyudang chŏnsŏ*, II, 33, *Ch'unch'u kojing* [An evidential analysis of the Spring and Autumn Annals], I, 10a–15a.

162. *Sishu jizhu*, 14 (Johnston and Wang, 445).

163. *Zhouli*, "Spring Offices," "xiaozongbo" in *Shisanjing zhushu*, I, 766.

164. *Zhouli*, "Autumn Offices, Minister of Justice," "qiuguan dasikou," in *Shisan-*

jing zhushu, I, 871. The Five Emperors are the legendary emperors who were believed to have ruled China in the 3rd millennium BCE.

165. *Guoyu*, "Discourses of Chu (Chuyu), B." Available at https://ctext.org/guo-yu/chu-yu-xia/zhs. Accessed June 14, 2019.

166. *Guoyu*, "Discourses of Zhou (Zhouyu), B." Accessed on June 14, 2019 at https://ctext.org/guo-yu/zhou-yu-zhong/zhs.

167. Legge, *Book of Rites*, II, 42, 60.

168. Guoyu, "Discourses of Lu, A." Accessed on June 14, 2019 at https://ctext.org/guo-yu/lu-yu-shang/zhs. Legge, *Book of Rites*, II: 201–202. Ku was one of the legendary emperors who supposedly reigned in the 3rd millennium BCE.

169. Legge, *Ch'un Ts'ew with the Tso Chuen*, 658 (Durrant, Li, and Schaberg, III: 1523).

170. Legge, *Book of Rites*, I, 225–226, II, 210.

171. *Analects*, III: 11. The translation of the relevant passage by Slingerland (on page 21) is as follows: "Someone asked for an explanation of the *di* sacrifice. The Master said, "I do not understand it. One who understood it could handle the world as if he had it right here," and he pointed to the palm of his hand. The line in this chapter of the *Zhongyong* says that if someone could understand these rituals, they would find it as easy to rule a kingdom as it is to place something in the palm of their hand.

172. In *Chungyong chajam*, II, 3: 19a, Tasan writes that the discussion surrounding the statement about ruling a kingdom makes a key point for this text. He does not go on to explicitly state what that point is, but he implies that you have to realize that these rituals are all directed toward the Lord on High in order to develop the moral strength to be a good ruler.

173. Legge, *Book of Rites*, I, 418.

174. Legge, *Book of Rites*, II, 210.

175. Legge, *Book of Rites*, II, 249–250.

176. Legge, *Book of Rites*, II, 271–272.

177. The only references to the *di* ritual in the *Analects* are in 3:10 and 3:11 (Slingerland, 21). This is where Confucius is cited as saying that he does not fully understand the *di* ritual.

178. "Shi" [示] is the Sinograph that precedes the phrase "in the palm of your hand" in the last line of chapter XIX. Some commentators read that Sinograph as "display." Zheng Xuan disagrees.

179. Johnston and Wang, 287.

180. Bao Xian (6 BCE–65 CE) was a Han dynasty official respected as an expert on the *Analects*. This statement by him is found in *Shisanjing zhushu*, II, 2467.

181. *Sishu jizhu*, 14 (Johnston and Wang, 445).

182. Kangcheng is the literary name of Zheng Xuan, the famous Han dynasty commentator (Johnston and Wang, 287).

183. Zhang Taizhan is the Qing Confucian philosopher Zhang Dalai. He is cited saying this in Mao Qiling's *Zhongyongshuo*, III, 21b.

184. "Lessons from the States," "Odes of Zhou and the South," "Juan Er." Legge, *Chinese Classics*, IV, *She King*, 8 (Waley and Allen, 7).

185. "Minor Odes of the Kingdom," "Decade of Lu Ming," "Lu Ming." Legge, *Chinese Classics, IV*, 245; Waley and Allen, 133. Waley and Allen translate that line as "will teach me the ways of Zhou."

186. *Xunzi*, chapter 27, "Grand Digest" (Hutton, 308).

Zhongyong XX

1. Lord Ai was a ruler of the state of Lu during the 5th century BCE.

2. Mao Qiling, *Zhongyongshuo*, IV: 1b. Mao Qiling's citation from the *Book of Etiquette and Ceremonial* can be found in Steele, I, 232.

3. Johnston and Wang, 293.

4. *Sishu jishu*, 14 (Johnston and Wang, 449). Shen Kuo (1031–1095) was a well-known philosopher, scientist, inventor, and statesman during the Song period. He served at one time as the chancellor of the Hanlin Academy.

5. *Sishu huowen*, 82 (Pak Wansik, 483).

6. *Dadai Liji* [Records of ritual matters by the Elder Dai] is available at https://ctext.org/da-dai-li-ji/xia-xiao-zheng, "Xiaxiaozheng" [The small calendar of the Xia]. Accessed June 14, 2019.

7. A bollworm wasp is a parasitic wasp that was believed to steal the larvae of bollworms to raise in its own nest and, in the process, transform that larvae into a wasp just like itself, rather than transforming itself into something else.

8. This entire exchange can be found at *Sishu huowen, 82* (Pak Wansik, 483).

9. A book by Ming dynasty official and poet Huangfu Fang (1497–1582).

10. This citation of *Some New Words for Breaking into Laughter* [Jieyi xinyu] is found in Mao Qiling, *Sishu shengyan* [Jottings on the Four Books], Vol. I. It was located via the Erudition database. Accessed on June 14, 2019.

11. The *Erya* section on insects (*shi chong*) can be found at https://ctext.org/er-ya/shi-chong. Accessed June 14, 2019. But that is not exactly what the *Erya* says. The *Erya* says the bollworm wasp (the *guoluo*) is also called *pulu*. A few lines above, it says that the mud wasp (which later came to be another name for the bollworm wasp, since it builds nests out of mud) is another name for the wood wasp. For more information on the bollworm wasp (the *guoluo*), see Mark Elvin, "Scientific Curiosity in China and Europe: Natural History in the late Ming and the Eighteenth Century," in Ts'ui-Jung Liu, ed., *Environmental History in East Asia: Interdisciplinary Perspectives* (New York: Routledge, 2014), 22–23. The bollworm wasp preys on the caterpillar larvae of the bollworm moth.

12. Legge, *Chinese Classics* IV, "Decade of Xiao Min," "Xiaowan," 334; Wiley and Allen, 176.

13. This is from Kong Yingda's subcommentary to the *Zhongyong*. Johnston and Wang, 297.

14. Mao Qiling, *Zhongyongshuo*, IV: 1b–2a. For Zhu Xi's claim that *pulu* should be read as "rushes and reeds," see Johnston and Wang, 440.

15. Yang and Song, ed. *Kongzi jiayu tongjie*, 208. This text is also available at https://ctext.org/kongzi-jiayu/ai-gong-wen-zheng. Accessed June 16, 2019.

16. Han Wo, 844–923. Late Tang–era poet.

17. Han's "Anbin shi" can be found in *Quantangshi,* vol. 681, available at https://ctext.org/quantangshi/681. Accessed July 4, 2020. I draw on the English translation of this poem in Beth Ann Upton, "The Poetry of Han Wo (844–923," unpublished doctoral dissertation, University of California, Berkeley, 1980, 106.

18. Mao Qiling, *Zhongyongshuo,* IV, 2a.

19. *Sishu huowen* 82 (Pak Wansik 483)

20. *Jinshu* (the history of the Jin kingdom, 265–420) was compiled in the seventh century by Tang dynasty officials.

21. *Jinshu,* vol. 26, "Food and Commodities. Available at https://zh.wikisource.org/wiki/晉書/卷026. Accessed June 16, 2019.

22. *Jinshu,* vol. 106, "Shi Jilong Part One." Available at https://zh.wikisource.org/wiki/晉書/卷106. Accessed June 16, 2019.

23. Liu Xin (46 BCE–23 CE), "Ganquan-gong fu" [Rhapsody of the Sweet Spring Palace] in *Yuding lidai fuhui* [Collection of prose poems by dynasty], vol. 72, available at https://zh.wikisource.org/wiki/御定歷代賦彙_(四庫全書本)/卷072. Accessed July 2, 2020.

24. *Huainanzi,* "Fanlunxun," 15. See John S. Major, Sarah Q. Queen, Andrew S. Meyer, and Harold D. Roth, trans., *The Huainanzi* (New York: Columbia University Press, 2010), 507.

25. "Kongque dongnan fei" 孔雀東南飛. A famous Han dynasty ballad by an unknown author.

26. Available at http://www.shicimingju.com/chaxun/list/15753.html. Accessed July 4, 2020. For more on this poem, including an English translation, see Hans H. Frankel, "The Chinese Ballad 'Southeast Fly the Peacocks,'" in *Harvard Journal of Asiatic Studies* 34 (1974): 248–271.

27. Cai Qing, *Sishu mengyin,* Vol. IV, at https://ctext.org/wiki.pl?if=gb&chapter=277936. Also available via the Erudition database.

28. Li Shizhen, *Bencao Gangmu,* vol. 39. Accessed via the Erudition database, June 16, 2019.

29. In *Chungyong chajam,* Tasan writes that *pulu* needs to be read as "bollworm wasp" instead of as "rushes and reeds" because the point this passage in the *Zhongyong* is making is that, just as a bollworm wasp can turn bollworm larvae into wasps, so too can a wise ruler ensure that governing is done properly so that people can reach their full potential as ethical beings. Just as bollworm larvae can never turn into wasps in the absence of the bollworm wasp, so, too, will good government fail to materialize in the absence of the proper ruler. In his view, the line in this chapter about "The Dao of the Earth stimulates plants to grow quickly" is so closely related to the preceding line about "The Dao of Humans is to govern properly" that the reading of *pulu* as "rushes and reeds" rather than bollworm wasps is incorrect (*Chungyong chajam,* II: 3: 19a).

30. In *Chungyong chajam,* II, 3:19a, Tasan elaborates further, saying that in the *Kongzi jiayu* we can see that material was lifted from the *Zhongyong* starting with this section all the way down to the section on the Nine Cardinal Rules and modi-

fied to make that material appear that all of it was one conversation Confucius had with Lord Ai.

31. *Sishu jizhu*, 15 (Johnston and Wang, 449). Also see Yang and Song, ed., *Kongzi jiayu tongjie*, 208. This line in the *Zhongyong* ends with "the right people are chosen by *shen*." Plaks translates this line as "the ground for selecting human capacity lies in the ruler's own individual character" (Plaks, 37). Ames and Hall have a slightly different translation: "one gets the right persons with one's own character" (Ames and Hall, 101).

32. *Yijing*, "Xici zhuan, xia." Lynn, *Classic of Changes*, 90.

33. Tasan is arguing that the line from this chapter, "故為政在人, 取人以身, 修身以道, 修道以仁" has to be read with the same meanings for the same Sinographs. For example, 身 in the second clause should be given the same meaning it has in the third clause, which is the self that is cultivated, and, therefore, the Sinograph for human being in the first clause must refer to a man who has cultivated his moral character. You cannot read the second clause as referring to the ruler [身] selecting the proper person and then read the very next clause as saying a person [身] cultivates his moral character by aligning with the Dao. Tasan demands consistency in the way Sinographs in phrases such as this are read and therefore sees Zhu Xi's reading as contorted.

34. *Sishu jizhu*, 15 (Johnston and Wang, 449).

35. This is line 5 of this chapter of the *Zhongyong*.

36. Tasan noted, in *Chungyong chajam*, II, 3: 19b, that cultivating the Dao [the Way we ought to behave] is called education. He goes on to point out that true education focuses on five areas: relations with our father, relations with our mother, relations with our older brothers, relations with our younger brothers, and relations with our children. That is why, he says, we can read both in Mencius (7B, 12; Van Norden 189) and in the "Biao Ji" chapter in the *Book of Rites* (*Liji*, "Biao Ji," 14; Legge, trans., *Li Chi*, II, 333) that "To be '*ren*' is to be truly human." He adds that no one in ancient times said anything about the term *ren* referring to that which begets all things.

37. *Sishu jizhu*, 15 (Johnston and Wang, 448). Zhu Xi reads this passage as referring to rulers. Tasan reads it as referring to anyone who wants to cultivate a moral character.

38. We found this statement attributed to an otherwise unidentified Chen in Hu Guang, *Sishu daquan*, "Zhongyong zhangju daquan-shang." Available at https://zh.wikisource.org/wiki/四書大全_(四庫全書本)/中庸章句大全上. Accessed December 11, 2022. As noted earlier, this is probably Chen Li.

39. *Liji*, "Xueji," 16: Legge, *Li Chi* II: XVI, 90–91.

40. Tasan is drawing here on the Confucian notion of the rectification of names, which says that a name is more normative than descriptive and therefore a human being is not a real human being unless he or she acts in the way a human being should act. In other words, only a human being who relates to other human beings appropriately is a true human being.

41. In *Chungyong chajam*, II, 3: 19b, Tasan writes that the *Zhongyong* tells us that understanding Heaven is the foundation for the cultivation of a moral character

since only after we truly understand Heaven will we be appropriately responsive and unselfishly cooperative. He adds that the *Great Learning*, on the other hand, tells us that we need a desire to be appropriately responsive and unselfishly cooperative in order to cultivate a moral character. He concludes that those two texts are actually saying the same thing, since, if we truly understand Heaven, we will know that Heaven can see everything we think and do. Such knowledge will motivate us to be watchful over our thoughts and actions at all times and in all places and that, in turn, will ensure that we are appropriately responsive and unselfishly cooperative.

42. Acting in a benevolent manner (being fully human and acting unselfishly), acting appropriately (acting righteously), acting in accordance with the principles of propriety (acting politely), and acting wisely are usually listed as the four fundamental ways of displaying ethical virtuosity.

43. These four trigrams are *zhen* 震 ☳ (the beginning of movement in the right direction), *dui* 兌 ☱ (achieving something good), *li* 離 ☲ (taking action in the right place at the right time), and *kan* 坎 ☵ (taking action to mitigate a potentially dangerous situation). *Yijing,* "Shuogua" IV-XVIII; Lynn, *Classic of Changes,* 121–124.

44. *Mencius,* 2A6.6 (Van Norden, 46–47). In that passage, Mencius links the Four Sprouts to benevolence, righteousness, propriety, and wisdom respectively.

45. In *Chungyong chajam,* II, 3: 19b, Tasan writes that to understand what it means to be a real human being means to understand what it is that makes a human being a real human being. A human being becomes a real human being by acting in accordance with the innate potential for acting appropriately Heaven has conferred on him or her. Understanding that what Heaven has conferred is the Dao and heeding what it tells you to do is what is meant by understanding what it means to be a real human being.

46. *Sishu jizhu,* 15 (Johnston and Wang, 448). Tasan truncates this passage to focus on the Five Cardinal Patterns of Appropriate Interactions mentioned in the *Book of Documents.* Legge, *Chinese Classics* III, *Shoo King,* "The canon of Shun," 31. The term "Five Cardinal Patterns of Appropriate Interactions" is not defined here but it is understood to refer to the five cardinal principles of interactions within the human community.

47. Legge, *Chinese Classics* III: *Shoo King,* 44.

48. Legge, *Chinese Classics* III: *Shoo King,* 580.

49. Xie is a legendary forerunner of the lineage that later established the Shang dynasty.

50. Legge, *Chinese Classics* III: *Shoo King,* 44.

51. Legge, *Chinese Classics* V, *Ch'un Ts'ew with the Tso Chuen,* 279 (Durrant, Li, and Schaberg, I, 565).

52. Ji Wenzi and Zang Wenzhong were officials in the state of Lu during the Spring and Autumn period.

53. This is a title of the legendary Emperor Diku, who is the legendary emperor Yao's father.

54. This story refers to an incident in which an evil ruler was killed by his own son, who then fled to a neighboring state. During discussion at court over whether to

give sanctuary to a man who murdered his own father, the five precepts were cited as the criteria by which to determine whether someone was moral (and worthy of sanctuary) or not. Scholars in Chosŏn Korea who had memorized the *Zuo Commentary* would immediately recognize this reference. Legge, *Chinese Classics* V, *Ch'un Ts'ew with the Tso Chuen*, 279–280 (Durrant, Li, and Schaberg, I: 571–573).

55. See *Mencius*, 3A 4 (Van Norden, 71).

56. Tang is the legendary emperor Yao, and Yu is the legendary emperor Shun.

57. An official in the state of Qi in the seventh century BCE. He is the reputed author of the book named after him, the *Guanzi*. In the tenth chapter of the *Guanzi*, "Wu fu" [The five aids], there is a reference to six important family roles (father, son, older brother, younger brother, husband, and wife). Available at https://ctext.org/guanzi/wu-fu. Accessed July 11, 2020.

58. Legge, *Chinese Classics* V, *Ch'un Ts'ew with the Tso Chuen*, 11–12 (Durrant, Li, and Schaberg, I: 27).

59. *Liji* "Wang zhi"; Legge, *Li Chi* I, 248.

60. Yan Ying (578–500 BCE) was a prime minister of Qi during the Spring and Autumn period. See Yuri Pines, *Foundations of Confucian Thought: Intellectual Life in the Chunqiu Period, 722–453 B.C.E.* (Honolulu: University of Hawai'i Press, 2002), 101–103. Though Yan Ying's ways of acting appropriately are called "Ten Forms of Etiquette/Ritual," they have nothing to do with either ritual or etiquette. Instead, they are statements of how people from the ruler on down to daughters-in-law should behave in a hierarchical social order. Also see Legge, *Chinese Classics* V, *Ch'un Ts'ew with the Tso Chuen*, 715 (Durrant, Li, and Schaberg, III: 1671).

61. *Liji*, Book VII; Legge, "Li Yun or Ceremonial Usages," *Li Chi* I, 379–380.

62. *Liji*, Book XXII: 13; Legge, "Ji Tong or a Summary Account of Sacrifices," *Li Chi* II, 245.

63. *Mencius*, 3A, 4 (Van Norden, 71).

64. See the commentaries by Zheng Zuan and Kong Yingda on this line. Johnston and Wang, 294, 298.

65. Mao Qiling, *Zhongyongshuo*, IV: 5b–6b.

66. Johnston and Wang, 294.

67. Johnston and Wang, 297.

68. The Five August Emperors are legendary figures from China's mythical ancient past. They are Huangdi, Zhuanxu, Gaoxin, Yao, and Shun.

69. Legge, *Chinese Classics III, Shoo King*, 31.

70. Kong Anguo was a direct descendant of Confucius who was active in the late second century BCE. He is best known for deciphering a version of the *Book of Documents* written in archaic script that was said to have been hidden in a wall of the home of Confucius to escape the anti-Confucian measures of the Qin dynasty.

71. *Shisanjing zhushu*, I, 125.

72. Legge, *Chinese Classics* III: *Shoo King*, 44.

73. Legge, *Chinese Classics* III: *Shoo King*, 44.

74. *Shisanjing zhushu*, I, 130.

75. Legge, *Chinese Classics* III: *Shoo King*, 73.

76. Legge, *Chinese Classics III: Shoo King*, 580.

77. Mao Qiling, *Sishu shengyan*, vol. 6, *Sishu shengyan bu*, vol. 2 [A supplement to Residual Remarks about the Four Books]. Accessed via the Erudition database, July 12, 2020.

78. Legge, *Chinese Classics V, Ch'un Ts'ew with the Tso Chuen*, 715 (Durrant, Li, and Schaberg, III: 1671).

79. *Discussions in the White Tiger Hall (Baihutong)* is a record of discussions on philosophical, political, and cosmological matters supposedly held in the White Tiger Hall in Han China in 79 CE. The discussion of the Three Major and Six Minor Principles (*sangang liuji*) is in chapter 7 of that text. Available at https://ctext.org/bai-hu-tong/juan-qi. Accessed June 21, 2019.

80. Mao Qiling, *Sishu shengyan*, vol. 6, *Sishu shengyan bu*, vol. 2 [A supplement to Residual Remarks about the Four Books]. Accessed via the Erudition database, July 12, 2020.

81. Zhang Dalai.

82. *Analects* 18:7; Slingerland, 218.

83. Cited in Mao Qiling, *Zhongyongshuo*, IV, 7a.

84. Mao Wenhui was a scholar-official in the late seventeenth and early eighteenth centuries.

85. *Liji*, Book XXII: 13; Legge, "Ji Tong or a Summary Account of Sacrifices," *Li Chi II*, 245.

86. Cited in Mao Qiling, *Zhongyongshuo*, IV, 7a–b. Mao Wenhui appears to be paraphrasing the commentaries in *Shisanjing zhushu*, 1604–1605. We were unable to find the exact statements he cites.

87. King Chŏngjo is referring to a line in Zhu Xi's commentary on *Analects*, 6: 3: "Lunyu," *Sishu jizhu*, 34. In that line, Zhu Xi defines the five core features of our moral nature as benevolence, righteousness, propriety, wisdom, and fidelity.

88. *Mencius*, IIA, 6: Van Norden, 46–47.

89. In *Chungyong chajam*, II, 3: 20a, Tasan says that, since the five aspects of the Dao everyone must conform to as well as the three character traits necessary for ethical virtuosity all refer to actions rather than innate traits, they can all be boiled down to one thing: acting with full "sincerity" (*cheng*), in other words acting in a manner that is appropriately responsive while also being unselfishly cooperative. Moreover, "sincerity" in this sense is the Dao of Heaven. You need to understand what Heaven is in order to align yourself with it and act in a manner that is appropriately responsive and unselfishly cooperative.

90. *Sishu jizhu*, 16 (Johnston and Wang, 450).

91. This passage says that whether you understand basic moral principles easily, have to vigorously study to learn them, or have to struggle to learn them, what you learn is one and the same. Similarly, whether you find it natural to act appropriately, you have to be driven by a desire to better yourself in order to act appropriately, or you find you have to struggle and exert a tremendous amount of effort to act appropriately, the end result is one and the same.

92. Tasan writes in *Chungyong chajam*: II, 3: 20b, that the phrase normally trans-

lated as "acting in order to gain personal benefit" [*lixing* 利行] is actually an older way of writing "make a strenuous effort" and should therefore be understood with the latter meaning in this ancient text.

93. *Analects*, 12:1; Slingerland, 125.

94. *Sishu jizhu*, 16 (Johnston and Wang, 450). The material within the parentheses are comments added by Tasan.

95. *Sishu huowen*, 83 (Pak Wansik, 485).

96. *Analects*, 4.2; Slingerland, 29. Our translation differs from Slingerland's translation because we reflect Tasan's reading of *lixing* as "making a strenuous effort."

97. *Liji*, "Biaoji" 14. Legge, *Li Chi (Book of Rites)*, II: 333.

98. *Record of Ritual Matters by Dai the Elder* is said to have been compiled during the former Han dynasty. It is said to be by Dai the Elder to distinguish it from a similar work by his nephew, known as Dai the Younger. It is available at https://ctext.org/da-dai-li-ji/ceng-zi-li-shi/zh. Accessed June 25, 2019.

99. An alternative name for Zhang Zai.

100. This may be a reference to the statement in *Zhangzi yulu zhong* [Records of what Zhangzi said-B] in which Zhang Zai is cited as saying that being fully human is like the peace and quiet in a mountain, and wisdom is like the ocean being inexhaustible. You cannot say one is better than the other. They complement each other. Available at https://zh.wikisource.org/zh-hant/張載集#張子語錄·語錄中. Accessed June 25, 2019.

101. *Hanshu*, 58: "Zhuan," "Gongsun Hong, Bu Shi, and Er Kuan." Available at https://ctext.org/han-shu/gong-sun-hong-bu-shi-er. Accessed June 27, 2019.

102. *Sishu jizhu*, 16 (Johnston and Wang, 452). Since most of the first sections of Chapter XX are presented as a part of a continuous reply by Confucius to a question from Lord Ai, Zhu Xi points out that there does not appear to be any need to stick "The Master said..." in the middle of that speech.

103. Scholar-official during the reign of Kangxi (r. 1661–1722). Adopted son of Mao Qiling.

104. *Kongzi jiayu tongjie*, "Aigong wen zheng," 209. Also available at https://ctext.org/kongzi-jiayu/ai-gong-wen-zheng. Accessed June 25, 2019. Mao Yuanzhong is trying to explain why the *Zhongyong* has an unnecessary "the Master said" phrase in the middle of what is presented in the *Zhongyong* as a continuous speech by Confucius. The text in *Kongzi jiayu* is identical to what we see in the *Zhongyong*, except for the addition of the statement by Lord Ai (cited by Mao) right before the second "the Master said..." Much of Chapter XX is identical to the "Aigong wen zheng" chapter in *Kongzi jiayu*, except that, after Lord Ai's initial question, there are three more places where *Kongzi jiayu* has Lord Ai ask Confucius a question. Each time, the question is followed by "The Master said" before the *Kongzi jiayu* gives the response of Confucius. However, in *Zhongyong* Lord Ai's subsequent questions are dropped. Moreover, the only place in Chapter XX we see "the Master said" is after the first question, which is cited in the *Zhongyong*. The subsequent questions which appear in *Kongzi jiayu* are left out of the *Zhongyong* account of this conversation between Confucius and Lord Ai.

105. Confucius replied, "To love learning brings one close to acting wisely."

106. This statement by Mao Yuanzhong is cited in Mao Qiling, *Zhongyongshuo,* IV, 8b.

107. *Zhuzi quanshu* [The complete works of Zhu Xi], vol. 1 (Taibei: Guangxueshe yunshu guan, 1977), 557, lays out Zhu Xi's argument that all but the last few lines in Chapter XX can be trusted as an account of a conversation Confucian had with Lord Ai. A shorter version of that claim can be found in *Sishu jizhu,* 20 (Johnston and Wang, 460). Tasan's disagreement with Zhu Xi on this point is spelled out in XX: 18.

108. That passage is at the beginning of Chapter XX.

109. Those three ways to be fully human are, first, being able from birth to easily act appropriately; second, to work hard to act appropriately after studying what to do; and, third, learning correct behavior with great difficulty and then having to exert tremendous effort to act in accordance with what has been learned.

110. *Sishu jizhu,* 16 (Johnston and Wang, 452).

111. See the previous chapter, in which Tasan criticizes Zhu Xi's interpretation of XX: 9.

112. Lou Zhaizhong, an associate of Mao Qiling. Mao frequently cites Lou in his commentaries on the *Zhongyong.*

113. *Shijing,* "Decade of Dang," "Sang Rou." Legge, *She King,* 523 (Waley and Allen, 268).

114. This statement by Lou Zhaizhong appears in *Xu liji jishuo,* vol. 88. We located this citation via the Erudition database. Though "benefit" and "power" are pronounced differently in Korean, with power pronounced *yŏk* and benefit pronounced *yi,* in Chinese they are pronounced exactly the same.

115. Tasan believes that Lou has got it backward. He believes that we should read 利 as "make a strenuous effort" rather than read 力 as "to benefit." Tasan writes in *Chungyong chajam,* II, 3: 20b, that the phrase read literally as "acting in order to gain benefit [利行]" is actually an older way of writing "make a strenuous effort [力行]" and should therefore be understood as including the latter meaning in this ancient text.

116. There are many works with this title, but this is most likely a work by the Song scholar Su Shi 1039–1101), also known as Su Dongpo, since Tasan links Su Shi with this title in other essays.

117. *Sishu jizhu,* 16 (Johnston and Wang, 452). Zhu Xi is citing Lü Dalin here. "Next" in this sentence means that treating relatives with proper affection comes right after the cultivation of a personal moral character and recognizing, and respecting, the worthy.

118. See the comments on *Zhongyong* XX: 7.

119. Tasan explains in *Chungyong chajam,* II, 3: 20b, that this is advice to a ruler to refrain from treating his officials ("the worthy") as mere officials and to treat all the members of the royal family with affection. He then explains that this is not a reference to serving your parents properly, since serving your parents properly is the core practice in cultivating one's own moral character and therefore comes first.

120. *Sishu jizhu,* 17 (Johnston and Wang, 452).

121. Mao Qiling, "*Zhongyongshuo*" [On the *Zhongyong*], IV: 11b–12a; 119.

122. *Sishu jizhu*, 17 (Johnston and Wang, 452).

123. *Zhouli*, "Dongguan: kaogongji" (Winter Ministry: the Artificer's Record) (*Shisanjing zhushu*, I: 909).

124. *Zhouli*, "Tianguan: zhongzai" (Celestial Ministry: the Prime Minister) (*Shisanjing zhushu*, I: 647).

125. Suiren is the legendary sage, from five thousand years ago, who was said to have been the first person to discover how to make fire.

126. *Sishu huowen*, 83 (Pak Wansik, 486).

127. *Zhouli*, "Tianguan: zhongzai" (Celestial Ministry: Prime Minister) (*Shisanjing zhushu*, I: 646).

128. Kang Shu, Dan Ji, Cheng Shuwu, and Mao Shuzheng were all younger brothers of King Wu.

129. *Sishu huowen*, 84 (Pak Wansik, 491).

130. Legge, *Li Chi: Book of Rites*, I: 375 (*Shisanjing zhushu*, II: 1418).

131. The reference to stipend lands being for the sons and younger brothers is in a commentary in the "estate manager" section of the "Ministry of Education" chapter of the *Zhouli* (diguan situ-xia, zaishi) (*Shisanjing zhushu*, I: 725). Tasan is relying on the *Xu Liji jishuo*, vol. 88, which uses the exact same language Tasan uses here in citing both the *Book of Rites* and the *Zhouli*.

132. This is Mao Qiling. Hang Shijun, the editor of the *Xu Liji jishuo*, has inserted a long commentary by Mao in vol. 88. Accessed via the Erudition database, July 2, 2019.

133. Johnston and Wang, 306.

134. We found this citation in *Xu Liji*, vol. 88, via the Erudition database. The *Xu Sishu jishuo* may have been a late Ming compilation of several commentaries on the Four Books. However, there appear to have been many works with this title. The *Xu Liji jishuo* attributes this statement to Kong Yingda, not to *Sishu jishuo*. See Johnston and Wang, 308, for a statement by Kong Yingda very similar to what Tasan cites here.

135. *Zuozhuan*, Lord Xi 28th Year; Legge, 206 (Durrant, Li, and Schabert, I: 425–428). This is part direct citation and part paraphrase and duplicates exactly what appears in vol. 88 of *Xu Liji jishuo* right after the statement attributed to *Sishu jishuo*.

136. Mao Qiling, "*Zhongyongshuo*" [On the *Zhongyong*], IV: 14b; 120.

137. Feng Weishou, a Song dynasty scholar. Tasan is repeating what Mao Qiling cites in "*Zhongyongshuo*" [On the *Zhongyong*], IV: 15a; 121.

138. *Daxue*, VIII, Legge, 369 (Johnston and Wang, 159).

139. *Sishu jizhu*, 18 (Johnston and Wang, 454).

140. We were unable to identify Chen Ziceng, other than that he was an associate of Mao Qiling, or find the original source of this citation. Tasan appears to be re-citing Mao Qiling's citation of Chen's words. Mao Qiling, "*Zhongyongshuo*" [On the *Zhongyong*], IV: 15b; 121.

141. Johnston and Wang, 306.

142. *Sishu jizhu*, 18 (Johnston and Wang, 454).

143. Mao Qiling, "*Zhongyongshuo*," IV: 15b–16a; 121.

144. "Wangzhi," *Liji:* III; Legge, *Li Chi (Book of Rites)*, I: 217.
145. *Zhouli*, "diguan situ," *Shisanjing zhushu*, I, 698.
146. *Zhouli*, "Tianguan dazai," *Shisanjing zhushu*. I: 646.
147. *Zhouli*, "Tianguan xiaozai," *Shisanjing zhushu*, I: 653.
148. *Zhouli*, "diguan dasitu," *Shisanjing zhushu*, I: 703.
149. Legge, *Chinese Classics V, The Ch'un Ts'ew with the Tso Chuen*, Lord Xiang 22th yr., 49 (Durrant, Li, and Schaberg, II: 1099). That does not imply that he was corrupt. He was awarded horses for his good work.
150. This appears to be Chen Li (1252–1334), a Song dynasty follower of Zhu Xi's approach to Confucianism. This statement is attributed to him in Hu Guang's *Sishu daquan*, "Zhongyoung huowen-xia." Available at https://zh.wikisource.org/wiki/四書大全_(四庫全書本)/中庸或問卷下. Acccessed December 11, 2022.
151. *Zhouli*, "diguan: junren" (Ministry of Education: treating people fairly) (*Shisanjing zhushu*, I: 730).
152. "Wangzhi," *Liji* III; Legge, *Li Chi (Book of Rites)*, I: 227.
153. The encampment constellation (*dingxing/yingshi*) is the thirteenth lunar lodge (one of twenty-eight such constellations in the vicinity of the celestial equator) in traditional Chinese astronomy. For information on lunar lodges [*xiu* 宿], see F. Richard Stephenson, "Lunar Lodges in Chinese Astronomy," in Helain Selin, ed., *Encyclopaedia of the History of Science, Technology, and Medicine in Non-Western Cultures* (Dordrecht: Springer Reference, 2016), 1237–1241.
154. This phrase is used many times in the *Zuozhuan*. One example is Lord Xi, 20th year. Legge, *Chinese Classics V, The Ch'un Ts'ew with the Tso Chuen* (Durrant, Li, and Schaberg, I: 347), where it is recorded that the southern gate of the capital fortress was rebuilt in the spring, which was not the right time to do so.
155. *Sishu jizhu*, 18 (Johnston and Wang, 454). This is a paraphrase of a statement in the *Xiaguan* [Ministry of War] volume, in the "Gaoren zhi" section, of the *Zhouli*. It can be found at *Shisanjing zhushu*, I: 857. Instead of 稱事, the *Zhouli* has 乘事, "to take the situation into account." 稱 and 乘 are pronounced the same in Chinese.
156. *Guoyu*, "Luyu" A: 16. Available at https://ctext.org/guo-yu/lu-yu-shang. Accessed July 2, 2019.
157. Zheng Xuan's note on this can be seen in Johnston and Wang, 310.
158. Mao Qiling, "*Zhongyongshuo*," IV: 17a (122).
159. Tasan must be referring to the explication of this line that appears in *Shisanjing zhushu*, "Yueling," *Liji*, II: 1381.
160. "Yueling," *Liji*, IV; Legge, *Li Chi*, I, 299.
161. *Sishu huowen*, 84 (Pak Wansik, 487)
162. *Sishu jizhu*, 18; (Johnston and Wang, 454).
163. *Sishu huowen*, 84 (Pak Wansik, 487).
164. *Sishu huowen*, 84 (Pak Wansik, 487).
165. *The Analects*, 16: 1 (Slingerland, 192).
166. *Shangshu*, "Book of Zhou," "Speech at Bi"; Legge, *The Shoo King*, 621.
167. Tasan appears to be referring to his commentary on the *Analects*, *Nonŏ kokŭmju* [Annotations old and new on the Analects], *Yŏyudang chŏnsŏ* II: 8, 29b. Both

the Yi from Huai and the Rong from Xu were considered barbarians since they were not sinicized.

168. *Shangshu,* "Book of Zhou," "Hounds of Lu"; Legge, *The Shoo King,* 349. The "Mei version" refers to a specific version of the *Shangshu,* a supposed earlier version with commentary by Kong Anguo that was presented to the Emperor of Eastern Jin by one Mei Ze but is now considered a forgery.

169. This is from the *Shangshu dazhuan* [Great Commentary on *the Book of Documents*] of Fu Sheng (268–178 BCE), IV, "dagao." Available at https://ctext.org/wiki.pl?if=gb&chapter=610685#p14. Accessed July 29, 2020. Yuechang was a state in what is now southern China. See Martha P. Y. Cheung, ed., *An Anthology of Chinese Discourse on Translation* (New York: Routledge, 2016), 47–48.

170. *Zhouli,* "diguan: Huaifang shi" (Ministry of Education: warmly welcoming foreigners) (*Shisanjing zhushu* I: 730), 864.

171. *Sishu jizhu,* 18 (Johnston and Wang, 454).

172. "Do not neglect stranger and travelers" is from *Mencius* VIIb, 7 (Van Norden, 166).

173. *Shangshu,* II, 1, 5; Legge, *Chinese Classics* 3: *Shoo King,* 42.

174. *Sishu huowen,* 85 (Pak Wansik, 494).

175. This line appears in two of the Thirteen Classics. It appears in *The Book of Songs* ("Major Odes," "Decade of Sheng Min," "Minlu" (Waley and Allen, 256; Legge, *She King,* 495). It also appears in the *Book of Documents,* "the canon of Shun," Legge, *Shoo King,* 42.

176. This is the pen name of Zhen Dexiu (1178–1235), a Southern Song official who eventually became Minister of Rites. He was an important promoter of Zhu Xi's ideas.

177. We found this statement attributed to Zhen Dexiu in *Sishu daquan,* "Zhongyong huowen-xia." https://zh.wikisource.org/wiki/四書全_(四庫全書本)/中庸或問卷下. Accessed July 4, 2019. "Restoring Legitimacy" is a phrase from this chapter. "Raising the fallen" is a phrase from *Analects* XX (Slingerland, 233).

178. Mao Qiling, "*Zhongyongshuo*" [On the *Zhongyong*] IV: 19a (123)

179. *Sishu huowe* 84 (Pak Wansik, 487). These are explanations of two short phrases in this chapter.

180. *Zhouli,* "xiaguan: da sima" (War Ministry: duties of the minister of war) (*Shisanjing zhushu,* I: 835),

181. *Sishu jizhu* 18 (Johnston and Wang, 454). Zhu Xi is citing "Wang zhi," *Liji,* III; Legge, *Li Chi,* I, 216.

182. "Pinyi," *Liji,* XLV; Legge, *Li Chi,* II, 460.

183. Tasan took this picture of five concentric rings around the ruler's personal domain from *Zhouli,* "xiaguan, zhifangsi." *Shisanjing zhushu* I, 863.

184. *Zhouli,* "qiuguan" (Ministry of Justice): "da xingren" (Senior Messenger); (*Shisanjing zhushu* I: 890–894). For more on the Senior Messenger, see Elman, Benjamin A. and Martin Kern, ed. *Statecraft and Classical Learning: The Rituals of Zhou in East Asian History* (Leiden: Brill, 2010), 92–93.

185. *Zhouli,* "quiguan" (Autumn offices): "da xingren" (Senior Messenger); (*Shisanjing zhushu* I: 890–894).

186. Mao Qiling "*Zhongyongshuo*" IV: 23b-24a (173).

187. *Shangshu*, "Zhougwan" Legge, *Shoo King*, 530-31. This passage says that all those persons holding a fiefdom were supposed to present tribute at court once every six years. And six years after that the king was supposed to make an inspection tour.

188. "Wang zhi" *Liji*, III and "Pinyi," *Liji*, XLV; Legge, *Li Chi*, I, 209-248 and II, 458-464.

189. *Zhouli*, "quiguan" (Autumn offices): "da xingren" (Senior Messenger); (*Shisanjing zhushu* I: 890-894).

190. *Shangshu*, "Zhougwan" Legge, *Shoo King*, 523-34.

191. "Maessi sŏp'yŏng" [*A Critical Look at Mei Ze's Book of Documents*], *Yŏyudang chŏnsŏ*, II: 19-32.

192. *Sishu jizhu*, 18; Johnston and Wang, 454.

193. Mao Qiling, *Zhongyongshuo* IV: 26b-27a (126-27)

194. Legge, Chinese Classics V, *The Ch'un Ts'ew with the Tso Chuen*, Lord Zhao 5th yr., 601-602 (Durrant, Li, and Schaberg, III: 1391).

195. In *Chungyong chajam* II, 3: 21a, Tasan notes that the phrase "the people of this world fast and purify themselves, and dress themselves in fine clothes in order to offer sacrifices" is used in both this chapter, in the midst of the discussion of the "nine cardinal rules," as well as in the chapter on the Spirit (XVI) with the same meaning: to always remind ourselves that the Lord on High is watching us. If we do that, we will do nothing contrary to propriety and we will discipline ourselves and become the human being we should be. We will have successfully cultivated a moral character.

196. *Sishu Huowen* 86 (Pak Wansik, 497-498).

197. In *Chungyong chajam* II, 3: 21a-b, Tasan says the notion that prior preparation is necessary for success is the core message of both the *Daxue* and the *Zhongyong*. "Prior preparation," explains Tasan, means making yourself unselfishly cooperative and appropriately responsive. But that requires more than simply investigating things to extend your knowledge. You have to also understand Heaven, since understanding Heaven is the foundation for watching over yourself even when no one can see what you are thinking or doing.

198. *Sishu Huowen*, 90-91 (Pak Wansik, 510).

199. *Zhongyong* XX: 7.

200. *Zhongyong* XX: 8.

201. *Zhongyong* XX: 9.

202. *Zhongyong* XX: 12.

203. *Sishu jizhu*, 20 (Johnston and Wang, 463).

204. See *Kongzi jiayu tongjie*, "Aigong wen zheng," 208-220.

205. Tasan argues in *Chungyong chajam*, II, 3: 22a, that the reference to human nature being the Dao of Heaven is a reference to the basic human nature of sages like Yao and Shun. The Dao of ordinary humans, the path they need to follow, is to put a lot of effort into studying and self-cultivation so that they can become wise enough to think and act in an unselfishly cooperative and appropriately responsive manner. He then notes, as he does in *Chungyong kangŭibo*, that what Zhu Xi labels as chapter 21 belongs with the chapter preceding it.

206. Zhu Xi says that human nature is the Dao of Heaven, and education is the Dao of human beings. *Sishu jizhu,* 20 (Johnston and Wang, 462).

207. Hu Bingwen (1250–1333). This citation can be found in *Sishu daquan,* "Zhongyong zhangju daquan-xia."https://zh.wikisource.org/wiki/四書大全_(四庫全書本)/中庸章句大全下. Accessed July 5, 2019.

208. *Mencius,* "Jin Xin I," 30; "Jin Xin II," 79 (Van Norden, 179, 193).

209. In *Chungyong chajam,* II, 3: 21b–22a, Tasan distinguished between someone who is born with the ability to perceive how he should act and act accordingly and someone who has to study and exert a lot of effort to reach that stage. It is the latter group that, Tasan believes, Zhu Xi is referring to when he says (in a line Tasan does not discuss in *Chungyong kangŭibo*) that "with enough effort, even the not-so-bright will learn to see clearly and even the weak will develop the strength to follow the Way." *Sishu jizhu,* 19 (Johnston and Wang, 460).

210. "Zhang Zai and the Unity of All Creation," De Bary, *Sources of Chinese Tradition,* vol. I, 688. Our translation is somewhat different to better reflect the way we believe Tasan understood this text.

211. *Er Cheng yishu,* vol. 23. https://zh.wikisource.org/wiki/二程遺書/卷23. Accessed July 6, 2019. This statement is by Cheng Yi (1033–1107). A similar comment by him on this chapter of the *Zhongyong* can be found in Wing-tsit Chan, *A Source Book in Chinese Philosophy,* 548.

212. Thanks to Erudition, we found these comments cited in *Sishu zuanshu* [A compilation of notes on the Four Books], "Zhongyoung zuanshu," 3. *Sishu Zuanshu* was compiled by Zhao Shunsun (1215–1276). It is also available in *Sishu daquan,* "Zhongyong huowen-xia," https://zh.wikisource.org/wiki/四書大全_(四庫全書本)/中庸或問卷下. Accessed July 6, 2019. Pak Wansik discusses this statement in a footnote on p. 514.

213. Thanks to Erudition, we found this statement in *Sishu zuanshu,* "Zhongyoung zuanshu," 3. It is also available in *Sishu daquan,* "Zhongyong huowen-xia," https://zh.wikisource.org/wiki/四書大全_(四庫全書本)/中庸或問卷下. Accessed July 6, 2019. Pak Wansik discusses this statement on p. 514.

214. *Sishu daquan,* "Zhongyong huowen-xia," https://zh.wikisource.org/wiki/四書大全_(四庫全書本)/中庸或問卷下. Accessed July 6, 2019. Pak Wansik discusses Yang's statement on p. 514.

215. *Sishu huowen,* 91 (Pak Wansik, 512).

216. "Zhongyong," *Liji, Shisanjing zhushu,* II: 1632.

217. *Zhongyong* V. Tasan doesn't discuss this one-line chapter.

218. *Zhongyong* IV.

219. *Yijing* hexagram I: Qian; Lynn, *The Classic of Changes,* 130.

220. *Zhongyong* XXVI.

Zhongyong XXII

1. *Sishu jizhu,* 20; Johnston and Wang, 464.

2. *Zhuzi yulei,* IV: 59. Accessed at http://ctext.org/zhuzi-yulei/4. A similar statement referring to human beings only can be found in the *Sishu hwowen,* 92 (Pak

Wansik, 519). For an English translation of a discussion by Zhu Xi of this topic, see Philip J. Ivanhoe, ed., *Zhu Xi: Selected Writings* (New York: Oxford University Press, 2019), 16–17. This translation draws on *Zhuzi yulei*, IV. Available at https://ctext.org/zhuzi-yulei/4. Accessed July 31, 2021.

3. *Zhuzi yulei*, IV: 59. Available at https://ctext.org/zhuzi-yulei/4, line 17. Accessed April 8, 2022. This is a reference to the discussion in *Mencius*, 7a: III:3 (Gaozi); (Van Norden, 145). The problem neo-Confucians ran into with this passage is that Mencius says that the *xing* of dogs and oxen is different, but neo-Confucians understood *xing* to be the same thing as *li* and therefore this passage appears to say that *li* is different in different sentient beings.

4. Hu Yunfeng (1250–1333) was a member of the Zhu Xi school who lived during the Yuan dynasty. Yunfeng is his literary name. His actual name is Hu Bingwen. He is cited on this subject in *Sishu daquan*, "Mengzi jizhu daquan," 11. Accessed July 7, 2019, at https://zh.wikisource.org/wiki/四書大全_(四庫全書本)/孟子集註大全卷11.

5. Zhu Xi explains that in this passage Mencius is using *xing* the way Gaozi does, to refer to the ability to perceive and move around, abilities human beings share with animals. However, Zhu goes on to say that if we think about our nature as our innate potential to act appropriately, human beings are clearly different from animals. *Sishu jizhu*, "Mengzi zhangju jizhu," 158.

6. That is because, in this case, *li* is a singular noun referring to the universal network of appropriate interactions and therefore all things partake in that *li*, though the way that *li* is expressed in different beings is different.

7. In this case, *li* is a plural noun, referring to the various specific patterns of appropriate behavior for different things. For example, the way we expect a human being to interact with us is different from the way we would expect an ox or a dog to interact with us.

8. These "four major ways" are filial piety, fraternal affection, loyalty, and trustworthiness. They are enumerated as such in *Dadai Liji* [The Rites of Dai the Elder], "Wei Jiangjun Wenzi" [General Wenzi of Wei]. Available at http://ctext.org/da-dai-li-ji/wei-jiang-jun-wen-zi, Line 8. Accessed July 7, 2019.

9. This is a reference to the Buddhist text *Śūraṅgama Sūtra*, or less likely, *Śūraṅgama Samādhi Sūtra*.

10. *Zhuangzi*, "The Revolution of Heaven" chapter. Zhuangzi says that wolves and tigers are benevolent in the same way that human fathers and sons show affection to one another. Available at http://ctext.org/zhuangzi/revolution-of-heaven. Accessed April 8, 2022.

11. 1014–1083. A native of Tianchang in the Song dynasty. His mother was a concubine, Madame Liu. Zhu's father sent her away, due to the jealousy of the primary wife, when Zhu was age seven. He later became a high official in the Song government, but suddenly abandoned his position to search for his lost mother, telling his family he would not return unless he was successful. Finally, when his mother was seventy years old, he successfully found her. He was famous as a paragon of filial piety.

12. *Sishu jizhu*, 20; Johnston and Wang, 464.

13. *Sishu jizhu,* 20; Johnston and Wang, 464.

14. Yi was a legendary minister of the equally legendary early emperor Shun. He was in charge of Shun's forests. See *Shangshu,* "Canon of Shun" (Legge, *Shoo King,* 46).

15. This hierarchy of being is similar to what is seen in *Xunzi,* chapter 9, "The Rule of a True King" (Hutton, 76), as well as in Matteo Ricci's Catholic catechism, *The True Meaning of the Lord of Heaven,* 119.

16. *Book of Songs,* "Lessons from the States," "Odes of Shao and the South," "Zou Yu" (Legge, *She King,* 36; Waley and Allen, 22).

17. *Liji* (Legge, *Li Chi,* "Li Yun," I: 384).

18. Erudition found this in *Xu Liji jishuo,* vol. 89. Accessed July 7, 2019.

19. *Zhouli,* "xiaguan: sima" (War Ministry: Overseer of Military Affairs) (*Shisanjing zhushu,* I: 846).

20. The phrase "something even Yao and Shun would find difficult to do" is from the *Analects:* 6:30 (Slingerland, 63).

21. *Mencius,* III: B, 9, "Teng Wen Gong II" (Van Norden, 84).

22. In *Chungyong chajam,* II, 3: 22a–b, Tasan writes that for individual human beings, actualizing their human nature means fully realizing their potential to live moral lives. Heaven has endowed them with the ability to cultivate their moral character so that they become the best person they possibly can. Actualizing the human nature of other human beings means governing them so that they realize their full potential to act appropriately and play their proper roles in society. Actualizing the full potential of plants and animals simply means helping them grow and multiply. This notion that human beings and animals have the same basic nature, he argues, is an idea that was picked up from Buddhists and is not a part of real Confucianism. How, he asks, can you possibly teach a tiger or a wolf to be benevolent or a jackal or an otter to perform proper rituals?

Zhongyong XXIII

1. This refers to those below the level of those discussed in the preceding chapter. In other words, it refers those who have not developed the ability to act in a fully unselfishly cooperative and appropriately responsive (*cheng*) manner.

2. *Sishu jizhu,* 21 (Johnston and Wang, 464).

3. *Mencius.* "Jinxin," II: 33 (Van Norden, 193).

4. Johnston and Wang, 326.

5. *Sishu jizhu,* 21 (Johnston and Wang, 464).

6. *Liji,* "Liqi" (Rites in the Formation of Character) (Legge, *Li Chi,* I: 404).

7. *Shangshu,* "Zhoushu," "Numerous Regions," II (Legge, *Shoo King,* 500).

8. Cited in *Sishu daquan,* "zhongyong huowen-xia." Available at https://zh.wikisource.org/wiki/四書大全_(四庫全書本)/中庸或問卷下. Accessed July 7, 2019.

9. *Zhuzi yulei,* "xingli-1," line 41. Available at https://ctext.org/zhuzi-yulei/4. Accessed July 9, 2019.

10. *Sancang* can refer to either the first Chinese character dictionary, named

after the legendary inventor of Chinese writing Cang Jie, or early dictionaries that were expansions of that pioneer dictionary.

11. In *Chungyong chajam*, II, 3: 22b–23a, Tasan wrote that extending your efforts to that which is most detailed and complicated means, for those at the level below that of the natural-born sages, to focus your whole heart-mind on not looking at, listening to, saying, or doing anything that is not in accord with the rules of proper interactions. If you can do that, then you will be able to act in an unselfishly cooperative and appropriately responsive manner, and that will influence both people and animals to act the same way so that they, too, will actualize their full potential.

ZHONGYONG XXIV

1. Tasan made a mistake by adding to Kong's reference to He Yin (446–531) that He Yin was from the state of Jin. Jin fell in 420. He Yin died as a subject of the Liang.

2. Johnston and Wang, 330–332.

3. This passage in which Chen Ziceng cites the *Zuozhuan* and the *Shuowen* can be found in Mao Qiling, *Zhongyongshuo*, V: 6 a–b. The same *Zhuzhuan* and *Shuowen* material can be found in Zheng Zuan's commentary, Johnston and Wang, 330.

4. *Zuozhuan*, "Lord Xuan 15th year." Legge, *The Ch'un Ts'ew with the Tso Chuen*, 328 (Durrant, Li, and Schabert, I: 680).

5. *Shuowen Jie Zi*, vol. 14, "insects." Available at http://ctext.org/shuo-wen-jie-zi?searchu=草木之怪. Accessed July 10, 2019.

6. Johnston and Wang, 330.

7. *Sishu jizhu*, 21 (Johnston and Wang, 466).

8. Tasan made a mistake here. This incident is recorded in *Zuozhuan* as occurring in the 15th year of Lord Ding's reign.

9. *Zuozhuan*, "Lord Ding, "15th year. Legge, *The Ch'un Ts'ew with the Tso Chuen*, 790 (Durrant, Li, and Duke Schaberg, III: 1823).

10. "Lord Ai, 7th year"; Legge, *The Ch'un Ts'ew with the Tso Chuen*, 813 (Durrant, Li, and Schaberg, III: 1872).

11. Mao Qiling, *Zhongyongshuo*, V: 6b.

12. *Sishu jizhu*, 22 (Johnston and Wang, 466).

13. *Sishu jizhu*, 30 (Johnston and Wang, 492).

14. Here we see Tasan breaking with mainstream neo-Confucianism by insisting that Heaven is separate and distinct from human beings and that, for human beings, the Dao of Heaven means acting the way Heaven intends us to act, not acting as Heaven. Heaven for him in this context is another way of referring to the Lord on High, which is his name for the supernatural personality who oversees us all and endows us with the spiritual insight and penetrating intelligence that makes it possible for us to determine how we should act and then to act in accordance with that determination. Tasan insists we must remain aware of the vast difference between the Lord on High and human beings below if we are to maintain the cautious apprehension and sense of awe that we need to inspire us to act appropriately rather than follow our selfish impulses.

15. *Er Cheng Yi Shu*, Vol. III. Available at https://zh.wikisource.org/wiki/二程遺書/卷03. Accessed July 27, 2019.

16. *Sishu huowen*, 93 (Pak Wansik, 523).

17. In *Hŭmhŭm sinsŏ* [A new guidebook for forensic medicine], *Yŏyudang chŏnsŏ*, V: 30, 3a, Tasan makes an interesting comment that draws on a line from this chapter of the *Zhongyong*: "The Dao of being perfectly selflessly cooperative and appropriately responsive makes it possible to see what lies ahead." He argues that this is telling us that if you are perfectly sincere, then your heart-mind will resonate with the heart-mind of the Spirit. It will be as though the Spirit is directly telling you what to do (in this instance, he is referring to deciding a legal case). Then he adds, "I have had such an experience myself."

18. *Yijing*, "Commentary on the Hexagram Qian." Lynn, *Classic of Changes*, 138.

19. The Duke of Zhou's brothers, Shu Xian of Guan and Shu Du of Cai.

20. Wu Geng was the son of the last Shang ruler.

21. 276–324. He was a Daoist who is credited with writing an early commentary on the *Shanhaijing* as well as early classics of geomancy.

22. 210–256. He was a diviner interested in astrology, fortune-telling, and physiognomy.

23. 602–670. He was an important mathematician and astronomer in early Tang China. However, he also is believed to have promoted astrology, which is why Tasan lists him among those who falsely claim to be able to predict the future.

24. In *Chungyong chajam*, II, 3: 23a, Tasan writes that a person who is unselfishly cooperative and appropriately responsive is able to see and understand the world around him with great clarity. Such a person will naturally be watchful over his thoughts and actions even when no one else can see what he is doing or thinking. Moreover, because of his penetrating intelligence, he is able to understand omens that ordinary people are unable to understand. Tasan goes on to give an example drawn from the *Discourses of the States* [Guo Yu] in which one wise man predicted the fall of Zhou by noticing changes in the rivers that flowed through it. (*Guo Yu*, "Zhouyu-shang. Available at https://ctext.org/guo-yu/zhou-yu-shang. Accessed August 8, 2020.) That same example is used by Zheng Xuan in commenting on this chapter (Johnston and Wang, 335).

Zhongyong XXV

1. *Sishu jizhu*, 22 (Johnston and Wang, 468).

2. *Daxue*, Plaks, 5 (Johnston and Wang, 134).

3. In the section called "Discussing Zhu Xi's Preface to Chapters and Phrases" found near the end of this text, after the chapters in the *Zhongyong* have been discussed, Tasan makes more explicit his objection to what Zhu Xi is saying here. He insists that Zhu Xi has it backward. As Tasan sees it, a thing or process must exist first before patterning principles can be applied to it. Rather than arguing that patterning principles are prior to the actual entity or process they define and direct, he insists that there must first be something for patterning principles to define and

direct before we can talk about those principles actually defining and directing anything. Tasan's argument is based on the assumption that potential precedes actualization. That is why he criticizes Zhu Xi for, in his view, conflating potential and actualization.

4. This appears to be a direct challenge to the Buddhist claim that the only thing that can be called real is something that is unchanging and uncaused. Instead, Zhu Xi is saying that the patterns of change and causation seen in interactions constitute reality.

5. *Sishu huowen*, 94 (Pak Wansik, 525).
6. *Daxue*, Plaks 5 (Johnston and Wang, 134).
7. *Li Chi*, "Yueling" (Legge, I: 277).
8. Mao Qiling, *Zhongyongshuo*, V: 9a.
9. *Mencius*, "Gongsun Chou I," 2 (Van Norden, 42).
10. Zisi was believed to be the author of the *Zhongyong*. This chapter of the *Zhongyong* says that fully actualizing your potential is called becoming fully human, and helping others actualize their full potential is called acting wisely.
11. *Sishu huowen*, 95 (Pak Wansik, 526). This Hu Bingwen citation can be accessed at *Sishu daquan*, "Zhongyong zhangju-xia." Available at hhttps://zh.wikisource.org/wiki/四書大全_(四庫全書本)/中庸章句大全下. Accessed July 11, 2019. Also available via the Erudition database, *Sishu daquan*, vol. 46.
12. *Sishu jizhu*, 22 (Johnston and Wang, 468). Here Zhu Xi is paraphrasing the last line in Chapter XXV of the *Zhongyong*.
13. This is a reference to *Mencius*, "Li Lou II," 57 (Van Norden, 112–113).
14. *Zhuzi yulei*, vol. 64, "Zhongyong III." Available at https://ctext.org/zhuzi-yulei/64. Accessed July 28, 2019.
15. In *Chungyong chajam* II, 3: 24a, Tasan writes that there is never a time when you should not act wisely or act in a way that does not show that you care for others. When a situation calls for your intentions to be selflessly cooperative and appropriately responsive, you should make them so. When you are rectifying your heart-mind, you should make sure it is selflessly cooperative and appropriately responsive. Whether you are managing your family, governing your country, or trying to bring peace to the entire world, you should act in an unselfishly cooperative and appropriately responsive manner according to the particular situation you find yourself in. There is no situation in which it is not appropriate to think and act in that manner. However, Tasan notes, your response has to be tailored to the particular situation you find yourself in. Then, repeating the many ways a moral person thinks and acts as listed in the first chapter of the *Daxue*, Tasan adds that, without striving to be unselfishly cooperative and appropriately responsive, you will not be able to have proper intentions, rectify your heart-mind, cultivate a moral character, manage your family, govern your country, or bring peace to the earth. The only item on the *Daxue* list Tasan leaves out is an initial item, "extending your knowledge," but he makes clear elsewhere that knowledge that the Lord on High is watching us is essential to cultivating a moral character and being motivated to act appropriately.
16. Tasan is quoting *Analects*, 4.2 (Slingerland, 29).

17. Tasan is citing *Analects*, 6.23 (Slingerland, 60). Tasan reverses the order in which these two clauses appear in the standard version of the *Analects*.

18. In *Chungyong chajam*, II, 3: 23b, Tasan points out the *cheng* (K. *sŏng* 誠), meaning acting in an unselfishly cooperative and appropriately responsive manner, is pronounced the same as a different *cheng* (K. *sŏng* 成), meaning to be complete or to become complete. He writes that this is not a coincidence because a person cannot become complete (the second *cheng*) without acting in an unselfishly cooperative and appropriately responsive manner (the first *cheng*). Nor can a person develop to the point where he does everything he is supposed to do in the way he is supposed to do it (the first *cheng*) without actualizing his full potential (the second *cheng*).

Zhongyong XXVI

1. "Pure power we see in King Wen" is a line from the *Book of Songs*, "Sacrificial odes of Zhou," "Decade of Qing Miao." "Wei Tian zhi Ming," 1 (Legge, *She King*, 570–71; Waley and Allen, 291).

2. This citation from You Zou can be found in *Sishu daquan*, vol. 46, "Zhongyong huowen-xia." Available at https://zh.wikisource.org/wiki/四書大全_(四庫全書本)/中庸或問卷下. Accessed July 28, 2019. Also available in the Erudition database. The reference to Yan Hui is from *Analects* 6.7 (Slingerland, 55).

3. *Sishu daquan*, vol. 46, "Zhongyong huowen-xia." Available at https://zh.wikisource.org/wiki/四書大全_(四庫全書本)/中庸或問卷下. Accessed July 27, 2019. Also available via the Erudition database.

4. *Sishu hwowen*, 95 (Pak Wansik, 530).

5. *Sishu jizhu*, 22 (Johnston and Wang, 470).

6. *Sishu jizhu*, 22 (Johnston and Wang, 470).

7. *Sishu jizhu*, 22 (Johnston and Wang, 470). For the original statement by Zheng Xuan, see Johnston and Wang, 338.

8. *Zhuzi yulei*, vol. 64. Available at https://ctext.org/zhuzi-yulei/64. Accessed July 27, 2019.

9. In *Chungyong chajam*, II, 3: 24b, Tasan argues that it is Heaven that never stops acting in an unselfish and appropriately responsive manner. When a sage studies Heaven for a long time, then his ethical virtuosity can come to resemble that of Heaven and what he can accomplish can also come to resemble what Heaven accomplishes. That is why it is said that the sage can transform things for the better without even taking any direct action to do so, as is seen in the seven odes that are the heart of the final chapter of the *Zhongyong*.

10. In *Chungyong chajam*, II, 3: 24b, Tasan noted that this particular chapter clarifies that the Dao of the *Zhongyong* has its foundations in the Dao of Heaven and that is why the Dao is never-ending. Citing Zhu Xi, Tasan goes on to say that the one word that encapsulates the Dao is "*cheng*," acting in a consistently unselfishly cooperative and appropriately responsive manner (*Sishu jizhu*, 23; Johnston and Wang, 470). Tasan adds that "not being of two minds" means acting consistently in that way.

11. *Sishu jizhu*, 23 (Johnston and Wang, 470).

12. This is Lou Zhaizhong (dates unknown), a disciple of Mao Qiling.

13. Ames and Hall translate the phrase in this chapter in which *chen* appears as "the sun, moon, stars, and **constellations**..." (Ames and Hall, 107).

14. *Zuozhuan*, Lord Zhao, 7th year, 11th month. Legge, *Chinese Classics V*: 614 (Durrant, Li, and Schaberg, III: 1432–1433).

15. This is a reference to Jupiter stations [*ci* 次], the twelve locations Jupiter was seen to pass through on a sky map on its apparent movement through the heavens.

16. *Han Shu*. Available at https://ctext.org/han-shu/lv-li-zhi. Accessed July 27, 2019.

17. *Shisanjing zhushu*, I, 119. "Shangshu zhengyi," II. Ma's order is the one that appears in Joseph Needham, *Science and Civilization in China, Volume 3: Mathematics and the Sciences of the Heavens and the Earth* (Cambridge: Cambridge University Press, 1959), 403.

18. As cited in *Xu Liji jishuo*, vol. 89. Accessed via the Erudition database, July 27, 2019. It can also be found in Mao Qiling, *Zhongyongshuo*, V: 11b–12a.

19. "Xiaguan Sima," *Zhouli, Shisanjing zhushu*, I: 862.

20. Mao Qiling, *Zhongyongshuo*, V: 12a. The Erya citation is from "shishan," *Erya*, as reprinted in *Shisanjing zhushu*, II: 2617. It is also available at https://ctext.org/er-ya/shi-shan. Accessed July 29, 2019.

21. The King would not consider it an orthodox classic, but there is a reference to water endlessly flowing out of the ocean without emptying it in the "Floods of Autumn" chapter in Zhuangzi. Available at https://ctext.org/zhuangzi/floods-of-autumn. Accessed August 14, 2020. The phrase the King uses here is 尾閭沃焦 [*weilü wojiao*]. *Wojiao* is the name of an imaginary mountain at the bottom of the Eastern Sea. *Weilü*, a term that appears in that chapter of *Zhuangzi*, is a reference to an opening in the ocean floor, believed by later generations to be at the foot of Mt. Wojiao.

22. *Zhuzi yulei*, chapter 2. Available at "liqi-xia," https://ctext.org/zhuzi-yu-lei/2. Accessed July 29, 2019.

23. *Sishu jizhu*, 23 (Johnston and Wang, 472).

24. This is a challenge to the traditional notion that the earth is flat, which Zhu Xi, among others, appears to have assumed. (See Yung Sik Kim, *The Natural Philosophy of Chu Hsi, 1130–1200* [Philadephia: American Philosophical Society, 2000], 140–141.) However, the possibility that the earth might be round was not unknown in Korea. (See Park Seong-rae, "Hong Taeyong's Idea of the Rotating Earth," *Korea Journal* 20, no. 8 (1980): 21–29.

25. Also known as the *Zhoubi suanjing*. Christopher Cullen, *Astronomy and Mathematics in Ancient China; The Zhou bi suan jing* (New York: Cambridge University Press 1996), translates its title as "The Gnomon of the Zhou Mathematical Classic." It is a Han dynasty collection of earlier Chinese astronomical and mathematical works.

26. See Cullen, 192. The original text is available at https://ctext.org/zhou-bi-suan-jing/juan-xia. Accessed July 29, 2019.

27. "Shidi," *Erya*, as reprinted in *Shisanjing zhushu*, II: 2616. Also available at https://ctext.org/er-ya/shi-di. Accessed July 29, 2019.

28. I was unable to locate this statement in the *Suwen*. However, I found a

similar statement in chapter 23 of *Zhuzi yulei*, at https://ctext.org/zhuzi-yulei/23. Accessed July 29, 2019.

29. This draws on a conversation recorded in the "Zengzi Tianyuan" [Zengsi answers questions about heaven being round] section of the *Dadai Liji* [Record of Ritual Matters by Dai the Elder]. That text is available at https://ctext.org/da-dai-li-ji/ceng-zi-tian-yuan. Accessed February 19, 2018.

30. *Sishu jizhu*, 23 (Johnston and Wang, 472). This Sinograph appears in the phrase "the Earth...can shore up the great rivers and seas without shedding a drop of water" (Plaks, 47). Zhu Xi reads that phrase as saying, "the Earth...collects the great rivers and seas...," as reflected in the translation by Johnston and Wang, 469.

31. "Sacrificial Odes of Zhou," "Decade of Qingmiao," "Wei Tian zhi Ming." Legge, *She King*, 570 (Waley and Allen, 291).

32. Zhu Xi cites this statement from Cheng Hao in *Zhongyong zhangju* (*Sishu jizhu*, 24, Johnston and Wang, 472). It can also be found in *Er Cheng yishu*, 5: 3b, available at https://zh.wikisource.org/wiki/二程遺書/卷05. Accessed July 29, 2019.

33. In *Chungyong chajam*, II, 3: 24b, Tasan says that this section is another case of clarifying that the Dao of the sage has its foundation in Heaven.

Zhongyong XXVII

1. *Sishu jizhu*, 24 (Johnston and Wang, 474).
2. *Li Chi* (Book of Rites), Legge, 1: 404; *Sishu jizhu*, 24 (Johnston and Wang, 474).
3. *Zhongyong*, XII.
4. *Sishu jizhu*, 24 (Johnston and Wang, 474).
5. *Zhouli*, "chunguan zongbo," 18: 1a–5b (*Shisanjing zhushu*, I: 757–761).
6. The *Zhouli* says the Three Omens are "jade omen," "tile omen," and "spring omen." According to Zheng Xuan, these are three different kinds of cracks that could appear in tortoise plastron divinations. *Zhouli*, "chunguan zongbo" (*Shisanjing zhushu*, I: 802).
7. In *Chungyong chajam*, II, 3: 25a, Tasan writes that it is human beings who make the Dao visible. The Dao cannot make human beings visible. He also remarks that we can see the utmost "sincerity" of Heaven in the way the sun, the moon, and the various stars stay in their assigned places in the sky and in the way grasses and animals populate the earth. We can see the utmost selflessness of a sage in the way he nurtures the flourishing of everything. He does that by abiding by the three hundred rules of ceremonial ritual and the three thousand rules of etiquette, which need human beings to carry them out.
8. This definition of *Dao* is this context is provided by Zhu Xi. *Sishu jizhu*, 24 (Johnston and Wang, 474).
9. *Yijing*, "Qian." Lynn, "The Classic of Changes," "The Sixty-four Hexagrams," 136.
10. Zhu Xi makes this argument in more detail in *Huowen* than in *Zhongyong zhangju*. *Sishu huowen*, 97 (Pak Wansik, 534).
11. *Sishu jizhu*, 24 (Johnston and Wang, 474).

12. *Sishu huowen*, 97 (Pak Wansik, 534).

13. *Sishu jizhu*, 24 (Johnston and Wang, 474).

14. Mao Qiling, *Sishu gaicuo*, vol. 16. Accessed via the Erudition database, July 28, 2019.

15. Hu Bingwen, cited in *Sishu daquan*, "Zhongyong zhangju-xia." Available at https://zh.wikisource.org/wiki/四書大全_(四庫全書本)/中庸章句大全下. Accessed August 4, 2019. Hu explains that the four sentences divided into two clauses linked by "and" do that to emphasize that the second clause refers to the inevitable result of what the first clause says we should do, but the fifth sentence, linking its clauses by putting "with" between them, emphasizes the attitude we need to work with in order to accomplish the action mentioned in the second half of that sentence.

16. *Sishu hwowen*, 97 (Pak Wansik, 534).

17. *Sishu jizhu*, 24 (Johnston and Wang, 474).

18. Tasan's point is obscured in English translation because I am forced to use the phrase "in an appropriately solemn manner" to translate what he says is a single word formed from two Sinographs. However, even though Tasan would not have used these modern grammatical terms, we can see that he has noticed that the other phrases are composed of nouns and verbs, and therefore can stand alone, while this phrase is adverbial, modifying the way ritual is to be performed. That is why it is linked to the clause that follows it by "with" rather than "and."

19. *Analects*, 12:15 (Slingerland, p. 133).

20. Wang Shouren (1472–1529), better known as Wang Yangming, was a Ming philosopher who famously argued for the unity of knowledge and action, insisting that you can only learn by experiencing in your own actions what you intend to learn. His insistence that knowledge is not prior to action was seen as a challenge to Zhu Xi's neo-Confucianism. Wang's philosophy was condemned in Korea as dangerously misleading.

21. In *Chungyong chajam*, II, 3: 25a–b, Tasan writes that action is important because ethical virtuosity refers to *acting* according to what your true heart-mind tells you to do. If you do not act properly, you cannot be called virtuous. Filial piety, fraternal affection, conscientiousness, trustworthiness, showing regard for your fellow human beings, acting appropriately, acting in accordance with propriety, and acting wisely, all these are different ways of displaying ethical virtuosity. If you do not embody them in your actions, how can you be said to be virtuous? As for the innate human potential to act appropriately, that means that you are born with a natural human tendency to prefer what is good and that tendency is actualized when you allow that tendency to direct your actions. He also says that our ability to act appropriately is something Heaven has given us. We are obligated to respect what it tells us to do, just as we are obligated to respect orders from our sovereign.

He goes on to say that the first Confucians understood that respecting your innate potential to act appropriately results in action, and that following the path of study and inquiry results in understanding. They both are important. We should not favor one over the other. He also explains here that "respecting our innate potential for acting appropriately" means fully actualizing our potential for acting in a totally unselfishly cooperative and appropriately responsive manner. See Chung So-Yi, "Tŏksŏngesŏ tŏkhaengŭro: kwadogi yullihagŭrosŏ ŭl Tasan sasang" [Virtuous nature vs. virtuous action: Tasan's ethical perspective], *In'gan, hwan'gyŏng, mirae* [Human beings, environment, and their future] 9 (2012): 43–62, for a lucid explanation of how Tasan distinguished between the innate potential for acting appropriately [德性], which we are all born with, and actually acting appropriately [德行], which few of us do consistently.

22. *Sishu jizhu*, 25 (Johnston and Wang, 474). Zhu Xi is explaining a line in Chapter XXVII a little after the line that provides the heading above. That line is "When the Dao prevails in his state, his words will be enough for him to prosper."

23. Tasan here is drawing on the implications of the lines from *Book of Songs*, "Daya," "Decade of Dang," "Zhengmin," which are quoted in this chapter of the *Zhongyong*: "Very clear-sighted was he and wise / He assured his own safety." Legge, *She King*, 543 (Waley and Allen, 276).

24. *Dadai liji* [Record of Ritual Matters by Dai the Elder]. "Wei jiangjun wenzi" [Wenzi, General of Wei], 21. Accessed at https://ctext.org/da-dai-li-ji/wei-jiang-jun-wen-zi February 24, 2018.

25. Tongti Bohua was an official in the ancient state of Jin in the sixth century BCE, during the Western Zhou period. He is also known as Yangshe Chi.

26. In *Chungyong chajam*, II, 3: 26a, Tasan writes that the warning in this chapter against arrogance and in the next chapter against being too self-confident go together. They both tell us how a wise person should act so as to maintain composure when confronted with the world's failure to adhere to the Dao. In particular, if he is in a lower position, he should not draw attention to himself by criticizing his superiors. He notes that this is how Confucius acted. He did not try to correct the mistakes he saw in the court music and court rituals of his day but instead concentrated on being clear-sighted and wise enough to assure his own safety.

Zhongyong XXVIII

1. This is a line from this chapter of the *Zhongyong*.
2. *Zhongyong*, XVII, XIX.
3. *Zhongyong*, XXX.
4. The contrast between personal ethical virtuosity and transforming the whole world for the better draws on *Mencius*, 7A: 9 (Van Norden, 173).
5. *Sishu jizhu*, 25 (Johnston and Wang, 476).
6. *Sishu jizhu*, 25 (Johnston and Wang, 476).
7. Cai Qing, *Sishu mengyin*, IV: 91. Available at https://ctext.org/wiki.pl?if=gb&chapter=277936. Accessed August 6, 2019. See the "Dianming" [Superintendent of ranks and titles] chapter in the "Spring Offices" section in *Zhouli*, "chunguan zongbo" (*Shisanjing zhushu*, I: 780–781).
8. It is found in the *Jinche* [Chariot decorator] section in the chapter on "Spring Offices" in *Zhouli*, "chunguan zongbo" (*Shisanjing zhushu*, I: 822–825).
9. This is found in the *Sifu* [Wardrobe overseer] section in the chapter on "Spring Offices" in *Zhouli*, "chunguan zongbo" (*Shisanjing zhushu*, I: 781–783).

10. This is found in the *Sichang* [Overseer of banners] section in the chapter on "Spring Offices" in *Zhouli*, "chunguan zongbo" (*Shisanjing zhushu*, I: 826–827).

11. This is found in the *Daxingren* section in the chapter on "Autumn Offices" in *Zhouli*, "qiuguan sikuo" (*Shisanjing zhushu*, I: 890–891).

12. *Wen* appears in the phrase "only the Son of Heaven can... standardize the written script."

13. A Tang dynasty commentator on the Confucian classics.

14. This is in the chapter on "Spring Offices" in the *Zhouli*, "chunguan zongbo," "waishi" (*Shisanjing zhushu*, I: 820).

15. Zhao De, *Sishu jianyi* [Notes on the meaning of the Four Books], "Zhongyong. vol. I," accessed on August 5, 2019, via the Erudition database.

16. *Analects*, 15.26 (Slingerland, 184). This statement from the *Hanshu* can be found in section 145 of the *Yiwen zhi* [Imperial Bibliography] chapter. https://ctext.org/han-shu/yi-wen-zhi. Accessed May 4, 2018.

17. An official during Emperor Xuan's reign who seems to have been knowledgeable about pre-Qin Sinographs.

18. *Zhouli*, "qiuguan sikuo, daxingren" (*Shisanjing zhushu*, I: 892).

19. *Zhouli*, "chunguan zongbo" (*Shisanjing zhushu*, I: 820).

20. Mao Qiling, *Zhongyongshuo*, V, 15a–b.

21. Lynn, *Classic of Changes*, "Xici zhuan, xia," 93.

22. The radical (meaning-signifying component) of both Sinographs is "tree" (木).

23. The radical for both Sinographs is "metal" (金).

24. Steele, *The I-li*, I: 232.

25. In addition to saying that the way Sinographs are written has been unified, this chapter also said that axle widths have been made the same through the realm.

26. A *chi* (K. *ch'ŏk*) is a little longer than a foot. A *cun* (K. *ch'on*) is a little longer than an inch.

27. *Zuozhuan*, Lord Yin 1. Legge, *Chinese Classics* V: 2 (Durrant, Li, and Schabert, I: 14).

28. *Zhouli*, "chunguan zongbo" (*Shisanjing zhushu*, I: 820).

29. *Zhouli*, "qiuguan sikuo" (*Shisanjing zhushu*, I: 892).

30. *Sishu huowen*, 95–96 (Pak Wansik, 539).

31. *Sishu jizhu*, 25 (Johnston and Wang, 476).

32. *Book of Songs*, "Daya," "Decade of Sheng Min," "Jiale." Legge, 482 (Waley and Allen, 251).

33. *Analects*, 16.2 (Slingerland, 193).

34. Yi Pyŏk.

35. *Sishu jizhu*, 25 (Johnston and Wang, 476). Zhu Xi is explaining why Confucius said that he followed the rites of Zhou rather than the earlier rites of Xia or Shang.

36. *Analects*, 3.9 (Slingerland, 20.). Song was a state in the time of Confucius in which descendants of the Shang ruling class were believed to live.

37. Mao Qiling, *Zhongyongshuo*, V: 16a–b. A man of Lu referenced in the *Analects* (and possibly a disciple of Confucius). "The Master said, 'Who says that Weisheng

Gao was upright? If someone asked him for vinegar, he would beg some from his neighbors and present it as his own.'" *Analects,* 5.24 (Slingerland, 49).

38. A line from this chapter of the *Zhongyong.*

39. The rest of this chapter of *Chungyong kangŭibo* is a discussion of passages in Chapter XXIX of the post-Song version of the *Zhongyong.* Tasan is following the original text of the *Zhongyong* as he believes it appears in the *Book of Rites.* There the last part of Zhu Xi's Chapter XXVIII, according to Tasan, is linked to the first few lines in Zhu Xi's Chapter XXIX, as it is in Zheng Xuan's commentary (Johnston and Wang, 358). See *Chungyong chajam,* II, 3: 26b.

40. Johnston and Wang, 360.

41. This is a reference to the *Jingdian Shiwen* of Lu Yuanlang (literary name Deming [556–627]). That text is available at https://zh.wikipedia.org/wiki/經典釋文. Accessed August 17, 2019. However, we were unable to locate this particular statement in the version of the text available to us. We did, however, find it (though not attributed to Lu Deming) in a Ming text, Ge Yinliang's *Sishu Hunanjiang,* "Zhongyong Hunanjiang," accessed via the Erudition database.

42. This is discussed in a footnote by Pak Wansik in his translation of *Huowen* (Pak Wansik, 541). It does not appear in *Huowen* itself. Master Cheng (either Cheng Yi or Cheng Hao) is relying on Zheng Xuan for this explication (Johnston and Wang, 360).

43. As cited by Zhu Xi. *Sishu jishu,* 26 (Johnston and Wang, 478).

44. Cai Qing. *Sishu mengyin,* IV: 109. Available at https://ctext.org/wiki.pl?if=gb&chapter=277936. Accessed August 17, 2019.

45. *Li Chi* (Book of Rites), Legge, 1I: 241. The "martial dance" is a dance in honor of King Wu, the "martial ruler."

46. Mao Qiling, *Zhongyongshuo,* V: 16a.

47. We found Cheng cited saying this in Hu Guang, *Sishu daquan,* "Zhongyong zhangju daquan-xia," at https://zh.wikisource.org/wiki/四書大全_(四庫全書本)/中庸章句大全下. Accessed August 17, 2019. The line in which those phrases appear can be read as saying that "that which is prior" cannot be authenticated and therefore the people do not trust it and, consequently, do not follow it, while "that which is later" is not respected and therefore the people do not trust it and, consequently, do not follow it. See Ames and Hall, 110.

48. Cited in Wei Shi, *Liji jishuo* [Collection of commentaries on the Book of Rites] 135: 24. Available at http://ctext.org/wiki.pl?if=gb&chapter=905505. Accessed August 17, 2019.

49. See the discussion in Pak Wansik, 542. Lü's interpretation is only alluded to in the primary text.

50. *Sishu jizhu,* 26 (Johnston and Wang, 478).

51. Tasan notes in *Zhongyang chajam,* II, 3: 27b, that the reason we can say the Dao is rooted in the personal behavior of a ruler worthy of the name is because the Dao is based in human nature, which is manifest in actual individual human behavior. If someone takes the human nature Heaven has endowed him with and actualizes it to its fullest so that he is filial, shows fraternal affection, is conscientious, is trustworthy, and is benevolent, then he will act appropriately, be polite, and act

with wisdom, and therefore will be fully human. This is not something imposed from outside but is the foundation of what makes human beings human.

52. This chapter says that people will recognize the Dao for what it is when spirits confirm it or when the sage, whom they have been waiting for, arrives. That is why, Tasan notes in *Zhongyang chajam*, II, 3: 27a–b, that although Confucius never held a high position in government, the exemplary kings of old respected his Dao, as do heaven and earth, all the spirits, and multiple generations of wise men. How could it be possible for the masses not to have confidence in his Dao and follow it?

53. A line in Chapter XXIX in Zhu Xi's version but in this chapter in Zheng Xuan's version.

54. *Zhongyong*, Chapter XXIV.

55. *Sishu jizhu*, 11 and 26 (Johnston and Wang, 480 and 436).

56. *Zhouli*, "Chunguan zongbo" (*Shisanjing zhushu*, I, 757).

57. The "Sayings of Zhou" and the "Sayings of Jin" are both included in *Guoyu* [Discourses of the States], a work assumed to have been compiled during the Spring and Autumn period. See "Zhouyu," I: 12, for the statements by the Royal Secretary Guo. Available at https://ctext.org/guo-yu/zhou-yu-shang. Accessed August 17, 2019. We were unable to find a reference to the scribe Yin in the *Guoyu*, but he is cited talking about spirits in *Zhuozhuan*, Lord Zhuang, 32. Legge, *Chinese Classics* V: 119 Durrant, Li, and Schabert, I: 222.

58. *Sishu jizhu*, 26 (Johnston and Wang, 480).

59. Zhu Xi, *Zhuzi yulei*, 64: "Zhongyong III," Chapter XXIX (IV: 1952). Accessed at https://ctext.org/zhuzi-yulei/64, August 17, 2019.

60. *Zhouli*, "diguan situ" (*Shisanjing zhushu*, I, 734).

61. Tasan concludes his note on this section, in *Chungyong chajam*, II, 3: 27b, by saying that the Dao spoken of here is nothing other than acting in accordance with the human nature Heaven has endowed us with. Those who act in conformity with their true human nature, he writes, will be consistently focused and cooperative in all their interactions.

ZHONGYONG XXIX

1. Cai Qing. *Sishu mengyin*, IV: 109. Available at https://ctext.org/wiki.pl?if=gb&chapter=277936. Accessed August 17, 2019.

2. *Sishu jizhu*, 26 (Johnston and Wang, 476). Tasan leaves out the rest of Zhu Xi's statement in which he says this passage is about the Dao of human beings.

3. Ames and Hall, 109–110.

4. *Sishu jizhu*, 27 (Johnston and Wang, 478). Tasan again leaves out the rest of Zhu Xi's statement in which he says this passage, as well, is about the Dao of human beings.

ZHONGYONG XXX

1. These descriptions of the conduct of Confucius come from the *Analects* 10: 8 and 10: 25 (Slingerland 103, 109).

2. This is in reference to what Confucius is cited as saying in the "Ruxing" [Conduct of the scholar] chapter of the *Book of Rites*. Legge, II: 402.

3. *Sishu huowen*, 99 (Pak Wansik, 544).

4. *Sishu huowen*, 99 (Pak Wansik, 544).

5. Here Tasan is drawing on the language in this chapter that immediately follows the references to "harmonizing with what is above" and "being in tune with what is below."

6. Mao Qiling, *Zhongyongshuo*, V: 18b (137).

7. In *Chungyong chajam*, II, 3: 28a–b, Tasan writes that, even though the sun, the moon, and other celestial objects in the sky all follow their own paths in the sky, those paths come together to constitute the one Dao of heaven, and they do not get in each other's way. And if people all concentrate on their own individual talent, some going into government, others focusing on literature, and others specializing in rhetoric, they are all doing what is appropriate for them, so together they are examples of following the Dao of human beings and do not come into conflict with each other. But if people all do whatever they want rather than what is appropriate for them to do, how could conflict be avoided?

8. *Sishu jizhu*, 27 (Johnston and Wang, 482).

9. This statement by Chen Li is from *Sishu daquan*, "Zhongyong zhangju-xia," available at https://zh.wikisource.org/wiki/四書大全_(四庫全書本)/中庸章句大全下. Accessed August 18, 2019.

10. In *Chungyong chajam*, II, 3: 28a–b, Tasan says that small acts of ethical virtuosity are actions in accordance with our moral nature and result in the actor leading some others in the right direction in accordance with the times. Great acts of ethical virtuosity build on those small displays of ethical virtuosity and, combining them with concern for others, lead to the betterment of everyone.

Zhongyong XXXI

1. In *Chungyong chajam*, II: 3: 28b, Tasan says "perfect sage" is a reference to Confucius himself.

2. Joseph A. Adler, *Reconstructing the Confucian Dao: Zhu Xi's Appropriation of Zhou Dunyi*, 168–69. Zhou does not explicitly mention acting with a sense of propriety and respect for ritual or acting wisely in connection with the *Taijitu*. That comes from Zhu Xi's comments on Zhou's comments. Adler, 190.

3. This line is based on Zhu Xi's comments on Zhou Dunyi's explication of the diagram. Adler, *Reconstructing the Confucian Dao*, 190.

4. In *Chungyong chajam*, II: 3: 29a, Tasan rejects the statement in this chapter that human beings, even one who is a perfect sage, can be the equal of Heaven. He says it makes no sense. He says they would be qualified to offer sacrifices to Heaven but could not be said to be the equal of Heaven. He does not even bother to discuss that line from this chapter in *Chungyong kangŭibo*. Nor does he discuss a similar statement made in Chapter XXII. Tasan assumes a much greater gap between the Lord on High and human beings than traditional Confucianism assumes between Heaven and humanity.

Zhongyong XXXII

1. King Chŏngjo is citing Zhu Xi here. *Sishu jizhu,* 29 (Johnston and Wang, 486).
2. *Zhuzi yulei,* "Zhongyong III, 25:39b. Available at https://ctext.org/zhuzi-yulei/64. Accessed August 19, 2019. Zhu Xi says here that the difference between a sage, as discussed in the previous chapter, and someone who always acts in a *cheng* [K. *sŏng*] manner is nothing more than a sage appearing to those who observe him to have a superior moral character and someone acting in an unselfishly cooperative and appropriately responsive manner appearing to those who observe him to transform the world around him. In other words, the difference is only in how that person is perceived.
3. *Sishu jizhu,* 29 (Johnston and Wang, 486).
4. *Zhuzi yulei,* "Zhongyong III 25:39b." Available at https://ctext.org/zhuzi-yulei/64. Accessed August 19, 2019.
5. *Sishu jizhu,* 20–29 (Johnston and Wang, 462–488).
6. *Zhongyong* XX: 18.
7. In *Chungyong chajam,* II, 3: 29a, Tasan writes that those who are completely unselfish and appropriately responsive watch over both their thoughts and actions even when no other human being is aware of what they are thinking or doing. And those who establish themselves on that which is the foundation of All-under-Heaven are totally focused and act in harmony with the people and things around them. To do that and not be drawn off-course is precisely what Confucius did.

Zhongyong XXXIII

1. This is similar to what we see in *Book of Songs,* "Guofeng" [Airs of the states], "Odes of Wei," "shuo ren" [a beautiful woman]; Legge, 94 (Waley and Allen, 48).
2. The "feng" ode is a reference to *Book of Songs,* "Guofeng," "Odes of Zheng," "feng" [a splendid gentleman]; Legge, 141 (Waley and Allen, 72). Both this ode and the "shuo ren" ode refer to a woman wearing an unlined plain coat over brocade garments. However, the last two Sinographs of this four-Sinograph phrase are synonyms of what we see in the chapters of the *Zhongyong* rather than the exact same Sinographs. Denying that this line was taken from the "shuo ren" or the "feng" ode, because of the difference in the last two Sinographs, is a direct challenge to Zhu Xi, who wrote that it had been. *Sishu jizhu,* 29 (Johnston and Wang, 490).
3. *Liji* XI: 2, 10 (Legge, *Li Chi,* II: 11). This is the *jiong* Sinograph (絅) that comes at the end of the four-syllable phrase that opens this chapter. A different Sinograph (褧) also pronounced *jiong* and also meaning "plain and unlined" appears as the third Sinograph in a similar phrase in the the *shuo ren* and *feng* odes.
4. Mao Qiling, *Sishu shengyan* [Residual remarks about the Four Books], II: 12a. Accessed via the Erudition database.
5. In *Chungyong chajam,* II, 3: 29b, Tasan writes, "Over her brocade garments she wore a plain coat with no lining" is actually a reference to behaving in an unselfishly cooperative and an appropriately responsive manner, which, he adds, means

the same thing as being watchful over your thoughts and actions even when no one else can know what you are thinking or doing. An exemplary person, Tasan states, is not noticed at first because he does not make a display of what he is doing but over time his moral excellance will be recognized. A petty person, on the other hand, may draw attention to himself at first but eventually people will realize he is all show and will stop paying attention to him. Tasan here shows that he is torn between his desire to read ancient texts literally, according to the way they were read at the time they were composed, and his assumption that those ancient texts impart the same moral message, which we can discern only when we go beyond their literal meaning.

6. Zhu Xi simply says "not monotonous" refers to the beauty of the embroidered garments worn under the plain, unlined coat. *Sishu jizhu,* 29 (Johnston and Wang, 490).

7. In *Sishu daquan,* "zhongyong huowen-xia," a Mister Chen (probably Chen Li) is cited as saying that "not monotonous" means "to not get tired of." Available at https://zh.wikisource.org/wiki/四書大全_(四庫全書本)/中庸或問卷下. Accessed August 23, 2019.

8. Cited in Wei Shi (?-1227), *Liji jishuo* [Collected comments on the Book of Rites] vol. 136. Accessed at https://ctext.org/wiki.pl?if=gb&chapter=570841 July 13, 2018; Pak Wansik, 552 (footnote 398).

9. Liaoweng is Chen Guan (1057-1124). Liaoweng is his literary name. He studied under Cheng Hao, and he was criticized for being overly influenced by Buddhism. We were unable to locate this preface by Chen Guan.

10. *Sishu huowen,* 101 (Pak Wansik, 549-550).

11. *Sishu jizhu,* 29 (Johnston and Wang, 490).

12. Lin Xiyuan (1481-1565). This is probably a reference to his *Sishu cunyi* [Harboring doubts about the Four Books]. We were unable to locate the exact citation.

13. *Shangshu,* "Yu Shu," "Counsels of Gao Yao"; Legge, *Chinese Classics III,* 69. The full statement is "From what is near he may reach what is distant."

14. In *Chungyong chajam,* II, 3: 29b, Tasan writes that "extrapolating from what is far away to what is near at hand" is a reference to the spirits appearing to be far away when they actually are all around you. In particular, he writes, this is telling us that Heaven may appear to be far away but actually Heaven is aware of everything you do, even if you are alone in a dark room.

15. *Zhuzi yulei,* 64 (*Zhongyong* III). Accessed August 23, 2019, at https://ctext.org/zhuzi-yulei/64.

16. *Book of Songs,* "Guofeng" [Airs of the states], "Odes of Bei," "Kaifeng" [gentle wind]; Legge, 50 (Waley and Allen, 28).

17. *Book of Songs,* "Guofeng" [Airs of the states], "Odes of Bei," "Beifeng" [Northern wind]; Legge, 67 (Waley and Allen, 35).

18. *Book of Songs,* "Xiaoya," "Decade of Qi Fu," "Zheng Yue"; Legge, *Chinese Classics IV,* 319 (Waley and Allen, 169).

19. *Sishu jizhu,* 30 (Johnston and Wang, 490). Zhu Xi is citing a line from *Zhongyong* 1:3.

20. *Sishu jizhu,* 2 (Johnston and Wang, 410).

21. In *Zhongyang chajam*, II, 3, 20b–30a, Tasan says that, since an exemplary person is watchful over himself even when no one else is aware of his thoughts and actions, if he engages in self-examination he will find nothing to be ashamed of.

22. *Book of Songs*, "Daya," "Decade of Dang," "Yi"; Legge, *Chinese Classics IV*, 514–515 (Waley and Allen, 264).

23. *Sishu jizhu*, 30 (Johnston and Wang, 490).

24. This statement by Chen Chun (1159–1223), also known as Chen Beixi, can be found in the *Sishu daquan*, "Zhongyong zhangju daquan-xia." Accessed on August 22, 2019, at https://zh.wikisource.org/wiki/四書大全_(四庫全書本)/中庸章句大全下.

25. Hu Bingwen, *Sishu Tong* [A comprehensive look at the Four Books], 28: 111 (*Zhongyong* tong III). Accessed via the Erudition database. Also available in *Sishu daquan*, "Zhongyong zhangju daquan-xia." Accessed on August 22, 2019, at https://zh.wikisource.org/wiki/四書大全_(四庫全書本)/中庸章句大全下. The literal reading of the line discussed here would be "not move but reverential/revered; not speak but trusting/trusted." Hu's interpretation is plausible because the original line, as is not uncommon in Literary Sinitic, lacks an explicit subject anywhere, and also because both Sinographs which immediately follow "but" can be read as either a verb or an adjective. Others who read those lines assumed that "exemplary persion" is the implied subject of the verbs before "but." Some of them also assumed that the object of the verbs after "but" was the "exemplary person," with the implied subject of the verbs after "but" understood as "the people." Hu, however, made the subject of both verbs preceding "but" the Dao, and made the "exemplary person" the subject of the verbs that follow "but." As Hu read that line, what some others saw as verbs following "but" functioned instead as adjectives describing the state of mind of the exemplary person. Hu's reading is grammatically defensible.

26. This statement is by Xu Qian (1270–1337) can found in *Sishu daquan*, "Zhongyong zhangju daquan-xia." Accessed on August 22, 2019, at https://zh.wikisource.org/wiki/四書大全_(四庫全書本)/中庸章句大全下.

Calling him Dongyang tells us that is the city in Zhejiang Province in which he lived.

27. Cai Qing, *Sishu mengyin*, IV: 126. Available at https://ctext.org/wiki.pl?if=gb&chapter=277936. Accessed August 24, 2019.

28. This statement by Lü Dalin can be found at *Sishu daquan*, "Zhongyong huowen juanxia." Available at https://zh.wikisource.org/wiki/四書大全_(四庫全書本)/中庸或問卷下. Accessed August 24, 2019. Pak Wansik cites this statement in his translation of *Zhongyong huowen*, 552 (footnote 400).

29. *Sishu huowen*, 100–101 (Pak Wansik, 549).

30. In *Chungyong chajam*, II, 3: 30a, Tasan writes that this ode is telling us to be watchful over our thoughts and actions even when no one can tell what we are thinking or doing. Even though he does not see the Dao of Heaven in action, an exemplary person does not let down his guard but instead maintains a mindful and respectful attitude, being cautious and apprehensive of what he cannot see. And even though

he does not hear the Dao of Heaven speak, an exemplary person does not waver in his belief in it but instead stays wary and apprehensive of what he does not hear.

31. *Book of Songs,* "Song," "Shang Song," "Liezu"; Legge, *Chinese Classics IV,* 635 (Waley and Allen 319).

32. *Sishu jizhu,* 30 (Johnston and Wang, 490).

33. In *Chungyong chajam,* II, 3: 30a, Tasan writes that someone who watches over his thoughts and actions even when no one else can see what he is doing or thinking will have a heart-mind that is on an even keel and therefore he will be able to interact harmoniously with everyone and everything he encounters. Such composure combined with harmonious interactions will then have the effect of stimulating everyone and everything he interacts with to reach their full potential. That is why this excerpt from the *Book of Songs,* Tasan argues, says that a ruler can inspire others to do what is right without promising them rewards for doing so and have his people hold him in respectful awe though they have no need to be afraid of him.

He also writes that in serving Heaven, an exemplary person is respectful even though he does not see Heaven doing anything and has complete trust in Heaven even though he does not hear Heaven utter a single word. That being the case, the people under him will serve him without needing the incentive of a reward or being concerned that he might get angry with them. This is a marvelous example of how attitudes toward Heaven influence attitudes among human beings.

34. *Book of Songs,* "Song," "Zhou Song," "Decade of Qing Miao," "Lie Wen"; Legge, *Chinese Classics IV,* 573 (Waley and Allen, 292). This reading is different than the way both Legge and Waley and Allen read it. They have this line say that there is nothing more distinguished than his ethical virtuosity. Legge, and Waley and Allen, base their interpretation on where that line fits into the poem in the *Book of Songs* of which it is a part. Zhu Xi, Hu Yunfeng, and Tasan understand this line within the context in which it appears in the *Zhongyong.* Ames and Hall, *Focusing the Familiar,* agree with Zhu Xi, Hu Yunfeng, and Tasan (115).

35. *Zhuxi yulei,* 64. Accessed August 24, 2019, at https://5ctext.org/zhuzi-yulei/64.

36. Hu Bingwen, *Sishu tong,* "Zhongyong tong III" [A comprehensive look at the Four Books], 28: 112. Accessed via the Erudition database, August 24, 2019. Also available in *Sishu daquan,* "Zhongyong zhangju daquan-xia." Available at https://zh.m.wikisource.org/wiki/四書大全_(四庫全書本)/中庸章句大全下. Accessed August 24, 2019.

37. Hu Bingwen, *Sishu Tong,* "Zhongyong tong III," 28:112–113. Accessed via the Erudition database, August 24, 2019. Also available in *Sishu daquan,* "Zhongyong zhangju daquan-xia." Available at https://zh.wikisource.org/wiki/四書大全_(四庫全書本)/中庸章句大全下. Accessed August 24, 2019.

38. In *Chungyong chajam,* II, 3: 30a–b, Tasan writes that "to not make a public display" means to act in an appropriately responsive and unselfishly cooperative manner. It also means to watch over your thoughts and actions when no one can see what you are thinking or doing. According to Tasan, this section is telling us the same thing preceding sections told us. The power of the Dao of Heaven is not obvious, yet an exemplary person is careful about what he thinks and does. And that is why,

though an exemplary ruler does not make a public display of his ethical power, his subjects follow his example. This is another marvelous example of how attitudes toward Heaven influence attitudes among human beings.

39. *Book of Songs,* "Da ya," "Decade of Wen Wang," "Huang Yi"; Legge, *Chinese Classics IV,* 454 (Waley and Allen, 238).

40. *Sishu jizhu,* 30 (Johnston and Wang, 492).

41. *Sishu jizhu,* 30 (Johnston and Wang, 492).

42. The *Zhongyong* is the only ancient text that attributes this statement to Confucius. In *Chungyong chajam,* II, 3: 30b, Tasan writes that King Wen of Zhou did not use a strong voice or a stern demeanor to govern. He simply was careful to serve the Lord on High properly. That caused his subjects to admire his moral authority. Being watchful over his own thoughts and actions even when he was alone was enough to transform his subjects into better human beings. In that respect, he resembled the Dao of Heaven, which also does not speak or take strong actions to ensure conformity to its Way. A sage, Tasan notes, serves the Lord on High by acting in an unselfishly cooperative and appropriately responsive manner and, in doing so, ensures that the people will in turn serve their ruler in the same way. This, Tasan writes, is a universal principle.

43. *Book of Songs,* "Guofeng," "Binfeng," "Chixiao"; Legge, *Chinese Classics IV,* 234 (Waley and Allen, 122).

44. This statement is attributed to Confucius in *Kongzi jiayu,* "haosheng," 18. See *Kongzi jiayu tongjie,* 121. Also available at https://ctext.org/kongzi-jiayu/hao-sheng. Accessed August 24, 2019.

45. *Book of Songs,* "Xiao Ya," "Decade of Durenshi," "Mianman"; Legge, *Chinese Classics IV,* 418 (Waley and Allen, 219).

46. This episode appears in the *Daxue.* See Andrew Plaks, *Ta Hsüeh and Chung Yung (The Highest Order of Cultivation and On the Practice of the Mean),* 7–8.

47. *Book of Songs,* "Day Ya," "Decade of Dang," "Zhengmin"; Legge, 544 (Waley and Allen, 276).

48. This last chapter of the *Zhongyong* follows the citation from the "Zhengmin" ode with a reference to a line from *Book of Songs,* "Daya," "Decade of Wen Wang," "Wen Wang"; Legge, 431 (Waley and Allen, 228). The line referred to here reads "The way Heaven on High operates has neither sound nor scent."

49. *Sizhu juzhu,* 30 (Johnston and Wang, 492).

50. In *Chungyong chajam,* II, 3: 30b, Tasan says that the reference to Heaven on High making no sound or giving off any scent clarifies how an exemplary ruler can transform his subjects for the better. Neither making a public display nor adopting a stern demeanor reflects an unselfishly cooperative and appropriately responsive manner. Moreover, to say that Heaven on High makes no sound and gives off no scent clarifies that the Dao of Heaven is not something that can be seen or heard but nevertheless we should maintain an attitude of caution and apprehension as though we can sense that it is both above and all around us.

51. See *Zhuxi yulei,* 64 (*Zhongyong* III), 66a. Accessed on August 26, 2019, at https://ctext.org/zhuzi-yulei/64.

52. Non-Polarity refers to what is thought of when we think of the universe as

quiet, calm, and undifferentiated. We need the concept of Non-Polarity, mainstream neo-Confucians argued, to understand Supreme Polarity, the dynamic division between Yin and Yang which is for them the metaphysical basis for all differentiation in the cosmos. Non-Polarity and Supreme Polarity are not thought of as two distinct states of existence which can be distinguished temporally. Instead, they are abstractions that imply each other and are therefore conceptually intertwined. Just as you cannot conceive of something being divided without being able to also conceive of it when it is not divided, similarly you cannot conceive of something as undifferentiated unless you can at the same time contrast that image with an image of that same thing differentiated. They represent two different ways of envisioning the same cosmos at the same time, either as undifferentiated or as differentiated, with each image a prerequisite for conceiving its opposite. You need both for a complete picture.

53. This argument by Hu Bingwen can be found in *Sishu daquan,* "zhongyong zhangju daquan-xia." Available at https://zh.wikisource.org/wiki/四書大全_(四庫全書本)/中庸章句大全下. Accessed October 4, 2020.

54. *Sishu huowen,* 54 (Pak Wansik, 383).

55. David R. Knechtges, trans., *The Han Shu Biography of Yang Xiong* ((Tampe: Center for Asian Studies, Arizona State University, 1982), 23. See the original at https://ctext.org/han-shu/yang-xiong-zhuan-shang/zh. Accessed September 4, 2020.

56. In *Chungyong chajam,* II, 3: 3a, Tasan says that exercising dominion over the myriad things is a reference to "the rule of Heaven on High over the myriad things."

57. Hu Bingwen is cited in *Sishu daquan,* "zhongyong zhangju daquan-xia" (available at https://zh.wikisource.org/wiki/四書大全_(四庫全書本)/中庸章句大全下; accessed October 4, 2020) as saying that ethical virtuosity that does not make a public display is a reference to a heart-mind in a state on non-activation and therefore being completely quiescent. Moreover, Hu goes on to say, a heart-mind in such a state is what is meant by Non-Polarity yet Supreme Polarity.

58. Kwangam is the literary name of Yi Pyŏk. Elsewhere in this text he is referred to as Yi Tŏkcho.

59. Adler, *Reconstructing the Confucian Dao,* 151–166, esp. 157. *Kan* [坎] and *Li* [離] are polar opposites, meaning not only water and fire but also descent and ascent, so they are used here to represent *yin* and *yang*.

60. An ancient alchemy text sometimes accredited to Wei Boyang 魏伯陽 (??–728) of the Eastern Han. The title is translated as *The Kinship of the Three, The Triplex Unity,* or *The Seal of the Unity of the Three.* See Fabrizio Pregadio, trans., *The Seal of the Unity of the Three: A Study and Translation of the Cantong qi, the Source of the Taoist Way of the Golden Elixir* (Mountain View, CA: Golden Elixer Press, 2011), esp. 37–38.

Discussing Zhu Xi's Preface to *Zhongyong zhangju*

1. "Master Cheng" here appears to be Cheng Yi. See *Er Cheng Yishu,* vol. 24. Available at https://zh.wikisource.org/wiki/二程遺書/卷24. Accessed August 28,

2019. Also see A. C. Graham, *Two Chinese Philosophers: The Metaphysics of the Brothers Ch'eng* (LaSalle, IL: Open Court, 1992), 64.

2. "Preface to the *Zhongyong zhangju*," Johnston and Wang, 400.

3. *Mencius*, 7b: XXIV, 1 (Jin Xin); Van Norden, 189.

4. This statement by Zhu Xi can be found in Cai Chen, *Shujing jichuan* [A collection of commentaries on the Book of Documents], vol. 6. Accessed via the Erudition database, August 28, 2019.

5. *Daodejing*, 39. Accessed at https://ctext.org/dao-de-jing August 28, 2109.

6. Yi I, *Yulgok chŏnsŏ* [The complete works of Yulgok Yi I], "Insim.Dosim tosŏl" [A diagram of the Human Heart-mind and the Dao Heart-mind], XIV: 4a–b.

7. *T'oegye sŏnsaeng munjip* [The collected works of T'oegye Yi Hwang], 16:32a.

8. Here Tasan uses language quite similar to what Ricci uses in *Tianzhu shiyi* [The true meaning of the Lord of Heaven], 83–84.

9. Yi I, *Yulgok chŏnso*, "Tap Sŏng Howŏn" [A response to a letter from Howŏn Sŏng Hon], X, 26a–27a. For more on Yulgok's thoughts on the relationship between *li* and *ki*, as expressed in his exchanges with Sŏng Hon, see Edward Y. J. Chung, *The Korean Neo-Confucianism of Yi T'oegye and Yi Yulgok: A Reappraisal of the "Four-Seven Thesis" and Its Practical Implications for Self-Cultivation* (Albany: State University of New York Press, 1995), 85–118.

10. Yi Pyŏk.

11. This essay is partially translated as "What the I/Ki Debate is Really All About," in Yongho Ch'oe, Peter H. Lee, and Wm Theodore De Bary, ed. *Sources of Korean Tradition* (New York: Columbia University Press, 2000), 200–202.

12. "Preface to the *Zhongyong zhangju*," Johnston and Wang, 400.

13. "Preface to the *Zhongyong zhangju*," Johnston and Wang, 400.

14. *Zhongyong*, XX: 18. In *Chungyong chajam*, II: III, 22b, Tasan writes that "to hold fast" means to be consistent in following through on that decision to act appropriately. For "consistent," he uses the Sinograph *yong*, the second syllable in *Zhongyong*, the title of this work.

15. Here the multilayered meanings of important Sinographs come into play. The Sinograph *zhong* [literally, "center"] in this text often means a composed and focused mental state. However, it can also mean to avoid extremes by following the path between extremes, which you can do if you keep your heart-mind composed and focused. Such a mental state will also allow you to evaluate the particulars of a situation you find yourself in and act appropriately. Such action is *zhong*, in this case meaning on-target. This reference to centered action is how Tasan interprets the first phrase the king asks about here. See *Chungyong chajam*, II, 3: 9b.

16. *Book of Documents*, "Counsels of the Great Yu," II: 2, 15; Legge, *Chinese Classics III*: 61–62.

17. *Zhongyong*, II.

18. *Mencius*, Jinxin 1: 26 (Van Norden, 178). Mencius compares Zimo to Yang Zhu, who exemplifies extreme selfishness, and Mozi, who called for loving everyone equally. He praises Zimo for remaining centered between those two extremes. However, he also warns that being too rigid without adapting to changes in the situations you find yourself in is as bad as going to one extreme or the other.

19. Hu Guang (91–172) was a scholar-official in Han China. He was supposedly an expert on the *Zhongyong*. However, he made a recommendation to the throne which backfired, which caused people to say that he actually did not know how to choose the appropriate way to act at a particular time in a particular situation. *Houhanshu* [History of the later Han dynasty], chapter 44, "Deng-Zhang-Xu-Zhang-Hu liezhuan" [A collection of biographies of Deng Biao, Zhang Yu, Xu Fang, Zhang Min, and Hu Guang]. Available at https://ctext.org/hou-han-shu/deng-zhang-xu-zhang-hu-lie-zhuan. Accessed January 1, 2020.

20. *Zhongyong*, II.

21. Huangfu Xi was a recluse during the Jin dynasty (265–420).

22. Feng Dao (882–954) was an important statesman during the Five Dynasties and Ten Kingdoms period and served different rulers in different states, which gave him a reputation for being an opportunist.

Discussing the Divisions of the Text

1. Available in Hu Guang, "Du Zhongyong Fa," *Sishu daquan* [A great collection on the Four Books], vol. 46, in *Siku quanshu* Wenyangge edition. Accessed via the Erudition database. It is also available at https://zh.wikisource.org/wiki/四書大全_(四庫全書本)/中庸章句序. Accessed September 1, 2019.

2. Wang Bo (1197–1274) belonged to an early generation of neo-Confucians who followed Zhu Xi.

3. "Li Sao" [Encountering Sorrow] is a long poem by Qu Yuan, said to been active in the late fourth century BCE. See David Hawkes, *Ch'u Tz'u: The Songs of the South* (Boston: Beacon Press, 1962), 21–34.

A Record of the Discussion of the *Zhongyong* at the Brilliant Governance Hall

1. The Brilliant Governance Hall [Hŭijŏngdang] is a building within Changdŏk Palace. This is a record of a discussion King Chŏngjo held there in 1790.

2. O Chae-sun (1727–1792) had a distinguished career under King Chŏngjo, serving in high posts in several government departments.

3. "He is appropriately composed and focused in whatever situation he finds himself in" appears in *Zhongyong* II. "Composed, focused, and cooperative" appears in *Zhongyong* I.

4. Yi Pyŏngmo (1742–1806) had a distinguished career under King Chŏngjo, serving as Second State Councillor on the State Council as well as serving as an ambassador to the Qing court and then rising to Chief State Councillor under King Sunjo (r. 1800–1834). He played a leading role in the persecution of Catholics and those believed to be associated with Catholicism, such as Tasan, in 1801.

5. *Zhongyong*, II.

6. *Zhongyong*, III.

7. *Analects*, 6.29 (63). Slingerland has: "among the common people few are able to practice it for very long," which is similar to the way Tasan reads this line.

8. *Zhongyong*, VII.

9. This is a reference to *Zhongyong*, XXXII.

10. In Chapter I of the *Zhongyong*, there is a line saying that equanimity ["being centered"] is the great foundation of All-under-Heaven. In Chapter XXXII, there is a line saying that those who are unselfishly cooperative and appropriately responsive are able to establish the great foundation for All-under-Heaven. Tasan seems to be saying here that maintaining equanimity and acting in an unselfishly cooperative and appropriately responsive manner are the same thing, in that they are what establishes the link between Heaven and humanity.

11. *Mencius*, Jinxin I: 1 (Van Norden, 171).

12. *Shangshu*, Shang Shu, Announcement of Zhong-hui; Legge, *Chinese Classics III*, 183.

13. See the discussion in *Chungyong Kangŭibo*, I: 4.

14. This is a reference to the first line in Chapter XXXI, which says a sage is discerning, intelligent, and wise.

15. *Book of Documents*, "Zhoushu," "Charge to the Count of Wei," 1; Legge, *Chinese Classics III*, 378. *Chunqiu Zuozhuan*, "Lord Wen," 18th year; Legge, *Chinese Classics V*, 282 (Durrant, Li, and Schaberg I: 572).

16. Tasan may be hinting here at his belief that human beings need to rely on the Lord on High rather than a sage to inspire them to exert the effort necessary to consistently act appropriately.

Works Consulted

Primary Sources

Ban Biao 班彪. *Hanshu* 漢書 [History of the Former Han dynasty]. Available at https://ctext.org/han-shu. Accessed April 24, 2020.

Ban Gu 班固. *Baihutong* 白虎通 [Discussions at the White Tiger Hall]. Available at https://ctext.org/bai-hu-tong. Accessed August 28, 2019.

Cai Chen 蔡沈. *Shujing jichuan* 書經集傳 [A collection of commentaries on the Book of Documents]. Accessed via the *Erudition Database of Chinese Classic Ancient Books* August 28, 2019.

Cai Qing 蔡清. *Sishu mengyin* 四書蒙引 [Introduction to the Four Books for beginners]. Available via *Erudition Database of Chinese Classic Ancient Books* and at https://ctext.org/wiki.pl?if=gb&res=745255. Accessed May 21, 2018.

Cheng Yi 程頤 and Cheng Ho 程顥. *Er Cheng yishu* 二程遺書 [Surviving works of the Cheng Brothers]. Accessed at https://zh.wikisource.org/wiki/二程遺書 July 7, 2019.

Chŏng Yagyong 丁若鏞. *Chŏngbon Yŏyudang chŏnsŏ* 定本 與猶堂全書 [The complete works of Chŏng Yagyong, the definitive version]. Seoul: Tasan Haksul Munhwa Chaedan, 2012. Also available online at http://db.itkc.or.kr and at http://tasan.or.kr. Accessed July 10, 2021.

———. *Yŏyudang chŏnsŏ* 與猶堂全書 [The complete works of Chŏng Yagyong]. Seoul: Tasan Haksul Munhwa Chaedan, 2001. (This is the version that provides the traditional pagination, the volume (*kwŏn*) and a–b page numbers, used in the citations.)

Chosŏn wangjo sillok 朝鮮王朝實錄 [Annals of the Chosŏn dynasty]. Available online at http://sillok.history.go.kr/main/main.do. Accessed April 6, 2019.

Dadai Liji 大戴禮記 [Record of ritual matters by Dai the Elder]. Available at https://ctext.org/da-dai-li-ji. Accessed July 29, 2019.

Dahui 大慧. *Dahui chansi yulu* [大慧禪師語 Records of Chan Master Dahui], cited in Shengyan 聖嚴, ed. *Chanmen xiuzheng zhiyao* 禪門修證指要 [Essential pointers to practice and realization through the Chan Gate]. Taipei: Fagu Wenhua, 1980.

Dallet, Charles. *Histoire de L'Église de Corée*. Paris: Victor Palmé, 1874.

Fan Ye 范曄. *Houhanshu*. 後漢書 [History of the Later Han dynasty]. Available at https://ctext.org/hou-han-shu/deng-zhang-xu-zhang-hu-lie-zhuan. Accessed January 1, 2020.

Gu Menglin 顧夢麟. *Sishu shuoyue* 四書說約 [Simple explanations of the Four Books]. Accessed via the *Erudition Database of Chinese Classic Ancient Books*. It was origi-

443

nally published in Beijing in 1640. It is also available at https://ctext.org/wiki.pl?if=gb&res=640342. Accessed June 20, 2019.

Guoyu 國語 [Discourses of the states]. Available at https://ctext.org/guo-yu. Accessed June 14, 2019.

Han Yu 韓愈. *Han Yu ji* 韓愈集 [Han Yu's collected writings]. Accessed May 22, 2019, at https://ctext.org/wiki.pl?if=gb&res=464031.

Hang Shijun 杭世駿. *Xu Liji jishuo* 續禮記集說 [Supplement to the commentaries on the Book of Rites]. Accessed via the *Erudition Database of Chinese Classic Ancient Books*. June 1, 2019. Also available in print. Shanghai: Shanghai Guji Chubanshe, 2002.

Hu Bingwen 胡炳文. *Sishu tong* 四書通 [A comprehensive look at the Four Books]. Accessed at *Erudition Database of Chinese Classic Ancient Books*. Accessed on August 22, 2019.

Hu Guang 胡廣. *Sishu daquan* 四書大全 [The complete collection on the Four Books]. Accessed at *Erudition Database of Chinese Classic Ancient Books*. A printed reproduction was published in Taibei, Taiwan, by Shangwu Yinshuguanin in 1978. It first appeared in China in 1415. It is also available https://zh.wikisource.org/zh-hant/四書大全_(四庫全書本) Accessed December 11, 2022.

Kang Mangil (강만길) et al., ed. *Ch'uan kŭp Kugan* 推案及鞫案 [Records of special investigations by the State Tribunal], vol. 25. Seoul: Asea Munhwasa, 1978 Also available at http://http://waks.aks.ac.kr/rsh/dir/rdirItem.aspx?rptID=AKS-2012-CAB-1101_DES&rshID=AKS-2012-CAB-1101&dirRsh=추안급국안$25권:권책$025. Accessed April 6, 2019.

Li Dingzuo 李鼎祚. *Zhouyi jijie* 周易集解 [Collected exegeses on the Zhou Book of Changes]. Available at https://zh.wikisource.org/zh-hans/周易集解/卷一. Accessed September 5, 2020.

Lu Deming 陸德明. *Jingdian shiwen* 經典釋文 [Explanatory writings on the Classical Canon]. Available at https://zh.wikipedia.org/wiki/經典釋文. Accessed August 17, 2019.

Lü Liuliang 呂留良. *Luzi pingyu* 呂子評語 [Master Lü's critical observations]. Available at https://ctext.org/wiki.pl?if=gb&res=205251. Accessed on May 19, 2019.

Mao Qiling 毛奇齡. *Sishu gaicuo* 四書改錯 [Correcting the errors in Zhu Xi's commentaries on the Four Books]. Accessed via the *Erudition Database of Chinese Classic Ancient Books*. Accessed June 13, 2019.

———. *Sishu shengyan* 四書賸言 [Residual remarks about the Four Books]. Accessed via the *Erudition Database of Chinese Classic Ancient Books*. Accessed on June 14, 2019.

———. *Zhongyongshuo* 中庸說 [A discussion of the Zhongyong], reprinted in *Siku quanshu cunmu congshu Jingbu* 四庫全書存目叢書經部 [A collection of works whose titles appear in the *Siku quanshu:* on the Classics], ser. 1. Jinan: Qi Lu shu she, 1997. 173: 84–140. Also included in Mao Qiling's *Xihe heji* 西河合集.

Mingxin baojian (K. *Myŏngsim pogam*) 明心寶鑒 [A precious mirror of an enlightened heart-mind]. Available at https://ctext.org/wiki.pl?if=en&chapter=523440. Accessed December 25, 2019.

Qu Ruji 瞿汝稷. *Zhiyue lu* 指月錄 [Record of pointing at the moon], compiled in 1595. Available at https://zh.wikisource.org/zh-hant/指月錄. Accessed December 11, 2022.

Shisanjing zhushu fu xiaokanji 十三經 注疏附校勘記 [Notes and annotations to the Thirteen Classics]. Reprint; Beijing: Zhonghwa Shuju, 1980.

Sima Qian 司馬遷. *Siji* 史記 [Records of the Grand Historian]. Available at https://ctext.org/shiji. Accessed June 3, 2019. There is also an English translation edited by William H. Nienhauser Jr., translated by Weiguo Cao, Scott W. Galer, William H. Nienhauser Jr., and David W. Pankenier, published in multiple volumes as *The Grand Scribe's Records*. Bloomington: Indiana University Press, 1994–2019.

Sŏ Chongt'ae 서종태 and Han Kŏn 한건, trans. *Chosŏn hugi Ch'ŏnjugyo sinja chaep'an kirok: ch'uan mit kugan* 조선후기 천주교 신자 재판: 推案 및 鞫案 [The record of the trials of Catholics in the latter half of the Chosŏn dynasty: The records of the special investigations by the State Tribunal]. Seoul: Kukhak Charyowŏn, 2004.

Wei Shi 衛湜. *Liji jishuo* 禮記集說 [Collection of commentaries on the Book of Rites], Qinding Siku quanshu [The complete collection of the Emperor's Four Treasuries]. Available at https://ctext.org/wiki.pl?if=gb&res=213863. Accessed May 21, 2018.

Wugouzi 無垢子. *Mohe banruo boluo miduo xinjing zhujie* 摩訶般若波羅蜜多心經註解 [A commentary on the Prajñaparamita Heart Sutra]. Available at http://buddhism.lib.ntu.edu.tw/FULLTEXT/sutra/10thousand/X26n0574.pdf. Accessed May 18, 2019.

Xu Qian 許謙. *Du Zhongyong congshuo* 讀中庸叢說 [A collection of accounts of reading the *Zhongyong*]. Accessed via the *Erudition Database of Chinese Classic Ancient Books*. Accessed June 9, 2019.

Xuandi chuixun 玄帝垂訓 [Instructions handed down on Mt. Wudang to humans by the Supreme Lord of Dark Heaven]. The full title of this text is *Wudangshan Xuantian shangdi chuixun* 武當山玄天上帝垂訓文. Available at http://www.taolibrary.com/category/category86/c86017.htm. Accessed December 25, 2019.

Yan Shigu 顏師古. *Kuangmiu zhengsu* 匡謬正俗 [Corrections of errors and rectification of vulgar readings]. Available at https://ctext.org/wiki.pl?if=gb&chapter=402955. Accessed May 19, 2019.

Yi Hwang 李滉. *T'oegye sŏnsaeng munjip* 退溪先生文集 [The writings of Master T'oegye Yi Hwang]. Seoul: Konggŭpch'ŏ Han'guk Ch'ulp'an Hyŏptong Chohap, 1997. Also available as *T'oegyejip* 退溪集 at http://db.itkc.or.kr. Accessed December 24, 2019.

Yi I 李珥. *Yulgok Chŏnsŏ* 栗谷全書 [The complete works of Yulgok Yi I]. Seoul: Minjok Munhwa Ch'ujinhoe, 1989. Also available at http://db.itkc.or.kr. Accessed December 24, 2019.

Yi Ik 李瀷. *Sŏngho sasŏl* 星湖僿說 [The humble discourses of Sŏngho]. Seoul: Minjok Munhwa Ch'ujinhoe, 1977–1978. Also available at http://db.itkc.or.kr. Accessed April 6, 2019.

Yi Kigyŏng 李基慶. *Pyŏgwip'yŏn* 闢衛編 [In defense of orthodoxy against heterodoxy].

Seoul: Kyohoesa yŏn'guso, 1979. This is the original *Pyŏgwip'yŏn* on which Yi Manchae's *Pyŏgwip'yŏn* is based.

Yi Manch'ae 李晩采. *Pyŏgwip'yŏn* 闢衛編 [In defense of orthodoxy against heterodoxy]. Seoul: Yŏlhwadang, 1971.

Zhao De 趙悳. *Sishu jianyi* 四書箋義 [Notes on the meaning of the Four Books]. Accessed at the *Erudition Database of Chinese Classic Ancient Books*, August 5, 2019.

Zhao Shunsun 趙順孫. *Sishu zuanshu* 四書纂疏 [A compilation of notes on the Four Books]. Available at https://ctext.org/wiki.pl?if=gb&res=804089. Accessed June 20, 2021.

———. *Zhongyong zuanshu* 中庸纂疏 [A compilation of comments on the *Zhongyong*]. Downloadable at https://archive.org/details/06079390.cn. Also accessible at https://ctext.org/wiki.pl?if=gb&res=579522. Accessed June 3, 2019.

Zhu Xi 朱熹. *Hui'an xiansheng Zhu wengong wenji* 晦菴先生朱文公文集 [Collected writings of Hui'an Zhu wengong]. Accessed via the *Erudition Database*, April 19, 2020.

———. *Sishu huowen* 四書或問 [Questions and Answers on the Four Books]. Shanghai: Shanghai Guji Chubanshe, 2001. Also available at https://ctext.org/wiki.pl?if=gb&res=256209. Accessed April 5, 2019.

———. *Yuzuan Zhuzi quanshu* 御纂朱子全書 [The complete works of Master Zhu Xi]. Available at https://ctext.org/wiki.pl?if=gb&res=363512. Accessed June 7, 2020. Also available as pdf files at https://archive.org/search.php?query=御纂朱子全書. Accessed June 7, 2020.

———. *Zhongyong jilüe* 中庸集略 [An abridged collection on the *Zhongyong*]. Accessed via the *Erudition Database of Chinese Classic Ancient Books*, April 21, 2020.

———. *Zhongyong Zhangju* 中庸章句 [The *Zhongyong* by chapter and phrase] as found in *Sishu jizhu* 四書集註 [Collected Commentaries on the Four Books], published by Dafu Shuju in Tainan, Taiwan 1991. Also available at https://ctext.org/si-shu-zhang-ju-ji-zhu/zhong-yong-zhang-ju/zh. Accessed April 5, 2019.

———. *Zhuzi wenji* 朱子文集 [Collected writing of Zhu Xi]. Taipei: Defu Wenjiao Jijinhui, 2000. Also available at https://ctext.org/wiki.pl?if=gb&chapter=149612&remap=gb. Accessed April 18, 2020.

———. *Zhuzi yulei* 朱子語類 [The classified sayings of Master Zhu]. Taibei: Zheng Zhong Shuju, 1962. Also available at https://ctext.org/zhuzi-yulei. Accessed April 19, 2019.

Translations of Primary Sources

Ames, Roger T., and David L. Hall, trans. *Focusing the Familiar: A Translation and Philosophical Interpretation of the Zhongyong*. Honolulu: University of Hawai'i Press, 2001.

Baker, Don. *Catholics and Anti-Catholicism in Chosŏn Korea*. Honolulu: University of Hawai'i Press, 2017.

Bang In [Pang In]. "Chŏng Yag-yong's Cosmogonic Idea and Matteo Ricci's Influence Shown in His Interpretation of the Zhouyi: A Compromise between Creationism and Evolutionism," *Tasanhak* 35 (2019): 281–328.

Birch, Cyril, ed. *Anthology of Chinese Literature from Early Times to the Fourteenth Century*. New York: Grove Press, 1965.

Chan, Wing-tsit. Compiler and Translator. *A Source Book in Chinese Philosophy*. Princeton, NJ: Princeton University Press, 1963.

Chan, Wing-tsit, trans. Lu Zuqian and Zhu Xi, *Reflections on Things at Hand*. New York: Columbia University Press, 1967.

———, trans. Ch'en Ch'un, *Neo-Confucian Terms Explained (The Pei-hsi tzu-i)*. New York: Columbia University Press, 1986.

Cheung, Martha P. Y., ed. *An Anthology of Chinese Discourse on Translation*. New York: Routledge, 2014.

Choi Byonghyon, trans. Chŏng Yagyong. *Admonitions on Governing the People: Manual for All Administrations*. Berkeley: University of California Press, 2010.

Chŏnju University Center for the Study of Honam 全州大湖南學研究所, trans. *Kugyŏk yŏyudang chŏnsŏ Kyŏngjip I: Taehak. Chungyong.* [國譯 與猶堂全書 經集 I. 大學•中庸 A Korean Translation of the Complete Works of Yŏyudang Chŏng Yagyong: On the Classics, volume I, the Great Learning and the Doctrine of the Mean]. Chŏnju, Korea: Chŏnju University Press, 1986.

De Bary, Wm. Theodore, and Irene Bloom, eds. *Sources of Chinese Tradition*, I. New York: Columbia University Press, 1999.

Durrant, Stephen, Wai-yee Li, and David Schaberg, trans. *Zuo Tradition: Zuozhuan Commentary on the Spring and Autumn Annals*. Seattle: University of Washington Press, 2016.

Ebrey, Patricia Buckley, trans. *Chu Hsi's Family Rituals*. Princeton, NJ: Princeton University Press, 1991.

Forke, Alfred, trans. Wang Chong. *Lun-Heng: Part 1, Philosophical Essays of Wang Ch'ung*. London: Luzac & Co., 1907.

Frankel, Hans H. "The Chinese Ballad Southeast Fly the Peacocks," *Harvard Journal of Asiatic Studies* 34 (1974): 248–271.

Gardner, Daniel K. *The Four Books: The Basic Teachings of the Later Confucian Tradition*. Indianapolis: Hackett, 2007.

Hawkes, David, trans. *Ch'u Tz'u: The Songs of the South*. Boston: Beacon Press, 1962.

Hucker, Charles O., trans. *Dictionary of Official Titles in Imperial China*. Stanford, CA: Stanford University Press, 1985.

Hutton, Eric L., trans. *Xunzi: The Complete Text*. Princeton, NJ: Princeton University Press, 2014.

Ivanhoe, Philip J., ed. *Zhu Xi: Selected Writings*. New York: Oxford University Press, 2019.

Johnston, Ian, and Wang Ping, trans. *Daxue and Zhongyong*. Hong Kong: Chinese University Press, 2012. This work includes the original text of Zhu Xi's *Zhongyong zhangju* as well as Zheng Xuan's notes and Kong Yingda's commentary on the *Zhongyong*.

Kalton, Michael C., trans. Yi Hwang. *To Become a Sage: The Ten Diagrams of Sage Learning*. New York: Columbia University Press, 1988.

Kim, Hongkyung, trans. Chŏng Yagyong, *The Analects of Dasan: A Korean Syncretic Reading* I–IV. New York: Oxford University Press, 2016–2021.

Knechtges, David R., trans. *The Han Shu Biography of Yang Xiong*. Tempe: Center for Asian Studies, Arizona State University, 1982.

Lancashire, Douglas, and Peter Hu Kuo-chen, trans. Revised by Thierry Meynard, S.J., Matteo Ricci, *The True Meaning of the Lord of Heaven*. Boston: Institute of Jesuit Sources, Boston College, 2016.

Lee, Peter H., ed. *Sourcebook of Korean Civilization* I-II. New York: Columbia University Press, 1993–1996.

Legge, James, trans. *The Chinese Classics, with a translation, critical and exegetical notes, prolegomena and copious indexes*. Reprint; Taipei: Wen Shih Che Publishing, 1972.

———. *The I Ching: The Book of Changes*. New York: Dover Publications, 1963.

———, with Ch'u Chai and Winberg Chai, trans. *Li Chi: Book of Rites. An Encyclopedia of Ancient Ceremonial Usages, Religious Creeds, and Social Institutions*. New Hyde Park, NY: University Books, 1967.

Liao, Wenkui, trans. *The Complete Works of Han Fei Tzu*. London: A Probsthain, 1959.

Lynn, Richard John, trans. *The Classic of Changes, a new translation of the I Ching as interpreted by Wang Bi*. New York: Columbia University Press, 1994. This is based on pre-Song understandings of the *Classic of Changes*. Since Tasan looked to earlier readings of the classics to find what he thought would be their real meaning, when Tasan cites this work, I rely primarily on Lynn's translation.

Major, John S., Sarah A. Queen, Andrew S. Meyer, and Harold D. Roth, trans. *The Huainanzi*. New York: Columbia University Press, 2010.

Milburn, Olivia, trans. *The Spring and Autumn Annals of Master Yan*. Leiden: Brill, 2016.

Miller, Harry, trans. *The Gongyang Commentary on the Spring and Autumn Annals: A Full Translation*. New York: Palgrave Macmillan, 2015.

Muller, Charles, trans. *Doctrine of the Mean*. Available at http://www.acmuller.net/con-dao/docofmean.html. Accessed June 20, 2021.

Pak Ilbong 朴一峰, trans. *Hyogyŏng* 孝經 [*Xiaojing* – Classic of Filial Piety]. Seoul: Yungminsa, 1992.

Pak Wansik 박완식, trans. *Chungyong* 중용. Seoul: Yŏgang Publishing, 2008. This contains Zhu Xi's *Zhongyong zhangju* and *Zhongyong huowen* in the original along with a Korean translation.

Plaks, Andrew. *Ta Hsüeh and Chung Yung (The Highest Order of Cultivation and On the Practice of the Mean)*. New York: Penguin, 2003.

Pregadio, Fabrizio, trans. *The Seal of the Unity of the Three: A Study and Translation of the Cantong qi, the Source of the Taoist Way of the Golden Elixir*. Mountain View, CA: Golden Elixer Press, 2011.

Rosemont, Henry, Jr., and Roger T. Ames. *The Chinese Classic of Family Reverence: A Philosophical Translation of the Xiaojing*. Honolulu: University of Hawai'i Press, 2009.

Sawyer, Ralph D., trans. *The Seven Military Classics of Ancient China*. New York: Basic Books, 1993.

Silsi Haksa Kyŏnghak Yŏn'guhoe 實是 學舍 經學 研究會, trans. Chŏng Yagyong, 丁若鏞 *Tasan ŭi Kyŏnghak Segye* 茶山의 經學世界 [The world of Tasan's studies of the Confucian Classics]. Seoul: Han'gilsa, 2002.

———. Chŏng Yagyong 丁若鏞, and Yi Chaeŭi 李載毅. *Tasan kwa Munsan ŭi insŏng nonjaeng* [다산 과 문산 의 인성 논쟁 [The discussion between Chŏng Yagyong and Yi Chaeŭi on human nature]. Seoul: Han'gilsa, 1996.

Slingerland, Edward. *Confucius: Analects, with Selections from Traditional Commentaries*. Indianapolis: Hackett, 2003.

Steele, John, trans. *The I-li or the Book of Etiquette and Ceremonial*. London: Probsthain & Company, 1917.

Van Norden, Bryan W., trans. *Mengzi, with Selections from Traditional Commentaries*. Indianapolis: Hackett, 2008.

Waley, Arthur, trans. *The Analects of Confucius*. New York: Vantage Books, 1989.

———. *The Book of Songs*. New York: Grove Press, 1960.

——— and Joseph Allen, trans. *The Book of Songs Translated from the Chinese by Arthur Waley*. New York: Grove Press, 1996.

Watson, Burton, trans. *Xunzi: Basic Writings*. New York: Columbia University Press, 2003.

Yang Zhaoming 楊朝明 and Song Lilin 宋立林, ed. *Kongzi jiayu tongjie* [孔子家語通解 A complete exegesis of the sayings of the Confucian School]. Jinan: Qi Lu shu she, 2009. *Kongzi jiayu* is also available online at https://ctext.org/kongzi-jiayu. Accessed June 14, 2019.

Yi Chihyŏng 李篪衡, trans. Chŏng Yagyong 丁若鏞. *Yŏkchu Nonŏ kogŭmju* [譯註論語古今註 Ancient and Recent Annotations to the Analects of Confucius, translated into Korean and annotated]. Seoul: Saam, 2010.

———. Chŏng Yagyong 丁若鏞. *Yŏkchu Tasan Maengja Yoŭi* [譯註孟子要義 An annotated translation of Tasan's the *Essential Points in Mencius*]. Seoul: Hyŏndai sirhaksa, 1994.

Yun Kugil 윤국일, trans. *Sinp'yŏn Kyŏngguk taejŏn* [新編經國大典 newly edited version of the Great Administrative Code]. Seoul: Sinsŏwŏn, 2005.

Secondary Sources

Some of the secondary sources listed below are not explicitly cited in this work. However, they all proved very useful for understanding the philosophical orientation of Chŏng Yagyong, particularly his distinctive approach to extracting lessons for moral cultivation from the *Zhongyong*.

Adler, Joseph A. *Reconstructing the Confucian Dao: Zhu Xi's Appropriation of Zhou Dunyi*. Albany: State University of New York Press, 2014.

———. "Varieties of Spiritual Experience: *Shen* in Neo-Confucian Discourse." Tu

Wei-ming and Mary Evelyn Tucker, eds., *Confucian Spirituality*, II, 120–148. New York: Crossroads, 2004..

———. "Zhu Xi's Spiritual Practice as the Basis of His Central Philosophical Concepts." *Dao* 7 (2008): 57–79.

Ames, Roger. *Confucian Role Ethics: A Vocabulary*. Honolulu: University of Hawai'i Press, 2011.

An, Yanming. "Western 'Sincerity' and Confucian 'Cheng.'" *Asian Philosophy* 14, no. 2 (July 2004): 155–169.

Angle, Stephen C., and Justin Tiwald. "Moral Psychology: Heartmind (Xin), Nature (Xing), and Emotions (Qing)." 361–387. In Kai-chiu Ng and Yong Huang, eds., *Dao Companion to Zhu Xi's Philosophy*. Cham, Switzerland: Springer Nature, 2020.

Baek Min Jeong (Paek Minjŏng). "Moral Success and Failure in the Ethical Theory of Tasan Chŏng Yagyong." *Acta Koreana* 19, no. 1 (June 2016): 241–266.

Baker, Don. "The Martyrdom of Paul Yun: Western Religion and Eastern Ritual in Eighteenth-Century Korea." *Transactions of the Royal Asiatic Society, Korea Branch* 54 (1979): 33–58.

Center for Research of Religious Issues, Seoul National University 서울대학교 종교문제연구소, ed. *Yugyo wa Chonggyohak* [Confucianism and Religious Studies]. Seoul: Seoul National University Press, 2009.

Cha Kijin 차기진. "Manch'ŏn Yi Sŭnghun ŭi kyohoe hwaldong kwa chŏngch'ijŏk ipchi" 蔓川 李承薰의 교회 활동과 정치적 입지 [Manch'ŏn Yi Sŭnghun's political stance and his activities for the church]. *Kyohoesa yŏn'gu* 교회사연구 8 (1992): 33–57.

Chen Feng-Yuan 陳逢源. "Cong 《sishu jizhu》 dao 《sishu daquan》 –Zhu Xi houxue zhi xueshu xipu kaocha" (從《四書集注》到《四書大全》—朱熹後學之學術系譜考察). *Chengda zhongwen xuebao* 成大中文學報 49 (June 2015): 75–112.

Cheng, Chung-ying. "On the Metaphysical Significance of Ti (Body-Embodiment) in Chinese Philosophy: Benti (origin-substance) and Ti-Yong (substance and function)." *Journal of Chinese Philosophy* 29, no. 2 (June 2002): 145–161.

———. "A Theory of Confucian Selfhood: Self-cultivation and Free Will in Confucian Philosophy," 124–147. In Kwang-loi Shun and David B. Wong, eds., *Confucian Ethics: A Comparative Study of Self, Autonomy, and Community*. Cambridge: Cambridge University Press, 2004.

China Biographical Database Project. Available at https://projects.iq.harvard.edu/cbdb/home. Accessed June 20, 2021.

Cho Sŏngŭl 조성을. "Chŏng Yagyong kwa Hwasŏng kŏnsŏl" 정약용 과 화성 건설 [Chŏng Yagyong and the construction of Hwasŏng], 173–228. In Yu Bonghak, Kim Tonguk, and Cho Sŏngŭl, *Chŏngjo sidae Hwasŏng sin dosi ŭi kŏnsŏl* 정조시대 화성신도시의건설 [The construction of the new city of Hwasŏng during the time of Chŏngjo]. Seoul: Paeksan sŏdang, 2001.

Ch'oe Sŏgu 崔奭祐. "Han'guk kyohoe ŭi ch'angsŏl kwa ch'och'anggi Yi Sŭnghun ŭi kyohoe hwaldong" 한국 교회의 창설과 초창기 李承薰의 교회 활동 [Yi Sŭnghun and his church activities during the founding of early years of Catholicism in Korea]. *Kyohoesa yŏn'gu* 교회사연구 8 (1992): 7–31.

―――. "Tasan Sŏhak-e kwanhan nonŭi" 茶山 西學의 관한 논의 [A discussion of Tasan's relationship with Western Learning], 19–80. In Ch'oe Sŏgu et al., *Tasan Chŏng Yagyong ŭi Sŏhak sasang* 茶山 丁若鏞의 西學思想 [The Western Learning Philosophy of Tasan Chŏng Yagyong]. Seoul: Tasŏt Sure, 1993.

Ch'oe Taeu 崔大羽. "Taehak Kyŏngsŏl ko" 大學經說考 [An examination of ideas about the *Daxue* as a Confucian classic], 11–43. In Ch'oe Taeu, Chŏng Pyŏngnyŏn, An Poo, and Yi Ŭlho, *Chŏng Tasan-ŭi kyŏnghak: Nonŏ, Maengja, Taehak, Chungyong yon'gu* 丁茶山의 經學: 論語, 孟子, 大學, 中庸 硏究 [Tasan's Studies of the Classics: The *Analects, Mencius, Daxue*, and *Zhongyong*]. Seoul: Minŭmsa, 1989.

Choi Jeong-yeon. "Reassessment of the Late Joseon Neo-Confucian Scholar Yi Ik's Attitude toward Western Learning: With a Focus on His Perception of the Lord of Heaven." *Korea Journal* 56, no. 2 (summer 2016): 111–133.

Choi Young-jin. "The Historical Status of Dasan's Inseongmulseongron: On the Horak School's Inmulseong-dongiron." *Sungkyun Journal of East Asian Studies* I, no. 1 (2001): 131–152.

―――and Hong Jung Geun. "Tasan's Approach to the Ethical Function of Emotion as Revealed in His Annotations of Chinese Classics: With a Focus on his Maengja youi." *Korea Journal* 53, no. 2 (summer 2013): 54–79.

Chŏng Ilgyun 鄭一均. "Tasan Chŏng Yagyong ŭi ch'ŏn kaenyŏm-e taehan chaegoch'al" 다산 정약용의 '천天' 개념에 대한 재고찰 [A re-examination of Tasan Chŏng Yagyong's concept of heaven]. *Tasanhak* 32 (June 2018): 61–120.

―――. *Tasan Sasŏ Kyŏnghak Yŏn'gu* 茶山四書經學硏究 [Studies of Tasan's classical learning focusing on the Four Books]. Seoul: Ilchisa, 2000.

Chŏng Pyŏngnyŏn 鄭炳連. "Chungyong haesŏk ko: Tasan ŭi sosahakchŏk chungyong haesŏk pangbomnon" 中庸解釋考: 茶山의 昭事學的 中庸解釋方法論 [An examination of Tasan's approach to explicating the *Zhongyong*: his focus on serving the Lord on High], 45–129. In Ch'oe Taeu, Chŏng Pyŏngnyŏn, An Poo, and Yi Ŭlho, *Chŏng Tasan-ŭi Kyŏnghak: Nonŏ, Maengja, Taehak, Chungyong yŏn'gu* [丁茶山의 經學: 論語, 孟子, 大學, 中庸硏究 Tasan's Studies of the Classics: The *Analects, Mencius, Daxue*, and *Zhongyong*]. Seoul: Minŭmsa, 1989.

―――. *Tasan sasŏhak yŏn'gu* [茶山 四書學 硏究 Studies on Tasan's scholarship on the Four Books]. Seoul: Kyŏngin munhwasa, 1994.

Chow, Kai-ling. *The Rise of Confucian Ritualism in Late Imperial China: Ethics, Classics, and Lineage Discourse*. Stanford, CA: Stanford University Press, 1994.

Chung, Edward Y. J. *The Korean Neo-Confucianism of Yi T'oegye and Yi Yulgok: A Reappraisal of the "Four-Seven Thesis" and Its Practical Implications for Self-Cultivation*. Albany: State University of New York Press, 1995.

Chung So-Yi. "Dasan's Moral Epistemology," *Korea Journal* 53, no. 2 (summer 2013): 105–123.

―――. "Kyŏnggi Southerners' Notion of Heaven and Its Influence on Tasan's Theory of Human Nature." *Journal of Korean Religions* 2, no. 2 (October 2011): 111–141.

―――정소이. "Tŏksŏngesŏ tok'aengŭro: kwadogi yullihagŭrosŏ ŭi tasan sasang" 덕성(德性)에서 덕행(德行)으로: 과도기 윤리학으로서의 다산 사상 [Virtuous

Nature vs. Virtuous Action: Tasan's Ethical Perspective]. *In'gan, hwan'gyŏng, mirae* 인간, 황경, 미래 [Human Beings, Environment and Their Future] 9 (2012): 43–62.

Clark, Kelly James, and Justin T. Winslett. "The Evolutionary Psychology of Chinese Religion: Pre-Qin High Gods as Punishers and Rewarders." *Journal of the American Academy of Religion* 79, no. 4 (2011): 928–960.

Cua, Antonio S. "On the Ethical Significance of the Ti-Yong Distinction." *Journal of Chinese Philosophy* 29, no. 2 (June 2002): 163–170.

Cullen, Christopher. *Astronomy and Mathematics in Ancient China; The Zhou bi suan jing.* New York: Cambridge University Press, 1996.

Eggert, Marion. "Text and Orality in the Early Reception of Western Learning within the Namin Faction: The Example of Sin Hudam's Kimunp'yŏn," 141–159. In Marion Eggert, Felix Siegmund, and Dennis Würthner, eds., *Space and Location in the Circulation of Knowledge (1400–1800): Korea and Beyond.* New York: Peter Lang, 2014.

Elman, Benjamin A., and Martin Kern, eds. *Statecraft and Classical Learning: The Rituals of Zhou in East Asian History.* Leiden: Brill, 2010.

Elvin, Mark. "Scientific Curiosity in China and Europe: Natural History in the Late Ming and the Eighteenth Century," 11–39. In Ts'ui-Jung Liu, ed. *Environmental History in East Asia: Interdisciplinary Perspectives.* New York: Routledge, 2014.

Eno Robert. "Was There a High God Ti in Shang Religion?" *Early China* 15 (1990): 1–26.

Feng, Youlan. Derk Bodde, trans. *A History of Chinese Philosophy.* Princeton, NJ: Princeton University Press, 1983.

Goossaert, Vincent. "Modern Daoist Eschatology: Spirit-Writing and Elite Soteriology in Late Imperial China." *Daoism: Religion, History and Society* 6 (2014): 219–246.

Graham, A. C. *Two Chinese Philosophers: The Metaphysics of the Brothers Ch'eng.* LaSalle, IL: Open Court, 1992.

Han Yŏng'u. 한영우 *Kwagŏ, Ch'ulse ŭi Sadari: Chokporŭl t'onghae pon munkwa kŭpche ŭi sinbun idong: Chŏngjo – Ch'ŏljong tae* 과거, 출세의 사다리: 족보를 통해 본 조선 문과급제자의 신분이동: 정조 – 철종대 [The civil service examination as a ladder of success: changes in the social status of those who passed the civil service examination from the reigning period of King Chŏngjo through that of King Ch'ŏljong, as seen in genealogies]. Seoul: Chisik sanŏpsa, 2013.

Han'guk ch'ŏrhaksa yŏn'guhoe 한국철학사연구회, ed. *Tasan kyŏnghak ŭi hyŏndaejŏk ihae* 다산경학의 현대적 이해 [A contemporary understanding of Tasan's studies of the Confucian Classics]. Seoul: Simsa Publishing, 2004.

Huang Yingnuan 黃瑩暖. "Zhuzi lun: Zhongyong-Weifa zhi yi ji qi gongfu" [朱子論《中庸》「未發」之義及其工夫 What Zhu says in the *Zhongyong* about the meaning of the "unactivated state" and its relationship to the effort to cultivate a moral character]. 興大中文學報 *Chung-Hsing Journal of Chinese Literature* 21 (2007): 1–20.

Huang, Yong. *Why Be Moral: Learning from the Neo-Confucian Cheng Brothers.* Albany: State University of New York Press, 2014.

Kalton, Michael. "Chŏng Tasan's Philosophy of Man: A Radical Critique of the Neo-Confucian World View." *Journal of Korean Studies* 3 (1981): 3–38.

Kim, Daeyeol. "Reviving the Confucian Spirit of Ethical Practicality: Tasan's Notions of Sŏng (Nature) and Sim (Heart/Mind) and Their Political Implications," 187–202. In Andrew David Jackson, ed. *Key Papers on Korea: Essays Celebrating 25 years of the Centre for Korean Studies, SOAS, University of London.* Leiden: Global Oriental, 2014.

Kim, Hansang A. "Freedom, Agency, and the Primacy of Li in Zhu Xi's Neo-Confucianism (Seongnihak)." *Review of Korean Studies* 16, no. 1 (June 2013): 121–135.

Kim, Hyoung-chan (Kim Hyŏngch'an) 김형찬. "Chosŏn yuhak ŭi li kaenyŏm-e nat'anan chonggyojŏk sŏnggyŏk yŏn'gu: T'oegye ŭi ibal-esŏ Tasan ŭi Sangje kkaji" 조선유학의 理 개념에 나타닌 종교적 성격 연구: 退溪의 理發에서 茶山의 上帝까지 [A Study of the Religious Character of the Concept of *Li* in Korean Confucianism: from T'oegye's "Li issues" to Tasan's "Lord on High"]. *Ch'ŏrhak yŏn'gu* 철학연구 39 (2010): 67–101.

Kim Sanghong 金相洪. "Tasan ŭi Ch'ŏnjugyo sinbong-e taehan pallon," 茶山의 天主教 信俸에 대한 反論 [Refuting the contention that Tasan was a Catholic], 11–68. In Kim Sanghong. *Tasanhak yŏn'gu: Pu Tasanhak yŏn'gu nonjŏ ch'ongmongnok* [茶山學研究:附 茶山學研究 論著 總目錄 Studies of Tasan: with a catalogue of works in Tasan studies] Seoul: Kyemyŏng munhwasa, 1990.

———. "Tasan ŭi Ch'ŏnjugyo sinbong-e taehan pallon: Ch'oe Sŏgu sinbu ŭi nonmunŭl ikko" [茶山의 天主教 信俸 대한 反論: 崔奭祐神父의 論文을 읽고 A refutation of the claim that Tasan believed in Catholicism: After reading the article by Fr. Ch'oe Sŏgu]. *Tongyanghak* 東洋學 20 (October 1990): 117–159.

———. "Tasanŭn Ch'ŏnjugyoin ida'-e taehan pallon: Ch'oe Sŏgu sinbu ŭi nonmundŭl ikko" 茶山은 天主教人이다'에 대한 反論: 崔奭祐神父의 論文을 읽고 [A refutation of the claim that Tasan was a Catholic: After reading the article by Fr. Ch'oe Sŏgu]. *Han'guk hanmunhak yŏn'gu* 韓國漢文學研究 13 (1990): 345–366.

Kim, Seonhee, and MinJeong Baek, "A Religious Approach to the Zhongyong: With a Focus on Western Translators and Korean Confucians." *Journal of Korean Religions* 6, no. 2 (October 2015): 27–60.

Kim, Shin-Ja. *The Philosophical Thought of Tasan Chŏng.* Translated by Tobias J. Körtner. New York: Peter Lang, 2010.

Kim Woo Hyung. "Moral Agent and Practical Functions in Cheong Yagyong's Theory of Mind," *Journal of Confucian Philosophy and Culture* 22 (August 2014): 49–66.

Kim Yŏngil 김영일. *Chŏng Yagyong ŭi Sangje sasang* 丁若鏞의 上帝思想 [The ideas of Chŏng Yagyong regarding the Lord on High]. Seoul: Kyŏngin munhwasa, 2003.

Kim, Yung Sik. *The Natural Philosophy of Chu Hsi, 1130–1200.* Philadelphia: American Philosophical Society, 2000.

Ko Sŭnghwan 고승환. "Tasan Chŏng Yagyong ŭi kwŏnhyŏngnon chaehaesŏk: sŏnjin munhŏn-e taehan kojŭngŭl pat'anguro" 다산 정약용 의 권형론權衡論 재해석: 선진문헌에 대한 고증을 바탕으로 [A re-evaluation of Tasan Chŏng Yagyong's theory of weighing alternatives, based on a careful examination of what he wrote]. *Tasanhak* 29 (December 2016): 197–248.

Ko Sŭngje 고승제. *Tasanŭl ch'ajasŏ* 다산을 찾아서 [Searching for Tasan]. Seoul: Chungang Ilbosa, 1995.

Kŭm Changt'ae 금장태. *Chosŏn sirhak ŭi Kyŏngjŏn ihae* [How Korean scholars of Practical Learning understood the Confucian Classics]. Seoul: Seoul National University Press, 2014.

———. *Silch'ŏnjŏk iron'ga: Chŏng Yagyong* 실천적 이론가 정약용 [Chŏng Yagyong: a practical theorist]. P'aju, Korea: Ikkŭllio Books, 2005.

———. *Tasan sirhak t'amgu* 다산 실학 탐구 [Explorations of Tasan's practical learning]. Seoul: Sohaksa, 2001.

Lee Seung-hwan. "Dasan's Metacritique on the Seongni Debate in Joseon Neo-Confucianism." *Korea Journal* 53, no. 2 (summer 2013): 10–30.

Liang Tao. "The Interpretation of *Shendu* in the Interpretation of Classical Learning and Zhu Xi's Misreading." *Dao* 13 (2014): 305–321.

Liu, JeeLoo. *Neo-Confucianism: Metaphysics, Mind, and Morality*. Hoboken, NJ: John Wiley & Sons, 2018.

Mabuchi, Masaya. "Quiet-Sitting in Neo-Confucianism," 207–226. In Halvor Eifring, ed., *Asian Traditions of Meditation*. Honolulu: University of Hawai'i Press, 2016.

Meng Peiyuan. Eric Colwell, and Jinli He, trans. "How to Unite Is and Ought: An Explanation Regarding the Work of Master Zhu," 273–97. In David Jones, ed., *Returning to Zhu Xi: Emerging Patterns within the Supreme Polarity*. Albany: State University of New York Press.

Miura Kunio. "Orthodoxy and Heterodoxy in Seventeenth-Century Korea: Song Siyŏl and Yun Hyu," 411–443. In Wm. Theodore de Bary and JaHyun Kim Haboush, eds., *The Rise of Neo-Confucianism in Korea*. New York: Columbia University Press, 1985.

Nah, Seoung. "Tasan and Christianity: In Search of a New Order." *Review of Korean Studies* 3, no. 2 (2000): 35–51.

Needham, Joseph. *Science and Civilization in China, volume 3: Mathematics and the Sciences of the Heavens and the Earth*. Cambridge: Cambridge University Press, 1959.

Ni, Peimin. "Moral Cultivation: Gongfu—Cultivation of the Person," 445–63. In Kai-chiu Ng and Yong Huang, eds., *Dao Companion to Zhu Xi's Philosophy*. Cham, Switzerland: Springer Nature, 2020.

Nylan, Michael. "Translating Texts in Chinese History and Philosophy," 119–148. In Ming Dong Gu and Rainer Schulte, eds., *Translating China for Western Readers: Reflective, Critical, and Practical Essays*. Albany: State University of New York Press, 2014.

Paek Minjŏng 백민정. *Chŏng Yagyong ŭi ch'ŏlhak* 정약용의 철학 [The philosophy of Chŏng Yagong]. Seoul: Ihaksa, 2007.

———. "Tasan ŭi chungyong kangŭi(bo) chodae naeyong punsŏk: Chŏngjo 'Kyŏngsa kangŭi. Chungyong' ŏje chomun mit kit'a chodae wa ŭi pigyorŭl chungsimŭro" [茶山의 中庸講義(補)』 條對 내용 분석: 正祖 『經史講義·中庸』 御製條問 및 기타 條對와의 비교를 중심으로 An analysis of Tasan's Answers to Questions on the *Zhongyong* as seen in his *Chungyong kangŭibo*: A comparison with the opinions of King Chŏngjo on the *Zhongyong* seen in his lectures on the Classics]. *Tongbang hakchi* 동방학지 147 (2009): 399–448.

Pak Chongch'ŏn 박종천. *Tasan Chŏng Yagyong ui ŭirye iron* 다산 정약용의 의례이론 [The ritual theory of Tasan Chŏng Yagyong]. Seoul: Sin'gu munhwasa, 2008.

Pang In [方仁 Bang In). *Tasan Chŏng Yagyong ŭi Yŏkhak sŏŏn: Chuyŏk ŭi haesŏksarŭl tasi ssŭda* 다산 정약용의 '역학서언': '주역'의 해석사를 다시 쓰다 [Tasan Chŏng Yagyong's *Introductory Remarks for the Study of the Changes*: Rewriting the history of the interpretations of the *Book of Changes*]. Seoul: Yemun sŏwŏn, 2020.

Park Seong-rae, "Hong Taeyong's Idea of the Rotating Earth." *Korea Journal* 20, no. 8 (1980): 21–29.

Patt-Shamir, Galia. "Li and Qi as Supra-Metaphysics," 243–263. In Kai-chiu Ng and Yong Huang, eds., *Dao Companion to Zhu Xi's Philosophy*. Cham, Switzerland: Springer Nature, 2020.

Pfister, Lauren. "Mao Qiling's Critical Reflections on the Four Books." *Journal of Chinese Philosophy* 40, no. 2 (June 2013): 323–339.

Pines, Yuri. *Foundations of Confucian Thought: Intellectual Life in the Chunqiu Period, 722–453 B.C.E.* Honolulu: University of Hawai'i Press, 2002.

Setton, Mark. *Chŏng Yagyong: Korea's Challenge to Orthodox Neo-Confucianism*. Albany: State University of New York Press, 1997.

Shim, Yoonjeong. *Affirming 'Civilization' in Exile: Chŏng Yagyong (1762–1836)*. Doctoral dissertation, University of Illinois at Urbana-Champaign, 2013.

Shin Jeonggeun. "Bridging Moral Individuals and a Moral Society in Tasan's Philosophy," *Korea Journal* 53, no. 2 (summer 2013): 80–104.

Sirhak Pangmulgwan 실학박물관, ed. *Tasan sasang kwa sŏhak* 다산 사상 과 서학 [Tasan's thought and Western Learning]. Seoul: Kyŏngin munhwasa, 2013.

Song Young-bae. "A Comparative Study of the Paradigms between Dasan's Philosophy and Matteo Ricci's *Tianzhu shiyi*." *Korea Journal* 41, no. 3 (Autumn 2001): 57–99.

Stephenson, F. Richard. "Lunar Lodges in Chinese Astronomy," 1237–1241. In Helain Selin, ed., *Encyclopaedia of the History of Science, Technology, and Medicine in Non-Western Cultures*. Dordrecht: Springer Reference, 2016.

Sterckx, Roel. "Searching for Spirit: Shen and Sacrifice in Warring States and Han Philosophy and Ritual." *Extrême-Orient Extrême-Occident* 29 (2007): 23–54.

Sung, Tae Yong. "The Heavenly God without Revelation in Tasan's Philosophy." *Tasanhak* 5 (2004): 87–126.

Tasan Haksul Munhwa Chaedan 다산학술문화재단, ed. *Tasanhak sajŏn* 茶山學辭典 [A dictionary for Tasan studies]. Seoul: Saam Books, 2019.

Theobald, Ulrich, ed. "ChinaKnowledge.de: An Encyclopaedia on Chinese History, Literature and Art." Available at http://www.chinaknowledge.de/index.html.

Tu Wei-Ming, *Centrality and Commonality: An Essay on Confucian Religiousness*. Albany: State University of New York Press, 1989.

Upton, Beth Ann. "The Poetry of Han Wo (844–923." Unpublished doctoral dissertation, University of California, Berkeley, 1980.

Wang Hui. *Translating Chinese Classics in a Colonial Context.* Bern: Peter Lang, 2008.

Wilson, Thomas. "Spirits and the Soul in Confucian Ritual Discourse." *Journal of Chinese Religions* 42, no. 2 (November 2014): 185–212.

Winslett, Justin T. "Deities and the Extrahuman in Pre-Qin China: Lesser Deities in the *Zuozhuan* and the *Guoyu.*" *Journal of the American Academy of Religion* 82, no. 4 (December 2014): 938–969.

Wu, K. C. *The Chinese Heritage: A New and Provocative View of the Origins of Chinese Society.* New York: Crown Publishers, 1982.

Yi Haeyŏng 이해영. "Chŏng Yagyong ŭi Chungyong haesŏk-e kwanhan yŏn-gu I 정약용의 중용해석에 관한 연구1 [A study of Chŏng Yagyong's explication of the Zhongyong, part 1]. *T'oegyehak* 退溪學 3 (1991): 203–232.

———. "Chŏng Yagyong ŭi Chungyong haesŏk-e kwanhan yŏn-gu II 정약용의 중용해석에 관한 연구2 [A study of Chŏng Yagyong's explication of the Zhongyong, part 2]. *T'oegyehak* 退溪學 4 (1992): 125–149.

Yi Hyangman 李香晚. "Tasan Zhongyong: chusŏk-ŭi in'ganhakchŏk ihae" 茶山 『中庸』 註釋의 人間學的 理解 [An interpretation of Tasan's notes on the *Zhongyong* from the perspective of philosophical anthropology], 289–313. In Han'guk ch'ŏlhaksa yŏn'guhoe 한국 철학 연구회, ed. *Tasan kyŏnghak ŭi hyŏndaejŏk ihae* 다산 경학의 현대적 이해 [A contemporary understanding of Tasan's studies of the Confucian Classics]. Seoul: Simsan Publishing, 2004.

Yi Kwangho 이광호. "Chungyong kangŭibo wa chungyong chajamŭl t'onghayŏ pon Tasan ŭi sŏng ŭl ch'ŏlhak" 중용강의보 中庸講義補 와 중용자잠中庸自箴을 통하여 본 다산茶山의 성誠의 철학 [Tasan's philosophy of *sŏng* as seen in his *A Discussion of the Meaning of the Zhongyong, Revised,* and his *Admonitions for Myself upon Reading the Zhongyong*]. *Tasanhak* 다산학 7 (2005): 51–79.

Yi Sukhŭi 이숙희. "Yongmang kwa yŏmch'irosŏ ŭi Chŏng Yagyong ŭi simsŏng: Sŏng.kihosŏl ŭi 'naksŏn ch'iak e taehan yŏn'gu," 욕망과 염치러서의 정약용의 심성: 성기호설의 낙선치악 樂善恥惡 에 대한 연구 [Chŏng Yagyong's notion of human nature and the heart-mind as a desire to act appropriately and a sense of shame when failing to do so: a study of his concept of human nature as the desire for the moral good and disdain for the moral bad]. *Tasanhak* 다산학 27 (December 2015): 41–76.

Yi Tonghwan 李東歡. "Tasan sasang esŏ-ŭi 'Sangje' toip kyŏngno wa sŏnggyŏk " 다산 사상에서의 '상제' 도입의 경로와 성격 [The origins of Tasan's concept of Sangje and its characteristics], 371–392. In Pak, Hong-sik 박홍식, ed., *Tasan Chŏng Yagyong: Han'guk ŭi sasangga 10-in* 다산 정약용: 한국의 사상가10人 [Tasan Chŏng Yagyong, ten Korean philosophers series]. Seoul: Yemun sŏwŏn, 2005.

———. "Tasan sasang esŏ-ŭi 'Sangje' toip kyŏngno-e taehan sŏsŏlchŏk koch'al" 다산 상상에서의 '상제' 도입경로에 서설적 고찰 [A preliminary inquiry into the origins of Tasan's concept of Sangje], 347–370. In Pak, Hong-sik 박홍식, ed., *Tasan Chŏng Yagyong: Han'guk ŭi sasangga 10-in* [다산 정약용: 한국의 사상가10人 Tasan Chŏng Yagyong: ten Korean philosophers series]. Seoul: Yemun sŏwŏn, 2005.

———. "Tasan sasang-e issŏsŏ ŭi 'Sangje' munje" 茶山思想에 있어서의 '上帝' 문

제 [The question of the role of the Lord on High in Tasan's thought]> *Minjok Munhwa* 민족 문화 19 (1996): 9–28.

Yoo Kwon Jong, "Dasan's Approach to Ultimate Reality." *Korea Journal* 53, no. 2 (summer 2013): 31–53.

You Tae Gun. "Metaphysical Grounds of Tasan's Thought." *Korea Journal* 34, no. 1 (Spring 1994): 5–19.

Index

actions: acting courageously, 90, 136, 228; appropriate, 208–209, 212, 411n91; because of caution and apprehension, 371n51, 421n14, 441n16; being fully human, 68, 199, 246, 413n109; consistency important, 18, 87, 124–126, 376n17; Dao, 67, 146; difficulty of, 34, 39, 41–44, 86, 364n50; emotions, 371n53; empathy and, 386n11; ethical virtuosity, 90, 362n34, 387n14, 409n42, 427n21; failure in, 377n29, 377n33, 379n4; five types of, 375n8; four ways of, 201; innate potential for, 72–76, 92, 126, 256–262, 298, 361n5, 367n1, 368n19, 427n21; inspiration for, 47; neither falling short nor going too far, 51–52, 66, 108, 132, 257, 361n14, 376n23; proper interactions among humans, 23, 36, 160, 268; result of being composed and focused, 66, 126, 381n7; righteousness as, 105, 201, 279; ten types of, 203–206, 410n60; traditional Confucian virtues, 24; *Zhongyong* as providing guidelines for, 88. See also *cheng (song,* "sincerity")

actualization of potential *(yong),* 88, 118; contrasted with *ch'e* (potential), 42–43, 72, 144, 146, 303, 422–423n3; defined, 63–65

Admonitions for Myself upon Reading the Zhongyong (Chungyong chajam), 16–17, 102, 143, 188

All-Under-Heaven, 116, 165, 230, 234, 433n7, 441n10; entire human community, 28, 34, 54, 188, 213; everything on earth, 34, 124, 188, 277; most subtle in, 159; most virtuous, 234, 279–280; nature, 156–157, 159, 273; ruling over, 136, 147, 193, 271, 275, 393; traveling throughout, 220

ancestors, 54, 68, 81, 92, 156, 165, 173, 193; ancestor ritual banquet, 181–186; family ancestor memorial ritual, 7–9, 10, 23, 53, 158, 160, 169; honoring imperial ancestors, 160, 166–168, 170–172, 177, 180–181, 188, 191–192, 402n128; impersonating, 172–173; mourning, 168–169; offerings to, 173–174, 224; position of descendants during rituals, 175–180, 187; respect for, 188, 264–265, 276, 288

apprehension, 50–52, 78, 97, 111; before other emotions have stirred, 113–120, 289; caution and, 3, 85, 287–293, 364n56, 369n27, 377n33, 421n14, 437n50; exemplary person, 287, 303; the heart-mind, in, 25, 52, 96–97, and *li,* 51, 71; the Lord on High, 16, 18, 25, 51, 78, 158, 163–164, 371n51, 374n89; reverence and, 111; of what he can neither hear nor see, 110–112, 284, 373n73, 435–436n30

artisans, 213–214

awe, 71, 133, 163, 287, 421n14; attitude toward an exemplary person, 287; attitude toward a ruler, 436n33; attitude toward the Lord on High, 16, 25, 78, 164

benevolence *(in),* 88, 90, 183; alongside wisdom and courage, 104, 143, 206; of heaven and earth, 198; humanity, 363n50; definition of, 67–68, 76, 368n8; primary virtue, 68, 84, 104–106, 206, 279, 409n44; of rulers, 222; of spirits, 18

Bi Gan, 165, 381n4, 393n4n5

459

Bo Yi, 142, 165, 381n3, 382n12, 393n5
Book of Changes (Yijing), 114, 117, 128, 142, 198; on an exemplary person, 125, 128, 256; Great Treatise on, 142, 266; and li, 45; on males and females, 144–145; Tasan's commentaries on, 12, 356n28; trigrams and hexagrams in, 191, 201; yin and yang as the Dao, 103, 105, 162
Book of Documents (Shangshu), 125, 134, 166–167, 220, 239, 305; commentaries on, 147, 204, 249; "Counsels of Gao Yao," 125, 129, 205, 284; Five Cardinal Patterns of Appropriate Interactions, 154, 202, 204–205, 409n46; the heart-mind, 33, 295, 360n83, 376n23; the imperial pivot, 94, 365n78; Lord on High, 25, 48, 107; Mei's version, 220, 223–224; people from afar, 220–221; Tasan's commentaries on, 12, 14; Yao and Shun, 144–145
Book of Etiquette and Ceremonial (I-li), 152, 185, 187, 195, 267; archery contest, 183; banquet ritual, 181–184; behavior while in mourning, 152, 168; drinking ceremony, 186; names on spirit tablets, 124
Book of Rites (Liji), 87, 145, 204, 238, 291, 396n22; "Ceremonial Uses" chapter, 106, 203, 215, 236–237; *Daxue* and *Zhongyong*, 22, 430n39; "Great Treatise" chapter, 166, 192; "Interchange of Missions" chapter, 222, 223; "King Wen as Son and Heir" chapter, 179, 180; "Meaning of Sacrifices" chapter, 159–160, 180, 192; "Meaning of the Banquet" chapter, 182, 185; "Meaning of the Ceremony of Archery" chapter, 181; "Places in the Hall of Distinction" chapter, 171, 180; "Proceedings" chapter, 174, 219, 245, 403n138; "Record of Examples" chapter, 108, 143, 209; "Record of Small Matters in Mourning Garments," 152, 192; "Record on the Subject of Education" chapter, 200; "Royal Regulations" chapter, 53, 171, 173–174, 190, 192, 203, 217, 218, 222; "Rules for Sacrifices" chapter, 168; Seven Emotions in, 31, 85, 122; "Single Sacrificial Animal" chapter, 192; "Summary Account of Sacrifices" chapter, 175–176, 186, 192–193, 203, 206, 270–271; "Summary of the Rules of Propriety" chapter, 185; "Tan Gong" section, 169; "Yuzao" chapter, 282; "Zhong-ni at Home at Ease" section, 193
Book of Songs (Shijing), 92–93, 109, 145, 194, 212, 236, 253, 269, 282–292; Chu Ci, 186; cry of the osprey, 144; Fu Yi, 18; Kong Yingda on, 122; Lord on High, 25; spiritual beings, 8; Tasan's commentary on, 12, 14

Cai Qing, 133, 197, 265, 287; emotions, 122; placement of spirit tablets, 175, 176, 397n33; three important things, 270, 275, 287
Catholicism, 6–11, 13–14, 17, 49, 382n16; Catholic books, 6–8, 14, 21, 25, 36; Lord on High, 8, 26; Yi Pyŏk, 5–6, 366n1
caution and apprehension, 3, 16, 18, 293, 371n51, 421n14, 437n50, 441n16; before other emotions are activated, 113–118, 289–290; cultivating, 52, 114–115, 364n56; essential to moral cultivation, 84–85, 371n51, 377n33; Lord on High, 51, 374n89, 421n14; stimulus to appropriate action, 50–51, 78, 96–97, 158, 163–164, 303, 369n27; of what is not seen, 159, 284, 373n73, 436n30; Zhu Xi on, 110, 113, 120, 287
centered, 54, 86–87, 118, 305–306, 441n10; defined, 51–52, 66, 139–140, 376n23, 439n15, 439n18; neither falling short nor going too far, 51–52, 66, 108, 118, 126–127, 132, 257, 306, 361n14, 376n23
Changzong, 153
Chen Ziceng, 180, 216
cheng (sŏng, "sincerity"), 63, 93, 364n56, 420n1, 436–437n38, 441n10; acting with, 89, 372n65, 423n15; actualizing your full potential, 244, 427–428n21; consistent, 246–248; core characteristic of acting appropriately, 92, 208, 258–259; Dao, 67, 229, 281, 418n205, 422n17, 424n10, 431n61; Daxue and

Zhongyong compared, 91, 244; definition of, 42, 54, 75–77, 363n44, 411n89, 420n1, 424n18, 433–434n5; emotions, 114; Heaven, 293–294; intentions, 95, 366n85; main point of Zhongyong, 52, 56, 96, 227–228; nature, 243, 249; one of eight stages to cultivating a moral character, 364n55; power of, 93, 242, 280, 421n11, 422n24; relationship of understanding to, 92, 226, 230–233, 238–240, 408–409n41, 417n197; sagehood, 54–55, 92, 229, 242–243, 247, 433n2, 437n42, 437n50; spiritual beings, 273

Cheng school, 113–114, 116, 147, 371n55; Cheng Hao, 253; Cheng Yi, 45, 78, 116, 230–232, 295. *See also* Master Cheng

Cheng-Zhu school, 28, 69, 128, 137, 353n2; emotions, 52; human nature, 37, 72; *li*, 29, 70; reverence, 69; spirits, 68. *See also* Cheng school

Chŏng Chaewŏn, 3–4

Chŏng Yachŏn, 4–6, 8, 10–11

Chŏng Yagyong, 101. *See also* Tasan

Chŏng Yakchong, 4, 6, 10–11

Chŏngjo, King, 39, 63, 94; Catholicism, 9–10; death of, 10; on emotions, 361n7; on the heart-mind, 78; on human nature, 361n5; Namin, 4; questions on the Zhongyong in, 1784, 7, 17, 57, 83, 101; questions on the Zhongyong in, 1790, 64, 303

Ch'unch'u kojing, 191, 192

chung (focused composure), 126, 253; action, focused, 90, 257–260, 303; before emotions are aroused, 64–65, 114–121, 289; being watchful over oneself, 115; *cheng*, 247, 372n65; consistency in maintaining, 86–88, 124, 126–129, 133–135, 139–140, 146, 262, 304, 380n17, 381n7, 387n18; definition, 66, 303, 361–362n14, 376n23, 377n30, 439n15; equanimity, 135, 441n10; equilibrium, 289; exemplary person, 145–146, 299–300, 373n73, 377nn32,33; harmony, 86–87, 113, 116, 121, 126, 129, 247, 253, 433n7; human nature, 431n61; imperturbability, 113; Lord on High, 70; main point of Zhongyong, 305; sagehood, 279; title of Zhongyong, 381n7; Yan Hui, 143, 380n3. *See also* centered

ch'ung (conscientious), 194, 256–257, 427n21, 430n51; combined with empathy, 89, 91, 149–151, 169, 385–386n8; definition, 66–67; serving your sovereign, 68, 216–218

Classic of Filial Piety (Xiaojing), 168, 191, 404n159

compassion, 68, 199, 204, 205, 207

composure. See *chung*

Confucius, 26, 95, 105, 146, 209, 271–272, 278, 428n26; advocating composure and focus, 299; on being consistently centered, 86–88; *Book of Changes*, 142; *Book of Songs*, 92–93, 291; cited from the *Analects*, 83–84, 129, 133, 134, 150, 193, 220, 266, 270; cited in the Zhongyong, 124, 126, 130, 141, 151, 166, 291, 449n42; Dao, 110; emotions, 119, 121; harmonizing with his surroundings, 276–277; on husbands and wives, 150–151; in *Kongzi jiayu*, 195–196, 210; personal name, 9; on a petty person, 111; rectification of names, 2; a sage, 92, 118, 165–166, 233, 393n6, 431n52, 433n7; spirits, 159–160; studying, 114, 131, 210, 262; talking with Lord Ai, 210, 227, 408–409n30, 412n104; Tasan's commentary on the Analects, 15; Yan Hui, 119, 135, 147; Yan Yuan, 89; Yao and Shun, 264–265, 276

conscience (*chŏnmyŏng*), 33, 41, 158, 163, 373–374n81; definition of, 65–66, 370n39

conscientiousness. See *ch'ung*

consciousness (*yŏngmyŏng*), 69, 72, 207, 297, 392n48; definition, 79; *li* as lacking, 71

consistency, 33–34, 86–88, 126, 129, 146–148, 253, 375n5, 381n7, 439n14. *See also* *yong* (*zhongyong*)

cooperative, unselfishly. See *cheng*

courage, 88, 90, 136, 206–207; of Zilu, 143, 209

Dao (the Way), 46, 84, 172, 244, 264, 426n7; aligning with, 213, 307; ancient past,

264; appropriate behavior, 83, 145, 149–151, 154–155, 202–206, 220, 227, 241, 256, 263, 369–370n32, 408n36, 422n17, 428n26; of Confucius, 92, 277, 431n52; conscientiousness and empathy, 91, 169; consistent composure and focus, 133, 135, 138, 257–258, 303, 386n11; cultivating, 107–108, 230, 408n33; defined, 67, 110, 431n61, 432n7; difficulty of following, 88, 143, 158, 209; of earth, 105, 195–196, 249, 407n29; essence of the classics, 23; everything plays its proper role, 121–122; of an exemplary person, 90, 112, 143, 144–145, 149, 165, 198, 232, 283, 357n18; fills the universe, 160; heart-mind, 33, 39, 66, 78–79, 125, 295–300, 359n59, 370n39, 376n23; of human beings, 38, 73, 85, 92, 109, 146, 201, 232, 288, 383n2, 387n18, 407n29, 417n205, 418n206; as more than ordinary behavior, 34, 124; near at hand, 89; of nature, 38, 86–87; not the same as *li* or human nature, 75, 369n27; pronunciation, 61; of a ruler, 270–275, 428n22, 430–431n51, 427n42; of a sage, 426n33; searching for, 105; subtle yet obvious, 93, 164, 254, 284, 291, 292, 435–436n30, 436n38, 437n50; understanding, 130, 200, 246, 409n45; of the *Zhongyong*, 96–97, 163, 259, 373n77, 424n10

Dao of Heaven, 65, 286, 289, 421n14; *cheng*, 227, 418n206; compared with *dao* of human beings, 77, 105–106, 195–196, 228–229, 231, 240, 242, 280–281, 357n18, 417n205; Confucius, 84; hidden and subtle, 64, 144–147, 284, 384n20, 435–436n30, 437n42, 437n50; nature, 159, 384n21; sages, 87, 233, 249; same as Dao of an exemplary person, 291, 357n18, 383n2; the way things naturally are, 67, 291; yin and yang, 103, 162

Daxue, 42, 131, 154, 214–215, 216, 366n85, 388n4, 423n15; compared with the *Zhongyong*, 15–16, 22, 89, 91, 136, 234, 244–245, 417n197

deference, 30, 203–205

desire, 5, 39, 43, 114, 295–296; base desires, 50; conflicting, 40, 74, 359n59, 368n19; and *ki*, 33; moral desires, 47–48, 66, 85, 105, 109, 110, 214, 409n41; one of the Seven Emotions, 31, 84, 122; personal, 53, 55, 73, 78, 95, 97, 137, 363–364n50

Diagram of the Arrangement in the Imperial Ancestral Temple, 168

Diagram of the Dao heart-mind and human heart-mind, 298, 300

Diagram of the Zhou Ancestral Temple, 178

Duke of Zhou, 168, 215, 222, 237; and King Wu, 166–167, 188, 194, 402n131, 402n132; as a sage, 147, 233, 243, 264, 268

earth, 50, 76, 103–104, 206, 241, 266–267, 277; abode for humanity, 27; bring peace to, 423n15; comparing heaven and earth, 147; feminine, 144–145, 151; gods of, 53–54, 71, 90, 156, 163, 189–191, 274, 390n9, 404n159; heart-mind of heaven and, 198–199, 249; heaven and, as the entire universe, 36, 121–122, 150, 165, 245, 274, 276, 431n52; home for animals and plants, 426n7; round, 250–252; sacrifices to, 158, 403n144; separate from the functioning of heaven and, 273; spirits of heaven and earth, 111, 163; transformations of, 55, 109; yin spirit, 160. *See also* Dao, of earth; Heaven, and earth

effort (at cultivating a moral character), 74–75, 95–96, 107, 290, 304, 373n76; incentive to exert, 16, 51–52, 71, 95–97, 116–118, 441n16; producing goods, 214; required for self-cultivation, 54, 107, 149, 382–383n19, 417n205; strenuous, 33–34, 140, 208–209, 211–212, 411n91, 412n92, 413n109, 413n115, 418n209; to achieve focus and composure, 86–87, 120–121, 299, 372n65, 373n73, 386n17; to maintain caution and apprehension, 163; to watch over yourself, 228; wasted, 45, 128

emotions, 71–72, 377n33; anger, 113–119, 121; caution and apprehension, 18, 52; control of, 5, 16; empty mind of, 18,

52, 114–119; generated by the body, 5, 29, 40, 52; grief, 115; harmful, 43, 75; helpful, 30, 66, 120, 126, 370n39; joy, 113–123; *li*, 46; not yet activated (stir), 116–117, 127, 289–290, 293, 373n76; number of, 84–85, 122–123, 361n7; pleasure, 113–123; self-centered, 19, 40, 42, 51, 137; Seven Emotions, 30–31, 45, 46, 84–85, 296–297; sorrow, 113–123

empathy *(sŏ)*, 54, 222; and conscientiousness, 67, 89, 91, 150, 169, 386n11; definition, 73

ethical virtuosity, 29, 88–90, 125–127, 220, 270–271, 427n21; achieving, 304–305; and cheng, 227–228, 411n89; consistency in, 33–34, 388n4; cultivation of, 75, 95, 153, 210–211, 256–260; defined, 77–78, 387n14, 389n1; and family relations, 154; five ways of displaying, 84; focused composure and, 129, 139, 253; four ways of displaying, 201–207, 409n42; great acts of, 278, 432n10; and human nature, 38–40; lacking, 141–142; power of, 162; quiet display of, 289–292; sages and, 233, 249, 264, 268–269, 306–307, 393n6, 424n9; small acts of, 278, 432n10; and wisdom, 88

exemplary person, 256–258, 291, 377n32; and focused composure, 124

Explanation of the Diagram of the Supreme Polarity, 279, 294

feudal lords, 217, 271; mourning rituals for, 167–171, 176–177; rites of, 183–187, 188; sacrifices to the Celestial Spirit, 53, 191; sacrifices to the gods of soil and grain, 158; visiting, 220–224

filial piety, 24, 188, 202–205, 256–257; acting in a fully human fashion, 68, 199, 430–431n51; animals and, 235–236; ethical virtuosity, 78, 154, 427n21; kings, 191; one of four major ways of acting appropriately, 419n8; one of the Five Precepts, 205; and sages, 165, 194; serving parents, 75, 106, 131, 149, 155, 162, 200, 213, 413n119

fish, 88, 90, 130, 146, 147, 286, 371n50

Five Fundamental Human Relationships, 89, 91, 150, 154–155, 203–207; defined, 363n37, 386n14, 388n5; as illyun, 67

Five Precepts, 125, 154, 205, 375n8; defined, 202–206, 375n8

Five Primary Virtues, 84–85, 104–105, 125, 204, 375n8

Five Processes, 8, 103, 106–107

Four Books, 12, 14, 22, 47–48

Four Sprouts, 35, 46, 102, 201; defined, 30–32, 409n44; *li*, 296–298

fraternal respect and affection, 68, 78, 202–205, 256–257, 388n4, 402n128, 430n51

fully human *(in)*, 68, 105, 200, 208–209, 246, 304–305; acting appropriately, 72, 210–212, 256, 279, 413n109; *cheng*, 247; concern for the common good, 136; defined, 67–68, 198–199, 363n50, 368n8; potential to become, 74, 91, 430–431n51; serving the Lord on High, 71

Gnomon, 127, 139–140, 306

gods, 122, 156–158, 390n9; as deified humans, 168, 190; offerings to, 173–174; of soil and grain, 158, 171, 189, 191, 389–90n7. *See also* earth, gods of; Gou Mang; Rushou

Gou Mang, 122, 156, 189, 390n10

harmony, 28–29, 44, 117, 202; cosmic, 32, 38, 55, 76, 84; failure to maintain, 35; with heaven and earth, 249, 276; of human nature and human feelings, 72; within human relations, 32, 202, 205; selfless actions, 65, 208; society, 26, 44, 53; with the way of the sages, 108. See also *chung*, harmony

hawks, 88, 90–91, 147

heart-mind, 40, 45, 105, 113–121, 143, 159, 231, 238–239, 283, 368n14, 376n23, 436n33; ability to make choices, 47, 75, 153, 207, 283–284; attitudes of awe and apprehension, 25, 52, 96–97; of common people, 288; as conscience, 370n39; conscientiousness, 66; cosmic power, 86–87; contrary tendencies within, 38–39, 43–44, 46, 359n59,

368n19; as the Dao, 125;Dao heart-mind, 31–33, 66, 78–79, 125, 295–300, 359n59, 370n39, 376n23; definition, 71–73; emotions and, 122, 126, 169, 228, 293; empty of specific content, 18, 52, 367n5; of an exemplary person, 135, 148, 247, 287, 386n17; of heaven, 198–199; human heart-mind, 31–33, 75, 295–300; as human nature, 85; knowledge, 260; *li* complete within, 29, 35, 45–47, 110, 153; the Lord on High, 51, 71, 77, 95–97, 111, 153, 228, 371n51; of a petty man, 127–128; rectifying, 23, 40, 42, 54, 89, 91, 372n65; of a sage, 64, 83, 123, 269; sincerity, 16, 55, 217, 248, 421n11, 422n17; unites human nature and human feelings, 84

Heaven *(ch'ŏn)*, 5, 45–46, 113, 123, 126, 147, 214, 245, 260, 292, 304–305, 307, 424n14; ability to act appropriately bestowed by, 92, 105, 163, 256–258, 296, 361n5, 370n39, 427n21; aligning with, 150, 243, 259, 276; ascend to, 160; as *cheng*, 262, 281, 295, 384n21, 411n89, 424nn9–10, 426n7, 432n7; Confucius and, 165, 277; Dao endowed by, 272–273, 409n45; definition of, 65; does not display empathy, 150; and earth, 36, 55, 92–93, 113, 145, 151, 272; as the foundation of morality, 8, 39, 41, 43, 47, 55, 65, 70, 78, 95, 97, 111; as the foundation of the material world, 103–106, 156; as the Lord on High, 25, 48–51, 74–75, 77, 79, 93–94, 96, 112, 156, 158, 161, 371n51, 388n6, 392n48, 434n14, 436n33; heart-mind of, 198–199; human nature bestowed by, 84–86, 107–109, 230, 256, 271, 359n59, 368n19, 430n51; power of, 158, 160, 162, 247, 280; recognition of the proper way to behave bestowed by, 119; sacrifices to, 53–54, 162, 189; as the sky, 76, 92–93, 104, 250, 251, 266, 277; understanding, 163, 200–201, 213, 226, 227, 242, 259, 408–09n41, 417n197; what is bestowed by, 113, 194, 234–236, 244–245, 253, 293, 296, 369n27, 420n2. *See also* mandate of Heaven; spirits

History of the Former Han Dynasty (Hanshu), 122–123, 131, 141, 210, 249–250, 266, 293–294
History of the Later Han Dynasty (Huhanshu), 125
Hou Shisheng (Hou Zhongliang), 129, 146, 153, 165, 208
Houji (Lord of Millet), 122, 168, 176, 246, 404n159
Hu Bingwen (Hu Yunfeng), 234, 245, 287, 289, 293
Hu Guang (Han official), 94, 300, 301, 365–366n82, 440n19
Hu Hong (Hu Wufeng), 189
Huang Xunrao (Huang Kuan), 154
human nature, 26, 32, 50, 84, 95, 235, 443n61; ability to act wisely, 201; Buddhist notion of, 283; and *cheng*, 231; conferred by Heaven, 48, 107, 271, 430–431n51; cultivating, 233; Dao mind and, 66; defined, 25, 38–39, 73–75; different from animal nature, 85, 105, 108–109, 236, 420n22; different from Dao, 110; and emotions, 72, 84, 113, 120; essentially moral, 8, 37, 68, 74, 207; innate ability to act appropriately, 200, 209, 230, 298; and *li*, 26, 35, 45–47, 369n27; moral side of, 109; natural inclinations, 85, 359n59; as our conscience, 33; of sages, 417n205; two sides of, 34, 41, 107, 368–369n19
Huowen, 57, 107, 132, 141, 148, 196, 215, 257, 260; being cautious and apprehensive, 110, 113, 115, 120, 373n73; being on target, 139; Buddhism, 119–120, 153, 242; *cheng*, 227, 231, 247; composure and harmony, 116, 258; Confucius, 276–277; Dao, 144; dealing with visitors, 219–222; emotions, 117, 137; the heart-mind, 153; petty men, 128, 377n29; the *pulu*, 195–196

intelligence, 79, 207; Heaven's, 51, 93, 371n51; in humans, 104–105, 359n59, 367n5, 368n19, 421n14, 422n24. *See also* moral insight

Jupiter stations, 249–250

ki, 20, 86, 103, 106, 292; animals and, 88, 104, 234; Dao and, 84; defined, 30, 68–69, 361n10; Four-Seven Debate, 31–33, 35, 45–46, 102, 296–298; heart-mind and, 71–72; human nature and, 107; *li* and, 13, 70, 234, 238–239; Non-Polarity, 94; of a sage, 5; spirits and, 44, 89, 91, 161–164; transformations of, 87, 157, 384n21

Kija, 165

knowledge, 122, 153, 158, 226, 257–260, 262, 417n197; action and, 378n1; of the Dao, 149, 220; effort to acquire, 211, 230–232; foreknowledge, 241–243; guide to appropriate behavior, 55, 66, 90, 114, 194, 196, 209, 228; of Heaven, 160, 200, 227, 286; how to rule, 193; innate, 153; of the Lord on High, 56, 75, 423n15; not enough for moral behavior, 34, 39, 51; of sages, 147, 254; teaching, 202, 205; useless, 95; of what is primary and what is secondary, 226; of what it means to be fully human, 161, 200; wisdom and, 98, 201, 209, 246, 295

Kong Anguo, 204, 410n70, 416n168

Kong Yingda, 122, 178, 195, 204–205, 241

Kongzi jiayu, 89, 91–92, 195–196, 198, 210, 229; Zhu Xi rejected, 196

kwisin, defined, 69, 389n2. *See also* gods; spirits

li, 29–33, 35, 273; appropriate behavior, 88–89, 91, 213; defined, 5, 21, 41, 46, 70–71, 124, 162, 244–245, 362n32; demoted, 44–47, 56, 369n27; endowed by Heaven, 103, 106, 108; Four-Seven Debate, 31–33, 35, 45–46, 102, 296–298; guiding principles, 50; the heart-mind and, 71–73; investigating, 92; manifestations of, 85–86, 206; not human nature, 75; not in ancient texts, 24, 47–48, 213; not the same as the Lord on High, 71, 75, 158; not the same as spirits, 161–163, 392n38; as a plural noun, 20, 37–38, 419n7; as a singular noun, 419n6; as unconscious, 51. *See also ki*, *li* and

Lord on High, 8, 26, 47–51, 441n16; awe and apprehension of, 16, 18, 25, 51, 78, 85, 371n51, 374n89; as the Celestial Spirit, 53–54, 156–157; conferred a moral sense, 107, 256; defined, 45, 65, 71, 392n48; far above humans, 421n14, 432n4; as Heaven, 25, 74–75, 77, 79, 93–94, 112, 371n51, 388n6, 434n14, 436n33; object of reverence, 69–70, 95–97, 114, 366n84; power of, 77–78, 156–164; sacrifices to, 53–54, 58, 160, 163, 188, 189–191, 403n144, 405n172; serving, 437n42; as the Spirit, 69, 228; supreme spiritual being, 156–157; various names for, 392n48; watching us, 16, 18, 23, 24, 52, 54, 56, 73, 79, 228, 374n89, 389n11, 417n195, 423n16

Lou Xiangming (Lou Zhonghuan), 141, 182

Lü Dalin, 119, 128, 129, 141, 208, 230–231, 270–271, 283, 287

mandate of Heaven, 274; definition, 65–66, 373–374n81; moral rules, 97, 133, 163; to rule, 166–167, 177, 243

Mao Qiling, 131, 134, 152, 155, 221, 236–237, 241, 245, 250, 259, 270, 277; on the *Book of Songs*, 282; criticizing Zhu Xi, 213; on the Five Precepts, 202–205; on the meaning of *pulu*, 195–196; on rituals, 170, 172–174, 180, 182, 184, 185–187, 270–271; on rulers and officials, 215–217, 219; on visits to the capital of a fief, 223–225; on writing Sinographs, 277–278

Master Cheng, 132, 148, 150, 270, 271; cited by Zhu Xi, 129; Buddhism and, 242, 283; on composure, 129, 136–137; on the heart-mind, 118, 295; on spirits, 156, 273; on the three important things, 270. *See also* Cheng school

Mencius, 22, 26, 48, 152, 165, 272, 305; consistency, 125; emotions, 119, 121; on the Five Precepts, 203–205; on the Four Sprouts, 30–31, 201, 207; on the heart-mind, 29, 114; on human nature, 39; on *li*, 45, 224; Tasan's commentary on, 12, 392n48; on the will, 42; on Zimo, 94

mindfulness, 33, 50; definition, 69–70; respect and, 287, 289. *See also* reverence

mirror, spotless, 64, 118–121
moral frailty, 17, 28, 30, 32, 33–35, 37, 45; overcoming, 47, 50–52, 78
moral insight, 22, 92, 97, 207, 230–233, 240, 297
morality, 27, 39, 71, 144–145, 298–300; Confucianism and, 7, 13, 36, 37, 95; defined, 30, 39–40, 44, 56, 73, 77, 78, 204, 386n15; inclination toward, 39, 44, 75; *li* and, 5, 29, 46–47, 70–71; reverence and, 50

Namin, 3–5, 9, 10, 32, 49
network, cosmic, 20, 29, 35, 36, 78, 159, 234, 238; of appropriate human interactions, 32, 37, 238; of *li*, 30, 44–45, 70, 234
Nine Cardinal rules, 89, 91–92, 210, 213–225, 229
Noron, 4, 9, 10, 11

potential *(ch'e)*, 36–37, 207, 238, 305; contrasted with *yong* (actualization), 42–43, 72, 144, 146, 303, 422n3; defined, 63–65, 374n92; of the heart-mind, 118–120; as human nature, 8, 73–75, 278; of plants and animals, 109
propriety, 39, 146, 169, 184, 220, 224, 234, 260, 279; defined, 23–24, 53–54; inspired to conform to, 417n195; Laozi and, 147; one way of four ways of acting appropriately, 40, 68, 78, 84, 105–106, 201, 206–207, 409n42; return to, 108; in ritual, 241, 279; three thousand rules of, 92, 94, 254–255; traditional Confucian virtue, 24, 427n21, 430n51; Yan Hui and, 208. See also *Book of Etiquette and Ceremonial*

quiet sitting, 33, 48, 52, 108–109, 111–112

Rao Lu, 147, 154, 166, 302
Record of Ritual Matters by the Elder Dai, 195, 209
Responsive, appropriately. See *cheng*
reverence *(kyŏng)*, 33, 50, 111, 241, 289, 373n76; defined, 69–70; for the Lord on High, 25, 77, 95–97, 163; for parents, 388n4; as respect, 13
Ricci, Matteo, 6, 8, 36, 49

right on target, 89, 118, 132, 136, 279, 284, 379n4, 439n15. See also centered; *cheng*
righteousness, defined, 199; *li* and, 45; one of four ways of acting appropriately, 68, 105–106, 201, 206, 279; one of the five primary virtues, 85, 104
rituals, 53–54, 105, 107, 241, 257; ancestral, 124, 170–181, 188, 191–193, 288; of ancient times, 270–272; for banquets, 181–187; barbarians and, 220; Catholicism and ancestral, 5–10; creating new, 268–269, 402n132; diplomatic, 223–225; for the Former Kings and Former Lords, 167–169; reverence and, 69, 259–262; rituals to the Lord on High, 58, 160, 163, 188, 189–191, 403n144, 405n172; rules of, 238, 254–255, 426n7; for spiritual beings, 158, 189–191, 273, 403n1; Tasan and, 23–24; Tasan's writings on, 12, 14, 22, 53
Rushou, 156, 189–190, 389–390n7, 390nn10–11, 403n138

Sangje. See Lord on High
selfishness, 31, 40, 41–45; *cheng* and, 76; desires, 51, 78, 95; emotions, 18, 28, 55, 66, 295–296; free from, 35, 47; the heart-mind and, 71–72; human nature and, 74; *ki* and, 30–33
selfless orientation. See *cheng*
Shang, 171–172, 178, 192, 221, 238, 243; ritual and music of, 268, 270–272
Shun, 132, 166, 202, 204, 228; as ruler, 122, 194, 235, 264; wisdom of, 87–90, 143, 208–209; and Yao as rulers, 121, 146–147, 237; and Yao as sages, 115, 127, 136, 158, 230, 233, 238, 269; and Yao revered by Confucius, 92, 165, 264–265, 276; as Yao's son-in-law, 144
Shuowen, 108, 152, 219, 241
Sishu jishuo, 215
Six Relationships, 154, 160, 388n5
son of heaven, 167–169, 171, 177, 187, 215, 269, 270; filial piety of, 188; lost rites of, 183–184; relations with feudal lords, 222, 224; ritual obeisance to Heaven, 53, 158, 190–191
Spirit, 53–54, 69, 156, 228; as Sangje, 73, 77–78. See also Lord on High

spirit tablets, 10, 124, 168, 172–173; Catholicism and, 8–9; placement of, 175–179
spirits, 6, 8, 48, 85, 111–112, 156–164, 273–274; defined, 69, 370n44; interactions with, 53–54, 157; neither *li* nor *ki*, 91, 161–162; power of, 44; sacrifices to, 189–191; types of, 71, 156. *See also* gods
Spring and Autumn Annals, 190, 191, 202, 218, 241; Tasan's commentary on, 12; Zuo Commentary on (Zuozhuan), 189, 192
Symposium in the White Tiger Hall, 122, 205

Tasan, life of, 3–14. *See also* Chŏng Yagyong
ten ways of acting appropriately, 203–206
terrestrial branches, 249–250
three levels of life, 236
Tianzhu shiyi, 6–8, 36. *See also* Ricci, Matteo
T'oegye (Yi Hwang), 10, 26, 30–33, 35, 46, 49, 296–297; admiration of Tasan for, 10, 28
transformation of things, 55, 78, 86–87, 92–94, 103, 145, 169, 284–285; *chohwa*, 65, 384n21; Heaven and, 159, 293–294; human beings and, 8; human beings can assist, 109; spirits as traces of, 156–158, 273–274, 390n16
trustworthy, 66–67, 68, 78, 160, 207, 257, 287; officials, 216–218

unselfish, 136, 143, 238; altruistic, 68; lacking in animals, 234–235; Yan Hui, 143. *See also cheng*

virtue. *See* ethical virtuosity

watchful over oneself *(sindok)*, 33, 113–115, 118, 227, 372n65, 422n24; because Heaven is watching you, 50–52, 70–71, 158, 377n33, 408–409n41; *cheng*, 54, 77, 433–434n5; defined, 73
water, 250–252; still, 64, 118–121
Wen, King, 166, 168, 171, 247; Confucius emulating, 92, 165, 264–265; descendants of, 176–177; reverence toward the Lord on High, 25, 114, 163; sage, 194, 228, 233, 269
wisdom, 201, 211, 279; act wisely, 27, 88, 90, 136, 206–208, 430–431n51; goal of philosophy, 22; knowledge and, 295; one of four ways of acting appropriately, 68, 84, 104–106, 201; sagely, 307; Shun, 143, 208–209; Zhu Xi, 165; Zigong, 245–246
Wu, King, 166–167, 168, 171, 180, 188, 194; Confucius emulating, 92, 165, 264–265; defeated Shang, 172, 221; descendants of, 176–177; sage, 230, 238, 269

Xia, 171, 221, 270–272

Yan Hui, 88, 90, 136, 208, 246, 380n3; acting unselfishly, 143; *cheng* of, 227; death of, 121, 147, 165; fully human, 209, 247
Yang Guishan, 119–121
Yangban, 3, 10
Yao: and Shun revered by Confucius, 92, 165, 264–265, 276; and Shun as rulers, 121, 146–147, 237; and Shun as sages, 115, 127, 136, 158, 230, 233, 238, 269; Shun's father-in-law, 144
Yi Ik, 5, 28, 32
Yi Pyŏk (Kwangam, Tŏkcho), 7, 17, 101, 164, 252, 300; Catholicism, 5–6; proofs of the power of Heaven, 160–161; stirring of emotions, 366–367n3, 373n78; Supreme Polarity, 294; validation of a sage, 272–273; virtuous nature and Heaven, 256
Yi Yŏhong, 367n5
yong (ch'eyong). *See* actualization of potential
yong (zhongyong), 152, 253, 375n5, 381n7, 439n14; defined, 33–34; in maintaining focus and composure, 86–88, 124–129, 133–135, 139–140, 262, 304, 380n17; ordinary, 152
You Zuo, 126, 231, 233, 239–240, 247
Yu, 122, 246
Yulgok (Yi I), 26, 30–32, 35, 46, 49, 296–300
Yun Chich'ung, 6, 8–10

Zeng Shen, 150
Zhang Taizhan, 152, 193
Zhang Zai, 35, 230–233
Zheng Xuan, 128, 152, 184, 193; *Book of Songs* commentary, 168; cited by Zhu Xi, 159; explaining *pulu*, 195; Tasan disagrees with, 141, 190–191, 241–242, 248; *yong* as consistency, 129; *Zhongyong* com-

mentary, 204, 215, 216, 219, 238, 265, 270; *Zhouli* commentary, 167, 170–171, 173, 180, 190–191

Zhong, defined, 51–52. *See also* centered

Zhongyong huowen, 52, 107, 128, 148, 215, 242, 260, 271; being on target, 132, 139; *Book of Changes*, 117; Buddhism, 119–120, 153, 242; caution and apprehension, 110, 113, 115, 120, 293, 373n73; *cheng*, 227, 231, 247; compared with Zhongyong zhangju, 116, 132, 139, 141–142, 257–258; composure and harmony, 116, 258; Confucius, 276–277; Dao, 144, 150; education, 231; emotions, 117, 137; heart-mind, 153; petty men, 128, 377n29; physical endowment, 137; *pulu*, 195–196; sages, 276, 277; Tasan disagreed with, 107–108; visitors from afar, 219–222, 257–258

Zhongyong zhangju, 121, 133, 257–258, 260, 280, 282, 302; *Book of Songs*, 282, 286; Cheng brothers, 147–148; compared to *huowen*, 116, 132, 139, 141–142, 257–258; Dao, 122, 144, 165; emotions, 113, 137; focus and composure, 136; human nature, 116; King Chŏngjo questions, 282; mourning rituals, 172–173, 175; preface to, 295–301; *pulu*, 195; ritual rules, 254; Tasan disagrees with, 128, 142, 170, 247; visitors from afar, 220–221; Zheng Xuan and, 219

Zhou, 166–169, 215, 267, 270; ancestral temple of, 178; Duke of, 147, 188, 194, 222, 233, 237, 243, 264; King Ding of, 192; King Jing of, 171; King Wen of, 25, 166; King Wu of, 166, 188, 221, 238; officials of, 205, 217–218; Qin and writing system of, 268; ritual interactions with subordinate fiefs, 220, 222–224; rituals and music of, 268, 275; Yellow River Diagram of, 170

Zhouli, 109, 157, 215, 216, 218; ancestral shrines, 168; artisans, 213–214; autumn offices, 187; celestial ministry, 173, 218; dealing with envoys, 221; dealing with fiefdoms, 222–223; market contracts, 274; military, 250; music, 129; protocol, 156, 170–171, 180, 189, 191, 254, 265; spirits, 157, 160, 273; summer offices, 179; taming animals, 237; treatment of officials, 219–220; writing, 266–267

Zhu Rong, 122, 156, 390n10

Zhu Xi, 124, 130, 136, 146, 153, 210, 263; on artisans, 213–214; on benevolence, 198; on becoming fully human, 200, 208, 210–211; Buddhism and, 119, 283; caution and apprehension advocated, 52, 111, 287; on *cheng*, 244–245, 247; on composure and harmony, 116; on consistency, 129, 208; criticized by Mao Qiling, 213; criticized by Tasan, 34, 47, 64, 126, 132–134, 138, 141, 143–144, 147, 149, 152, 159, 170, 213, 221, 228–229, 230, 238–240, 242, 247–248, 250, 252, 258, 275, 281, 283–284, 286, 288, 289, 291, 291, 363–364n50, 369n27, 381–382n1, 408n33, 422–423n3, 433n2; on Dao, 110, 202, 254; on emotions, 113–121; on family relations, 214–215; *Family Rituals*, 23; floating earth, 250; Four Books and, 22; on Four Primary Virtues, 105; on governing, 198; on heart-mind, 295; on Heaven, 103, 147, 249; on human nature, 107–109, 234–236, 238, 278; on investigating things, 226, 232; on *li*, 29, 234; meaning of *Zhongyong*, 124, 129; on officials, 216–217, 219; positive impact of appropriate behavior, 154, 213; praised by Tasan, 127, 142–143, 164, 165, 188, 233, 242, 271, 293, 402n128; on *pulu*, 195–196; on ritual, 167–186, 189, 191–194, 241, 265, 270–271; on social hierarchy, 268; on spirits, 159, 161–162, 271, 273; visitors from afar, 221–222, 224; on wisdom, 209, 246; on Zhou, 267–268; *Zhuxi yulei*, 280. *See also Zhongyong huowen*; *Zhongyong zhangju*

Zhuangzi, 108, 121, 149, 235, 298

Zigong, 83–84, 241; wisdom of, 245–246

Zilu, 138, 206; courage of, 143, 209

Zisi, 83–84, 87, 95, 118, 245; earth, 250; *Kongzi jiayu*, 210; Mao Qiling on, 155; Mencius and, 204–205; writing *Zhongyong*, 86, 124, 154, 270, 279

Zixia, 121

Zonggao, 148

About the Translator

Don Baker is professor of Korean civilization in the Department of Asian Studies at the University of British Columbia. He earned his PhD in Korean history from the University of Washington in 1983 and has been teaching at UBC since 1987. He has published widely on Korean religion, philosophy, traditional science, and history. *Korean Spirituality* (2012) and *Catholics and Anti-Catholicism in Chosŏn Korea* (2017), both from the University of Hawai'i Press, are among his many publications.

Korean Classics Library: Historical Materials

Imperatives of Culture: Selected Essays on Korean History, Literature, and Society from the Japanese Colonial Era
edited by Christopher P. Hanscom, Walter K. Lew, and Youngju Ryu

A Chinese Traveler in Medieval Korea: Xu Jing's *Illustrated Account of the Xuanhe Embassy to Koryŏ*
translated, annotated, and with an introduction by Sem Vermeersch

Seeking Order in a Tumultuous Age: The Writings of Chŏng Tojŏn, a Korean Neo-Confucian
translated and with an introduction by David M. Robinson

Korea's Premier Collection of Classical Literature: Selections from Sŏ Kŏjŏng's *Tongmunsŏn*
translated, annotated, and with an introduction by Xin Wei and James B. Lewis

A Korean Scholar's Rude Awakening in Qing China: Pak Chega's *Discourse on Northern Learning*
translated and annotated by Byonghyon Choi, Seung B. Kye, and Timothy V. Atkinson

Tales of the Strange by a Korean Confucian Monk: *Kŭmo sinhwa* by Kim Sisŭp
translated, annotated, and with an introduction by Dennis Wuerthner

The Encyclopedia of Daily Life: A Woman's Guide to Living in Late-Chosŏn Korea
translated, annotated, and with an introduction by Michael J. Pettid and Kil Cha

Record of the Seasonal Customs of Korea: *Tongguk sesigi* by Toae Hong Sŏk-mo
translated, annotated, and with an introduction by Werner Sasse

Korean Classics Library: Philosophy and Religion

Salvation through Dissent: Tonghak Heterodoxy and Early Modern Korea
George L. Kallander

Reflections of a Zen Buddhist Nun
Kim Iryŏp, translated by Jin Y. Park

A Handbook of Buddhist Zen Practice
translated by John Jorgensen

Korea's Great Buddhist-Confucian Debate: The Treatises of Chŏng Tojŏn (Sambong) and Hamhŏ Tŭkt'ong (Kihwa)
translated and with an introduction by A. Charles Muller

A Korean Confucian Way of Life and Thought: The Chasŏngnok (Record of Self-Reflection) by Yi Hwang (T'oegye)
translated, annotated, and with an introduction by Edward Y. J. Chung

Numinous Awareness Is Never Dark: The Korean Buddhist Master Chinul's Excerpts on Zen Practice
translated, annotated, and with an introduction by Robert E. Buswell, Jr.

Doctrine and Practice in Medieval Korean Buddhism: The Collected Works of Ŭich'ŏn
translated, annotated, and with an introduction by Richard D. McBride II

The Foresight of Dark Knowing: Chŏng Kam nok and Insurrectionary Prognostication in Pre-Modern Korea
translated, annotated, and with an introduction by John Jorgensen

A Place to Live: A New Translation of Yi Chung-hwan's T'aengniji, the Korean Classic for Choosing Settlements
translated, annotated, and with an introduction by Inshil Choe Yoon

The Master from Mountains and Fields: Prose Writings of Hwadam, Sŏ Kyŏngdŏk
translated, annotated, and with an introduction by Isabelle Sancho

A Korean Confucian's Advice on How to Be Moral: Tasan Chŏng Yagyong's Reading of the Zhongyong
translated, annotated, and with an introduction by Don Baker